Tommaso Campanella

Ritratto a olio eseguito in Roma, intorno al 1630, dal pittore stilese Francesco Cozza
(Roma, Palazzo Caetani di Sermoneta).

TOMMASO CAMPANELLA

Renaissance Pioneer of Modern Thought

by

BERNARDINO M. BONANSEA, Ph.D.

THE CATHOLIC UNIVERSITY OF AMERICA PRESS

Washington, D.C. 20017

Contents

PART THREE

PHILOSOPHY OF BEING

Introduction

Tommaso Campanella is one of the most controversial figures of the Italian Renaissance. His complex personality and the syncretic nature of his thought have for centuries perplexed historians and commentators, with the result that the most divergent judgments have been passed on him both as a man and as a thinker. The number and extent of his works, which were written at different periods of a troubled life, have no doubt contributed to present confusion in Campanellian studies. Moreover, it can hardly be denied that doctrinal prejudices and inferior scholarship have often adversely influenced the opinion of critics. Only in comparatively recent times has a more objective approach to the primary sources shed new light on the nature of Campanella's thought and personality. This revival of Campanellian research has taken place especially in Italy.

Italian thinkers of different philosophical positions, including some eminent scholars, have subjected Campanella's thought to careful study. A critical edition of all his works together with an Italian translation of the original Latin text is being prepared by Professor Luigi Firpo of the University of Turin. The first of the three volumes containing Campanella's literary works appeared in 1954. This extensive project will include an imposing series of volumes dealing with subjects that range from grammar and rhetoric to philosophy and theology, from apologetics to politics, and from medicine to magic and astrology. It will also include Campanella's letters, poems, and best known work, *The City of the Sun*.

A study of Campanella is both interesting and rewarding for the historian of philosophy. It enables him to understand better a leading figure of the Italian Renaissance, and it also presents an opportunity to broaden his view of Renaissance thought as a whole. Campanella represents in effect all the cultural trends of his age. The vast extent of his knowledge, in which he was helped by an extraordinary memory, makes it evident that he was acquainted not only with most of the philosophers of ancient times, as well as the scholastics, but also with the leading thinkers of his own day. Many of the latter exerted a definite influence on the formation of his doctrine.

Gilson observed that prejudices against Renaissance philosophical systems are many and persistent and that Campanella is perhaps the

most ill-treated of the thinkers of that epoch.[1] There is some truth
to this statement. We hope that the present study will help to dissipate many erroneous ideas about Campanella and correct false judgments in regard to his philosophy.

A chief concern in the preparation of this work has been to support
our statements with Campanella's own words or references to one or
more primary sources. This exacting method has the double advantage
of assuring the reader of a faithful rendering of Campanella's thought
and of acquainting him with original material not easily available.
Indeed, much of the material used in this study is contained in books
scattered throughout the libraries of the entire nation. In some cases
the books are so rare that there is only a single copy in the United
States and very few elsewhere.

We have not intended to give equal coverage to all the aspects of
Campanella's philosophy. Thus we have omitted his logical treatises
and have considered only tangentially his psychology and philosophy
of nature, two fields in which he shows little originality. Emphasis
has been placed on his theory of knowledge, his metaphysics, and his
moral and political doctrines. A discussion of these areas of his thought
provides the three principal parts of this study. Each one of these parts
is followed by a critical evaluation in which the main positions are
summarized and judgment is passed on them in the light of what
we consider to be sound philosophical principles. Thus a distinction
has been kept between the presentation of Campanella's thought and
our own appreciation of it.

This is the first work on Campanella's philosophy to appear in
English. It is also one of the few comprehensive studies in which
Campanella's thought is systematically presented and critically evaluated on the basis of his entire philosophical production. To provide
the reader with the necessary background and with a better perspective the study will be prefaced by a brief survey of Italian Renaissance
thought and a chapter on Campanella's life and historical position.

The writer expresses his gratitude to all who have helped him in
the completion of this work during several years of painstaking
research. Special thanks are due to the Right Reverend Msgr. John
K. Ryan, Ph.D., LL.D., former Dean of the School of Philosophy of
The Catholic University of America, for his constant encouragement
in the pursuance of a study undertaken at his suggestion, for his
reading of the manuscript, and his constructive criticism. Grateful
appreciation is also expressed to Mr. George C. Hill, M.A., Sr. Dorothy
A. Haney, Ph.D., and Mrs. Robert J. Fitzpatrick, who carefully read

the manuscript and offered many helpful suggestions, and to Professor Luigi Firpo for generously donating the frontispiece copies of Campanella's portrait.

Acknowledgment of permission to use certain published material is gratefully made to *The Catholic University of America Press, The American Catholic Philosophical Association,* and *The Franciscan Educational Conference.* The writer is indebted to the many libraries throughout the country that have kindly placed material at his disposal. In addition to the Library of Congress and the New York Public Library, the libraries of the following universities have been particularly helpful: The Catholic University of America, Columbia University, University of Michigan, University of Chicago, Harvard University, Cornell University, and Yale University.

The Catholic University of America
Washington, D. C.

PART ONE

The Man and His Period

CHAPTER ONE

Italian Renaissance Thought*

All philosophers are to some degree the product of their times. Their own cultural environment and the spiritual legacy of the men who preceded them cannot fail to exert an influence on the shaping of their thought or the molding of their system. Even the greatest minds and the most original thinkers are subject to this law of continuity in intellectual development which is at the basis of all progress in philosophy as well as in the other fields of human endeavor. Tommaso Campanella was no exception. His system was so indebted to the then contemporary philosophies and the philosophies of his immediate predecessors that many of their ideas were absorbed into and became an essential part of it. Consequently, as an introduction to our study on Campanella, a survey will be made of the schools of philosophy prevailing at his time, with a special view to their bearing on the formation of his thought. The survey will be preceded by a short discussion of the Renaissance as a distinct philosophical movement.[1]

1. *Meaning and Nature of the Renaissance.* The period of transition from the Middle Ages to the modern era stands out in European history as the distinctive cultural movement called the Renaissance. There is no agreement among historians on the exact chronological delimitations of this period or its specific nature. The two subjects are correlated, inasmuch as we cannot set the time limits of any intellectual movement unless we know first its specific nature and characteristics. The diversity of views depends to a great extent on the meaning we attach to the term "Renaissance," and especially on whether or not we include the humanistic movement. If we hold that humanism was simply the preparation or beginning of a rebirth of classical antiquity,[2] then the whole period of the Renaissance will extend approximately from the middle of the fourteenth century to the earliest part of the seventeenth century, having at one end Francesco Petrarch, "the father of humanism," and at the other end Tommaso Campanella, "the last philosopher of the Renaissance."[3] But if we consider humanism as a distinct although not altogether separate movement, then the Renaissance period must be dated roughly from the fifteenth

---

* This chapter was written primarily for the reader who is not sufficiently acquainted with Italian Renaissance thought and wishes to have an overall picture of the philosophical trends prevailing in Italy at Campanella's time. Many of the sources used in the preparation of this chapter are not available in English.

century and will have a life-span of about two hundred years.[4]

For the purpose of this study we shall adopt the former view and use the term "Renaissance" in a broader sense to include the humanistic movement. In this sense we can speak of a Renaissance humanism, an expression that has long been used by historians and applied especially to the Italian Renaissance, the object of our most direct concern. Care must be taken, however, not to confuse the two terms, humanism and Renaissance, whenever their specific traits are to be stressed. In general, one may say that "humanism" emphasizes the study of man through the revival of Greek and Latin classics, or what has become known as the study of humanities;[5] whereas "Renaissance" has the more general connotation of revival of classical antiquity by a greater concentration on the study of nature.[6]

A point that deserves emphasis is that neither the humanistic movement nor the Renaissance represents a break with the culture of the Middle Ages, as if the Renaissance brought light and luster to an age of darkness and intellectual stagnation. The debt of the Renaissance to the medieval tradition has become increasingly evident with the advancement of studies on the cultural relationship between the two periods. Many scholars now agree that what best distinguished the Renaissance from the Middle Ages was not so much an increase in learning on the part of Renaissance men—the reverse is rather true—as it was a shift of interest. Whereas medieval man, especially the philosopher, was mainly concerned with God and eternal verities, Renaissance man was more interested in himself and the world around him. Contrary to what has often been asserted, the Renaissance was not in itself a pagan movement. Still, much of the appeal that religion and the spiritual values held for medieval schoolmen was lost for the Renaissance man.[7] This fact leads to the more specific question of Renaissance philosophy.

2. *Aristotelianism.* Among the great variety of philosophical schools in the Italian Renaissance, two major trends stand out as most representative—Aristotelianism and Platonism. The intrinsic value of the thought of Plato and Aristotle, who had been held in such high esteem by medieval schoolmen, and the growing knowledge of their writings through the many new translations and commentaries are the principal reasons why these two Greek philosophers became the center of attention in the Renaissance. Yet precisely because of the many commentaries written on the Greek masters, different groups began to form around the centers of learning in Italy, each group

claiming to represent the genuine thought of its preferred master. This is particularly true in the case of Aristotle, whose system involves many controversial issues, especially in regard to creation, divine providence, and the immortality of the soul. Thus in his *Discussionum peripateticarum libri XV* (1571) Francesco Patrizi could mention ten different groups of interpreters of Aristotle's thought. Only three of these groups, however, have gained official recognition by historians of philosophy, namely, the *Averroists,* who interpreted Aristotle according to the mind of the great Arabian commentator; the *Alexandrists,* who interpreted him according to the principles laid down by the Greek commentator Alexander of Aphrodisias (flourished c. 200 A.D.); and the *Thomists,* who followed the lead of St. Thomas Aquinas and tried to fit Aristotelian thought into a Christian theological framework. The three groups represent the Arabic, the Greek, and the Christian traditions, respectively.

The principal seat of Averroism was the University of Padua, while Alexandrism had its center in the University of Bologna. Heated controversies were carried on between the two factions in the rival cities. Padua had become such a stronghold of the peripatetic school that when Antonio Persio, a disciple of Bernardino Telesio, was on his way to Venice in 1575 for a three-day disputation directed against Aristotle's doctrine, he did not dare enter the city for fear of a personal attack. The cult of Aristotle had reached such a point that the Spanish Dominican Melchior Cano (1509-1560) could write, not without some sarcasm, that "the Peripatetics consider Aristotle as Christ, Averroës as St. Peter, and Alexander as St. Paul."[8] The main difference between the Averroists and the Alexandrists, or at least the difference that most aroused contemporary attention, was found in their attitudes toward the nature of man's intellect. While the Averroists stood for the doctrine of one immortal intellect for all men, the Alexandrists contended that man possesses no immortal intellect at all. Both positions led to the denial of personal immortality, a pivotal doctrine of Thomistic Aristotelianism and one in which Campanella was to be particularly interested.

The chief representatives of the Averroistic school were Nicoletto Vernia, Agostino Nifo, Alessandro Achillini, and Marco Antonio Zimara. Vernia (d. 1499) first held the doctrine of one immortal intellect for all men, but later retracted it for the orthodox view of an immortal soul for each individual man. In like manner Nifo (1473-1546), his disciple, later rejected the Averroistic doctrine of the unicity of the intellect which he had held in an early work, *De intellectu et daemonibus* (Padua, 1492). Nifo became famous because of his *Tractatus de immortalitate animae contra Pomponatium* (Venice, 1518), in which he defends the Thomistic interpretation of Aristotle's doctrine against the interpretation of Alexander of Aphrodisias. Achillini (1463-1512) also took a stand against Pomponazzi, but at the same time tried to avoid the difficulty inherent in the Averroistic doctrine of the unicity of the intellect by introducing the notion of *virtus* or *anima cogitativa* as a principle of multiplication and corruptibility. Zimara (1460-1532) devoted all his writings to commentaries on Aristotle and Averroës and enjoyed such a reputation that his followers called him "a new Averroës." However, he managed to stay within the limits of Catholic orthodoxy by interpreting Averroës' doctrine of the human intellect as meaning the unity of the most universal principles of knowledge recognized by all men.[9]

The Alexandrist group had its main exponents in Pietro Pomponazzi and his pupils Gaspare Contarini and Simone Porta. Pomponazzi (1462-1525), who taught successively at Padua, Ferrara, and Bologna, stirred a controversy lasting for about a century by his treatise *De immortalitate animae,* published at Bologna in 1516. In this work he presents the Aristotelian doctrine of the soul as the form or entelechy of the body and uses it against the Averroists as well as the Thomists. Just as he rejects the existence of a separate human intellect, so he denies the immortality of the soul on the ground that according to Aristotle the human soul depends on the body for all its operations, both in the sensitive and the intellectual orders. A separate soul could not operate, and so there is no reason why it should exist apart from the body. Pomponazzi does not draw this conclusion explicitly, but his teaching very definitely leads to it. To the objection that sanctions in a future life are required for preservation of the moral order, he answers, in anticipation of Immanuel Kant, that virtue is its own reward and vice its own punishment. Yet, in spite of his philosophical teaching, Pomponazzi holds to the doctrine of the immortality of the soul as a Christian believer. In this respect he accepts the Averroistic principle of the double truth.

The first to criticize Pomponazzi's views on the soul was his disciple, the future Cardinal Gaspare Contarini (1483-1542). At one time Contarini had accepted the Alexandrist interpretation of Aristotle, and for this reason he is sometimes listed as a representative of the Alexandrist group. On the question of the immortality of the soul, however, he sided against his former master by showing that even though the soul depends on the senses for the attainment of knowl-

edge, it can go beyond sense knowledge and understand first principles
and pure abstract forms. Furthermore, the intellect can understand
itself, an act that is impossible for a faculty essentially dependent
on matter and phantasm. These are basically the arguments used in
Thomistic philosophy to prove the spirituality of the soul and consequently its immortality. Only with certain qualifications, therefore,
can Contarini be considered an Aristotelian of the Alexandrist group.
His place is rather within the Thomistic school.

Another figure of the Alexandrist group was Simone Porta (1496-
1554), also called Porzio, from the Latin *Portius*. Basically he shares
Pomponazzi's views on the human soul but shows a greater knowledge
of the original Aristotelian texts. In his *De humana mente disputatio*
he distinguishes between the possible intellect, which he makes part
of human nature and thus mortal, and the agent intellect, a divine
power that makes things intelligible in the same way that the light
of the sun makes things visible. In other words, as a recent Renaissance
historian puts it,[10] in Porta's view man has a capacity for understanding but the intelligibility of things is in the things themselves. The
capacity for understanding is not dependent on any bodily organ, nor
is it determined by any particular object. To this extent it is impassible,
but this impassibility has nothing to do with the notion of immortality. It is merely a functional immutability, inasmuch as the intellect never operates without the phantasm and cannot be conceived
as having a separate existence.[11]

Such were the leading champions of Averroism and Alexandrism
during the Italian Renaissance. But not all Renaissance Aristotelians
belonged strictly to one of these two groups. Men like Andrea Cesal-
pino, Giacomo Zabarella, and Cesare Cremonini did not take sides
in the controversies between Averroists and Alexandrists, but tried
to reconcile the two parties or else left many disputed points unde-
cided. In addition, there were the Thomists, whose best exponent was
Cardinal Thomas de Vio, commonly known as Cajetan (1468-1534).
Cajetan's views on the immortality of the soul are startling, since it
was unusual for a Thomist of his stature to depart from the teaching
of Aquinas on such an important issue. Cajetan is skeptical about the
ability of the human mind to produce a strict demonstration of the
immortality of the soul. This, he says, is a truth that we can know
with certainty only by revelation. It does not seem likely that Cajetan
reached this conclusion as a result of his study of Aristotle, although
he was firmly convinced that the Stagirite denied the doctrine of
immortality. Whether Cajetan's teaching on the soul when he was

lecturing at Padua had any influence upon Pomponazzi, who was then a student there, is not certain.[12]

To complete this survey of the Aristotelians of the Italian Renaissance, we must also mention the Occamists and the Scotists, since they represented two very influential currents of thought that seem to have been even more active and more widely spread than the Thomistic school.[13] This fact must be kept in mind in order to understand Campanella's position on several issues about which Dominicans and Franciscans adopt opposing views.[14]

3. *Platonism.* In Platonism, the other major trend of thought in Renaissance Italy, we are faced once more with such a variety of interpretations that, in the words of a contemporary scholar, "hardly a single notion which we associate with Plato has been held by all Platonists."[15] Platonism, or more accurately, neo-Platonism had its seat in the Platonic Academy of Florence, founded by Cosimo de' Medici at the suggestion of George Gemistus Plethon (d. 1450), who had gone to Italy from Byzantium on the occasion of the Council of Florence (1438-45). Plethon is the author of numerous commentaries and a treatise in Greek in which he discusses the principal differences between the Platonic and Aristotelian doctrines. This treatise was attacked by the Aristotelian George of Trebizond (1395-1484) in his *Comparatio Aristotelis et Platonis,* which in turn was attacked by Cardinal Bessarion (1403-1472). A follower of Plethon, Bessarion rose to defend his master and Platonism in his opuscule *Adversus calumniatorem Platonis.*

The most prominent member of the Florentine Platonic circle was Marsilio Ficino (1433-99).[16] He became the leader of the Academy and gave to the Western world the first complete Latin translation of the works of Plato and Plotinus, which he enriched with ample commentaries. His most important work is the *Theologia platonica* (Florence, 1482), a valuable treatise in which the teachings of Plato are fused into a synthesis that includes neo-Platonic and Christian as well as original elements. In it Ficino portrays the universe as a harmonious system with degrees of being that extend from corporeal things to God. Man is the bond between spiritual and material substances. The main theme of the treatise is the immortality of the soul, which he proves by man's inner tendency to union with God, a goal to be achieved only in a future life. Ficino owes much of his philosophy to St. Augustine, whom he follows in the interpretation of the Platonic theory of ideas, in the doctrine of illumination, and in other doctrines. He identifies the love of which Plato speaks with Christian love as described by St. Paul. Ficino's philosophy of love, especially as developed in his commentary on Plato's *Symposium*, inspired many poems in the later Renaissance. It also became the subject of many academic lectures and discussions and gave rise to several treatises on love, among which is the *Dialoghi d'amore* of Leone Ebreo (c. 1460-1530), a Portuguese Jew. This work deals with the intellectual love of God and contains views that inspired Renaissance literature on the subject. It is thought that Leone Ebreo's idea of the love of God had some influence on the philosophy of Spinoza.

A member of the Florentine Academy directly influenced by Ficino was Giovanni Pico della Mirandola (1463-94). Possessing a knowledge of Greek and Hebrew, he conceived a synthesis in which the entire school of Aristotle, the Arabian philosophers, and the Jewish Cabala would be joined in a Platonic-Christian system. Pico speaks of God in terms that remind us of the negative theological approach of Pseudo-Dionysius. He maintains that, as far as we are concerned, God is darkness, and we know Him only by denying the limitations of the perfections we find in creatures. In Pico's conception of the universe man occupies a special place. He stands between the celestial beings and the earthly creatures, and because of his freedom he is the master of his own destiny. Man is the head and synthesis of lower creation, while Christ is the head of the human race. Although Pico acknowledges with Ficino the superiority of Christianity, he maintains that all religions and philosophical systems contain at least some partial truths and share therefore in one universal truth. "These ideas," it has been observed, "imply not only a philosophical justification for the eclecticism of the sixteenth century, but they also contain the seeds of later theories of tolerance and of natural religion."[17]

Pico's nephew, Giovanni Francesco Pico della Mirandola (1470-1533), did not show too great an enthusiasm for his uncle's efforts to reconcile Platonism with Aristotelianism. In his *Examen vanitatis doctrinae gentium et veritatis Christianae disciplinae* he sharply criticizes the Aristotelian theory of knowledge for placing too much emphasis on sense experience and blames philosophy in general for the decay of Christian morality. He is credited with having called the attention of his contemporaries to the urgent need for religious reform within the Catholic Church, just as Campanella, among many others, would do after him.

A thinker usually associated with the Platonists, even though he occupies a place of his own, is Nicholas of Cusa (1401-1464), who studied at the universities of Heidelberg and Padua and became cardinal and bishop of the Church. A learned man, he wrote treatises on mathematical, philosophical, and theological subjects, such as *De concordia catholica* (1433), *De coniecturis* (1440), *De Deo abscondito* (1444), *De quaerendo Deum* (1445), *Idiotae libri* (1450), *De visione Dei* (1453), and *De mathematica perfectione* (1458). His best known work is the *De docta ignorantia* written in 1440. Following Platonic-Augustinianism, he distinguishes three stages in human knowledge. The first stage is sense-perception *(sensus)*, whereby we grasp the external objects of our experience but form no judgment about them. The second stage is represented by reason *(ratio)*, which proceeds discursively and affirms or denies on the basis of the principle of contradiction or incompatibility of opposites. Discursive reasoning may produce scientific knowledge, or that kind of knowledge that is characteristic of the Aristotelian school; but it cannot give us anything more than an approximate knowledge of God and even of creatures, the truth of which is hidden in God. Hence all science is "conjecture." The last and most advanced stage is intuitive or intellective knowledge *(intellectus)*, which surpasses or rather denies the oppositions of reason and apprehends God as the *coincidentia oppositorum*. This means that God is the synthesis of opposites in a unique and absolutely infinite being. Whereas creatures are multiple and distinct, God transcends all distinctions and oppositions by uniting them in Himself in an incomprehensible manner. Our knowledge of God is necessarily limited; but, to the extent that we recognize our mind's limitations when confronted with God's infinite and transcending nature, we surmount our own ignorance and become learned men. We acquire in knowledge that kind of "learned ignorance" already mentioned by St. Augustine and St. Bonaventure, which is the theme of Nicholas's treatise *De docta ignorantia*.

To prove his assertions, Nicholas argues that in the acquisition of knowledge our intellect proceeds by comparisons. But no comparison is possible when the object we try to understand is the absolute infinite. Yet if we cannot comprehend God who is the absolute maximum, we can at least know that He is beyond the power of our understanding. We can even go further and know that the absolute maximum is also the absolute minimum. In fact, the absolute maximum is actually all that it can be; it is both as great as it can be and as small as it can be. This is tantamount to saying that God can be neither greater nor smaller than He is. And since the maximum and the minimum considered in themselves, and not as the maximum or minimum of a certain matter or quantity, are both infinite, and since the infinite is unique, it follows that God is at once the greatest and the smallest in a perfect *coincidentia oppositorum*.

A competent mathematician, Nicholas makes use of mathematical analogies and symbols to illustrate his point. The symbols that he finds most useful in describing the nature of the absolute maximum are the line, the triangle, and the circle. Thus, if one side of the triangle is extended to infinity, the other two sides will coincide with it. In like manner, if the diameter of a circle is extended to infinity, the circumference will coincide with the diameter. Hence the infinite straight line is at once a triangle and a circle. These are, of course, mere analogies which cannot give us a real insight into the nature of the absolute infinite. Yet in Nicholas's view, they suggest that entities disparate in character are such that, when taken to infinity, they become indistinguishable. This is an illustration of God as the *coincidentia oppositorum*.

The relation between God and the world is expressed by Nicholas in terms that may suggest pantheism. Such an interpretation is definitely against Cusa's mind, as he disavows any pantheistic implications. When he states that God contains all things because all things are in Him and that He is the reason for all things because He is in all things, he simply means that God as the cause of all existing realities is immanent in all things and all things essentially depend on Him. The world is the unfolding of the absolute and most simple, divine being; it has no limit, at least no potential limit, as to time and space; it possesses unity and plurality in that it includes a multiplicity of finite things, each one reflecting the entire universe. Although Nicholas speaks of a world soul, apparently he does not understand it in the Platonic sense. The *anima mundi* is for him a universal form that contains all forms; it does not seem to be a being distinct from God and the world but rather God himself, who "works all things in all things."

Man is endowed with a soul. In him the spiritual and the material join together to form a "perfect little world," which is a part of the great world and a finite representation of the divine *coincidentia oppositorum*. The perfect union between God and creatures is to be found in Christ, the *maximum contractum*, that is, the maximum that is at once absolute and restricted. Christ is also the necessary link *(medium absolutum)* between man and God, since through Him man can be united with God and thus achieve his eternal happiness.[18]

While from this résumé of Nicholas's thought it appears he is indebted to earlier philosophers, such as Pseudo-Dionysius, Meister Eckart, and perhaps John Scotus Eriugena, he advanced views that were adopted and developed in their own way by later Renaissance thinkers, especially Giordano Bruno. There is no clear indication of Nicholas's direct influence upon Campanella. Nevertheless, the two philosophers move on a common ground, their Platonic-Augustinian heritage, and show a mutual interest in the study of nature as the work and manifestation of God. The Christocentric doctrine as the synthesis of all philosophical speculation is another instance of the similarity of the two doctrines.

4. *The Humanistic Movement.* While Aristotelianism and Platonism were the two major schools of philosophy of the Italian Renaissance, the humanistic movement, originating early in the fourteenth century and reaching its climax in the sixteenth century, also exercised a considerable influence upon the philosophical thought of the time. Typical humanists were classical scholars mainly interested in literary and philological studies, but they touched on philosophical questions in their writings, and in many instances they formally discussed philosophical problems. This was only natural in an age in which philosophy still played a fundamental role in classical education and was considered an essential part of the university curriculum. At this time also the *studia humanitatis* included, among other subjects, courses in rhetoric and moral philosophy, and the humanist professors of moral philosophy were accustomed to base their lectures on Aristotle.[19] The impact of humanism on Italian Renaissance thought makes it necessary to examine briefly the principal figures in the movement and point out their particular contributions to philosophy. To complete this survey, we shall investigate the meaning and extent of the naturalistic movement which appeared in the late Italian Renaissance and thus prepare the way for our study of Tommaso Campanella.

The chief initiator of the humanistic movement in Italy was Francesco Petrarch (1304-1374), whose literary and poetical works are far better known than his philosophical writings. In his *De sui ipsius et multorum ignorantia* (1367) Petrarch argues against the Aristotelian Averroists and opposes to their empty dialectics the richness of Plato's thought and the treasures of Christian wisdom. For him Plato is the prince of philosophers, just as Cicero is the prince of classical writers. Drawing his inspiration from St. Augustine, whom he considers his master, Petrarch cherishes the vision of a harmonious blending of

Christian wisdom with the teaching of the ancients. In his *Secretum* or *De secreto conflictu curarum multarum*, completed in 1356, he describes the dramatic conflict raging in the inner part of his own soul between a craving for human glory and an inclination toward the ascetic life. This conflict reflects to some degree the nature of Petrarch's thought, which was torn between the desire for self-affirmation, a characteristic of the humanistic spirit, and his adherence to the perennial truths of Christian philosophy inherited from the Middle Ages.

Petrarch's humanistic movement was carried on by Coluccio Salutati (1331-1406), known especially for his moral treatises in which he extols the active life and defends the doctrine of the supremacy of the will. These ideas are dominant in his *De fato, fortuna et casu*, completed in 1399, while in an earlier treatise, *De saeculo et religione* (1381), dedicated to a friend who had joined a religious order, he contrasts the evils of the secular life with the many advantages of the religious life. The treatise shows an approach to life in its concrete reality and centers on the idea that man is like a gladiator thrown in the world arena where he has no choice but to fight. And fight he must for the sake of justice, truth, and honesty, to attain everlasting peace in the future life. In another work, *De nobilitate legum et medicinae*, Salutati affirms the superiority of law over medicine and the natural sciences.

Another representative of humanism was Leonardo Bruni of Arezzo (1374-1444), a follower of Salutati, who is credited with the translation of several Platonic dialogues and some of Aristotle's works. He wrote the *Isagogicon moralis disciplinae*, a moral treatise aiming to prove the compatibility of classical culture with the Christian doctrine. The treatise was meant to be an introduction to Aristotle's ethics. Still another contemporary writer who followed the pattern of Salutati in praising the merits of active life was Matteo Palmieri (1406-1475), author of *Della vita civile*, a series of dialogues where love of family and love of country are reckoned among the greatest virtues.

The dignity of man, a favorite theme of humanism, was the subject of *De excellentia et praestantia hominis*, a short treatise written by Bartolomeo Fazio between 1448 and 1450 and dedicated to Pope Nicholas V. The author places man's dignity in his spiritual and immortal soul, which makes him similar to God. The same theme was developed by Giannozzo Manetti in his *De dignitate et excellentia hominis*, written between 1451 and 1452 as a result of his discussions with King Alphonse of Aragon, who apparently was not satisfied with Fazio's work. While taking a critical view of Pope Innocent III's *De contemptu mundi,* Manetti stresses man's accomplishments in his control over inanimate nature and in many fields of intellectual endeavor and attributes these successes to the superior nature of his soul, the object of God's special concern. Thus with Manetti, as well as with Fazio, the dignity of man is traced back to its rightful place, the soul.

A very different figure from those just named was Lorenzo Valla (1405-1457), the greatest philologist of Italian humanism. In his *Dialecticae disputationes contra Aristotelicos* Valla attacks Aristotelian logic as an abstract and artificial scheme that does not lead to real knowledge. Logic, he maintains, must be subordinated to rhetoric, which is not merely the art of expressive speech, or discourse, but rather the linguistic expression of the real. He assails the empty dialectics of contemporary Aristotelians and their blind adherence to the word of their master. In his *De voluptate* Valla discusses man's supreme good, a timely topic for those days when Leonardo Bruni had just completed his translation of the *Nicomachean Ethics* (1414). Valla's solution of the problem is that pleasure (*voluptas*) is man's supreme good, for that is what man seeks above all and toward which he tends by his natural inclination. However, for Valla pleasure has a much broader meaning than it has in ordinary usage. It includes not only material and sensuous satisfaction in all its forms but also satisfaction of a purely intellectual and spiritual order, which man apprehends as an additional good to be enjoyed. Furthermore, it includes satisfaction derived from the possession of God in the celestial beatitude, the only type of pleasure that completely fulfills man's aspirations. Thus, while founding his moral theory on a hedonistic basis similar to that of Epicurus, Valla raises it in the last analysis, although not quite consistently, to the high level of Christian doctrine by proclaiming God as man's ultimate end. Valla's adherence to Christian teaching is more evident in his *De libero arbitrio,* a minor work completed in 1439, in which he discusses the difficult problem of the compatibility of God's foreknowledge and human freedom. He first attempts to clarify the issue by distinguishing between *praescire* and *scire* and by making God's knowledge coextensive with His own eternity; then he concludes by saying that such a truth is a mystery for the human mind and must be accepted on faith.

Valla's attitude toward the Aristotelian logic found a supporter in Rodolfo Agricola (1443-85), who renewed the attacks against the Stagirite in his *De inventione dialectica.* The man, however, who most strongly defended Valla's views on rhetoric as a general science was Mario Nizolio (1498-1576), better known for his *Thesaurus Ciceronianus* than for his philosophical treatise *De veris principiis et vera ratione philosophandi contra pseudophilosophos*, first published in 1553 and reprinted by Leibniz in 1671 under the title *Antibarbarus philosophicus, sive Philosophia scholasticorum impugnata*. Nizolio stands for complete independence in philosophy, especially in regard to Plato and Aristotle, and asserts that a philosopher should rely only on his external senses, experience, mind, and memory. He is convinced with Ramus (Pierre de la Ramée) that Aristotle's logic has done irreparable damage to humanity. Rhetoric as the general science of meaning should take the place of logic and be kept free from the abstractions of metaphysics since they do not attain to the real essence of things. Reality is individual and particular; hence knowledge, to be true, must also be of individuals and particulars. The Aristotelian universal is only a fiction of the mind, as are the Platonic ideas. This amounts to saying that metaphysics as a science has no value, for it deals only with universal terms or concepts and not with things in themselves. Evidently, the confusion between logical and metaphysical universals obscures Nizolio's presentation of Aristotle's thought. This confusion was common at his time, and even Campanella is not free from the anti-Aristotelian prejudices of his contemporaries.

5. *The Naturalistic Movement*. With the development of the physical sciences, brought about by new discoveries and more effective means of observation, a new direction taken by the philosophers of sixteenth-century Italy resulted in the naturalistic movement. It was so called because of the growing interest that its representatives had in the study of nature. It would be wrong, however, to think of this movement as an homogeneous and well-determined pattern of thought, since each individual philosopher had his own distinctive and often quite different approach to nature. Moreover, there was no agreement among the representatives of this movement on the idea of nature, which for some was a self-sufficient unity comprising all reality, and, for others, the visible world as the external manifestation of God's glory. Another point to be kept in mind when treating this group of thinkers is the difficulty in deciding whether a given author spoke strictly as a philosopher or merely as a scientist. As has been observed, a number of philosophers of the time were interested in science and in scientific investigation, while many scientists were not at all averse to philosophical speculation.[20] It is necessary, therefore, to study each

individual thinker separately and view his thought in the whole context of his works, as well as in the cultural setting that led to its
formation. This will be done in the present section, where attention
is given to three main figures of the naturalistic movement who, besides being contemporaries of Campanella, contributed either directly
or indirectly to the shaping of his thought.

The first and certainly most influential man in this respect was
Bernardino Telesio (1509-1588) of Cosenza, in Calabria, the author
of *De rerum natura iuxta propria principia* in nine books (1586), and
of several other short works collected and published in 1590 by his
disciple Antonio Persio under the title *Varii de naturalibus rebus
libelli*. Telesio studied philosophy at the University of Padua, where
he became acquainted with the teaching of Aristotle and with the
two main Aristotelian schools, the Averroist and the Alexandrist.
Following contemporary interests, he devoted himself especially to the
study of nature, but, far from accepting the Aristotelian doctrine, he
reacted vigorously against it. He proposed to interpret nature following the lead of the senses, rather than to attempt to explain it through
the "abstract and preconceived ideas" of the Aristotelians. Nature
must be studied in itself and in its own principles, which are matter
and the two active forces of heat and cold. Matter is the passive, inert
substratum of all physical changes; it is substantially the same everywhere. Unlike the Aristotelian prime matter which is pure potency,
it is concrete and actual, so that it can be seen and felt by the senses.
Heat and cold are the two opposing forces responsible for all natural
events and are represented by heaven and earth, respectively. Heat is
also the source of life in plants and animals, as well as the cause of
the biological operations and of some of the lower psychological functions in man. The whole of nature is animated and endowed with
sensation in varying degrees *(panpsychism)*. In addition to the vital
principle, there is present in man and animals the "spirit," a very
subtle material substance that emanates from the warm element and
is generated with the body. The spirit is properly located in the brain
and has the function of receiving and anticipating sense impressions.
It has both an appetitive and an intellective power of its own which
correspond to the sensitive appetite and the *vis cogitativa* or *aestimativa* of the Aristotelians.

Besides body and spirit man has a *mens* or *anima superaddita*,
which is created by God *(anima a Deo creata)* and informs both body
and spirit. This is roughly the spiritual soul of Platonic-Augustinian
tradition, whose operations transcend those of the spirit and reach out

to the divine. For, apart from the natural drive or instinct of self-preservation, which Telesio attributes to all beings including inorganic matter, man can also strive after union with God and contemplate the divine. This inner tendency of the *mens* and the need for proper sanctions in a future life are some of the arguments used by Telesio to prove the immortality of the soul, a doctrine that is known by revelation but can also be demonstrated with arguments from reason (*humanis etiam intelligere licet rationibus*).

Telesio does not give a formal treatment of the problem of God's existence, which is beyond the scope of his study, but incidentally criticizes Aristotle's argument from motion on the ground that movement is an intrinsic property of heat, the first active principle of material beings. Accordingly, there is no need for an extrinsic agent to set the bodies in motion. Besides, an immovable mover that sets the heavens in motion, as conceived by Aristotle, is a contradiction. The existence of God is better proved from the wonderful order of the universe, which can only be the work of a divine mind.

Telesio's thought, as revealed in this summary, is not strictly naturalistic if the term "naturalism" is taken to mean a purely materialistic approach to reality. Telesio does not deny the existence of spiritual substances, such as the soul and God. Furthermore, he admits in man an intellectual faculty and a rational appetite or will that transcend the sensitive level of the "spirit" and raise him to a superior order. He likewise acknowledges the existence in man of spiritual values, such as the virtues of the *mens,* among which wisdom occupies a prominent place inasmuch as it enables man to attain to the knowledge of God, his creator and his supreme beatitude. Yet, it must be admitted that in his *De rerum natura,* a pioneering work of unquestionable value, Telesio often discusses scientific problems with a philosophical method. The result is that his work is neither a scientific study nor a philosophical treatise, but a hybrid combination of science and philosophy not quite in agreement with the rigorous empirical method he professes to follow.[21]

This weakness in Telesio's system was pointed out by Francesco Patrizi (or Patrizzi), who was born at Cherso, in Dalmatia, in 1529. Like Telesio, he studied at the University of Padua, where he learned the peripatetic doctrine only later to turn against it. He favored instead Platonism, which he taught first at the University of Ferrara and then at Rome until his death in 1597. His main works are the *Discussiones peripateticae* in fifteen books (1571-81) and the *Nova de universis philosophia* in fifty books (Ferrara, 1591; Venice, 1593; Lon-

don, 1611), which he dedicated to Pope Gregory XIV. Patrizi's attacks
on Telesio are directed against his method as well as against some of
his doctrines. In his appraisal of the *De rerum natura* he says that
the author is not faithful to the experimental method he claims to
follow in the study of nature. Thus the work appears to be more of a
metaphysics than a treatise on physics *(magis metaphysica videtur
quam physica)*. Telesio's notion of matter as a universal substratum
of physical changes and the object of our senses is hard to grasp. If
sensible, matter must be physically determined; if undetermined, it
cannot be perceived by the sense. The conception of heat as the
principal cause of all natural events is likewise unacceptable, for it
does not account for the large variety of beings in nature. Moreover,
there seems to be no reason, observes Patrizi, why the same substantial
heat should produce from the same material substratum such diverse
parts as hair, skin, flesh, nerves, and bones in a mouse.

These and other similar objections do not prevent Patrizi from
sharing Telesio's anti-Aristotelian attitude in his *Discussiones peripateticae,* where he compares Aristotelianism with Platonism and
shows the superiority of the latter. After discrediting Aristotle both
as a person and a scholar, he engages in a relentless polemic that drew
upon him the sharpest and crudest criticism of Giordano Bruno.[22]

The destructive and somewhat negative character of the *Discussiones peripateticae* is counterbalanced by Patrizi's bulky work *Nova
de universis philosophia,* where he opposes to Aristotle's theory his
own conception of nature based on Platonic and neo-Platonic principles. For this reason many historians place Patrizi among the Platonists rather than among the naturalistic philosophers. The work is
divided into four parts, each one covering one aspect of Patrizi's
philosophy. They are the *Panaugia* or treatise on light; the *Panarchia*
or treatise on God as the first principle; the *Panpsychia,* which discusses living beings and man; and finally, the *Pancosmia,* a treatise on
the corporeal world. Characteristic of Patrizi's approach to nature is
his doctrine on light, which goes back ultimately to Platonic and neo-
Platonic tradition. In his view, throughout the entire universe there
is spread a visible light that proceeds from God and is the active and
formative principle in nature. This light is neither corporeal nor incorporeal, but something intermediary between the two orders of
being. It is most simple, and while not composed of matter and form,
it is both matter and form. It is infinite, as are the space which it fills
up and the world that occupies the space. Patrizi's description of space
as an incorporeal body is even more confusing than his notion of light.

Besides light and space, Patrizi admits two other principles in the constitution of the world, warmth and fluidity (fluor). The four principles permeate all beings in nature.

One cannot fail to notice that Patrizi's conception of nature is not free from that strange mixture of physics and metaphysics which he condemns so strongly in Telesio. To confine ourselves to the last point of our discussion, it appears that light is both a material and metaphysical principle, since it emanates from God, the most pure spirit, and at the same time it is not something really distinct from visible natural light.[23] This confusion of the material and spiritual found in Patrizi is even more evident in Giordano Bruno, the third and last exponent of the naturalistic movement that we propose to consider.

One of the best known thinkers of the Italian Renaissance, Bruno had much in common with Tommaso Campanella. Born at Nola, near Naples, in 1548, he entered the Dominican order at an early age. Intolerant of religious discipline and dissatisfied with scholastic teaching, he left the order and began to wander through Italy and other parts of Europe. Upon his return to Italy in 1591, he was denounced by John Mocenigo, a Venetian nobleman, who had invited him to Venice, where he was arrested by the Inquisition on charges of heresy. He was then sent to Rome and imprisoned by the Holy Office for eight years. Because of persistent refusals to retract his theological errors, he was handed over to the court of the Roman governor and, in accordance with the law of the time that considered heresy a social crime, he was burnt at the stake in 1600.

Bruno left many writings, some in Italian and some in Latin. Among the Italian works, written in dialogue form, the following may be mentioned: *La cena delle ceneri* (1584), *De la causa, principio e uno* (1584), *De l'infinito, universo e mondi* (1584), *Spaccio della bestia trionfante* (1584), and *Degli eroici furori* (1585). The Latin works include *De umbris idearum* (1582), *De minimo* (1591), *De monade* (1591), and *De immenso et innumerabilibus* (1591).

Bruno's philosophy is characterized by a marked tendency toward neo-Platonism and by a new approach to nature inspired by the heliocentric theory of Copernicus. Cosmology plays a chief role in his system. He conceives the universe as infinite and made up of infinite worlds, the celestial bodies, all animated by one infinite power, nature, "the living mirror of the infinite deity." Because of its infinity, the universe does not have a fixed center or a circumference. Every point may be considered as a center, while a circumference is only possible in a finite universe, which for Bruno is a contradiction. An infinite power can only produce an infinite effect. The universe, which proceeds from God and is His expression, must be one and infinite like God himself.

Bruno is convinced that he has destroyed the Aristotelian notion of a finite universe moved by a first, unmovable mover. The world and the celestial bodies possess an intrinsic power that moves them in the same way that the soul moves our body. This universal power or world soul is endowed with an equally universal intellect, which is "the artificer of the world" and its "universal form." Matter, the other constitutive principle of the universe, is also universal, for from it all things are made and formed. It is not Aristotelian prime matter, a formless and potential substratum, but rather the receptacle and fountainhead of all forms; ultimately, it is pure act. Yet, as has been observed,[24] matter and form are not for Bruno two distinct substances, but only two aspects of a unique substance or nature which is universal and infinite. His is a monistic doctrine that will greatly influence, if not Spinoza, certainly many other philosophers from the seventeenth century to the present time.

The relationship between God and the world is not clear in Bruno's philosophy. Although in *De la causa, principio e uno* he affirms God's transcendence and incomprehensibility and the creation of things distinct from Him, he seems to be primarily concerned with the principles and causes in the world and the idea of a world soul as an immanent causal agent. In *De l'infinito, universo e mondi* he makes a distinction between God as *totally* infinite and the universe as an infinite *whole*. God is totally infinite because He is wholly in the whole world and infinitely and totally in each of its parts; the universe is an infinite whole because it has no limit or surface, but each part of it is finite, just as each of the innumerable worlds that it contains is finite. However, according to Bruno's own observation, one can hardly speak of parts in relation to an infinite world. Finite things are rather accidents that surround the one infinite substance. God, he states elsewhere, is called *natura naturans* insofar as He is the principle and active source of all things; He is called *natura naturata* when considered in His self-manifestation in the totality of things.

Bruno does not present a single view of the universe and the relationship between God and the world. While the general trend of his thought is in the direction of monism, he does not discard pluralism altogether. Thus in his *De minimo* he speaks, in anticipation of Leibniz, of the world as a composite of an infinite number of units or "monads," which he conceives on the mathematical, physical, and metaphysical planes and as inclusive of the human souls. Moreover, like many of his contemporaries, he seems to accept the principle of a twofold truth. As a philosopher, he can discuss nature in itself and its principles; as a believer, he retains the doctrine of a transcendent God. Hence it is not correct to label Bruno's system as outright pantheism. His philosophy admits of more than one interpretation.[25]

6. *The Political Thought of Machiavelli.* An important phase of Renaissance thought was the new political theory that developed in Italy as a result of the writings of Niccolò Machiavelli (1469-1527), the famed Florentine Secretary who has been called the founder of modern political science. Because of his deep interest in politics, Campanella could not remain indifferent to the new ideas advanced by Machiavelli, whom he often attacks vigorously in his writings. A thorough understanding of Campanella's political philosophy makes it necessary, therefore, to analyze the basic principles suggested by Machiavelli in his two main political works, *The Prince* (1513) and the *Discourses on the First Ten Books of Titus Livius* (1513-21).

The Prince is dedicated to Lorenzo de' Medici, Duke of Urbino, and contains advice to rulers on how to be successful in winning and retaining power. The *Discourses* is a broader work and deals with problems common to principalities and republics. Because of the different treatment of government in the two works, the former being concerned with monarchies and the latter with republics, it may be thought that their author contradicts himself. But this is not the case. Both books, as has been observed,[26] present aspects of the same subject: the causes of the rise and decline of states and the means by which statesmen can make them permanent. Both books are in substantial agreement that immoral means can be used for political purposes and that force and craft are at the basis of successful government. But, whereas *The Prince* depicts an absolute monarchy as the only form of government that under the circumstances could save Italy from the oppression of the foreign powers and bring about its unification, the *Discourses* makes it clear that a popular republic, molded upon the early Roman Republic, is the author's preferred form of government.

Machiavelli was not a political philosopher and did not pretend to write a political treatise. He was a diplomat who was more concerned with the mechanics of government and the practical means by which states may be preserved and strengthened than with moral and political principles. Throughout his writings the assumption is implicit that politics is an end in itself and that no other consideration should pre-

vail against what he calls "ragion di stato," which may be freely translated as "political expediency." A ruler, Machiavelli suggests, must be
guided in his decisions solely by practical consequences, which is but
another way of saying that in politics what counts is success, no matter
how this is achieved. This is the famous Machiavellian principle that
the end justifies the means.

Machiavelli was perfectly aware that a morally degraded nation is
doomed to destruction and lamented the moral condition of Italy at
the time of his writing. Thus it would be wrong to interpret his teaching as favoring corruption and immorality among the people. Nevertheless he seems to admit a double standard of morality, one for the
ruler and another for the private citizen. This is not because, ideally
speaking, a good ruler is not to be preferred to a ruthless and un-
scrupulous one; but because the wickedness and selfishness of men
make it impossible for a ruler who wants to preserve his power to be
good and virtuous. Hence Machiavelli's cynical advice to the prince:
"He need never hesitate to incur the reproach of those vices without
which his authority can hardly be preserved. For if he well considers
the whole matter, he will find that there may be a line of conduct having the appearance of virtue, to follow which would be his ruin, and
that there may be another course having the appearance of vice, by
following which his safety and well-being are secured."[27]

Yet, in Machiavelli's view, a prince should try to win the love of his
subjects by simulating virtue even if he does not actually possess it.
But if situations arise in which a choice has to be made between being
loved and being feared, the latter course must be chosen. "Since love
and fear can hardly exist together, if we must choose between them,
it is far safer to be feared than loved."[28]

A prince, to be successful, must know how to mingle the fox's cunning with the lion's strength, that is, he must have the ability to avoid
traps and the capacity to fight enemies. It is true that success in politics
does not depend entirely on one's craft and power (virtù); a great deal
is also due to luck (fortuna), the aggregate of those events and circumstances that do not depend on man's free will. However, fortuna can
be resisted, or at least her damage can be prevented by man's organized
power and strength. For fortuna is like a wild torrent that "displays
her might where there is no organized strength to resist her, and
directs her onset where she knows that there is neither barrier nor
embankment to confine her."[29] Fortuna is also likened by Machiavelli
to a woman "who to be kept under must be beaten and roughly
handled," for "she suffers herself to be more readily mastered by those

who so treat her than by those who are timid in their approaches."[30]
Thus, for Machiavelli, show of power and strength of character best
qualify a good and successful ruler. This same conception prompts
him to praise in the *Discourses* the religion of antiquity for its emphasis on building up these qualities; while the Christian religion, by
laying stress on humility and contempt of the world, renders men
weak and effeminate.[31]

Such are the basic principles of Machiavelli's political theory. The
theory may be new, but its practice is as old as political society itself.
It has been said that, more than any other political thinker, Machiavelli created the meaning that has been attached to the state in modern political usage.[32] This may be true; but the fact remains that
"Machiavellism" has become synonymous with treachery, intrigue,
subterfuge, and tyranny. Campanella, as we shall see, did not think
otherwise of his renowned contemporary.[33]

With Machiavelli we conclude our survey of Italian Renaissance
thought. This account of the main philosophical trends that characterized the period is brief and incomplete but sufficient to show the
cultural climate of the time in which Campanella lived. It also enables
us to judge the influence that his contemporaries and his immediate
predecessors may have exerted upon him. Its relevance will become
more evident as we investigate Campanella's life and thought.

CHAPTER TWO

Tommaso Campanella and His Historical Position

I. LIFE AND WORKS

"I live as I write," said Tommaso Campanella in a letter written from his French exile to Cardinal Antonio Barberini,[1] meaning that his thought and his life are inseparable. Yet, if we except a few autobiographical notes and a chronological report on his writings up to 1632,[2] his works throw little light on events in his life. Hence an account of Campanella's career must be constructed from other sources.

Among his biographers the first in order of time is Ernest S. Cyprianus, whose work contains a certain amount of information but is not exempt from prejudice and arbitrary interpretations.[3] More objective is the life of Campanella written by his Dominican confrere, James Echard, included in *Scriptores Ordinis Praedicatorum*.[4] His list of Campanella's published works and manuscripts is particularly valuable and for more than a century and a half constituted the best reference source for Campanellian bibliography. It remained for Michele Baldacchini to give a more critical and systematic account of Campanella's life and thought. He refutes various unjustified attacks and corrects false judgments that had been passed on by earlier writers.[5]

In 1844 Mme Louise Colet published a selection of Campanella's works, preceded by an extensive introduction on their author.[6] She writes: "Our generation should not be indifferent to the writings of this generous man, who two hundred years ago had a presentiment of those truths which, although obscure at that time, afterward became very radiant and were transformed into beliefs for all the noble intelligences of our epoch."[7] A much longer and by far much more important study of Campanella's life and doctrines is that of Alessandro D'Ancona,[8] whose interpretation was severely criticized by Bertrando Spaventa.[9] Domenico Berti should also be mentioned in this connection, since he made public for the first time some of Campanella's letters and other writings and composed a new catalogue of Campanellian works.[10]

Campanellian studies had progressed thus far when Luigi Amabile, a physician and professor, gave up his profession and academic

23

career in order to devote himself exclusively to the study of Campanella's life and activities. The results of his studies are five large volumes which, in spite of their shortcomings, are still the basic and indispensable source of biographical information on Campanella.[11] In addition to Amabile's works, lesser but very important contributions have been made toward a better understanding of Campanella. Chief among them are the works of Jan Kvačala,[12] Enrico Carusi,[13] Rodolfo De Mattei,[14] and Luigi Firpo.[15] For a more comprehensive view the monograph of Léon Blanchet,[16] that of Cecilia Dentice D'Accadia,[17] and more recently the excellent works of Giovanni Di Napoli[18] and Romano Amerio,[19] both written in 1947, are all valuable. Campanellian bibliography has been accurately presented by Luigi Firpo, whose studies are authoritative.[20] It is on the basis of the foregoing sources that the life and literary activity of Campanella will be described in the pages to follow.

Tommaso Campanella was born at Stilo, in Calabria, on September 5, 1568, and was baptized Giovanni Domenico. His father, Geronimo, was a shoemaker, and his mother was Caterina Martello. At a very early age he showed remarkable mental powers. His memory was particularly good. When he was only five years old, he could remember everything he had been told by his parents or had heard from the priests in church. At the age of thirteen he had already mastered all the Latin authors available to him, both poets and prose writers.[21]

Attracted by the preaching of a Dominican friar and by reading the lives of St. Albert the Great and St. Thomas Aquinas, he entered the Dominican order in 1582. Having completed his novitiate, he was sent to the monastery of San Giorgio Morgeto for the study of philosophy, which at the time was limited mainly to the teaching of Aristotle, especially his logic, physics, metaphysics, and *De anima*. While at San Giorgio, he transcribed in the light of his own thought the lectures of his professors;[22] but unfortunately these *Lectiones logicae, physicae et animasticae,* which are his first philosophical writing, are lost. Not satisfied with Aristotelian philosophy, he devoted himself to writing poetry, for which he had a special talent.[23]

Following a reorganization of studies in the Dominican order, Campanella was transferred to Nicastro in 1586. There he became even more discontented with the doctrines of Aristotle and with his own teachers with whom he was constantly arguing.[24] His professors began to dislike him because of the boldness of his remarks and also because of his determination to read all available books of ancient philosophers, and the encouragement he gave to his classmates to do the same.[25] It is at this time, or perhaps before, that one night he burst into tears at the thought of the weakness of the proofs for the immortality of the soul.[26]

In 1588 Campanella was sent from Nicastro to the theological house of studies at Cosenza, where a friend gave him the first two books of *De rerum natura iuxta propria principia* by Bernardino Telesio.[27] This was a happy discovery, for at the time he was anxiously searching for truth, which he had hoped to find in the study of nature rather than in what he considered purely abstract notions. In Telesio he had finally met a thinker who shared his own views on science and philosophy, and could possibly become his leader.[28] He began to read the work with the utmost interest and joy and found it to be in perfect agreement with his own principles. So consistent was it, he claimed, that after reading the first chapter, he already understood the content of succeeding chapters even before actually going through them.[29] Telesio's freedom of expression as well as his appeal to nature rather than to authority delighted him. He wanted to meet the well-known humanist immediately, but before he could do so Telesio died at the age of seventy-nine. Campanella was only able to see his body as it lay in state in the Cosenza cathedral and to compose a Latin elegy in his honor which he placed on the coffin.[30]

Campanella's interest in Telesio's philosophy, which he defended in both private and public debates, and apparently also his general behavior were a cause of great concern for his superiors, who decided to send him to a small rural monastery in Altomonte.[31] There he found himself surrounded by a group of friends who shared his enthusiasm for Telesio and who provided him with philosophical and medical books, from Plato to Galen and the Stoics, and from Democritus to Raymond Lully, which "he devoured rather than read."[32]

Eventually, his attention was drawn to a new work written by an Aristotelian against Telesio. It was the *Pugnaculum Aristotelis adversus principia B. Telesii* by Giacomo Antonio Marta.[33] As soon as he procured the book and read it, he became so indignant at its author[34] that he decided immediately to write a refutation of it and vindicate Telesio, "the prince of philosophers,"[35] from the attacks of his adversaries. Hence, on the first day of January 1589, at the age of twenty-one, he began to write the *Philosophia sensibus demonstrata*,[36] which he finished in the following August, "destroying in seven months what had cost seven years of sweat" to the composer of the *Pugnaculum*.[37] In his work Campanella makes use of various argu-

ments to discredit Aristotle, whom he calls "impious" and "extremely
ignorant," because of his denial of the doctrines of creation, God's
omnipotence, providence, and freedom.[38] Furthermore, he claims,
Aristotle contradicts himself in his philosophy of nature and refuses
to admit the doctrine of the immortality of the soul which he had
learned from Plato. As far as his personal conduct is concerned, Aristotle was ungrateful, cruel, and lascivious.[39] Pure Peripatetics, Campanella goes on to say, are heretics, whereas Telesio is a Christian philosopher who can be followed.[40]

The freedom and boldness of these attacks upon the traditional
peripatetic school as well as upon the established authority of his
order, an alleged association with a Jewish rabbi named Abraham,[41]
and a suspicion that he was practicing magical arts made his life in
the monastery impossible. He therefore resolved to leave Altomonte
and go to Naples. There he found hospitality with the Del Tufo
family.

Campanella's residence in Naples was far from being fruitless. He
completed the De investigatione rerum, which he had started a few
years before;[42] wrote the De sensu rerum et magia, occasioned by his
discussions with Giambattista Della Porta, the author of the famous
Physiognomia;[43] published the Philosophia sensibus demonstrata (at
the beginning of 1591); set about drawing up the outline of a new
metaphysics;[44] composed some other small treatises; and, finally,
compiled the first of a projected series of twenty books on the philosophy of nature to be entitled De rerum universitate.[45] In May, 1592,
while in the midst of this intense activity, Campanella was denounced
by one of his confreres. He had to stand trial before a tribunal of
Dominican friars set up by the Minister Provincial and was temp-
orarily imprisoned in the monastery of St. Dominic in Naples.

The charges against Campanella are not clear. If we are to believe
the dedicatory letter of his Atheismus triumphatus, he was suspected
of being possessed by evil spirits because of his extraordinary knowledge. In answer to this accusation, he told his judges that he had used
more oil than they had wine, and that when he was ordained a deacon
he was told, "Receive the Holy Ghost," who teaches all things. Of
this, he added, we can be sure on St. John the Evangelist's word; as
to his being possessed by the devil, no proof could be brought forth.[46]
Whatever may have been the real reason for his denunciation and
imprisonment, it was known for certain that in his ardent desire for
knowledge of occult sciences, Campanella frequented in Naples the
circle of Della Porta, who was believed to be in communication with

evil spirits. This fact, along with his preference for Telesio's teaching over the traditional Thomistic doctrines of the Dominican order, and his departure from religious discipline by living outside the monastery in a private house, constituted sufficient grounds for his denunciation. That these were the main points of accusation against Campanella can be deduced from the sentence issued by the Dominican Provincial at Naples on August 28, 1592, in which he ordered the fugitive friar to return to his province of Calabria within eight days, to reject Telesio and accept St. Thomas, and to do some penitential work as a punishment for his unlawful dwelling in secular houses.[47]

In spite of the Provincial's command, Campanella did not return to Calabria but went to Rome. He next went from Rome to Florence, in the hope of obtaining from the Grand Duke Ferdinand I a professorship in philosophy either at Pisa or at Siena. Disappointed in his expectations, he set out for Padua and Venice, where he planned to publish his books. On his way to those cities he made a short stop at Bologna, where certain "false friars" robbed him of all his manuscripts, including the *De sensu rerum et magia*.[48]

At Padua, in 1593, Campanella made friends with Galileo and other learned men at the University. Having successfully defended himself against a charge of immorality,[49] he had a year of relative peace and worked hard on the composition of the *Nova Physiologia iuxta propria principia*, the *Apologia pro Telesio*, the *Rhetorica nova*,[50] the *De monarchia Christianorum*, the *Discorsi ai Principi d'Italia*, and the *De regimine Ecclesiae*.[51] He had scarcely finished these works when early in 1594 all his manuscripts were seized, and he was arraigned before the Holy Office in Padua. The charges were that he had discussed matters of faith with a Jewish sympathizer, that he was the author of the book *De tribus impostoribus* (Moses, Christ, and Mohammed), that he accepted the philosophy of Democritus, and finally, that he had been critical of the constitution and doctrine of the Church.[52] He had therefore to stand a trial. It was easy for him to defend himself against the charge of being the author of the infamous work *De tribus impostoribus*, since the book had been written thirty years before he was born. Likewise it was not difficult to reject the accusation of being a follower of Democritus: he simply called the attention of the judges to his various writings in which he attacked Democritus' atomistic theories. However, he did not succeed in freeing himself entirely of the other charges, and the case was referred to the Holy Office in Rome, where he was taken with two other accused men.

During his trial and imprisonment Campanella was subjected twice to physical torture.[53] Nevertheless, his difficulties did not prevent him from writing new works in an effort to defend himself and to explain his ideas in the various fields of his concern. Among these works are the *Physiologia compendiosa* (1594), the *Ars versificatoria* (1594), and the *Defensio Telesianorum* (1595), in which he defends his doctrines of the *De sensu rerum et magia*. All these works have been lost. In addition he wrote the *Compendium de rerum natura* (1595) and part of the *Epilogo magno* (1595).[54] Toward the end of 1596, sentence was passed and he was condemned to make a public abjuration in the church of *S. Maria sopra Minerva* because of the strong suspicion of heresy held against him (*de vehementi haeresis suspicione*). After his release from prison, he was confined to the monastery of St. Sabina, where he wrote the *Dialogo contro luterani, calvinisti ed altri eretici,* the *Poetica,* and other works.[55]

On March 5, 1597, a fellow countryman who was about to be hanged at Naples, brought a new charge of heresy against Campanella. Again thrown into jail, he remained there until December 17 and was released only on the condition that his superiors would confine him to some monastery. They decided to send him back to Calabria. On August 15, 1598, after he had finished the *Epilogo magno* during a prolonged stay in Naples, Campanella returned to the monastery of his native town of Stilo. There he wrote the *Quaestiones contra Molinam,* in which he defends the Thomistic position against the Jesuits in the famous controversy on the doctrine of grace. Whether the *Monarchia di Spagna* should also be assigned to this period is a point of discussion among his biographers.[56]

Campanella's restless spirit could not find peace in the quiet of a monastery. The social, political, and religious upheavals of the time, the sudden occurrence of floods, earthquakes, and other natural disturbances, as well as the supposed appearance of ominous signs in the sky and his belief in astrology and prophecies, convinced him that the time for great changes in the world was near at hand. A reform was necessary. He was to be preacher of this reform, and this would lead to a universal republic under the leadership of the Pope. To effect this politico-religious reform, Spanish rule in Naples and Calabria had to be ended. Campanella did not keep these ideas to himself but began to preach them publicly, although it is not clear whether he really meant to start a revolution or form a conspiracy against the Spanish government.[57] On September 6, 1599, upon denunciation by Fabio di Lauri and Giambattista Biblia and betrayal by a man who had given him hospitality during his flight from the monastery, he was arrested, taken to Naples in chains, together with other friars and over a hundred laymen, and committed to prison under the double charge of heresy and conspiracy.

Campanella had to stand one trial after another. The hatred and threats of the judges helped to extort false confessions from witnesses. A jurisdictional dispute arose between the Holy See and the Spanish authorities and made the case even more complicated. Four times he was subjected to physical torture. On the first two occasions, on February 7 and 8, 1600, he yielded to the torture and admitted that he had preached on coming political upheavals, but rejected charges of rebellion or conspiracy.[58] The third time, on May 18, 1600, under torture by rope, he uttered some incoherent sentences accompanied by strange gestures but did not confess to heresy.[59] Finally, between June 4 and 5, 1601, he was subjected for thirty-six straight hours to the terrible torture called "la veglia," which was considered at that time as the last means of obtaining a confession from criminals.[60] Even in such horrible pain Campanella did not give in or confess to any crime or heresy. He feigned madness, as he had already done since April 2 of the preceding year when he set fire to the mattress of his bed and began to act in a strange way, and was declared insane. This device, along with his extraordinary strength of will, probably saved him from the death penalty. Later he would use the experience to prove the freedom of human will.[61] On November 13, 1602, the Holy Office pronounced Campanella's sentence of imprisonment with the clause "with no hope for liberation." On January 8, 1603, the sentence was read to him. He had stopped feigning madness in June of the year before.[62]

Whether justly or not, the unfortunate philosopher was kept in prison at Naples for almost twenty-seven years (1599-1626) and suffered great misery. Yet his spirit was unbroken, and he fought continuously for his freedom by writing letters and appeals to the Pope, to cardinals, and to anyone who could possibly be of help to him. He was convinced that his detention in prison prevented him from carrying out a universal reform, which he promised to accomplish as soon as he was set free. While he was thus working for his freedom, he composed sonnets and prepared a series of philosophical, theological, and political works that reveal the powers of his fertile mind and his extraordinary strength of will. It must be remembered that Campanella was working under the most unfavorable and discouraging circumstances. He had no books to read or consult, and his only source of information was his prodigious memory, a real storehouse of knowledge. Often he had to write the same works several times, either in Latin or in Italian, as previous copies had disappeared or had been taken away from him. Worst of all, the physical and moral sufferings of his confinement were far from conducive to that peace of mind which is indispensable for any serious intellectual work.

The results of his literary activity in the Neapolitan prison of Castel Nuovo up to July 1604 are the *Aforismi politici* (1601), which he considers as the basis of a new political science;[63] the famous *Città del Sole* (1602), a dialogue on the lines of Plato's *Republic* and St. Thomas More's *Utopia,* in which he describes an ideal state for citizens guided only by the light of reason;[64] the treatise *De astronomia* (1604), and his most important work, the *Metaphysica,* in fifteen books, to which three books were added later. There are five known drafts of the *Metaphysica,* some in Italian and others in Latin.[65]

Having failed in an attempt to escape from the prison in July, 1604, Campanella was transferred to the dungeon of Castel Sant'Elmo. Living conditions there were almost unbearable. The cell was dark and damp and the food very scarce. Campanella used to compare himself to Prometheus bound to Mount Caucasus[66] and called his life worse than a thousand deaths.[67] During these four terrible years at Castel Sant'Elmo he went through a spiritual crisis which, through the providential assistance of his adviser and confessor, Don Basilio Berillario,[68] ended in a sincere repentance for his past mistakes.[69] The *Monarchia del Messia* (1605) and the *Atheismus triumphatus* (1605-1607)[70] are, among others, works written during this period of his life.

In April, 1608, Campanella was removed from the dungeon and was transferred to better quarters in Castel dell'Uovo. Taking advantage of his new situation, he devoted himself to more writing, translated into Latin certain of his Italian works, rewrote some of the others, and composed the *Medicina* (1609-1613), the *De gentilismo non retinendo* (1609),[71] and the *Historiographia* (1612). He also began in 1613 one of his largest works, the *Theologia,* in thirty books,[72] and wrote a substantial part of the first six books of the *Astrologicorum libri 7.*[73]

Meanwhile new suspicions arose concerning Campanella on account of his many outside contacts. As a result, in October, 1614, he was again thrown into the dungeon and kept there in strict confinement, except for a short period of time, until May, 1618, when he was sent to Castel Nuovo, the least severe of the Neapolitan prisons. In the meantime, having read Galileo's *Sidereus Nuncius* and written a very favorable letter to its author as soon as the work appeared,[74] he undertook to defend him in his *Apologia pro Galilaeo* (1616).[75] Another important book written about this time is the *Quod reminiscentur,* which he dedicated first to Pope Paul V, then to Pope Gregory XV, and finally, to Pope Urban VIII.[76] The book is a message to the representatives of the four great religions, the Christian, the Jewish, the Gentile, and the Mohammedan, to remind them that the peoples of all nations should be converted to Christ and be united into one fold under one shepherd.[77]

In Castel Nuovo, Campanella was allowed considerable freedom. There seem, indeed, to have been great doubts even in the minds of those who had imprisoned him that he had done anything deserving such long punishment, for neither heresy nor treason had ever been definitely proved against him. In spite of his spiritual conversion, he was still looked upon as dangerous and therefore kept in custody.

Campanella's eight years in Castel Nuovo were spent in revising and developing his earlier works, as well as in writing new ones. However, his main activity consisted in taking all possible steps to bring about his liberation. Through the help of certain cardinals and upon the request of the Dominican Fathers of the Calabrian province, the Spanish authorities finally released him on May 23, 1626, and allowed him to live with the friars in the Neapolitan monastery of St. Dominic.

His liberty did not last long. By order of the Apostolic Nuncio, he was arrested in the following month and was ordered to stand trial before the ecclesiastical tribunal in Rome, where he was imprisoned in the palace of the Holy Office. Obliged to defend himself against eighty suspected propositions that were found in his *De sensu rerum et magia* and *Atheismus triumphatus,* he apparently went through the trial without too much difficulty. However, not being completely satisfied with his oral defense, he wrote the *Defensio libri sui De sensu rerum* in 92 pages (1627). In it he develops arguments from science, philosophy, and theology in defense of his doctrine of universal sensation in created things.[78]

It was part of Campanella's character to have an opinion on every subject, and he did not fail to take part also in the great controversy between the Dominicans and the Jesuits on the doctrine of grace. His contribution was the treatise *De praedestinatione et reprobatione et auxiliis divinae gratiae* (1627-28),[79] in which he attempts to offer a compromise between the two diverging opinions but actually favors the Jesuit position. The book was not well received in his order, and when he obtained permission to leave the Holy Office and stay in the monastery of *S. Maria sopra Minerva,* first as a prisoner (July 27, 1628) and then as a completely free man (January 11, 1629), many fiery discussions arose between him and his confreres, especially Father Niccolò Riccardi, Master of the Sacred Palace.[80] In answer to Father Riccardi's accusations, Campanella selected sixty-four propositions from a devotional book that Riccardi himself had published some time before and denounced them as heretical to Pope Urban VIII. The result was that the Pope himself, who had been sympathetic to him, became disgusted with the imprudent friar.

At this point, one of Campanella's former disciples, Fra Tommaso Pignatelli, was arrested and imprisoned in Naples on a charge of conspiracy,[81] and suspicion immediately fell upon Campanella as being involved in the same crime. Recognizing the danger of his situation, and profiting from experience and the advice of the Pope, he fled from Rome. Disguised as a Friar Minimite and passing under a false name, he left Rome on the night of October 21, 1634. Sailing from Leghorn, he arrived at Marseilles toward the end of the same month. From Marseilles he proceeded to Aix and Lyons, and finally Paris, where he arrived on December 1, 1634, and was received with marked favor by Cardinal Richelieu.

Campanella spent the last years of his troubled life in working for the conversion of Protestants and preparing the edition of certain of his works, such as the *Philosophia realis* (1637), the *Philosophia rationalis* (1638), and the *Metaphysica* (1638). Taking advantage of royal favor, he tried to influence French politics by means of an anti-Spanish campaign. This action only served to revive the opposition of Church leaders and his own order against him.

From his exile Campanella wrote on December 4, 1634, to Cardinal Francesco Barberini: "I shall try to end all my miseries in peace."[82] His desire was not entirely fulfilled, for he fought till the end against what he considered an unjust persecution. When he realized that his last hour was approaching, he made a desperate attempt to prolong his life by having recourse to the astrological practices that he had described in his treatise *De fato siderali vitando.*[83] The stars failed to come to his help. On May 21, 1639, after receiving the last sacraments "with the greatest piety,"[84] the seventy-one-year-old friar died in the quiet of the Dominican monastery on the Rue St. Honoré in Paris, surrounded by the sympathy and affection of his confreres. He was buried the following day in the Dominican cemetery. His remains were lost during the French Revolution.

II. CAMPANELLA'S PERSONALITY AND THOUGHT IN
THE LIGHT OF HISTORY

The first impression that the reader receives from Campanella's life is that he was both a very interesting and a very complex figure of the late Italian Renaissance. Such an impression is confirmed by the study of his thought, which will be the object of the following chapters. In this section the writer intends to make a brief survey of the judgments passed on Campanella in the course of history and point out the main interpretations of his thought. But first let us outline the principal traits of his personality.

1. *Personality*. As far as physical traits are concerned, Campanella is said to have been a tall man with a very strong body. His large head was divided, as it were, into seven segments; hence the nickname of "Settimontana Squilla," or "Seven-hilled Bell," that he gave to himself by playing on the shape of his head and his family name. As a matter of fact, he considered himself the announcer and forerunner of a new age. Luigi Amabile has said that Campanella's head would have been an interesting object of study for a phrenologist,[85] and, it may be added, for a more serious scientist as well. He had shaggy hair, his eyes were chestnut-brown and very sharp, and he had a powerful voice.[86]

Campanella possessed a brilliant mind and a knowledge of many subjects. He himself tells us in various passages of his works that he studied all the philosophers—ancient, medieval, and contemporary. He examined the laws and customs of all peoples, including Hebrews, Turks, Persians, Moors, Chinese, Japanese, and Mexicans. Furthermore, he delved into all the sciences, both human and divine,[87] and read most of the classical Latin writers.[88] He had a great craving for knowledge; the more he read, the more he wanted to read.[89] What was even more amazing was his power to retain everything. Thus he was able to quote in his works authors he had come across in his reading by relying entirely on his prodigious memory. "When I read a book," he says, "I am so affected by its reading that the very words and content of it remain impressed into my memory almost indefinitely."[90] In addition, he had a powerful imagination, which was partly responsible for many of his troubles and miseries. He has been aptly compared to a volcano in continuous eruption.[91]

Campanella had a powerful will and was tenacious in pursuing his purposes, but, at the same time, he was exceedingly proud and stubborn. He was convinced of his mission as a reformer of society, religion, and the sciences. "Since my childhood," he wrote, "my aspirations have always been to reform the present century."[92] In one of his poems he boasted: "I was born to defeat the three greatest evils, tyranny, sophistry, and hypocrisy."[93] His opinion of his own philosophy will be seen later; meanwhile, it is worth noting that he really thought he had reformed the sciences. Appealing to the future centuries for a correct judgment, he proclaimed: "I have reformed all the sciences according to nature and Holy Scripture, the two divine codices. The centuries to come will judge us, for the present century always crucifies its benefactors. But they will rise again on the third day, or the third century."[94] Shortly before his death, he wrote to Cardinal Barberini: "The Church has no better defender than myself."[95] Campanella had an intense love for his native land and for the people of Calabria.[96] He likewise had an ardent zeal for the spreading of the kingdom of Christ, whom he calls the eternal reason.[97]

Campanella's fiery nature and spirit of insubordination are well known. Was he also insincere, as Amabile, Blanchet, and other writers seem to believe? Apparently not. In any event, it is unwarranted to interpret Campanella's thought, as some writers do, on the basis of a few scattered statements of doubtful meaning or of minor works like *The City of the Sun,* and to lose sight of much larger and much more important productions where his genuine thought is fully expressed.

2. *Judgments on Campanella.* More than a century ago Baldacchini remarked that the judgments passed on Campanella were so many and so varied that any attempt at harmonizing them was hopeless.[98] This statement holds true both for Campanella's life and for his thought. Scholars since Baldacchini's time have not yet reached a final interpretation of his work, although it must be admitted that many points of his doctrine have been clarified in recent years. Whatever the final word on Campanella may be, it is important to see how he was regarded by his contemporaries and by writers of the following centuries. Their judgments can help us to understand his personality and obtain a more realistic view of his philosophy. The opinions that follow are most representative, and a special effort has been made to present them as faithfully as possible.[99]

Among Campanella's contemporaries, Luigi Bresci, in the verses placed at the beginning of our philosopher's first work, the *Philosophia sensibus demonstrata,* published when he was only 23 years old (1591), states that Campanella had been Minerva's most favored man, for by his talents and abilities he surpassed all living persons.[100]

Giulio Battaglino, on September 4, 1592, writes as follows: "To judge from the books that I have seen and from his widespread reputation, I think that Campanella is one of the rarest geniuses of Italy. He is certainly a prodigy of nature to know all that he does at the age of 24. This is so true, that he has been suspected of having a familiar spirit with him."[101]

In 1609, Cesario Brancadoro speaks of Campanella in these terms: "With regard to this man, it seems that the demon of nature has tried to show how much a human genius can do. In him all fiery and most subtle powers are glowing and excel in the utmost degree."[102]

Tobias Adami, Campanella's close friend and the editor of many of his works, says that "he is to be admired for his genius and memory as well as for his powers of discernment."[103]

Another friend, Gabriel Naudé, in an epigrammatic description of our philosopher, asserts that "the man who surpasses all others by the sharpness of his mind also has an external appearance different from that of everyone else."[104]

To these judgments we might add those of many other contemporaries of Campanella. With very few exceptions, they recognize in him a superior mind with a vast amount of knowledge. However, many of them take issue with some of his doctrines, which they call fantastic, contrary to common sense, and even heretical.

Thus Gaspar Schopp, a German who took an active part in the publication of Campanella's works, puts this question to him: "How is it possible that you, who attribute common sense to all things, are yourself completely deprived of it?"[105]

Marin Mersenne, the well-known French philosopher and friend of Descartes, passes this severe sentence: "I think that the book *De sensu rerum et magia* and all others of the same kind should be burned and reduced to smoke."[106]

Samuel Sorbière, commenting on Campanella's *Atheismus triumphatus*, makes the following statement: "Although nothing is more precious to me than time, which I always hate to throw away, I confess that I wasted time and labor in reading the very unsatisfactory book called *Atheismus triumphatus*, written by the most inefficient and ignorant monk, Tommaso Campanella . . . From reading this book I learned only one thing, that if I wish to make good use of my time, I will never again read any work by the same author."[107]

An even more severe judgment is pronounced by Theophilus Raynaud, S.J. He writes: "Campanella is an extremely ignorant man, who does not even understand philosophical and theological terminology. . . In his books there are so many and such inexcusable crass heresies that one wonders how a dull writer like him could find in the past years someone to praise him."[108]

More objective is the statement of Cardinal Sforza Pallavicino, also a Jesuit, who gives in a few words the essential traits of the philosopher of Stilo: "A man who read everything, remembered everything, and had a very powerful mind, but was completely beyond control."[109]

When we pass from Campanella's contemporaries to later writers, we find much the same diversity of opinions about him, although a tendency toward a more objective attitude gradually becomes noticeable.

Despite prejudices against Campanella because of his strong defense of Catholicism, Ernest S. Cyprianus recognizes his genius and vast learning and classifies him among the most prominent sons of Calabria.[110] At the same time he presents him as something of an atheist who mocks the Christian religion.[111]

James Echard, a Dominican, defends his confrere from the accusations of the Protestant biographer. However, he does not approve of all Campanella's doctrines, especially those expounded in the *De sensu rerum et magia*.[112]

Pietro Giannone shows no sympathy for Campanella and speaks of him in the following terms: "[Campanella] wrote an infinite number of books . . . that show the vast extent of his knowledge and the variety of his doctrines, but indicate at the same time that he is a cheat, a strange character, and a restless and troubled spirit."[113]

Michele Baldacchini undertakes a defense of Campanella against what he calls Giannone's shameless attacks.[114] The same attitude is adopted by Colet,[115] and D'Ancona, whose work[116] gave Spaventa occasion for a sharp criticism and an interpretation of Campanella's thought that will be considered later.

To conclude this survey, we report statements made on Campanella's philosophy by four thinkers of worldwide reputation, not so much because of their intrinsic value but mainly because of the renown of their authors.

Leibniz classes Campanella with Francis Bacon. He then compares both men to Hobbes and Descartes who, he claims, merely follow the footsteps of the two earlier masters "who seem to raise themselves to the clouds and to reach what appears to be beyond human power."[117]

Hegel calls Campanella an Aristotelian and says that he is a mixture of all possible characters. He made a contribution to philosophy, Hegel goes on to say, by bringing up new problems, but did not produce anything of positive value.[118]

Victor Cousin writes that "the philosophical undertaking of Campanella was undoubtedly above his power; there was in him more ardor than solidity, more extensive than deep knowledge."[119]

Finally, Antonio Rosmini maintains that in the Campanellian system of philosophy, "whether true or false, everything is well united and closely connected. This harmony of parts and self-consistency in Campanella's system are due to its very simple origin, namely, Campanella's opinion on the origin of human knowledge."[120]

3. *Recent Interpretations of Campanella's Thought.* In our survey of the judgments passed on Campanella in the course of history we have reached the point where the Campanellian thought as a whole is made the object of a more serious consideration and is evaluated on the basis of a more extensive knowledge of the sources. Only from this vantage point can we really speak of an interpretation of Campanella's philosophy as such. What has been quoted so far consists in broad statements which are the result of easy generalizations and betray a superficial knowledge of Campanella's works. In most instances, the judgments passed have direct reference to his personality rather than to his works. Because of these considerations, instead of reviewing all the opinions on Campanella from the middle of the nineteenth century, which would be beyond the scope of the present survey, we shall group them under a few names, each representing a special way of interpreting Campanella's thought.

As previously stated, Alessandro D'Ancona wrote in defense of Campanella against the attacks of those who tried to discredit him by misrepresentation. D'Ancona reclaimed the philosopher of Stilo for the Catholic religion. There is nothing, he says, in his life or behavior that deserves the charge of conspiracy, and his teaching is far from being heretical. After a detailed exposition of Campanella's doctrine, D'Ancona concludes:

> We are now able to establish that at the summit of Campanella's edifice is God. . . He reveals himself to our intellect in two ways, namely, by the means of the ancient revelation contained in the sacred books, and by the means of the actual revelation, which is sensible nature. Man, who lies at the bottom of this high ladder, needs two instruments so that he can rise to, or at least approach as best he can, the first being. These two instruments are revelation and nature. The first rests on faith, which is incorporeal and rational; the other is the senses and sensible experience. . . Hence

one can see that at the basis of his system Campanella is not a sensualist, as some hold him to be. He himself states this explicitly when he says that the soul does not perceive *with* the organs, but *through* the organs *(non organis, sed per organa)*.[121]

D'Ancona's interpretation was shared later by the French scholar Charles Déjob[122] and, to a great extent, by other writers.

Bertrando Spaventa considers Campanella as one of the greatest Italian Renaissance philosophers,[123] but in contrast to D'Ancona he admits a double element in the Campanellian system, the element of the Middle Ages and the modern element, the supernatural and the immanentistic. Campanella, he writes, never succeeded in reconciling these two contradicting elements.

> In him, there is a man of the middle ages, the Dominican, the disciple of St. Thomas, and also a new man with new instincts and tendencies, who is always afraid to contradict the former. He constantly aims at reconciling this opposition that had already arisen before his time, and which is one of the main features of the emancipation of the spirit from the middle ages, namely, the opposition between the new science, especially the knowledge of nature, and the doctrines of the Church.[124]

Campanella, Spaventa goes on to say, is truly the philosopher of the Catholic restoration. However, his main contribution consists in an attempt to reconcile the old with the new, that is, the traditional scholastic philosophy with the new free thought.[125]

Spaventa's interpretation set a pattern for Francesco De Sanctis, who speaks of contradicting elements in the philosopher of Stilo,[126] and Francesco Fiorentino, who emphasizes in Campanella immanentistic and idealistic trends at the expense of traditional scholastic teaching.[127] A similar attitude can be noticed in varying degrees in Ernst Cassirer, who maintains that in Campanella one can find all the philosophical trends of the Renaissance;[128] in Giovanni Gentile, for whom Campanella is the most mature fruit of the Italian Renaissance[129] and to some extent the forerunner of modern idealism;[130] in Guido De Ruggiero, whose Campanella, although in some ways the philosopher of the Catholic restoration, is confusedly both the Descartes and the Locke of Italian philosophy;[131] and, more recently, in Giuseppe Saitta, whose presentation of Campanella is in decidedly idealistic terms.[132]

In his monumental works,[133] Luigi Amabile makes the conspiracy the central point of Campanella's life as well as the clue to the interpretation of his philosophy. In his opinion, Campanella tried to start a revolt in Calabria in order to establish a communistic republic on a purely deistic basis. The religious naturalism that inspired the attempted revolution also inspired his writings, particularly *The City of the Sun,* which embodies, as it were, all his philosophical and religious beliefs. *The City of the Sun* is claimed to be Campanella's principal work, and all other works have to be interpreted according to the doctrines contained in it. (In size, it must be remembered, *The City of the Sun* is less than a thousandth part of Campanella's literary production.) The so-called orthodox works, particularly those of the last period of his imprisonment, must have been written under external pressure and for purely pragmatic reasons. In other words, Campanella simulated orthodox ideas in order to regain his own freedom, while to the end of his life he held to his naturalistic and heretical doctrines.[134]

Amabile's fundamental conclusions were accepted by Giovanni Sante-Felici, who developed them and applied them to Campanella's religious doctrines.[135]

Amabile's "simulation theory," which prevailed in the field of Campanellian studies till the beginning of the present century, became less tenable as a better exploration of Campanella's biographical sources and a more careful examination of his doctrines were made. A French scholar, Léon Blanchet, replaced Amabile's theory with what has been called a theory of syncretism of naturalistic doctrines, as expressed in *The City of the Sun,* and the Catholic doctrines.[136] According to Blanchet, Campanella first had in mind a general reform inspired by motives contrary to the spirit and the tenets of the Catholic Church. However, because of the impossibility of realizing such a plan, he later tried to use the Church itself as an instrument for the establishment of the naturalistic republic of *The City of the Sun.*[137] In Blanchet's opinion, "the discrepancy in Campanella would no longer be between his thought and his words, as in Amabile's amphibological exegesis, but only between his thought and reality. The philosopher's sincerity would thus be saved, but the solidity of his doctrine is compromised."[138]

Blanchet's interpretation was expounded by Cecilia Dentice D'Accadia, who presents Campanella's philosophy as an attempt to reconcile his religious naturalism with Catholicism.[139] Francesco Olgiati also accepted substantially the position of Blanchet.[140]

In strong reaction against both Amabile and Blanchet, Romano Amerio proposes a new interpretation of Campanella's philosophy with the aid of the *Theologia* and the *Quod reminiscentur,* which he

studied in the original manuscripts. Amerio admits a gradual development in Campanella's thought from the naturalistic tendencies of
his earlier period to a real Christian philosophy of his later years.
The metanoia would have been determined by a spiritual crisis during
the years 1603 and 1606 from which a new man emerged. There are,
therefore, two different philosophies in Campanella, but not to the
extent that the one is a complete rejection of the other. The second
philosophy is rather the realization of the exigencies of the first philosophy in the light of new metaphysical and theological principles, such
as the doctrines of the primalities or first constituents of being, and
of Christ as universal reason. This explanation clarifies Campanella's
effort to justify the Catholic religion as the fulfilment of the exigencies
of natural religion, which in his mind does not mean the positive
content of religion but rather its "naturality" or rational character.[141]

Amerio's theory of a metanoia in Campanella's thought is shared by
another eminent Campanellian scholar, Luigi Firpo.[142]

A more recent interpretation is that offered by Giovanni Di Napoli,
in whose judgment Campanella is the greatest Italian philosopher of
the Renaissance.[143] He agrees with Amerio in many fundamental
points, but refuses to admit a philosophical metanoia, and consequently a double philosophy, in Campanella. Di Napoli agrees with
certain other interpreters in recognizing the unity and continuity of
Campanella's thought and work, but he parts company with them
over the real meaning of the formative principle of this unity. Whereas
some scholars speak of a naturalistic and deistic philosophy, Di Napoli
states in very clear terms the Catholic principles inspiring all of
Campanella's thought and activity, even though some doctrines are,
as it were, extraneous to the orthodox synthesis conceived by him
and can hardly be fitted into it. In the Campanellian philosophy there
is certainly not a static unity, or one that does not admit of any change
in the smallest particulars; it is rather a unity that continuously
gains in clearness and profundity, but remains within the frame of
orthodoxy.[144]

> The [Campanellian] synthesis had to be radical and total. It had
> to start out from the least of the elements not subject to doubt and
> to comprehend all the branches of culture, wherefrom the descent
> to life was to be made. Such Campanellian philosophy wished to be
> essentially, decidedly, and clamorously Christian . . . Nature,
> which the Renaissance used to exalt so much, had to be manifestly
> respected and taken into due account. Thus, the Thomistic intuition
> of a fusion of reason and faith, abandoned by the unilateral view

of Averroistic naturalism as well as by the Lutheran and Calvinistic fideism, could be reaffirmed and enriched.[145]

Thus Di Napoli's interpretation, which could be called "the ortho-dox-synthetical theory," differs from all former interpretations, even though it has some resemblance to D'Ancona's view. While D'Ancona conceives Campanella's thought as within the frame of orthodoxy, he is far, however, from presenting it as a synthetic unity embracing all the fields of knowledge.

Since Di Napoli's work, three comprehensive studies of Campanella's thought have appeared which deserve special mention. The first in order of time is Antonio Corsano's new revised edition of his 1944 book, *Tommaso Campanella*. In it the author modifies substantially his previous position on Campanella's philosophy in the light of the findings of Firpo and Amerio and through a direct contact with Campanella's *Theologia*.[146] While he does not fully endorse Di Napoli's view of Campanella's unfailing orthodoxy, he discards Ama-bile's simulation theory and sees no reason for denying "the Catholic thesis of Campanella's total or quasi-total loyalty to the Church and her doctrine, provided no violence is done to the factual truth of his adventurous manifestations at the time of the Calabrian conspiracy."[147]

The work of Nicola Badaloni is of a different nature. He holds that Campanella's philosophy is but a gradual development of the early naturalism he inherited from Telesio which he coupled with a theory of magic that pervades his entire speculation.[148] Badaloni maintains that Campanella had a purely naturalistic conception of religion which found its best expression in *The City of the Sun*.[149] "In the light of Campanella's philosophical convictions," writes Bada-loni, "to raise the problem of the truth of Christianity is an absurd-ity."[150] Thus in manifest contrast with the findings of Amerio, Firpo, Di Napoli, and Corsano whose studies are analysed in the introduc-tion—significantly enough, Di Napoli's work is disposed of at the very beginning of the introduction in a few negative sentences—Badaloni concludes by saying that Campanella's thought is "an im-posing witness to the decisive historical moment in which science and religion, technology and social justice seek in magic their last meeting point"(!)[151]

A far more serious study has been undertaken by Salvatore Femiano. His two-volume work on Campanella's metaphysics and philosophy of God shows an extensive knowledge of both primary and secondary sources and a well-balanced critical judgment.[152] Femiano accepts

Amerio's thesis of Campanella's conversion but does not expound on the extent and exact nature of his unorthodoxy.[153] Convinced that an objective study of an author's thought ought not to be influenced by any preconceived view about his intentions, he concentrates his study on Campanella's most significant writings, which in his view are those that followed his conversion.[154] According to Femiano, four characteristics distinguish Campanella's metaphysics: (1) its spirituality, inasmuch as metaphysics is conceived as a search for the ultimate foundation of reality which Campanella finds in an absolute, transcendent Being; (2) its interiority, insofar as truth is said to be attainable by interior illumination rather than by syllogistic reasoning; (3) its denunciation of the abuses of reason due to fear, ignorance, and bad will; (4) its autonomy in the study of the world of our experience as a most effective weapon against atheism.[155] Any other interpretation of Campanella's metaphysics, affirms Femiano, whether idealistic or pantheistic, naturalistic or deistic, Aristotelian-Thomistic or heretical, is groundless, arbitrary, and superficial.[156] In Femiano's view, Campanella's spiritualistic approach to reality becomes even more evident in his treatise on God, where doctrinal elements from Plato and Aristotle, Augustine and Thomas Aquinas are integrated in a new and original synthesis and reconsidered in the light of the first divine Reason.[157]

It is not our intention to evaluate critically all the judgments passed on Campanella and the various interpretations that his thought has received in the course of history. Such an evaluation at this point would be premature. We will limit ourselves to making a few general observations on the principal views and ideas expressed by Campanella's commentators.

First, many writers, especially earlier ones, never had the opportunity, or never took the trouble, to investigate all the sources of Campanellian thought. Thus, in many cases, we have mere repetitions of earlier statements without any critical study of the primary sources.

Secondly, in preparation and general background several commentators, including some of the best known scholars, were not equal to the task. This lack of preparation applies particularly to the field of scholastic philosophy and theology, a knowledge of which is absolutely indispensable to the understanding of Campanella's doctrine.[158]

Thirdly, prejudice and bias seem to have so blinded some writers that they were concerned not so much with finding what was Campanella's real thought as with reconciling it with their own preconceptions. This is a dangerous proceeding at anytime and particularly in the study of a complex personality like Campanella, whose statements, when separated from their context, may lead to quite different interpretations.[159]

Fourthly, in the interpretation of Campanella's philosophy care must be taken not to force the texts beyond their literary meaning, as has sometimes been done, in order to obtain a clear and simple statement of a particular point of doctrine that most likely was not altogether clear to Campanella himself. This lack of clarity is understandable in a man who planned a general reform of all the sciences and wrote on countless subjects often without books to consult.

These considerations, we hope, will help us avoid the errors of the past so that Campanella's thought may be faithfully presented and objectively judged.

PART TWO

Theory of Knowledge

CHAPTER THREE

Theory of Knowledge and Doctrine of Self-Consciousness

I. NATURE, SCOPE, AND METHOD OF CAMPANELLA'S PHILOSOPHY

Campanella conceives philosophy, which he also calls metaphysics, as an all-embracing science, the ultimate source and foundation to which all other sciences should be referred. The title of his work, *Universalis Philosophiae, seu Metaphysicarum rerum iuxta propria dogmata, Partes tres, Libri 18,* points to the universal character of his philosophy. Moreover, he explicitly states this point in many passages. "This philosophy," he writes in his dedicatory letter, "which I call universal and metaphysical, may be referred to as the workshop and source of all arts and sciences that have been discovered or will be discovered."[1] It is called metaphysics because it goes beyond physics and deals with the first principles and final ends of things. It is called universal philosophy because it reaches out to the primary causes, and even to the supreme cause, by which we can understand the reasons of all things.[2] Whereas subsidiary sciences deal with all things only insofar as they appear to us,[3] metaphysics deals with all things inasmuch and insofar as they are. It does not presuppose anything besides the appearance of something, which may be true or false. Hence metaphysics is clearly distinct from all other sciences, principally because it deals with the first being, its proprinciples and attributes.[4] All sciences are related to metaphysics as orations are to rhetoric, and poems to poetry.[5] Consequently, metaphysics is the "mistress of all the sciences,"[6] and occupies a place between physics and theology,[7] assisting the latter as *magistra ancillarum.*[8]

Campanella is proud of his book on metaphysics, which he calls "the bible of philosophers" and "the ark of all sciences, human and divine." The book contains, so he claims, the solution to all problems. It provides all nations with a code on the basis of which they can discover what is right and what is wrong in their sciences and in their laws.[9] The work is so good and so wonderful that in comparison with it other human books seem childish.[10] In truth, it seems to be the work of an angel rather than of a man.[11] Campanella goes on to say that just as the works of Galen, St. Augustine, St. Thomas Aquinas, and other great writers are widely read, so it will be with

46

his *Metaphysica*.[12] The book is worthy of Caesar[13] and excels his previous works as the sun excels the stars in brightness.[14] Indeed, no comparable book has ever been written in the whole world.[15]

After this appraisal of his own work on metaphysics, Campanella defines more specifically its content and purpose as being an inquiry after the truth of both human and divine things, based on the testimony of God, who reveals himself either through the world of created things or by direct teaching. It is necessary, therefore, to overthrow all human schools that are opposed to God and to call men back to God's school.[16] It is imperative to reject pagan and atheistic philosophy and to restore Christian doctrine, which is the only really true doctrine.[17]

This program had already been outlined in *De gentilismo non retinendo*, where Campanella discusses certain questions pertaining to a general reform of knowledge, particularly in relation to the prevailing Aristotelian philosophy of his own days that was interpreted along the lines of the Alexandrist and the Averroistic schools. He does not doubt the need of a new philosophical synthesis based on Christian principles in opposition to the philosophy of the Gentiles, who, in his words, are but children when compared to Christians.[18] It is a fact that the Gentiles have expressed many truths which we should accept as a participation of God's wisdom to all men; but such truths belong by right to the followers of Christ.[19] In any event, it would be heretical to say that Aristotle found the whole truth and that we have nothing more to say about it.[20]

To the question of whether or not it is permissible to contradict Aristotle, Campanella answers by distinguishing three types of Aristotelian teachings. Some of them must be absolutely rejected by those who care for the salvation of their souls; certain of them may be profitably contradicted; many others may be licitly rejected.[21] He inquires further into the correct method of philosophizing and denies any kind of intellectual servitude to a particular master, even if this master happens to be St. Thomas Aquinas.[22] There is only one teacher that must always be followed because of his infallibility, Christ, the eternal wisdom.[23]

Campanella kept to this program in the composition of his *Metaphysica*. Convinced that Aristotelian philosophy is anti-Christian, he directed his attacks against the Stagirite at the very beginning of his work, thus preparing the way for his new Christian philosophical synthesis. Aristotle's metaphysics, he says, is no metaphysics at all. It proves neither the first principles and final ends of things, nor the principles of sciences or their connections. When Aristotle deals with being and its properties, he speaks more as a grammarian than as a philosopher. Furthermore, he has no order in the exposition of his doctrine.[24] While proposing to deal with the ultimate causes, he actually expends eleven books on his introduction. The twelfth book, which is metaphysical, contains as many blasphemies and stupidities as there are propositions.[25] Accordingly, a new metaphysics is necessary, and Campanella will attempt to write it on the basis of the two divine codes, nature and Scripture, as he had already proclaimed in his *De gentilismo non retinendo*.[26]

We read the code of nature and learn from it by means of our external senses. Their impressions are stored up in memory. When the impressions are repeated, there results what is called experience. By piling up and interpreting these experiences we can proceed to the formulation of universal rules, which rest finally on the truth and faithfulness of the senses.[27] This process is in accordance with the general principle that Campanella had already laid down in his *Prodromus philosophiae instaurandae*. In the beginning of this work he states that a philosopher should follow the lead of the senses, for sense knowledge is absolutely certain, as it is acquired through the presence of its objects. As a matter of fact, we have recourse to the senses when we want to ascertain something of which we are not sure.[28] However, since we can never be sure that every sense reads correctly the code of nature, either because of some physical impediment, or because of the distance of the object in time or place, it is necessary sometimes to make use of sense perceptions of others as is the case in history.[29] Even then we must not give a blind assent to everybody, but only to those who deserve it. In conclusion, our guiding principle in philosophy must be as follows: "Assent must be given to witnesses and not to mere theorists, even if these happen to be very holy men. However, when both witnesses and theorists bear witness through the senses, then those are to be believed who are holier, for they will not wilfully deceive us."[30]

With regard to the second code, God's revelation of hidden things both in the natural and supernatural order, we have to adopt a respectful attitude and accept it as a valid source of information even for philosophy. The content of revelation is not merely a matter of opinion, but a solid doctrine that must be received on the authority of God, no matter whether He speaks to us directly or through well qualified witnesses.[31] Thus, in Campanella's opinion, philosophy cannot be cut off from Christian revelation. Such a dichotomy would deprive us of one of our best sources of knowledge, which is also the most certain and authoritative. It is only by combining the study of the two codes, nature and divine revelation, that we can attain to a real synthesis of knowledge.

The theory of knowledge occupies a pivotal place in Campanella's philosophy and has a clear relation to his metaphysics, taken in the classical sense as the science of being. The fact that he divides his philosophy into three parts, *principia sciendi, principia essendi,* and *principia operandi,*[32] and assigns the first place to the treatise of the principles of knowledge shows his keen and original mind. He has advanced beyond his predecessors in philosophy and has anticipated a common trend among later philosophers. Campanella is the first philosopher to feel the need of explicitly stating the critical problem as an introduction to philosophy.[33] In this respect he brings to philosophy a very definite and important innovation. He was fully aware of the new task that he imposed upon himself and wrote:

It is difficult to know the nature of things, but it is far more difficult to know the method of knowing. Hence many men have talked about things, but few have discussed the method of knowing. When they did discuss it, they were greatly deceived, either because they created a method of their own without any foundation, or because they simply relied on the authority of others. . . . Thus a great amount of labor has been left to us, *in explaining and establishing the foundation of science.*[34]

Campanella was convinced that before a philosopher builds his metaphysics, he must prove the possibility of science with all its implications and must establish the rules of knowing what cannot be grasped primarily by the senses.[35] In other words, philosophy must start with epistemology and its first inquiries are about the possibility and the form of knowledge. In this connection Campanella could not be more explicit. Long before Descartes produced his famous *Discours de la méthode,*[36] Campanella began his philosophical investigation with a *universal theoretical doubt* of all the determinations of thought which might or might not have a real correspondence outside the mind. "Metaphysics," to quote a passage already mentioned, "deals with all things inasmuch and insofar as they are. It does not presuppose anything besides the appearance of something, which may be true or false."[37] In another place he states: "The metaphysician does not take anything for granted, but begins his inquiry about all things with doubt. He does not even presuppose himself to be what he appears to be to himself; nor will he say whether he is living or dead, but he will doubt."[38] These two texts contain in germ all that Campanella expounds in his *14 dubitationes,* or doubts, which are the problems that every philosopher must face and solve before starting any metaphysical speculation. The *14 dubitationes* represent the various forms and aspects that the theoretical doubt may assume in relation to scientific knowledge. They embody all the objections that a sceptical mind can possibly advance in order to undermine the very basis on which knowledge is built.

We will state briefly all the *dubitationes* which, together with the *responsiones,* make up a large portion of the first section of Campanella's *Metaphysica* and constitute an essential point in the inquiry about his theory of knowledge.[39]

First Doubt. "That man is to be called wise who knows things as they are in themselves" *(Sapiens est, cui res sapiunt, prout sunt).* This principle of St. Bernard is very helpful for a correct understanding of our knowledge of the external world. By it our capacity of knowing is measured and judged, and consequently our knowledge of the world is seen to be very limited. Neither God, nor the angels, nor anything that exists outside of our world and is inaccessible to our sense powers, can be the object of our knowledge. We do not know the future, and we know the past only by the report of other people. We are very much like a worm in a man's body which knows neither the entire man nor its dwelling place and itself.[40]

Second Doubt. In order to know the universal we ought to know all the particulars, since the universal is made up of particulars. But the particulars are infinite in number and cannot all be known: hence neither can the universal be known. Moreover, the particular and the individual are constantly beginning and passing away, whereas science is of things that are permanent and everlasting. The universal is a mere thought, and so it cannot constitute the object of science, the aim of which is to know the real.[41]

Third Doubt. All knowledge is by the senses and through the senses. Hence, since the senses do not attain to the essence of things, there can be no real knowledge or science. Wisdom *(sapientia)* takes its name from savor *(sapor),* which perceives things as they are, i.e., not only their external appearance and operation, but also their intrinsic and intimate nature. But even savor does not give us true science, since it often takes for sweet what is bitter, and for bitter what is sweet. Wherefore, an objective knowledge is absolutely impossible.[42]

Fourth Doubt. Since we must philosophize according to the perceptions of the senses, and since, on the other hand, our senses are so uncertain that no philosophy can be based on their perceptions, it would seem more correct to philosophize according to the senses of the lower animals. Their senses, in fact, surpass our own because of the greater number of their objects and because of their sharpness. Animals, moreover, have been in many ways teachers of men, who have often worshipped them. They also have been endowed with the gift of prophecy. It seems better, then, to philosophize according to the senses of animals than according to the senses of men.[43]

Fifth Doubt. Nevertheless, even the acute senses of animals do not perceive things as they are in themselves but only their images *(simulacra).* The specific properties of human and animal senses show the uselessness of all philosophy. Thus, considering the activity of the senses, we are right in saying that *non sapiunt nobis ipsae res,* for the senses do not give us the things themselves but only their accidental images. These are of no use for the knowledge of the essence of things or for philosophy.[44]

Sixth Doubt. But even the images of things that our senses receive in themselves from the outside cannot reach our soul purely and completely, since they are altered and falsified by the perceiving organs and by the medium through which images enter the soul.

We cannot perceive God and the angels through a proper image of them but only through their effects. Nor are the heavenly bodies and the stars perceivable by us in their proper substance, because of their great distance from us. It is true, then, as the Platonists and Augustine teach, that all our perceptions are images of other real things existing in the world of the angels and God. We are so far away from a knowledge of them, that we are like people who are held in a cavern and contemplate the shadow of things that pass by.[45]

Seventh Doubt. Things and their images cannot be known in their reality because they are in a continuous change and flow and are never the same. When a man wants to know something through the senses or the intellect, this thing has already been changed into another, like the water in a river, before he comes to know it. When I say, for instance, that Peter is white, the Peter that I mention has already been changed into another before I finished my statement. Hence Origen compares man to a leather bottle into which and out of which different water is continuously flowing. Heraclitus comes to the conclusion that there is no knowledge of anything, for, before we come to know a thing, that very thing has already been changed.[46]

Eighth Doubt. Even on the supposition that things do not change, we still have no real knowledge, for we ourselves are continually changing and are never the same. Our sensory organs are constantly changing through the inflowing and outflowing of their parts; and the perceiving spirit is continually exhaling and being refilled with new blood, just as the flame of a lamp is always changing, although it apparently remains the same all through the burning of the oil. A new spirit follows without interruption the spirit that preceded it, so that no communication of knowledge is possible. We are the same only through succession, just as the people of a town succeed to one another but the town remains the same, for the following generation keeps the customs and the laws inherited from the former one.[47]

Ninth Doubt. We do not perceive anything by which we are not affected and by which we are not changed. I feel warmth when I become warm; I perceive sound when a sound strikes my ear; I see color when a color affects my eye. So every sensation is through assimilation. The agent makes the passive subject similar to itself through assimilation, not merely by perfecting it, as Aristotle teaches, but also by corrupting it, in the way that intensive heat destroys a body. Sensation is a kind of passion *(sensus est passio)*. When we perceive something, we are in some way alienated and changed into something else, so that we know when we become something else. But this is insanity, for when man is changed into something else he is said to be insane. Thus knowledge is self-alienation and loss of one's self, even if something better is acquired, as is the case with the saint during an ecstasy.[48]

Tenth Doubt. Our knowledge is folly, for our soul does not know anything about its own nature. The soul looks for itself but does not find itself, like the fool who looked for the donkey on which he was riding. Philosophers hold contradicting views on the nature of the soul and dispute a great deal about it as if it were a completely extraneous thing. If a man does not know himself, how can he be expected to know other things?

The soul lives and operates in the body where it performs many activities without seeing itself and its work. It looks through the windows of the eyes and asks other people what it really is, why it is enclosed in the body, and who has put it there. It is like a drunkard who awakens from his sleep and inquires about himself, about what he did while intoxicated, and how he happens to be in somebody else's room.[49]

Eleventh Doubt. That knowledge is a kind of madness is proved by the contradictory statements of philosophers with regard to things that should afford no doubt whatsoever. Aristotle holds that the sun is neither warm nor bright and—which is most absurd—that it generates heat and light by striking the air. Heraclitus believes that everything is in motion and that nothing is at rest, whereas Zeno says that nothing moves and that there is no such thing as motion. Parmenides asserts that all things are one, while Democritus says that no being is one but merely a concrete union of atoms. Epicurus thinks that only what we perceive through the senses is real, whereas Plato holds that the things we see do not exist and that only the ideas are real beings. Pythagoras affirms that he remembers having been in existence before and passing from one body into another, while the poet Ennius remembers having been Homer. If these are not insane beliefs, one may wonder what insanity is.[50]

Twelfth Doubt. The same confusion exists in regard to the principles of the sciences, especially metaphysics. Some philosophers hold with Pythagoras that the principles of metaphysics are the one and the many; others admit with Aristotle that they are the infinite and the finite. The Peripatetics deny any metaphysical principles, and other philosophers deny even the possibility of metaphysics.[51]

Thirteenth Doubt. That science is impossible has been recognized by the philosophers themselves. Some of them, like Heraclitus, Democritus, and Socrates, deny absolutely the possibility of attaining certitude in knowledge, while Plato considers science as an art of telling stories and handed down his philosophy in the form of dialogues. Empedocles says that the ways of our senses are so closed that wisdom has no access to them. The sceptics go to extremes in their doubt and denial of any science when they affirm that man does not even know whether he knows or does not know. Sextus Empiricus says, "This, too, I do not know, namely, whether I know or I do not know that I do not know anything."[52]

Fourteenth Doubt. The names that men give to things are a demonstration that there is no science. In fact, man communicates his knowledge of things to others in the way he understands them and, for this reason, he indicates things by names, whose formation is due partly to chance, partly to convention, and partly to a manifest lack of knowledge.

Sciences are often more mistaken in naming their objects than in explaining them. Examples may be found in theology which ascribes human attributes to God, and in astronomy which names the stars after the names of animals. However, the most important thing to be noticed in this connection is that no word indicates the thing itself, but only an external and accidental property of it or some likeness that it has to other things.[53]

The fundamental themes of this long series of objections against our knowledge can be summarized as follows: first, the imperfection, limitation, and subjectivity of our knowledge, which is knowledge of phenomena rather than of reality; second, the deception of our senses; third, the relativity and instability of knowledge because of the changeableness of things and of ourselves; fourth, the difficulty inherent in the very act of knowing, insofar as it is a passion or information whereby the subject, in perceiving the object, becomes the object itself and consequently is annihilated as a subject; fifth, the same difficulty looked at from the point of view of the subject, which, being what it is, cannot *become* another than itself, so that in the process of knowledge of the self through its own passion, the other term of the cognitive act, the object, is necessarily lacking. Hence the soul's ignorance of itself.

Campanella deals with these points in his answers to the *14 dubitationes* where each objection against the possibility of knowledge is taken up separately and given a proper solution. However, in order to arrive at a solution he immediately saw that he first must have clear and definite ideas concerning the problem of knowledge itself. It was only on the basis of well established epistemological principles that he could take the field and destroy all the arguments of his adversaries by showing their inconsistency. Accordingly, he set about writing the *praeambula responsionum,* in which he laid down the basic principles of his theory of knowledge, to be expounded later in the course of his entire metaphysics. We shall follow him and highlight the main points of his discussion.

III. SCEPTICISM AND BASIC PRINCIPLES OF KNOWLEDGE

1. *Refutation of Scepticism.* In his approach to the epistemological problem, Campanella first deals with absolute scepticism. When a philosopher admits the possibility of absolute doubt, the transition to the negation of knowledge is very easy. This procedure, Campanella sees, has disastrous implications. It undermines not only any system of Christian philosophy but also the very basis of religion, since religion cannot be built upon truths that we do not know or that we cannot even possibly know. He reacts to the attacks of the sceptics by meeting their objections and answering their doubts in a very decisive way.

The first argument in the refutation of scepticism consists in extracting an implicit admission of the existence of truth from the very fact of its negation by the sceptics, or from their doubtful attitude toward it. This argument, of course, derives from St. Augustine, who states that it is enough for a person to understand that he doubts in order for him to be certain of something, namely, of the truth of his doubt. No one can rightly deny the existence of truth, since his very denial implies the possession of truth in himself.[54] But Campanella has his own way of reasoning upon this subject, and it is worthy of consideration.

To know *(sapere)*, he says, is to perceive a thing as it is. Anyone who thinks that he knows something, does so because he is convinced that he knows the thing as it is. Those who think that they know nothing do so because they are convinced that they do not know anything as it is. Likewise, those who claim that they know only one thing, namely, that they know nothing, do so because they think that they have at least attained to the truth that they know nothing. The same principle holds for those who affirm that they know they are partially cognizant of something and partially ignorant of it. Therefore, since those who think that they know claim that they know the truth, and those who think that they do not know claim that they do not know the truth, it must be asserted that truth is the entity of a thing as it is, while falsehood is the entity of a thing as it is not. The entity of a thing insofar as it is unknown is not called falsehood but ignorance.

Those who hold that they do not even know whether they know or do not know anything do not speak correctly. They necessarily know that they do not know this, and this is to know something. Obviously, this is not knowledge in the strict sense of the word; for it is knowledge through negation, just as the vision of darkness is not

a vision proper but privation of vision. Nevertheless, the human mind
has this peculiar characteristic: it knows in that particular case that
it does not know, just as it understands that it does not see in the dark
or does not hear when everything is silent. If the mind did not have
this kind of perception, it would be like a stone, to which the presence
or absence of light is absolutely indifferent. Hence no argument is
possible with those who refuse to admit that they know that they do
not know, for by so doing they destroy all sound principles of reasoning. Furthermore, how do they come to know that they are not even
aware whether they know or whether they do not know, unless they
first understand that things cannot be perceived as they are? This
fact at least is known to them, and if they deny it, they deny their own
position. Likewise, they know what is truth and what is knowledge;
otherwise they would not be able to say that they do not know the
truth. To say something is implicitly to admit that they do know
something, if their statement has any meaning.[55]

The practice of sceptics is inconsistent with their own theory. In
ordinary life sceptics follow their opinions, rely on sense perceptions,
utilize their experiences, and adopt prevailing customs. Thus in practice they admit that they not only know what they are doing, but that
a certain amount of knowledge is possible to man. However, when
sceptics start to philosophize, they find so much imperfection and confusion in the science that they deny their achievement, their method of
knowing, and their end. Yet they cannot deny science, art, and sense
experience as such. How could they possibly deny that they walk, eat,
and talk? Even if they assert that these actions are only external appearances, they must concede an already implicit recognition of the
possibility of knowledge.

The best way to deal with a sceptic who persists in denying the
reality of all sensations is to beat him until he no longer says, "I do
not feel any pain! It is only imagination!," but cries out, "I really
suffer!" In this way, he will admit that he actually perceives something,
and, since perception is a form of cognition, knowledge then is possible.[56]

2. *Self-consciousness.* Having justified against the sceptics the possibility and reality of knowledge, Campanella immediately realizes
that this is only a partial cure for the wounds caused by scepticism.
He seeks a remedy so powerful that it will not only heal the wounds
inflicted on knowledge but will prevent their occurrence. He wishes
to establish absolute and immediately evident principles which will

provide a solid foundation for all the sciences and about which no one can possibly be deceived.[57] Confronted with this problem, the solution of which was to have a decisive bearing on his whole theory of knowledge, he goes back to St. Augustine and lays down the *principle of self-consciousness* as the basis of knowledge and certitude.

> Three things are absolutely certain for us, namely, that we are, that we know, and that we will. For we know without any doubt or error that we are, and we delight in our being and in our knowledge. Moreover, in these things no true-seeming illusion disturbs us; for we are subject to error only with regard to those objects that we know through their images, or through the changes that they produce in us. Since these images and changes are similar to those of other objects, they can deceive us either because we may get confused by taking one for another, or because they do not represent the object in its entirety. However, with regard to our being, our knowing, and our willing, there is no image or impression whatsoever of the phantasy, but only one perennial presence. Therefore, we cannot be mistaken with regard to them.[58]

At this point Campanella anticipates an objection that the Peripatetics would likely raise against his teaching of the soul's direct knowledge of itself, since they admit only the soul's knowledge of itself through its acts, or reflex knowledge. He simply mentions the objection and says that he will answer it later. Meanwhile, he remarks that St. Thomas Aquinas also agrees with St. Augustine in admitting a *notitia praesentialitatis* of the soul.[59] Then, still quoting St. Augustine, he goes on to say:

> I am most certain that I am. If you admit it, I have this certitude; if you deny it and say that I am deceived, you plainly recognize that I am; for I cannot be deceived if I am not. What is not can neither know truly nor be deceived. Hence, I am not deceived in knowing that I am. Likewise, I know that I know, and am not deceived. As I know that I am, so I know that I know that I am. Moreover, I am delighted in, and love, these two things, namely, that I am and that I know. So I add a third thing, i.e., the love of my being and of my knowledge. No one can say that I am deceived when I say that I love my being and my knowing, since it has already been demonstrated that in these things which I love, namely, my being and my knowledge, I am not deceived. However, even if these were false, it would still be true that I love false things. For how could I be blamed for, and prohibited from, loving false things, if it were false that I love them? It is true, then, and beyond any doubt, that I love those things, since whether they are true or whether they are false, my love is true. Further, as there is no one who does not wish to be happy, so there is no one who does not

wish to be. Thus love is most certain, just as my being and my knowing are certain.[60]

From the fact of one's own existence Campanella proceeds to infer the possibility of existing, for to be necessarily involves to be able to be. Since then it is absolutely certain that I am, it is likewise certain that I can be, or that I have the power to be. Thus *esse* is equivalent to *posse,* and power, or *potentia,* goes along in me with knowledge and love.

By extending this notion of man to every being, in accordance with his metaphysical doctrine that he will expound later, he proceeds to the unwarranted conclusion that being, together with its "primalities," *potentia, sapientia,* and *amor,* is the most certain and evident thing to us and that no one can deny or be ignorant of it.[61]

The concept of being as power, knowledge, and love is admitted both because it is in accord with our nature and because of the general consent of men. It is the first and most certain principle of science: *Nos esse et posse, scire et velle est certissimum principium primum.* But this principle is not universally valid. It is restricted by a second principle, *viz.,* that we are something, but not all things, and that we can do, and know, and desire something, but not all things nor absolutely: *Nos esse aliquid et non omnia, et posse, scire, velle aliquid et non omnia vel omnino.* Finally, we can do, know, and want other things, because we can be, know, and desire ourselves: *Nos possumus, scimus et volumus alia, quia possumus, scimus et volumus nosipsos.* I perceive heat, because I feel myself heated; I love the light, because I wish to have light within me. Every being does, knows, and desires a thing, because it feels itself affected by that thing. We cannot acquire, we do not know, and we do not love things that do not affect us. A confusion of *innate* and *illate,* or acquired, knowledge is the source of all doubt and error, whereas knowledge of ourselves, as identified with our own being, is the absolute principle of certitude.[62]

3. *Innate and Acquired Knowledge.* For a deeper penetration of Campanella's doctrine of self-consciousness it is necessary to develop his concepts of innate and acquired knowledge. There are two kinds of knowledge in things: innate knowledge, or *notitia innata* or *indita,* whereby things know that they are, delight in their being, and hate not to be; and acquired knowledge, or *notitia illata,* whereby they know things outside themselves, inasmuch as they are acted upon by them and become similar to them.[63] Innate knowledge belongs to the very essence of things by reason of their primalitarian structure

and is nothing but the *notitia praesentialitatis*. It is also called *notitia abdita* because it is hidden, as it were, in the thing itself, and also because it is darkened on the occurrence of knowledge of external reality.[64] Acquired knowledge is the *notitia obiectiva* insofar as it is knowledge of external objects. It can be acquired only accidentally, since it does not proceed directly from the very essence of the thing. Another name for it is *notitia addita,* because it is an addition to innate knowledge.

The soul, like every other being, and even more than other beings, has a primalitarian structure. By its essence it has power, knowledge, and volition as co-principles of its being. Therefore, because of the identity of its being and knowledge, it has the *notitia praesentialitatis*. On the other hand, by getting in contact with what is outside itself, it acquires the *notitia obiectiva*. The soul's self-cognition is also objective, but only in a secondary way, when through reflection the soul makes itself present to itself as an object.[65] This kind of self-cognition Campanella calls *notitia sui addita* or *reflexa*. Over the *notitia addita* of the external things it has the advantage of being a representation of an innate knowledge.

The following scheme shows the various kinds of the soul's knowledge according to Campanella.

	NOTITIA PRAESENTIALITATIS (Self-cognition of the soul through self-presence)	—*Notitia innata, indita,* or *abdita* (Innate or hidden knowledge)
NOTITIA	NOTITIA OBIECTIVA (Knowledge of external objects)	—*Notitia illata* or *addita* (Illate or acquired knowledge)
	NOTITIA SUI ADDITA or REFLEXA (Self-cognition of the soul through reflection)	

Leaving aside objective knowledge, which will be discussed later, we shall consider briefly the soul's cognition of itself either through self-presence or through reflection.

When Campanella speaks of the soul's knowledge through self-presence, he does so, as already pointed out, on the ground that self-cognition belongs to the soul's essence. It is enough, then, for the soul, and indeed for every other being, to be what it is in order to know itself.[66] In other words, to understand itself the intellect does not need to be acted upon by any external object, or be the subject of any outside passion, as Telesio had taught.[67] Nor does it need be the subject of its own passion or becoming; it is an intellect, that is, a self-intelligent power, and what already is, does not need to become. Accordingly, it knows itself through its very essence, which includes knowledge and the act of knowing. Hence, with regard to innate knowledge, there is no essential difference in the soul, just as there is no difference in the angel, between the intellect, the act of knowing, and the knowing subject.[68] Here again Campanella appeals to the teaching of St. Augustine, whose viewpoint on this particular matter he declares to hold firmly.[69]

The identification of the soul with the intellect and its act of knowing is contrary to the tenets of the peripatetic school, which admits a real distinction between the soul and its faculties, the faculties themselves, and between the faculties and their operations. Hence Campanella, anticipating the objection of the Aristotelians that the intellect is only in potency with regard to its object and therefore cannot have an intuitive or direct knowledge of itself, answers that it is only by misunderstanding Aristotle's doctrine that such an objection can be raised. For Aristotle taught that the intellect is in potency only to understand things outside, not to understand itself. Being immaterial, the intellect can better understand itself than the sensible species after they have been stripped of their material elements.[70] Campanella was evidently misled in his interpretation of Aristotle, who maintains that it is of the nature of the intellect to know itself only insofar as it comes into contact with an intelligible object, so that any self-knowledge of the intellect without passing from potency into act is inconceivable.[71] Hence Campanella's attempt to reconcile his own teaching with that of Aristotle, while unsuccessful, shows that he was concerned with putting his doctrine under the patronage of the Stagirite so as to make it more acceptable.

Campanella could not deny the fact that we know our own being only in a very imperfect way. If the soul's cognition through self-presence were true, would not the self reveal itself without the slightest possibility of doubt? His answer to this question is that the knowledge of the manifold external objects obscures the self-transparency of the soul to such an extent that under their pressure the soul becomes almost oblivious of itself.[72] The *notitia praesentialitatis* would be more natural to the soul in the ideal state of absolute independence of the external world. In the real state of things, the soul is alienated from itself and is forced to return to itself by reflection. Accordingly, reflex knowledge is more proper to the soul in its present state.[73]

It is little wonder, then, that after having considered God, the angels, the substance of the world, and the beginning and end of things, the soul inquires with a certain anxiety about its own nature, origin, and purpose. In doing so, it is moved by its desire to know the place that it occupies among beings in order to direct all its activities to the attainment of its final end.[74] However, it should be clear that in spite of its own inquiry and the different opinions that may be held about its nature and operations—differences due to acquired knowledge[75]— the soul is never entirely ignorant of itself, for it possesses an essentially knowing nature.[76] The soul is considered here not as an animating principle, but as a being with the primalitarian structure of power, knowledge, and will.[77]

This leads to a final conclusion about the soul's self-cognition. Innate knowledge, being part of the soul's essence, which is from God, has the characteristic of being superior to and more certain than acquired knowledge. We can be mistaken about many things but not about the essential principles of being.[78]

IV. CAMPANELLA AND DESCARTES

In a fine passage in her *Notice* on Campanella Mme. Colet wrote:

The star that was going to spread an immortal light on the dawn of [modern] philosophy had arisen. Descartes had just published his *Méthode*. Campanella was undoubtedly deeply impressed by this work that caused a revolution in Europe. In spite of his age, in 1638 he left France and went to Holland to find Descartes; but Descartes was in hiding, and even his friends could not find the town where he was living . . .

Without doubt, if these two great minds had met, they would have understood each other, and Descartes would have talked with less contempt of the Italian philosopher. If Campanella was not one of the great founders of modern philosophy, one cannot forget the fact that he suffered for it, and has therefore a right to our admiration and respect.[79]

Whatever view we may take of this observation and of Descartes' attitude toward Campanella, we cannot fail to recognize that the latter's *Metaphysica*, conceived in the darkness of a Neapolitan dungeon, has a striking resemblance to the *Discours de la méthode*, written by Descartes in the solitude of his voluntary exile in Holland.[80] Both works are the fruit of long meditation in an attempt to solve the critical problem that arose when they made the thinking subject the center and starting point of their philosophical speculation.

The main reason these two philosophers, so distant from each other in background, environment, training, and purpose, focused their efforts on the rehabilitation of knowledge is to be sought in the cultural climate of the time. On one side, the humanists, with an excessive enthusiasm for the revival of the study of Greek and Roman classics, had conducted a bitter campaign against the scholastics, whose teaching in certain instances had unfortunately degenerated to the point that they became subject to criticism and ridicule. On the other side, the representatives of scepticism, a natural outcome of the intellectual confusion of the period, attacked the foundations of knowledge in such manner as to make fruitful philosophical speculation impossible. In addition, the revival of Platonism was a strong incentive to the subjectivistic tendencies of both Campanella and Descartes.

Whatever may have been the full causes of their origin, the fact remains that the Cartesian and Campanellian systems have many points of contact. Hence, with the new emphasis on the Campanellian studies, it is not surprising that the question of the relationship between Campanella and Descartes has been raised and given various solutions. Perhaps on only one point is there general agreement, namely, the recognition of the spiritual heritage that both philosophers received from St. Augustine. For the purpose of this study we shall confine ourselves to a short discussion on the nature of Campanella's doubt and his doctrine of self-consciousness in comparison with Descartes' methodic doubt and his *Cogito, ergo sum*.

As previously stated, the metaphysician, according to Campanella, must start his speculations with a universal doubt, which goes so far as to include even doubt about one's own existence.[81] We find evidences of this teaching in several passages of his works, especially the *Metaphysica*. Campanella is emphatic in stressing this point and takes care to make it clear whenever the opportunity presents itself. Thus, in dealing with the object of the sciences and distinctions between them, he writes that metaphysics inquires about the essence and existence of all things, and particularly of those things that are not immediately evident to all our senses. It also inquires about the evidence of things, as well as about the meaning of sensation and understanding, so that we may know whether we really possess knowledge or not. More specifically, metaphysics presupposes the existence of many things—although not of all things—that appear to the senses, but at the same time tries to find out whether those things which do so appear to us are true or false. If they are true things, then metaphysics inquires what they really are and whether they are such in nature or only in appearance.[82]

These statements, along with similar ones previously mentioned, clearly indicate Campanella's understanding of the task of the metaphysician at the very beginning of his philosophical speculation. He goes on to show the difference between metaphysics and the other sciences. For metaphysics he claims the privilege of condensing and establishing the principles of all the sciences, of naming things according to their nature, and of making manifest the order and end of all things.[83] Unquestionably Campanella's doubt has the same characteristic of universality as the Cartesian doubt, and in the Campanellian systematization of the sciences the solution of the critical problem has absolute priority over metaphysics proper.

It might be objected that in certain passages of his works Campanella seems to place basic metaphysical concepts at the root of his methodic doubt. Thus, just before the passage in his *Syntagma* where he proclaims that the metaphysician does not presuppose anything (*nihil praesupponit, sed omnia dubitando perquirit*), he writes: *Qui autem inventivas tradit scientias, modum quo ad eas pervenit viamque aperiet, nec aliquid praesupponet nisi universalissimum esse* (*Syntagma*, p. 67). Likewise, immediately after the list of the *14 dubitationes* in the *Metaphysica* we find the following statement: *Sternenda est via ex certissimis et notissimis nobis et naturae infallibilibusque. Haec autem sunt universalissima ut Ens, Entisque Primalitates: Potentia, Sapientia et Amor, quae nec ignorari nec per deceptionem incerta fieri posse, ex iam dictis notum est* (*Metaphysica*, I, p. 32a). Hence the concepts of being and its primalitarian dialectic apparently escape the doubt and are presupposed as fundamental truths that manifest themselves as such to the reflecting mind and offer the key to the solution of the doubt itself.[84]

If this were so, we could not help admitting some inconsistency in Campanella's teaching, for it is evident from all the pertinent texts that his metaphysics does not presuppose or take anything for granted. A careful study of the two passages in question, however, shows that there is no such inconsistency in Campanella. When he teaches on the one hand that the metaphysician presupposes at the beginning of his speculation at least a most universal being (*universalissimum esse*) and when, on the other hand, he states immediately after and just as emphatically that the metaphysician does not presuppose anything at all (*nihil praesupponit, sed omnia dubitando perquirit*), he is manifestly speaking of two different persons. In the first case, he speaks of the one who is dealing with what he calls *scientiae inventivae* or the investigative sciences; in the second case, he speaks of the metaphysician proper. The *scientiae inventivae,* according to Campanella, are the sciences concerned with singulars, which are a preparation for the *scientiae doctrinales,* dealing with universals.[85] Since the *scientiae inventivae* are, as it were, a preliminary step to philosophy,[86] it is only natural that they presuppose the existence of some kind of being or the *universalissimum esse.* Indeed, the object of their inquiry is not being as such, but only certain aspects of being as they are known to us mainly through the senses.[87] Metaphysics, on the contrary, which is concerned with philosophical principles underlying every science *(metaphysicus, qui communem cunctis scientiis philosophiam tractat),* does not presuppose anything at all, not even one's own existence.[88]

In the *Metaphysica,* where Campanella seems to state that the metaphysician presupposes not only the concept of being but also the concept of its "primalities," namely, power, knowledge, and love, these notions are not laid down by Campanella on a purely metaphysical basis prior to any epistemological investigation. For him to do this would be out of keeping with the general plan of his work. They are rather the result of an inquiry that begins in sceptical doubt and ends in the affirmation of self-consciousness. Campanella himself seems to imply this when he refers the reader to his previous discussion on the possibility and limitations of knowledge and cites a passage from St. Augustine where the doctrine of self-consciousness as the first and most evident knowledge is clearly stated.[89]

It should be emphasized that the foregoing discussion leaves intact the question of whether or not the Campanellian doubt implies *by its very nature* a metaphysical concept. The writer is quite willing to admit that the doubt implies both an attitude of the self and an object, even if this object is only the self-reflecting thought. For to doubt is to think, and a thought must be a thought of something, if it is going to be a thought at all. Therefore, some sort of reality is implied even in Campanella's methodic doubt, just as a certain amount of metaphysics is always implied in epistemology. But this point has nothing to do with the problem under discussion, which is whether or not Campanella explicitly placed any metaphysical concepts at the basis of his doubt. This is what we have denied.

Just as Campanella's doubt is similar to the Cartesian doubt because of its character of universality, it is likewise similar in its lack of absoluteness. In other words, Campanella's doubt is not the universally real doubt to which scepticism is supposed to lead. It is rather an artificial and hypothetical attitude adopted at the threshold of his philosophical system in order that he may provide it with a critical foundation.[90] This is evidenced at the very outset of his epistemology when he conducts a destructive campaign against the sceptical theses.

There is another point of contact in the teaching of the two philosophers. Neither Campanella nor Descartes pretends to extend the doubt to the first self-evident principles, such as the principle of noncontradiction, whose denial would make all thinking impossible.[91] But whereas Descartes' doubt bears almost exclusively on the existence of things, Campanella's doubt, as previously indicated, includes also their essence or quiddity.[92]

Thus far the nature and characteristics of Campanella's doubt in relation to the Cartesian doubt have been considered, but no treatment has been given of the subject from the historical point of view. Moreover, the doctrine of self-consciousness, which offers the key to the solution of the critical problem, has been touched upon only incidentally. It is therefore necessary to face the historical aspect of the question and study more closely the principle of self-consciousness as it is presented by Campanella and Descartes.

In his critical study of the relationship between the philosophy of the two men, Léon Blanchet establishes that because of his position on the universal methodic doubt and doctrine of self-consciousness Campanella was a forerunner of Descartes.[93] He then proposes the question of whether Descartes was actually influenced by Campanella and answers as follows. If we think of a possible influence through the *Universalis Philosophia* or *Metaphysica,* which was published only in 1638 and consequently one year after the *Discours de la méthode,* the answer is evidently negative. However, Campanella had already outlined and stated his doctrine clearly in some of his earlier works, especially the *De sensu rerum.* Descartes referred to this work with some indifference, but admitted that he had read it. In Campanella, Descartes read that only knowledge of the soul through itself is an intuitive knowledge, that this innate knowledge is the source of all other knowledge, and that it is the only knowledge not subject to the uncertainty of the senses. All these theses, apart from their compromising panpsychist implications, appear to be fundamental tenets in Descartes' system. The French philosopher revised the doctrine that he took from Campanella and restated it in a completely new way. This statement of the methodological doubt, so used for the first time in history, prepared the way for modern idealism.

Yet Descartes held fast to the concept that the absolute identity of the intellect and the intelligible is the best guarantee of truth and that it confers upon the *Cogito* its value of certitude. For this reason, Descartes feels the need for recourse to God as a guarantee for truth when thought is no longer identical with the object of its affirmation. This is exactly what happens in the case of knowledge of the external world. Thus, by accepting fully the Augustinian criterion of certitude and by keeping more faithfully than his predecessors to the spirit of that doctrine, Descartes laid down the foundation of later idealistic systems.[94] This, in brief, is the result of Blanchet's inquiry on the relationship between Campanella and Descartes with regard to the methodological doubt.

Etienne Gilson takes exception to Blanchet's view and writes that, in spite of its solidity of doctrine and rich findings, his work contains many uncertainties and other shortcomings. He holds that the entire second part of the book concerning Campanella seems to be of doubtful value, if not completely wrong. In his opinion, a brief comparison of Descartes' *Cogito* with that of Campanella will justify this statement.

The *Cogito* of Descartes, Gilson says, has two essential features. First, it establishes, or at least it stresses, a real distinction between the soul and the body. When Descartes says, *Cogito, ergo sum,* he means that spirit is conceived as something subsistent and that nothing material is to be attributed to it, and that the body is likewise conceived as something subsistent and that nothing spiritual is to be attributed to it. The entire *Méditations métaphysiques* is an argument for this doctrine. The second essential feature of the Cartesian *Cogito* is that it is posited as clear knowledge, which furnishes us directly with the criterion of certitude. This cannot be otherwise, since we posit the *Cogito* to define the two concepts of thought and extension by opposing them one to another.

On the other hand, Gilson continues, the most characteristic feature of Campanella's metaphysics is panpsychism. What Descartes found in the *De sensu rerum* is the statement of a universal animism and a systematic confusion of soul and body. This doctrine was to be even more detestable and unacceptable to Descartes than that of Aristotle and the scholastics. Instead of saying, "I think, therefore I am," i.e., "I am a thought," Campanella tells us that "Everything thinks because of the sole fact that it exists." Consequently, the *Cognoscere est esse* of the Renaissance philosopher finds its radical negation in the *Cogito, ergo sum* of Descartes. Campanella's principle, far from meaning clear knowledge aiming to define and separate two substances, seeks to establish everywhere a secret or hidden cognition *(notitia abdita)*, a kind of instinct of conservation to which as much consciousness is attributed as is required for the functions of the body: "All the parts of the material world, as well as their particles, are endowed with sense perception, which is either clear or obscure according to their need for conservation."[95] Therefore Campanella's statement, "Everything that exists, thinks," is in direct opposition to the Cartesian concept, "I think, therefore I am."[96]

In his study of Campanella's doctrine of self-consciousness, Romano Amerio makes some pertinent observations that may throw light on the entire issue. Campanella, he says, arrives at certitude not only through thought but also through love. It would seem, therefore, that he does not attain to the strict concept of self-consciousness, such as we find in Descartes, and that he gives us nothing but an enthymeme of the principle of causality. In this case the profound meaning of thought as a basis for certitude would have escaped Campanella, whose philosophy, like that of St. Augustine, would have no relation to Descartes' philosophy, which on the contrary it really anticipated. It is true that in the formal expression of Campanella's reasoning the three primalities of being—power, knowledge, and volition—are put on the same level as the Augustinian *vivere, nosse,* and *velle.* Yet the strength of the Campanellian demonstration prescinds from that triad as a triad of abstract primalities. It consists in this, that, given the soul as a synthesis of those three constitutive principles (our power, knowledge, and volition), the content of the demonstration is grasped immediately by our consciousness and constitutes the datum of a primary and definite knowledge. The primalities are not *res* or *essentiae,* but transcendental constitutive principles, *realitates* or *essentialitates,* of one and the same essence, in which they are one *per toticipationem.* Hence the principle of self-consciousness is founded by Campanella not upon three acts—in which case it would be a spurious concept—but upon the primalities of one sole act, which is the concrete act of the thinking soul.[97]

Annibale Pastore agrees with Amerio in considering Campanella a link between St. Augustine and Descartes in the affirmation of the principle of self-consciousness, but claims that Campanella and Descartes follow two different ways. Campanella follows the way of the senses, which leads to individual self-consciousness; Descartes follows the way of reason, which leads to universal self-consciousness. Descartes' *Cogito* is a principle of thought, whereas Campanella's *notitia sui* is a principle of consciousness, or rather of self-consciousness. Accordingly, the whole difference between the two *Cogito*'s can be summed up this way: Descartes says, "I am, because I think," while Campanella says, "I am, because I think of myself," or, "My being has its foundation in the thinking of myself."[98]

Di Napoli emphatically rejects Pastore's interpretation and accepts in substance the views expressed by Gilson in his criticism of Blanchet. However, he remarks that the differences between the self-consciousness of Campanella and that of Descartes are essential because they stem from a different concept of the reality that underlies the doubt and the self-affirmation in the two philosophers. In Descartes the reality, reduced to an idea as a psychical fact, causes the doubt and the self-certitude of both the idea and the soul, which is nothing but thought. In Campanella the doubt is of an historical and common character for the purpose of achieving a universal systematization of knowledge; it finds its way out in the concept of reality as being *(ens)* with its primalitarian structure. Thus if one takes doubt and self-consciousness in the sense that they are understood in modern philosophy, the French philosopher may be considered their first proponent; but if one takes doubt and self-consciousness in the sense of an attitude of suspension of judgment in the face of all possible problems for the purpose of a critical foundation of knowledge, then the first truly critical philosopher is Campanella.[99]

The foregoing opinions represent the main views that have been expressed on the relationship between the philosophy of Campanella and that of Descartes. Blanchet deserves most of the credit for the large amount of information that he has condensed in his work in regard to both the historical and the critical aspects of the question. However, as Gilson has pointed out, Blanchet overstresses the points of contact between the two philosophers and underrates the influence exerted on Descartes by the Augustinian tradition.[100] Gilson's criticism has certainly helped to mark the difference underlying the two systems of philosophy. Nevertheless, it seems that Gilson overemphasizes the metaphysical approach to the two types of self-consciousness and does not give sufficient consideration to the purely epistemological aspect of the question. As has already been remarked, Campanella does not base his doctrine of self-consciousness on the metaphysical concepts of being and its primalities, but finds in it a radical solution to the universal critical doubt, thus paving the way for his metaphysics proper. This interpretation is also in conformity with Campanella's standpoint that a systematic organization of philosophy would require

that the *principia sciendi* precede the *principia essendi*. If Gilson had
approached the study of the relationship between the two types of
self-consciousness from the epistemological viewpoint, perhaps he
would not have stated that Campanella's affirmation, "Everything that
exists, thinks," is in direct opposition to the Cartesian concept, "I
think, therefore I am." The simple fact is that Campanella does not
posit the principle of self-consciousness in those terms. On the contrary, in Campanella's thought one's own existence represents already,
as it were, a secondary moment in the intuitive act of the self-knowing
soul. Hence Amerio's observation that the principle of self-consciousness is founded by Campanella upon the primalities of only one act,
the concrete act of the thinking soul, is completely relevant.

Pastore's interpretation of Campanella's *Cogito* as meaning, "I
am, because I think of myself," can be accepted only if properly understood, namely, on the condition that self-consciousness necessarily implies self-existence. It cannot be accepted in the sense Pastore attaches
to it, as if Campanella were making one's own existence depend on
the thought that he has of himself. In other words, for Campanella
thought is not the basis of the thinker's being. Rather being, and
especially the human soul, is an essential composite of thought, power,
and volition. These two distinct positions should not be confused,
as unfortunately has been done by those who interpret Campanella's
thought on the principles of the idealistic system.[101]

Since Di Napoli's interpretation of the Campanellian critical doubt
agrees with that of Gilson, our criticism of Gilson's view may also be
applied to him. It is the writer's conviction that in spite of the
emphasis placed by Di Napoli on the metaphysical impact of the
Campanellian doubt and doctrine of self-consciousness, his conclusive
statement concerning the relationship between Campanella and
Descartes is sound. Thus, if doubt and self-consciousness are conceived
along lines common to modern philosophy, then Descartes is their
first proponent; but if doubt and self-consciousness are only considered as a preliminary step to the systematization of philosophy on a
critical basis, then Campanella is truly the first critical philosopher.

The *Cogito*'s of the two philosophers have many common features,
and they show, even if there were no historical proofs, that both have
St. Augustine as their common source. Yet their metaphysical bases
are not the same, nor are their metaphysical implications. The
Cartesian *Cogito, ergo sum* amounts only to the affirmation of the
existence of a thinking substance or thought, while the Campanellian
Cogito means the never-failing consciousness that the soul has of itself

as a being which is essentially power, knowledge, and volition. By reducing reality to the content of a clear and distinct idea, Descartes makes thought the basis of his philosophy and renders impossible any passage from the ideal to the real order. The real is not grasped in the absoluteness of its intrinsic structural constitution but only on the basis of our subjective ideas. It is little wonder, then, that his system has been called a rationalistic phenomenalism.[102] On the contrary, by making knowledge a transcendental constituent of being itself, Campanella keeps an intimate connection between being and knowledge. Thus the Campanellian system is not based on thought as a mere phenomenon but on thought as a reality. For this reason, as well as for the others mentioned, Campanella's principle of self-consciousness cannot be identified with the *Cogito* of Descartes, although the two doctrines unquestionably have many striking similarities.

CHAPTER FOUR

Sense and Intellect
In Knowledge

The knowledge the soul has of itself, as evidenced in self-conscious-ness and innate ideas, does not account for the whole of human knowledge. Campanella was aware of this fact. If in his theory of knowledge, as set forth in the *Metaphysica,* the doctrines of self-consciousness and innate knowledge occupy first place, it is only because he wanted at the very outset to establish certain fundamental principles on. which knowledge could be founded. But the knowledge of the external world was his main concern. It is treated extensively in his *Metaphysica* and *Del senso delle cose* and is touched upon in many of his other works.

The many questions that arise in regard to the character and the process of our knowledge of the extramental world are not treated by Campanella in a systematic way, and it is difficult to follow his train of thought. An effort will be made in the following pages to set forth the essential points of his doctrine. By way of introduction there will be a brief exposition of his notion of man, a necessary prerequisite to an understanding of his epistemology.

I. THE HUMAN COMPOSITE

Man, according to Campanella, is a composite of three substances, body, spirit, and mind or *mens.*[1] The body is the organ of the spirit and is made of moist and solid matter.[2] The spirit, also called sensi-tive soul, is the corporeal principle that animates the body and serves as a vehicle or medium of communication between body and mind.[3] It dwells in the head, as in a fortress, and moves throughout the nervous system, as a pilot travels in the ship.[4] It is the principle of activity and sensation in man as well as in animals, and it takes the place of the Aristotelian "common sense," which has no need to exist.[5] The spirit is united to the body by means of the blood, and in turn it links the blood to the *mens.*[6] It is a mobile, tenuous, bright, warm substance in accordance with the nature of the objects. It participates in the primalities; hence it is sensitive, appetitive, and endowed with power.[7] Being mobile, it hears the sounds that shake the ears; being bright, it perceives light through the eyes; being warm, it feels the cold from which it suffers and the heat that exceeds its own heat.[8]

The sense organs are not instruments of sensation in the way that a pen is the instrument of writing. They are only ways and canals through which sensible objects are brought into contact with the spirit. If it was not enclosed in the body, the spirit would not need such doors and windows.[9]

Because it is corporeal the spirit is not the form of the body in the sense in which Aristotle defines form. It moves from one sense organ to another and is not attached to any organ in particular. It performs various tasks, like sailors in a ship or people in a town. If we should say that the spirit is the form or act of the organic body, we would be forced to admit that the body is its organ and instrument. But no being informs its own instrument; it merely moves and regulates it. It is clear then that the spirit is not the form of the body.

Furthermore, the body is composed of many parts which differ in temperament, color, disposition, and operations; it has bones, viscera, nerves, arteries, flesh, and various members, each one having its own form. How could one single form inform all of them?[10]

Campanella anticipates an objection from the Aristotelians that in his theory the body would continue to exist as such even after the departure of the intellective soul, just as the ship continues to be a ship after the departure of the pilot. He approves the consequence and points out to this effect the identity of Christ's body before and after his resurrection. This is also true of the bodies of others who have miraculously risen from the dead. Experience, he adds, shows that the body of a dead man is not reduced to primary matter.[11] Thus, insofar as the relationship of the sensitive soul and the body is concerned, he rejects the Aristotelian-Thomistic doctrine of a substantial union of primary matter and form. Yet, he does not admit a purely accidental union, for he speaks of a natural and substantial composition in which the parts converge into one form for the achievement of a common end. In this composition, he says, there is a greater unity than between water, millstone, and miller in a mill.[12]

Although the spirit is merely one and not threefold as the followers of Galen hold,[13] and although its substance is thinner than air,[14] still, since it is corporeal,[15] it can be divided, and is subject to dissolution.[16] The main reason the spirit is corporeal is that the sensitive soul is the subject of bodily sensations, which would not be possible unless the spirit were a corporeal substance.[17] Sensation, in fact, is an assimilation of the sensible objects with the sensitive principle, and this requires a real passion from the objects. Hence a likeness between subject and objects, the sensitive soul and bodies, is absolutely necessary.[18]

It could be objected that a corporeal or material substance cannot be the subject of a passion or sensation properly speaking. Faithful to his pansensistic theory, Campanella would answer that the sensitive soul does not perceive an object because it is corporeal but because it shares the primalities of every being, one of which is knowledge or sensation.[19] However, he carefully avoids the mistake of attributing to the sensitive soul the power of thinking and understanding proper to mind (mens), as we shall see presently.[20] If he sometimes speaks of the sensitive or animal soul as though it were endowed with the power of understanding, he does so only because of the lack of precision in his terminology. Whenever he formally discusses the question, he takes care to distinguish between the so-called intelligence of brute animals and the intellectual power of man as a rational being.[21]

As previously stated, the third component of man is mind (mens),[22] created and infused by God into the body already organized by the spirit. Thus mind becomes the form of the whole man and perfects his nature and operations.[23] It is possible for mind to inform both the spirit and the body because of its incorporeal nature, which makes it fit to become the form of all substances, whether they are thick, soft, or tenuous.[24] Mind joins the body by means of spirit and blood. It would not be possible for mind to join the body immediately, because its nature contrasts too much with the material qualities of the body. Hence the spirit is truly the vehicle of the mind.[25]

In an attempt to explain how the intellective soul permeates the spirit, Campanella makes use of the following analogy. Mind is in the spirit as light is in a mirror and in the air. Just as light disappears when the mirror is broken, so the soul disappears when body and spirit are destroyed. It departs from them and goes wherever God has destined it to go.[26] As light is the form of the air, yet does not depend on it but on the sun from which it originates, so the soul does not depend on the corporeal subject which it informs, but on God, the first eternal principle.[27]

From the foregoing statements there seems to be no doubt that in Campanella's opinion the intellective soul is the form of body and spirit in man, or, to be more exact, of the body by means of the spirit. Another passage from Del senso delle cose may throw further light on this point and explain Campanella's attitude toward the Catholic

Church's doctrine on the union of soul and body. He writes:

> I do not deny . . . that the mind which God gives to man may be the form of the human animal, for the Clementine definition so determines. However, that definition was directed against Averroës, who admitted only one intellect for all men, the function of this intellect being one of assistance rather than of information, just as St. Augustine placed divinity in Christ. In order to dispel this error the Pope stated that every man has his own informing soul. Although this has been variously interpreted, I believe it is as he states it, because the soul that God bestows does not depend on matter or temperament but on God in the way that the light depends on the sun. Thus, just as light informs and activates at one time the mirror, the cloud, and the air, so the soul can inform [things of] various temperaments. Such is the soul known to Aristotle, who states that nothing has been produced by God except the motion of the first sphere, which motion has thenceforth been imitated by the other movers.[28]

In this text Campanella's submissive attitude toward the Church's authority is worth noting. However, he is not accurate in his statement of the Church's definition and is arbitrary in his interpretation of the motive behind it. The Council of Vienne (1311-12) does not say that mind is the form of the *human animal,* but it states that the rational or intellective soul is *per se* and *essentially* the form of the human body, thus implicitly condemning the trichotomic theory.[29] Furthermore, it is not true that in defining this doctrine the Council intended to condemn the Averroistic error of one agent intellect for all men. It is commonly admitted that the Council's definition was directed against the doctrine of the information of the soul as propounded by Peter J. Olivi.[30] The weakness of Campanella's position in this matter is evident, and so is his inconsistency, since on one hand he accepts the doctrine of the Church and, on the other, he holds to a theory that is in contradiction with it.

Further confirmation of his apparent reluctance to accept the precise teaching of the Church on the substantial union of soul and body can be found in his *Theologia.* Much later in date than *Del senso delle cose,* this work represents Campanella's definitive opinion. "The human mind," he says, "is not a form except in a broad sense; moreover, it is not rooted [in the body and spirit], but independent."[31] Even supposing that the soul's independence here refers only to the independence of certain acts, the fact remains that Campanella speaks of the *mens* as a form in terms that can hardly be harmonized with the Council's definition.[32]

The nature of the intellective soul, Campanella states, is essentially different from that of the spirit. Because of his soul man is constituted in an order of beings far above mere animals and is able to unite himself with God more intimately.[33] It is precisely because of his soul that man may be called divine;[34] for he inquires about God and the angels and discusses divine things;[35] he tends toward a superior end and strives to attain a happiness that excels all bodily goods.[36] It is because of this supernatural end that the soul is united to the body.[37]

In scholastic fashion, Campanella proves the spirituality of the soul from its acts and operations. If the soul were only the product of the elements, like the spirit in the lower animals, it would never rise above the elements. No corporeal form or power can extend its action outside the body in which it inheres; nor can any effect be higher than its cause, or any part greater than the whole.[38] But man's soul extends its acts beyond the body and the corporeal world;[39] it transcends the heavens and understands other worlds and other suns and divine things *in infinitum*.[40] Hence it cannot be said to be either material or dependent on matter.[41]

On the relation of the soul to its faculties and the relations between the faculties themselves, Campanella sides with St. Augustine and the Scotistic school. He rejects the Thomistic teaching that intellect and will are only accidents of the soul[42] and that the two faculties are really distinct from one another.[43]

II. SENSE KNOWLEDGE AND INTELLECTUAL KNOWLEDGE

The emphasis that Campanella puts on the material elements in the composition of man has a definite bearing on his theory of knowledge of the extramental world. In accordance with a common trend of the philosophy of his time, he reacts strongly against the tendency of a decadent Aristotelianism to exaggerate the power of the intellect and reduce almost everything to abstraction, with a consequent neglect of sense knowledge. Under the influence of developments in the empirical sciences, he wishes to vindicate, along lines laid down by his master and guide, Telesio, the power of the senses by stressing their positive contribution to knowledge. As often happens in reactionary movements of this kind, he goes to the other extreme. Just as in his psychology he sacrifices some of the functions of the intellective soul for the spirit, so in his theory of knowledge of the extramental world he makes the intellect surrender some of its powers to the senses.

1. *Pre-eminence of Sense Knowledge.* With Telesio Campanella claims that all knowledge starts with sense[44] and rests on sense.[45] Sense is the principle of knowledge and certitude. Nothing we imagine, think of, or inquire about with our reason is held by us for certain until we verify it by sense experience.[46] Truth is in fact the entity of a thing as it is, not as we imagine it, and it is sense that bears witness to things as they are. Imagination represents things only insofar as we believe them to be.[47]

Each sense knows the external part of an object through evidence and the rest by reasoning and judgment.[48] One can never say that knowledge acquired by reasoning is true unless it is confirmed by sense experience. Thus St. Augustine and others, relying on their reasoning, denied the existence of the antipodes; the sense experience of Christopher Columbus proved that all their reasonings were groundless. To reason is to proceed to the knowledge of an unknown thing by means of something similar to it and known to the senses. Very often reasoning may become a source of deception because there is only remote likeness between the two things in question.[49]

Man does not reason or argue about things that are certain but only about the uncertain, and in so doing he bases his reasoning on the things that he experiences to be certain. Hence sense is the light through which he sees what is in the dark. When anyone knows a thing by sense, he no longer looks for reasons or arguments. Since Columbus discovered a new world, nobody argues any more about its existence. No one inquires whether the sun is bright, or whether man has the power of locomotion. No one asks whether fire is hot. All these things are known to sense. Aristotle is therefore wrong when he states that sense is less certain than reason, because reason gives the causes of things whereas sense does not. The truth is that sense is certain and does not require any proof, since it is a proof in itself. On the contrary, reason is uncertain and needs proof. When it looks for proofs or causes, it takes them from sense data.[50]

Needless to say, when taken separately, the senses may be wrong in their perceptions, but they may be corrected by new sensations. For example, by sight I see what looks like a broken oar in the water; I then correct my wrong impression by looking at it and touching it out of the water.[51] The report of all the senses taken together gives us the knowledge of the whole thing, for all sense impressions are collected by the single original sense, which is the sensing spirit.[52]

Campanella's efforts to vindicate the validity of sense perception against certain contemporary Peripatetics glow with an ardor that leads him astray. Thus he states that he would only accept what is taught by sense and Holy Scripture: *quae sensus docet et sacrae litterae.*[53] However, this statement and similar ones in the *Philosophia sensibus demonstrata* should not be taken too seriously. They represent only the beginning of his philosophical career, when in an outburst of youthful enthusiasm he threw himself into the midst of the campaign in defense of his favored master, Telesio. The very fact that in the same work he frequently mentions reason in conjunction with sense as a means for obtaining knowledge[54] shows clearly enough that he does not let himself be led into the excesses of the naturalists who discredit reason entirely. In other words, in emphasizing the importance of sense knowledge Campanella does not deny the part exerted by reason, but wants only to demonstrate that all cognition derives from the senses, and that true knowledge is that which is supported by the data of sense experience.[55]

So much for the role that sense plays in Campanella's theory of knowledge. How does he conceive sense? This question deserves special consideration because of the importance he attaches to sense and sensation. His teaching in this connection can only be understood in the light of his notion of man and the trichotomic theory with which we are already acquainted.

In the same place in the *Epilogo magno* where he states that all knowledge rests on sense, Campanella gives us the key to the understanding of what he means by sense. He says that by sense he does not mean the sense organs, but the spirit that perceives through them and is capable of retaining and comparing what it has grasped.[56] In the *Metaphysica* he repeats the same idea in more detail. The five external senses do not differ in their relation to the perceiving substance since they are one and the same with it, but only in regard to the organs and the objects that are attained by the organs. Various organs require various modes of acting and perceiving. In turn various modes require various faculties, which are one in the substance of the sensitive soul but many in relation to the objects. Hence it is not true that there are only five senses in man, as claimed by Aristotle.[57] Because of the plurality of the objects, there are in man as many senses and modes of sensation as there are parts or organs. Yet, radically, there is only one sensitive substance, and therefore one sense, and that is the sensitive soul or spirit.[58] The organs are merely ways or channels of the spirit.

Just as external senses are fundamentally reduced to one sense, i.e., the sensitive spirit, so also are internal senses and their various forms of knowledge. These Campanella classifies as follows: sense proper, memory, reminiscence, faith, discourse or reason, intellect, and imagination.[59] As previously stated, Campanella has no room for the Aristotelian common sense.

Sense knowledge is that gained by touch or from the actual presence of the object.[60] It is real and true knowledge, in contrast to memory, which is a sort of weak cognition[61] by sensation of the past.[62] Memory must be distinguished from reminiscence, which is but a renewed sensation.[63] Both memory and reminiscence are knowledge by real passion and are second only to sense as far as the degree of certitude is concerned.[64] Faith means to sense and to understand through the senses and intellect of others.[65] Discourse or reasoning is to sense things by way of their similarity or likeness[66] and constitutes the basis for science. It is impossible for us to have actual sensation of all things. The closer reason is to sense, the greater is its certainty.[67]

The task of the intellect is to penetrate within a thing and gather information that knowledge of externals, with which the preceding forms of cognition are concerned, cannot reveal to us.[68] Imagination builds up new images by separating and joining together previous images; sometimes it attains its aim, but occasionally it goes astray.[69]

Campanella's description of the functions of spirit may easily convey the impression that everything in his system, including the operations of the intellect, is reduced to sense knowledge. The fact that he frequently insists on the fundamental identification of those functions may help support this impression. Moreover, in terms that seem to leave no doubt as to his standpoint in this matter, he proclaims that the imaginative soul is the same as the sensitive, the memorative, and the rational soul;[70] that the sensitive soul can understand;[71] that the intellect is not to be distinguished from the spirit;[72] and that sense and intellect, as they were known to Aristotle, are one and the same thing.[73] To further increase the confusion caused by such statements, he adds that even the lower animals have all the faculties attributed to the sensitive soul. They are endowed with sense, memory, reminiscence, discourse, and reasoning, as well as with intellect by which they grasp the universal.[74]

It is therefore necessary to penetrate further into the study of sense as Campanella sees it and point out its relationship to intellect in his system of knowledge.

2. *Sense Knowledge and Supersensible Knowledge.* The foregoing paragraph has made it clear that Campanella uses the term *sensus* to

mean different things. It stands either for the sense organs and the knowledge acquired through them or for the spirit as the root and source of all activities connected with the external and internal senses. There is still another meaning that he attaches to sense and sensation. This third meaning signifies the knowledge obtained by direct and immediate contact of the knowing subject with its object. The object may be either the subject itself, in which case we have knowledge through self-presence, or an extramental object present to the subject. It is thus that we have *sapientia,* or intuitive knowledge, which belongs to every being, but particularly to God, angels, and man. In man intuitive knowledge belongs both to the spirit and to the mind. *Sapientia* is the basis for *scientia,* or knowledge through discourse and reasoning, and all other forms of knowledge. Because it is obtained through the presence of its object, *sapientia* is also most certain and most evident knowledge, although not as extensive as the knowledge acquired through science. Let us substantiate our statements with Campanella's own words.

Sense, he writes, is the intuitive knowledge of the theologians.[75] It is a delectable knowledge *(sapientia)* from which discursive knowledge is derived, since we are unable to have an intuition of all things at one time, as God has.[76] Only God has true and active knowledge without passion. On the contrary, our knowledge consists primarily in the sense that one has of himself independently of any process of reasoning. It consists secondarily in the sense of external things, which is passion, from which we know what is good for us; for we have not our own good within ourselves, as God has, but we must seek it outside.[77]

Wisdom *(sapientia)* in man belongs first to the senses, since they are in immediate contact with reality and can better savor things, for *sapientia* is from *sapor.* The mind also has wisdom insofar as it senses, but not insofar as it reasons.[78] Hence it is not true that the principles of the sciences belong to the intellect, as Aristotle claims; they pertain rather to sense. As a matter of fact, whenever a doubt arises about them, it is to sense that we have recourse in order to dispel the doubt.[79] In like manner, sense knows the causes of things.[80] Yet, in spite of its privileged position in regard to knowledge, sense does not possess the knowledge of a thing in its entirety. This is the task of science *(scientia),* reason, and syllogizing, which go from the partial data of sense to the knowledge of the whole thing as well as of its essential and integral parts.[81]

Should we say that science is better than wisdom? By no means, answers Campanella, giving the following proof. Wisdom, or *sapientia innata,* is a primality and comes from God. Hence it is nobler, truer, and more certain, since no error is possible with regard to primalities, being, and the universals. But we may fall into error with regard to the particularities of a thing and to nonbeing, which are the objects of science, or *scientia illata.* Needless to say, science is wider than innate wisdom, but science could not be broadened without wisdom, for we know other things only insofar as we know ourselves to be moved and affected by them.[82] In other words, wisdom essentially inheres in us and is given us by the author of nature, just as power and love are, whereas science is acquired accidentally through an outward reaching wisdom.[83] To sum up, we may say that all knowledge has some relation to wisdom,[84] and that wisdom in turn is based mainly on sense and sensation.[85]

To reduce Campanella's essence of knowledge merely to sensations and sense impressions along the lines of the systems of Locke and Hume is not to do him justice. Moreover, this interpretation completely misrepresents his notion of knowledge. The least we could say of such an interpretation is that it does not take into consideration one of the most important elements of Campanella's psychology, namely, the presence in the human composite of *mens* as its informing principle. *Mens* has in effect the specific task of raising knowledge to a higher level than that of the senses. A few pertinent texts, selected and arranged according to the dates of Campanella's works, will help support our statement and defend him from the charge of naturalism.[86]

In the *Philosophia sensibus demonstrata,* after stating that intelligence belongs to spirit and remains in it, he writes: "The divine soul is united to the perishable spirit, by which it is moved, in order to perfect its operations and to rule over it."[87] The same thought is expressed in the *Prodromus philosophiae instaurandae:*

> Knowing that the spirit senses and understands, we think it is useless to admit that the intellect is a different substance from it. Yet we believe that the intellect called *mens* is infused by God in order to perfect the operations of the body and the spirit, and make them serve to [eternal] happiness.[88]

In the *Quaestiones physiologicae* Campanella emphasizes the fact that in man there are many tendencies and vital operations, such as desire and understanding of the divine and the determination of mortifying one's own flesh, which not only do not agree with the spirit, but are repellent to it. He draws the conclusion that "it is evident that the soul has its own operations by which it does not communicate with sense."[89] The same attitude is adopted in *De sensu rerum*, which was written with the explicit purpose of stressing the role that sense plays in knowledge. He writes: "It is therefore its task [*mens'*] to control and to perfect all knowledge and operations."[90] Likewise in the *Epilogo magno* he states: "To contemplate the ideas, which are various participations of the first idea, is a property of the divine mind infused into man."[91] A further and even more explicit text in the *Metaphysica* defines the *mens'* role in knowledge and its relation to the sensitive faculties in the following terms:

> *Mens* performs together with the sensitive soul all that the latter does: it senses, remembers, reminisces, and reasons about natural things. Furthermore, it has operations of its own in regard to things that by themselves transcend nature (*transnaturalia per se*), to which it also lifts up the sensitive spirit.[92]

In another comprehensive passage in the *Metaphysica*, Campanella specifies the operations of the human soul as distinguished from those of the spirit and reduces them to three. First, the soul knows that things are not such as they appear to be; second, it understands divine things; and third, it has the capacity for ecstasy or rapture.[93] When in rapture, the soul enters into conversation with the world above. This state is called contemplation and in it the soul feels God within itself and is united to Him in a very special way. In so doing, the soul acquires the understanding of the divine, which is its second operation.[94] The other special operation of the human soul, namely, the power to know that things are not such as they appear to be, seems to refer to the so-called *discursus mentalis,* or mental reasoning, whereby *mens* disengages itself from the subjectivity of sensation and grasps the things in their very essence, the truth of which is guaranteed by the resemblance of the things to the ideas.[95]

These same operations of the soul are classified more accurately in the *Quaestiones physiologicae* under the names of *consideratio, contemplatio,* and *meditatio* or *ideatio. Consideratio* is a kind of reasoning that helps greatly in the formation of the judgment. *Contemplatio* is a concentrated intuitive understanding of many things at a single time. *Meditatio,* which is better called *mentis ideatio,*[96] is an operation of the imaginative mind by means of which the soul builds up ideal things and worlds, just as God would create real ones. It corresponds to *cogitatio* on the sensitive level, since both, in Campanella's classification, pertain to the *imaginativa.*[97]

Thus it seems well established that Campanella admits in man a type of knowledge that rises far above sense and reaches up to the realm of the supernatural. Accordingly, all the functions and operations that he attributes to the spirit, and hence also to animals, are to be understood as being essentially different from the functions and operations of the intellective soul.

In a special appendix to *Metaphysica*, I, 1. VI, c. 1, Campanella discusses the differences between man and the lower animals in the fields of knowledge and points out that, although animals are endowed with reason and intelligence, they cannot be compared to man. They do not possess reason and intelligence as a part of their essence, but merely participate in them insofar as their corporeal spirit participates in the primalities. Because of their corporeal nature, animals have neither pure reasoning nor pure understanding. They do not grasp the intimate nature of things but perceive solely what appears externally to their senses. Since both man and the animals have been produced by the same God through His eternal wisdom, the animals, too, partake to a certain extent of our knowing power. Indeed, God's created beings cannot differ entirely from one another. But, in preference to the animals, we have been endowed with an immortal soul. It is because of this soul that man's operations excel those of brutes and are of a superior order. Unlike the sense, mind can act independently of the body and the bodily organs, since it does not need the phantasm to attain to its object, as the intellect does. It can reach the infinite, in both space and time, and it can savor the divine. It is also through mind that the operations of the spirit acquire a higher degree of perfection.[98]

3. *The Double Intellect.* The same inaccuracy in Campanella's use of the word "sense" is found in connection with his use of the word "intellect." For a clear understanding of what he means by intellect, a twofold observation is in order. First, many representatives of the Thomistic tradition during the Renaissance wrongly interpreted the thought of St. Thomas and held that the intellect does not know particular things. The natural consequence was that, by considering the intellect as the faculty of the universal, emphasis was placed on the universal to the detriment of knowledge of concrete and immediate objects. On the other hand, some interpreters of Aristotle had concluded that intellectual knowledge does not go beyond the senses. Telesio pushed this theory to extremes and taught that all knowledge of nature can be reduced to sense knowledge.

Campanella saw difficulties in both systems and took an independent position. On the one hand, he accepted the empirical interpretation of Aristotle's universal and degraded the intellect almost to the level of the senses. On the other hand, he rose above this position by raising the very foundation of the so-called Aristotelian intellect.[99] Campanella used the term "intellect" to signify two different faculties. One does not transcend the senses and belongs both to men and to lower animals. This he calls the *intellectus sensualis,* identifies it with the Aristotelian intellect, and endows it with the power of grasping the universal as well as the particular. The other transcends the senses and belongs exclusively to men, angels, and God. He calls it the *intellectus mentalis* and says that it enables us to attain to the invisible and eternal things. This is the intellect *par excellence,* recognized as such both by theologians and by the best philosophers.[100]

The act of the intellect, Campanella observes, is to read inside the nature of a thing. If it can grasp the whole nature as such, we have the *intellectio intuitiva* by which the intellect becomes similar to the part-perceiving sense. If it does not grasp the whole nature as such, but only insofar as it resembles something else, then we have the *intellectio abstractiva.* Thus, when I know Peter to be a man merely because he resembles Paul, I know him abstractively, or by discursive reasoning. But when I know this man, Peter, with all his particular characteristics, I know him intuitively. Therefore, the difference between intellectual knowledge and sensitive knowledge consists in the fact that the intellect knows the whole nature of a thing, while sense knows only a part of it.[101]

The special connotation that Campanella gives to intuition and abstraction is worth noting. By intuition he means immediate knowledge of a thing in its concrete reality, so that nothing of the object escapes the penetrating and all-embracing act of the intellect. The analogy with sense knowledge in this case goes only as far as the immediate presence of the object to the knowing subject is concerned. By abstraction is meant an operation of the intellect, whereby one aspect of the object is considered without the others, so that an indistinct image of a thing is obtained merely because of its external appearance that makes it similar to another. While the human intellect is not required for this kind of abstraction, it may well be required for intuition, although lower animals also have some sort of intuitive and discursive knowledge.

A passage from the *Physiologia* throws some light on the whole question of Campanellian abstraction and intuition as well as on the nature and function of the twofold intellect. He writes:

> To understand *(intelligere)* is to read within *(intus legere)* sensible things what is not known from their exterior and to reason from what is known. This is something obscure in animals, but very clear in men. However, by understanding *(intellectio)* men usually mean imperfect cognition obtained by the process of abstraction. It is not the kind of abstraction that is made by the active mind purifying the objects, as some people believe—this can only be had by God— but the kind of abstraction that means a diminution of knowledge as well as impotence on the part of the knowing subject. This may be exemplified by the eye, which has the power to perceive the color of an apple without perceiving its taste: not because it actually abstracts the color from the taste, but simply because it cannot perceive the taste, or retain it when it is perceived. Such knowledge is proper to children and animals, as well as to those who perceive a thing from a distance. The intellect, in its capacity as understanding, reads whatever is within a thing *(intus legit omnia)*, not only its universal notes, but also its least particularities. (If this were not so, the angelic intellect and the divine intellect would not grasp such particularities.) It grasps the universal idea, no less than the ideated universal *(universale ideatum)*. All this belongs to man. Abstraction, on the contrary, is a weakness in the animal spirit. It is called intellect but incorrectly, because we do not read fully through it what is hidden within a thing, as an angel does, but only the external common notes, as a child does. Therefore, it should rather be called an apprehensive power *(apprehensiva virtus)*.[102]

In this text Campanella speaks of three acts, or rather three operations, that he attributes to the intellect. The first is to read within the sensible things and to reason from what is known from their exterior. This operation belongs to men as well as to animals, but to the latter only in an obscure way. It is an act of the reasoning spirit, and its perfection is in proportion to the perfection of the spirit itself. The second operation of the intellect is the imperfect cognition obtained through the process of abstraction, whereby only the external common notes of an object are known. It is proper to children and animals, being an act of an apprehensive power rather than an act of the intellect itself. The third operation is what we would call the operation of the true intellect as a spiritual power and consists in grasping the universal idea and the content of this idea in all its particular and universal characteristics. This ability belongs exclusively to men, angels, and God.

We can roughly reduce the two former kinds of operation of the intellect to sense knowledge and the third kind to intellective knowledge, so that the distinction already mentioned between the *intellectus sensualis* and *intellectus mentalis* still holds true.

Campanella himself seems to confirm this fundamental distinction when he sums up in the *Epilogo magno* the discussion on the intellect's operations by saying that "the understanding of the idea as a seal [or archetype] belongs to the mind; the understanding of the idea as being sealed [or as being participated in things] belongs to the interior sense."[103]

A key to the understanding of Campanella's notion of the interior sense, which he mentions in connection with the mind as an inferior species of intellect, may be found in the *Metaphysica*. Relying on the authority of St. Thomas and other philosophers as to the sensitive knowledge of the immaterial, Campanella claims for sense also the knowledge of the universal. The passage reads:

> Averroës, Avicenna, and St. Thomas admit that sense, that is, the interior sense, which is the cogitative or estimative power, perceives the immaterialities. Why then, I say, do they require an unnecessary intellect as a distinct power from the interior sense, since the alleged reason for the distinction between the intellect and the interior sense is none?[104]

In the appendix to *Metaphysica*, I, 1. I, c. 7, he emphasizes the point that St. Thomas calls the cogitative power intellect and reason,[105] and then, speaking of the animals, he writes:

> We are willing, therefore, to acknowledge in animals reason and sensitive intellect, but not the mental intellect. To be sure, the sensitive intellect does not deserve the name of intellect, but only that of estimative power, as the Christian philosopher [St. Thomas] teaches.[106]

On the exact meaning that he attaches to estimative power, a text from *De sensu rerum* is illuminating: "We endow animals with the sensitive reason, called by St. Thomas estimative power, *which is sense by essence, reason by participation.*"[107]

There seems to be no doubt, therefore, that Campanella identifies the interior sense or *intellectus sensualis* with the Thomistic *vis cogitativa*, the highest sensitive power in man, which is immediately linked to the intellect and takes on something of its rational nature. It is this cogitative power which Aquinas calls particular reason, because it compares individual intentions, i.e., unsensed qualities of objects, just as intellective reason compares universal intentions.[108] The *vis cogitativa* has its corresponding faculty in the *vis aestimativa* of the animals, to which Campanella often alludes.

Yet the analogy between Campanella's sensitive intellect and the Thomistic cogitative power should not be extended too far. In the Thomistic economy of knowledge, cogitative power has special tasks to perform with reference to our intellectual knowledge of singulars.[109] On the other hand, in the Campanellian theory of knowledge the sensitive intellect apprehends singulars just as well as the universal. Hence Campanella ridicules philosophers who attribute knowledge of singulars to one faculty and knowledge of the universal, which is but a conclusion from the singulars, to another.[110] This attitude may sound puzzling and somewhat misleading to one who has been formed in traditional scholastic philosophy, for which the knowledge of the universal belongs of its very nature to the supreme cognitive power of the human soul, the intellect. However, it is not altogether inconsistent with Campanella's system if one considers his peculiar notion of the universal.

4. *The Universals.* Campanella distinguishes three kinds of universals: (1) the universal *in causando,* (2) the universal *in essendo,* and (3) the universal *in praedicando.* Of these three kinds, only the first and the third are separately treated by him.[111] The universal *in praedicando* is the Aristotelian universal, which is obtained by abstracting the common notes from the particulars. It is always predicated univocally of individual subjects and not merely accidentally. Thus "man" is predicated univocally of Peter, Martin, and other men, because our intellect grasps the essential similarity among them and conceives the idea of this similarity for which it coins a name. Since our intellect in so doing is somehow acted upon by the objects, this universal is said to be caused and not to be a cause.[112]

The idea with the power to cause is the Platonic universal, which is not a universal in predication but *in essendo* and *in causando.* Whenever this universal is reduced to a mode of predication, it becomes so analogically, not univocally. Thus "man," taken for humanity, is predicated analogically of the ideal man in the mind of God, of man in his existing nature *(in rerum natura),* and of man in our mind; for the idea of man is the formal cause and, as it were, the stamp or model of all existing men. Consequently, the idea of man is also the cause of the concept of man in our mind. Just as the universal *in praedicando* is always something concrete, like man, horse, and white, so the universal *in causando* is always expressed by abstract terms, such as humanity, equinity, and whiteness.[113]

Further developing his thought, Campanella stresses the point that

the universal, i.e., the idea from which the similarity in things and
the concomitant unity of the particulars are derived, is real, while
the particulars have merely the capacity to be in many things through
the idea. Thus a man generates another man by multiplying himself
in the diffusion of the idea, just as through one single idea in the
mind of the architect a plurality of buildings is constructed. Indeed,
no particular building has the capacity to be in many buildings, but
only the building in the mind of the architect. Hence St. Thomas is
no less right in abstracting from the singularity of things than is
Scotus in admitting universality in nature. Yet the latter does not
know the correct term for it. Man, for instance, is not, strictly speaking,
in the nature of things, but he is either singular *in re* or singular
in the intellect, although universally he represents many men: just as
a carving of â crocodile represents many crocodiles. But man as such
is in the mind of God, in relation to which all things are to be
considered, as St. Augustine says. It is therefore more correct to say
that in God he has both unity and universality, whereas *in re* and
in the intellect man, like every other being, is particular. This, of
course, should not prevent us from asserting that every being is universal in its representation, as the same man *in re* and in the intellect
represents many other men whom he resembles. For the universal *in
repraesentando* is everywhere, namely, *in re* and in the intellect, but
it is predicated formally as it is in the intellect, and fundamentally
as it is *in re*.[114]

The foregoing statements contain substantially the Campanellian
doctrine on the universal, which appears to draw a sharp distinction
between the universal of the Platonic type and the Aristotelian universal. Making this distinction even more clear, Campanella writes in
the *Theologia* that the Platonic universal is the idea of the individuals and a cause that precedes material things, and not something
that comes after them. Using the same analogy as in the *Metaphysica*,
he says that it is like a house in the mind of the architect. On the
contrary, the Aristotelian universal is like a house impressed on the
senses of a man who looks at it from a distance, after the house has
been built according to the architect's idea. The former produces
being and knowing; the latter, although a representation of the idea, is
merely the effect of inspection and imperfect knowledge.[115] The
Platonic universal, he insists in the *Quaestiones physiologicae,* is the
eternal idea and the cause of the things as ideated; the Aristotelian
universal is like a common notion that we get from the likeness of
existing things as they are perceived by our senses.[116] In his admira-

tion for Plato and his contempt for Aristotle, Campanella remarks:

> Plato raises man to perfect knowledge, and from the sensible
> things lifts him up to the notion of the divine . . . Aristotle, on
> the contrary, clings to sensible things, like a man who is always
> learning and never understanding anything.[117]

Granted this notion of the Aristotelian universal, it is little
wonder that Campanella does not postulate the agent intellect to
grasp it by the process of abstraction from the phantasm, as the
Stagirite teaches. "Rightly Durandus did away with the agent intellect,
for to abstract the universal species is not the act of any cause, but
rather the result of a weak perception of the object's singularities,
with concentration on its common notes."[118] This is tantamount to
saying that the universal of the Aristotelian type is "weak and poor
knowledge,"[119] or "knowledge from a distance."[120] Thus it follows that
"to know in universal is to know in a confused and imperfect way."[121]
Otherwise stated, the Aristotelian universal can be compared to the
knowledge of a child who calls every man "father" simply because he
cannot grasp the distinctive features of his own father but only the
common notes that make him similar to any other man.[122]

By reducing the Aristotelian universal to an indistinct sensible
image, Campanella deprives it of its real character of supersensible
universality and makes it the object of a sensitive faculty.[123] One
should not be surprised, then, to read in his works statements like
these: "It is evident that the understanding of universals that Aristotle
attributes to men belongs more properly to animals,"[124] and "Dogs
and horses know universals better than particulars."[125] That dogs and
horses know universals is proved by the fact that dogs bark at night
at man in general, while horses eat any kind of barley, not merely a
particular type of it.[126]

A concrete example often mentioned by Campanella shows his
notion of the Aristotelian universal as a confused image of a thing:

> When the sense perceives a man coming forward from a distance,
> it says firstly, "It is an animal"; then, as the man approaches, it says,
> "It is a man." As he draws nearer and nearer, it says, "It is a
> monk"; and finally, "It is the monk Peter."[127]

This example indicates once more that, in Campanella's opinion, the
Aristotelian universal is not so much the result of abstraction as it is
the effect of the imperfection of the knowing subject.[128]

The Platonic universal, however, is entirely different. Campanella
grants the understanding of the Aristotelian universal to animals

but not the understanding of the Platonic universal, which is of a superior order and far above their knowing power.[129] Indeed, the peripatetic universal can be grasped by rude and dull minds that are unable to reach the particularities of things; but only the subtle and pure spirits can grasp the Platonic universal and the ideas of things with their singularities, and at the same time be elevated by the mind to the understanding of divine things.[130]

On the basis of his notion of the Aristotelian universal, Campanella assigns to both sense and intellect the power to grasp the universal as well as the particular.[131] Actually, he says, there is no distinction between the universal and the particular from the standpoint of the object: Peter is a man, just as he is this particular man. Why, then, should there be a distinction in the perceiving faculty, since the object is one and the same for both sense and intellect? If we say that the universal can be known without the particular, we are wrong; for the intellect does not grasp the objects extrinsically but intrinsically, as reported by the sense. Hence, the sense must perceive both the universal and the particular previously to the grasping of the intellect.[132] Aristotle himself teaches that the universal is obtained by induction through the senses, which perceive the universal and the particular alike.[133]

On the other hand, how could the intellect abstract the universal from singulars without first knowing the singulars? To hold this is to make abstraction a pseudo-operation, such as it would be if the intellect attempted to abstract the species of a pear or of a pumpkin from many singular apples.[134] Moreover, the soul separated from the body knows the singulars just as God and the angels do. Why then would our intellect in its present state be different from the sense which perceives the singular, since it is not against its nature to know singulars? Rather, because of its inherence in a singular body, it is proper for the intellect in its present state also to know singulars.[135] This may explain why two great theologians, Scotus and Durandus, hold that the intellect knows singular things directly. Thus, having already proved that sense knows also the universal, it is logical to conclude that both sense and intellect, being rooted in the same soul, know the singular as well as the universal.[136]

To the question whether science is of singulars or of universals, Campanella answers by distinguishing between *scientia inventiva* and *scientia doctrinalis*. Investigative science deals with singulars, while doctrinal science is concerned with universals gathered from the study of many singulars.[137] The universal, however, can only be such in

virtue of the idea which unifies the particulars because of their similarity.[138] This fact shows how foolish it is to believe that science is
of universals only. What do I know if I understand that Peter is a
rational animal but am not cognizant of his individual qualities and
properties? Since it is impossible to know all the particulars, it is
necessary to learn the sciences in terms of universals and in a confused
way. However, God knows the most minute particularities of all
things, and this is true and certain knowledge.[139]

The following diagram may help illustrate the contents of the
present chapter.

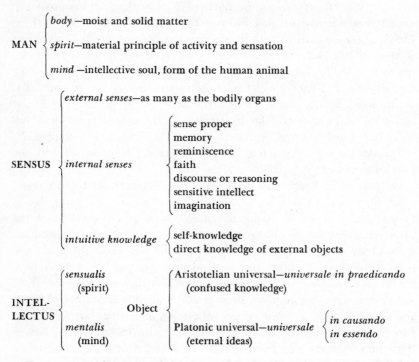

From a consideration of Campanella's doctrine on sense knowledge
as compared to intellectual knowledge, certain conclusions may be
drawn.

First, it is clear that sense occupies a pivotal position in Campanella's system, since all the functions of the spirit are but various
forms of sense and sensation.

Second, the external senses are a more reliable source of information than the internal senses, for they are in more direct contact with
their object and, consequently, less exposed to deception.

Third, although sense performs a very important role in knowledge, there is in man a spiritual power which is superior to the senses and enables him to reach the supersensible. This power is what is commonly known as the human intellect.

Finally, a materialistic interpretation of the Aristotelian intellect, which Campanella lowers to the sense level, is understandable only in terms of his notion of the Aristotelian universal and his peculiar theory of abstraction.

CHAPTER FIVE

The Essence of Knowledge

Our inquiry about knowledge of the extramental world in Campanella's philosophy has thus far been directed to establishing the roles
played by sense and intellect in relation to their objects. The meaning
attached by him to sense and intellect and their respective domains
in the field of knowledge have also been discussed. Problems that must
be faced are the nature of knowledge and the process whereby in the
Campanellian system knowledge is acquired.

To make as clear an exposition of Campanella's thought as the subject demands, discussion will be divided into four sections: (a) the
nature of truth; (b) the empirical explanation of knowledge; (c) the
metaphysical approach to knowledge; and (b) the doctrine of illumination.

I. THE NATURE OF TRUTH

No one can understand the essence of knowledge unless he first
knows what knowledge is concerned with or, more precisely, what is
the object of knowledge. For Campanella the object of knowledge is
truth, which he defines as "the conformity of reality with the intellect,"[1] or better, "of the intellect with reality."[2] There are two intellects: the divine intellect, which knows and produces truth, and the
created intellect, which does not produce but knows truth. All things
are said to be true insofar as they are adequate to the divine intellect,
which is the cause of their being. Insofar as they are adequate to our
intellect, they are not true, but they produce truth in us. We are right
when we understand a thing as it is, and we are wrong when we understand a thing as it is not. Therefore, in the nature of things there
is no falsity, but only truth; for things cannot be otherwise than God
wills them to be.[3]

If we say that there is falsity in things, we will have to admit
falsity in God from whom things proceed, which is a blasphemy. Consequently, truth is the entity of a thing as it is produced by its cause.
The more being a thing has, the truer the thing is; the less being a
thing has, the less true the thing is. This explains why things that
partake of nonentity have also their part of falsity; not in regard to
God, who knows them as they are, but inasmuch as their being does
not correspond to the perfection of God's idea.[4]

92

To say that falsity is in things insofar as they do not correspond to their ideas is not the same as to say that God is the cause of falsity. He merely permits things to participate in nonbeing. But there are falsity and error in us because we do not know things as they are.[5] Hence Aristotle does not seem to be right in admitting falsity only in the human intellect. Falsity is also in things to the extent that they do not have the fullness of being.[6] Thus truth and falsity in things are always mingled together for the reason that no being corresponds entirely to the idea.[7] On the other hand, since our intellect is true when it is conformed to things, and false when it is not, there can be no truth in the intellect without being first in the thing itself.[8]

The concept that truth in created things depends on their conformity with the idea of God is developed more extensively in the *Theologia*. In this work Campanella states that truth is the conformity of the thing "ideated" with the idea, just as a house is said to be true when it is perfectly similar to the idea in the mind of the architect and false when it is not so.[9] Natural things are true when they imitate the divine ideas from which they derive; and since God cannot be wrong in His works, all things are true. Hence being and truth are convertible.[10] Truth, however, adds to being its conformity with the intellect. Because God is not ideated, but is eminently the idea and entity of all things, as well as the cause of all ideated and known entities, He cannot properly speaking be called true. He is the very truth *per se* and essentially, after which all things are said to be true analogically.[11] In conclusion, there is one primary and unchangeable truth, and all things are true insofar as they are modeled on that truth.[12]

From the foregoing statements it is clear that Campanella speaks both of truth of things as related to the mind of God or to our intellect and of truth of knowledge, whereby the conformity of our mind with reality is expressed. Thus truth is attributed by him both to things and to knowledge. In the first case we have what scholastics call *ontological truth;* in the second case, *logical truth.* For Campanella as well as for scholastics the reason that reality has ontological truth is that, antecedently to the perception of our mind, things are already essentially in accord with the divine mind from which they derive their intelligibility. Although ontological truth is for us proximately and immediately the conformity of reality with our intellect, it is primarily and fundamentally the essential conformity of all reality with the divine mind. This conformity is said to be essential, in the sense that reality depends on the divine mind for its intelligibility. The conformity of reality with the human intellect is also essential in that the potential conformity with the latter is inseparable from reality; but inasmuch as the actual conformity of reality with our mind is contingent on the existence of human intelligences, this conformity is sometimes spoken of as accidental to reality.

Bearing this in mind, we can understand why Campanella, in agreement with scholastic philosophy, writes that

> the human intellect does not measure things, of which it is not the author, but it is measured by things. It is true when it is made absolutely similar to them, so that it understands things as they are; not otherwise. Things are true not so far as they are understood by us, but inasmuch as they are understood by God and have received being from God. They are false, when they are otherwise.[13]

If ontological truth is grounded in real being and implies a transcendental relationship of reality to the mind, it follows that there can be no such thing as transcendental falsity. Likewise, if whatever is real is ontologically true, then the ontologically false must be the unreal, or nothingness. This is basically Campanella's doctrine of nonbeing as cause of falsity and error in our mind.

With regard to logical truth or truth of knowledge, things are different. Whereas in the real order, Campanella states, truth and falsity are the being and nonbeing of a thing, in the logical order truth has to be placed in the conformity of the intellect with things. Whenever we understand something, we are changed into the object of our understanding, so that we receive, as it were, the object's being into ourselves. In the very moment that this change takes place, we form a judgment about the object by which we have been changed. If the judgment is in accord with the nature of the thing, the intellect is right; if it is not in accord with the nature of the thing, the intellect is wrong.[14]

Although these statements contain a notion of the process of knowledge that needs further clarification, they seem to point out that Campanella follows Aristotle and St. Thomas[15] in placing the essence of logical truth only in the second operation of the mind, i.e., in judgment. Perhaps the same conclusion can be reached by reading some of the texts quoted above, as when he says that in order to be right the intellect must *understand* things as they are, thus implying a conscious awareness of its own conformity with reality. Yet Campanella explicitly denies this. Relying on his own theory that truth and falsity can be found in things themselves, namely, in their own being and nonbeing, he maintains that the intellect may be right or wrong even in the simple act of apprehension. He writes:

> We admit that truth and falsity are in the intellect as well as in the knower, but not formally, as they [the Aristotelians] hold them to be. Truth and falsity are formally in things. . . They are likewise in things causally, insofar as they make our speech and intellect right or wrong. Furthermore, we assert that truth and falsity are in the intellect and in sense as something real *(quatenus sunt res quaedam)*. In this sense truth and falsity are in them causally and formally, and not merely as they are known *(non modo cognoscitive)*. Just as a thing is true insofar as it is adequate to the idea and false when it is not, so the intellect is right when it is adequate to the thing and wrong when it is not so. However, the intellect has this advantage, *that it can also know the true and the false* [in things] *directly,* and its own [truth and falsity] reflexively. This belongs also to sense (italics added).[16]

In a further attempt to reject the Aristotelian doctrine that truth consists only in the judgment or in that process of analysis and synthesis of reality called *actus componendi et dividendi,* Campanella writes that to know or to speak the truth makes the intellect truthful, but it does not constitute the truth of a thing.[17] He comes therefore to the conclusion that "the intellect is true when it is adequate [to reality], not when it knows its adequation [to it]."[18] The reason he gives is in direct opposition to the reason alleged by the followers of Aristotle and St. Thomas in defense of their doctrine. Whereas they hold that if truth consisted in the mere apprehension of a thing there would be no place for error, for reality, insofar as it reveals itself to mind leads necessarily to a conformity of mind with reality, Campanella maintains that if the intellect is assumed to know its conformity with reality in order to attain truth, there can be no question of error on the part of the intellect. Likewise there can be no question of error in the intellect in knowing its lack of conformity with reality.[19]

Summing up his discussion on the nature of truth, Campanella says that truth is threefold: truth of judgment, truth of things or reality, and truth of conformity of the knower with the object known. This last kind of truth, however, is also truth of reality, for, as will be seen more clearly in the next section, it implies a *real* change in being.[20]

II. EMPIRICAL EXPLANATION OF KNOWLEDGE

If from the epistemological point of view truth means the conformity of the mind with reality, how is this conformity attained in Campanella's theory of knowledge? Before an answer is given to this question an observation is in order. Whereas Campanella's approach to this problem is fundamentally the same in all his works to the extent that it everywhere shows an anti-Aristotelian attitude, the solution that he gives in *Del senso delle cose,* the *Epilogo magno,* and especially the *Metaphysica* and the *Theologia,* is considerably different from the solution that is found in the *Philosophia sensibus demonstrata,* the *Prodromus philosophiae instaurandae,* and other minor works of an early date. While in these early works Campanella proves himself to be a faithful adherent of the main body of Telesio's naturalistic theories, in the more mature works he rises far above the empiricism of his master and envisages knowledge from a higher position. His metaphysical doctrine of primalities, i.e., power, knowledge, and will, as transcendental principles of being, offers him the key to the solution of the problem of knowledge of the extramental world, just as it made it possible for him to solve the problem of knowledge of the intramental world through the doctrine of self-consciousness.

Campanella's discovery and adoption of this new theory does not mean, however, that he completely rejects his former empirical theory, which had been inspired mainly by Telesio's doctrine. He admits substantially both points of view at the same time, and he tries to harmonize them in such a way as to make them essential parts of a unique system. Whether his attempt has been successful remains to be seen. Our present task will be to outline the main features of his empirical approach to knowledge.

1. *Refutation of the Aristotelian Doctrine of Knowledge by Information.* As was pointed out in the preceding chapter, Campanella holds that all knowledge, apart from knowledge of the purely intellective type proper to mind, can be reduced to sense and sensation. It is not surprising, therefore, to see that in his empirical approach to the question of the cognitive process he deals almost exclusively with sensation. He accepts, on the one hand, Telesio's doctrine of the spirit as a corporeal principle in man; and he shares, on the other hand, his philosophy of nature based on the conception of matter or *moles corporea,* heat, and cold as concrete principles of being, in opposition to the hylomorphic doctrine of Aristotle.[21] Hence Campanella cannot offer a better theory of sensation than that of his master. Yet, in an effort to justify his own position against the so-called Aristotelians of his day, he goes much further in the explanation of sensation itself and raises a number of challenging issues.

Aristotle, as is well known, taught that sensation is the act by which we receive the form of sensible things without the matter, as the wax receives the figure of the seal without the metal of which the seal is composed. This form is a likeness or representation of the object and was called *species sensibilis* by the scholastics. It is not the object itself, nor is it something we first perceive and by means of which we are able to infer the object. It is rather a means by which the object itself is known. The sensible species has also been given the name of *intentional form* by the scholastics. It has been called *intentional* for two reasons: first, to distinguish it from those forms which give things their physical entities, i.e., substantial and accidental forms; and second, to indicate that it is not something absolute but something essentially relative determining the knowing subject in his "reaching out towards" the object.

In sensation, according to Aristotle, neither the object nor the subject undergoes any change or destruction as far as its nature is concerned. Furthermore, as the sense must be acted upon by the object in order to act, so distinction must be made between the sense in potency and the sense in act. Sense, however, is alive and responsive. It is not merely acted upon by the sensible object, but it also acts in its own way. Hence "from one point of view," as Aquinas puts it, "sensation is a passion, from another, it is an operation. Thus, in respect to the reception of sensible species, sensation is something passive; but in relation to what follows upon the perfecting of the sense by species, sensation is something active."[22]

In the actual process of sensation, whereby the sensible object is brought to bear on the organ of sense, the sensible in act becomes identical with the sense in act. This means that object and subject become one in the act of knowing. Yet this assimilation, or intentional identification of the object with the subject, is completed only when the subject is actually made aware of the external reality through perception by the internal senses.

The process of sensible knowledge "by information" through the species is applied by Aristotle also on the intellectual level, where the intellect, distinguished into active and passive, takes the place of the sense, and the *species intelligibilis* substitutes, or more exactly, succeeds to, the *species sensibilis.* Just as in sensation the sensible in act becomes identical with the sense in act, so in the act of understanding the intelligible in act becomes identical with the intellect in act. The intelligible forms of corporeal substances, however, are received by the intellect not only without matter, as in sensation, but also without the appendages of matter, since such forms determine and specify a power that is intrinsically independent of matter.[23]

Unfortunately, Campanella understood Aristotle's theory of knowledge by information as the process by which the substantial form of the object to be known is shifted, as it were, from the object to the sense and the intellect.[24] Such an interpretation of Aristotle's doctrine can be explained only by taking into account the complete misrepresentation of the Stagirite's teaching by many Renaissance philosophers. From this misstatement of Aristotle, Campanella drew the natural conclusion that the process of knowledge by information is impossible. It would in effect reduce sense and intellect to pure potencies to be actuated by the form of the object, just as primary matter is actuated by the form. The object itself would be stripped of its substantial form, and it would either be reduced to primary matter or it would perish altogether.

Another absurd consequence from such a conception of Aristotle's teaching is the impossibility on the part of the sensitive power to receive more than the form of a single object without being itself destroyed. By the testimony of all the Peripatetics, the union between the sensitive power and the form of the object in the process of information is greater than the union existing between matter and form. Therefore, just as a being is destroyed when it loses its form, so the sensing power would also be destroyed by taking on a new form.

It is true, Campanella remarks, that in the process of knowledge, as explained by some Peripatetics, it is not the form that comes from the object into the sensitive faculty but only its likeness. However, he states erroneously that this is not Aristotle's teaching. But even on the assumption that only the form's likeness comes from the object and not the form itself, it still remains to be explained, argues Campanella, how this likeness is produced, how it is transmitted from the object to the sensitive power, and finally, how this power after sensing one object will be able to perceive another object. How can a stone, for example, send forth its likeness and still remain a stone? Who is going to extract the stone's image and impinge it on the eye? Moreover, in order to be able to project constantly innumerable images of itself to numberless eyes, the stone should be endowed with almost an unlimited power, which is absurd. Our experience, Campanella claims, contradicts the Aristotelian doctrine of information, as can be evidenced from the fact that it is not necessary to take on the whole form of fire in order to sense the fire, but only a part of it.

Another difficulty that confronts Aristotle's theory is its inability to explain how sense, conceived merely as a passive and incorporeal power, can perceive at one time several objects with different and even opposite qualities, such as cold and heat, black and white. This difficulty does not exist, of course, for a corporeal spirit which is capable of change in its various parts and can receive and sense different species at the same time. But how an incorporeal power like that of Aristotle can perceive a body is unthinkable. Therefore sensation is not by information but solely by change. The only thing that Aristotle states correctly is that sensation is impossible without assimilation.[25]

To avoid all the difficulties involved in their theory the Peripatetics have recourse to the agent sense, which they place either within an animal or outside of it. The agent sense would strip the forms of the matter and carry them in an immaterial way to the sensitive power. But this is evidently false with regard to the sense of touch, in which the object itself impinges upon the recipient, precisely as a pen does in writing or a needle in sewing. The same thing must be said of the other senses. Hence the so-called agent sense is no less fictitious and imaginary than Aristotle's agent intellect as distinct from the possible intellect.[26]

Since he rejects the doctrine of knowledge by information, Campanella also refuses to admit the *intentional* or *universal* species as a means of communication between the object and the cognitive power. His teaching on this point is very clear.

> When they [the Peripatetics] state that the intentional species are received in the senses, they deceive themselves. For these species are called intentional either because they are merely the object of our intention, and then it is a nonsense: we and the animals sense without this peripatetic intention; or they are called so because, although real, they are very thin and unstable like the colors of the rainbow: and this is exactly what we maintain. However, this is not always the case, for certain objects are so strong that they impinge themselves on the senses in such a way that they [i.e., their impressions] can hardly be expelled.[27]

In a passage of the *Epilogo magno* Campanella is even more explicit in discrediting what he considers Aristotle's intentional forms. He affirms that "if the universal species is not the form of things, then it is only an intellectual fiction which will never lead to knowledge of intelligible things."[28]

The reason is that the so-called intentional species (*simulacra intentionalia*) are received only immaterially and intentionally in an immaterial faculty; whereas things do really exist in nature and do really affect our senses in a concrete fashion.[29] Aristotle himself could not deny, for example, that sound is something real and that it concretely moves our hearing power.[30] What deceived him is the phenomenon of sight. Having noticed that the image of the external object is reflected on the pupil of the eye, he was induced to believe that sensation is by information, in contrast to the wise teaching of Plato that sensation is through movement and change.[31]

Yet in Campanella's opinion neither Plato, nor Galen, nor Democritus has given the correct explanation of sight, and hence of sensation in general. Plato, he says, teaches that in sight the rays of light come out of our eyes and catch the visible object. Galen claims that it is not the rays of light that come out of the eye, but the spirit. Democritus states that corporeal images, made of atoms, are shed off the objects and penetrate the eye.[32] None of these explanations is satisfactory to Campanella. In fact, Plato will never be able to tell us how the little amount of light dwelling in the eye or the spirit can be so powerful that it reaches up to the stars, in spite of their brightness. Galen's opinion can be easily refuted on the ground that the spirit, being volative, once it has gone out, does not return to report on the object seen. The wind must carry it away! Finally, Democritus' theory of corporeal images is not a satisfactory solution. Were this theory true, every time a thing is seen by the eye, its surface would be reduced in size; so that an apple, for instance, would gradually lose its skin. Furthermore, vision would be distorted and the atoms would be dispersed by the winds, thus making vision impossible.[33] Hence a new solution of the whole problem of sensation is necessary. Following in Telesio's steps, Campanella claims that he will give it.

2. *Theory of Sensation.* In sensation, Campanella says, we have a two-fold operation. We have on one side the action of the sensible object, which consists in the diffusion of its own essence and likeness; on the other side we have the passion of the perceiving subject, which is the reception of that essence and likeness. The result of this combined operation is an assimilation of the agent and the recipient, both of which contribute their share of activity, although in a different way.

As far as we are concerned, sensation is a sort of passion. Thus we feel heat when we receive heat in us and become hot; we feel cold when we become cold; we feel color when our eyes become colored; and so on. This is so true that even Aristotle and most of the ancient philosophers agree with it. They teach, in effect, that sensation and understanding are possible only when sense and intellect become the perceived and known object.[34]

A confirmation of what has just been said can be found in the absence of any sensation whatsoever when the object cannot act upon our perceiving faculty. Thus in Italy people do not perceive things that are in America, because such things do not act upon them. On the contrary, we feel to the utmost degree what acts upon us very strongly, for example, a very severe cold or an intense heat. It seems, therefore, that sensation is a sort of passion through which we know what acts upon us, for the perceived object produces in us an entity similar to itself.[35]

But sensation is not merely a perfective passion, as Aristotle thinks; it is also a corruptive passion. In fact, every sensation is either pain or pleasure. Since pain is corruptive and pleasure preservative, sensation is both corruption and perfection.[36] From this it follows that sensation, and hence knowledge, involves a real change in the perceiving subject, whereby the latter becomes partly similar to the acting object. Without this assimilation knowledge is impossible.[37]

Moreover, sensation is perception of passion and a judgment of the sentient subject about the perceived passion.[38] From the little that we perceive of the object, we judge the rest of it and other things as well.[39] By some this is called sensation by similarity; by others it is called discourse, because the perceiving spirit moves from one thing to another similar to it.[40] Perception and judgment about passion, and consequently about the object producing passion, give rise to formal knowledge, which cannot be obtained by passion alone.[41]

All these ideas on sensation are condensed in a key text of the *Epilogo magno.*

Because the spirit of an animal does not sense all the things by which it is acted upon, but only those which have the power to change it . . . we maintain that sensation is perception of passion. It is not knowledge by information in such wise that the spirit has to be transformed into the substance of the object and take on the form of it; otherwise it would become sun by sensing the sun, earth by sensing the earth, and so on. Being corporeal, it is not necessary that the whole spirit be transformed, but only a part of it; and even this part does not have to be transformed entirely, but only to the extent that from the little by which it is affected, it can infer the rest of the power of the object acting upon itself. Thus by sensing a certain amount of heat in the presence of fire, and by realizing that the closer it comes to it the more it is transformed by it, it infers the great power of fire. Accordingly, sensation implies also a judgment about the sensible object.[42]

This passage clearly shows that for Campanella there can be no real sensation without perception of passion on the part of the sentient subject. As he will say later in the *Metaphysica,* when a hair of our head is burned, we do not feel it, for we do not perceive the passion, nor do we judge about the object that has caused the burning, just as a man who is sleeping does not feel the bite of a flea on his hand. Thus sensation cannot be separated from perception of passion.[43] The passage affords further evidence for his teaching that in sensation there is always a partial alteration of the subject through assimilation, and that from this partial alteration the sense, or rather the sensitive intellect, infers by discourse the whole nature of the object.[44]

At this point we may ask how sensation is actually brought about or, in other words, how the spirit which perceives through the sense organs, as previously shown, can actually get in touch with sensible objects. Campanella answers this question by saying that all sensation is by corporeal contact, although the organs and the modes of sensation are different.[45] For sensation is the process by which the action of the sensible object is received into the sensitive faculty. Since action and passion do not take place unless there is contact, it is evident that sensation is by contact.[46]

One may ask further how this contact is effected. The spirit, Campanella will answer, is endowed with a sensitive capacity that functions through the bodily organs by means of which external objects are introduced to it. Since in assimilation there must be some likeness between the assimilating power and the object assimilated, the spirit, under the guidance of God, has constructed as many sense organs in the body as there are entities to be communicated by things. These entities are similar in nature but not in degree. Thus, because the spirit is bright, subtle, warm, and mobile, certain organs, like the eye, have been produced by means of which simple and colored light is introduced. There are other organs, like the ear, through which movement and the objects causing movement are received. There are still others, like the nose and the tongue, by means of which the tenuous exhaling substance or the substance tempered with heat is perceived. Finally, the whole body has been constructed in such a way that heat and cold, the ever-acting agents, are sensed everywhere by touch. No other impression from things outside is possible; and if there is any, it is not perceived by us. Hence certain things are of themselves sensible, like heat, light, smell, taste, and sound; other things are sensibly perceived through things other than themselves, like things that are warm, illuminated, odoriferous, savory, and audible; while still others are accidentally mingled with all of these, like a man, a bell, a tree, the sky, a body, a substance, or the soul, which we sense by inference from other sensed things in such wise that we have the impression of sensing them directly.[47]

The passage just quoted from the Paris edition of the *Physiologia* is extremely important, because it contains in germ Campanella's teaching on the process of sensation, and shows once more his dependence on Telesio's doctrine. Reporting his master's teaching, he says in the *Metaphysica* that

> objects impinge on the sentient soul, either because they are active in themselves, such as heat, cold, and light, or because they are commingled with the action of another. For example, an illuminated quantity and a substance which is warm, cold, mobile, or exhalant, are brought to the sensory organs by heat or by cold, by light or by the air which communicates the motion to the ears. It may also be that the tenuous substance of the objects affects the nostrils. Therefore, every sensation is through touch and corporeal change.[48]

This text and the one from the *Physiologia* are complementary to one another. Whereas in the *Physiologia* the role played in sensation by the spirit is carefully described, in the *Metaphysica* the action of the objects is given special consideration. In this latter text the idea is also emphasized that, in addition to touch or contact, sensation involves a *corporeal change*. That this is not merely a Telesian concept, as the text may seem to imply, can be demonstrated by all the passages in which Campanella speaks of *a real change* in sensation, in opposition to the intentional assimilation of the Peripatetics.[49] This fact can also be proved by those passages in which he emphasizes the idea that the spirit, a corporeal substance, by sensing and knowing things, is actually transformed by them.[50]

It would be erroneous, however, to conclude from this discussion that things themselves, or even their accidental qualities, are received by the spirit in their physical entity. This would be a materialistic interpretation that Campanella had already dismissed as absurd when dealing with the Democritean species.[51] The spirit, as the two passages clearly indicate, is affected in a different way according to the different kinds of objects by which it is acted upon and also according to the different structure of each sense organ. Thus, in sight, light is the medium between the eye and the object, so that what the spirit sees through the eye is not the object itself but the light dyed with color of the object and brought to the eye by means of the air. By this partial sensation the spirit infers the nature of the object. Hence sensation is real, because the sense is really moved; yet the object itself moves the sense only accidentally.[52]

What has been said of the sense of sight can be said analogously of the other senses. However, in some of them, especially taste and touch, there is usually an immediate contact between the object and the sensory organs, which makes sensation more intense.[53]

Here we may appropriately ask whether Campanella allows room for the *sensible species*. More specifically, we may ask whether, in spite of his campaign against the species of the Aristotelian and Democritean types,[54] he still maintains that some sort of species is involved in sense knowledge. His teaching on this point seems to be extremely confused, or even contradictory. Shall we say then that Campanella is inconsistent in his attitude toward the sensible species, or shall we admit in him an eventual change of opinion in this respect, so that he accepted later what he had rejected in his earlier works? The second hypothesis seems to be supported by the fact that most of the statements favorable to the admission of some sort of species in knowledge are found in the *Theologia*. In the earlier *Del senso delle cose,* and for that matter even in the *Metaphysica,* his attitude toward species is rather negative.

After a careful study of all pertinent texts, the present writer has come to the conclusion that neither contradiction nor change of opinion is necessarily involved in Campanella's teaching, provided we interpret the texts according to their own context and do not place undue emphasis on their verbal expression. Our claim is that, with the exclusion of knowledge by immediate contact, Campanella admits sensible species as something that the spirit perceives first as its direct and immediate object, and by means of which it derives by inference the nature of external objects. These species are neither the intentional species of the Aristotelians nor the corporeal images of Democritus. As previously stated, they may assume as many different forms as there are sensations. They are either illuminated air dyed with the color of the object, as in sight; or vibrating air, as in sound; or air tempered by heat or any odoriferous and savory substance, as in touch, smell, and taste. In all cases, they are always something material which impinges on the senses and represents to a certain extent the external object.

Keeping this in mind, we can understand why Campanella sometimes writes as if he would reject altogether the theory of the species,[55]
while at other times he seems inclined to accept the species both as
id quod is perceived in sensation and as *id quo* we attain the object.[56]
Moreover, we must remember, on the one hand, his usual lack of
accuracy in writing, and recognize, on the other hand, that the species
he admits are after all mere representations of things. On the basis
of these considerations, we are more likely to explain, in a way to
exclude any contradiction, certain statements of the *Theologia* and
Del senso delle cose which, taken separately, may lead to an implicit
acceptance of the *species of things* in the process of sensation.[57] It is
inconceivable that Campanella would contradict himself in a matter
that he had already thoroughly discussed in many places in his works,
and even in the works where the supposedly diverging statements are
to be found, and on which he had taken a definite stand.[58] Nor can we
legitimately admit a change of opinion unless there is clear evidence
for it.[59]

Thus, it is logical to conclude that Campanella's doctrine on the
species as expounded in the course of this study reflects his thought
throughout all his works and that it did not undergo any substantial
change.

III. THE METAPHYSICAL APPROACH TO KNOWLEDGE

The main conclusions to be drawn from Campanella's empirical
explanation of knowledge are: first, that knowledge, which is reduced
chiefly to sensation, is not by information through Aristotelian species;
second, that knowledge is not only passion but also partial assimilation
through bodily change, as well as perception of passion; and third,
that this assimiltation is made by contact between the knower and
object known through a special type of sensible species. In this
approach to knowledge Campanella does not rise about Telesio.

Yet the naturalistic doctrines of his master could not offer an
adequate solution of all the difficulties involved in the complex problem of knowledge. Hence Campanella felt a need to face the problem
from the standpoint of being itself, conceived as an essentially knowing nature. Knowledge of the extramental world is thus raised from
Telesio's empirical level to the level of metaphysics proper. It becomes
part, as it were, of the very essence of the soul, in an analogous way
with the knowledge that the soul has of itself through self-presence.
It is with this metaphysical approach, which represents a new and

original phase of Campanella's theory of knowledge, that we are now concerned.

1. *The Meaning of "cognoscere est esse."* In *Del senso delle cose* Campanella lays down his new fundamental principle of knowledge in these terms:

> Everything knows itself to be, is contrary to nonbeing, and loves itself. Therefore, everything knows itself through itself, and it knows other things not through itself, but inasmuch as it becomes similar to them. This similarity is so great that one thing perceives other things by perceiving itself changed into, and made, the other things, which are not what it is itself.[60]

That is to say, one thing knows another inasmuch as it becomes, so to speak, the other thing, whereby knowledge of external things is also knowledge of itself.

This concept of knowledge, which is stated only briefly in *Del senso delle cose,* is fully developed in the *Metaphysica* to which the original Latin text of *Del senso delle cose* refers.[61] In the second part of the *Metaphysica* Campanella again discusses the Aristotelian and Telesian systems of knowledge. He then states his own point of view, different from both Aristotle's and Telesio's, and holds that sensation and knowledge belong to the very essence of things. Each thing is sensed and known, insofar as it is itself, as it were, a knowing nature. For sensation is assimilation, and all knowledge is possible because of the fact that the knowing essence of a thing becomes the object to be known. Thus, it knows the object perfectly, for it already is the object. Therefore to know is to be: *cognoscere est esse.* A being that is many things knows many things; a being that is only a few things knows only a few things.[62]

The new trend of thought as well as the metaphysical significance contained in these statements cannot escape the attention of the reader. It would be an exaggeration to see in their author a definite break with his former empirical approach to knowledge, but it would also be a lack of understanding not to recognize the striking development that Campanella's theory of knowledge has thereby undergone. In this new approach, knowledge is still called sensation and assimilation; but the assimilation is broadened to mean a real transformation of the knower into the object known. For example, when the soul, in virtue of its essential vital activity,[63] knows other things, it does not know the things, but it knows itself as changed into them.[64] Hence knowledge is the entity of the thing known into which the knower is changed; or, rather the other way around, it is the entity of the knower that becomes the object known.[65]

Campanella was well aware of the innovation that he was thus introducing into his theory of knowledge. In a passage in the *Metaphysica* he is anxious to tell us that, in contrast to what had been held by many philosophers, and incidentally by himself too, knowledge is neither an action nor a passion, but something much more divine. He calls it a *pre-eminence of the entity,* or a *primality,* a term of his own coinage, and holds that knowledge belongs to the very nature of being.[66] Therefore every being, from the very fact that it is a being, has knowledge as its essential principle.

We are already acquainted with this doctrine insofar as it refers to self-knowledge or *notitia innata* of a being, but Campanella seems to extend the identification of being and object also to acquired knowledge or *notitia illata.* St. Thomas himself, he says, has already cautiously suggested the idea of the identity of knowledge and being, when he states that the difference between beings that know and beings that do not know consists in the fact that the former are not only their own being but also the being of other things, i.e., of the things known, while the latter are only their own nature.[67]

Campanella holds that Telesio is wrong in reducing all knowledge to perception of passion from outside. The cause of his error is that he considers only the imperfect and partial knowledge of things and not their complete knowledge. Moreover, he thinks merely of knowledge as obtained through passion and reasoning, instead of thinking of it also as an actual part of being. Were knowledge not an essential part of being, God, who is in no way affected by things, could not know Himself; nor could angels know themselves, for they are not subject to passion.[68] However Telesio's doctrine, if properly understood and carried to its logical conclusion, leads equally well to the recognition of knowledge as an essential part of being. For if passion really causes knowledge by making the knowing thing become the thing known through assimilation, it necessarily follows that knowledge belongs to being and is not merely a passion.[69]

Campanella no doubt realized that his doctrine savored of a dangerous novelty and could mislead his readers. Just as he had appealed to the authority of Aquinas to support it, so he now brings on the scene Aristotle and Averroës. Well, indeed, he states, does Aristotle say, and Averroës repeats in even better fashion, that the union between the knower and the known is greater than the union between matter and form, since the intellect becomes the very object known and no third entity results from them as from matter and form. However, they are wrong in affirming this of the external intelligible object, which indeed is only partially known. Telesio states it in a better form. Yet Averroës' teaching is correct with regard to the internal intelligible, which is known in its totality and not only in part.[70]

Having established a connection among himself, Aristotle, and Averroës, Campanella then gives a more concrete explanation of human knowledge. He compares it to divine knowledge. In God, he says, and in God alone, all that is intelligible is absolutely identical with His mind. In creatures, on the contrary, nothing knowable is identical with the knower except the being of the knower himself. An adventitious being can only be identified with the knower when it is powerful enough as to transform the knower into its own nature, just as fire can transform wood into fire.[71] In this case, however, we no longer have an identification of object with subject, but a substantial change in which the nature of one thing is transformed into the nature of another.

From these statements it is evident that Campanella clearly distinguishes in creatures self-knowledge from hetero-knowledge. In the former there is a perfect identification of intellect with object; in the latter the identification is only partial in both extent and form. How then can this teaching be brought into agreement with his former affirmation that *cognoscere est esse*? Between the two positions there seems to be a contradiction, for in one place is denied what is affirmed in the other. If the knower is not to be identified with the known, how can one maintain that *cognoscere est esse*? Nor can one shirk the difficulty by saying that this latter is only a casual or incidental statement. Its constant recurrence throughout the *Metaphysica* makes it the distinctive label of Campanellian epistemology, just as *esse est percipi* is the label of Berkeley's theory. Furthermore, Campanella insists so much on the identification of knowledge with being that any doubt about this point seems to be out of question. More evidence is provided in the following texts.

> . . . I do not see what can prevent us from affirming the identity of knowing and being. Indeed, if knowledge is by information, it is manifest that in the opinion of all the Peripatetics it must be identified with the being of the intellect itself . . . Therefore, not only the understanding of one's self is one's own being, but also the understanding of other things.[72] . . . If, on the other hand, knowledge is produced by partial transformation, as Telesio claims, then, in this case too, the knowledge of external things belongs to being. In fact, just as in a total change whatever is transformed

goes entirely into the nature of the transforming subject, so also in a partial change the thing transformed becomes partly the subject.[73]

Since this is the case, an explanation of this apparent contradiction must be sought elsewhere. Because of the impossibility of attaching any ambiguous meaning to the statement that "nothing knowable is identical with the knower except the being of the knower himself,"[74] it is necessary to turn to the statement that *cognoscere est esse* and to see if it can be interpreted to agree with his former position. The whole question comes to this: What is the real meaning of *cognoscere est esse?*

Before an answer is given to this question, it must be made clear that we are not discussing the relationship in Campanella's philosophy between the knowing subject and the object in its extramental reality. To be more definite, there is no question in our opinion of the objectivity of the external world, which is postulated beyond any doubt in Campanella's very notion of truth, as already expounded.[75] The problem here is the relationship between the knowing subject and the external object *as known,* or between the soul and the intelligible object *as such.* In other words, it is the problem of the relationship between the Campanellian *cognoscere* and *esse* from an epistemological as well as from a psychological point of view, prescinding entirely from either its physical or metaphysical aspect.[76]

In the passage in the *Metaphysica* where Campanella's principle that *cognoscere est esse* is first stated, we also read that just as sensation is assimilation, so "all knowledge is possible because of the fact that the knowing essence of a thing *becomes* the object to be known. Having *become* the object itself, it knows it perfectly, for it already is the object."[77] We have underlined the verb *become* in its double occurrence, for it seems to us that this verb offers the key to the solution of the problem under discussion. The statement that the knowing essence *becomes* the object to be known is indicative of a process in which two distinct factors are involved, the knower and the knowable object. Since this process, whereby "all knowledge is possible," is compared by Campanella to sensation, which "is assimilation," we can assume that in the process of *becoming* something takes place which is also very close to assimilation. The least that can be said is that in this process the distinction between the knowing essence and the object known is not entirely suppressed, as in self-knowledge, and that our mind does not create its object or the world of objects, as the followers of transcendental idealism teach.

This view is supported by other passages in the *Metaphysica* where knowledge through *becoming* is presented as something different from knowledge inherent in the very essence of being. Thus the heading of one of its articles reads: "That knowledge, sensitive, imaginative, intellective, and memorative, consists in this, that the knowing subject *is* or *becomes* the being of the known object" (italics added).[78]

Granting then that in the process of becoming there is something akin to assimilation, one may further inquire about the extent of this assimilation. Is this assimilation to be understood in such a way as to mean the complete disappearance of the being of the knowable object as such, so that *cognoscere* is ultimately and exclusively the *esse* of the knower himself? Campanella warns against this misunderstanding by remarking that because something passes into another being its own being is not thereby destroyed. For "the knowledge of one's self is the being of one's self; the knowledge of other things is the being of other things."[79]

This latter statement is illuminating. While giving a definite clue to Campanella's idea of the relationship between subject and object in the process of extramental knowledge, it throws further light on the meaning of the doctrine that *cognoscere est esse*. Its main point is that although to know is to be, yet a distinction has to be admitted in the very act of knowledge between the being of the subject and the being of the object known. This distinction, which is thus explicitly stated, is of course already implied in Campanella's endeavor to show the fundamental identity of his teaching with that of Aristotle and Telesio. In addition there is Campanella's own statement on the reality and extent of this distinction. The fact that this statement is a conclusion in the same article where he proclaims that all knowledge belongs to being makes it even more relevant. He writes:

> It is clear, then, that all beings sense themselves because they are themselves and have no need to become. Therefore, *really* and *fundamentally*, to know is the being [of the knower]; *formally*, it is distinct, for it is a being inferred by reasoning.[80]

Thus a distinction is introduced between knowledge that a being has of itself in virtue of its own nature and knowledge that a being acquires from outside. To use Campanella's terminology, a distinction is made between *notitia innata* and *notitia illata*. Both types of knowledge are said to belong to being; but in one case the being referred to is the original being of the knower, while in the other case it is the being inferred by reasoning and formally distinct from the being of the knower.

This explanation, which is sometimes quoted by Campanella's commentators as his final word on the difference between self-knowledge and hetero-knowledge,[81] no matter how helpful it may be, still does not entirely solve the problem at issue. To reduce all knowledge to knowledge of one's self and knowledge of a being inferred by reasoning is to oversimplify the matter. It leaves no room for the type of knowledge obtained through real change and assimilation, the object of our particular concern here. We feel then the need of supplementing Campanella's own statement by distinguishing, on the basis of his doctrine otherwise known, a double kind of knowledge of the extramental world: the knowledge of the object acquired through a partial assimilation and some sort of impressed species, and the knowledge of the object obtained through the process of reasoning from the partial entity assimilated by the knowing subject.[82] Keeping in mind this distinction, we can easily answer in Campanella's own words that it is only in an imperfect and analogical way that the subject is said to become the being of the object inferred by reasoning.[83] What remains to be explained is the nature of the knowledge obtained through partial assimilation. For this explanation, appeal is made to further texts in the *Metaphysica*. In one of these texts Campanella specifies that the soul and all other beings know themselves primarily and essentially and know other things only *secondarily* and *accidentally,* insofar as they know themselves changed into, and made *in a certain way* the things by which they are changed.[84] This very concept is repeated later in the same work when he states that we know only what we are either essentially, that is, ourselves, or *accidentally,* that is, things outside of us into which we are changed.[85] It is clear, therefore, that knowledge of the external objects is only *accidental* to us.

What is the precise nature of this accidental knowledge? Is it called accidental in the sense that it merely *happens* to be our knowledge on the occasion of the presence of the objects; or is it called accidental because of its very nature that makes it opposed to essential knowledge? This question seems to have troubled Campanella himself when he was confronted with the task of defining the specific character of the soul's reflexive knowledge and of the soul's knowledge of the external objects. He answers in the following terms:

> I admit that in all created things such a reflexive knowledge [of the soul], as well as the knowledge [that the soul has] of other beings, is only an accident. It comes from the outside, and the intellect understands them [i.e., other beings] insofar as it knows

itself changed into, and made, them. But as far as the essential and original knowledge of one's self is concerned, I firmly hold with Augustine that the intellect, in its act of understanding, does not differ in any way from the object of its understanding.[86]

This passage seems to dissipate all doubt as to the entitative accidental character of hetero-knowledge. Yet this fact does not exclude the accidental nature of hetero-knowledge in its mode and origin, as will be shown. Are we then allowed, on the basis of this text, to admit a real distinction between the soul's knowledge of itself through self-presence and its knowledge of the external world through assimilation, such as we find in Thomistic philosophy between two distinct realities? The text does not warrant such an inference, which, in any event, would impair the notion of identity of knowledge and being so much emphasized by Campanella throughout his *Metaphysica*. The present writer is rather inclined to apply here the *formal* distinction mentioned by Campanella in this connection,[87] which is therefore extended not only to knowledge of external objects obtained by inference but also to knowledge obtained through assimilation of the object. This formal distinction, which is similar to the Scotistic formal distinction,[88] seems to be appropriate here, since it preserves the essential identity of knowledge and being, and allows at the same time for a certain degree of distinction between self-knowledge and hetero-knowledge on the part of the subject.

2. *Knowledge by Specification.* In addition to the nature of knowledge and the relationship between knowledge and being, another aspect of Campanella's metaphysical approach to knowledge must be studied. This concerns the process by which the subject attains to the object.

Campanella denies that in the process of knowledge the subject is merely a passive potency receiving in itself the species of things, as Aristotle is asserted to have taught. Nor does he admit with Plato that the knower possesses in himself the innate species or ideas in a sort of dormant state from which they are awakened by things and brought to a knowledge of the individual. How, then, does he explain the process whereby the knowing subject becomes partly the being of the object and is consequently able to attain by reasoning to the rest of the being? In other words, what is the action of things upon the knowing subject? In accord with his own tenet that, properly speaking, a being of inferior order cannot act upon a being of a superior order,[89] Campanella says that things do not produce knowledge; they are only the *occasion* whereby knowledge, already existing in a confused way in the intimate structure of the soul, becomes exactly this or that kind of knowledge, or knowledge of this or that thing. We have thus a cognitive process that may be called knowledge *by specification*.[90] To use an illustration,[91] just as he who possesses light possesses all the colors contained in it and is able under certain circumstances to distinguish them, so the soul has in itself, as it were, all the objects as a whole *(per modum unius)*, but does not distinguish them unless it is moved to do so by "ideated," i.e., concrete objects from the outside.[92]

In this process by specification, Campanella goes on to say, we can still speak of passion, but only to the extent that a flowing being *(esse fluens)* is added by the objects to the knowing subject. This "flowing being" does not give rise to knowledge; it merely offers to the radical knowledge of the subject the occasion of revealing itself, as a stone when struck emits fire.[93] Objects powerless to produce knowledge (for instance, how could an unknowing stone instruct me about its own nature?[94]) give the primalities of being the opportunity to act in that particular way which corresponds to the objects. To be more explicit, intelligible objects do not move the intellect to understand, nor do they cause its understanding. They merely furnish intellect an occasion for understanding each object in particular.[95] Hence it is not knowledge that is acquired but only knowable objects.[96] Just how this phenomenon occurs seems to have been somewhat mysterious even to Campanella, who concludes his explanation by saying that there is something in this process that cannot be explained in human words.[97]

It has been suggested that Campanella's teaching on the process of knowledge, if properly understood, is not too far removed from the Aristotelian-Thomistic doctrine of information. His campaign against *species*, it has been said, is merely "a campaign against the deformation that such elements of the Thomistic gnoseology had suffered during the Renaissance." If we change the name, "the *esse fluens* expresses nothing but the Thomistic doctrine of intentionality." In other words, according to this view the Campanellian *esse fluens* corresponds to St. Thomas's *esse intentionale*. What Campanella adds to the Thomistic theory of knowledge is "a universal and systematic affirmation of its interiority through the doctrine of the primalitarian structure of being."[98]

This interpretation has the advantage of putting in its proper light Campanella's dependence on St. Thomas and his school in the explana-

tion of the process of ideogenesis. The following considerations seem
to support it: (1) Knowledge is said to be a "communication of an
entity," implying thereby some means of communication between
the knower and the known.[99] (2) In the act of knowing, the intellect
is represented as becoming the intelligible object: a process that
recalls the Thomistic *esse intentionale,* even if its meaning is somehow
distorted.[100] (3) Campanella appeals to the information doctrine of
Aristotle and St. Thomas to support his own opinion on the identity
of knowledge and being.[101] (4) He asserts, in connection with the
cognoscere est esse, that "the more we know, the more we are," and
consequently, "the one who is all things, knows all things," whereas
"the one who is only a few things, knows only a few things."[102] (5)
Finally, he explicitly mentions the *species* in the process of knowledge.[103]

These considerations, which carry weight in favor of Campanella's
Thomistic tendencies, are counterbalanced by other considerations of
no less value: (1) It is true that in the process of knowledge a "communication of an entity" is said to take place; but the entity so communicated is far from representing the whole object, as is the case
in the Aristotelian-Thomistic doctrine of intentional species. The
knowledge acquired by the subject through the so-called *esse fluens*
is only a partial cognition or the beginning of the knowledge of the
object.[104] Furthermore, Campanella quotes approvingly the *Liber de
causis as* saying that "every intellect understands in its own way, and
not as things really are,"[105] a teaching that he repeats in many other
places.[106] St. Thomas states, on the contrary, that the intelligible
species are a faithful representation of the object as it really is,
although only in the intentional order. (2) In Campanella's teaching,
the external objects are not the cause of our knowledge but only the
occasion of its accidental specification. The cause is the soul itself
in virtue of its primalitarian structure.[107] Here again we are in conflict with the Thomistic teaching that the objects exert a real causal
action in the process of knowledge.[108] (3) Whereas Aristotle and St.
Thomas teach that the soul before the reception of the species is like
a *tabula rasa,* Campanella states that the soul, even before its actual
contact with objects, has already a confused knowledge of things.[109]
(4) Since Campanella denies the active and possible intellects as such,
the formation of the intelligible species in the Aristotelian-Thomistic
sense seems to be impossible. (5) Finally, whenever Campanella discusses *ex professo* the problem of knowledge, he rejects emphatically
the doctrine of information through the species.[110] His incidental

mention of the species in the *Theologia,* as reported above,[111] does not seem to weaken his many arguments against the admission of the species or indicate any change of attitude from his former position.[112]

In conclusion, the writer cannot accept the opinion that identifies Campanella's *esse fluens* with St. Thomas's *esse intentionale.* The points of contact between the two do not go beyond the limits of a mere external appearance. Furthermore, he believes that, while Campanella explicitly rejects the doctrine of the philosophers that preceded him, he himself does not have a clear idea of the process of knowledge on the intellectual level. His recourse to the *esse fluens* is only an attempt to reconcile the objectivity of the extramental world with his basic tenet that all knowledge is fundamentally knowledge of the self, either through self-presence or through self-representation of the external objects.

IV. THE DOCTRINE OF ILLUMINATION

By asserting that external objects do not cause knowledge but are simply occasions by which the soul's radical knowledge receives specification, Campanella does not offer a satisfactory solution to the problem of knowledge. He fails to explain adequately the inner and transcendental vitality of the soul, which, even before its actual contact with external objects, already has a radical, although confused, knowledge of all things. Also, an adequate reason must be given for the soul's capacity to infer, from the partial assimilation of being, notions and principles of universal value. Here he feels the need of appealing to St. Augustine's doctrine of illumination by the eternal reasons, which he adapts to his own system.

In a fundamental text in the *Theologia* Campanella tells us that the human mind is capable of reaching unknown realities and of knowing all things because it participates to a certain degree in God, who is everything and who knows all things. Therefore, the mind has in itself the reasons of things *(rationes rerum)* and the light of God *(lumen Dei)* containing them, so that it understands things in the eternal reasons *(in rationibus aeternis).* Telesio, he says, is right when he teaches that knowledge is in the soul and that learning is nothing but recalling the soul's attention from other concerns to the consideration of knowable objects. Plato and Augustine also teach that learning is a kind of recollection. Hence the soul can acquire knowledge of things, because it already possesses them in the eternal reasons which it shares by participating in the all-embracing God.[113]

It would be wrong to infer from this, Campanella reminds us, that the soul possesses in itself ideas of things in the same way that God possesses them. The soul does not create things but is merely an imitation of God in whose nature it participates.[114] Nor does the soul, as previously stated, have in itself Plato's innate ideas as such; it only somewhat confusedly participates in the divine ideas, inasmuch as the human intellect is a participation of the divine intellect which knows all things in itself.[115] The light of God through which all things are intelligible can be compared to air and light, the means of all perception in the sensible order.[116]

How does assimilation take place if, for lack of similarity, there is no means of contact between light dwelling in the soul and external objects? Here the doctrine of primalities, extended to all beings because of their essential dependence on God, comes to Campanella's aid. Were the eternal reasons only in the soul, knowledge would be impossible. But throughout the whole universe there is divine radiation of the primalities that makes all things knowable by making them similar to the knower.[117] It is on the basis of this fundamental similarity of things by their participation in the nature of God that knowledge is possible.

God, continues Campanella, is therefore the active intellect outside of us in the light of which our own intellect sees, just as the eye sees through the light of the sun. Accordingly, sensation and understanding, although belonging to us, are effected by our actual communication with external things under the light of God participated in through the primalities.[118]

With certain philosophers of the Augustinian school, Campanella admits that God plays the part of the active intellect in relation to the human soul. The divine intellect, nevertheless, is said to be essentially different from the human intellect. Unlike our intellect, it does not need to be acted upon by things, nor does its knowledge need to be specified or aroused from a supposed state of lethargy.[119]

It is worth noting that in Campanella's teaching our soul is not in immediate contact with the light of the divine intellect, since that would make our knowledge similar to the knowledge of the blessed in heaven. Its contact with the divine light is only through the medium of its essence, insofar as it is a participation of that light. In other words, although our soul understands everything in God,[120] to whom it is united as is a plant to the soil or a fish to the sea,[121] yet it does not have in this life a direct intuition of the eternal ideas.[122]

Thus, in Campanella's opinion, the problem of knowledge as a basis for truth and certitude may be considered to be solved. On the one hand, through the soul's illumination by the light of God and its own participation in the eternal reasons, our knowledge shares in the latter's infallibility and necessity. On the other hand, by avoiding a direct intuition of God's essence, the distinction between our present knowledge and the knowledge in the next life is duly preserved.

As a conclusion to our discussion of Campanella's theory of knowledge, a brief exposition will be made of his answers to the *14 dubitationes* or objections mentioned at the beginning of this study.

Answer to the First Objection. The first objection states that our knowledge is very little if compared with what we do not know. But even this little knowledge is of the greatest value for us in our present life. It provides such riches that from this little amount of knowledge we can, by the process of reasoning, reach out to an almost infinite number of things. Thus, in the science of nature, from a small particle of heat we can know all heat by its similarity. From one world we can know innumerable other worlds. We know the past and the absent by means of the senses of other men, just as we know the future in the causes that produce similar effects. Effects manifest their hidden causes because of the likeness that exists between cause and effect.[123]

Answer to the Second Objection. A partial knowledge is certainly very imperfect. Still it is not necessary to know all the particulars in order to conclude to a universal. If Peter and John are animals, it follows that every man is such. If this fire and that fire are hot, we conclude that every fire is hot. Some things are always connected and some things always separated; some things are usually such, and some things are rarely such. In the first case, we have a demonstration; in the second, an opinion; and in the third, only a conjecture.[124]

Answer to the Third Objection. Sense perceives when it is affected or acted upon by things. In other words, sense is passive and things act upon it. But every action is a flowing out of the very essence of a thing; therefore, sense is not deceived when it receives the action of the thing, because it is truly acted upon and things are truly acting. That the same thing appears different to different men is not because things do not exist or because they are continually changing, but because of the different disposition of those who are affected by things themselves. To know this is the real concern of science.[125]

Answer to the Fourth Objection. To the fourth doubt or objection, namely, whether it is better to philosophize according to the senses of the lower animals or the senses of man, the answer is that it is not the goodness of the organ but the excellence of the spirit perceiving through the organ that affords a better sensation. The capacity of a being to philosophize does not depend on its physical constitution or on the properties of its body, but on the nature of the spirit that philosophizes. By means of his intellect man knows much more than can be known through the senses. Science and the arts are the exclusive dominion of man.[126]

Answer to the Fifth Objection. The senses perceive not only the images of things but also their real entity, or a sufficient part of the entity to enable the spirit to know the whole thing and all like things. The little that we perceive is a measure for the knowledge of other things. Therefore, we are first measured by things as we become partly like them, and then we measure things through the part by which we have been made similar to them.[127]

Answer to the Sixth Objection. No answer is possible to the sixth objection, since science rests upon knowledge of things as they are. Our knowledge is a conclusion drawn from what is known to us in the modified subjective form of things to what we do not know of their being. Things that do not act strongly enough upon us so as to destroy our own being and do not have a nature similar to ours are perceived with a somewhat greater amount of certainty. On the contrary, the essence of things that are more or less similar to us is known only by a conclusion of our reason and with a lesser amount of certainty.[128]

Answer to the Seventh Objection. It is true that things are in a continuous flow, and thus they cannot easily become the object of our knowledge; yet the changeableness of things is not so great that it is impossible for us to know and to define them. Thus stones and metals retain almost the same weight, and man remains the same while undergoing minor changes in his body. We admit that our knowledge is very imperfect because of the continuous change of things. Nevertheless, we still recognize an individual being as the same according to its form, in spite of the fact that it increases or decreases in its volume and is continually changing in its parts.[129]

Answer to the Eighth Objection. This objection also contains some truth, for we forget and lose our knowledge very easily. In fact, our spirit is always changing and remains the same only through succession, just as other things do. Yet our knowledge is still of great value. Since we are in the midst of this succession of things, we can either coincide with, or accompany, them in the change. Stability is to be found only in immortal beings and in the intellect *(mens)* given to us by God.[130]

Answer to the Ninth Objection. Knowledge is not merely a passion but also a perception and a judgment of the passion, and consequently of the object that evokes the passion. As a matter of fact, every agent pours forth, as it were, its own entity. A being first knows itself, for it is itself; then it perceives other things, as it feels itself changed into these other things. As a result of these continuous changes, a being becomes so used to knowing other things that it loses cognizance of itself.

Knowledge is certainly a partial alienation, but we cannot call it *insanity* unless someone becomes so estranged from himself that he is unable to pass judgment on himself or on others.[131]

Answer to the Tenth Objection. The soul infused into the body is really apart from its source, just as is the heat of the sun when it is inside the earth. As long as the soul is moved and acted upon by things, it falls into forgetfulness and ignorance of itself. But as the heat of the sun—which becomes a part of the essence of the stone, the plant, and the animal—strives continually to get back to the sun, so the soul sent by God into the body never ceases from turning to God as soon as it is even a little free from the weight of the body and from the passions.

Differences of opinion in regard to the essence and the functions of the soul come from *illate* (acquired) knowledge and not from *innate* knowledge.

It is true that we are like men in a tomb, the region of death; but to know this is science, and whoever denies it is a fool.[132]

Answer to the Eleventh Objection. Philosophers are deceived when they try to reach conclusions by their own reasoning and do not base their doctrines on the senses and the sensations of the spirit. This approach is due either to a wish to appear learned or to the weakness of spirit, which is easily affected by any kind of argument. It may also be the result of a superficial observation of things, or of the fact that they philosophize on the sense perceptions of others. Whoever wishes to be a philosopher must be free from ambition, love of controversy, fear, and covetousness. He must build his doctrine not on men's schools but on the divine book of nature, not on opinion but on definite proofs and testimonies.[133]

Answer to the Twelfth Objection. Science is of two kinds. The first considers things according to the use that we can make of them and includes what we call arts, such as medicine, oratory, poetry, music, astrology, politics, and grammar. The second is science in the strict sense of the term. It includes physics and metaphysics. Mathematics partakes of both kinds. The man dealing with the arts does not inquire about the essence of things, but only about the use he can make of them. The physicist considers things in their physical constitution, while the metaphysician considers them as they are in themselves and in relation to all other things with special emphasis on primary causes. Although the metaphysician does not penetrate into the intimate nature of a thing, he comes very close to it. To understand that a thing cannot act upon us in its totality and perfection is already great scientific knowledge.[134]

Answer to the Thirteenth Objection. The opinions of scholars and philosophers concerning the value of human knowledge, as set forth in the thirteenth doubt, find their confirmation in our previous statements. It is evident, in fact, that we know only in part and nothing perfectly. We know inasmuch as we are affected by things; and because this affection or passion is different in each individual, knowledge is also different. But even if things did not change, our own change would nevertheless affect knowledge or the way of knowing. Nothing can be known perfectly. Yet to conclude from this, as sceptics do, that we know nothing at all, is not justifiable. As a matter of fact, we know, for instance, whether at the present moment we are writing, eating, or doing something else. To be conscious of such actions is to have some knowledge.[135]

Answer to the Fourteenth Objection. The arbitrary determination of the names of things is no indication of a complete lack of knowledge but only of its variety and imperfection. The very existence of words is a proof that they mean something and that whoever utters them knows what he is talking about. Stated otherwise, names are signs of things which we use for the specific purpose of communicating our knowledge to others. As the spirit perceives things, so it tries to imitate its sensations and to express at least something of the things perceived. The correct name of a thing is that which corresponds to the nature of the thing itself. When something cannot be perceived directly but only through its effects, such as the divine substance, the use of analogies is permitted. Philosophers must however be very careful in their denomination of things, for this has to be in agreement with the nature of the things so named.[136]

CHAPTER SIX

Evaluation of Campanella's Theory of Knowledge*

It has been claimed that Campanella's theory of knowledge displays the inconsistency characteristic both of his whole philosophy and of his personality. In his system, it has been further stated, one can see for the last time a blending of all the currents of Renaissance thought.[1] No doubt these statements contain a great deal of truth. They also give us an explanation why Campanella's theory of knowledge, as well as his philosophy in general, has given rise to almost as many interpretations as there are systems of philosophy. Each interpretation claims to be correct. By some he has been represented as an empiricist and a materialist; by others, as a rationalist or an idealist; still others hold that he is an ontologist. Finally, some claim that he is a scholastic of a particular type. Yet no one has ever said that his doctrine belongs to just one system of philosophy to the exclusion of all the others. To hold this opinion would be to disregard entirely the eclectic character of his philosophical synthesis.

Since this is the case, it seems difficult to attempt a new evaluation of Campanella's theory of knowledge without risk of repeating what has already been said. However, since investigations into Campanella's thought are far from complete and since each individual is guided in his approach by his personal opinions, it is of value to offer a general appraisal of Campanella's epistemology. This will not be a complete critique covering all the phases of his theory of knowledge, since much of that has already been done in the exposition of the theory itself. It will rather be a complementary critique, in which Campanella's main positions are summed up and certain points are brought out which for one reason or another were omitted in the course of our study.

Campanella's conception of philosophy as an inquiry after truth, based on the testimony of God and the study of nature, is an attempt to reconcile in a new synthesis Christian teachings and the naturalistic tendencies of his time. By stressing the fact of God's revelation to man through the Scriptures, he shows the Christian character of his sys-

---

*This chapter may be omitted without breaking the continuity of this presentation of Campanella's thought.

tem, in contrast to certain Renaissance philosophers who held with Averroës that Aristotle represents the ultimate perfection of human nature and that his teaching is the supreme truth.[2] On the other hand, Campanella's emphasis on the study of nature, which he calls the second divine code, shows his reaction against that exaggerated abstractionism which had many followers even among scholastics.[3]

It is incorrect to state with Spaventa that Campanella's emphasis on the study of nature as the book of God is in "open opposition to the [philosophy of the] middle ages which sought God outside of nature and human consciousness."[4] There is no real opposition between Campanella and medieval scholastics in their inquiry about God. Like them, Campanella rises from nature to the existence of almighty God, whose perfections are reflected in the created world. Indeed, for Campanella no less than for scholastics, as Spaventa himself is forced to admit,[5] creatures carry within themselves the image and vestige of God. However, it must be recognized that Campanella extends farther than scholastics the concept of the vestige of God in irrational and inanimate creatures.

Did Campanella, who insists so much on the need to study nature, practice his own experimental method? Since most of his works were written in prison, where he had scarcely any chance for experimentation, the answer must be negative. Blanchet states in this connection that most of Campanella's writings do not show much concern for scientific observation.[6] Galileo himself seems to have reproached Campanella for his method of making long discussions without any solid experimental basis.[7]

As has been pointed out, by stating the critical problem as an introduction to philosophy, Campanella anticipated a common trend among later philosophers. In his opinion, the long series of objections raised against the possibility of scientific knowledge represents the basic problems that a philosopher must face and solve before starting any metaphysical speculation. In other words, in Campanella's system epistemology has priority over metaphysics. Herein is seen the modernity of Campanella.[8]

It may be objected that the method of positing doubt as an introduction to philosophical reflection is almost as old as philosophy. It is implied in the Socratic irony; it finds explicit application in the works of Plato and Aristotle. It is likewise used by St. Augustine. Furthermore, scholasticism makes constant use of methodic doubt, as is seen in the well-known *sic et non* and in the tripartite method itself. In his commentary on Aristotle's *Metaphysica,* St. Thomas discusses how doubt can be an introduction to science and, in agreement with the Stagirite, requires at the beginning of the science of being a "universal doubt about truth."[9]

Such observations, which are usually made in connection with Descartes' methodic doubt in order to show its lack of originality, also apply to Campanella, who in many respects anticipated Descartes' method. Yet they do not invalidate our claim that Campanella set a new pattern in philosophy. He made methodic doubt the starting point of a systematic treatise of knowledge and applied it so universally that it included even one's own existence. In this is found his originality as a philosopher.

Campanella's first argument in refutation of absolute scepticism, which consists in extracting an implicit admission of truth from the very fact of its negation or doubtful attitude toward it, is certainly effective, but it does not represent any real contribution to philosophy. It is the traditional argument against scepticism, and Campanella derives it directly from Augustine.

His use of self-consciousness as the fundamental principle of knowledge and certitude is admittedly of Augustinian origin. Apart from the debated issue of whether Campanella's doctrine of self-consciousness had any actual influence on the *Cogito, ergo sum* of Descartes, it cannot be denied that the teachings of the two philosophers have many features in common. Hence, just as Campanella is the forerunner of Descartes in positing a universal methodic doubt at the beginning of his system of philosophy, so also he anticipates Descartes in considering the principle of self-consciousness as the basic principle of knowledge and certitude.

The doctrine of the soul's self-cognition by reason of its primalitarian structure leads Campanella to admit in man two distinct kinds of knowledge, innate knowledge and illate or acquired knowledge. Innate knowledge is part of the very essence of the soul and is nothing but a *notitia praesentialitatis*. Illate or acquired knowledge is the soul's knowledge of external objects. In his effort to reconcile his own teaching with that of the Angelic Doctor, he quotes St. Thomas as holding on the authority of St. Augustine that the soul and things know themselves *praesentialiter* by an innate knowledge. This is evidently a misrepresentation of Aquinas's thought. It is true that St. Thomas teaches that the soul knows itself by reason of its own presence; but at the same time he states clearly that such knowledge is only through its acts and not by reason of its essence.[10]

Campanella again seriously misrepresents St. Thomas's teaching, and St. Augustine's as well, when he ascribes to Aquinas the doctrine that there is some kind of innate knowledge in all things, on the ground that all things love themselves and love presupposes knowledge.[11] Nowhere in St. Thomas's works is self-love said to belong to inanimate nature. The extension of the primalitarian structure to all creatures, whether they are rational or nonrational, as though all of them were an image of the Holy Trinity, is another weak point in Campanella's theory.

The notion of innate knowledge in relation to illate or acquired knowledge is left obscure by the philosopher of Stilo. On the one hand, he states that self-knowledge, which he identifies with one's own being, is the absolute principle of certitude. On the other hand, he affirms that knowledge of manifold external objects obscures the soul's self-cognition to the point that it almost becomes oblivious of itself. Hence the soul must discover its own nature, origin, and purpose. Hence also arise various opinions among philosophers about the soul's nature and operations.[12] It is true that he distinguishes between the soul's ideal state of absolute independence of the external world and the soul's real state in which it is forced to return to itself by reflection. However, this distinction does not help solve the problem at issue, which is the nature of the soul's self-knowledge as the absolute principle of certitude in the real state of things and not merely in an imaginary state which can never be realized in this world. It seems that Campanella is at a loss in reconciling his preconceived theory of innate ideas with the fact of our daily experience that knowledge is only through contact with external reality. He tries to make the self the center of all knowledge and certitude, but he exaggerates in the direction of egocentrism with inevitable consequences of inconsistency and obscurity.

As previously stated, Campanella fails in his effort to prove the conformity of his own teaching with the doctrine of Aristotle on the way the intellect understands itself. In Aristotle's teaching, as Campanella admits, the intellect is in potency not only to understand outside things but also to understand itself. To ascribe any self-knowledge to the intellect without its passing from potency to act is absolutely contrary to Aristotle's principles of philosophy.

Campanella's trichotomic theory is an attempt to explain the union of a spiritual soul with the body in the human composite. The spirit, which partakes to a certain degree of the nature of both the soul and the body, is supposed to fill the gap between the two substances, and is responsible for the lower tendencies in man. There is nothing original in this theory, except a detailed description of the nature and operations of the spirit, which is the product of Campanella's fertile imagination rather than the result of a serious investigation. The attribution of the trichotomic doctrine to St. Augustine stems from a superficial interpretation of some passages where Augustine mentions three components in man, namely, spirit, soul, and body.[13] Campanella fails to notice that the term *spiritus* has different connotations in St. Augustine, depending on the context and derivation. When used in the sense attached to it by Porphyry, it means approximately what we now call reproductive imagination or sensible memory. It is superior to life *(anima)* and inferior to thought *(mens)*. When used in the Scriptural sense, it means the rational part of the soul and becomes a special faculty in man which lower animals do not possess.[14] Furthermore, since in many passages St. Augustine speaks only of soul and body as components of man,[15] we cannot say that he teaches the trichotomic theory.[16]

The difficulty encountered by St. Augustine in explaining the unity of the human composite by admitting the soul as a substance in its own right is experienced by Campanella on an even larger scale. By multiplying the number of substances in man, he only complicates the problem of their relationship. The union between the spirit and the body, and between the mind *(mens)* and the other two components, becomes in his system a union which is neither substantial nor accidental. It is a kind of compromise between the Church's doctrine and his own trichotomic theory and is far from both the Thomistic and the Scotistic explanations of a substantial and immediate union of soul and body.

Campanella's teaching on the spiritual nature of the human soul is in keeping with scholastic philosophy. Its main arguments are the soul's rational activities independent of the body and the bodily organs, and especially the soul's tendency toward God and divine things. It has been claimed that Campanella's doctrine of the spirituality of the soul is only developed in his second period of philosophical speculation as a result of a spiritual crisis which occurred in the first years after 1600.[17] Whether or not there was a spiritual crisis in our philosopher's life is not a matter of concern here.[18] The important fact in this connection is that the existence in man of a spiritual soul *(mens)*, infused directly by God and with operations of its own, is taught by Campanella in his early works no less than in his later writings.[19] Hence to present Campanella's early works as a mere repetition of Telesio's naturalistic doctrines is not correct.

In his opposition to exaggerated intellectualism, Campanella defends the superiority of sense knowledge to intellectual knowledge. Sense is used by him to mean not so much the external and internal senses in man as the direct and immediate contact of the knower with reality. His statement that "the principles of the sciences are for us nothing but histories,"[20] is an indication of the importance that he attaches to sense experience. However, to conclude from this statement that Campanella is a sensist or sensationalist for whom all knowledge is merely sensory would be incorrect. Unlike Locke and Hume, he admits in man a spiritual power capable of reaching up to supersensible ideas and realities. This power belongs to the mind and is entirely different from sense and sensitive intellect. The failure to distinguish between the various meanings of sense and intellect in Campanella's philosophy has been the source of great confusion among his interpreters.

While many charges against Campanella are perhaps due to a lack of understanding of his peculiar terminology, yet it is hardly possible to excuse him of his constant abuse of philosophical terms. It is an elementary rule of logic that throughout a discussion terms must be used in their accepted meanings, unless it be otherwise stated. Campanella flagrantly violates this rule by indiscriminately using "sense" for "intellect," and vice versa, and by attributing entirely arbitrary meanings to such philosophically important terms as "science" (scientia), "wisdom" (sapientia), "abstraction," and "universal." From this practice come shocking statements such as those paradoxically summarized by Spaventa:

> Sense is intellect; intellect is sense. The intelligible is the sensible; the sensible is the intelligible. Sense is passion (at least in part); therefore intellect is also passion. Sense is knowledge of the particular, and science consists in sensing; hence science consists in the knowledge of the particular, not of the universal. Therefore God is most wise, not because He knows the universals, but because He knows the minutest particulars.[21]

One might point to Campanella's further confusion in designating as sense all the alleged functions of the spirit, including memory, imagiation, discourse and reasoning, which he also attributes to animals; in stating that the imaginative soul is the same as the sensitive, the memorative, and the rational soul; and finally, in claiming that dogs, horses, and all the animals can grasp the Aristotelian universal. All this may give an indication of the distortion to which he subjects accepted philosophical terminology.

Another defect in Campanella's doctrine of intellectual knowledge in relation to sense knowledge is the role he assigns to mind. He states indeed that the mind performs in conjunction with spirit all the spirit's operations. Thus the spirit's operations acquire a higher degree of perfection. At the same time, he endows spirit with such power that the soul's intervention is almost incidental. At least, he does not define clearly the part that the mind plays in sense knowledge, since the mind's proper operations belong to an order high above the senses and reach what he calls ecstasy or rapture. Such a split between sense and mind is the natural consequence of his trichotomic theory, which does not provide for an adequate interaction between soul, spirit, and body.

The distinction between the *intellectus sensualis* and the *intellectus mentalis* is helpful to an understanding of Campanella's thought. The *intellectus sensualis* is what he calls the Aristotelian intellect and corresponds to St. Thomas's cogitative power or particular reason. The *intellectus mentalis,* on the contrary, is the intellect as a spiritual power of the soul. Whereas the former intellect can grasp the Aristotelian universal, conceived as a confused knowledge obtained by abstracting the common notes of the objects from the particulars, the latter can grasp the Platonic universal or eternal ideas.

It is evident that Campanella's degradation of "the Aristotelian intellect" to merely a faculty of the sensitive soul, no less than his reduction of "the Aristotelian universal" to an indistinct image, is open to criticism. Aristotle distinguishes between sense and intellect on the basis of the difference of their objects. Sense is concerned with singular and concrete entities, which by their very nature are measured in terms of space and time; intellect deals with universal and abstract entities, which transcend all spatial and temporal dimensions. Sense knowledge, moreover, is intrinsically dependent upon material organs; intellectual knowledge is intrinsically free of matter or material organs.[22] Since this is the case, Campanella completely misconceives the notion of intellect and universal in the Stagirite when he states that "the Aristotelian universal is not so much the result of abstraction as it is the effect of the imperfection of the knowing subject,"[23] and that "the peripatetic universal can be grasped by rude and dull minds that are unable to reach the particularities of things."[24]

This misconception of the Aristotelian universal leads Campanella to claim that sensible being and the universal are the first objects of a confused knowledge, inasmuch as they represent many things alike;

while the quiddity of a sensible thing is the first object of distinct knowledge, whenever such distinct knowledge can be obtained.[25]

Campanella's notion of truth is substantially the same as that of the scholastics. He borrows from them the definition of truth as "the conformity of the intellect with reality" (logical truth), or "of reality with the intellect" (ontological truth).[26] He also agrees with the scholastics that the divine intellect is the cause and measure of all things; whereas the human intellect is measured by things, of which it is not the cause. Things, then, produce truth in us.[27]

Certain discrepancies between Campanella and the scholastics are found in the explanation of the nature of truth and falsity and in the operation of the mind in which truth has to be located. Starting out with his metaphysical concept of finite reality as a composition of being and nonbeing,[28] Campanella maintains that truth and falsity in things correspond to their being and nonbeing. Just as a thing is true insofar as it is a being, so it is false insofar as it partakes of nonbeing, or does not share the fullness of being. Hence he claims that Aristotle errs in placing falsity only in the human intellect, and not in things themselves.

The basis of Campanella's whole argument is the assumption that nonbeing as such may help to compose reality. This assumption is obviously false and unjustified. Reality is equivalent to being, and to state that being is composed of being and nonbeing is to violate the principle of identity and admit the identification of two contradictories. Aristotle is therefore correct in holding that falsity is not in things but solely in the human mind, which may be deceived in its judgment about the object because of the object's external appearance. In this case, however, as St. Thomas observes, the object is not the cause but merely the occasion of our deception. The fallibility and limitation of our mind in interpreting reality are the real causes of our erroneous judgments.[29]

Whatever may be Campanella's reasoning, his assumption that falsity belongs to nonbeing no less than to the mind may perhaps be brought close to the scholastic doctrine by saying that the knowledge of something as it is not—the Campanellian concept of falsity—is the knowledge of its nonbeing, which is thus incidentally the cause of falsity in our mind.

Campanella again reveals his personal viewpoint on the problem of the exact operation of the mind in which truth has to be placed. Contrary to the tenets of Aristotle and most of the scholastics,[30] he maintains that truth is not to be found exclusively in judgment but also in the first operation of the mind, i.e., simple apprehension. The reason he alleges in support of his opinion is this: were the intellect supposed to know its conformity with reality in order to attain truth, there would be no question of error on the part of the intellect, just as there would be no question of error in the intellect in knowing its lack of conformity with reality.

Campanella's reasoning seems to imply that in the act by which the mind, either by an explicit or an implicit judgment, becomes aware of its conformity with reality, there can be no place for error. This is not correct; for a judgment may be true or false according to its actual conformity with the object. His mistake consists in confusing judgment as such with *true* judgment. While a true judgment is always and necessarily true, the judgment as such is subject to error.

In his empirical approach to knowledge Campanella reflects the naturalistic philosophy of his time as represented by Telesio. His critique of the Aristotelian process of knowledge, based on the wrong premise that information means the shifting of the substantial form of the object to the sense and the intellect, is an indication of his complete misunderstanding of Aristotle. Such a mistake is not easily excused in a man like Campanella, who boasted he had studied all the philosophical systems of the past as well as of his own day. A reading of just a few of the many valuable commentaries on Aristotle's *Metaphysica* written by medieval scholastics would have been sufficient to dispel many wrong ideas about the Stagirite and clarify other points essential to the understanding of his doctrine of information. We can only regret that Campanella's failure to get to the heart of the Aristotelian doctrine and his consequent lack of appreciation for it are the result of a prejudiced attitude toward the Stagirite and a superficial study of his works.

Just as Campanella fails to understand Aristotle's doctrine of information, so he also fails to grasp the real meaning of the Aristotelian species as a representation of the object in the cognitive faculty. He says in effect that a species which does not affect our senses and our intellect in a concrete way—and by concrete he means material—is either nonsense or an intentional fiction. Thus it is evident that he confuses, or rather identifies, the concrete and material with the real, as though the Aristotelian species were not something real or having a necessary relation to reality. However, the main reason underlying his whole argumentation against the Aristotelian process of information is his conviction that an incorporeal power, such as the intellect recognized by Aristotle, and a material object cannot be brought together in the unity of the cognitive act because of their different natures. This explains why Campanella, in trying to bridge the gap between spirit and matter, on the one hand reduces the Aristotelian intellect to a sensitive faculty and on the other hand makes the spirit a corporeal substance. How this concept can be reconciled with his doctrine of an intellect as a spiritual faculty, whose existence and operations with the spirit he never denied, remains to be explained.

Campanella's teaching on sensation, which accounts for his empirical explanation of knowledge, is mainly a repetition of Telesio's views contained in the *De rerum natura* and shares the weaknesses of his master's doctrine. Sensation is said to be a partial assimilation made by contact of the knower with the object known and involves a bodily change. Assimilation presupposes passion as well as a perception of passion.

As previously stated, in spite of his campaign against the Aristotelian species, Campanella admits in the process of knowledge through sensation some sort of *sensible species* which the spirit perceives first as its direct and immediate object, and by means of which it infers the nature of the external reality. The species, in other words, is not only the element of a psychic, perceptive process, a means by which *(id quo)* the perceiver apprehends the external reality, but also a direct object of awareness *(id quod percipitur)*, and at the same time a medium in which *(medium in quo* or *per quod)* he perceives the external reality. This amounts to what psychologists call "representationism" or the theory of mediate or representative sense perception, in contrast to "perceptionism" or "intuitionism," or the theory of immediate or presentative perception.[31] It should be emphasized, however, that Campanella's *sensible species* is always something material which impinges on the senses and is caused directly by the medium between object and sense and only accidentally by the object. Accordingly, the value of knowledge through sensation rests not merely on the fidelity of the senses but also on the quality of the medium connecting the senses with their specific object.

No matter how important a role sensation plays in his philosophy, the originality of Campanella's theory of knowledge does not consist so much in his doctrine of sensation as in his identification of knowledge with being, of which *cognoscere est esse* is the characteristic expression. This new phase of Campanella's epistemological theory, which takes its starting point from being as an essentially knowing nature, is what we have called his metaphysical approach to knowledge. Far from being a rupture with his empirical approach, the new conception of knowledge retains most of its elements. For this reason, a clear-cut distinction between the two approaches is almost impossible, and certain problems that had already been dealt with in his empirical explanation of knowledge had to be faced again in the exposition of his metaphysical approach.

In our critical account of Campanella's doctrine that *cognoscere est esse* most of the points that make up this theory havè been covered. Certain questions have been raised and answered in a tentative way, to clarify aspects of his thought that are not fully developed, while seemingly contradictory statements have been brought into harmony. If we have not agreed with those who wish to present Campanella's theory of *cognoscere est esse* as an anticipation of modern idealism, it has been our constant effort to keep to Campanella's texts and to avoid forcing upon them a meaning that would bring their author closer to scholastic philosophers than the texts themselves warrant.

The results of our inquiry into what can be truly called the essence of Campanella's theory of knowledge show that in regard to the soul's self-knowledge he carries the identification of knowledge with being to the utmost degree. Since for him the soul, and to a certain extent every being, is essentially a knowing substance, to suppress the soul's self-knowledge is to destroy the soul itself. For power, knowledge, and volition are the soul's "essentiating principles" or "coprinciples." They are not three distinct things, but rather three entities of one and the same thing.

Knowledge of external objects is also identified by Campanella with the being of the knower, but the identification in this case is not as perfect as that which is proper to self-knowledge, in regard to both its extent and its form. This has been proved by showing the analogy of his notion of hetero-knowledge, or knowledge through becoming, with his doctrine of sensation, or knowledge through assimilation. It has also been demonstrated by studying the extent of the assimilation involved in the process of hetero-knowledge. The assimilation does not go so far as to suppress entirely the difference between the being of the knower and the being of the object known. Evidence for this has been found in Campanella's own statement that "the knowledge of one's self is the being of one's self; the knowledge of other things is the being of other things." The distinction between self-knowledge and hetero-knowledge has been further shown to be implied in his recourse to Aristotle's and Telesio's theories in order to demonstrate the similarity of his own teaching with the teaching of those two philosophers. Finally, the existence of such a distinction has been documented by his explicit declaration that "really and fundamentally, to know is the being of the knower; formally, it is distinct, insofar as it is a being inferred by reasoning."

As far as the cognitive process of extramental reality is concerned, an attempt has been made to outline the basic principles underlying the implications of Campanella's new approach to knowledge, which, it is worth repeating, does not do away with his former empirical approach but rather completes it. The discussion led to the conclusion that for him hetero-knowledge, already existing in a confused way in the intimate structure of the soul, acquires its determination by becoming specifically the knowledge of this or that thing. We have thus a cognitive process that may be called knowledge "by specification." It involves some sort of a flowing being *(esse fluens)* that comes from the objects and offers to the radical knowledge of the subject the occasion of revealing itself. Whether the Campanellian *esse fluens* is to be identified with St. Thomas's intelligible species, or *esse intentionale,* is open to discussion. In our opinion, the points of contact between the two *esse*'s are not strong enough to counterbalance their differences, which seem to exclude the possibility of a real identification.

The doctrine of illumination through the eternal reasons is Campanella's explanation of the soul's radical knowledge of all things prior to its actual contact with them. It also provides an adequate reason for the objective value of knowledge and its character of certainty and necessity. Because of a divine radiation of the primalities throughout the whole universe, whereby all things participate in the nature of God, a basis for the similarity between the light dwelling in the soul and the objects outside is established. This fundamental similarity makes knowledge possible and excludes at the same time the soul's direct intuition of God and the eternal ideas. It is only through the medium of its own essence that the soul communicates with the divine light of which it is a participation.

A simple reflection on Campanella's theory that *cognoscere est esse,* whose basic elements have just been summarized, will show how deeply it is influenced by the metaphysics of being modeled after the doctrine of the Holy Trinity. Reversing the usual process of going from creatures to their creator, he tries to illustrate the soul's knowledge by showing its similarity with the divine wisdom. The result is that instead of helping to illustrate God's mysteries, he brings God's mysteries down to the creatural level.

Another observation to be made in this connection is that, apart

from the fact that the relationship between self-knowledge and hetero-
knowledge in man is not clearly defined, it is hard to understand how
the soul can have a radical knowledge of all things and not possess
at the same time innate ideas. What is even more difficult to understand is how external objects can be said to be merely the occasion
whereby the soul's radical knowledge receives its specification. This
concept is evidently against our own experience and the nature of
our intellect and its way of knowing things. We are not conscious of
having knowledge of things, not even in a confused way, before our
direct or indirect contact with them. On the other hand, it is of the
nature of our intellect to acquire knowledge of things through the
senses. As the traditional principle states, *nihil est in intellectu quod
prius non fuerit in sensu.*

Campanella's recourse to the doctrine of illumination through the
eternal reasons to support his own theory can hardly be justified. We
are willing to grant that our intellect understands things in the eternal
reasons, insofar as the light of our intellect is a participation in the
uncreated light of God in which the eternal reasons are contained.[32]
One can even go so far as to admit that a certain beginning of the
knowledge of the first principles is given us by nature.[33] But this is
only a habit, disposition, or power to form first principles; it is not,
as Campanella claims, actual knowledge, even in a confused way. The
powers that the creator gives the human intellect are sufficient to obtain, together with God's ordinary cooperation, knowledge of basic
principles and other truths without any special divine illumination.[34]
However, to attain this knowledge, an active principle of intellection,
such as the *intellectus agens* of scholastic philosophy, is required in
each man. Campanella's denial of an active intellect in man is but
another instance of the discrepancy between his teaching and scholastic philosophy. Yet he must be given credit for having preserved
the essential distinction between created and uncreated intellect, no
less than for severing all ties with later ontologists, who taught that
the soul has a direct intuition of the eternal reasons even in its present
state of union with the body.

In conclusion, Campanella's theory of knowledge is far from any
particular system of philosophy as such. He is not a pure Thomist,
nor is he a strict follower of St. Augustine or Telesio. Yet St. Thomas,
St. Augustine, and Telesio influenced him and on different levels
contributed largely in making his philosophy a peculiar combination
of some of their fundamental tenets. In Campanella's theory, to know
is the *esse* in the intimate structure of self-revealing being, whereas it

becomes the *esse* in the possession of the external reality. This is the meaning of his *cognoscere est esse*. If it is true that his overemphasis on self-knowledge is prejudicial to the knowledge of extramental reality, it cannot be denied that the objectivity of the external world independently of our mind is sufficiently maintained. Likewise, while his tendency toward concreteness and intuitionism explains the important role that he assigns to sensation, yet he does not limit cognition to sense knowledge. The intellect, as a spiritual faculty of the soul going beyond the appearances of things and reaching the supersensible and the supernatural, is never rejected by Campanella who indeed identifies it with the intellective soul. Hence, just as Campanella is far removed from pure idealism, so also he is far from pure empiricism or sensationalism.

PART THREE

Philosophy of Being

CHAPTER SEVEN

Being and Its
Metaphysical Structure

I. THE CONCEPT OF BEING

Campanella holds that metaphysics is concerned with all things as they are and insofar as they are.[1] Since all things are endowed with some sort of existence,[2] and since everything that exists is called being,[3] it follows that the object of metaphysics is being as an existing reality. What does not exist either internally or externally, or at least as a concept of our mind, cannot affect our soul; it cannot even appear to us as something. Sometimes we are deceived about the actual existence of things, such as objects in dreams. However, this is not because these objects do not exist but because we believe that they exist also externally, whereas they exist merely as objects of our imagination. In like manner, we may be deceived about things outside of us, because we think that their being as it is in nature is the same as the being that is known to us.[4] Being, therefore, insofar as it is the object of metaphysics, always has the connotation of some kind of existence. It cannot be defined, for being is a first and universal concept that applies to everything,[5] and every definition has to be made in terms of being. It is rather a self-defining term that means "that which has *to be*," or "that which is."[6]

The term "being" can be taken either as a noun or as a verb. As a noun, it stands for the essence or quiddity of a thing, and it refers both to finite and infinite essence, but more properly to the latter. As a verb, it stands for existence, and it refers to finite things only, for existence means to be outside of one's cause and thus applies exclusively to finite things. Actually, the term "being," when used as a participle, means a finite essence actuated by existence.[7]

There are two kinds of being, *real being* and *being of reason*. Real being is what is found in nature prior to any operation of the mind; being of reason is the product of our mind or skill and consists in something practical either in the logical order, such as nouns, verbs, and syllogisms, or in the order of artifacts, such as a dress, a house, or handwriting. All the works of God, or anything that exists outside of God, are beings of reason in regard to Him, because they are the products of His mind; but in regard to us they are real beings.[8]

138

The distinction between real being and being of reason is, of course, a familiar distinction of scholastic philosophy. Campanella, however, understands it in a way that shows once more his arbitrary use of scholastic terminology.

Campanella has another classification of being which is worth mentioning. He considers being from five different points of view: *Singularly,* as the efficient principle of all things. This applies exclusively to God, who is the first efficient cause of all things. *Ideally,* as the ideal principle or universal idea according to which all beings are made and in which they all participate. *Materially,* as that out of which things are made. In this case it is a metaphysical principle. *Formally,* as the very idea causing things, or as the product of such an idea. *Universally,* as a predicate, or as the concept that the human intellect forms of things, insofar as they are or exist. Being, in this case, is a common term that refers first to created things and then to the idea which is the cause of things. It is predicated *univocally* of all things insofar as they are, as Scotus teaches, but *analogically* of cause and effect, as St. Thomas holds.[9]

This point leads to a celebrated question, the problem of univocity or analogy of being, which has been for centuries a center of controversy between the Thomistic and Scotistic schools of philosophy. As usual, Campanella has his personal opinion on the matter, and tries to settle the dispute by clarifying certain points. As is well known, Aquinas teaches that being is analogous, i.e., its concept is simply *(simpliciter)* different and somewhat *(secundum quid)* the same. His followers, in a further development of his thought, hold that the analogy in question is *formally* a proper analogy of proportionality, and *virtually* an analogy of attribution. It is a proper analogy of proportionality, inasmuch as being is predicated of God and creatures, substance and accidents, on the basis of a certain proportional similitude that is found intrinsically in these various subjects. It is virtually an analogy of attribution, inasmuch as the notion of being is found in higher degree in substance than in accidents, and in God than in creatures, since accidents are dependent on substance for their existence, and creatures on God both for essence and existence.

Scotus and his school, on the contrary, maintain that being is a univocal concept, i.e., a concept that is one and the same when predicated of God and creatures and of substance and accidents. Or to put it in Scotus's own words, the concept of being possesses such a unity that to affirm and deny it simultaneously of one and the same thing would result in a contradiction.[10] This does not mean that

God and creatures, or, for that matter, substance and accidents, belong to the same order of being. There is no doubt that in Scotus's teaching God and creatures are radically different from one another, the perfections of God being infinite and those of creatures finite. Nor does it mean that being is a universal concept logically attributable both to God and creatures; for this is admitted by everyone, provided the sense in which the concept is thus attributable is first determined. What Scotus's doctrine really amounts to is that the very essence of being, taken apart from the modalities which determine the different modes of existence, is always apprehended by the intellect as the same. Hence there is no real contradiction between Scotus and Aquinas. They both agree in admitting that being is a transcendental concept, but they consider being from different angles. While in Aquinas's teaching the concept of being includes the concrete modes and determinations of the being in question, in Scotus's theory no such modes and determinations are included. They are distinct entities or modalities. The two positions are solidly consistent with their respective systems of philosophy and rest finally on their different notions of being itself.[11]

The highest unity of being, Campanella says, may be considered from the standpoint either of its extension or of its quiddity. From the standpoint of extension, being includes everything that exists, has existed, or will exist, both in nature and in our mind. It is a sort of community (communitas) rather than a unity. From the standpoint of quiddity, being is absolutely one and is the source of existence as well as of unity in things. It is called unity of essence and belongs to God alone. Community may be equivocal, univocal, analogical, or denominative, this latter term being used exclusively in logic. Equivocation gives rise to ignorance, for it claims as similar, things that actually are not so. Univocation produces partial science only, for it does not account for the numerical distinction of things. Analogy, on the contrary, contributes greatly to science, for it asserts a relationship in the nature of things that is not expressed by their names, such as beween ideas and the "ideated," between cause and effect, and between the first goodness and unity and all things that are good and one.[12]

Whether the unity in things with respect to their being, goodness, and truth, continues Campanella, is the same as the unity we find, for example, in man and beast as far as their animality is concerned, is a matter of great dispute. Scotus affirms univocity, Moses Maimonides equivocation, and St. Thomas analogy. St. Thomas speaks better as a metaphysician, Scotus as a logician, and Moses Maimonides as a physicist.[13] It should be clearly understood, however, that nothing can be said equivocally, analogically, or univocally of a contraction of being, unless equivocation, univocity, or analogy is first admitted in being taken in its most universal meaning (in ente communissimo). If man is univocal with the ass as an animal, he will also be so as a being; for he is a being as well as a sensitive substance, and so is the ass. Likewise, if health is predicated analogically of animal and medicine, and dog is predicated equivocally of the star and the fish, the same will be true of their being; for things are considered first as existing and then as having such and such a nature.[14]

After this introduction, Campanella faces directly the problem of the univocation of being and discusses it at length both from the negative and the positive side. The first thing that strikes him is the incommensurable difference that separates certain kinds of being, like motion and shadow, which scarcely contain any entity, from other kinds which carry within themselves a maximum of entity, such as heaven, angels, and God. To apply univocity to these various types of being, as the Scotists do, seems to him to be sheer nonsense. This is particularly true when one of the beings in question is infinite and the others finite.[15] On the other hand, he argues, it seems that being is predicated univocally of God and creatures for the reason that every effect bears the imprint of its cause; and because, on the Apostle's authority, we understand the invisible attributes of God through the things that are made (cf. Romans, 1:20). This fact is not possible without admitting a close similarity between God and creatures.[16] Furthermore, being is predicated of all things inasmuch as they are, either in potency or in act. Hence a concept can be formed in our minds of what these things have in common, and this becomes a univocal concept. That much the Thomists are willing to admit.[17] Their objection that Scotus writes as though he were making being a genus is comparable to Aristotle's campaign against Plato. Those who are free from all prejudice are not afraid to proclaim that being is a most common notion that is predicated of its species in quid, not otherwise than animality is predicated of rational beings.[18] Hence, since being is predicated of its specific differences, there is no reason that it should not be a genus. However, since genus is physically a series of things having common notes among themselves and distinct from others, it would be wrong to extend it to include God. Nevertheless, God falls within the range of the logical universal; otherwise, as St. Thomas himself acknowledges, nothing could be said in common of God and creatures.[19] It is in this sense that being can be called univocal. The intellect considers in things only that aspect which makes them alike, and regardless of what they are—God, substance, or accident—calls them all beings.[20]

In Campanella's opinion the intellect may arrive at this pure notion of being *qua* being by a twofold process, one following the opposite direction of the other. The first consists in removing from a subject all its perfections, concentrating entirely upon the concept of its being. Thus we may consider God as *He who is,* prescinding entirely from the fact that His essence is His existence. Likewise, in substance and accident we may leave aside the consideration that substance is *per se* and *in se* and accident *in alio,* and concentrate exclusively on their aspect of being as opposed to nothing.[21] The second way of arriving at the pure concept of being as univocal and attributable both to God and creatures consists in removing from creatures all their imperfections, so that the difference between finite being and infinite being no longer exists. This idea may seem difficult to understand, but it is consistent with Campanella's system wherein all created things are composed of finite being and infinite nonbeing. Thus, if in our mind we remove from a stone all the limitations of its entity, the stone will be left with its being in an infinite degree. Indeed, if nonbeing is the principle of limitation, once nonbeing is removed from any finite entity, only infinite being will remain.[22] Campanella contends that if Scotus had understood univocation in this sense, his teaching would have been more correct,[23] just as he would have been more correct in admitting that being is a genus.[24]

In conclusion, Campanella seems to teach univocation of being only from the standpoint of a logician who considers being merely as an *ens rationis,* irrespective of its relationship to reality. Being is thus reduced to a sign or to a logical universal, whose essence is predicability, in the same manner as genus, species, and the other predicables. In addition to the texts previously quoted, evidence of this teaching is found in the following passage of the *Theologia:*

> Univocation with regard to us and God also takes place when we consider being *logically* as severed from God and creatures. The same must be said of the primalities. However, since logic is fictitious and does not correspond to reality, I cannot accept this kind of unity. For God, as a being, is that which has *esse,* and a creature is likewise that which has *esse;* but a creature participates its *esse* in God, whereas God is He who has *esse* of His very nature *(per se).*[25]

It is inevitable, then, that when he deals with being as a metaphysical concept, Campanella parts company with Scotus.

> When Scotus argues that in our concept of being we can prescind from the being of God and the being of man, perhaps he is right. However, this concept is one by analogy, not by univocation.[26]

It is only by a mistake at the beginning of our investigation, he adds, that to arrive at the notion of God we use such names as "being" and "wisdom" univocally in metaphysics. As soon as we perceive, for instance, that God's wisdom by far exceeds our own wisdom and that no univocation is possible, we become wiser and correct our mistake.[27]

These last statements should leave no doubt about Campanella's position on Scotus's and St. Thomas's differences on the univocation and analogy of being. Although his presentation of Scotus's thought is not always accurate,[28] he definitely sides with St. Thomas, "the metaphysician who weighs and considers everything, and noticing the points of resemblance and difference in things, calls being neither equivocal nor univocal, but analogous."[29]

Granting that being is analogous, we may ask further what type of analogy Campanella holds. Will it be an analogy of proportionality and attribution, as most of the Thomists seem to admit, or will it be something different? In an article in the *Metaphysica*, he states

> that being, one, and good are said of God and secondary beings by an analogy of proportionality and attribution, and that every analogy is basically radicated in attribution.[30]

Developing his thought, he says that the analogy of proportionality in the concept of being is to be admitted on the ground that being lies at the basis of all things, of God as well as creatures. It is true that strictly speaking there is no proportion between a creature, which is finite, and God, who is infinite; but there is proportion between a creature and God inasmuch as both are being, good, one, and the like. By the very fact that things are, they are similar to God; and this is enough to establish a proportion and an analogical resemblance between them. It is this kind of analogy which is called analogy of proportionality and gives rise to mutual predication.[31]

There is another type of analogy, Campanella goes on to say, which holds when a predicate is attributed to a certain subject *per se* and to others because of their relation to that subject, or, as we would say in scholastic terminology, because of their relation to the primary analogate. This is the analogy of attribution. To illustrate it he has re-

course to the familiar example of health as attributed to animal
per se and to medicine insofar as it is the cause of health in the
animal. Arguing against Cajetan[32] and certain "shortsighted theologians,"[33] Campanella asserts that the analogy of attribution must
also be admitted between the primary being and secondary beings, for
being and the other transcendentals are affirmed of God *per se* and
simpliciter, and of creatures inasmuch as they are the effects of God,
their first cause.[34] Being is thus predicated of God and creatures
analogically as of cause and effect,[35] or rather, of God properly and
of creatures analogically.[36] Imitation is at the basis of the analogy
of proportionality[37] for the reason that everything that exists is an
imitation of God.[38] On the other hand, participation is at the basis
of the analogy of attribution, from which the analogy of proportionality is derived,[39] because creatures participate their being from
God who is being *per se.*[40]

To sum up the foregoing discussion, we may say that in Campanella's opinion being, from the metaphysical point of view, is neither
equivocal in the sense of Moses Maimonides,[41] nor univocal in the
sense of Scotus, but analogous by an analogy of proportionality and
of attribution. Although no explicit statement is made, Campanella
also implies that, as far as being is predicated of God and creatures, he
admits the proper analogy of proportionality of the Thomistic school.
Likewise, he indicates, at least by implication, that his analogy of
attribution is only virtually such, or such as is generally admitted by
the Thomists.

II. THE PRIMALITIES OF BEING

Being, it has been shown, is a very broad term that stands always for
some sort of existing reality, whether it is finite or infinite, internal or
external to us. What does not exist at all cannot affect us, nor can it
be the object of metaphysics. At this point Campanella's notion of
reality itself must be investigated. We must find out what in his
opinion is the intrinsic structure or essential constitution of being.
Here we meet his original doctrine of "primalities" which has already
been mentioned, but has not yet been made the object of a particular
study. Since the primalities of being play a fundamental role throughout his entire system of philosophy, they must be discussed thoroughly.
We shall study first their nature and general characteristics, and then
we shall consider each primality separately.

The doctrine of the primalities of being is contained substantially in Campanella's statement that all things consist of power, sense or knowledge, and love, like God himself, of whom they are but imitations.[42] This theory holds true not only for rational and sensitive beings, like men and animals, but also for the material world and all its elements.[43] The whole of nature, as a matter of fact, together with each minute part of it, would not last even for one moment had it no power to be, no sensation, and no love.[44]

A first proof in support of this theory is based on the nature of God, in whom all beings participate.[45] Campanella holds that God, who is most powerful, most wise, and most lovable, in effusing Himself into creatures, communicates to them power, knowledge, and love, so that they may exist. Hence power, knowledge, and love are the first principles of all things, without which no being is possible.[46]

A second proof is derived from the very nature of being. Every being is what it is, insofar as it can be, or has the power to be an entity. But what can be, knows that it is. If it did not know that it is, it would not avoid an enemy that seeks its destruction; nor would it strive for its own conservation, as every being does. Knowledge emanates from power: we do not know what we cannot know. Moreover, what beings know they likewise love. Hence all things wish to be forever and everywhere. This volition flows from knowledge and power.[47]

A third proof advanced by Campanella in support of his thesis may be called an inductive argument. It consists in the claim that no principles of being have been found by philosophers and confirmed by theology that are as universal and intimate to things as power, knowledge, and love.[48] In fact, all other principles either presuppose, or can be reduced to, these three. The Platonists and the Pythagoreans make *being, one,* and *good* the center of their study. But *being* is such insofar as it can be, knows that it is, and wants to be what it is. *One* is being itself undivided, for division implies nonbeing, that is to say, this being is divided from that being inasmuch as this being is not that being. *Good* is being insofar as it is loved; but evidently a thing must be before it can be loved. *True,* or *truth,* which is also mentioned in connection with the one and the good, is not a principle of being but being itself insofar as it is known. However, a thing has to be before it can be known.[49] Briefly, one, good, and true cannot be the first principles of being, for they are merely different aspects of being itself. They are what scholastics call the attributes or properties of being, which already presuppose being as essentially constituted by power, knowledge, and love.

Aristotle's theory of act and potency as metaphysical principles of being must be met. Here we are not confronted, as in the preceding theories, with mere attributes of being. Act and potency are claimed to be the metaphysical constituents of finite beings no less than the supposed primalities. Would not, then, the Aristotelian theory of act and potency be a better and more simple explanation of finite reality? Campanella anticipates the objection and gives his answer. It is true, he observes, that Aristotle makes act and potency the metaphysical principles of being. However, act may be taken to mean either the act of being, where it stands for existence, or it may be taken to mean action and operation. Now, action and operation flow from the agent's power, and therefore they cannot be the principles of being. Act, on the other hand, although preceding passive potency, does not precede active potency; for, as Aristotle teaches, it is active potency itself. Hence potency, or rather power, remains as the only principle of being. But since it has already been proved that power cannot be a principle of being without knowledge and love, the conclusion is that all things consist ultimately and fundamentally of these three principles, i.e., power, knowledge, and love.[50]

Campanella's method of reasoning away the Aristotelian theory of act and potency betrays a lack of understanding of the profound meaning of the theory itself. One cannot fail to remark how easily he confuses the Aristotelian act as principle of being with act as principle of operation. Hence he oversimplifies the matter when he identifies act with active potency and reduces act and potency to potency alone.

Valid or not, the three arguments based on the nature of God, the nature of being, and the inefficiency of all other theories lead Campanella to the conclusion that power, knowledge, and love are the three essential principles of being. Since the constitution of every being can ultimately be reduced to these principles, which are constantly found in all things prior to any other principles, it follows that power, knowledge, and love are truly the proprinciples of being and may be called primalities, first entities (*primordia*), and pre-eminences of being.[51] Although our knowledge and love are only accidental and transitory, Campanella insists that the primalities are not mere accidents. In effect, not all love, knowledge, and power are said to belong to the essence of things, but only those which are innate and hidden, as it were, in being itself.[52] Nor are the primalities physical principles which can be separated from their own effects. On the contrary, they are metaphysical principles inherent in the very effects which they produce.[53] In short, a primality is that by which a being is primarily "essentiated."[54]

The primalities are equally first in time, dignity, and nature and are one by reason of a real and essential identity. They are not essences but entities or "essentialities" of the same essence. Their identity results in a supreme unity: were they not one, they would not have one and the same essence. They might well be called "unalities" of one and the same thing.[55] That the primalities are essentially the same is manifest from the double consideration that they cannot be outside the essence of things and that the essence of things cannot be without them. For no essence can exist, unless it has the power to be, and also knows and wills its own being.[56] They are also the same because, although one proceeds from another, they are equally proprinciples of being. In their procession there is no division or separation of essence. Each primality is essentially contained in each one of the others in such wise that that which proceeds is already contained in the primality from which it derives, and this latter is communicated totally to the proceeding primality. Hence, the primalities are coprinciples of being.[57]

Such a process is not one of participation, whereby one primality is shared partially by another, but one of totication and coessentiation, so that one primality is totally and essentially communicated to another.[58] To give a concrete example, love proceeds from wisdom and power, for what is unknown and incapable of being loved cannot be loved. At the same time love already is in wisdom and power, otherwise it could not proceed from them; for nothing can come from nothing in act, and no being can give to others what it itself does not have. Furthermore, in proceeding from power and wisdom, love does not recede from them.[59] That is to say, even though love proceeds from power and wisdom, these latter do not cease to be essentially love, any more than love is essentially power and wisdom.[60]

Campanella does not hesitate to tell us that this doctrine is not only hard to understand, but far more difficult to discuss, and extremely difficult to describe or represent in imagination.[61] He attempts, nevertheless, to give some sort of explanation by anticipating and answering certain objections that are likely to be raised against it. He writes:

How is it possible, it may be asked, that they [the coprinciples of being] exist together at one and the same time, and that they proceed one from another? If power is both wisdom and will, how will it be able to produce wisdom and will? My answer is that it produces them because it already has them. If it did not have them within itself, it would not be able to produce them. But if it already has them, why should it give what it already has? To this I reply that it does not give it to others, but to itself. But why and how does it give to itself what it already possesses within itself? My answer is that it does not give to itself in order to be what it is giving, but in order to be what it is given.

Yet, [one may insist], if it itself already was that which is given, why would it still have to be produced? I reply to this by saying that just as it always was, so it always was being produced. For this is exactly [the kind of] being that proceeds from another being: because it is not by itself, it is necessary that it always be given and produced by the producing subject.

But what is the reason for not being by itself? My answer is: it is not because of any external being, but because being has such a nature that it contains both that which proceeds and that from which it proceeds without receding. It is thus that being is integrated as a whole.[62]

The whole discussion amounts to this: the three primalities are essentially the same, and as far as their function of proprinciples of being is concerned, there is no difference among them as to time or perfection. Moreover, they so intimately penetrate one another that each one shares with the others its whole nature. This is the meaning of the so-called process of toticipation, which Campanella describes in terms that remind us very closely of the mystery of the Holy Trinity. It is perhaps because of its mysterious nature that essentiation of being is called a wonderful process, but incapable of being expressed in human words.[63]

Campanella's explanation of the primalities shows one thing, that although they are essentially the same, they are not absolutely identical under every respect. Were they absolutely identical, why would he speak of three primalities instead of one? A first difference among them is one of origin.[64] Love is from wisdom and power, wisdom is from power only, and power is from neither wisdom nor love, since it is the source of both of them.[65] This difference gives rise to a distinction of real relationship,[66] which again, it may be observed, is but an imitation of the relationship existing among the persons of the Holy Trinity. A second difference among the primalities refers to their specific entity, since the *ratio* of one primality is different from the *ratio* of the other two. This difference, Campanella remarks, is not great enough as to justify a real distinction, but on the other hand it is not so negligible that it can be accounted for by a mere distinction of reason. The only type of distinction that would account for such a difference among the primalities is Scotus's formal distinction *ex natura rei,* inasmuch as they are not three different things but three different realities of the same thing.[67] This distinction, while providing an objective basis for our concepts of the primalities as distinct entities, does not destroy the essential unity of being. It is precisely to save the objectivity of the primalities and the unity of being that Campanella adopted the Scotistic formal distinction.

Yet, in his quest for originality, and in his desire to obviate any misunderstanding on the part of the Thomists who might accuse him of introducing a composition in being, Campanella changed in his logic the name of *formal* distinction to *ideal* distinction.[68] The ideal distinction is substantially the same as the Scotistic formal distinction, the main difference between the two being one of emphasis. Whereas in Scotus's formal distinction stress is laid upon the formalities of being as different entities, in Campanella's ideal distinction the concept that such formalities produce in our mind is better emphasized.[69] This explains why in his *Theologia,* while defending the Scotistic formal distinction among the primalities, Campanella states that such a distinction is *ex natura rei* or *idealiter terminative tantum:* two expressions that seem to be contradictory to one another but which are not so. For it appears from the text that *idealiter terminative tantum* is opposed to a distinction that is found *totaliter* and *fundamentaliter* in the thing itself, and not merely to the formal distinction *ex natura rei.*[70]

In closing his discussion of the nature and mutual relationship of the primalities, Campanella seizes the opportunity to make an earnest appeal, both to Scotists and Thomists, to desist from their centuries-old dispute about the primacy of intellect or will. For just as radical will is not superior to radical intellect, so intellect is not superior to will, nor will to power, the three primalities of being. They are all so united together and so connected with one another that they are but one thing and constitute only one being.[71] Moreover, they also constitute one single principle of operation *ad extra.*[72] All the questions in dispute between the two schools, adds Campanella, can therefore be solved by distinguishing between *res* and *realitas,* which unfortunately they have failed to do.[73]

Such being the nature and general characteristics of the primalities, we shall now consider their specific and individual features. Some repetitions are inevitable, but they will help us to obtain a better insight into this doctrine which dominates Campanella's entire philosophy of being.

III. THE FIRST PRIMALITY: POTENTIA

1. *Potentia essendi*. The term *potentia* is used by Campanella to mean power rather than mere potency or potentiality. It has three different connotations: power to be *(potentia essendi)*, power to act *(potentia activa)*, and power to be acted upon *(potentia passiva)*. The power to be precedes any other power.[74] It is the constitutive principle of being,[75] or that in virtue of which a being exists.[76] No being can be unless it has the power to be; what has not the power to be does not exist at all, simply because it cannot exist.[77] Just as power is needed for acting, so it is needed for being.[78] A being that always is has its power to be *ab intrinseco,* or else it would have to depend on another being for its existence. Such is the first being, whose power to be is its own *esse*.[79] Beings that now are but at one time were not, i.e., contingent beings, have their power to be *ab extrinseco*. They are called possible insofar as they can be made through their causes, and actual inasmuch as they actually exist outside of their causes. In the first case they have only an imperfect power to be, since this power rests with a cause outside of themselves; in the second case they have a perfect power to be within themselves, because they already exist.[80]

One might think that in contingent beings the power to be precedes their own existence; in fact, many things are possible that do not exist yet. However, this is not true; for what is possible already has some sort of existence. It exists causally in its cause, virtually in the agent, potentially in its power, and really, that is, existentially, in the thing itself when it is out of its cause. No matter how a thing can be, somehow or other it already is. If it can be perfectly, it is perfect; if it can only be in an imperfect way, it is imperfect.[81] To state that something has the power to be and not to assign to it any sort of being or existence is highly inconsistent. Power to be is therefore an "essentiality" of being.[82] It is being itself insofar as it is or will be.[83]

When the *potentia essendi* is said to be the entity or being of a thing, Campanella reminds us, this has to be understood *essentially,* not modally.[84] A being that is only potentially in its cause is not the same, as far as its mode of existence is concerned, as when it actually exists; but as far as its intrinsic entity is concerned, there is no essential difference. Thus a little boy is said to have the power to become a man because he already is potentially a man. A stone has not such a power. Likewise, rain is said to be possible because the forces of nature already are potentially and essentially rain, although they are not so existentially, i.e., in their modified act. Actual rain has of course its power to be to the utmost degree, but not in regard to its essence. The latter is much more so in its causes, since it is there in a state of communicability, which it loses by becoming individualized in existence. Hence one is no more justified in saying that things exist because they are possible, than when he says that things are possible because they already exist, be it in a different manner.[85] In other words, regardless of a thing's actual or potential existence, the *potentia essendi* is to be identified with its essence.[86]

Given such a notion of the *potentia essendi,* one may wonder how Campanella conceives the relationship of potency to act. Aristotle and his followers teach that potency and act are transcendental principles of finite beings: potency is the principle of limitation and multiplicity; act is the principle of perfection and determination. These two principles complete each other and together constitute the actually existing beings. They are so mutually dependent that their relationship is said to be a transcendental relation. Act and potency are really distinct from each other, and the composite that results from their union is called a metaphysical composite.

Since Campanella makes being a transcendental composite of power, knowledge, and love, he cannot accept the Aristotelian notion of act and potency. Potency, as a mere potential principle of being, could hardly find place in his system of philosophy. He rejects the real distinction of act and potency[87] and states that the *potentia essendi* is essentially the act of being. The only difference between them is a difference of mode.[88] Consequently, it is not true that potency precedes act; it must rather be affirmed that an imperfect act precedes a perfect one, just as in the process of human generation the seed precedes the embryo, and the embryo, the fully developed human being.[89] If one wishes to say that potency precedes act, he may do so, but only in the sense that potency, or rather power, is itself an act, and its precedence is to the extent that it is a constitutive principle of being.[90] In other words, the *potentia essendi* is a self-perfecting entity with an inner act whereby it is. This inner act is inherent in the *potentia* itself and forced upon it, so to speak, by its very nature. It is an entitative act, which is so called not because of an active power, but because of the entity itself of the *potentia essendi,* which, being a perfection, is necessarily and automatically an act.[91]

2. *Potentia activa.* Just as the *potentia essendi* is the power to be, so the *potentia activa* is the power to act. Since there are two kinds of action, one immanent and one transient, the power to act, says Campanella, is also twofold: the *potentia operandi,* which is characterized by an operation *ad intra* and is exclusively a conservative power, and the *potentia agendi,* which manifests itself through an action *ad extra.* To a certain extent this latter is also a conservative power, for, as we shall see presently, it is through its action that the recipient agent keeps up its own being in the recipient of its action. In this respect the *potentia agendi* can be reduced to the *potentia operandi* and action to operation, this latter being exclusively an internal process.[92]

The *potentia activa,* considered both as a principle of operation *ad intra* and as a principle of action *ad extra,* is essentially the same as the agent.[93] As the power to heat is nothing but heat in its heating capacity, so there is no reason, Campanella remarks, why the power of an agent should not be identified with the agent itself.[94]

Not only is the *potentia activa* one and the same as the agent, but it is also identical with its operation. This Campanella defines as "the innate act whereby things keep themselves in existence."[95] For, as soon as operation ceases, being itself, which is actuated and kept in existence by it, ceases to be.[96] It is because of its immanent character that operation is more properly called act[97] and identified with active potency.[98]

One cannot fail to notice the perfect analogy between Campanella's teaching on this point and his doctrine of the soul's self-knowledge. The soul, and to a certain extent any other being, knows itself through a vital act which is part of its own essence, so that, as far as innate knowledge is concerned, there is no essential difference between intellect, the act of knowing, and the knowing subject. In like manner, there is no essential difference between a being's innate act of self-preservation, the active potency from which this act is flowing, and being itself as the source of both of them. The perfect identification of innate power with being is but another application of the doctrine of primalities as constitutive principles of all reality.

What is to be said about action, which, in Campanella's conception, is no more an immanent act of being than is the soul's knowledge of external objects? Will there be the same relationship between action and acting power as between soul and illate knowledge? This is a very pertinent question which has to be answered in Campanella's own words. "Action," he says, "is the act of the agent insofar as it extends itself into the recipient."[99] It consists properly speaking in the effusion of the agent's likeness into something that is either contrary to, or different from, itself; for no passion, and therefore no action, is possible between two things which are absolutely the same.[100] To act is to communicate the likeness of the active cause to something else precisely because it is something else.[101] The likeness that is thus communicated through a kind of effluence is not to be understood as a mere external resemblance; it is rather a similitude of essence, form, action, figure, operation, etc., according to the different kinds of cause.[102] In brief, action is essentially the active power and active cause; it differs from them only accidentally inasmuch as it means an added influence upon, and relation to, the recipient.[103] For instance, calefaction in itself is nothing but heat that is being effused; the fact that it is being effused into this particular stone is only accidental.[104] Hence we can understand how Campanella's statement that *operari est esse* falls in line with his other saying, so characteristic of his theory of knowledge, that *cognoscere est esse*.[105] As knowledge of one's self is the being of one's self and knowledge of other things is the being of other things, so act, as an immanent activity of being, is being itself as it is in itself, while, as a transient action received in another, is the being of that other.[106]

Shall we say, then, that the construction of a building is the same as its architect or that generation, and therefore the man who is generated, is the same as the man who generates? Campanella answers these questions by stating that construction obviously is not the architect; it is nevertheless the architect's idea that is gradually being effused into a concrete building. This flowing process needs time and effort on the part of the agent because of his limited power and the difficulties he encounters in the environment of his activity. Yet all of these are only accidental circumstances that do not affect the idea of the building as such, which remains essentially the same in the building as it is in the architect's mind. The only distinction between the two is a numerical distinction determined by the matter in which the architect's idea is received.[107] Something similar must be said in regard to the process of generation. Here, however, we have not only a communication of the idea but of the whole being. The man who generates is causally the man that is generated, but insofar as the latter recedes from his cause, he becomes numerically distinct from it. He keeps with his cause an identity of essence but not of existence.[108] Briefly, whereas being and its immanent act are absolutely identical, being and its transient act are essentially identical but numerically distinct.[109] They are essentially identical because of the principle that formal essence of created things is from the idea;[110] they are numerically distinct because of the different matter in which the act is received, and consequently, of the different mode of existence.

3. *Potentia passiva.* Something remains to be said about the third and last species of *potentia,* namely, the *potentia passiva* or *potentia patiendi.* This again is divided by Campanella into *potentia receptiva* and *potentia perditiva.* The *potentia perditiva* is not properly speaking a power, but an impotence. It results from a lack of power, just as cold results from the lack of heat.[111] The *potentia receptiva,* on the contrary, is the power to receive something and is proper to matter.[112] Matter, as Scotus teaches, is endowed with an entitative act.[113] Were it not so, it would not be potency at all.[114] In the same way that the *potentia perditiva* is the *res impotens,* so the *potentia receptiva* is the *res potens.*[115] However, it would be wrong, observes Campanella, to draw from this the conclusion that being consists of matter as one of its substantial principles. Being consists of the idea. Matter is somewhat extraneous to the true essence of things, since it is only its receptacle. It enters as potency to compose material things only to the extent that it is upon matter that images and shadows of true things are impressed, so that they may affect our senses. The principle, however, holds true that potentiality in matter is such only because of its relationship to the idea and the active cause.[116]

That Plato's doctrine of ideas plays an important role in this teaching will become even more clear when Campanella's doctrine of ideas is discussed. Meanwhile, to complete our exposition of his teaching on passive potency, a final question must be asked. Is receptive potency to be identified with reception in the same way that active potency is identified with action? Fundamentally, that is, as it is in itself, answers Campanella, receptive potency is not reception; but from the standpoint of its relation to the receptible, it becomes both reception and the recipient.[117] In this sense the *potentia patiendi* is to be identified with the *actus patiendi.*[118]

To sum up this rather lengthy discussion, the first primality is divided by Campanella into *potentia essendi, potentia activa,* and *potentia passiva.* The *potentia essendi* is a constitutive principle of being either *ab intrinseco* or *ab extrinseco.* When it is *ab intrinseco,* it refers to primary being which has in itself the reason for its own existence; when it is *ab extrinseco,* it refers to secondary beings which depend on the first being for their existence. Secondary beings either exist out of their causes or they are in a mere state of possibility. In the first case their power to be is *perfect,* because it is actually a part of their being; in the second case their power to be is *imperfect,* because it still remains within the potentiality of the causes. However, in both cases the *potentia essendi* is essentially the same, although the mode of existence is different.

The *potentia activa* is the power to act. As a principle of activity or operation *ad intra,* it is called *potentia operandi;* as a principle of action *ad extra,* it is called *potentia agendi.* In accordance with the principle that *operari est esse,* there is no distinction between active potency and the agent; nor is there any distinction between the agent and his operation, since this is an immanent act whereby things keep themselves in existence. However, between the agent and his action *ad extra* there is a numerical distinction caused by the different matter in which the agent's act is received and the different mode of existence of the recipient. This numerical distinction does not prejudice in any way the essential identity of the agent and his transient act as it is in the recipient, for essence is from the idea, and the idea is essentially the same both in the agent and in the recipient.

In direct opposition to active potency is the *potentia passiva,* or capacity of being acted upon in its double aspect of *potentia receptiva* and *potentia perditiva.* The former is the *res potens* and corresponds to matter, which is therefore endowed with an entitative act. The latter can hardly be called a potency, for it is a mere negation and is equivalent to impotence. Considered in itself, passive potency is not reception; but it becomes reception as well as the recipient in its actual relation to the receptible.

The following diagram will show the main divisions and subdivisions of *potentia* according to Campanella.[119]

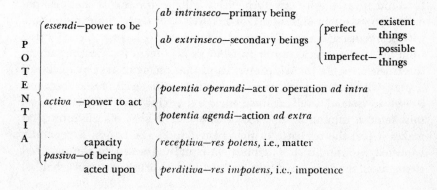

IV. THE SECOND PRIMALITY: SAPIENTIA

Campanella's treatise of the second primality, as contained in the *Metaphysica,* is in many respects a development of his theory of universal sensation propounded in *Del senso delle cose e della magia.* As a matter of fact, he refers to this work for a confirmation of his pansensistic doctrine.[120] In the *Metaphysica,* however, sense or sensation is considered more specifically as a primality of being. It is identified with knowledge and wisdom *(sapientia)*[121] and ranked along with power and love as "a primordial principle of being."

> All things have the sensation of their own being and of their conservation. They exist, are conserved, operate, and act because they know.[122]

Wisdom is "a constitutive essentiality of being." Whether the being in question is divisible or not does not make any difference,[123] for wisdom is "a pre-eminence of being as a being."[124] It is on the basis of this notion, as has been previously demonstrated, that Campanella builds up his theory of knowledge. Not wishing to go any further into the epistemological aspect of *sapientia,* we shall confine our discussion to *sapientia,* or rather sensation, as a primality of being. Here *Del senso delle cose e della magia* will be particularly useful.

The subtitle of this work reads as follows:

> A remarkable tract of occult philosophy in which the world is shown to be a living and truly conscious image of God, and all its parts and particles thereof to be endowed with sense perception, some more clearly, some more obscurely, to the extent required for the preservation of themselves and of the whole in which they share sensation. The causes of all the secrets of nature are also herein disclosed.[125]

It would be a lengthy task to mention all the arguments that Campanella brings forth in support of his thesis.[126] Only those arguments will be mentioned that Campanella believed to have a special value from the philosophical standpoint. A first argument in favor of pansenism is the struggle for self-preservation that seems to take place in all beings, whether rational, animal, or purely material. Every being is forced to defend itself against enemies seeking its destruction, and this defense cannot be effected without some sort of sensation that makes it feel the presence of the enemy. Such a sensation is generally admitted in animals; but it must be equally granted to the material elements, for their existence is no less threatened than that of animals.[127] A second argument in support of universal sensation is based on the principle that whatever is in the effect is in the cause. Since animals have sensation and are composed of elements as their cause, the elements too must have sensation.[128] A third argument rests on the doctrine that all beings, no matter how imperfect they may be, carry within themselves the image or vestige of God and are essentially related to one another.[129] Hence, just as everything that is in inferior beings is found more eminently in beings of a superior order, so everything that is in superior beings is also to be found, though more imperfectly, in beings of an inferior order.[130] Sensation is therefore to be extended to all beings. A fourth argument runs like this. In all things there are appetite and love; but appetite presupposes the perception of something appetible, and love, the knowledge of the thing loved. Therefore, all things are endowed with sense perception imprinted in them by the first wisdom.[131]

If adequately proved, any of these arguments could lead to the recognition of sense perception in things. The first and the fourth arguments are closely related to each other, insofar as the alleged struggle for self-preservation is the natural outcome of innate appetite and love in being. Once such appetite and love are demonstrated, there is no reason why a fight in self-defense against an outsider aiming at its destruction should be denied to being. On the other hand, once a natural and conscious instinct for self-preservation is admitted, innate appetite and love must be granted to being as a basic root for such an instinct. The second argument is evidently based on the premise, which is far from being proved, that purely material elements are the formal, as well as the total, cause of beings of a superior order like animals. The third argument likewise assumes without foundation that everything that is in superior beings is also to be found, although in a lesser degree, in inferior beings. The weakness of these two arguments may perhaps explain why Campanella, in his attempt to gain full recognition for the pansensistic theory, did not elaborate on them as he did on the first and the fourth arguments. He actually devotes large portions of *Del senso delle cose, Defensio,* and *Metaphysica* to the study of things in nature in order to discover in them some sort of instinct for self-preservation as well as an innate appetite and love. It is worth following him in his endeavors, which remind us of a similar effort on the part of his immediate predecessors, Donio and Telesio, and of some members of the early Ionian school in ancient times.

That all things in nature have sensation can be demonstrated, affirms Campanella, by the unceasing struggle that goes on between heat and cold, the two active principles which preside at the formation of all things. Heat acts against cold and pursues it to death. When possible, it drives it out of the place where it is entrenched and destroys it; when that cannot be done, it flees. Cold acts in the same way in regard to heat. Had heat and cold no sensation at all, they would not feel each other, nor would they mind being killed and destroyed.[132] Without sensation the whole world would be chaos. Fire would not rise upward; water would not run down to the sea; stones would not fall downward; all things would stay where they were originally placed, unaware of any form of destruction or conservation. Generation itself and corruption would be impossible.[133] Thus the order of the world, the production of things, and their mutual struggle are very powerful arguments in favor of universal sensation.[134]

Plants, continues Campanella, are endowed with sense perception, for they nourish themselves and vegetate.[135] They are imperfect animals which, in contrast to other animals, do not have to prowl about for their food. They feed themselves by sucking through their roots the humor of the soil to which they adhere.[136] Stones have sensation, for they do not remain still, but move around in search of a proper ground for growth and nourishment.[137] Bones, hair, nerves, blood, and spirit, all have sense, contrary to the teaching of Aristotle.[138] Even those things which we call dead have some sort of sensation, as is evidenced by the movement of a dead man who pours out blood in the presence of his murderer, as though he were still seized with fear and with anger against the killer. To die is merely to change the manner of sensing and to lose the spirit in which life is chiefly manifested; it is by no means the loss of all sensation. This loss only occurs when being itself is entirely destroyed.[139]

Matter and space have a sensing power. This power belongs to matter in virtue of its capacity to receive and support the forms. Having, as Plato and Aristotle teach, a craving for form, like the desire of female for male, matter must know what it craves for.[140] Space is likewise endowed with sensation, because all beings hate a vacuum and tend toward space, which has therefore a sense of attraction for them.[141] In conclusion, all beings have sensation.[142] Sensation is spread throughout the world like the solar rays of the first wisdom, which directs everything most wisely.[143] The world itself is a huge animal.[144] Its spirit is the heaven, its body the earth, its blood the sea, and its mind the soul.[145] As worms are within our body, so are we within the world,[146] whose soul is extremely refined and superior to the souls of all men as well as to the angels.[147]

Campanella foresaw that his pansensism would be an easy target for the attacks of scholastics. They would no doubt object to a doctrine that is so far from traditional teaching and contrary to the data of common sense. Sensation, in their teaching, is a distinct characteristic of the animal world. It requires specialized receptors or sense organs, which plants and much less purely material beings do not possess. Although sometimes it may be difficult to determine precisely where the line of demarcation between plants and animals is to be drawn, the principle remains true that plants and animals are two specifically different orders of beings, with specifically different operations. To confuse the two orders, or worse than that, to extend their common characteristics as living substances to purely material beings, as Campanella does, could not fail to disturb the convictions of scholastics and of other philosophers. A clarification was needed, and Campanella did not hesitate to supply it.

Everything, he states—and in so doing he takes up once more the general theme of *Del senso delle cose*—has as much sense as is required for its preservation. But not everything has sense in the same degree.[148] As there are different degrees of being,[149] so there are different kinds of sense. One is the *natural* sense, which belongs to elements and things in nature, and consists in touch alone. Another, the *vegetative* sense, which belongs to vegetables, adds taste to touch, as evidenced in plants which nourish themselves from a particular type of food in preference to others. A third is *animal* sense, proper to animals, and consists not only in touch and taste but also in hearing, smell, and sight. A fourth type is *rational* sense, whereby man's reason draws conclusions of a universal character from the perception of sensible objects. In addition to these four, there is the *intellective* sense proper to angels, who perceive all things in nature by an intuitive act. Finally, there is the *divine* sense which pertains exclusively to God and is the source of all other senses.[150]

Every being has one of these different kinds of sense, for every being participates in the Word, the incarnate wisdom consubstantial with God, from which all wisdom derives to creatures.[151] Sense, therefore, is essentially the same in all created beings, although they share it in different degrees. Further, because of the primalitarian structure of all beings, each sense is also contained to some degree in each one of the others. Thus natural sense is natural in virtue of its essence and vegetative by participation; vegetative sense is vegetative of its nature and animal by participation; animal sense is essentially animal, but it is rational by participation; and so with the other kinds of sense. Hence, all kinds of sense of an inferior order participate in those of a superior order, and all kinds of sense of a superior order contain eminently those of an inferior order. God alone has all sense knowledge essentially and supereminently.[152] This doctrine is in accordance with Campanella's teaching, to be expounded later, that all created beings are essentially related to one another and participate, through their primalities, in the essence of the infinite being, God, who transcends them all.

Such an explanation of the various meanings of sense may help to clarify Campanella's thought about universal sensation. Yet one fundamental point remains to be clarified, namely, how material things have natural sense, or, which amounts to the same, what is the basis for sensation in things of the physical order. It is true that Campanella reduces natural sense to touch; however, he makes it clear that by touch he does not mean a mere physical contact—which everybody is willing to admit—but a *sensed* contact. It is a contact that entails the perception of a passion from the external object, as in animals, although in them sensation is more vivid because they have also a spirit.[153] The difference between material things and animals, as far as sensation is concerned, is not one of essence but one of mode. It is caused by the different qualities of their matter.[154] Accordingly, it is not necessary to be an animal in order to sense; [155] nor are organs required for sensation.[156] For "all sense is touch, and he who has touch cannot be called senseless."[157]

It seems beyond question that Campanella attributes to all things in nature something like an embryonic consciousness, whereby they have a confused knowledge of themselves and of their activity. While this kind of consciousness is considered to be inferior to the sensitive perception proper to animals, it is none the less a vital action that makes material things belong in the realm of living substances.[158] Precisely what type of life Campanella attributes to material things, it is hard to say. On the one hand, he makes them inferior to plants; on the other hand, he makes them participate in sense knowledge proper to the animal kingdom.[159] This is but another instance of the difficulties he encountered in the application of his doctrine on the primalities of being.

Another serious objection threatened to destroy Campanella's pansensistic theory. This objection is not based on sensation as an exclusive property of animals, but on the nature itself of the action of a being in the physical order. Scholastic philosophers maintain that physical bodies have determined natures and consequently determined modes of acting. Such modes are commonly called the laws of nature and owe their origin to God, the author of nature. No sense or cognition whatsoever is required for such physical actions because material bodies are incapable of such a cognition and because cognition in them is useless, since the same effects can be obtained equally well through the laws of nature.

Campanella no doubt felt the weight of this objection. He answers it together with the objections of those philosophers who make the actions of physical bodies dependent on the world-soul, the agent intellect, the "colchodea,"[160] angels, fate, or necessity.[161] All these objections, he proclaims, stem from opinions that are either erroneous or based on a misunderstanding. If the works of God are perfect, as Moses tells us they are, God must have bestowed upon all things those powers requisite for their preservation. But no power is more necessary to them than the knowledge of what can save them from an enemy seeking their destruction. Hence one must say that all things have sense perception.[162] God, of course, operates in things as a first cause by producing their being and giving them the power to be and to act; but this does not prevent the forms of things from acting on their own, as, for instance, fire from heating or earth from being cool and heavy. Accordingly, things act in virtue of their own power, which they received from God by creation.[163]

It is not enough, argues Campanella against the scholastics, to admit in things a natural instinct impelling them to act in the way horses are guided with spurs and bridles.[164] Natural instinct is an impulse of nature, and nature, says Aristotle, works toward an end. It must therefore have first a knowledge of the end. Hence instinct is the impulse of a conscious nature.[165] Nor can it be objected that things are directed by God to act without any knowledge of their own, such as an arrow which reaches its goal without sensing it. This analogy is misleading. God, as St. Augustine says, is intrinsic to things even more than their forms. He bestows upon them not only the power to reach their goal but also the power to know how to reach it.[166] Yet things act in virtue of their own nature, which, in Aristotle's teaching, is nothing but matter and form.[167] Briefly, the operations of things through which sense is manifested are neither from God nor from any other external agent. They are from the natural forms of things themselves, although not without divine concurrence.[168]

V. THE THIRD PRIMALITY: AMOR

In the preceding pages love *(amor)* has often been referred to as
a primality of being. As a matter of fact, it is from love that Campanella deduces the second primality, knowledge or wisdom, for no
being can love itself unless it first know itself. Love is thus a manifestation of knowledge, just as knowledge is a prerequisite of love.
Love and knowledge are complementary to one another and share
many elements in common with the first primality, power. This
consideration provides the reason for our comparatively short discussion of *amor*. Campanella himself set the pattern in the *Metaphysica*
by devoting much less space to *amor* than to the other two primalities.
He introduces his doctrine on love with the following statement:

> Beings exist not only because they have the power to be and
> know that they are, but also because they love [their own] being.
> Did they not love their own being, they would not be so anxious
> to defend it, but would instead allow it to be destroyed immediately
> by their opponent [i.e., nonbeing]. They would not seek the
> friendship of beings helping to keep themselves in existence, nor
> would they disdain their enemies or generate a being similar to
> themselves in which to be preserved. All things would either be
> chaos or they would be entirely destroyed. Therefore love, not
> otherwise than power and wisdom, seems to be a principle of being
> as well as of its preservation, operation, and action.[169]

Love may be considered either as the act of him who tends toward
a good or enjoys it, or as the essential power from which that act
flows. Taken in this latter sense, love belongs to the essence of a
thing.[170] Hence to love oneself is to be oneself, just as to know oneself
is to be one's own being. Between self-love and being there is only
a distinction of reason or a conceptual distinction.[171] To love something else is to become something else.[172] This involves the process
of an effluent being whereby the subject becomes imperfectly the
object loved. Since whatever is added to the essence of a thing is
called accident, so to love other things is to be accidentally other
things.[173] Accidental love, no less than essential love, belongs to being:
amare est esse.[174]

Love is to be distinguished from knowledge because of its origin
and relation: because of its origin, for self-love is the product of
self-knowledge, and love of other things is the product of knowledge
of other things; because of its relation, for love tends to the object
loved.[175] As in our present state self-cognition of the soul through
reflection is more evident to us than innate or hidden knowledge, so

reflex and acquired love is more evident to us than hidden love.[176] Essential love proceeds internally from essential wisdom and power. It does not proceed from external causes but from God, who is the intrinsic cause of all things. Accordingly, the external object does not move the appetite to desire it, but it specifies the act of the appetite by converting general love into the love of this particular good. The external object is but an occasion of the specification of love, which, as an ever-acting principle of being, moves itself to action, if one can so speak of an intrinsic emanating act of being.[177]

Our love for God, remarks Campanella, is not accidental but essential. We love ourselves because we love to be. But God is being *simpliciter,* whereas we are only beings *secundum quid.* Hence we love God to a much greater extent and much more essentially than we love ourselves. Likewise, we love not merely to be here and now in a limited manner; we wish to be always and everywhere; to be able to do, to know, and to will everything, in such a way that nothing will interfere with our will. We want to be like God. Therefore, we love God by an innate and essential love even more than we love ourselves, for what we love in us is what God really is.[178]

Faithful to his principle that a definition is the conclusion of a science,[179] Campanella concludes his discussion of love by attempting to define it, not without a warning that strictly speaking love cannot be defined, for it completely transcends our knowledge. We may call love, he says, "a pre-eminence, that is, a primality constituting being and emanating from power and wisdom, in which it pre-exists and on which it overflows." Just as *potentia* constitutes being through power, and *sapientia* through knowledge, so *amor* constitutes being through complacence.[180]

In conclusion, power, knowledge, and love are the three constitutive principles of being;[181] for being is what it can be, what it knows to be, and what it loves to be.[182]

CHAPTER EIGHT

Transcendentals, Predicaments, And Causes

I. THE TRANSCENDENTALS

The primalities of being are not something static. The very notion of power, knowledge, and love conveys the idea of some kind of activity proper to each one of them. They have an intrinsic as well as an extrinsic dynamism that makes them principles of action and operation, no less than principles of being. It is because of their operation *ad extra*—of exteriority of nature rather than of place—that the primalities are called principles and correspond to what philosophers call faculties.[1] Just as there are three primalities, so there are three principles, i.e., the potential principle *(principium potestativum)*, the cognitive principle *(principium cognitivum)*, and the volitive principle *(principium volitivum)*,[2] which are one in their operation *ad extra* but distinct among themselves by a distinction of reason.[3] Every faculty and every organ in created beings belong to one of these principles, and although none of the three principles can be found without the other two, the action of one principle may be more evident in a certain faculty or organ than in another, because of its particular relation to it. Thus the potential principle is more evident in bone, the cognitive principle in the eye, and the volitive or appetitive principle in the stomach.[4]

1. *The Supreme Transcendentals.* a) *Existence, Truth, and Goodness.* The operations of the three principles are but an extension of the principles themselves through an internal process, which, for lack of better terms, Campanella calls respectively passion, notion, and affection.[5] Through passion the potential principle attains to being or existence, the object of power; through notion the cognitive principle attains to truth, the object of wisdom; and through affection the volitive principle attains to goodness, the object of love. Existence, truth, and goodness are thus the three supreme transcendentals in the metaphysical order *(transcendentia transcendentalissima)*, because they can be predicated of both the creator and creatures and of everything that is a being. To these three a fourth transcendental must be added, namely, unity or oneness, the object of all the primalities together.[6]

164

Existence as the object of power is evidenced by the very nature of the object. An object is that toward which a power or faculty tends primarily and *per se,* and on account of which other things are attained.[7] Thus we say that the object of sight is light, because light is seen primarily and directly and through it colors and colored objects become visible. Since *esse* (to be) is that to which power as a primality of being is primarily directed and through which other things are attained, so existence is the object of power.[8] It cannot be essence, for essence is power itself in Him in whom it is primarily contained. The essence of things is therefore in the mind of God, the primary being whose essence is the essence of all things.[9]

That the object of the second primality is truth has been amply demonstrated in discussing the theory of knowledge. It will suffice to recall here that, from the metaphysical point of view, truth is being itself insofar as it is adequate to the divine intellect, which is the cause of truth in things, or to the created intellect, which is made true by things.[10]

Just as truth is the entity of a thing as known, so that the greater amount of being has a thing the more it can move our intellect and the better it can be known, so is goodness the object of love; and those things that possess a greater amount of goodness have a greater appeal to us and are better loved.[11] As St. Augustine says, the good, like the true, seems to be good in itself even before it is such to the lover. For although a thing is not loved by us, it may nevertheless be good. Hence goodness is the entity of a thing.[12] Love on the part of the first cause is what makes things to be good; love in creatures, not being creative, does not make things good any more than their knowledge makes them true. We must therefore conclude that our love becomes good by loving things which are good in themselves, and that things move us to love them precisely because they are good.[13]

b) *Beauty.* Closely related to the good is the beautiful, to which Campanella devotes a long article in the *Metaphysica.* His personal approach to the beautiful is worth considering, especially because in recent times the beautiful has become the object of wide discussion among philosophers. Even if his doctrine on the nature of the beautiful cannot be held to be a real contribution to philosophy, its originality makes it interesting to the historian of philosophy.

Beauty, writes Campanella, is not something that is in itself lovable, for beauty is not goodness but the sign or appearance of goodness, which may be true or false.[14] As there is natural, useful, and artificial goodness, so also there is natural, useful, and artificial beauty, for beauty follows goodness.[15] All things, inasmuch as they manifest a hidden goodness, are said to be beautiful; and they are even more beautiful to those for whom they are good.[16] Indeed, not all things have the same degree of beauty,[17] nor are they beautiful to everybody but only to those for whom they are good.[18]

Since the intrinsic goodness of a thing consists in power, wisdom, and love, the manifestation of these three primalities is what makes a thing beautiful to us. Light, for instance, is very beautiful because it is extremely powerful and diffusive of itself. Likewise, fire, the lion, the eagle, and whatever is strong are beautiful. Yet beauty is not power or fortitude, but merely the sign and manifestation of it.[19] As a sign, it is only the object of knowledge from a distance.[20] Hence God is not beautiful to Himself, since he is present to Himself; nor is He beautiful to us, since we cannot see Him as He is in Himself. However, His beauty is reflected in creatures as the radiation of His goodness.[21]

The Peripatetics are wrong, remarks Campanella, in saying that beauty relates to sight and consists in a certain proportion between sense and things in such a way that sense loves beautiful things not because they are good but because they are similar to itself. The essence of the beautiful is not proportion but the appearance of goodness. A snake, for example, is well proportioned and much more similar to us than a flower; yet a snake is not beautiful to us, whereas a lily and a rose are.[22] Plato states more correctly that beauty is like the blossoming of the divine goodness. Just as created goodness is the fruit of the divine goodness, so its sign is, as it were, the flower that manifests it.[23]

Campanella's presentation of the peripatetic theory of the beautiful may have been inspired by one of the passages in the *Summa Theologica*, where St. Thomas affirms that "those things are beautiful which being seen please. Hence the beautiful consists in due proportion; for sense delights in things duly proportioned, as in what is similar to itself."[24] But evidently this does not reflect Aquinas's complete notion of the beautiful. Although St. Thomas did not develop a theory of beauty as such, he nevertheless laid down a few principles which sufficiently indicate the orientation of his thought in this respect. From these texts one thing appears certain, namely, that in his estimation beauty is founded objectively on the form of a being[25] and is only logically distinct from goodness. The good is that which quiets the appetite when it is *possessed*, whereas the beautiful is that which quiets the appetite when it is *seen* or *known*.[26] For "the beautiful is that whose apprehension pleases."[27] Accordingly, proportion, properly speaking, is not the essence of beauty but merely an objective condition of it. Nor is it the only condition. Integrity or perfection and clarity or splendor are also mentioned by Aquinas as necessary requirements for beauty.[28] Further, the beautiful does not relate exclusively to the sense, but also to the intellect; for the beautiful is both a thing's intelligibility and desirability taken together. It is the good of the intellect.[29]

Aristotle, whose notion of beauty St. Thomas completed with elements taken from Pseudo-Dionysius,[30] teaches in the *Metaphysics* that the chief forms of beauty are order, symmetry, and definiteness,[31] while in the *Poetics* he stresses magnitude and order as essential factors of the beautiful.[32] Plato had taught before him that beauty, whether of soul or body, and whether of animate or inanimate creatures, is not the result of chance, but of order, rectitude, and art.[33] On the metaphysical level both Plato and Aristotle agree in identifying the beautiful with the good,[34] as do the Platonists and the Peripatetics after them. Thus Campanella's criticism of the peripatetic theory of the beautiful, as though the Peripatetics considered beauty as a mere matter of proportion between the object and the sense of sight, is not well grounded.

In addition to *natural* beauty, or beauty inherent in things by their nature, there is also what Campanella calls *useful* beauty. This second type of beauty pertains to what is good for us independently of the intrinsic nature of the object.[35] In this sense a scythe is beautiful if it is good for cutting grass, and an iron scythe is better than a gold one, for it better serves our purpose. Likewise, a mirror, whether made of gold or not, is beautiful if it reflects our image well.[36]

A third kind is *artificial* beauty which corresponds to the perfection attained by an artist in his work of art.[37] Artistic beauty consists in the imitation of nature. Hence Dante's *Inferno* is more beautiful than his *Paradiso* simply because it is closer to reality. By imitating nature an artistic genius makes a beautiful work of art to the likeness of the divine ideas, of which nature itself is but an imitation. Thus the beautiful, whether natural or artificial, is in the last analysis the blossoming of divine goodness.[38]

After this digression on the nature of the beautiful, Campanella returns to the discussion of the three supreme transcendentals and studies them from the standpoint of their mutual relationship and predication. Though existence, truth, and goodness are respectively

the objects of power, knowledge, and love, all of them are also predicated cumulatively and reciprocally of each one of the primalities.
Accordingly, every power, wisdom, and love is existence, truth, and
goodness; and every existence, truth, and goodness is power, knowledge, and love. Because of this mutual predication, no real distinction
exists between the primalities and their objects; there is only a logical
or formal distinction and a distinction of relation as among the
primalities themselves.[39] Moreover, contrary to the teaching of the
Peripatetics, the transcendentals are predicated of all things, both in
the real and the logical order. For metaphysics is concerned with being
of reason no less than with real being; it governs all the sciences,
including the logical sciences, and discusses all the principles on
which sciences and arts are built.[40]

c) *Unity*. The fourth supreme transcendental is unity or oneness,
the object common to the three primalities taken together. The relationship between being and "the one" has been a controversial issue
among the philosophers of all times. The divergency of opinions on
this matter has often been the result of a confusion of two utterly
different concepts: "the one" as a transcendental unity of being, and
"one" as the unit of measurement.[41] The discussion has also been
shifted sometimes from the question of the relationship between being
and "the one" to the problem of "the one and the many," which is
one of the fundamental problems of metaphysics as well as of all
philosophy. An example of this method of combining the two issues
under the same heading is offered by Campanella, whose explanation
of the plurality of beings follows naturally from his peculiar notion
of being as a transcendental unity. His opinion, which is presented
as a solution to the problem of the one and the manifold that puzzled
Greek philosophers from the time of Parmenides, helps throw some
light on the whole issue concerning the relationship between God
and creatures.

The ancient philosophers, writes Campanella, teach that no being
can exist without being one, and that a being exists precisely because
it is one. The identity of being and "the one" is also taught by
Aristotle. Plato, on the contrary, says that "the one" precedes being,
for every being is one but not every "one" exists, or else it would
be composed of existence and unity and would no longer be "one"
simpliciter.[42] It may be observed incidentally that Campanella attributes to Plato that which is actually more in conformity with Plotinian
doctrine. It is Plotinus who stresses the idea of God as the *One* rather

than that of God as being, even though he does so by developing a Platonic theme. Apart from this slight inaccuracy, there is no doubt that Parmenides and the Eleatic school identify being and "the one." Aristotle also says that being is one, but he considers "the one" as a transcendental property of being, not as something absolute absorbing all reality, as Parmenides seems to teach. The two theories are entirely different.

Having indicated what he considers to be the main trends of Greek thought concerning the unity of being, Campanella advances his own opinion. Essence, he states, is neither one nor manifold. For instance, if the idea of man were one *per se,* it could not be multiplied in many individuals; were it manifold, it could not be preserved in a single individual. Likewise, there would not be just one sun or one world, but an infinite number of suns and worlds; nor would there have been only one man at one time, i.e., Adam, but many men at all times. It seems, therefore, that the very being from which all beings are is neither one nor many.[43]

It is not hard to understand, although Campanella does not elaborate the point, that the first being cannot be simultaneously many beings: it would no longer be the first, nor would it be the source of all other beings. But just why the first being cannot be one remains to be explained. For this we refer to Campanella's text.

. . . the very being from which all beings are does not seem to be either one or many. Were it one, never a multiplicity [of beings] would have been originated from it. That much Parmenides proves in Plato by saying that if it is one it cannot be many. Aristotle himself seems to affirm that from "one" as such no multiplicity can come . . . But it seems to me that not even one [single being] can come from "one," for "one" as such cannot be multiplied [at all]. Therefore, God cannot be otherwise than one, for He is truly "the One."

However, nothing can prevent a unity from producing other minor and similar unities. For if the same thing proceeds [from "the one"], it does not recede [from it] so as to make two [out of one]. To be sure, being cannot produce nonbeings; nor can unity produce nonunities. Yet only the infinite is one, and it cannot make another infinite outside of itself. Multiplicity is therefore a number of unities.

Now since number implies division, and division is from nonbeing, . . . [it follows that] unity, which is the supreme being, is infinite. Further, such a unity does not admit of any number, for it does not admit of any division, either actually or potentially.[44]

... [On the contrary], the kind of unity that is not the whole being admits of division and number, and therefore of limitation and finiteness. Finiteness is from nonbeing. Thus supreme unity is supreme being; it is purely divine and absolutely first.[45]

A study of these difficult and seemingly contradictory statements makes it clear that Campanella uses the term "one" to mean two different things. He uses it, in the first place, to mean the first of a series of finite and limited beings, and in this sense he is perfectly justified in saying that the first being from which all beings are is not one; for God, as an infinite and transcendent being, is above all series. Nor can He, as Campanella states, produce another infinite being outside of Himself, so that He would be first in regard to this other being; for two infinite beings are exclusive of one another. The other meaning that Campanella attaches to the term "one" is that of absolute unity, or such a unity as to exclude any actual or potential division or composition. It is also a unity that entails an absolute priority in virtue of the very essence of the being to which it belongs.[46] Taken in this latter sense, "one" can only be referred to the supreme being, with which it is identified, for it implies "divinity and a very sublime entity."[47]

Shall we say, then, that on the basis of such a notion of "one," unity is solely a transcendental attribute of the infinite being, and a finite being is called "one" only insofar as it represents a numerical entity? Campanella's texts seem to preclude such an inference, which, in any event, would be incompatible with his classification of "one" among the supreme transcendentals of both finite and infinite beings. He writes:

The primacy of unity is not the same as the primacy of the pro-principles, i.e., power, wisdom, and love. These, in fact, make up being not insofar as they are things or beings, but inasmuch as they are realities and essentialities. And since essence is such because it is one, *unity is both what is essentiated and the essentiation of the primary being and of the secondary beings, no matter how this essentiation may be,* for being is composed of these primalities.

Thus unity refers to the whole being as it is essentiated by the primalities and adds to it a [concept of] priority over other beings, either *simpliciter* or *sui generis* . . . Just as all things participate in the *esse* of the first being, so they also participate in something of its unity and primeness . . . They are almost *per se* as God is *per se.*[48]

From this text it appears that Campanella, while maintaining the transcendental character of unity, distinguishes between a unity that bears with it the concept of primeness, divinity, and supreme entity *simpliciter*, and a unity that implies these prerogatives only relatively, i.e., inasmuch as they are participations in the supreme being.[49] For "such is unity in things as in their entity. Suppress unity, and neither one being nor a manifold will remain. A manifold is in effect nothing but a composition of many unities."[50]

2. *The Subaltern Transcendentals and Their Predicaments.* Thus we are introduced to the second class of transcendentals, which Campanella calls subaltern transcendentals *(transcendentia subalterna).* Unlike existence, truth, goodness, and unity, which are predicated of every being, whether infinite or finite, real, logical, or imaginary,[51] the subaltern transcendentals are limited in their predication. They are *res, aliquid,* and the *terminus infinitatus. Res* is predicated of every real being, but not of a chimerical or logical one; *aliquid* is predicated of all finite beings, but not of the infinite being; the *terminus infinitatus* is predicated of all beings except one. Thus not-man is predicated of every being except man, for man alone cannot be called not-man.[52]

Both the supreme and the subaltern transcendentals have different categories or modes of being. The categories of the supreme transcendentals are the various modes in which existence, truth, and goodness can be contracted in finite things. The infinite being, precisely because it is infinite, cannot be contracted into any category.[53] The categories or predicaments of the subaltern transcendentals relate exclusively to finite beings. To each one of these transcendental predicaments corresponds a generic predicament. Indeed, Campanella distinguishes between the generic predicaments and the transcendental predicaments. Beginning with his notion of genus as "a community of communities,"[54] he maintains that diversity in things gives rise to different genera and consequently to different generic predicaments. Diversity exists among those things that have a mode of being so opposed to one another that it cannot be mutually predicated except in an accidental and denominative manner.[55]

The generic predicaments are ten in number,[56] as are the transcendental predicaments. The latter are more properly metaphysical, and in contrast with the generic predicaments which are predicated univocally, they are predicated analogically of their inferiors.[57] Just as diversity is the basis for the distinction of the generic predicaments, so disparity, which is a dissemblance of a second degree, is the basis for the distinction and classification of the transcendental predicaments.[58]

The first transcendental predicament is *essence.* It is not the essence of being as such, but of a participated being; it is a finite essence. God, who is infinite and immense, cannot be reduced to a particular mode of being.[59] Essence has as its corresponding generic predicament *substance,* the nature of which is to be the substratum of the properties of being.[60] Thus it is only improperly that God is called substance.[61]

Essence is limited in its entity by *finitude,* the second transcendental predicament, to which *quantity* corresponds among the generic predicaments.[62] Indeed, all things outside God are finite because of their composition of being and nonbeing. The limit between being and nonbeing quantifies the essence.[63] Quantity is therefore that by which matter is determined in its length, width, depth, and so forth;[64] but quantity as such does not make one being distinct from another, especially if the being in question is of a spiritual nature, such as angels and the human soul. This distinction comes from *quality* alone, i.e., from the mode of quantity and finitude that corresponds to the generic predicament of *form* or *figure.*[65] Quality and quantity differ between themselves inasmuch as the former determines the mode of being, while the latter determines its measure.[66] Quality in turn has its proper way of existing that entails a *power (vis, virtus)* to be and to operate. This constitutes the fourth transcendental predicament and is matched in the order of the generic predicaments by *faculty,* the *potentia* or principle of operation of the Peripatetics.[67] Power is exercised by *act,* whereby something is and operates *ad intra.* The correspondent of act in the generic predicaments is *operation.*[68]

Since a finite being is necessarily surrounded by other beings limiting its own entity, it cannot act without communicating to them its own likeness. This process of communication of one's own likeness to another is called *action* in the generic predicaments and can be called *communication, emanation,* or *effusion* in the order of transcendental predicaments.[69] On the other hand, a finite being, when acted upon by others, becomes passive. We have thus the generic predicament of *passion* and its corresponding transcendental predicament of *reception, change,* or *alienation.*[70] Moreover, many things may happen to a finite essence by way of a complementary determination. This gives rise to the generic predicament of *accident.* No term exists for its corresponding predicament in the transcendental order, although it could be termed *addition, existentiality,* and *circumstance.*[71] Accident, remarks Campanella, is not something opposed to substance and divided into nine genera, such as quantity, quality, relation, etc., as the Peripatetics claim, because these are not primary genera, and not every accident is necessarily inherent in, and added to, a substance. Further, it is not precisely correct to say that accident is that which is beyond substance, since accident is that which is beyond power, intention, will, and order.[72] In brief, accident is either a being in its own right, having its own essence and cause, or a composition of beings by the concurrence of many causes, including a metaphysical one.[73]

The last two transcendental predicaments are *unity* and *plurality* or *number*, having as their correlative predicaments in the order of genera *similarity* and *dissimilarity* or *opposition*. Every being is in effect one in itself and similar to others because of its substance, quantity, or existence, while it is opposed to them because of division and distinction.[74]

A brief consideration of the foregoing predicaments makes it obvious, in the first place, that their classification is rather arbitrary and no better than Aristotle's traditional classification, which Campanella pretends to improve upon. Secondly, the generic predicaments, as compared to the transcendental predicaments, are less universal. In most instances, a generic predicament is only a further determination of its corresponding transcendental predicament. Finally, in both classes of predicaments, if we except the last two couples, a regressive order can be observed whereby being, considered either as an essence or as a substance, becomes more and more particularized by widening the sphere of nonbeing. This idea will be better understood in the next section, where the notion of being vs. nonbeing is discussed.

II. BEING AND NONBEING

In addition and prior to dissimilarity or opposition as a generic predicament and every other predicament, there is, in Campanella's opinion, a more fundamental dissimilarity and opposition which he considers the greatest of all. Such is the dissimilarity and opposition existing between being and nonbeing.[75] There is nothing in common between being and nonbeing, since their very ideas are diametrically opposed to one another. To be sure, in all oppositions there is at least some sort of agreement between the two things opposed inasmuch as they both are beings. But between being and nonbeing even this agreement is impossible. Further, there is nothing that can serve as a medium between them; for they differ in everything. This difference is the metaphysical basis for the principle of noncontradiction.[76]

In spite of their radical opposition, Campanella says, being and nonbeing are found together in created things; for they are the principles, or rather proprinciples, of all finite beings.[77] All things are in effect composed of an affirmation and a negation. Affirmation is finite and means being; negation is infinite and means nonbeing. Thus man is essentially and necessarily a rational animal, which is a limited entity; but he is also essentially and necessarily a nonass, a nonstone, a non-God, and so forth, which is an infinite nonentity.[78] Such a composition of being and nonbeing gives rise to something that is neither pure being nor nonbeing, as instanced once more in man, who on the one hand is not nothing, and on the other hand is not being absolutely. He is this being, or a certain being. How does he happen to be just a certain being and not all beings? Because nonbeing, no less than being, makes him to be so. More precisely, it is not being as such that makes him limited and modified; for being as such is infinite and immense like God. What makes him limited is nonbeing. Should man not participate in nothingness, he would be all things. He would be omnipotent, omniscient, and omnivolent like God himself.[79]

However, Campanella remarks, one should not conceive the composition of being and nonbeing as the union or mingling of two things. It is not a physical but a metaphysical and transcendental composition.[80] We might question the possibility of a composition of an affirmation and a negation, being and nonbeing, on the ground that a composition means the putting together of at least two realities, whereas nonbeing is the negation of reality. Campanella does not overlook the difficulty, and attempts an explanation which helps clarify his notion of nonbeing.

> When we compose things of being and nonbeing, we may seem to conceive nothingness as something positive. In this we are both wrong and wise. We are wrong, because nothingness does not exist in reality; we are wise, because, like God, we make use of nothingness as though it were something really existing. Man, for example, is not an ass; but this is not just because he is rational. Indeed, humanity is not the only God-given thing; there is also angeleity, asineity, and stoneness. Hence, the lack of stoneness in man is neither from God nor from man's power to reason; it is from the distinction of rationality from stoneness, angeleity, and other things alike. This distinction is the influx of nonbeing.[81]

In other words, it is true that, essentially speaking, nonbeing is not a reality, since it is of its very nature not to be. In this sense we can never say that nonbeing enters into the composition of things. Man, to use Campanella's example, can never be said to be composed of humanity and nonhumanity, because the two terms are contradictory, the latter taking away what is posited by the former. But we may consider nonbeing in the existential order as that which limits a finite being and separates it from other finite beings by removing their entities. In this sense nonbeing enters into the constitution of a finite being as a metaphysical principle, for it posits, as it were, the nonbeing of all other finite beings by which a being is surrounded. Hence man can be said to be composed of his own being and of the nonbeing of an ass, a stone, and an infinite number of other things, insofar as this nonbeing actually limits his own entity as a man.[82]

In a further attempt to explain nonbeing, Campanella distinguishes between pure nothing *(nihilum simpliciter)* and nothing as a negation of the entity of a thing *(nihilum secundum quid)*. Pure nothing never existed, unless we admit that all beings, including God, have come from nothing. In fact, pure nothing means absolute negation of being. Had pure nothing existed, God, who is pure being, would never have existed. Had God never existed, the world would never have come into existence either. Thus, when we say that the world was created from nothing, we simply mean that its being succeeded upon its nonbeing, or that the world was made without any pre-existing matter.[83]

From pure nothing one must distinguish relative nothingness, which is the essence of a thing prior to its actual existence.[84] This explains why God, who is pure existence, does not admit of nothingness.[85] This is also the reason for saying that the nonbeing of finite things preceded their being; otherwise they already would have been something even before coming into existence.[86]

The following scheme may help to illustrate Campanella's notion of the different types of nonbeing.

NONBEING
- Essentially
  - Pure nothing —absolute nothingness
  - Relative nothing —possible essence
- Existentially—The entities of other things vs. a particular existing being

Where was the nonbeing of the world before creation? If it had been in God, then God was composed of being and nonbeing; if it had been outside God, then God was limited by nonbeing. Campanella answers this question by stating that the nonbeing from which the world was made was neither in God nor outside God. It was not in God, because God is the fecundity of all entity and does not admit of any nonbeing. In His essence and mind the world was already pre-existent in the most eminent manner, just as it exists now and will exist forever. It was not outside God, because God could not be limited by nonbeing. Hence nonbeing was nowhere, for such is the nature of nonbeing, not to be anything and not to be anywhere. In God, however, there was causally and radically the creating, governing, and sovereign power, so that the nonbeing of the world merely meant in Him the lack of an exterior and actual sovereignty over the world itself. This kind of sovereignty constitutes only a logical relation in God; in creatures it introduces a real relation.[87]

It should be noted, however, that God is in no way the efficient and effusive cause of the nonbeing of created things. He is merely its permissive and ordinative cause. Evidently God, the absolute being, cannot effuse the nonbeing which He does not possess. In the concrete, by creating man as a rational being, God does not deprive man, so to speak, of the essence of a stone and of an ass, but simply allows him to be the nonbeing of a stone and of an ass.[88]

Two more questions are raised by Campanella in connection with his doctrine of nonbeing. One concerns the intelligibility of nonbeing and the other the possibility of a composition between an infinite nonbeing and a finite being, such as is found in created things. For on the one hand, he asserts, nonbeing is terminated by being; on the other hand, it is infinite.[89] As to the intelligibility of nonbeing, we are told that this is only possible in terms of being itself, since no species of nothingness can ever be obtained. By totally removing being we simply obtain its opposite, which is nonbeing.[90] Thus we know the nonbeing of man in the beast of burden by removing its being from man, just as we know darkness through light.[91] In so doing, we attribute to nonbeing an essence and existence of reason whereby it becomes intelligible.[92] Likewise, we form propositions about nothing as though it were really something, and despite the fact that truth is a property of being, these propositions are true.[93]

The second point at issue, namely, the apparent contradiction involved in the composition of an infinite nonbeing with a finite being, presents a more serious problem. To avoid any misunderstanding, it should be emphasized that we are not concerned here with a composition of pure nothing (nihilum simpliciter) and a finite being; for pure nothing as such excludes the presence of any entity whatsoever.[94] Neither are we concerned with a composition of relative nothingness *(nihilum secundum quid)* in the essential order with a finite being; for relative nothingness, which in Campanella's system is the essence of a thing prior to its existence, does not enter into the composition of any actual being. What we are here concerned with is something that has an actual bearing on the existential order, i.e., the composition of an infinite nonbeing with a finite being in existing realities. This is the point at issue, and this Campanella tries to illustrate by means of an analogy. Just as we can conceive a line stretching from the center of the earth beyond the circumference of the sky *in infinitum,* so, he says, man, like any other creature, is but a little dot where infinite nonbeing is terminated. Man is in effect the negation of an infinite number of other things and of God himself, being surrounded, as he is, by an infinite nonbeing.[95] This explanation, however unsatisfactory it may be, has the advantage of representing Campanella's effort to establish on a rational basis his Platonic doctrine of finite being and infinite nonbeing,[96] which he substitutes for the Aristotelian theory of act and potency.

By raising nonbeing to the rank of a metaphysical component of finite things, Campanella develops a theory of nonbeing and its primalities parallel to that of being. Nonbeing, he claims, is constituted of impotence *(impotentia),* insipience or ignorance *(insipientia),* and dislike or hatred *(disamor, odium)* as of its three primalities.[97] In fact, what does not exist at all, has no power, knowledge, or love; it has only their opposites. Since, however, nonbeing can only be understood through being, one can say that nonbeing has power, knowledge, and will not to be, not to exist, not to operate, not to receive, and so forth. The more of being a thing has, the more of power, knowledge, and love it has; the less of being a thing has, the less of power, knowledge, and love it has, and consequently, the more of impotence, ignorance, and hatred. Thus, the composition of the primalities of being and nonbeing in creatures is in direct proportion to their degree of entity and nonentity.[98]

As it is of the essence of nonbeing not to be, so is it of its primalities. Like nonbeing, they have an existence of their own to the extent that they deny and remove being.[99] The primalities of nonbeing are also called principles, i.e., *principium impotestativum, principium incognitivum,* and *principium involitivum,* and have as their objects nonexistence, falsity, and negation or privation of goodness. From these nonbeing, falsehood, and evil are derived.[100] Evil, to confine ourselves to this last, may be considered absolutely and relatively. Absolutely speaking, it is the object of unwillingness *(noluntas);* relatively speaking, it is either an imperfection by excess or defect, or a privation. As such, evil cannot be the object of desire, for it is nothing. It is therefore the object of inappetency, the third constitutive principle of nonbeing. It is because of their mixture with evil that things are bad.[101]

The doctrine of nonbeing is Campanella's solution to the problem of limitation and multiplicity of finite beings. It aims, in the last analysis, at an explanation of the celebrated antinomy of the one and the many, and by implication, of the so-called paradox of being and becoming.[102] His position derives from his rejection of the monistic system of Parmenides and the Eleatic school, according to which everything that exists is one, absolute, and immutable being; of the dynamic theory of Heraclitus, who reduces all reality to change and becoming; and of the dualistic theory of Aristotle, who explains both being and becoming through act and potency.

By way of conclusion, we present Campanella's doctrine of being and nonbeing in the following scheme.

PRIMALITIES   PRINCIPLES   OBJECTS

BEING	Power Knowledge Love or Will	Potential Cognitive Volitive	Existence —Being Truth —True **ONE** Goodness —Good
NONBEING	Impotence Ignorance Hatred or Unwillingness	Impotential Noncognitive Unwilling	Nonexistence—Nonbeing Falsity —Falsehood Lack of —Evil goodness

Infinite Being: GOD; finite being and infinite nonbeing: CREATURES

III. ESSENCE AND EXISTENCE

Creatures are not only distinct from God because of their composition of being and nonbeing, but also because of the contingency of their being. Unlike God, whose essence is to exist, creatures come into existence only at the moment they emerge from their causes. For, properly speaking, to exist is to be out of one's causes.[103] The question now arises: what is the relationship between essence and existence in finite beings? This question, which has caused a great deal of controversy among scholastics of all periods, could not leave Campanella indifferent. He took sides on it, and established a position of his own at variance with the traditional teaching of the Dominican order.

Essence, he claims, is that which a being is properly, principally, and eminently in regard to itself and not to another.[104] Essence refers always to being. That which is not cannot be called essence, although it may terminate essence. Moreover, essence is said to be "that which a being is properly, principally, and eminently in regard to itself," in order to exclude from the concept of essence anything that does not belong to the intrinsic nature of a being.[105]

Essence is not related to existence as potency to act, for essence is itself an act. That is why we can speak of the act of being, just as we can speak of the act of existing, the act of operation, and so forth. Between essence and the act of being there is only a logical distinction.[106]

Essence may be considered as it is in its causes, in our mind, and in the reality of things. In the first case, we have causal or potential essence; in the second case, we have mental essence; in the third case, we have real essence. But whenever and however it is, essence has an existence of its own, for existence is but a mode of essence. In other words, both essence and existence either are or are not simultaneously, and no distinction is possible between them, except of course in the mind.[107]

The existence of which Campanella here speaks is *intrinsic* existence, which is distinguished from what he calls *extrinsic* existence, or the existence of a thing insofar as it is related to its environment and other external beings. It is one thing to be this man, and it is another thing to be in this particular place and time, under such a sky, and in such and such a circumstance. Taken in the latter sense, existence is really distinct from essence.[108] Before it exists essence is pure; by coming into existence it loses its purity. An essence, in fact, whenever it comes to exist outside of its causes, becomes necessarily involved with other existing things among which it happens to be *(quae sibi accidunt)*. In this sense, existence is called a transcendental predicament and corresponds to the generic predicament of accident. Take for example, says Campanella, the letter A. As it stands in my mind, it is pure; it is neither large nor small, neither white nor black; neither hard nor mortal or changeable. But whenever it loses its purely mental state and takes on a material shape on a sheet of paper or elsewhere, it becomes either white, black, or red; large or small, papery or igneous. All these additions are mere accidents of the essence of the letter A.[109]

The relationship between essence and existence and the distinction between intrinsic and extrinsic existence in finite things are further developed by Campanella in a text where he argues against Scotus, not for the real distinction between essence and existence, which he also denies, but for the need of admitting, in addition to an intrinsic existence logically distinct from essence, an extrinsic accidental existence really distinct from it. He writes:

> To [Scotus's] second and third arguments we answer that existence is the limit of essence. Since it cannot be distinguished from what is limited and modified, any more than the extreme end of a line can be really distinguished from the line itself, it follows that existence belongs to the same predicament of essence, or better, to the predicament of quantity which is the measure of substance. I mean transcendental quantity; for the angel, too, has a limited quantity of power, and this limit is from his own existence. However, if one considers the extrinsic terminating factors, existence must be said to be an accident. Indeed, although time, place, and all the surrounding beings are also essences, yet they do not belong to the quiddity of a thing that is thereby circumscribed and located in a particular place and time. They are but accidents which contract a thing into such and such an existence.[110]

Existence is, therefore, neither matter, nor form, nor their composite, but their extreme and ultimate mode. It is a transcendental measure that implies a real relationship to external things. It is the end of being and the beginning of nonbeing; or rather, the connecting link between being and nonbeing. Insofar as it has being, it belongs to essence; insofar as it has nonbeing, it belongs to nothingness.[111]

In these statements we have, we believe, the exact meaning of Campanella's notion of extrinsic existence as something distinct from intrinsic existence. This notion enables us to understand why the existence of a finite being can be said to be identical with essence and at the same time really distinct from it. In the first case, existence stands for the actual intrinsic entity of a thing; in the second case, it stands for the beings outside of an individual essence which is thereby limited by its own nonbeing. For, it should be noted, although in Campanella's philosophy existence limits essence no less than essence limits existence, the actual limitation or contraction of both essence and existence is from nonbeing.[112]

Returning to the relationship between essence and intrinsic existence, Campanella affirms that such a relationship can only be one of identity, whether the being in question is considered in its potential, mental, or real state. A being is in potency to be when it can exist but does not exist yet.[113] In such a potential state, a being has no essence or existence of its own. It exists only insofar as it is in its cause, or rather, insofar as the cause has the power to bring it into existence. It is the cause itself, or more precisely, the exemplary idea according to which the cause will produce it.[114] Evidently, then, one cannot speak of a real distinction between essence and existence in a potential being, since they coincide with the essence and existence of their cause.

Nor can one speak of a real distinction between the essence and existence of a purely mental being: certainly not of a being in the mind of God, because of God's absolute simplicity; but not even of a being in our own mind. For it is not because we think of a thing as possible, that this thing can exist; it is rather the other way around, i.e., a thing can exist because it is possible or has the power to be.[115] Our mind, in effect, does not measure things, but is measured by things.[116] Accordingly, our thoughts have always some sort of relation to existence, just as they have a relation to essence: the two cannot be separated.

In regard to real or actual being, i.e., being that has been actualized by its causes, the same principle of a real identity of essence and existence holds true.[117] In a real being essence and existence are not only inseparable, but a real distinction between them seems to be altogether out of question. There is no such thing as an essence without existence, anymore than there is an existence without an essence. Essence and existence are simultaneous and from the same causes. When they are in their causes, they are in a potential state; when they are out of their causes, they are in an actual state.[118] Because existence follows essence outside of its causes, it does not follow that it is something intrinsically and really distinct from it as one thing is distinct from another.[119] In other words, essence and existence are so closely related to each other that just as a thing cannot be conceived as existing unless it has an essence, so it cannot be conceived as having an essence unless it exists.[120] The difference between a thing as it is in the mind of God and the same thing as it is in its actuality consists in this, that in the latter case its being is contracted to a definite concrete existence. This amounts to saying that by its creation a thing does not acquire a better existence, but only an existence that contracts to a particular and concrete essence the essence that exists in the mind of God in the form of a universal and nobler idea. Since existence is in turn also contracted to a certain particular essence, no distinction can be admitted between essence and intrinsic existence in finite things, just as no distinction is to be admitted between them as they are in the mind of God.[121]

To the objection that something can be conceived as an essence, prescinding entirely from the fact of its existence, Campanella answers that existence is presupposed in all notions as the basis for any discussion. It is true, he remarks, that existence does not enter into the definition of an essence; but this does not mean that it is really distinct from it. The purpose of a definition, which is always the conclusion of a science, is to reveal something or say something new. Now, we do not say anything new when we state that something exists; for whatever we talk about is always in terms of being, and being implies existence, whether potential, mental, or real.[122]

One of the conditions Campanella lays down for his denial of a real distinction between essence and intrinsic existence is that both of them must be within the same order of being. If, for instance, we consider the essence and existence of a thing in the purely potential or mental order in relation to the essence and existence of the same thing in the actual and concrete order, then, of course, we have to admit a real distinction between them. "The act of existing," he states, "is really distinct from essence in common [i.e., universal essence in the mind of God], but not from a personated [i.e., individualized] essence, that is, an essence brought into existence."[123] Also, "the existence outside the mind of God is distinct from the essence in the mind of God."[124] Again, "this [ideal metaphysical] essence is really distinct from the exterior existence." By the latter, as is evident from the context, he means the existence of an individualized physical essence.[125]

This teaching shows once more how Campanella, though in disagreement with the traditional Thomistic tenet of a real distinction between essence and existence in finite things, is far from any pantheistic or idealistic conception of reality. His position is admittedly very close to that of Scotus. However, he differs from the Subtle Doctor in distinguishing between intrinsic and extrinsic existence and in making intrinsic existence identical with essence. How far Campanella's notion of extrinsic existence approaches some modern existentialist conceptions of existence could be the object of an interesting study.[126]

IV. THE CAUSES OF BEING

1. *Causes in General.* The exposition of Campanella's metaphysics would not be complete without an analysis of his doctrine on the causes of being. Since a finite being does not exist by itself, it must have a reason for its coming into existence, as well as for its intrinsic constitution. This is what, after the manner of Plato and Aristotle, we call the ultimate causes of being. They will be discussed here from the Campanellian point of view.

Cause, says Campanella, is that from which something is made.[127] Whereas primality refers to the essence of being and principle refers to the same essence as a source of intrinsic activity, cause or causation bespeaks a production and is necessarily connected with an effect.[128] Cause is to be distinguished from element, occasion, and condition. Element is the primary constituent of a thing; occasion is that which prompts the motive for the cause to operate; and condition is the proper setting or necessary requirement for operation.[129] The complex of all the causes, principles, elements, and primalities, as manifested in the production of a numerically distinct being, is called the seed (*semen*).[130] As all the causes are in the seed by participation, so all the principles are in the causes, and all the primalities in the principles. Hence the primalities contain in an eminent way the principles, the causes, and the seed; the principles contain the causes and the seed; and the causes contain the seed. Thus every seed is a cause, every cause is a principle, and every principle is a primality; but not vice versa.[131]

There are three genera of causes, namely, one genus for each principle of being. Every genus comprehends a twofold cause: one, the interior, pertains to the essence of being; and the other, the exterior, pertains to the object. Thus we have not only four causes, as Aristotle taught, but six.[132] The self-extension of the potential principle gives rise to the *agent* or *efficient* cause. From the combined activity of the efficient cause with the object of its extension the effect is produced, which is a new being numerically distinct from the causes. Hence to the efficient cause a *material* extrinsic cause has to be added on the part of the object. Likewise, in the operation of the cognitive principle through self-extension a twofold cause is involved, the *ideal* cause *ad intus* and the *formal* cause *ad extra*. Both of these causes have reference to the idea and operate in conjunction with one another. Finally, the extension of the volitive principle gives rise to the *final* cause inherent in the essence of being, inasmuch as every being wills for itself whatever it wills; and to the *perfective* cause, which is the finality or perfection of the effect.[133] Briefly, there is the agent or efficient cause, that by which something is made *(a qua aliquid fit);* the material cause, that out of which something is made *(de quo fit);* the ideal cause, that according to which something is made *(instar cuius fit);* the formal cause, that by means of which something is made *(quo fit);* the final cause, that for the sake of which something is made *(propter quod fit);* and the perfective or perfectional cause, that according to which something is perfected *(secundum quod per fit, seu perficitur).*[134]

Every cause may be considered in four different stages according to its ultimate effect. Let us take the example of a plant. The most remote cause of a plant is God; its remote cause is the sun; its less proximate cause is the heat received by the earth and the plant; and its proximate cause is the seminal heat that goes into the substance of the plant.[135] What is true of the efficient cause is also true of the other causes. Thus, to mention only the interior causes, the most remote ideal cause of a plant is its exemplar in the mind of God; its remote ideal cause is its exemplar in the vault of heaven and the intellect of the ideating angels; its less proximate ideal cause is its image in the generating tree; and its proximate ideal cause is the same image as it is in the seed.[136] Likewise, the final end of a plant is God; the remote end is the use that a plant has for man; the less proximate end is the generated plant itself; and the proximate end is the plant's own existence.[137] The seed is the synthesis of all the causes, i.e., the participation of all the causes at one time and proximately.[138] However, this does not prevent us from saying that the proximate cause is a participation of the less proximate cause, the less proximate cause of the remote, and the remote of the most remote cause.[139]

A cause may be total or partial, universal or particular. There can be only one total and proximate cause of one single effect. Two writers, for instance, cannot be at one time the principal causes of the same writing. However, there can be many partial causes or causes of a different order cooperating in the production of one and the same effect, like two men rowing the same boat.[140]

From each cause emanates a different category of being. From the efficient or active cause emanates action, which is the diffusion of the agent's likeness into the passive subject. From the material cause proceeds quantity, i.e., number and measure. The ideal cause gives rise to similarity and opposition; the formal cause to quality, and the final cause to act. Act differs from action insofar as it is immanent in the essence of a thing; action entails an effusion to the outside. Act stands to action as self-calefaction to the heating of a piece of wood. Perfection also comes from the final cause. When something is made according to its end, it is said to be perfect for the purpose of its existence. Finally, use and ornament follow from the perfective cause.[141]

The following scheme may well represent Campanella's doctrine of causes in relation to their principles and effects.

	PRINCIPLES	CAUSES	EFFECTS
	Potential	Interior —efficient	Action
		Exterior—material	Quantity
BEING	Cognitive	Interior —ideal	Similarity and opposition
		Exterior—formal	Quality
	Volitive	Interior —final	Act and perfection
		Exterior—perfective	Use and ornament

2. *Causes in Particular.* a) *The Efficient Cause.* Having mentioned the nature and division of causes, Campanella goes on to describe each one of them in particular. The causation of the agent or efficient cause, he states, is threefold, *material, active,* and *metaphysical.* The first two types of causation belong properly speaking to the realm of physics. Material causation, in fact, consists in the commingling of two elements, whereby the active element loses in most of the cases part of its own entity. Such is the case of dampness penetrating dryness, and vice versa.[142] Active causation—otherwise called formal causation[143]—takes place when an agent effuses its own likeness into a passive subject by producing a numerically distinct being. Thus fire generates fire by amplifying and multiplying itself.[144] Metaphysical causation, in contrast to the two preceding ones, is the result of the action of the primalities,[145] which is far more powerful than that of a merely material or physical action. Moreover, no material or physical action is possible without the premotion of a primality.[146] Whether the mode of acting of the primalities is by a commingling process as in material causation, or by multiplication as in active causation, or finally by a better process, it remains obscure.[147] One thing, though,

seems to be certain. Whereas in material causation the active and passive causes have to come into direct contact with one another for the production of the effect, and in active or formal causation a contact has to be established at least through a medium,[148] a metaphysical action can take place even without a medium of communication. In other words, it can be exerted also through a vacuum; for a vacuum, too, has its own primalities.[149]

b) *The Final and Perfective Causes.* Starting off with the principle that "every agent acts for an end, either in himself or in another,"[150] Campanella affirms that the first and primary end of a being is its own good and conservation. All other things are willed and intended only insofar as they lead to that end, which is of the very essence of a being. That which represents the terminus of one's operation cannot properly speaking be called *finis* or end; it should rather be called finality or perfection.[151] Hence arises the distinction between final and perfective cause, which is analogous to the distinction between agent and material cause, or ideal and formal cause.

Finality is the final entelechy of a thing. Thus navigation is the finality of a ship, while the construction of the ship is the finality of the shipbuilder. The end, on the contrary, is the shipbuilder's own conservation by means of the ship's construction.[152]

The distinction between end and finality, one pertaining to the self and the other to the object of its operation, can be proved by comparing our actions with the actions of God. Just as God does everything for Himself, since the final end of His actions cannot be the usage and operations of creatures, so it must be conceded that all beings imitate God and act for themselves. Therefore, the end lies within oneself; finality is in something distinct from the self.[153]

The distinction between final and perfective cause in being, it has been observed, is not motivated in Campanella's system by reasons of a purely architectonic structure; it corresponds to the anti-immanentistic inspiration of his metaphysics.[154] This is true, yet such a distinction is merely another way of expressing the scholastic distinction between the *finis operis* and *finis operantis.* The former is the end realized by the act itself in virtue of its very nature; the latter is the end expressly intended by the agent. Campanella, however, emphasizes the aspect of one's own good, that is, self-preservation, in the *finis operantis.*

c) *The Ideal Cause and the Doctrine of Ideas.* The final cause leads necessarily, in Campanella's opinion, to the admission of an ideal cause distinct from all other causes. If it is true that all things act for an end, and the end is only possible through an idea, it must be admitted that the existence of an end implies the existence of an idea. Hence, just as the end constitutes a cause distinct from the agent, so the idea, which is the cause of the end, its knowledge and realization, is also distinct from the agent. Aristotle is therefore wrong in identifying the ideal cause with the efficient cause. Were he right, there would be no distinction between a principal cause and an instrumental cause. The principal cause would not even be able to act, because of its lack of knowledge of the effect.[155]

Having justified, to his own satisfaction, the existence of the ideal cause as a prerequisite for the final cause and as something distinct from both the final and the efficient cause, Campanella proceeds to establish more firmly the existence and nature of exemplary ideas.

The marvelous construction of the world makes it clear to us that it cannot be the product of chance or the outcome of a blind struggle between the opposite forces of nature. It must be, on the contrary, the work of a most powerful, most wise, and infinitely good architect. But every agent that does not act blindly knows what he intends to do, and carries out his plan according to an idea of his mind. Thus the idea is the form present in the agent's intellect as the model or pattern of things to be done. It concerns both intellect and will, for one does not execute everything he conceives, but only those things he wills to do. Moreover, since the model of one thing is different from the model of other things, there must be in the primary architect as many ideas as there are things.

The primary architect differs from the secondary architects insofar as he is an inventor and has the model of his artifact in his mind, whereas the secondary architects are only imitators who observe and copy the inventor's artifact. That is why we maintain, remarks Campanella, that the ideas of all things are in the mind of God. They are the very essence of God as capable of imitation and participation by creatures.[156]

The idea is the quiddity of a thing to be made. Accordingly, essential predication is basically a predication of the idea. Peter, for instance, is a man to the extent that he comes close to the idea of man; a house is a true house inasmuch as it corresponds to the idea of its builder. In brief, formal essence is from the idea.[157] It is true that we define a thing principally from its form; but that is the form of the whole that comes from the idea of the principal agent, who makes such a thing according to the specific end he has in mind. The parts

within the whole are the effects of partial ideas. The universal idea
neither generates nor is generated as a principle *ut quod;* however, it
both generates and is generated as a principle *ut quo.* Thus, it is
through the idea that Peter generates this particular man, John.
Likewise, it is through the idea that an architect builds a house. Yet
the being of this particular house depends on this matter, this agent,
and this ideation; not on the idea.[158] For the idea is not a form that is
already formed, but a forming form, i.e., that according to which
formation takes place. The idea is in the "ideated" thing, not in the
fullness of its essence, but to the extent that it participates in it.[159]

The distinction between idea and form is more clearly indicated
in the *Theologia,* where the idea is called *forma effundibilis* and the
form *forma effusa* or *ideata;* the idea is said to be intellectual, the
form material; the idea is described as something communicable, while
the form is incommunicable.[160] To sum up, the idea is the form
existing outside of things, through which the architect knows things,
and which he imitates in his productions.[161]

It is hardly necessary to point out the close relationship between
this teaching and Plato's doctrine of forms. Campanella openly
acknowledges his indebtedness to the Greek philosopher. Along with
St. Augustine, he tries to reconcile Plato's views with the Christian
conception of God. After reiterating his statement that God is the
author of the ideas and that the ideas are in God, he appeals to
Plato's *Parmenides* and *Timaeus* for a confirmation of his doctrine.[162]
Then he adds:

> The Peripatetics are therefore mendacious, as usual, when they speak
> of Plato's ideas as though he placed them in the hollow of the
> moon or somewhere else, immovable and abstract from material
> things. If God is the cause of things and knows things before they
> are made, the ideas must be placed in God. This is what all scho-
> lastics teach.[163]

In the light of recent critical studies it is very doubtful whether
Campanella's interpretation of Plato's doctrine of ideas, however at-
tractive it may be to a Christian philosopher, reflects Plato's authentic
thought.[164] It is indicative, nevertheless, of a frame of mind common
to many Renaissance philosophers and of the high esteem in which
the founder of the Academy was held by the representatives of the
Platonist current of thought. Apart from his interpretation of Plato's
theory, it can hardly be denied that Campanella's doctrine of exemplary ideas is substantially in agreement with the traditional scholastic philosophy of the Augustinian school.

With this observation, we close the exposition of Campanella's teaching on the causes of being. No special mention has been made of the formal and material causes. They will be considered in the following section, when matter and form are discussed.

V. BEING AND NATURE

Campanella's philosophy of nature is inspired by Telesio's *De rerum natura,* a work that aims to explain nature through itself *(iuxta propria principia)* and on the basis of mere empirical observation. We have already indicated how enthusiastically Campanella welcomed Telesio's revolutionary work and how violently he defended it from, the attacks of G. A. Marta. The principles laid down by Campanella in his *Philosophia sensibus demonstrata* were to become the mold of his whole philosophy of nature, characterized by a definite reaction against Aristotle's hylomorphic system. This doctrine can be better understood in the light of his cosmogony.

1. *Space and Matter.* In the beginning of time God created an almost infinite space in which the world was placed.[165] Space or place is a primary, immovable, and incorporeal substance having the capacity to receive all bodies.[166] It is the mathematical world, interior and anterior to all systems of the corporeal world.[167]

Space is a substance, because it is the substratum or basis of all things *(substat omnibus).*[168] Being incorporeal, it penetrates all things and is penetrated by all beings.[169] Space, which is endowed with the primalitarian structure,[170] attracts all beings to itself, especially those offering less resistance because of their thin and rare nature. Like all bodies, it abhors an absolute vacuum.[171]

In this space God placed matter, a body which is formless and inactive, but capable of being molded into many forms and acted upon as wax is acted upon by a seal. Matter is infinitely divisible in our imagination; actually, its division terminates in the minutest atoms that appear in a sunbeam. Matter is the passive principle of composition in things. Being inert, it exerts no action upon our sight. It is black like darkness, which can be seen neither by open nor by closed eyes.[172]

That matter is a body, from which it is distinct only by name, is for Campanella a fundamental principle of sense experience.[173] Were matter not a substantial body, we would have to admit that corporeal bodies are made of incorporeal principles, i.e., an incorporeal matter and an incorporeal form, which is a contradiction.[174] If matter is a principle of being, it must itself be a being. If it is a being, it is so not because of the form, but because of its own material entity. From the form it has formal being, not material being. Therefore, since it is from matter or *moles corporea* that things are made and into which they can be dissolved, it is of the nature of matter to be a universal, formless, inert body, apt to receive all forms and operations.[175]

By calling matter a universal body Campanella intends to emphasize, in the first place, its character of unity and adaptability in regard to the many forms it can receive. For matter is not the same as an element: an element is manifold, matter is one. Yet, he observes, matter cannot take up all the forms indistinctly, but only the physical forms of the order to which it belongs. Otherwise, there would be just one type of matter for men, angels, and the brutes.[176] In the second place, Campanella wishes to stress the concrete nature of matter in contrast to the so-called Aristotelian matter. This, he says, is neither a substance nor anything else, but merely a construction of the mind.[177] Matter without a body, he asserts even more emphatically, is only Aristotle's chimera.[178]

When matter is described as a formless body, Campanella insists, the expression should not be taken to mean that the matter can be without a form; it means simply that matter is not limited to any particular form. It is possible that matter be without any active form, such as heat, cold, and the like; but it cannot be without a passive form, unless it be infinite or extended *in infinitum*. As it is limited in its existence, it must necessarily be terminated by a form.[179] This distinction between active and passive form will be discussed later.

To complete the inquiry about matter, we wish to refer to other passages of the *Metaphysica,* where Campanella's notion of matter appears to be even more at variance with Aristotelian doctrine. He rejects the idea of matter as pure potency actualized by form and asserts that matter is endowed with a reality of its own distinct from the form. It gives to form its material being, which is more than it receives in terms of formal being.[180] Matter has, therefore, a considerable amount of entity, since it is the basis and substance of things. It has many advantages over form, which is determinate to a particular mode of being and cannot receive all the perfections of matter. All things, in fact, can be made from matter without its being destroyed. This is not true of form, which is subject to destruction whenever a change is made in things.[181] Accordingly, Scotus attributes to matter an entitative act, and Plato stresses the being of matter somewhat to the detriment of form; for matter always remains, whereas form disappears.[182]

2. *Form and the Active Principles of Being.* From the foregoing discussion it is clear that Campanella does not speak of form in the same sense that scholastics do. He explicitly rejects the scholastic notion of form as a substantial principle of being on the ground that the peripatetic form, like primary matter and privation, is a chimerical entity that can never enter to compose real beings.[183]

Form, he claims, represents the idea as it is actualized in things outside the mind. It distinguishes things and their natures. The knowledge of the external form of a thing enables us to understand by analogy its interior form, and through it, the entire thing.[184] Analogically considered, form is the mode or quality of a thing.[185]

Every finite being includes an essence as its matter and the limit of this essence as its form or qualification of matter. Through this limit a being is constituted in its own *esse* and distinguished from other beings. Thus, form participates in being and nonbeing: as a constituent of being it is an entity, as a principle of distinction it is a nonentity.[186]

Considered as a cause, form is that whereby something is made and constituted in its essential or accidental specific being.[187] One and featureless, matter can only be multiplied and distinguished by form, which does not give being *simpliciter* but merely specifies it. In other words, form is the principle of distinction as well as of individuation of being, whereas matter has only the capacity of being distinguished and individualized.[188]

Campanella sometimes speaks of *haecceitas* or thisness as a principle of numerical unity.[189] However, to the notion of *haecceitas,* as conceived by Scotus, he adds something that "Scotus did not know."[190] What makes a thing to be numerically identical with itself, he asserts, is its singularity or *haecceitas* as it is manifested by extrinsic existence, namely, that type of existence that makes a thing to be that particular thing, located in that particular place, and surrounded by that particular environment.[191] Indeed, it is not because of its essence that an individual is numerically distinct from another of the same species; its numerical distinction is only from its existence. Peter and Paul, to give concrete examples, are not distinct from each other because of their essence, which they share in common; their distinction is from their actually different participation in the same essence outside of their cause. They are like two prints of the same seal.[192]

By rejecting the scholastic notion of form as a substantial principle of being, Campanella also rejects the identification of form with act. Form, he states, is called act, and whatever acts is called form. But this does not mean, as is commonly understood, that form makes one thing pass from potency to act. It is not the form that causes this passage, but the agent that produces the form. Form may be called act of its matter, but only analogically. Just as operation is called act because it is the action of an agent in accordance with the agent's nature, so form may be called act but only insofar as the action of a thing is in direct relation to the thing's intrinsic constitution of an essence modified by a form.[193] This is the active form, in contrast to the passive form which is a quality or disposition enabling the active form to act. Thus heat in fire is the active form, whereas the tenuity of fire and the solidity of earth are the passive forms.[194]

That form is not the act of matter as an essential principle of being can also be demonstrated by the fact that no form is limited to a particular matter, unless God in His infinite wisdom has a special use for it which is unknown to us.[195] The essence of a thing is, therefore, quite different from the form of it. This latter is only a part of the thing, not its entire entity.[196]

As Campanella does not agree with the Peripatetics in identifying form with act, so he does not agree with their teaching that form is educed from the potentiality of matter.[197] Matter is a passive principle that can receive forms when they are given to it; it can never give out forms which it does not possess. It is simply impossible that a passive nature become an active one without the intervention of an agent. What is true of a corporeal form is much truer of an incorporeal one, such as a vegetative and sensitive form.[198]

What are the agents that produce form in matter and consequently are responsible for the actual composition of physical reality? This question presents no problem to Campanella. His study of nature by means of the senses provides him with an easy answer.

It is most evident that heat and cold exist and perform everything in nature, and that all contrarieties can be reduced to them. We must, therefore, establish these [two] as principles [of physical beings] and place them within the first two bodies called elements.[199]

Heat and cold are thus the two active principles that God introduced into the corporeal but formless mass of matter so that they could organize it and give it shape. These two principles are not substances,[200] but incorporeal agents endowed with a diffusive power of an opposite nature that in the beginning of time produced heaven and earth, the first two bodies or primary elements of the world from which all things are made.[201] Nor are heat and cold accidents, in the sense that they just happen to be after a being is already in existence.[202] They are real components of being. They are principal agents and not the instruments of any form or being, except God, the first architect of the world. Being endowed with sense, they also produce plants and animals.[203] Briefly, material beings are the product of two active principles, heat and cold, and one passive principle, matter. Form is intrinsically the heat that comes from the sun and unites itself to matter; extrinsically and passively, it is the external configuration of material beings that results from the action of heat on matter.[204]

If we compare this notion of physical reality with Aristotle's hylomorphic system, we see immediately that the two doctrines have very little in common.[205] Both of them aim at explaining inanimate nature through its intrinsic causes; but here agreement ends. The Stagirite approaches nature from the metaphysical standpoint and reaches out to the ultimate causes of being. In so doing, he makes use of reason without discarding the data of the senses. Campanella, on the contrary, relying exclusively on sense experience, approaches nature from a purely physical viewpoint and does not penetrate to the core of reality. What he offers is not a philosophy of nature, but a very questionable theory of the physical constitution of bodies commingled with elements of his somewhat fantastic cosmogony.[206] The result is that his explanation of nature *iuxta propria principia* deprives cosmology of its metaphysical foundation, following a trend in philosophy that had been initiated by Telesio without being aware of it.[207] Through his theory of nature Campanella also contributed to the revival of certain naturalistic doctrines of early Greek philosophers which had already been successfully refuted by Aristotle. In this sense Campanella's theory of nature appears to be a step backward in the philosophical speculation.

3. *Time.* A last point to be discussed in connection with Campanella's philosophy of nature is his notion of time. Scholastics in general accept Aristotle's definition of time as "the number of movement in respect of before and after."[208] According to this definition, time includes two distinct elements: a formal element which is number or measure, for all quantity is measurable and measure is expressed by number; and a material element which consists in the continued existence of motion or change. Both of these elements are

essential to time. Time exists, however, neither as a duration nor as a measure. The only element of time which has an extramental existence is the instant. To measure in terms of present, past, and future is an act of our mind. Hence Aristotle can affirm that if there were no soul or mind there would be no time.[209]

Campanella is fully acquainted with the Aristotelian notion of time, but claims that Aristotle is wrong in defining time as the measure of movement. Rather we measure time by movement. Besides, time is the measure of rest no less than of movement, even though we come to know time through movement.[210] Hence it is not of the essence of time to be a measure. Indeed, to measure is to attempt to find an unknown quantity through a quantity that is known. Further, what we call measure, apart from being a measure, is also something concrete. A foot, for instance—Campanella speaks of a palm—in addition to being a standard unit of length, is also a part of our body. Hence, when defining time in terms of measure of movement Aristotle does not indicate the essence of time, but rather the usage we make of it.[211] In other words, time is not something ideal and subjective but something real; so that, contrary to Aristotle's teaching, even if no soul or mind existed, there still would be time.[212]

But precisely what is time? Time is the successive duration of things having a beginning and an end.[213] It is different from eternity, which is duration of something altogether unchangeable and without beginning or end, like God.[214] It is also to be distinguished from aevum, the duration of a thing which is unchangeable in its substance and has no end but is not without a beginning, like angels and the human soul.[215] Time is likewise to be distinguished from perpetuity and vicissitude, one belonging to the mathematical world of universal space and the other to the material world of the *moles corporea*.[216] Time belongs to transient things, namely, those things which are not only subject to change, like matter, but also cease to exist and eventually are brought back into existence.[217]

Time stems from nonbeing or impotence. Thus, because one cannot be simultaneously at home and on the public square, a period of time elapses in the transition from one place to the other. Had one the power to go from home to the public square instantly, there would be no lapse of time. Succession, then, and consequently time, implies a lack of power.[218] Time, to be more precise, is a composition of being and nonbeing, one succeeding to the other.[219]

It is of the nature of time to be a succession in change whereby one thing succeeds to another, or the same thing changes its own state. Change, in turn, involves a flux and a flowing form. Time is this flux, which is a comparatively slow process depending on the nature of the succeeding thing,[220] while the flowing form is the actual instant (*ipsum nunc*).[221]

From the identification of time with flux and of the actual instant with the flowing form, Campanella concludes to the relativity of time and even of the instant.[222] However, he admits that there is a universal time which is the cause of all changes, and this is the movement of heaven.[223]

In summary, time for Campanella is not the measure of movement, as Aristotle taught, but the movement or change of a thing insofar as it is the measure of the movement of other things; or, more objectively, the thing itself considered in its successive duration through change.

CHAPTER NINE

Treatise on God

The notion of God plays such an important role in Campanella's philosophy that his whole system seems to rest on it as on its foundation. Since every creature carries within itself the image and vestige of its creator, God is not only the primary being in which all beings participate but also the model upon which all reality is fashioned. The very notion of primalities of being is based on God's nature as revealed to us in the mystery of the Holy Trinity. It is no wonder, then, that God occupies a prominent place in Campanella's metaphysics. Indeed, in his system of philosophy metaphysics deals principally with the first being.[1] Hence the problem of whether the philosophical study of God constitutes a distinct and separate discipline from general metaphysics or ontology has no meaning for Campanella.[2] As his treatise on God is contained mainly in his *Metaphysica* and *Theologia,* we shall refer to these two works as the principal sources of information for his doctrine on the existence, nature, and operations of the divine being.

I. THE EXISTENCE OF GOD

1. *The Demonstrability of God's Existence.* The first question that Campanella raises in connection with the philosophical knowledge of God concerns the possibility of proving His existence. Taking as a starting point his distinction between innate and acquired knowledge, he argues that God's existence is both self-evident in itself and self-evident to us by innate knowledge *(notitia innata)*. On the contrary, by acquired knowledge *(notitia illata)* it is only self-evident in itself and not to us, and so it can be demonstrated.[3]

Knowledge of God is so inherent in the essence of our soul that it is a part of our self-consciousness. For every created being in the very act of knowing itself also knows its creator, in whom it participates.[4] Furthermore, the knowledge that it has of God is greater than the knowledge of its own being. Just as all creatures love God more than themselves because God is absolute goodness, whereas their own goodness is necessarily limited, so also they know God more than themselves.[5] God's existence is so evident that no rational being can fail to see it. God himself, as the supreme and most active being, directs us in such wise that the soul comes to know Him even before it knows anything else. In fact, every kind of knowledge, whether it is natural, animal, or mental, presupposes knowledge of God.[6] To the objection that we have no experience of an innate knowledge of the divine being, Campanella answers:

> The science by which we know God is primordial and hidden even to us, in the same way as is the natural love by which all things love God more than themselves. First, because, in spite of the fact that through innate knowledge we always tend to the first true [being], we are alienated from the knowledge of ourselves and God by the action of external objects that assimilate us to themselves. Second, because the divine object, which exceeds our faculties as the sun exceeds the faculties of the bat, is not proportionate to us.[7]

We are thus referred again to the doctrine of self-consciousness in its double aspect of *notitia praesentialitatis* and *notitia reflexa*. Because of the obtrusion of external reality upon the senses, the knowledge that our soul has of itself is, as it were, hidden and darkened. Hence the soul in its present state of union with the body has to return upon itself in order to understand its own nature. So it is with its knowledge of God.

By admitting an innate knowledge of God, Campanella takes sides with St. John Damascene and St. Augustine against St. Thomas Aquinas. St. John Damascene teaches that "the knowledge of God is naturally implanted in all men, so that the knowledge of God's existence is not only self-evident in itself but also to us."[8] St. Augustine reaches a similar conclusion by inquiring about the nature of truth.[9] However, Campanella agrees with Aquinas in stressing the need of a demonstration of God's existence from the observation of the visible world. For even though God is intrinsic to all things, He is invisible and cannot affect us in a sensible way. It is only by reasoning from visible things that we can argue to His existence. We, like all other created things, are in God and within God as worms are within our body. Just as these worms because of their tiny dimensions live within us without perceiving us, so we live in God without perceiving Him. This is true because of His infinite nature which incommensurably exceeds our limited faculties.[10]

2. *Proofs of the Existence of God.* Having paved the way for a demonstration of God's existence based on empirical knowledge, Campanella proceeds to the exposition of his arguments, which he divides into two categories: arguments of a metaphysical order *(rationes*

metaphysicales) and arguments of a physical order *(rationes ex physicis petitae)*. Let us consider them briefly.

a) *Arguments of a Metaphysical Order.* These are called metaphysical proofs because they are based on the primalities of being and their objects. They lead to the demonstration of the existence of a first being, who is at the same time the first power, wisdom, and love, as well as the first existence, truth, and goodness. They show further that this first being possesses all such properties essentially and infinitely and is the source of being for all creatures.[11] The proofs based on the primalities are as follows:

1) In every coordination of things there must be one thing that has a particular perfection by its very essence and *simpliciter,* while other things have it only by participation. Thus fire is by its very nature hot, and heat has essentially the power to heat; whereas other things produce heat only to the extent that they participate in heat. Therefore, in the series of beings there must be a first being which is being by its very essence and *simpliciter,* while other beings are only beings by participation. That first being is God.[12]

2) Whatever exists has the power to exist either in itself or in something else. But contingent things, being changeable and corruptible, do not have the power to exist in themselves. Moreover, some of them are endowed with greater power to exist than others. Hence there must be a first subsisting power which is power *per se* and of whose power all other beings partake.[13]

3) All created beings are endowed with sense knowledge. This knowledge is not the same in every being, for some beings sense more clearly than others. Consequently, a first subsisting wisdom must be admitted from which sense knowledge is derived by all finite beings, although in different degrees.[14]

4) From the observation of things in nature we can see that in all of them there is order and design. But order and design are the effects of wisdom. Therefore, whether these things are self-moving or are moved by an intelligence outside of them, we must admit a first wisdom in which they participate, or by which they are directed in their actions.[15]

5) All things love their own being and hate not to be. This love is not self-existent but is participated, just as heat is participated in by iron. Hence there must be a first love in which all things participate.[16]

The objects of the primalities lead also to the demonstration of God's existence.

1) Whatever is in the world is finite and has only a limited existence: a man exists only as a man, a stone as a stone, the world as a world; none of them has the fullness of being. Hence, since certain things have more existence than others, one must conclude that there is a first being which exists *per se* and absolutely.[17]

2) Likewise, whatever exists is true. But a being is said to be true to the extent that it approaches, or departs from, the supreme truth. Thus a man is more or less perfect to the extent that he comes close to, or departs from, the idea of man. Therefore, all beings are true because of their participation in the first immutable truth.[18]

3) The same kind of reasoning applies to the good, which is found in creatures in different degrees and is a participation in infinite goodness.[19]

These metaphysical proofs for the existence of God have in common the Platonic principle that beings with limited perfections presuppose the existence of a supreme and absolutely perfect being from whom all perfections are derived.[20] This being, Campanella says, is God.

b) *Arguments of a Physical Order*. This second series of proofs for God's existence arises from consideration of the world. Although less profound, they are easier to understand than the metaphysical proofs and are equally convincing.[21] The reason is that they rest on sense experience, and, like the metaphysical proofs, lead to the demonstration of the existence of a first being, God, who is the primary cause of all existing reality.[22] These are the arguments of a physical order as listed in the *Metaphysica*:

1) In the order of causes one cannot proceed to infinity. Now secondary causes act either of themselves or because they are moved by other causes. Evidently they do not act of themselves. Therefore, there must be a first cause that moves all other causes.[23] The impossibility of proceeding to infinity in the series of seecondary causes is proved by the fact that in such a supposition there would be no first cause, and consequently no cause at all.[24] On the other hand, an infinite regress in the series of causes would make the action of posterior causes depend on the causality of a first hypothetical cause from which they would be separated by an infinite distance. This also is an absurdity, for an infinite distance can never be overcome.[25] Since, then, no cause can be the cause of itself and since no infinite regress

in the series of causes is possible, one is bound to admit a first efficient cause whose causality is responsible for all the effects of the secondary causes.[26]

2) All things act for a particular end. Yet, although they are in conflict with one another, they all converge toward a final common end. Hence there must be a single universal cause directing their actions toward the attainment of this end.[27]

3) The visible world is composed of matter, heat, and cold, the three conflicting principles that give rise to contrary elements and constitute through them the universal structure of the world. But all contrary principles and elements aim only at their own conservation and at the destruction of their opposites and would never join together on their own to form the world. Thus it is necessary to admit a most powerful and intelligent being, who coordinates all the opposite tendencies of the physical components of the world in such a way that one is within the other without destroying it, and all contribute to the world structure.[28]

4) The world around us did not always have its present structure, for composing parts, especially if they have opposite characteristics, precede their composite. Therefore, since these parts, as previously stated, cannot exist or join together on their own, who else but a most powerful and intelligent being could have made them and put them together?[29]

5) Certain things are generated and subject to corruption. This process of generation and corruption either had a beginning or has gone on from all eternity. In either case, it can only be understood if we admit a first and most perfect cause, which is God.[30] The same conclusion must be drawn from the observation of the structure of an animal,[31] its sensory system,[32] and the elements that make up that system.[33]

6) The human soul's knowledge of something infinite and the desire for it are not possible unless there exist an infinite being. For an effect cannot exceed its cause, and our soul, which is only a small particle of the world, cannot conceive or desire anything greater than that which exists in reality. Hence an infinite being must exist.[34]

With the exception of this last, all the so-called *rationes ex physicis petitae* can be reduced to St. Thomas's second, third, and fifth ways of demonstrating God's existence. Special emphasis is placed on the argument from order and design in creation. The last argument is worth considering, for it corresponds basically to Descartes' first theistic argument as laid down in his *Third Meditation*.[35] Both

Campanella and Descartes take as their starting point the existence in the mind of the idea of something infinite, from which they argue by means of the principle of causality to the existence of an infinite being. The difference between the two philosophers consists in this: that, whereas Descartes speaks of the idea of an infinite substance and supremely perfect being,[36] Campanella speaks only of the idea of, as well as of the desire for, something infinite. Campanella does not state expressly, as Descartes does, that the idea of the infinite must be produced in us by an infinite substance.[37] It remains true, nevertheless, that from the simple idea of the infinite he concludes to the existence of an infinite being along the line of Descartes' argument, i.e., through the principle of efficient causality.[38] On the basis of the foregoing considerations, is one not justified in claiming for Campanella the honor, if any, of having been the forerunner of the great French philosopher on this point also? The striking similarity between the two arguments indicates at least the pertinence of such a reflection.

c) *Criticism of Aristotle's Argument from Motion.* In going through the theistic proofs of both the metaphysical and the physical order, one looks in vain for the argument from motion, called by St. Thomas "the first and more manifest way of proving God's existence."[39] The reason is that Campanella denies any philosophical value to such a proof. This argument, which was first proposed by Aristotle, has been the object of serious attacks since Duns Scotus.[40] Campanella states in his *Theologia* that those who pretend with Aristotle to prove the existence of God by showing that He is the first mover commit a two-fold paralogism. First, they take for granted that everything that is in motion is moved by a distinct and separate mover. This is only true of those things that are moved mechanically and artificially. Things having within themselves their own principle of motion need not be moved by an external agent. Second, they pretend to prove the existence of God from the eternity of motion. Once eternal motion is denied, as it is by Christian thinkers and many other philosophers, the argument automatically loses all its strength.[41]

This statement represents only the conclusion arrived at by Campanella in the *Metaphysica,* where the problem is discussed at considerable length. There he accuses the Aristotelians of failing to distinguish between act and action, as though in every movement both action and passion were involved. This is not true; for every being has an act or operation of its own. Act or operation is immanent and inherent in the nature of a being in virtue of its own constitution. In animated beings, act is represented by the soul, which rules over the body like a captain in a ship. In purely material things, act is the intrinsic form by which they are actuated. Thus heaven is naturally moved by its own form, and no separate mover is needed to explain the celestial movements, since the heavenly bodies have been endowed by the creator with such a power. Aristotle's objection to the self-movement of things on the ground that it implies the identification of agent and patient, act and potency, has no foundation. For the soul or form is always in act, and what Aristotle calls potency is but active power. Action, on the contrary, is an act or operation *ad extra*, which involves an active agent and a passive subject, or, in the case of motion, a mover and a thing moved. Only in this sense does Aristotle's principle *quidquid movetur ab alio movetur* hold. However, his argument from motion does not lead to the demonstration of a first unmoved mover; for no one can give motion to other things unless it itself possesses motion. Such an argument may at most lead to the admission of a first mover, i.e., heaven, that moves itself essentially and in virtue of its own nature. Being the cause of heat, heaven is a much better mover than any other mover in the physical order.[42]

II. THE NATURE OF GOD

1. *The Cognoscibility of the Nature of God.* Having proved the existence of God, Campanella proceeds to the consideration of His nature. The first problem he faces is whether God's nature can be the object of our knowledge at all. Were the divine nature entirely beyond the reach of our intellect, or the way of knowing it undisclosed, it would be useless to attempt any discussion of it.[43] He is no doubt aware of the negative attitude of certain philosophers toward this problem. Plotinus maintains that God is beyond all the things that are attainable by our mind and that no concept of a finite being can help us to understand Him.[44] Dionysius likewise states that God is beyond all determinations and human expressions; He is beyond all concepts and ideas. Not to know God is the highest knowledge we can have of Him.[45] St. Thomas himself affirms that we know that God is, but not what He is.[46]

Taking his lead from Aquinas's distinction between knowledge of God's existence and knowledge of His essence, Campanella argues that even if our knowledge of God were limited to His existence, it still would be a quidditative knowledge, for in God essence and existence are one and the same thing.[47] Further, we must distinguish between essence and existence as they are in God and as they are in their effects. While essence and existence in God will never be fully understood by men, they can be known by us in their effects, inasmuch as effects resemble the cause in which they participate.[48] Just as we first know things to exist and then inquire about their nature, so do we first know God's existence and then rise to the knowledge of His nature by discussing whether He is corporeal or incorporeal, finite or infinite, temporal or eternal, and the like. To inquire about these attributes is to inquire about the quiddity of God.[49] However, the quidditative knowledge we obtain of God by means of our natural reason is so imperfect that it is almost nothing in comparison with the knowledge that, absolutely speaking, could be had of Him.[50]

God, of course, is in no way the object of our external senses,[51] and what we know of God in the light of our reason is by inference from His effects. It consists in attributing to Him all the perfections we find in creatures and in removing from Him all the imperfections thereof.[52] This can be done in three different ways, namely, by attributing to Him *causal, negative,* and *supereminent* predicates. By causal predicates *(praedicata causalia)* are meant those predicates asserting that God is creator and Lord, the final, exemplary, and efficient cause of all things. The negative predicates *(praedicata negativa)*, such as immaterial, incorporeal, infinite, and immortal, remove from God the imperfections found in their opposites. The supereminent predicates *(praedicata supereminentia)* affirm a pure perfection, such as being, one, true, wise, good, and just, i.e., the transcendentals or objects of the primalities, the primalities themselves, and their participations.[53] Although all these perfections are predicated of God analogically,[54] they are in Him formally and substantially. Thus we do have a positive, although imperfect, knowledge of the divine essence.[55]

In addition to natural reason, there is a better and quicker way of arriving at the knowledge of God. It consists in the direct intuition of God or contemplation, which can be obtained by the purification of the soul in faith and love. This is the way used by saints, like Moses, Paul, Bernard, Catherine, and Denis the Carthusian.[56]

It would be wrong to maintain that God is entirely hidden from us or that His light does not affect us at all. On the contrary, God is clearly manifest to us. We do not see Him because, lying as we do in the dark, we think that He hides Himself from us. Likewise, we are far from speaking truly when we say that God is hidden by His own light. Light does not hide; it makes things clear. It is our inability to sustain the radiance of the divine light that makes us believe that

God is hidden from our sight. We should rise above syllogistic reasoning and try to contemplate God in His own light. This can only be done by repeated exercise, whereby we develop the inner potentialities that constitute our very nature, namely, the primalities, and especially love. God, who is never outdone in love, will certainly assist us in this effort.[57]

This thought, which reveals a deep philosophical and theological insight, shows how greatly Campanella's philosophy is influenced by the mystical trend of the Augustinian school. Whereas in his approach to the problem of the cognoscibility of God by the light of natural reason he goes only slightly beyond St. Thomas's position,[58] he completely departs from Aquinas in holding the possibility of a direct intuition of God through the self-revealing act of our soul in virtue of its primalities. In so doing, he goes even further than St. Augustine and many of his followers; although he does not suggest a direct intuition of God in the sense that ontologists after him will advance.

2. *Negative Knowledge of the Nature of God.* To discover what God is, one must first see what He is not. This negative knowledge gives us a hint of the essence of God, which surpasses the power of all our faculties.[59] It is obvious, in the first place, that God is neither body nor matter. These are merely passive principles, whereas it belongs to God to be in act and to give.[60] Likewise, God is not the universal space in which the world is located,[61] nor the form of bodies,[62] nor the world soul, although He is intrinsic to, but not mixed with, all things.[63] Further, God is neither a composite of matter and form, nor the world, the sun, the air, or any other corporeal being.[64] In Him there is no composition of substance and accident. An accident is that which happens to be outside the essence of a thing, or it is something that is unintentional, involuntary, abnormal, unusual. Nothing of this sort can be said of God, the supreme being and the first cause of all things. His essence does not admit of anything new, either internally or externally.[65]

Nor is God a composite of *suppositum* and nature. Common nature is so called from the common idea that is in the mind of God, as a house is in the mind of its architect. By participation in the idea particular things are derived, and these are called individuals, since they are undivided in themselves and divided from others. Thus Peter is in Peter as a whole, not in a divided being; man, on the other hand, is in Peter, Paul, and every other man, just as the form of a seal is in all things that have been impressed thereby. Common nature, therefore, is not to be found in the nature of things as such, but only in its contracted form, which is a composite of nature and "thisness." Hence, unless we want to admit a plurality of divine beings, such a composition cannot be attributed to God. To be God and to be this God is one and the same thing; to be man and to be this man is not the same thing, since it implies a composition.[66]

God is not a composite of genus and difference, for both genus and difference are modes of being, and God, who is being *per se* and essentially, cannot fall into any of these modes. He is above all predicaments.[67] Being, one may object, applies both to God and creatures, and it is only through some difference that the being of God can be distinguished from the being of creatures. Hence God must be composed of genus and difference.[68] Campanella's answer to this objection is that God is all things without their imperfections and limitations. He is not all things formally, for this would imply that He is constituted by their limited forms; but He is the ideal and causal form of things, having within Himself the being of all things virtually and eminently.[69] Accordingly, being is predicated of God and creatures analogically, as of cause and effect, and not univocally, as Scotus claims. The difference between God and creatures does not contract God; on the contrary, it elevates Him by taking away from Him all contractions. For He is being *per se,* whereas creatures are beings by participation.[70]

In God there is no composition of essence and existence.[71] Whether existence be taken to mean the act of essence, as the Thomists teach, or simply a distinct formality, as the Scotists maintain, or whether it be taken to mean the extrinsic adjacency in which things find themselves, as Campanella asserts,[72] essence and existence in God are one and the same thing. Since God is pure act, excluding any potentiality, it is clear that His essence cannot be actuated; it is rather His own act. Being one *per se,* He is neither a whole nor a part. He excludes any participation in act; otherwise He would be actuated and would no longer be pure act. In other words, God is being *per essentiam,* who neither receives His *esse* from others, nor gives His *esse to* Himself. Were He to give His *esse* to Himself, He already ought to possess it beforehand. Whence else would He receive it? If He already possessed His *esse,* He would have been an actual being even before existing, which is a contradiction. But not even extrinsic existence can enter into a composition with God; for He is an infinite being and no other being can be adjacent to Him. He does not need any place or time to exist. His existence is in Himself; it is Himself.[73]

From the absence of composition of essence and existence, and of common nature and "thisness," it follows that abstract and concrete are also identical in God. He is deity, justice, greatness, and all other perfections; and the only difference between concrete and abstract in Him is a difference of meaning due to the limitations of our mind and the imperfection of our terminology.[74]

Being infinite, God cannot be composed of being and nonbeing. When we say that God is all things, it must be understood that He is so in a most eminent way. When we deny that God is all things, we do not deny anything of Him except the nonbeing of creatures. For every creature is a composition of being and nonbeing. More specifically, God is not all things insofar as they are imperfect and participate in nothingness and contraction; but He is all things inasmuch as they all participate in being and perfection.[75] Imperfections, such as impotence, pain, fragility, death, contrariety, insipience, stupidity, hatred, limitation, and numberless others are the product of nonbeing and can be reduced to the primalities of impotence, ignorance, and hatred. By removing all imperfections from things, we have power, knowledge, and will, although in a limited degree because of the very nature of finite things. If we further remove this limitation, which is from nonbeing, we obtain pure power, pure wisdom, and pure love, i.e., God, in whom all perfections are united.[76] Indeed, even among the primalities in God there is no composition. The primalities do not make any composition in secondary beings, where they are fundamentally and absolutely the same;[77] a fortiori, they make no composition in God.[78] In God one primality is perfectly identical with each of the other two, because of the eminence of the first being in which there is the utmost unity.[79]

Scotus teaches that among the perfections of God there is a formal distinction *ex natura rei*. Such a distinction, Campanella says, cannot be admitted, for in God every perfection is infinite, each one including whatever is in the others. Accordingly, the Thomistic school is right in saying that the divine perfections, although giving rise to different formal concepts in our mind, are not formally distinct.[80]

Is there, then, no distinction whatsoever among the primalities in God? Here Campanella seems to contradict himself. On the one hand, he rejects the Scotistic distinction *ex natura rei,* asserting that they are formally and fundamentally indistinct from one another;[81] on the other hand, he seems to admit such a distinction, for he proclaims, in the very title of the article of the *Metaphysica* where the distinction among the primalities is discussed, that in the first being the proprinciples are distinct from one another *ex natura rei* formally and fundamentally.[82] This apparent inconsistency may perhaps be explained in terms of mere inaccuracy in terminology. The title of the aforesaid article has to be taken in a rather broad sense and made to agree with the content of the article itself, and not vice versa. In other words, while the "formal distinction" of the title may be explained through the different formal concepts *(rationes formales)* that God's primalities produce in our mind, the distinction *"ex natura rei and fundamentally"* should be understood as actually corresponding to the Thomistic logical distinction *cum fundamento in re.* The fact that in the article's title Campanella tries to minimize the distinction among the primalities in God as compared with the primalities in creatures, confirms the validity of this interpretation.

3. *The Divine Attributes.* From the absence of any composition in God Campanella derives God's first attribute, His infinite simplicity. Following St. Augustine, he says that God is neither a whole nor a part, except in our mind. For whatever is in God is God.[83]

Being absolutely simple, God is also one. Thus unity follows from simplicity.[84] It is true that every being is one, and that unity is a supreme transcendental; but no other being is simply and infinitely one like God. In fact, a being is one to the extent that it is a being; the more it has of a being, the more of unity it has. Hence God, who is the supreme being, is also one in the highest degree.[85] Further, a being *per essentiam* cannot but be one. But God is such a being. Therefore, God is one, and all things participate their being in Him.[86] Unity or oneness is the essence of God no less than goodness, wisdom, power, and love. Yet, although infinite, unity in God does not exclude other unities depending on it.[87] For all things, insofar as they are, are one; insofar as they are not, that is, insofar as their being is contracted to this particular entity through the nonbeing of other things, they are many.[88] Indeed, just as unity indicates a positive entity, so multiplicity implies division, and division privation of being.[89]

Once the unity of God is established, and all the imperfections of creatures are removed from it, it follows that God is being properly, substantially, and in a supreme degree. In saying that God *is* being, we do not destroy the divine unity; for the copula "is" does not connect really different things, but only different notions or *rationes formales* invented by us in order to better understand the nature of God. For whatever we predicate of God, we predicate of Him essentially.[90]

God, as previously stated, is neither a genus nor merely something; He excels everything. Hence the term "being," when applied to Him, prescinds from all modes and determinations of existence and admits of infinite extension.[91] Creatures, on the contrary, are beings by participation. Properly speaking, they are not beings; they rather *have* being. To be more specific, although in common usage *being* is predicated both of God and creatures, as a noun it refers to God alone, who is being *per se* and absolutely; as a participle it refers to creatures, who are only beings in relation to God.[92]

If God is being in the most absolute sense of the term, He must be infinite. Whatever is limited is so either because of being or of nonbeing. But God, who is all beings eminently, cannot be limited by any being outside Himself; nor can He be limited by nonbeing, having in Himself the fullness of entity. Hence He must be essentially infinite.[93]

Another argument for the infinity of God is deduced from the very notion of finite being. A finite being is in fact a being by participation. Now, unless we want to fall into the absurdity of having beings by participation without a being in which to participate, parts without a whole, or effects without a cause, we must admit a being *per essentiam,* which is an infinite being.[94] Likewise, our soul has the idea of the infinite. But this idea cannot be the product of our soul, which is by nature finite and limited. It must therefore be produced by a being that is infinite. Were it not so, we would have to admit an effect superior to its cause, which is against the principle of causality.[95] This argument, which is fundamentally the same as the one already mentioned in connection with the proofs for the existence of God,[96] is considered by Campanella as the best argument for the demonstration of God's infinity.[97]

The notion of infinity leads to that of omnipresence. A being that has only a limited entity is necessarily confined to a definite place; but a being that is simple and has no limits whatsoever must be everywhere.[98] God's omnipresence must not be understood in the way that a supposedly infinite body or the soul of an infinite world would be understood. In neither of these ways would God be everywhere in the fullness of His being, as is proper to a being who is everywhere *simpliciter.*[99] God, affirms Campanella in agreement with St. Gregory the Great,[100] is everywhere by His presence, because He knows all things; by His power, because everything is subject to Him; by His essence, because He is the cause of the being of all things.[101] If we identify essence with power, and add another kind of presence to

God, i.e., presence by love, we have exactly what corresponds to the doctrine of primalities.[102]

God is intimately present in every being, and yet we do not see Him. We inquire about Him just as we inquire about our own soul.[103] God is more intimate to us than we are to ourselves; for He is the cause of our very essence and of our conservation in existence.[104] He penetrates everything and is not penetrated by anything.[105] In spite of God's intimate presence in creatures, all things are outside Him. Evidently this does not refer to place, knowledge, power, and will, for all things are in Him and by Him. However, they are outside Him as far as their essence and nature are involved. For God is supreme and infinite being, and no finite being can enter to compose Him. A finite being is limited by nonbeing, and in God nonbeing has no place whatsoever. Accordingly, we are considered as being outside God.[106] These statements, whereby God's transcendence over the finite world is openly proclaimed, may dispel any doubt about the pantheism with which Campanella is often charged.[107]

Another attribute that follows from God's infinity is eternity. An infinite being can never be produced. It cannot be produced by itself, because nothing can be the cause of its own being: it would have to exist before being what it is. It cannot be produced by another, for this other being would have to be either finite or infinite. A finite being cannot be the cause of an infinite power which it itself does not have, and an infinite being cannot produce another infinite being, for the simple reason that two infinite beings exclude each other. Therefore, an infinite being must have always existed, and if so, it will never cease to exist. What must always exist, will never be able not to exist.[108]

The eternity of God can also be demonstrated by His immutability. In every change there is a transition from potency to act, which implies some sort of intrinsic composition in the changing being. But God is incorporeal, absolutely one, and indivisible. He is pure act without any potentiality. Hence in Him no change is possible either in His essence or in His operations. Moreover, change implies the loss of something and the acquisition of something else. But God can neither lose nor acquire anything without ceasing to be God. He is therefore immutable and eternal.[109] To be eternal is to be above time, for time is essentially change.[110] Now God is not only eternal, but He is *the* eternal.[111] He is eternity itself,[112] which, in Boethius's definition, is "the simultaneous whole and perfect possession of interminable life."[113] For just as it is a property of omnipotence to be wholly and totally everywhere, so it belongs to eternity to be totally and identically the same in every moment.[114]

4. *The Primalities in God*. After discussing the attributes of God Campanella turns to the divine essence itself. Starting from the notion of God as supreme being, he asserts that God is power, wisdom, and love in the highest degree, to the absolute exclusion of any kind of nonentity.[115] The primalities and their perfections make up the perfect essence of God.[116] They are not in God in the same way they are in creatures; for He is most perfect, and all perfections of creatures are in Him in an eminent degree and analogically. They are infinite.[117]

a) *Power*. To begin with the first primality, God has the power to be, or *potentia essendi*, the power to act intrinsically, or *potentia operandi*, and the power to act extrinsically, or *potentia agendi*. Being pure act, He has no passive power.[118] In God the power to be is different from that of creatures. In creatures, the power to be is a constitutive principle of their essence; but the essence of created things is not the same in its cause as it is in its actual existence. In other words, we can distinguish in creatures between a potential essence and an actual essence. In God there is only one actual essence, and hence only one power to be.[119]

God's power to be is the same as His power to operate or act intrinsically. If we distinguish in Him the *potentia essendi* from the *potentia operandi*, it is merely because the former refers to His essence *simpliciter* and the latter to His essence insofar as it is in act, i.e., as it lives, understands, and wills.[120] But what of His power to act *ad extra*? Is this also the same as His essence and operation *ad intra*? It does not seem so. The reason Campanella gives is that God's power to be and to operate is simply infinite, whereas His power to act *ad extra* is not infinite. Indeed, God cannot make an infinite being.[121] Another reason he gives—and this is very important because it shows how careful he is to avoid all forms of theistic determinism—is that God's power to exist is the same as His will. For, as far as His intrinsic dynamism is concerned, whatever God can do, He wills; and whatever He wills, He can do. But in regard to His operations *ad extra* it is not so. He could, for example, create many worlds, or for that matter, a better world than the present one; but He does not do so, simply because He does not want to. This shows that His power to act *ad extra* and His will are not absolutely identical.[122]

It should be noted, however, that the action of God, insofar as it is in God, is just as infinite as His operation; for both action and operation, i.e., extrinsic and intrinsic acts, stem from God's essence. But insofar as this action is received into the effect, it shares the limitation of the effect itself.[123] It is no more an action, but a passion.[124] It would be inaccurate, then, to argue from the limitation of the effect to the limitation of the divine power. God does not cease to be infinite or to have an infinite power simply because He cannot produce an infinite effect. The reason for this apparent impotence is to be found not in God but in the effect, which by its very nature is limited. Besides, an infinite effect outside God would imply the existence of two infinite beings, which is a contradiction.[125]

This leads us to another question, namely, whether the power of God is limited because He cannot make two contradictories both be true. While Campanella sides with scholastic philosophers in denying such a power to God, he gives a reason consonant with his own system.

> God cannot make two contradictories come true, i.e., that the same thing be and not be, that I write and do not write at one and the same time, for the same reason that He cannot produce nonbeing.[126]

The reason God cannot produce nonbeing is stated in another passage:

> . . . it must be said absolutely that God can neither give nor produce nonbeing. He is in fact the supreme being, having no part in nothingness *(nullius particeps nihilitatis)*. What He has not, He cannot give.[127]

A contradiction, in other words, implies that something is and is not at the same time (and we would add, under the same respect). This leads to the identification of being and nonbeing. Now God, who is pure being, has the power to cause and to produce whatever is being,[128] but He cannot produce nonbeing without going against His own nature. Hence He cannot make two contradictories become true.

Campanella, as we recall from his philosophy of being, assigns to each primality an object. In speaking of the object of the first primality, he distinguishes it from the standpoint of the threefold power in God which is as follows. The object of God's power to be is His *esse;* the object of His power to operate is the intrinsic act whereby He lives, understands, and loves; the object of His power to act *ad extra* is the producible *(ipsum factibile)*. Because God's *esse* is the same as His life, and because life is conceived as prior to His other operations, namely, understanding and love, it follows that life is properly speaking the object of God's power to be and to operate.[129] Again, since God is being in the highest degree, He is also life in the highest degree. He is life itself and the source of life for all other beings.[130]

b) *Wisdom*. The wisdom diffused throughout the works of creation leads us to the recognition of a first wisdom, which follows from God's omnipotence[131] and constitutes God's second primality. God is not only wise, but wisdom itself. A wise man has wisdom in a limited degree, because he participates in wisdom. God does not participate in the wisdom of any other being; on the contrary, all other beings participate in His wisdom.[132] He is the supreme being, and therefore He is supremely wise and intelligent.[133]

It will be recalled that Campanella admits two types of knowledge, innate knowledge and acquired knowledge. Innate knowledge is self-knowledge, in which the knower *is* the very object known; acquired knowledge is hetero-knowledge, whereby the knower *becomes* the object known. This is true of creatures, which depend upon things for their knowledge of the extramental world. But God, who is the cause of all things, cannot depend on things for His knowledge of them. He knows them even before they are.[134] Hence in Him there is only one type of knowledge, that is, innate knowledge, whereby He understands His own essence, and in His essence, all other things. This is how Campanella explains the identity of God's knowledge with His essence:

> . . . it is very easy to prove that God's knowledge is His own substance. Indeed . . . innate knowledge is the direct knowledge of one's self, which would belong to all things were they not alienated by the knowledge of external objects. But in His act of knowing, God is the same as the object known. Therefore [in Him] to know is to be. God's knowledge of things other than Himself is also His own substance. When I understand other things, I become similar to the things I so understand. But God does not become similar to them; He already is [similar to them], for He is the cause and the creator of all things. Unlike a disciple who learns from the artifact of his master, He is the master who invents His own artifact. If, then, He is similar [to things], as cause is to effect, and does not have to become so, His understanding is not a passion, but His own very being [*esse ipsissimum*].[135]

Thus God has a perfect knowledge of Himself because knowledge, like power and love, is His very essence. He also knows things in His own essence because He produced them. Accordingly, His knowledge of things is active knowledge, not merely passive like ours. He measures things instead of being measured by them.[136]

Aristotle, who denies God's creation of the world from nothing, does not admit the ideas of things in the mind of God, lest God debase Himself by looking at things outside. In so doing, Campanella observes, he is consistent with his own teaching; but his doctrine is impious.[137]

God knows all things also because He is all things in an eminent way; for everything that exists was made by Him and is a participation in His being. The plurality of things does not in any way affect the unity of the divine knowledge.

> All things are in the divine essence not as many images or species but as God's single idea of Himself, which is capable of being participated in an infinite number of modes. These participations constitute the ideas of things, which are therefore the very essence of God, not as such, but insofar as it is understood as capable of being participated in by numberless things. Hence the idea includes in itself something absolute and something relative. It is not something that is made by God outside Himself; nor is it something that is made within God after the act of the intellect understands things or the ideas of things; it is rather the product, so to speak, of the very act by which God understands Himself as capable of being participated in.[138]

This teaching throws further light on Campanella's doctrine of ideas and gives new evidence of his effort to save God's transcendence, even though all things participate in His essence.

The problem, however, arises as to the exact way God knows things in Himself: whether He knows them in His essence immediately or mediately. St. Thomas, Campanella says, teaches that God sees things only in His essence and through His essence, never directly in themselves. Scotus, on the other hand, holds that God, in the act of understanding His own essence, produces things in their *esse cognitum*, and thus He knows them. This *esse cognitum* is something between the being of things as it is in nature and the essence of God as capable of being participated in.[139] Taking exception to both views, Campanella claims that God knows things immediately in His essence, insofar as this essence is capable of being participated in a certain degree by things, which in turn are only shadows of the divine essence itself.[140]

In a system where the formal essence of things is the idea in the mind of God, one should not be surprised to see that God knows things immediately in His essence by the very act He knows Himself. Campanella is thus able to maintain the immediacy of God's knowledge of things and safeguard its independence from them. Whether these things already exist or still are in the mind of God, and whether they are in their actual state or still in their potential state, does not make any difference. In both cases they are beings, and as beings they are in God, who as their cause is intrinsic to them.[141]

With regard to the characteristics of God's knowledge, Campanella remarks that such a knowledge is intuitive, not discursive; it is of universals as well as of singulars. It embraces in one single act all actual and possible things, not only in general and as they are in their causes, but in all their details and as they are in themselves.[142] Being above time, God knows things from the standpoint of eternity.[143]

As for the objects of the divine knowledge, Campanella mentions the scholastic classification of knowledge of vision (scientia visiōnis) and knowledge of simple intelligence (scientia simplicis intelligentiae). The former extends to all existing realities, past, present, and future; the latter includes all possible things that will never come into existence. To this classification he adds what "more recent theologians," namely, Molina and his followers, have called middle knowledge (scientia media), because it occupies a position between the other two types of knowledge and comprises those free acts of an intellectual creature which would have been elicited had the creature been placed in certain definite circumstances. These acts are called the free futurables or conditional acts, and their knowledge is also called scientia conditionalium.[144]

In Campanella's opinion, the distinction between knowledge of vision and knowledge of simple intelligence is not completely justified. For although the knowledge of vision refers exclusively to the external effects of the creative act of God, it can be reduced in the last analysis to the knowledge of simple intelligence. Knowledge, in fact, precedes the act of will whereby something is brought into existence. Whether or not a thing is going to exist, has nothing to do with divine knowledge as such.[145] For the same reason, the scientia media, or knowledge of the conditionals, does not constitute for him an altogether distinct type of knowledge. However, he adds, this classification can be accepted for practical purposes: it helps solve certain problems that will be better understood when dealing with God's providence and predestination.[146]

A question arises as to God's knowledge of future contingent things. Before investigating this problem, Campanella discusses the related issue of whether God's knowledge is the cause of things. St. Thomas takes a positive stand on this question and, following in the steps of St. Augustine,[147] asserts that it is not because things are or will be that God knows them, but rather because He knows them and wishes them to be, that they are or will be. He adds, however, that God's knowledge is the cause of things insofar as His will is joined to it.[148] Therefore, when Aquinas affirms that the divine knowledge is the cause of things, he does not mean that the divine knowledge alone is the adequate extrinsic cause of existing creatures, but knowledge to which the act of the will is annexed. Nor does he mean that the divine knowledge as such is the efficient cause of things; for the divine knowledge merely determines or specifies the nature of the effect, of which it is the formal extrinsic cause. What actually causes things to come into existence is the act of the divine will.

In failing to distinguish between formal and efficient causality, Campanella blames St. Thomas for having exaggerated the role of the divine intellect in the production of things at the expense of the will. The will, he says, has the first part in the creative act of God. Accordingly, it is more correct to say that things are known to God because they exist, rather than the other way around. Since, however, Sacred Scripture often attributes the works of God to His power—and this is in conformity with the nature of things and with our own nature in particular, which, besides knowledge and will, presupposes power for its operations—it follows that the causality of things has to be ascribed to all three primalities together. In God, it belongs to the three Persons of the Holy Trinity.[149]

Having determined the relationship between divine knowledge and causality, Campanella proceeds to discuss the thorny question of God's knowledge of future contingent events and especially of free future actions. Not wishing to enter into the details of this lengthy discussion, we shall confine ourselves to a summary of his thought.

God knows future contingent events because He has in Himself from eternity the ideas of all things, whether in act or still in the potentialities of their causes. Because of their coexistence with eternity, which is above time and succession, all things and events, present, past, and future are known to Him by a knowledge of presentiality. This does not mean that future things exist simultaneously in every moment of time. Future things are part of a temporal series, and a temporal series necessarily implies a succession in time, otherwise there would be no distinction between today and tomorrow. It only means that they coexist in the actual now of eternity, so that, in contrast to our way of knowing things, God sees them as eternally present to Himself.

How is it possible that God knows free future events in their causes, since, as St. Thomas says, only a conjectural knowledge can be had of the effect of a cause which is not determined to any particular effect?[150] Here Campanella departs once more from the teaching of Aquinas, and in accordance with his own theory that every effect already has some sort of existence in its causes—for nothing can come from sheer nothingness—he maintains that future contingent things are already known by God in their causes by a knowledge of vision. God, indeed, knows the fecundity of the principal cause as well as of all other auxiliary causes in regard to the effect. He knows the tendency of each particular cause, its reaction to the impediments arising from all sides, and, therefore, its determination under the influence of all the surrounding causes to produce or not to produce any particular effect.[151]

This explanation is, of course, not completely satisfactory. It fails to consider the part that man's will as a self-determining power plays in free future acts. There is no doubt that God knows the way a secondary cause, including man, will act under any particular circumstance. But just *how* God's foreknowledge can be reconciled with human freedom is the problem at issue. This Campanella leaves unsolved.

Like power, wisdom also has its object, which consists in the adequation of the ideated thing with the idea.[152] In God, who is the first unchangeable truth on which all things are modeled,[153] there is a perfect identity of intellect and object. Hence truth in God is the identity of Himself as a knower with Himself as the object of His own knowledge.[154]

c) *Love.* From power and wisdom proceeds love or will, the third primality of God.[155] Love consists in complacence in one's own being, and constitutes, together with power and wisdom, the very essence of God. God is His own love, and love is God's being.[156] God loves Himself for His own sake, and He loves other things because of the exuberance of His love. It is God's love that causes things to be. Divine love is also the source of all love in creatures.[157]

Since God's love is infinite, both intensively and extensively, it would seem that nothing can be added to it. How, then, can God love things outside Himself? Will not such a love add something to God's infinity, and consequently be a contradiction?[158] The following explanation, which is in accord with the explanation of God's knowledge of things, is offered by Campanella in the *Metaphysica*. God, he says, loves things because He loves Himself who is every being causally and eminently. Inasmuch as all beings participate in God, He loves them with the love He has for Himself, but in a modified manner. As far as the act of the will is concerned, God loves all things equally, embracing in one and the same act His own being and the being of all things. But as far as the object and terminus of love are concerned, a difference has to be admitted. If God did not love one thing more than another, there would be no degrees in being, and therefore no degrees in goodness, since His love is the cause whereby all things exist. Likewise, were things lovable in themselves with an infinite love, as they are in God, they too would be infinite like God. Since this is impossible, a modification must be recognized in God's love of things as they are in themselves. This modification is due to the limitation in being which is proper to every creature. By giving things a limited entity, God loves them only to the extent that they are similar to Himself, namely, to the extent that they have being.[159]

This explanation does not seem to have completely satisfied Campanella,[160] who in the *Theologia* returns to the same subject and calls it mysterious and impervious to our mind. All we can say, he adds, is that God's exuberance of goodness and perfection must be placed within God himself. Because God's love is active and free, it seems to be of its nature to give things love as well as being.[161]

The object of love is goodness. Being the cause of all things, God possesses goodness in its entirety. His goodness is diffusive of itself. Just as it is of the nature of fire to heat and of sun to shine, so it is of the nature of God to spread out the rays of His own goodness. From Him must come not only what constitutes the essential goodness of all beings, namely, their very *esse,* but also all their accidental perfections. God is therefore supremely good in Himself and supremely appetible to creatures.[162]

III. THE DIVINE OPERATIONS

From the nature of God Campanella proceeds in his *Theologia* to deal with God's operations *ad extra.* He discusses in the first place divine providence, not because providence is before creation—a thing has to exist before it can be taken care of—but because providence follows directly from God's primalities.[163] We shall not follow his order, but will discuss creation first and then providence, since this seems to be a more logical sequence. The fact that the *Metaphysica,* and not the *Theologia,* furnishes us with a complete doctrine on creation from the philosophical point of view is another reason for departing from the order of the *Theologia*.

1. *Creation*. a) *Creation and Eternity of the World*. Long before Campanella, the scholastics and other philosophers had expressed different opinions concerning the origin of the world. These philosophers are classified by Campanella into three main groups: 1) those who admit that the world had an origin in time; 2) those who claim that the world was made from eternity; and 3) those who proclaim the eternity of the world and deny to it any origin whatsoever. The defenders of the first opinion are again divided into groups, depending on their explanation of the world's origin either by a casual meeting of the atoms, or from the ruins of a pre-existing world, or from an original chaos.[164] After mentioning all the arguments advanced by each group in support of its opinion,[165] Campanella states and proves his own doctrine in no less than twenty-one points, refuting at the same time the arguments of the opposite theories. In short, he holds with scholastic philosophers that the world was made by God from nothing in the beginning of time.[166]

Creation from nothing, he explains, is difficult for us to understand, since we do not have any experience of it: all we see is partial changes in matter already existing. Reason, however, convinces us of the necessity of admitting that all beings come from one universal principle. Matter as such does not have any active part in creation; it rather receives the act of the creator. In this respect it is not a being, but it becomes one. Yet it is not correct to say that matter is merely a passive principle. For passion consists in receiving a likeness or similitude that a thing does not have. It is essentially a negation, and as such it cannot come from God who is pure act. Matter is therefore from God to the extent that it has an entitative act.[167] When God created the world and all other existing beings, He did so through the Word. Creation may be called an accidental production in order to distinguish it from the essential production taking place within God himself, and also because things happen to exist almost accidentally.[168] Properly speaking, God does not create things from absolute nothingness but from His own ideas in which things participate.[169] God is, in effect, not only the active cause of all things but also their formal, final, and ideal cause, having in Himself the entities of all things in a most eminent way.[170]

All things come from God by some sort of emanation. Just as light emanates from the sun but is not the sun, so things emanate from God but are not God; they are like rays reflecting God's magnificence.[171] Limitation in things is not from God but from nonbeing. Since on the one hand an infinite being cannot be limited in its operations, and on the other hand an infinite being outside God is a metaphysical impossibility, the source of limitation as well as of multiplicity is to be found in the very nature of a finite being which includes nonbeing as a metaphysical component.[172]

A question that is discussed by Campanella at considerable length is whether the world could have been created from all eternity. As is well known, Aristotle admits the eternity of the world. Lacking the notion of creation from nothing, he teaches that the world was formed by God from an eternally existing matter. In his effort to minimize the discrepancy between Aristotle's teaching and Christian revelation, St. Thomas maintains that from the philosophical point of view there is no contradiction between creation and eternity.[173] Campanella takes exception to Aquinas's teaching on this score and claims that creation and eternity are mutually exclusive terms.[174] Creation means transition from nonbeing to being; eternity excludes such a transition and makes a finite being, in our case the world, similar to God who is pure and infinite being. Moreover, had the world existed from eternity, an infinite number of days would have elapsed before the present day, which means that no present day is possible. For no matter how far back we go into the past, we would never be able to reach a first day, since the notion of eternity excludes any beginning. Without a first day, no present day is possible either.[175]

Granting, therefore, the impossibility of the world's creation from eternity, would it at least be possible that the world had come into existence before the time it actually did? This question, says Campanella, is not so easy to answer. However, before the world there was neither time nor succession but only eternity, which is a perpetual now (nunc). Hence it seems that just as motion could not have started before its first movement, or a line before its first dot, so the world had to be created in the first instant of time that marked its transition from nonbeing into being.[176] Campanella's reasoning comes down to this. Creation and time are two correlative terms that cannot be conceived independently of one another. Hence the question of whether the world could have been created before the time it came into existence is meaningless. The "before" and "after" have a meaning only insofar as there is succession or change. But before the world there was only God, who is the eternal now and does not admit of any succession or change. The nonbeing of the world which preceded creation does not admit of any succession either, since no succession is possible where there is nothing to succeed. One must therefore conclude that the world could only have been created in the very first moment of time in which it came into existence. To hold the contrary is to confuse real time with imaginary time.[177]

b) *The Doctrine of the Five Worlds.* When from creation Campanella goes on to describe the structure of the world and its relationship to God and all other superior beings, he develops what may be called "a theory of the five worlds." He divides all beings into five orders, and to each order he assigns a particular world. Thus in the first being, God, he places the *archetypal world,* namely, the world of ideas. This world is infinite like God himself and contains the archetypes of all possible worlds.[178] For in God, as in their cause, are all things even prior to their existence.[179] The archetypal world is eternal.[180] Within it, but distinct from it, is the *mental world* of angelic and human minds. It is a metaphysical world, because the only composition of these minds is from the primalities. The mental world has a beginning but no end; it is eviternal.[181] Closely related to the mental world is the *mathematical world* or universal space, the basis and substratum of all bodies. Space does not change, and so its characteristic is perpetuity.[182] The bodily mass *(moles corporea)* makes up the fourth world, namely, the *material world,* which is the source of heat and cold, the two active principles that produce all bodies. Because of the regular alterations that take place in matter, "vicissitude" belongs to this world. Vicissitude is something that is above time and participates in the perpetuity of the mathematical world.[183] Finally, just as matter is in space, so there is within the material world the *localized world* or *mundus situalis,* which is the product of the two active principles in their struggle for the possession of matter. This is the physical world in its actual organization, and to it belongs time.[184]

The five worlds are so linked to one another that whatever is in an inferior world is eminently in the worlds above, and whatever is in a superior world is by participation in the lower worlds. Thus heat, which is one of the agents in the lowest world, participates in the bodily mass of the immediately superior world in such a way that without it, it could not exist. Matter, in turn, participates in space which is its support; space or the mathematical world participates in the mental world, and the mental world in God, who is eminently all beings and in whom all beings participate. It is because of this essential relationship linking one world to another that all beings are, like God, made up of power, knowledge, and love as their ultimate constitutive principles.[185]

c) *Man and Angels.* In the vast plan of creation man occupies a privileged position, for God made him "the epilogue of all the worlds." He is a microcosm, a little world of his own, where the five worlds join together in a wonderful harmony. Because of his composition of soul and body, he belongs to the physical and mathematical worlds as well as to the world of angels, and thus is able to contemplate the archetypal world of ideas in God.[186]

Campanella does not doubt the existence of angels, which he tries to demonstrate with arguments from reason, experience, and authority. The entire twelfth book of his *Metaphysica* is a treatise on the angels. The fundamental reason for the existence of such pure intelligences is the harmony that must reign in the world of existing reality. Between God, supreme and absolutely perfect being, and a corporeal nature, even if animated by a spiritual soul, there is such a gap that it is possible to conceive of an intermediate class of beings that do not share in the imperfections of matter and participate more closely in the essence of God. That such a class of beings should exist is demanded by divine wisdom. Their existence follows also from the principle that, whenever it is possible or convenient, an agent acts in a way that is most suitable to himself. Now God can produce pure intelligences that resemble Himself more perfectly than any others among His creatures. Therefore angels must exist.[187]

Another proof for the existence of angels is derived from the fact that man often thinks of, and desires, things that never occurred to him before. The cause of such thoughts and desires must be a spirit outside him but in communication with him. Further, since not all inspirations are toward the good, there must also be conflicting intelligences striving for the possession of man's faculties. There are then what theologians call good and evil angels, whose external manifestations have been witnessed by men of unquestionable sanctity of life and wide learning.[188]

Although the existence of angels can be established on solid grounds, very little is known about their nature. The conviction that they are incorporeal substances is purely a negative factor, and as such, it does not give us any real knowledge of the angels' nature. However, the exclusion of any physical element from their constitution places them in a superior category where only power, wisdom, and love join together in a metaphysical composition. This same composition is found in all beings, but in higher creatures it is far more perfect.[189] Yet, despite their superior nature, angels are not eternal. They are finite beings, and as such they cannot have existed from all eternity. Once created, they continue to exist forever, since it would be against God's wisdom to destroy such noble and highly refined beings.[190]

2. *Providence*. a) *Providence vs. Necessity, Fate, and Harmony*. God did not create the world and then abandon it to itself. He also directs it to its ultimate end and disposes all things for the realization of it. This is what is commonly understood by divine providence, a doctrine based on the primalities of God, and therefore following directly from God's nature.[191] A being that is most powerful, most wise, and supremely good must also be most provident. Otherwise our God would not differ from the Aristotelian God, who is concerned only with the world above and does not pay any attention to this world of ours.[192] The providence of God appears in all things, no matter how tiny these things may seem to us. It manifests itself in the formation of little animals, like ants and mosquitoes, no less than in the formation of heaven, man, or the elephant.[193] Furthermore, God disposes all things in such a way that every one of them exists directly or indirectly for the benefit of all others, just as any letter is for the entire composition and all letters taken together are for the expression of a certain point of doctrine.[194]

The order that exists in the world is thus the effect of divine providence, which in turn is the result of *necessity, fate,* and *harmony,* the three great influences *(influxus)* following from God's primalities.[195] Necessity flows from God's power to produce and to move the causes to their end.[196] It must not be understood in the sense that God is bound to produce something outside Himself, or that creation and providence are God's necessary acts. Necessity means that whenever God decides to do something, the effect will necessarily follow, for He has the absolute power to do whatever He wants. If anything stands between cause and effect, or power and its exercise, there is no longer necessity but contingency, which is the opposite of necessity and proceeds from impotence. This pertains to creatures, whose composition of being and nonbeing makes them subject to all the limitations of a finite being.[197]

Fate, the second influence, is the organized series of causes that proceeds from God's wisdom.[198] Here again Campanella warns us against taking this term in its usual meaning of a blind decree of heaven, as though heaven itself were not subject to the laws of its creator. Fate is the order among the secondary causes established by divine wisdom for the production of effects which are certain and definite, not in regard to the causes as such which may be contingent and free, but in regard to God himself who directs all the causes to their end.[199] Hence another name for fate is coordination.[200] Opposed to fate is chance, which means lack of order and proceeds from ignorance.[201]

Harmony is the influx of God's third primality, love. It is the adaptation of things to their particular ends and of all particular ends to the supreme end, God. Just as love proceeeds from wisdom, so harmony proceeds from order.[202] The negation of harmony is fortuitousness (fortuna). An event is said to be fortuitous when it has not been willed. Accordingly, fortuitousness is the product, as it were, of unwillingness, and, like contingency and chance, is found only in creatures.[203]

b) *Providence and Human Freedom.* By excluding contingency, chance, and fortuitousness from God's providence, Campanella was confronted with the difficult task of explaining human freedom. If everything that happens in the world follows necessarily from God's power, and if order and harmony must prevail in the world because of their dependence on God's wisdom and will which are not subject to change, how is it possible to maintain, as experience teaches, that we are free to act and not to act, to act one way rather than another? To provide a tentative solution to the problem, Campanella distinguishes three kinds of necessity. The first kind is a quidditative necessity that follows from the very nature of a thing and makes it unalterable, even by the absolute power of God. Such is, for example, the necessity for a triangle to have three angles, or for the will to be free. The second kind of necessity is based on the decree of the divine will which makes something inevitable, for nothing can prevent God's decree from having its course. The rising of the sun tomorrow morning, the coming of the antichrist, and like things, are events that follow from this type of necessity. The third and last kind of necessity is the one based on contingent causes, once the events have been determined. Thus, in the moment I am writing, I am necessarily writing, even though I am a free and contingent cause. For a thing or event, whenever it is or happens, is necessarily what it is, with a necessity that may be called infallible. Hence free and contingent events, although avoidable in themselves, are infallibly necessary as far as God's knowledge is concerned, because they coexist with eternity.[204]

On the basis of this distinction Campanella states that all things act necessarily, but of a necessity of infallibility. This is a necessity of coaction and love at one and the same time. It is a necessity of coaction, because the act is forced by an external agent; it is a necessity of love, because the coaction does not violate the internal structure of things, nor of man, who is naturally free. Things do not do what they want to do, but they do what they are forced to will.[205] More specifically, God does not move the will physically, but neither does He move it only morally; He moves it metaphysically.[206] Under such a motion the will retains its power to resist, but for all practical purposes it does not exert it.[207] In this way the infallibility of divine providence can somehow be reconciled with the contingency of things and human freedom.[208] However, if a choice has to be made between the opinion of those who deny God's predetermination and the theory of those who deny human freedom, our preferences, observes Campanella, go to the first group of philosophers. Nothing is so clear and evident to us as the fact of human freedom. We should be willing to confess our ignorance of the nexus existing between divine providence and human freedom rather than reject the data of common sense and reduce man to a mere brute.[209]

c) *The Problem of Evil.* A second and even more challenging problem that Campanella faced in his teaching on divine providence is the presence of both physical and moral evil in the world. Physical evil, he says, God simply permits but in no way is He directly responsible for it. Physical evil results from the conflict of things in nature because of their composition with nonbeing. God allows such defects in things in view of a greater good which is not always manifest to us.[210] We should therefore abstain from judging about goodness and evil in things. Sometimes what we call physical evils, like monsters, are only evils in regard to the end of a particular cause, but not in regard to the universal order of creation.[211] Whether God could have created a better world than the present one, is a matter of discussion among philosophers. It seems more reasonable, however, to hold with St. Thomas that God's infinite wisdom cannot be limited to the world of existing things.[212] Why God did not create a better world, nobody knows.[213]

So much for physical evil. But what about moral evil? Will God also permit it in view of a greater good? If not, how is it possible for man to sin if God does not permit it? In his answer to this question, Campanella points out that sin is a defect of free will, inasmuch as the will recedes from the law by choosing what is forbidden instead of what is prescribed. Sin is a nonbeing; it participates in nothingness. Since on the one hand God cannot have any part in the production of nonbeing, and on the other hand He cannot act against His own law, He cannot permit sin either, not even in view of a greater good, as St. Thomas teaches. In fact, God forbids sin by all of His laws. When we say that God permits sin, we mean only that He allows man to exercise his freedom and sustains him physically in the act of sinning by virtue of the universal concurrence whereby all things exist and operate. In other words, God's permission to sin does not affect sin as such, but only the necessary prerequisite for man's use of his freedom.[214]

Explaining his thought, Campanella affirms that in the act of sinning God cooperates with man *in opere* but not *in velle,* for He does not determine man's will to sin. From this it does not follow that an entity exists without God. Sin, as previously stated, is not an entity but a privation, a nonbeing, and God is not the author of nonbeing. When the will determines itself to a guilty action, it does not need any one to impel it to do so; its determination is a defective one, and as such it requires no efficient cause but only a deficient cause. Yet, in its physical entity, the guilty action cannot exist without God's general concurrence.[215]

d) *Immortality of the Soul and Predestination.* Predestination is another doctrine that Campanella discusses in connection with divine providence. This doctrine rests, of course, on the conviction that the human soul is immortal, a fundamental tenet in Campanella's entire system of philosophy. The proofs he brings forth in support of the immortality of the soul are as follows:

1) The soul is neither a body nor a composite of dissoluble parts. It has no contrary agent seeking its destruction, nor a subject in which to necessarily inhere. It is incorruptible. On the other hand, God, the author of nature, will not deprive the soul of the being that belongs to it in virtue of its nature. Therefore, the soul is immortal.[216]

2) No form of a body extends itself beyond the subject by which it is possessed. But the soul's intellectual operations transcend the body and the corporeal world. Therefore, the soul does not depend on the body or any other corruptible element but only on God, the infinite and immortal principle from which it has immortality.[217]

3) The soul has a notion of the infinite and no limitations in its desires. But an infinite act manifests an infinite power, if not entitatively at least in duration. Therefore, the soul must be immortal.[218]

4) The soul understands universal ideas. Such an understanding is only possible in a being that is similar to the ideas themselves. Hence the soul is immortal like the ideas.[219]

5) The soul inquires about God and other superior beings whose company it anxiously desires. But nature would not give man, the most perfect of animals, an aspiration that could not be fulfilled. Hence a good must be awaiting him in the next life which is proportioned to his aspiration and desire.[220]

The natural exigency that the soul has for immortality is not in itself a sufficient guarantee for its actual predestination to eternal life. A positive act of God is required. This is a common teaching among scholastics. But just how God's predestination of man is to be conceived, is a subject of heated discussion. The main point of controversy is whether God's predestination of man to eternal glory is in view of man's future merits (post praevisa merita), as the followers of Molina hold, or whether it takes place before the prevision of such merits (ante praevisa merita), as the Dominicans and Augustinians generally maintain. Campanella takes his own stand on the controversy. He asserts that by an antecedent act of His will (voluntate antecedenti) God predestined all men both to natural and supernatural beatitude, even before their foreseen merits or demerits. That is why God created man for Himself and to His own image and likeness. Just as a father would not generate sons for the gallows, so God, who is supremely good, would not create man out of hatred. It is only by a consequent act of His will (voluntate consequenti) that God condemns, not all sinners but only those whom He foresees as willing to die obstinately in their sins.[221]

Predestination, continues Campanella, does not do away with human freedom. It does not impose any necessity upon man to do good,[222] anymore than it forces him to do evil. If some men are going to be damned, it is entirely through their own fault,[223] whereas the salvation of the others is due principally to God and His efficacious grace.[224] Predestination is a somewhat misleading term, for it implies a past act. We know on the contrary that, as far as God is concerned, there is no past or future. He is above time. Hence predestination is co-existing with us and our works, so that no one should complain and say that he is not predestined, or that he is damned, and therefore cease to do good.[225] There is no such thing as an inevitable predestination. There is, however, one divine providence, and that provides here and now for every individual thing and man. Whether you understand this doctrine or not, concludes Campanella, does not make any difference. All in all, it is better not to understand it than to attempt to judge the mysterious ways of God with a shortsighted mind. Best of all, one should endeavor to act so that he may avoid the danger of being erased forever from the book of eternal life.[226]

CHAPTER TEN

Evaluation of Campanella's Metaphysics*

In our critical appraisal of Campanella's metaphysics we will follow the same method as in the evaluation of his theory of knowledge. His fundamental positions will be examined and a judgment will be passed on them as well as on his philosophy of reality as a whole.

To begin with his concept of being, one cannot fail to notice how at the very threshold of metaphysics Campanella seems to depart from traditional scholastic teaching. Whereas for St. Thomas being is "that whose act is to be,"[1] or "that whose due it is to be,"[2] Campanella states that being is "that which *has* 'to be,' " or "that which *is*." Being for him is a self-defining term that always connotes an existing reality, even if this reality is only a product of our mind. For just as existence without essence is a metaphysical impossibility, so, he claims, essence without existence, be it a mental existence, is no essence at all.[3] For St. Thomas and scholastics in general the object of metaphysics is real being, which may be actual or possible; for Campanella it is both real and logical being. Further, real being is never merely possible, for whatever can be, somehow or other already is.[4] Do we have here a real contradiction between the teaching of Campanella and that of St. Thomas? It does not seem so. What we have is an equivocal use of the term "existence," which for Aquinas is the act of an essence, while for Campanella it is simply the act by which something is out of its cause, or that which is opposed to nothing. Hence arises his concept of being as that which exists either internally or externally, or at least as a concept of the mind. One might say that Campanella is an essentialist who uses the language of an existentialist.

Being, continues Campanella, may be called a univocal concept from the standpoint of the logician, who considers it merely as an *ens rationis.* From the standpoint of the metaphysician, being is analogous by an analogy of proportionality as well as of attribution. This is substantially the teaching of the Thomists. However, in contrast to both the Thomistic and the Scotistic schools, Campanella claims that being is a genus which is predicated of its specific differences in the same

---

*This chapter may be omitted without breaking the continuity of this presentation of Campanella's thought.

sense that animality is predicated of rational beings. This is evidently incorrect, for all the inferiors of being are being, and no specific difference can be predicated of being which is not being. It would have to be not-being, or nothing, and a predication of nothing is no predication at all.

When we pass from the concept of being to Campanella's teaching on the intrinsic structure of reality, we meet his original doctrine of primalities. To establish his theory that all beings are essentially composed of power, knowledge, and love, he makes use of three arguments: the nature of God, in which all beings participate; the nature of being itself, whose self-preservation requires power, knowledge, and love as its constitutive principles; and the supposed inefficiency of all other theories to explain reality. None of these arguments is convincing. Not the first, because a being that exists as an effect of God's creative act does not necessarily have to share in God's power, knowledge, and will, anymore than an artifact has to share in its maker's capacity to produce it. The action of a cause in the production of an effect demands that cause and effect, although immediately present to each other, nevertheless be absolutely distinct realities. In the case of God and creatures, there is in addition an essential distinction: God is distinct from the world by His very essence.

The second argument, based on the nature of being, is even less convincing than the first. A created being is not kept in existence by an intrinsic power but by God. He also brought it into existence, and He alone can preserve it from being destroyed. It is not correct, as Campanella seems to say, that the power to be or to exist belongs to being as an active and essential principle of it. If this were the case, every finite being would be able to exist in virtue of its own nature like God: it would be necessary and eternal. This is evidently false. One should rather say that a finite and contingent being has the capacity or potentiality to exist, insofar as its nature does not imply a contradiction. However, in order that such a being actually exist and continue in existence, a positive act on the part of God is required.[5] Just as power as an intrinsic active principle of being is not essential to a being's constitution, neither is knowledge or love. To admit the reality of knowledge and love in purely material beings is also contrary to the testimony of common sense and experience.

To refute the third argument advanced by Campanella to establish his doctrine of primalities, namely, the assertedly futile attempt of all other philosophers to explain the ultimate constituents of reality, we may recall how easily he pretends to reason away the Aristotelian theory of act and potency. He wrongly identifies act with active potency and reduces act and potency to power. He further confuses act as principle of being with act as principle of operation.

Once the doctrine of primalities of being has been established on more or less questionable grounds, Campanella does not spare any effort in defending it against possible attacks. In so doing, he stresses the metaphysical character and essential identity of the primalities, which he calls coprinciples of being and the "unalities" of one and the same thing. For lack of adequate terms, the process by which one primality derives from another is called a process of "totication" and "coessentiation," whereby one primality is totally and essentially communicated to another. It is hard to understand precisely what this process is; nor does Campanella find it easy to explain. He tells us that "it is a wonderful process, but such that cannot be expressed in human words." Evidently, he has in mind the mysterious nature of the relationship existing among the persons in the Holy Trinity, but he fails to convince us that the Trinitarian doctrine can and must be applied to creatures. A slight modification of Ockham's razor may be made. The reader can say that *mysteria non sunt multiplicanda sine necessitate* and refuse to accept a doctrine that is wrapped in mystery and has all the appearances of a gratuitous assertion. Hence Campanella's appeal to Scotists and Thomists to desist from their centuries old dispute concerning the pre-eminence of intellect or will on the ground that the doctrine of primalities makes such a controversy useless and outmoded appears to be naive and ineffective.

The treatise on the specific features of each primality shows how carefully Campanella worked out his doctrine. The division of the first primality into *potentia essendi, potentia activa,* and *potentia passiva* offers him the opportunity to clarify his thought about the various meanings of *potentia*. A point to be noted is his distinction between the power to be *ab intrinseco,* proper to primary being, and the power to be *ab extrinseco,* proper to secondary beings, which depend on God for their existence. However, his teaching that a thing's power to be, regardless of its actual or potential existence, is to be identified with its essence is misleading. Existence cannot be considered simply as a different mode of an essence, that is, an essence in its potential state; for no real and essential distinction would then be possible between the divine mind in which all possible essences are contained and the world of concrete reality, i.e., between God and creatures. Even though Campanella would be the first to disavow pantheistic implications, his teaching on this score logically leads to pantheism.

Another characteristic of Campanella's treatise on the first primality is the absolute identification of the agent with the *potentia activa* or active power, considered in its double aspect of principle of operation *ad intra* and principle of operation *ad extra*. Likewise, no distinction is admitted between the agent and its immanent act, while only a numerical distinction is held to exist between the agent and its transient act. The clue to the explanation of this doctrine, noticeably in contrast with Thomistic philosophy, is to be found, first, in Campanella's teaching that the formal essence of created things is from the idea, which prevents any real or essential distinction between cause and effect; and second, in his principle that *operari est esse,* whereby act, as an immanent activity of a being, is being itself as it is in itself, while, as a transient action received in another, is the being of that other being. This doctrine, of course, does not allow for any real distinction among agent, its power to act, act itself, and the effect of the act or operation. Consonant with his other doctrine that *cognoscere est esse,* it is open to the same criticism.[6]

In regard to the first primality and the *potentia passiva,* the close relationship between Campanella and Plato in the doctrine of primary matter is to be noted. Both philosophers conceive matter as a mere receptacle of the true essence of things, and therefore as something extraneous to it. This does not prevent Campanella from holding with Scotus that matter is endowed with an entitative act. It is a *potentia receptiva:* as such it must be something positive, although not a substantial principle of being in the sense that Aristotle teaches.

The second primality of being is *sapientia* or wisdom, which is shared by all beings in different degrees proportionally to their amount of perfection. For Campanella the existence of some sort of wisdom, even in purely material beings, is a necessary postulate of his pansensistic theory. To be more exact, his pansensism rests on the principle that all beings are endowed with sense or sensation, which is improperly called wisdom. Pansensism, or what is very close to it, panpsychism, is not a doctrine original to Campanella's system. It began as an hylozoic theory with the Greek cosmologists of the Milesian school, who reportedly maintained that all matter is alive.[7] Hylozoism, or the doctrine of universal animation, soon developed into the theory of the world soul, which Plato conceived as the proximate cause of life, order, motion, and knowledge in the universe.

Later, the Stoics identified the world soul and the universe with God, giving rise to that materialistic pantheism that was to be revived, under one form or another, by many philosophers of later times, including the Renaissance.[8] Although Campanella did not fall into the excesses of materialistic pantheism, he accepted the pansensistic theory of nature that he found substantially in Telesio's *De rerum natura iuxta propria principia,* and took upon himself the task of defending it with all the weapons of his dialectic.

The arguments with which Campanella builds his demonstration are no stronger than their premises, and these are far from being proved. The alleged struggle for self-preservation that takes place in all beings, whether living or nonliving, is a gratuitous assumption. So also is his claim that all things have appetite and love. It is easy to admit the existence of some sort of self-defense mechanism or instinct in living beings, whereby they resist the attacks on their life; but there is no evidence whatsoever that such a mechanism or instinct is also to be found in inorganic beings, unless one wants to equate self-defense with inertia. Campanella's basic mistake is his failure to distinguish between organic and inorganic beings, and among the former, between vegetative and sentient beings. To attribute sensitive qualities, the characteristic of animals, to beings of the vegetative and mineral worlds, such as plants and stones, is to disregard completely the principles on which the distinction among the orders of beings is founded. The same observation holds true, *mutatis mutandis,* for Campanella's attribution of sensation to his supposed elements of nature, such as fire, heat and cold, and for his claim that even a corpse is not entirely without sensation. His raising of plants to the rank of animals is another weak point in his philosophy. So also is his Platonic theory that the world is a most perfect animal, with its own body, spirit, and soul.

Campanella's other argument in support of universal sensation, namely, that what is in the effect is in the cause, so that elements must have sensation because they are the cause of animals, is another instance of his arbitrary assumptions and misconceptions. He assumes that purely material elements are the formal as well as the total cause of animals, whereas they are solely their material and partial cause. As such, they do not have to share in animal nature, since this derives principally from the form.

Still another argument is his contention that all beings are essentially related to one another and that they all participate in the wisdom of God, whose image or vestige they carry. To refute this argument it is enough to recall the earlier observation that a real distinction exists among the different orders of beings in the world, and a real as well as an essential distinction exists between created beings and God. Such a distinction does not warrant an essential relationship among the various orders of beings, anymore than it allows for a substantial identity of their properties. In other words, a being of an inferior order does not have to participate *formally* and *intrinsically* in the nature of a being of a superior order, and much less in the nature of God. For God is the efficient, final, and exemplary cause of all existing beings, but not their formal intrinsic cause. Had Campanella made a careful distinction between *intrinsic* and *extrinsic* formal cause, much confusion and misunderstanding would have been avoided.

Campanella must be given credit for his distinction among the different kinds of sense or sensation. This is particularly helpful in determining the precise meaning he attaches to sense and wisdom in beings of the physical order. Although sense and wisdom are said to be essentially the same in all created beings because of their primalitarian structure, *natural* sense, that is, the kind of sense proper to elements and things in nature, is basically touch. Yet touch—and this is Campanella's weak point—is not merely a physical contact, but a *sensed* contact. The difference between sensation in animals and sensation in purely material things is of mode or degree, not of essence.

Evidently, we cannot agree with Campanella on this score. The comparison of the whole world to a living statue of almighty God, made for His glory and endowed with power, knowledge, and love,[9] is perhaps a daring and even fascinating figure of speech, but it rests on a philosophical theory that is both unreal and superfluous. It is unreal, because it is incompatible with the existence of countless beings in the inanimate world that give no sign of life or sensation. It is superfluous, because God can just as well attain His glory and the purpose of creation by the instrumentality of His physical laws directing nature to its end, without the impact of a sensitive and conscious matter.

As for the third primality, love, very little remains to be said, since its treatment follows along the lines of the first two primalities. Basically, the same observations made in connection with power and wisdom apply to love, which is also conceived as an essential principle of being. Although love proceeds from power and wisdom, it is from the love that a being has for itself that Campanella endeavors to prove its knowledge and wisdom. Hence the particular importance of the third primality in the inquiry about the ultimate constituents of being. The statement that our love for God is an essential love, because it is part of our nature which tends to a being *simpliciter* more than to a being *secundum quid* like our own, is contradicted by the fact that many people love themselves more than God. This fact is enough to show that our love for God is neither an essential part of human nature nor a necessary property of it. It is only an accidental act depending on our free will, although our will has a natural inclination toward God as its supreme good.

The primalities, says Campanella, have a dynamic nature that makes them principles of operation as well as principles of being, each one with its own object. The objects of the primalities are existence, truth, and goodness, to which unity must be added as the object of the three primalities taken together. They are called supreme transcendentals, because they can be predicated of both the creator and creatures.

Scholastics would agree with Campanella that truth, goodness, and unity are predicated of all beings, of God no less than of creatures. However, they would call them transcendental properties of being rather than transcendental entities or objects of the so-called transcendental principles. Furthermore, they would not consider existence on the same level as truth, goodness, and unity. Existence is for them the last actuality and perfection of a being. To conceive existence as a supreme transcendental of being along with truth, goodness, and unity is to make the same mistake that has already been pointed out in connection with "the power to be": it leads, at least by implication, to the identification of creatures with God, whose essence, according to Campanella, "is the essence of all things."[10]

The treatise on beauty, which Campanella calls "the sign and manifestation of goodness," and which he distinguishes into natural, useful, and artificial, does not manifest any metaphysical insight. Actually, he seems to insist more on the subjective aspect of the beautiful than on its objective and transcendental character. His presentation of the peripatetic teaching on the nature of the beautiful as a mere matter of proportion between the object and the sense of sight is not correct. His own treatment of the beautiful is far from attaining the heights of Plato's metaphysical speculation. Plato, under whose patronage Campanella places his own doctrine, identifies ontological beauty with the good, as do Aristotle and his followers after him, especially St. Thomas Aquinas. Hence Campanella's attempt to contrast Plato's doctrine with the peripatetic theory of the beautiful is groundless and futile; it betrays, in addition, a lack of understanding of the two systems.

Unity, the last of the supreme transcendentals, is the object of Campanella's special consideration. Unfortunately, two different questions are treated under one heading, namely, the question of the relationship between being and "the one," and the problem of "the one and the many." The confusion is unavoidable. Despite the complexity of the problem, we believe we have successfully delineated the essential traits of Campanella's teaching on unity as a transcendental. We distinguished in his system a unity that includes the concept of primeness, divinity, and supreme entity *simpliciter,* and a unity that implies these prerogatives only relatively and by participation. The first kind of unity is found in God alone; the second is found in creatures, who participate their being and, therefore, their unity in God, the supreme being. This is altogether a sound teaching based on Plato's doctrine of participation.

The second class of transcendentals is constituted by *res, aliquid,* and the *terminus infinitatus.* They are called subaltern transcendentals because, unlike the supreme transcendentals, they are limited in their predication. It is worth noting that *res* and *aliquid* have in Campanella different meanings from those found in St. Thomas's *De veritate,* where they are thoroughly discussed.[11] For Aquinas *res* or thing is *being* taken as a noun; hence it is synonymous with being. In Campanella's system *res* stands only for real being, which he contrasts to chimerical and logical being. This fact explains why *res* cannot be predicated of being as such but only of a certain kind of being. Likewise, St. Thomas explains *aliquid* as *quasi aliud quid,* or being insofar as it is opposed to nonbeing: in this sense *aliquid* is a property of being. Campanella, on the contrary, takes *aliquid* in its literary meaning of *something;* he can, therefore, state consistently that *aliquid* cannot be predicated of the infinite being.

With regard to Campanella's doctrine on the predicaments of being, which he distinguishes into two series, each one having ten distinct predicaments, the conclusion reached at the end of the discussion of the transcendentals must be repeated. It is an arbitrary classification and certainly not an improvement upon that of Aristotle.

The discussion of the last two generic predicaments, similarity and dissimilarity, leads us naturally into what Campanella terms the greatest dissimilarity of all, namely, the dissimilarity existing between being and nonbeing. The relationship between being and nonbeing can be summarized as follows: (1) Whereas God is pure and infinite being, creatures are a composition of a finite being and an infinite nonbeing. (2) Just as a creature is essentially and necessarily a particular and limited entity, so also is it essentially and necessarily the nonbeing of all other things and of God himself. (3) Being and nonbeing concur to make up finite things not as physical components but as metaphysical principles.

Thus affirmation and negation lie at the core of all reality in the created world. To the extent that a thing is its own entity, it is being; to the extent that a thing is not the entities surrounding it, it is nonbeing. Being and nonbeing join together in a transcendental composition that makes things limited in their entity and distinct from God, who is pure and infinite being. Being is not in itself the principle of limitation, for limitation means precisely the opposite of being; limitation is from nonbeing. It is not true, argues Campanella against the Aristotelians, that essence limits existence, just as it is not true that potency limits act. Potency is itself an act, and existence is but a mode of essence. The nonbeing that enters into the composition of finite things as a metaphysical principle is not absolute nothingness. That would be absurd. Nor is it relative nothingness, or the essence of a thing prior to its actual existence. That again would imply a contradiction, for an essence cannot be a self-limiting principle. It is instead the nonbeing in the existential order, i.e., the being of all things and of God himself insofar as their entity limits a particular existing being to its own reality. It is in this sense, and in this sense alone, that creatures are a composition of a finite being and an infinite nonbeing. This explains Campanella's statement that nonbeing terminates being and his other affirmation that a finite being participates in nonbeing.

In spite of this explanation, which must be stated in order to present Campanella's position in its proper light, one may wonder how nonbeing, whose nature is "not to be," may enter a metaphysical composition with finite being and still retain its own nature. What seems to be even a greater source of wonder, is the paradoxical expression of Platonic origin that being participates in nonbeing. To say that the nonbeing in question is the entity of other things, inasmuch as it limits an existing being to its individual reality, does not solve the problem. The problem is basically metaphysical; it concerns the very nature of finite being, and its solution must be sought in a principle intrinsic to being itself. In other words, nonbeing, no matter how it is understood, cannot be a principle of limitation of being, anymore than it can be something in which being participates. To hold the contrary is to contradict oneself or, at least, to expose oneself to a verbal contradiction that gives rise to equivocation.

The relationship between essence and existence in finite beings provides another opportunity for Campanella to display his own position. He rejects from the very beginning the Thomistic tenet that essence is related to existence as potency to act.[12] Essence is itself an act having an existence of its own; existence, on the other hand, is only a mode of essence. They cannot be separated from each other, nor is there any distinction between them except in the mind. A being that is in a potential state has only a potential essence and existence, insofar as its cause has the power to bring it into actual existence; a being that is in the mind has only a mental essence and existence; and finally, a being that has already been actualized by its causes has an actual essence and existence. Accordingly, essence and existence are always found together in their respective order of being, for, to repeat Campanella's statement, just as no existence can be conceived without some sort of essence, so no essence is possible without some form of existence. A real distinction, however, must be admitted between essence and existence in a different order of being, such as the existence of a purely mental being and the existence of a being in its concrete reality. Likewise, a real distinction has to be admitted between essence and "extrinsic" existence, or that kind of existence which consists in the limiting factors of an essence in its existential order, such as time, place, and all the surrounding beings. For extrinsic existence is only accidentally related to essence.

The same equivocation in the use of the term "existence" that has already been pointed out in the beginning of this chapter will be noticed throughout the foregoing discussion. By refusing to admit a real distinction between essence and existence in finite things, Campanella not only departs from the Thomistic point of view, but he goes even further than Duns Scotus. He simply identifies essence with intrinsic existence. Furthermore, he conceives extrinsic existence as a predicamental accident of being. This notion of existence as an accident of being may well remind us of what Averroës erroneously presents as Avicenna's doctrine.[13] Yet the two theories have but a verbal similarity. When Avicenna speaks of existence in finite beings as an extrinsic element added to essence,[14] he does not mean that existence is merely an external factor like Campanella's extrinsic existence. This latter is grounded in the doctrine of nonbeing as a limiting principle of being. Does Campanella's notion of extrinsic existence also share in the weakness of his doctrine of nonbeing? This does not seem to be the case. The reason is that extrinsic existence is not presented as a metaphysical constituent of being, but only as an accident of being in the predicamental order.

The doctrine of the causes of being is developed by Campanella along the lines of his primalitarian theory. A being that is essentially power, knowledge, and will, and that contains a threefold principle of activity, i.e., the potential, the cognitive, and the volitive, has also three sets of causes, one set for each principle. Thus, in addition to the four causes of Aristotelian philosophy, Campanella's etiology provides for two more causes, namely, the ideal cause and the perfective cause. The ideal cause is conceived as something distinct from both the efficient and the final cause. The perfective cause, on the other hand, represents the terminus or finality of an operation apart from the agent's personal end in his acts and operations. While the distinction between the perfective and final cause can be reduced to the Aristotelian distinction between the *finis operis* and the *finis operantis* within one and the same final cause, great emphasis is placed by Campanella on the ideal cause of Platonic origin. The ideal cause is the form present in the agent's intellect as the model or exemplar of things to be done. Hence formal essence is from the idea. More specifically, the idea is the *forma effundibilis,* while the form is the *forma effusa.* This latter is found in the "ideated" things in various degrees, according to the extent of participation in the ideal or exemplary cause.

Following St. Augustine, Campanella places Plato's ideas in the mind of God, with which they are identified. However, his claim that this is the correct interpretation of Plato's thought can hardly find support in the latter's works. Hence also his sarcastic criticism of the Peripatetics, as though they were trying to discredit Plato by placing his ideas somewhere between God and the world of material things, or, as he puts it, in the hollow of the moon, is far from being justified.

Our discussion of the material and formal causes of being gave us the opportunity to study Campanella's fundamental positions on the philosophy of nature. Because of his dependence on Telesio's naturalism, this part of his system is perhaps the least original and certainly not very profound. What he offers us is not so much a philosophy of nature, as it is an interpretation of nature in the light of physical theories that have long been superseded. Here the spirit of the Renaissance thought, aiming at the concrete and the individual, is especially noticeable. To confirm this statement it is sufficient to recall that Campanella substantializes space by making it the substratum of all material bodies; that he identifies matter with a universal, formless body, and makes it a being in its own right, even though, less consistently, he calls it the passive principle of all corporeal beings; that finally he dismisses the scholastic notion of form as a substantial principle of being and confines it, together with primary matter, to what he calls "Aristotle's chimerical world." In short, he rejects the Aristotelian hylomorphic system and substitutes for it Telesio's naturalistic theory of heat and cold as the active principles, and matter as the passive principle, from which all material beings are derived.

In such a system of nature it is not surprising that even the notion of time loses the abstract character attributed to it by Aristotle. Rather than being the number of movement in respect of the before and after, as Aristotle defines it, time becomes for Campanella movement itself. It is the movement of a thing insofar as it is the measure of the movement of other things. Or, more precisely, it is the thing itself considered in its successive duration through change.

The treatise on God as the author of nature and the model upon which all existing reality is fashioned is the logical conclusion of Campanella's philosophy of being. Indeed, his whole system of philosophy is centered on the idea of God and moves within the framework of a conception of reality based upon the mystery of the Holy Trinity. In his theodicy, more than in any other part of his system, the natural and supernatural elements join together to form a philosophical synthesis that is decidedly Christian in its inspiration. Taking the lead from his theory of an innate knowledge whereby the soul knows itself essentially, and in itself knows the creator in whom it participates, Campanella affirms that God's existence is not only self-evident in itself but also to us. Our soul is so made that it cannot obtain any knowledge, not even of the external world, prior to the knowledge of God. The knowledge of God, in other words, is part of its own self-consciousness. Yet, because of the disproportion existing between our faculties and the divine nature, and especially because of the present union of soul and body, the soul's knowledge of God is hidden and darkened by the knowledge of external objects. It is only by returning upon itself that the soul acquires knowledge of its own nature and God.

A first point of criticism of this doctrine is the contradiction existing between a supposedly self-evident knowledge of God's existence and the fact that we can attain to it only by a process of reflection. Furthermore, how can something be self-evident to us when we have no experience of it? We may ask Campanella an even more embarassing question. God's existence, as he will be ready to admit, is absolutely identical with the divine essence. Now, were the existence of God self-evident to us, would we not have an intuitive knowledge of God himself even in this life? Why then encumber the mind with so many arguments, as Campanella does, in order to prove what would otherwise already be known by the soul's simple reflection upon itself?

The *rationes metaphysicales* for the existence of God are for Campanella the proofs based on the primalities of being and their objects. They lead to a supreme and absolutely perfect being from whom all perfections in creatures are derived. The *rationes ex physicis petitae*, on the other hand, take their start from a consideration of the world and also lead to the existence of a first being, who is the primary cause of all existing reality. Basically, the two long series of arguments can be reduced to St. Thomas's *quinque viae* for the demonstration of God's existence. However, the fourth way, that of Platonic origin, is particularly developed, while the first way, of Aristotelian origin and based on motion, is completely omitted. The reason for this omission, states Campanella, is that the argument from motion leads only to a first mover but not to an unmoved mover; hence, it has no value. This attitude toward St. Thomas's "first and more manifest way of proving God's existence" should not surprise anyone with even a slight knowledge of the attacks made on the argument soon after its formulation. That Campanella should take a critical view of it because of the Aristotelian principle on which it rests, namely, *quidquid movetur ab alio movetur,* should be even less surprising. Yet, his main objections against Aristotle's argument from motion do not constitute anything new in the field of philosophy. Long before him, Duns Scotus had already restricted the Aristotelian principle of motion to nonliving beings. On the other hand, St. Bonaventure, for one, had already raised serious objections against the possibility of eternal motion, and consequently of an eternal world. However Campanella goes somewhat further than Duns Scotus in his limitation of the Aristotelian principle of motion. He claims, in effect, that even purely material beings have an immanent principle of act and operation by virtue of their form. He is thus consistent with his own theory of the dynamic nature of being, but he fails to account for the essential difference between organic and inorganic beings.

The possibility of attaining a positive knowledge of God's nature even in this life is defended by Campanella against Plotinus, Dionysius, and other philosophers. He exaggerates, however, the extent of such a knowledge when he attributes to our soul a direct intuition of God, not in the sense that ontologists will claim after him, but through the soul's self-revealing act in virtue of its primalitarian structure. Indeed, our soul is so far from having an intuitive cognition of God, that it does not even know its own nature except by reflecting upon its own acts and operations.

The discussion of the negative knowledge of God obtained by removing from Him all the imperfections of creatures is well conducted and is in harmony with scholastic teaching. It tends to emphasize the absolute simplicity of the first being, a being *per se,* in contrast to all other beings, which are only beings by participation. God's simplicity, affirms Campanella, not only does not allow for any composition, but it excludes even the formal distinction *a parte rei* introduced among the divine attributes by Duns Scotus. This, at least, is our interpretation of Campanella's seemingly contradictory statements. How consistently he can hold this view and make the primalities of God the model and pattern of all creation, is a matter of doubt.

Campanella's treatment of the divine attributes affords no special basis for criticism. It moves within the framework of sound philosophical reasoning by logically inferring one attribute from another in a sequence that starts from God's simplicity and reaches out to His eternity. Exception may be taken to what he calls the best argument for God's infinity. To infer the attribute of God's infinity from the idea that we have of an infinite being, as though an infinite being alone could be the cause of such an idea, is to disregard the abstractive power inherent in our intellect as a spiritual faculty. Credit must be given to Campanella for stressing one aspect of God's omnipresence that is often overlooked even by some of the best scholastic philosophers. Reference is made here to God's presence in the world by love. It is most fitting that in a prevailingly Platonic-Augustinian system this aspect of God's omnipresence should be duly emphasized.

God is more intimate to us, writes Campanella, than we are to ourselves. Yet He so transcends us and all created things that no composition, much less any identification, of God with creatures is possible; nor is it conceivable. Thus God is both immanent and transcendent. Campanella would readily agree with the author of an old Latin hymn, who so characteristically describes God as *Intra cuncta, nec inclusus; Extra cuncta, nec exclusus.* God is within the universe, but not enclosed in it; He is outside the universe, but not excluded from it. True, God's immanence in the world is overemphasized by Campanella somewhat to the detriment of His transcendence; but the two doctrines are substantially saved and are kept distinct one from the other.

The doctrine of the primalities finds its application in God, the supreme being. Indeed, it is the essence of God as power, wisdom, and love that constitutes for Campanella the basis and model of all finite reality, which is the effect of the creative act of God and must bear the imprints of the divine nature. The primalities are in God in a most eminent way; hence God is infinite power, infinite wisdom, and infinite love. This statement is only logical, since in Campanella's philosophy every limitation is from nonbeing, and God, who is pure act, cannot contain any nonbeing. The distinction between the primalities in God and their operations *ad extra* is well made. Campanella attempts to explain how an infinite act can have a limited effect. This is not because of the limitation of the act itself, which, of its nature, is unlimited, but because of the contradiction that would follow from the admission of an infinite effect outside God. There would be two infinite beings, one limiting the other, which is evidently absurd.

In regard to the objects of the divine knowledge, Campanella seems to have little use for the scholastic distinction between knowledge of vision and knowledge of simple intelligence. For him all divine knowledge is fundamentally knowledge of simple intelligence, since knowledge in God precedes the act of will whereby things exist. The fact of their actual existence has nothing to do with divine knowledge as such. If this were true, we may object, how would one be able to account for the distinction between knowledge of actual things and knowledge of possible things in God? There would be no distinction between them. But this is certainly not the case, for actual existence is a perfection, and the knowledge of a being with this perfection must be different from the knowledge of a being having only the potentiality to receive such a perfection. In other words, God must know existing things, present, past, and future, in their actual existence, and not only as they are potentially in Himself or in other secondary causes.[15] Knowledge in God, explains Campanella, precedes the act of His will. This is true, but such a priority is only a priority of nature, for in one and the same act God knows all things, possible and actual. The fact remains that the knowledge of things to which the act of God's will is joined, or, as St. Thomas puts it, practical knowledge, is distinct from the knowledge of things to which such an act is not joined, that is, speculative knowledge.[16]

Campanella makes no special contribution in his tentative explanation of God's knowledge of free futures. He simply agrees with those thinkers who see the solution of the controversial issue in God's exhaustive knowledge of all secondary causes, including man's free will, and of all the circumstances that might affect a cause in the production of its effect. This explanation, while emphasizing the fact of the universality of divine knowledge, which must embrace all events and hence also man's free acts, does not account for the equally basic fact that man is essentially free in his acts and that only a conjectural knowledge can be had of the effect of a cause which is not determined to any particular course of action. The solution must, then, be sought elsewhere. Campanella's statement that God has in Himself from all eternity the ideas of all things and events, which He knows by a knowledge of presentiality, whether they are in act or still in the potentiality of their causes, may offer a better clue to the solution of the problem. Because things and events are intelligible, i.e., have truth, they must be known in the exemplarity of the divine essence from all eternity, even though creatures place their free acts in time. This is basically the solution of St. Thomas Aquinas,[17] from which Campanella does not seem to be very far. It is not, however, the solution of the real problem at issue, which concerns the medium of God's knowledge of free futures rather than the mode of the latter's presentiality to the divine intellect.

God created the world from nothing. This doctrine, asserts Campanella, is difficult for us to understand, because we have no experience of it. Yet, the world could not have had any other beginning; and it had to begin, for an eternal world is a contradiction. Creation, in effect, means the transition from nonbeing to being, and eternity excludes such a transition. Moreover, in the supposition of an eternal world there would be no first day, and consequently no present day either. To ask whether the world could have come into existence before the time it actually did, Campanella adds, is to forget that time is coexisting with the world, of which it marks the beginning. In other words, time and the world are so related to one another that neither one could exist alone; they must exist simultaneously. Hence to speculate about a creation before or after the present world came into existence, is to confuse real time with imaginary time.

In general, this reasoning is sound and in line with St. Augustine's philosophy.[18] However, there seems to be a misunderstanding of the real meaning of creation. Campanella calls it the production of something from nothing, but then goes on to describe it in terms of a transition from nonbeing to being which implies a succession of one after the other. Once this transition is proved, the possibility of an eternal world is automatically ruled out. Yet, as St. Augustine had indicated,[19] as St. Anselm after him explained,[20] and as St. Thomas demonstrated,[21] creation from nothing does not mean that being came after nonbeing in the order of time or duration, but only in the order of nature. Thus, a causal subordination of the world to its creator is sufficient. More precisely, creation and eternity are not in themselves mutually exclusive terms. Hence, if God cannot create an eternal world, as Campanella and many scholastics maintain,[22] it is not because of the nature of creation itself, which is an instantaneous act and involves no time,[23] but rather because of the intrinsic contradiction that a supposedly eternal world involves. The whole question rests, in the final analysis, on the debated issue of the possibility of an infinite series of accidentally subordinated causes. St. Thomas raised the problem and solved it in the affirmative;[24] Campanella, on the contrary, took a negative stand with regard to it.

The theory of five worlds, namely, the archetypal world of God and the eternal ideas, the mental world of angels and human minds, the mathematical world of universal space, the material world of bodily mass, and the localized world of organized bodies, is Campanella's ingenious and well-devised plan to classify all reality. By making the five orders of beings essentially related to one another, the theory strengthens the doctrine of primalities. Yet, no matter how ingenious the scheme of the five worlds may appear, its foundation is questionable. There seems to be no need, for instance, for a mathematical world distinct from the material world. Space, in fact, is not in itself something real but merely abstract extension considered as receptacle for bodies. Nor is there a need for distinction between a material world and a localized world or *mundus situalis,* since one cannot be separated from the other except in our mind.

The privileged position assigned by Campanella to man in the world of creation is in keeping with scholastic teaching and the humanistic tendencies of the Renaissance. However, he seems to overemphasize the philosophical arguments for the existence of pure intelligences like angels as a link between man and God. The part that good and evil spirits play in man's life is likewise exaggerated.

Like creation, divine providence is extensively treated by Campanella. He would hardly miss such an opportunity for renewing his attacks against Aristotle, who rejects the doctrine of God's governance of the world. Campanella states that divine providence is manifest in the order reigning in the world and stems from necessity, fate, and harmony, the three great *influxus* or influences flowing from God's primalities. Admittedly, necessity and fate are not the best terms to characterize divine providence. Campanella is the first to see this. Accordingly, he tries to make these terms more acceptable by explaining them, yet, because of the resulting ambiguity, their use cannot be entirely justified.

The problem of providence and human freedom is also thoroughly discussed by Campanella. His proposed solution that God does not move our will physically or morally but metaphysically, in such a manner that our will retains its power to resist but will not exert it, is no solution at all. It does not explain how metaphysical motion is possible and exactly what it is. Philosophers, in their attempt to solve this problem that has perplexed human minds for centuries and may very well be above the capacity of man's understanding, do not look merely for a new term. Rather they look for an explanation that avoids the difficulties involved in physical premotion and takes into account the infallibility of God's plan for man and the undeniable fact of human freedom. In our opinion, Campanella's solution does not meet these requirements.

Another challenging problem that Campanella tries to solve in his treatise on providence, is the relationship between divine providence and evil. He maintains that God cannot be held responsible for any kind of evil, whether physical or moral. God permits physical evil in view of the universal order of creation, but He cannot permit moral evil or sin. He simply allows man to exercise his freedom and sustains him physically in the act of sinning. Campanella is thus more radical than the Angelic Doctor in limiting God's part in evil. First, he does not accept Aquinas's teaching that God *wills* physical evil *per accidens,* and second, he explicitly disagrees with St. Thomas's other teaching that God *permits* moral evil. Carefully examined, the two doctrines of Campanella and Aquinas seem to contain only a verbal conflict. Indeed, just as Campanella does not deny the fact that physical evil exists in the world as part of God's plan, so he does not disavow the other equally evident fact that man sins and God allows him to go on sinning. Whether in the first case one should speak of God's simple permission rather than of God's will *per accidens,* and whether in the second case one should say that God allows man to use his freedom in the act of sinning, or rather that God permits sin itself as necessarily following from man's abuse of freedom, is merely a verbal question that does not affect the substance of the teaching.

The last point Campanella discusses on divine providence is his notion of man's eternal predestination. This question, which is strictly speaking a theological issue but which is discussed by Campanella in his *Metaphysica* no less than in his *Theologia,* again puts him in the midst of heated controversy. In Campanella's day, predestination concerned not only Catholic philosophers and theologians but also thinkers of different beliefs.[25] Campanella had to decide whether to side with the disciples of Molina (1535-1600) who held that God's predestination of man to eternal glory is in view of man's future merits, or to follow the opposite view which maintained that God's predestination takes place even before the prevision of man's merits. Here again, on a vital question like this, where his solution could well decide his good standing with the Dominican order, Campanella goes his own way and breaks with the tradition of his order. The only concession he makes to his confreres—and this is not a real concession because the Molinists would have no difficulty in getting along with him on this score—is that by an antecedent act of His will God predestined all men both to natural and supernatural beatitude, even before their foreseen merits or demerits. Having granted this, he states positively that there is no such thing as an inevitable predestination on the part of God. God's predestination coexists with us and our works; it is not, therefore, prior to, but only in consideration of, our merits or demerits.[26]

Campanella's standpoint on the difficult problem of man's predestination may be criticized, as it was in his own time by those who did not share his opinion. Yet one thing that stands out clearly in the midst of the dispute is his intellectual honesty. In a time when bias and school prejudices were influencing the opinions of many thinkers almost to the point that from the color of a man's habit one could tell the trend of his thought, it is refreshing to see a man that has the courage to state his own position frankly and honestly, even though in so doing he would hurt the feelings of his confreres and colleagues. Will this attitude also be justified from standpoints other than those of a purely academic character? This is not a matter of concern to us, and we prefer not to venture any judgment.

Campanella's whole system of reality rests on a concept of being modeled on the mystery of the Holy Trinity. All things, whether spiritual or material, consist ultimately, although in different degrees, of power, knowledge, and love as their transcendental principles. These are called primalities. In creatures, they are mingled with nonbeing, which is the principle of their limitation; in God, they exist to the utmost degree and constitute the divine nature, in which all things participate. Thus God is pure and infinite being; while creatures, who depend on God for their essence as well as for their existence, are a metaphysical composition of a finite being and an infinite nonbeing. This system reflects no doubt an original and keen mind, but it lacks solidity and consistency.

PART FOUR

Moral Philosophy

CHAPTER ELEVEN

Ethical and Social Doctrines

Campanella divides moral philosophy into three parts: ethics, politics, and economics. Ethics is concerned with individual acts and operations, politics with the state, and economics with the family. Strictly speaking, he says, there is only one moral science. However, because of the mind's limitations, it is customary to divide moral science into three distinct branches. Just as man is part of the family, and the family of the state, so ethics is part of economics, and economics of politics. The principles on which these three distinct branches of moral philosophy rest arise from an understanding of man's actions and passions and tend to man's conservation, either in himself, in the state, or in his reputation. Whatever contributes to man's conservation is good and useful; whatever is opposed to it is evil and useless.[1]

The best way to study moral philosophy, says Campanella, is to begin with fundamental principles, and first of all, with the discussion of the ultimate end of man, which is also man's supreme good.[2] Once this end has been established, the means to attain it must be discussed by considering man as an individual being, as a member of the family, and as a citizen of the state. This is also the division we shall follow in our treatment of Campanella's moral philosophy. It will include three sections, dealing respectively with what may be called Campanella's ethical, social, and political doctrines. Because of the special importance of the Campanellian political theory, we shall discuss it in a separate chapter.

I. GENERAL ETHICAL DOCTRINES

1. *Man's Supreme Good.* It is a well-known principle of scholastic philosophy that man, as a rational being, always acts for an end. The question then naturally arises, "What is man's ultimate end?" Following a common trend in philosophy, Campanella discusses man's supreme good at the very outset of his *Quaestiones morales,* which serves as an introduction to his *Ethica.*[3] Man's supreme good is in effect the ultimate end of man.[4] The reason he gives is this: "Since that which is the last in the order of attainment is the first in the order of knowledge, the question of the supreme good must come first."[5] Yet, he rightly remarks, the supreme good to be considered in ethics is not

250

the same as the supreme good that is discussed in metaphysics. It is not the supreme good in the ontological order, which everyone knows to be God, but the supreme good in which man's happiness consists.[6]

What is man's supreme good? This question has received many answers in the history of human thought. Campanella reduces them to six. (1) The Romans thought that the supreme good of man consists in glory, for it is to glory that all acts and operations of virtuous men are directed. Personal glory was considered by the Romans as something even more important than their own lives. (2) Modern politicians and the followers of Machiavelli think that power is the highest good of man. Those alone are believed to be really happy who rule over a country and are independent in their acts and operations. (3) Bias, one of the Seven Wise Men of Greece, places man's supreme good in wealth, for he is convinced that power without wealth is useless. (4) Some ancient philosophers, among them Eudoxus and Epicurus, claim that pleasure is the greatest good, since it is what all men seek. (5) Aristotle distinguishes among useful, honest, and pleasant good, and teaches that contemplation of truth is what constitutes man's supreme and ultimate good. (6) Finally, the Stoics, observing that virtue is what makes a man respectable, assert that man's highest good consists in a virtuous and honest life.[7]

All these theories, affirms Campanella, are faulty. They contend that the supreme good is either something extrinsic to man, like glory, power, and wealth, or something that is only good partially and relatively, like sense pleasure.[8] Aristotle's notion of the supreme good is puerile and based on very weak grounds.[9] Although he assumes that happiness is the last end of man, he is greatly mistaken—Campanella states bluntly that he lies—when he asserts that the supreme end of man consists in one of man's operations, i.e., contemplation, rather than in man himself. An operation is always ordered to something else. In our case, operation is ordered to man, not man to operation.[10] Furthermore, mere contemplation of the truth cannot be the supreme end of man, for contemplation leads to the union of soul with the object known and consequently to the love of it. And we love for our own enjoyment. Hence mere knowledge, i.e., knowledge without love, will never cause any real happiness in us. It is not because we know the good that we are happy, but because we enjoy it. Contemplation is always directed to the possession of the good; it is never an end in itself.[11] If contemplation of the truth were the supreme good of man, as Aristotle claims, then the only happy men in this world would be the philosophers. But this, observes Campanella, is absurd;

for there are scarcely ten real philosophers in a thousand years. The rest are either dupes, tricksters, or sophists.[12] Nor is the Stoic opinion that man's highest good is virtue the correct doctrine. Virtue is only a means to the attainment of eternal life, not the end toward which men must tend.[13]

Having rejected all other theories on the nature of the supreme good, Campanella states his own doctrine.

> All beings desire their own happiness, which is undoubtedly the reason for all their acts and operations. Since these acts are performed for the conservation of one's own being, it follows that happiness consists in one's own being or life. It consists in the full and complete possession of the good of which a being is capable . . . Obviously, happiness must be found in oneself and not in another; for if it were to be found in another being rather than in oneself, all beings would seek their own destruction and look forward to being changed into that other being.[14]

Thus the supreme good of man is happiness, and this consists in self-conservation. Will man find his supreme and ultimate end in himself to the exclusion of God? This seems to be the logical conclusion to be drawn from some of Campanella's statements just mentioned. Indeed, if happiness is to be found exclusively in oneself, then man is so shut up within his own little ego that all his aspirations for an unlimited and transcending good are thwarted. Campanella's doctrine would be no better than a purely naturalistic ethics with no opening on the infinite, let alone on the supernatural.

Against such an interpretation of his thought, Campanella warns that man's conservation may be understood in four ways. It may be understood as meaning the conservation of one's person, of one's children, of one's reputation, and finally, it may also be understood as meaning the conservation of one's existence in God in the next life.[15] Conservation taken in this last sense is what actually constitutes man's ultimate end and happiness. It also makes man distinct from God. Whereas God is His own supreme good and does not look to another being outside Himself for His conservation, so that to be and to be happy is for Him one and the same thing, man depends entirely on God for his own conservation. God is therefore the supreme good toward which man must direct all his acts and operations.

Indeed, such are the qualifications of the supreme good that it must exclude any admixture of evil; it is most perfect and constitutes the end of all man's desires and aspirations. Briefly, the supreme good must be such that beyond it nothing more remains to be desired. Such is God, who is simple and absolute goodness, while other beings are good only analogically and insofar as they are related to God. Hence God alone is man's supreme good.[16]

Is there a conflict between this statement and the affirmation that man's supreme good consists in self-conservation? Campanella says that there is none and takes great pains to show that the two statements, far from being contradictory, complement one another. The desire for self-conservation, which constitutes man's happiness, is also the desire for God. By the very fact that man wants to live forever and to be everywhere, he wants to do everything, to know everything, and to enjoy everything. In other words, he wants to be God. Not being able to be God essentially, he aspires to be God by participation, i.e., by sharing in his divinity.[17]

In Campanella's *Metaphysica* and *Theologia* the same concepts are expressed even better than in his *Ethica*.[18] "Happiness,"—so reads the heading of an article on the nature of happiness—"which is the conservation of the human entity, consists in the union with the supreme being through power, wisdom, and love, and can only be enjoyed by fruition. This presupposes possession and knowledge."[19] The article further states that happiness does not consist in possession alone, or possession to which knowledge is joined; nor does it consist merely in fruition and love. It rather consists in the possession of that which conserves us, as well as in the knowledge and fruition of it. In contrast with the supreme being, which, on account of its extensive and intensive infinity, is its own beatitude, the human soul can only find its happiness in its union with God. This does not mean that the soul must be transformed into God and become one with Him, as wood becomes fire, in which case it would lose its own individuality; it means only that the soul must become God-like, just as iron becomes ignited and still retains its own nature as iron.[20] It is thus that self-love becomes the love of God in whose essence every being participates.[21] This thought may also explain how God, who is formally and objectively His own beatitude, is also truly and objectively the beatitude of all beings, for He is the efficient and exemplary cause of all existing good.[22] In conclusion, God is man's supreme beatitude *ut quod;* virtue and grace are man's beatitude *ut quo;* the conservation of his own being is man's beatitude *formaliter,* while his acts and operations are the *necessary condition* for man's attainment of God.[23]

To the question whether beatitude consists principally in vision and contemplation, as St. Thomas maintains, or in fruition and love, as Scotus teaches, Campanella answers that neither theory makes

sense. Beatitude consists primarily in neither contemplation nor fruition, but equally in power, knowledge, and love, the three primalities
of every being.[24] More specifically, beatitude begins with power, is
accomplished by knowledge, and is consummated in love.[25] Otherwise
stated, beatitude is attained by comprehension, perfected by understanding, and completed by fruition.[26] However, if one primality
must be singled out for a more direct bearing on beatitude as such,
that primality is the will. For it is the good, the formal object of the
will, that makes one happy. The good, as known, is more properly
called beautiful than good.[27]

2. *The Virtues.* The preceding discussion makes clear the following
points: (1) man's ultimate end is his supreme good; (2) the attainment
of this supreme good constitutes man's greatest happiness; (3) the
supreme good as well as the greatest happiness of man consists in
self-conservation; (4) the desire for self-conservation is the desire for
God as the cause of one's own being and the only good that can fully
satisfy man's infinite aspirations. The question now arises: How can
the supreme good be attained? This, says Campanella, is possible only
through the practice of virtuous acts.[28] Hence the treatise on virtue
follows naturally upon the discussion of the nature of the supreme
good.

a) *Virtue in General.* Various opinions have been advanced by
philosophers on the nature of virtue. Campanella evaluates them, and
in doing so paves the way for his own theory. Aristotle teaches that
virtue is an elective habit dictated by right reason that enables man
to follow a middle course between two extremes.[29] Galen and those
who believe with him that the soul is mortal maintain that virtue is
essentially a bodily quality.[30] Telesio asserts that virtue is purity of
nature, insofar as a being is what it is and what it ought to be, having
nothing extraneous to its nature.[31] The Stoics claim that virtue is
nothing but knowledge.[32]

These theories, affirms Campanella by way of a general appraisal,
contain no doubt many good points. Yet, they fail to give us the real
nature of virtue as a conservative power of being in its threefold primality. A being's good is its own conservation both in regard to its
esse and its operations. This good is the effect of virtue. Accordingly,
virtue is a quality that derives directly from a being's power, knowledge, and love. It is improper to call virtue an active power. To be
perfect, virtue must be integrated with knowledge and will, the other

two constitutive principles of being.[33] Therefore, virtues are inherent in us by nature, although God may also infuse them.[34]

To really define virtue we must say that it is a natural power, directed by wisdom and strengthened by will, which governs human affections, passions, and operations for the attainment of the supreme good.[35] Thus virtue is immediately grounded in the primalities. It is a directive norm discovered by the cognitive principle of being. Powers inherent in the primalities apply this norm practically; operations make it manifest.[36] When a man deviates in his actions and operations from the right path indicated to him by his natural directive norm, the result is no longer virtue but vice.[37] Vice stems from the animal spirit that affects the superior part of man, his intellective soul.[38]

Since this is the concept of virtue, all other theories must be rejected. First of all, virtue is not an operative habit, as Aristotle teaches. A habit is the effect of virtue rather than its essence.[39] Nor is it of the essence of virtue to be a mean between two extremes, since in certain things we can go to one extreme and still be called virtuous, as in the case of a man who practices virtue in a heroic degree. Moderate anger, on the other hand, is not a virtue; only the norm imposed upon anger is virtue.[40]

Just as it does not belong to the essence of virtue to be a habit, so it is not of its essence to be a mere quality of the body or of the animal spirit. Galen's definition of virtue is therefore wrong; it ignores completely the fact that virtue is primarily a mental quality and norm.[41] Telesio's opinion that virtue is purity of nature is only partially true. Fundamentally, virtue is purity, since it is grounded in the nature of a being with no mixture of other entities; formally, however, virtue is the decree and norm of a will that knows, and has the power to attain to, its good.[42] Finally, the Stoic opinion that virtue is knowledge has a certain amount of truth, but it is incomplete. While no virtue is possible without knowledge, one must admit that knowledge alone cannot make a man virtuous, any more than will alone can. All three primalities must concur, each in its own way, in making a man virtuous.[43]

A corollary of Campanella's treatise on virtue is his discussion of the relationship between man's freedom and morality. If virtue flows from man's nature, how can man still be free in his actions and operations? What distinguishes a natural act from a moral act? These are two different aspects of one and the same problem, and we confine ourselves to Campanella's general statement at the beginning of the article in *Ethica* where the problem is discussed. A moral act, we are told, is so called because it causes in us a way of living (*morem*), i.e., a way to be followed in relation to ourselves, other men, the state, God, and all things with which we come in contact. Hence the difference between a moral act and a natural act consists in the fact that a natural act is rooted in our nature, while a moral act can only be acquired by practice. A natural act becomes moral when it is performed in accord with the standard of morality dictated to us by our manifold relations to ourselves, our neighbor, and God, and when by repetition it becomes a habit. The same act is both natural and free; for freedom is not only a property of the will but also of intellect and power.[44]

b) *Classification of Virtues.* Campanella's classification of virtues is another instance of the originality of his system. He discards Aristotle's distinction between moral and intellectual virtues, and between virtues of the speculative intellect and virtues of the practical intellect, on the ground that such a distinction is too subtle and serves no purpose. All virtues having reference to knowledge are intellectual virtues; all virtues directed to operation are practical virtues.[45] Likewise, he says that the distinction of virtues made by the Stoics and the Peripatetics is unsatisfactory. The Stoics base their distinction on the function of a virtue, while the Peripatetics base it on the object with which a virtue is concerned. Neither of these is a good criterion for distinguishing virtues, since many virtues function more or less in the same way and are concerned with the same object.[46] The best criterion for distinguishing virtues is the different way by which the primalities tend to their objects. This, says Campanella, is also the viewpoint of Aquinas, who affirms that from the nature of an object we may infer the particular nature of a virtue. Since the object of virtue is the good, and the good is what keeps man in existence, virtues will be classified according to their way of preserving man in God, himself, his children, and his good name. Vices, on the other hand, are to be classified according to the way in which they cause man's destruction and are opposed to virtues.[47]

On the basis of this principle, Campanella classifies in his *Quaestiones morales* all virtues in different groups. The first group includes the virtues that contribute to our preservation in God. These are faith, hope, and charity in the supernatural order, each one corresponding to a primality of being; religion, which is the direct effect of the theological virtues; justice, through which religion is put to practice; and sanctity, which sums up all virtues directed to the ultimate end as known by natural reason. Among the virtues in the second group are those which contribute to our own conservation, such as probity, studiousness, prudence, industriousness, manliness, fortitude, liberality, parsimony, magnificence, sobriety, and the like, all of which stem from the volitive, cognitive, or potential principle. To these the virtue of physical exercise *(exercitium)* must be added, as the one which helps man to be strong in soul and body. Neither Aristotle nor Telesio speaks of it, but St. John Chrysostom mentions it in a very special way. The third group includes only one virtue, chastity, which alone helps preserve ourselves in our children through a proper use of marriage. Magnanimity and wisdom are the two virtues necessary for the preservation of our good name among men; hence they make up the fourth group. Finally, in order to be able to preserve ourselves in our own being, in our children, and in our reputation, we must live in peace and harmony with other people. To do this we need benevolence, "beneloquence," and beneficence. Each of these virtues has its own species. Other virtues mentioned under this heading are equability, meekness, gratitude, and hilarity. These virtues help us to practice the three preceding ones, while commutative justice is necessary for anyone who wishes to lead a good social life. The list closes with incidental mention of three virtues of a general character, namely, modesty, penance, and humility. All other virtues mentioned by the Stoics, concludes Campanella, can in some manner be reduced to certain of the virtues indicated above. Hence this list may be considered complete.[48]

Despite this observation, the classification of virtues found in Campanella's *Ethica* is far more complete and systematic than that in the *Quaestiones morales,* even though in the ensuing treatise on individual virtues a different order is followed.[49] It is not our intention to make a detailed description of each virtue along the lines of Campanella's treatise. To do so would be beyond the scope of the present study. We shall rather attempt to highlight certain aspects of his doctrine on individual virtues that deserve special consideration, either because of their importance or because of their originality. Although reference will be made to the section on ethics contained in the *Epilogo magno,* our main source of information will be the *Ethica,* as the one treatise that best represents Campanella's final standpoint on the subject under consideration.

c) *Virtues in Particular.* Since God is the final end toward which all things tend by their nature, the first and most important virtue is *sanctity*. This virtue makes us recognize *(sancit)* God as our Father and helps us direct all things to Him.[50] Unknown to Aristotle and not very well understood by Plato, it sets not only the final goal to be pursued, but sanctifies us by purifying our affections and operations. Man acts according to his convictions. If God is his great concern, his life will also be modeled upon the divine life. The love of the supreme good surpasses the love of all other goods and affects one's life more intensely than any other love. Hence, from the time man attains the use of reason, his main concern ought to be his own sanctification.[51]

While sanctity helps us love God, *probity* sets the norm for self-love. By nature, and hence by innate knowledge, the love of God is prior to self-love. Yet, in the order of acquired and reflex knowledge, self-love is prior to the love of God. The virtue of probity helps man love God more than himself. When the object of love is one's parents, wife, or children, then the virtue of probity takes up the names of piety, charity, and affection.[52]

Once the norm for pursuing man's final end has been established, and the love man has for himself has been channeled in the right direction, the means to best attain this goal must be sought. This is the task of the virtue of *studiousness*.[53] *Prudence,* on the other hand, puts to use the results of this latter virtue by determining who is qualified for study as well as his particular field of study.[54] *Vigilance* preserves us from frustration in our actions,[55] while *discipline* provides for the correct performance of our duty.[56] A very practical virtue is *industriousness*. It contributes to the development of our ability for mechanical arts, so that we may profitably use external things for our own conservation.[57] *Moderation,* as commonly understood, is opposed to cupidity; it teaches us to be satisfied with a small amount of wealth and material goods. Moderation is truly the virtue of philosophers. Being satisfied with their own rectitude, they do not place their happiness in external things but in themselves and in God.[58] *Parsimony* is the virtue that limits the use of the goods obtained by one's industry.[59] *Liberality* consists in the good use of money for oneself and for others and manifests a free spirit.[60] Finally, *sobriety* prescribes proper amounts of food and drink and helps us avoid sensuous pleasure, gluttony, and drunkenness.[61]

All these virtues can be practiced without too much effort, but it is in the performance of arduous things that virtue shines the most.[62] Among the virtues of this latter type are reckoned virility, alacrity, strenuousness, longanimity, perseverance, zeal, tolerance, fortitude, and physical exercise.[63] *Chastity* is an altogether different kind of virtue, for, unlike the preceding ones, it aims at self-preservation in our children. It teaches the sanctity of generation, which is an imitation of God's creative act. The act of generation is a natural sacrament and partners in marriage are its ministers.[64] There are other virtues that aim at the conservation of our good name, such as benevolence, emulation, eloquence, veracity, beneficence, gratitude, equability, meekness, and joy.[65] Finally, we need the virtue of *justice* for our own conservation in the state or republic. Justice teaches men to live together, to help one another, and to perform those tasks for which they have a natural ability. It also decrees proper sanctions for the citizens of the state.[66]

In both the *Ethica* and the *Epilogo magno* Campanella closes his treatise on virtue by praising the magnanimous and generous efforts of a man who practices the virtue of *sublimity*. This he calls the summit and sum total of all virtues. Through it man understands that honors are worthless unless they are a testimonial to an honest and virtuous life. Riches are no concern of a man endowed with the virtue of sublimity, for he knows that riches are equally shared by evil and dishonest people. Rather he cultivates the loftiness of the spirit that makes him happy. If he likes to be honored, it is only inasmuch as he is a living image of God.[67]

II. ETHICS OF THE FAMILY

1. *Nature and Purpose of the Family.* Man has a natural tendency to live in society.[68] The first and most simple society is the union of husband and wife; the second is the union of parents and children; the third is the union of parents, children, and servants, both rational and irrational. This last form of society is, in Campanella's opinion, what we call family in the usual sense of the term. It includes not only men and women servants, but also domestic animals, such as the ox and the dog.

Other more complete forms of society are the union of a plurality of families into a village, of several villages into a township, of several towns into a province, and of several provinces into a nation. Finally, we have the union of several nations into an empire, of several empires into a monarchy, and of all men under the Pope.[69] Between family and state there is no specific difference, for the family possesses in a lesser degree everything found in the state, and both family and state are governed by one ruler. But specific differences exist between a family and a school and between an army and a religious community, since their ends, as well as their subjects, are different.[70] Like the state, the family can be compared to the human composite, with the soul represented by man and woman and the body by their home.[71]

Just as the nature of the family does not differ specifically from the nature of the state, so also its end is essentially the same. A part cannot have a different end from the whole of which it is a part. Hence the family, as a part of the state, must also concur in the attainment of the end for which the state exists. This end is ultimately a happy and eternal life in the possession of God, our supreme good.[72] God is therefore the supreme extrinsic end, not only of the individual but also of the family and the state,[73] even though the way to attain Him may be different. Generally speaking, this is done through self-preservation, as explained when the nature of man's supreme good was discussed. But, whereas in the state self-preservation means more specifically the preservation of the individual, in the family it means the preservation of both individual and species. Thus the family is a more natural society than the state.[74]

2. *Formation and Government of the Family.* After defining the nature and purpose of the family, Campanella goes on in his *Quaestiones oeconomicae* to discuss certain practical points concerning the formation of the family and the proper way to run a household. In so doing, he touches upon fundamental notions of marriage, education of children, and rights and duties of the family members. His discussion contains many interesting and original points.

The good and evil of society depend to a great extent on the formation of the family. Husband and wife are the primary elements of society and upon them rests the responsibility of shaping future generations. The marriage contract, instituted by God and raised by Christ to the dignity of a sacrament, must be entered upon with great care and consideration. Man and woman ought to join together on the basis of certain natural qualities that will insure a strong and healthy offspring, since marriage was instituted primarily for the begetting of children. Thus it is befitting that a thin man marry a heavy-set woman, and that a woman of an irascible temperament be joined with a quiet and peaceful man.[75] However, it is not advisable for a pretty woman to marry an ugly or deformed man. Such a marriage cannot be successful. As far as possible, the beauty of one partner should match the beauty of the other.[76] In general, when a husband or wife is chosen, the qualities of soul and body should rank first, not wealth or any other material good. For such a choice the advice of prudent and experienced persons must be sought.[77]

That marriage is a contract of the natural law is Campanella's teaching throughout all his works.[78] Does he also maintain that unity and indissolubility are essential properties of marriage? This is a very pertinent question, since the inhabitants of *The City of the Sun*, who are supposed to live according to the law of nature, are described by Campanella as practicing community of women.[79]

Leaving aside the question of the interpretation of Campanella's teaching in *The City of the Sun*, which will be discussed in the next chapter, there seems to be no doubt about the orthodoxy of his teaching in his philosophical works. In the *Quaestiones oeconomicae* he devotes the entire first article of the second question to the discussion of the unity of marriage. The title of the article reads: "Whether it is advisable to take one wife or several according to nature and apart from [positive] law."[80] In the body of the article he lists the reasons favoring polygamy; and then, after stating that such a system is against the tradition of the Church and God's wisdom, he says that polygamy is not against the primary purpose of marriage, which is the procreation and education of children—indeed, where there are more wives there will also be more children and more mothers to take care of them—but against its secondary purpose, namely, the mutual support and welfare of the spouses. Polygamy breeds jealousy and bitterness among the wives, each one striving for the husband's love. Hence polygamy is somehow against the secondary precepts of the natural law.[81] This same teaching is repeated in the *Oeconomica*[82] and in other works of Campanella whenever the subject is discussed.[83] We shall return to it in the next chapter and see how it can be reconciled with Campanella's political theory.

Husband and wife are not only united in one flesh, but, says Campanella, they have also equal rights to the act of generation, since both contribute on an equal basis to the perpetuation of their lives through eternity. The husband is obliged to treat his wife as his companion; yet, as head of the family, he possesses a natural dominion over her and the children. The wife shares the husband's right in ruling over the children and the family.[84]

Since procreation and education of children are the primary purposes of marriage, Campanella gives some practical advice to the spouses concerning the act of generation, the duties of pregnant women, the nursing of infants, and the rearing of children. Conception should be preceded by a period of six or seven days of continence. During this time the spouses will nourish themselves with veal and meat of other strong animals. They will also offer special prayers to God, perform good deeds, and occupy their minds with pious and religious thoughts, since the animal spirit to be transmitted in the husband's seed is influenced by the imagination.

After conception has taken place, the woman should rest for a few days, then she will gradually perform certain bodily exercises to strengthen her offspring. Further, she will walk to church after sunrise and endeavor to discuss matters relating to virtue and honesty, for her imagination has a strong bearing on the offspring's temperament and character.

It will be the mother's duty to nurse her children, since her traits and moral dispositions are transmitted with milk. It is also fitting that the newly born baby be gradually exposed to cold and hardships. These will tend to make the baby stronger and healthier.

Children must be trained in the fear of God. After they have reached the age of six, they may be lightly spanked for any misdeed, bad word, or failure in the fulfillment of their religious duties. However they should never be whipped or subjected to excessive punishments and fear, lest they develop a timid and fearful nature.[85] For other practical hints concerning the training and education of children, which he calls an undertaking of the greatest importance for the welfare of society, Campanella refers to his teaching in the *Politica* and *The City of the Sun*.[86]

As previously stated, in Campanella's notion of the family servants are also included. They may be either rational or irrational beings, and these latter are further distinguished into animals, tools, and natural goods, such as soil, plants, vines, and the like. All servants are like instruments in the hands of the head of the family, but all do not depend on him in the same way. Whereas man's dominion over rational servants is limited and subject to the law of the state, a *dominium politicum,* his dominion over irrational servants is complete and absolute: it is a *dominium despoticum.* Great care should be used by the head of the family in choosing his rational servants, since it is through them that his power reaches out to the instruments of the inferior order.[87]

Campanella is not satisfied with laying down general principles concerning the nature, purpose, formation, and government of the family. He is convinced that without a wise administration of material goods the family will not be able to attain to that temporal happiness which is its immediate goal. Hence in the *Oeconomica* he devotes long sections to administrative problems, such as the preparation of a proper home, which is to be located on a convenient site with plenty of sunshine and air;[88] the rational cultivation of animals and plants;[89] and the art of best administering the family goods.[90] He teaches how these goods can be acquired,[91] how they should be preserved,[92] and how they can be enjoyed in this life and disposed of at the time of death.[93]

All these problems directly concern the branch of science that today goes under the name of economics. For our purpose it suffices to have mentioned them.

CHAPTER TWELVE

Political Theory

Boasting that he had been called to reform society, religion, and all the sciences, and posing as a champion of freedom and justice against the social and political evils of his time, Campanella could not fail to include in his ambitious plans of reform a treatise on political science. In fact, his political writings are so numerous that they make up a very considerable portion of his literary work. Their subjects range from particular problems of a social and administrative nature to a bold and grandiose conception of a universal monarchy headed by the Pope.

The number and length of Campanella's political treatises and the fact that they were written years apart under many adverse circumstances make it difficult to reduce his political thought to a unified system.[1] The difficulty is increased by the fact that the critical edition of Campanella's works is still incomplete, and his political writings, which are known to contain many interpolations by other hands, are perhaps those in greatest need of revision.[2] However, we are fortunate to have at hand either a critical edition or the original text of certain fundamental works, and on their basis it is possible to reconstruct and evaluate Campanella's political theory. We refer especially to Professor Firpo's critical editions of Campanella *De politica*[3] and *The City of the Sun,* and to the *Monarchia Messiae,* a work that has come down in its original Latin version.[4] This trilogy of works may well represent three phases of Campanella's political thought, as well as three different, although not altogether contradictory, conceptions of the state.

The *De politica* is the most important of the three treatises, since it contains Campanella's mature thought and discusses questions of a general character rather than problems arising from particular situations. It is an objective approach to the state in its concrete reality. Although less original than some of his other works, it ranks first among Campanella's political writings. This seems to be the opinion of Campanella himself, who rates it highly and calls it "the foundation of political science."[5]

A work of a quite different nature is *The City of the Sun,* a new and original version of Thomas More's *Utopia* built along Platonic lines. It does not deserve to be taken too seriously as it is a product of

Campanella's fertile imagination rather than of solid thought. However, because it is his best known production and because it is often misunderstood and misrepresented, we make it the object of our special study.

The *Monarchia Messiae* is an important treatise in which Campanella discusses the doctrine of a universal monarchy under the leadership of the Roman Pontiff as its supreme temporal and spiritual ruler. This treatise, together with the *Quod reminiscentur* and the *Discorsi universali del governo ecclesiastico,*[6] a short but valuable document containing practical suggestions for the realization of the author's long cherished dream described in the *Monarchia Messiae,* serves as a basis for discussion of the third and final phase of Campanella's political theory, his conception of a theocratic state.

Other primary sources, such as *Metaphysica, Theologia, Atheismus triumphatus, Monarchia di Spagna, De regno Dei,*[7] and especially the *Quaestiones politicae,*[8] an important commentary on the *De politica* and *The City of the Sun,* will also be used. Thus, with the aid of some special studies on the subject,[9] it is possible to present an adequate view of Campanella's political thought within the limits of this study.

I. THE REAL STATE

Accepting a familiar definition, Campanella calls politics the science of governing the state.[10] It is a science, and not merely an art, since an art may or may not be grounded in sound ethical principles. Politics is in effect a branch of ethics,[11] on which it depends and to which it is subalternate.[12] It is a science given to men by God.[13] Hence politics cannot be divorced from religion, for a state without religion is a state that lacks foundation and support.[14]

Since this is the true nature of politics, Machiavelli's theory of the state must be discarded as a vicious and pernicious doctrine.[15] No state or empire based exclusively on human prudence or political expediency can last.[16] To build a political system on cunning and mere personal ability, as Machiavelli tries to do, is to show the utmost ignorance of political science.[17]

The state, with which political theory is concerned, is a natural community resulting from the union of several provinces into a kingdom, of several kingdoms into a monarchy, and of all mankind under the Pope.[18] The inner tendency that impels a man to join his fellow men and form a state comes from the First Mind, which disposes things in such a way that a man cannot attain his final end except by living in society.[19] Accordingly, the final cause of the state and the last end of man are one and the same, namely, God, from whom all happiness derives. The state does not exist for the ruler's private good or even for the temporal welfare of the citizens, since wealth and exaggerated freedom lead to tyranny.[20]

Three causes concur to form a state: God, prudence, and occasion. Sometimes the operation of one cause is more evident than that of the others. Examples of this are God, in the formation of the Jewish kingdom; prudence, in shaping the Roman empire; and occasion, in the establishment of the Spanish monarchy. However, God is always behind all secondary causes.[21] The priesthood takes God's place in the formation of a state; its role is so important that no state can exist without it.[22] Priests should be commissioned to shape and direct state policy, which rulers enforce, and soldiers and public officers execute.[23]

It is fitting that the Pope, as supreme priest, should have his own army to be used for the preservation of peace in the world and the defense of true religion.[24] To deny the Pope the use of the temporal sword along with the spiritual sword is not only imprudent but also heretical.[25] Once the various sects and different religious denominations, as well as all forms of government, have undergone a radical change and lost their right to exist as separate entities, then all men will return to the state of original innocence, a golden age in which there will be one ruler who is both king and priest. He will be chosen from among the members of the senate, a body composed of the best men whose task is to assist the king-priest, that is, the Pope, in governing the monarchy. This is described in the *De monarchia Christianorum*.[26]

The second cause in the formation of the state is prudence, a virtue of true kings, in contrast to cunning, the characteristic of a Machiavellian tyrant. Prudence wins even by losing; cunning loses even when it obtains an apparent victory. Prudence dictates laws suitable to all the people; cunning dictates laws that benefit only one man. The commonwealth is best served by the appointment of officers naturally gifted for the particular tasks they are called upon to perform. Material wealth should have no consideration in such appointments. The common good must prevail over the private good. Hence there will be community of goods, culture, and religion. Furthermore, things pertaining to God must have priority over those pertaining to man.[27]

The third and last cause of a state is occasion, i.e., those factors and circumstances that contribute to the acquisition of power over a territory or its extension over a new land. Such factors may be the weakness of an enemy, dissension among princes in a divided land, corruption of the reigning ruler, and all external evils and vices that lead the subjects to submit to a new ruler.[28]

Campanella has no doubt that authority in the state or society comes ultimately from God, who by His very nature is absolute owner of all things.[29] Man can share in God's power only to the extent allowed by God, to whom all creatures tend as to their supreme and final cause. A man cannot dispose of himself, his limbs, or other men, much less heaven and earth and the natural elements, in whatever way he wants, but only for the end established by God through natural and positive law.[30]

The person to exercise authority in the state may be chosen in different ways. By nature he is fit to command who excels others in good qualities of soul or body or both.[31] In practice, the selection of a ruler may be made by election, drawing lots, succession, census (polls), or two or more of these methods combined.[32] The best way is when the king is appointed directly by God, rather than by choice of the people.[33] Yet the system of election is better than mere hereditary succession.[34]

Monarchy is Campanella's preferred form of government, as is evident from his teaching in the *Monarchia Messiae,* where he states that it is more natural for men to be governed by one ruler.[35] He repeats the same doctrine in the *Metaphysica,*[36] the *Theologia,*[37] and *The City of the Sun.*[38] In the *Politica* he discusses this point more specifically and affirms that the government of one man is better in wartime, while the government of many is to be preferred in time of peace. To support his view, he appeals to the Romans, who turned to a dictator whenever a dangerous war threatened, so that he could make quicker decisions for the safety of the country. In time of peace, however, they set up consuls and a senate. All things being equal, the government of one good ruler is better than the government of many good rulers, just as the government of one bad ruler is worse than the government of many bad rulers. But since it is easier to get rid of one bad man than of many, it seems that the government of one bad man should be preferred.[39]

Campanella lays down some good norms to help the citizens in choosing their leader. Any leader of a large group or society should first prove himself to be a good leader of a small community. Thus the ruler of a universal monarchy embracing all mankind should give sufficient evidence that he is a good king. A king, in turn, must first show himself to be a good governor of a province, and prior to that, a good ruler of a town, a village, and his own family. Most important of all, he must have learned how to rule over himself by subjecting his lower appetites to reason and will and by letting these two higher faculties be directed by God. Thus, Campanella concludes, there can be no good ruler without divine law; otherwise, a ruler would be the scourge of God *(flagellum Dei)* and a hangman.[40]

If a nation is to prosper and flourish, each citizen must be assigned the task for which he is naturally fit, or else there will be chaos and ruin.[41] Who are the real citizens of a state? Campanella's idea of citizenship is somewhat different from notions prevailing both in his time and in our own. For him a citizen is not merely a man who happens to be the subject of a particular state or government, but one who resides in the state and does something useful for it. Those who merely live within the state and in no way contribute to its welfare should be considered as guests or the scum of society *(hospites aut reipublicae excrementa)*. Such were, in Campanella's opinion, many members of the nobility at the time he wrote.[42]

To emphasize this point, he goes on to say that it is the duty of nobles to defend the nation, while the common people ought to support it, and the learned rule over it and instruct the citizens. Those who do not perform any of these duties should be called scum and drones. On the contrary, mediators between men and God are to be considered the most honorable members of a society, just as they are its most learned and virtuous men.[43]

Having discussed the nature of the state, the qualities of a good ruler, and the right type of citizen, Campanella takes up the question of law, which he calls a basic requirement for a community.[44] The function of the law in society is compared to virtue in the individual. Just as virtue is the norm an individual man must follow in his acts and operations to attain to his supreme good, so law is the norm of acts and operations of a community for the achievement of the supreme common good as decreed and promulgated by the superior.[45] Only God, the state, and those empowered by them can make laws.[46] As a result, there are eternal law, natural law, and divine positive law, all of which are directly from God. Positive civil law is from state authorities, and is a further determination and adaptation of the *jus gentium*. The *jus gentium,* in turn, is the law common to all peoples and is derived, by way of conclusion, from the natural law.[47] Thus all positive laws depend on the natural law, and natural law is simply a participation in the eternal law which is Christ, the wisdom and reason of God. Stated differently, every law worthy of the name is from Christ as the author of nature and the First Reason.[48]

The eternal law is identical with the divine primalities considered in their relation to the governance of the world. As such, it is immutable and necessarily attains to the end predetermined by God. The natural law is also unchangeable in its primary precepts; however, God can dispense man from its secondary precepts when conditions concerning the matter of the law are changed. In such a case God does not act as lawgiver but as Lord.[49]

To be effective, laws must be worded in short and simple terms. They must be few in number and adapted to the customs of the people for which they are made. Laws should not be changed easily, and punitive laws must not outnumber disciplinary laws. A frequent change of laws and an excessive number of punitive laws are indications of a bad government. The best law is that of Jesus Christ.[50]

A final point to be mentioned is Campanella's teaching on the means to be used for the acquisition and conservation of the state, or what in scholastic terminology is called the instrumental cause of the state. This, Campanella says, may be threefold: the tongue, the sword, and money. The tongue is the instrument of religion and prudence, i.e., of the goods of the soul; the sword is the instrument of the body and all corporeal goods; money is the instrument of the external goods that are useful both to soul and body. Of these three instruments, each one corresponding to one of the three kinds of goods that make up the state, the most important is the tongue; the sword comes in the second place, while money is only an accidental means.

To use the sword alone is the quickest way to establish a state, but, as history teaches us, it is also the quickest way to lose it. By using only the tongue a ruler will succeed in getting control over men's minds, and sooner or later he will also obtain political control. Yet many times preachers pay with their lives for the truth they preach, while their successors acquire a temporal empire by reaping the fruits of the preachers' campaign. In order to obtain a solid and lasting empire, it is necessary to use the sword as well as persuasion.[51] Thus the tongue seems to be the most effective means of conquering a state; the sword, of defending it; and money, of preserving it.[52]

We have presented the general lines of Campanella's notion of a real state. In the following section we shall describe his ideal or imaginary state.

II. THE IDEAL STATE

The City of the Sun, which in its Latin edition appears as an appendix to the treatise *Politica in aphorismos digesta,* is a fictional dialogue. In it a Genoese Sea Captain tells a Grandmaster of the Knights Hospitalers about his journey to the island of Taprobane under the equator.[53] While there, he met a large group of armed men and women, many of whom understood his language, and they took him to the City of the Sun.[54] The city, in the Captain's report, is largely built on a hill which rises out of an extensive plain, but its rings extend far beyond the base of the hill. The diameter of the city is over two miles and the circumference seven miles. Yet, because of the humped shape of the mountain, the area contains more buildings than it would if the city were built on a plain.

The city is divided into seven huge rings or circles named for the seven planets, and each ring is connected by four streets and gates facing the four points of the compass. The city is so built that if the first circle were stormed, it would take much more effort to storm the second, and still more to storm the others. Thus anyone wishing to capture the city must storm it seven times.

On top of the hill there arises a splendid temple built in the form of a circle and standing on thick columns beautifully grouped. It has a large dome containing in its center a small dome with an opening right over the altar. There is only one altar, and on it there is nothing but a large globe with the painting of the sky and a small globe with a representation of the earth.

The small dome at the top of the temple is surrounded by several small cells, while larger cells are built behind the level space above the enclosures or arches of the inner and outer columns. These larger cells are occupied by priests and other religious officers.

The temporal and spiritual ruler of the city is a priest called Hoh or Sun, although in our language, the Captain remarks, he would be called Metaphysic. He is assisted by three princes, Pon, Sin, and Mor, names standing for *Potentia, Sapientia,* and *Amor,* that is, Power, Wisdom, and Love. Power takes care of all matters relating to war and peace and the military arts. He directs the military magistrates and the soldiers, and has the management of munitions, fortifications, and the storming of places. Wisdom has charge of the liberal and mechanical arts and all the sciences. He has as many magistrates and teachers under him as there are disciplines to be taught. To foster education, he has had the outer and inner walls of the city adorned with fine paintings and with illustrations of all the sciences. Love attends to the improvement of the race by providing that men and women unite to bring forth the best kind of offspring. Indeed they laugh at us for devoting so much care to the breeding of dogs and horses while neglecting the breeding of the human race. The education of children, along with stock raising, medicine, and agriculture, falls also under the care of Love.

Metaphysic treats all these matters with the three rulers, and nothing is done without him. Thus all the business of the state is discharged by the four together, but whatever Metaphysic says is always favorably accepted.

The inhabitants of the City of the Sun came originally from India, as they fled from the sword of the Moguls. Many among them were philosophers, and they decided to lead a philosophic life in common. There is among them a community of wives as well as of property. They hold, in fact, that private property is acquired because each man wants to have his own home and wife and children. This gives rise to self-love. Once self-love is abolished, there remains only love for the state.

They receive whatever they need from the community, and the magistrates take care that no one has more than he deserves. Yet no one is deprived of what is necessary. All young men call themselves brothers; those who are fifteen years older are called fathers, and those who are fifteen years younger are called sons.

They have magistrates corresponding to the name of each of our virtues, such as Magnanimity, Fortitude, Chastity, Liberality, Justice, and the like. Their selection is based on the excellence shown in the practice of the particular virtue they represent. Among them there is no robbery, murder, rape, incest, adultery, or other crimes that exist among us. They accuse themselves only of ingratitude, indolence, scurrility, lying, etc., for which they are duly punished.

Men and women wear almost the same kind of garment, which is suitable for war. The only difference is that the women's toga extends below the knee, while men's ends above the knee. Both sexes are educated together in all the arts. They learn the language when they are very young, and they are drilled in various kinds of gymnastics, so that their body is fully developed. They always go barefooted and bareheaded until they are seven years old. They are introduced to different trades, so that each one's talent may be discovered. After the seventh year they begin more serious and more specialized studies by attending lectures, engaging in disputations, and visiting the countryside with their teachers and judges. He who has learned several trades and knows how to practice them well is considered noble and superior to others.

Management of the race is for the good of the commonwealth and not for the benefit of private citizens. They maintain, in effect, that children are bred for the preservation of the species rather than for individual pleasure. Hence infants, by order of the physicians, are nursed by their mothers until they reach the age of two or more. Then girls are handed over to mistresses and boys to masters appointed by the state. As they grow older, their education is committed to the care of the magistrates, who also have charge of mating the best endowed male and female breeders according to the rules of philosophy. Women are forbidden under the death penalty to use cosmetics, high heeled shoes, or gowns with train.

Labor and other duties are so distributed among the inhabitants that each one works only for about four hours a day. The rest of the time is spent in study, reading, writing, walking, and lawful recreation. All citizens are rich because they desire no more than they have; at the same time all are poor because they own nothing in private. They have no fear of death, since they believe in the immortality of the soul and a future reward.

The inhabitants of the City of the Sun place great emphasis on agriculture, and no piece of ground is left uncultivated. They observe closely the winds and propitious stars, and attach great importance to the science of navigation. They travel abroad in order to become acquainted with other countries and peoples.

In diet, they make a distinction between useful and harmful foods, using them in accordance with medical science. They eat the most healthful foods which vary according to the different seasons of the year. They are very temperate in their use of wine, which is never given to the young until they reach nineteen, unless the state of their health demands it. After their nineteenth year they take it diluted with water, as do the women. When fifty or older the men take wine without water, except when they have to attend meetings. There are very few diseased among them, and for these they have special remedies, many of which are known only to them.

The rulers of the city hold regular meetings to decide on matters pertaining to the public welfare. Judges are constituted by the first masters in each trade. They observe the *lex talionis* or law of recompense and punish serious crimes with the death penalty. Secret confession is practiced in such a way that the citizens tell their sins to the magistrates, the magistrates to the three supreme chiefs, and these to Hoh himself, who offers sacrifices and prayers to God, but only after he has confessed publicly in the temple all the sins of his people. Human sacrifice is practiced on a voluntary basis. A man who volunteers to die for his country is treated with great benevolence and much honor; however, God does not require the death of the victim.

Priests, all of whom are over twenty-four years of age, offer prayers and sing hymns to God four times a day. They also observe the stars and note their motions and influences upon human affairs. In most cases, it is from among the priests that Hoh is elected.

The inhabitants of the City of the Sun regard the sun and the stars as living representations of God, which they honor but do not worship. They believe that the world is a huge animal in which men live just as worms live within men. They claim that it is not easy to know whether the world was made from nothing, from the ruins of other worlds, or from chaos; but they hold that it was made and did not exist from eternity. Hence they dislike Aristotle. They admit the existence of two physical principles: the sun as the father and the earth as the mother. Likewise, they admit two metaphysical principles: being, which is God; and nonbeing, which is the lack of being and the necessary condition for all created things. It is their conviction that evil and sin stem from a tendency toward nothingness. Sin has no efficient cause but only a deficient one; it shows a defect of the will, for it is in the will that sin resides.

They believe in the Trinity and say that God is Power, Wisdom, and Love. However, they do not distinguish the three divine persons by name, as Christians do, for they are not acquainted with revelation. They also say that all things are made of power, wisdom, and love inasmuch as they have being; of impotence, ignorance, and hatred inasmuch as they have nonbeing. They know that there is great corruption in the world, and from this fact they argue to the existence of some serious disorder in the past, but they do not believe it is due to Adam's sin. They acknowledge the freedom of the will and say that heresy is the work of the flesh. Finally, they teach that the true and holy law is the law of the First Reason.[55]

As might be expected, many questions have been raised about *The City of the Sun*. Some of these questions concern the general theme of the work in the light of Campanella's entire literary production, and some concern particular issues, such as the practice of common use of goods and community of wives. There have been interpreters who claim to see in Campanella's ideal republic the model of state socialism and communism and hold that he is a forerunner of those doctrines.[56] Others prefer to see in *The City of the Sun* a bold conception of a rationalistic state, in which man knows all faiths and religions, including the Christian religion, but accepts none of them.[57] In this view, Campanella's ideal republic would show once more the heretical and rebellious spirit of its author, whom the Church never ceased to persecute.[58] The fact that in many of his writings Campanella refers to *The City of the Sun* as a "dialogue on his own state" (*dialogo di propria repubblica*), is believed to lend support to the view that he stood for his own personal rationalistic theory even when he was contemplating a universal monarchy under the Pope, as described in the *Monarchia Messiae*.[59]

Neither of these interpretations is acceptable. We believe that a great injustice is done to the author of *The City of the Sun* by those who like to present him as a harbinger of modern socialism and communism or as a champion of a purely rationalistic state theory. There is sufficient textual evidence in Campanella's works to support the contention that *The City of the Sun* is only a "poetical dialogue," as the subtitle of the work indicates,[60] which depicts an imaginary community of men and women *in the pure order of nature*. Following the light of reason but unaided by Christian revelation, they organize themselves into an ideal society where all abuses—with due reservation for some questionable practices to be examined later—are eliminated and all citizens contribute effectively to the common welfare. To prove our point, we shall let Campanella speak for himself and present his case in his own terms. We shall add only those comments and observations that may help the reader better to understand Campanella's thought.

Anticipating the objections that the highly provocative character of *The City of the Sun* would raise among its readers, Campanella wrote a defense of the work to which he refers possible inquirers. This defense makes up the entire fourth question of the *Quaestiones politicae*,[61] and is divided into three articles. In the first article he discusses the truth and usefulness of his political dialogue, while in the second and third articles he deals respectively with the controversial issues of community of goods and community of women. Answering the question whether the work would serve any purpose, since it is hardly conceivable that an ideal state like his could ever be brought into existence, he appeals to the authority of Thomas More, whose *Utopia* served as a blueprint for his own dialogue. Plato is also brought on the scene as the creator of an ideal republic that could not be fully realized in the state of corrupt nature but could have been in the state of innocence. Legislators are likewise known to issue laws that will never be fully observed; yet such laws serve their purpose, inasmuch as they set a pattern of action to be followed by the citizens in pursuing the common good of the state.[62]

The ideal republic described in *The City of the Sun,* continues Campanella, is not like the Mosaic and Christian laws, which have been revealed to man by God. Rather, it represents the best form of government that philosophers can achieve by the light of reason alone. If in certain matters, such as the community of women, the inhabitants of the City of the Sun differ from the teaching of the Gospels, this is not due to ill will but to the weakness of the human mind, which considers as permissible certain practices that revelation proves to be faulty. The republic reflects the conditions of a people that is still *in gentilismo,* that is, in paganism, and looks forward to the revelation of a better way of life. They are, as it were, in a state of preparation for Christianity *(in Catechismo ad vitam Christianam),* since, in the opinion of St. Cyril, it is the function of philosophy to prepare the gentiles for the evangelical truth.[63]

These statements are so clear that they leave no doubt about the real nature of Campanella's dialogue. To see in *The City of the Sun* the realization of a naturalistic society that knew but rejected Christian revelation, is to distort Campanella's doctrine completely.[64] One might object that he presents his ideal republic as a model also for Christians who have been enlightened by supernatural revelation and restored by Christ to the state of original innocence.[65] He even expresses the hopes that such a republic may some day, after the downfall of the Antichrist, be established throughout the entire world.[66] These statements, however, which follow almost immediately upon those we have just mentioned, should be interpreted in the light of the entire context and made to harmonize with the preceding doctrine rather than contradict it.

The point Campanella wants to make is that although his ideal republic can best be achieved by philosophers who have never come in contact with Christian revelation, it represents also the idealization of human nature in its striving for a perfect natural society. By restoring man to the state of original innocence and raising him to the supernatural order, Christ did not destroy human nature, which remains essentially the same even after Christ's redemption. Rather, He made it easier for men to organize themselves into an ideal society that, with the aid of grace and the sacraments, would help them better to attain their final end, both in the natural and supernatural orders. It is in this sense that Campanella can speak in the same article, and without contradicting himself, of an ideal state *in gentilismo,* modeled after Plato's *Republic* and Thomas More's *Utopia,* and an ideal state for all Christendom, inspired by the community system of early Christians and the monastic life of contemporary religious orders. It becomes likewise understandable how he can say that the Anabaptists, a contemporary religious sect of people living in common, cannot expect to make any real progress unless they decide to accept the teaching of the Catholic Church and rid themselves of their heretical beliefs.[67]

Campanella has no doubt that the system of community of goods is in conformity with the natural law and that it contributes to the welfare of the state and its citizens. He defends this thesis in the second article of the fourth question of the *Quaestiones politicae,* where he argues against Aristotle and all philosophers who stand for the natural right of private property. To establish his position, he makes use of arguments from authority and from reason. Among the arguments from authority he cites statements by Pope St. Clement the Roman, St. Augustine, St. John Chrysostom, St. Ambrose, St. Thomas Aquinas, and others. However he takes some of these statements out of context and twists them to suit his own purpose.[68] He also brings forward the teaching of the Apostles, the example of early Christians and churchmen, and the actual system of community life of the religious orders to show that the community of goods is a much better system than that which allows private property. In his opinion, the Church relaxed this law of nature at a later date, especially for the clergy, to avoid greater evils. It amounts in effect to a permission rather than to a real law.[69]

The main reason for the abolition of private property is to prevent abuses that inevitably creep into society once the goods are divided among the citizens. Avarice, which is the root of all evils, fraud, theft, robbery, pride, egoism, jealousy, enmity and the like are only the most common abuses. To avoid them, goods must be distributed among the citizens on the basis of their natural talents and abilities. This will also help to uproot the social evils that result from a system based on heredity or an elective system in which ambition plays an important role.[70] In conclusion, the doctrine of the community of goods, affirms Campanella, is definitely according to the law of nature.[71] To hold the contrary is nothing short of heresy.[72] Nor can it be said with Duns Scotus that the community of goods was of natural right in the state of innocence but not after Adam's fall. Original sin deprived man of the goods of the supernatural order, not of those which belong to the order of nature.[73]

Thus, according to Campanella, community of goods is an ideal system for man both in the order of grace and the order of nature. Shall we say that his theory is an anticipation of modern socialistic and communistic collectivism? There are no doubt points of contact between the two doctrines, inasmuch as both defend some sort of state absolutism in regard to material goods. However, the doctrinal background and inspirational motive of the two systems, as well as the methods suggested for their establishment, make them very different. The state absolutism advocated by scientific socialism, and especially by Marxist communism, is a completely materialistic and atheistic conception of society that makes the state the supreme and absolute ruler over the goods and destinies of the citizens. It admits no spiritual or moral values and controls the citizens, who are reduced to almost insignificant units in the state machinery, by flashing before their imagination the mirage of an ideal temporal happiness that will never materialize.

Campanella's community system, on the other hand, is based on a completely different ideology. It is modeled after the system of early Christian communities and fashioned along the general lines of monastic life in the religious orders, where the abolition of private property is only a means to help the monks detach themselves from earthly goods and attend more completely to the things of the spirit.[74] Furthermore, in *The City of the Sun* there is no indication whatsoever of violence or compulsion in enforcing the laws of the state. On the contrary, everything is done smoothly and in a most reasonable manner, since every citizen is asked to do what suits him best.[75] Briefly, while Marxist communism attempts to achieve its purely materialistic ends by brute force, class warfare, and hatred, Campanella's collectivism aims at helping man to attain better the end for which he was created by fostering love and mutual understanding.[76]

A second thorny question that Campanella discusses in his *Quaestiones politicae* is "Whether the community of women is more in agreement with nature and more helpful to generation, and hence to the state, than the possession of one wife and children."[77] Here he faces the obvious objection, raised throughout the entire history of philosophy from Aristotle to his own time, that the community of women is against the natural law and destructive of marriage, the essential properties of which are unity and indissolubility.

Campanella is aware of the seriousness of the objection and proceeds carefully to justify the conduct of the dwellers in the City of the Sun. To avoid any misunderstanding, he cautions the reader at the beginning that not all kinds of community of women are legitimate, but only the particular type he describes in his political dialogue. There are, in effect, several ways of understanding the community of women. First of all, there is the so-called *concubitus vagus,* whereby a man is allowed to have sexual intercourse with any woman, at any time, with no restrictions whatsoever, as do certain animals. Promiscuity of this kind must be condemned, as it is against man's rational nature and leads to various abuses. There is another kind of promiscuity, continues Campanella, which consists in allowing a legally wed man to have sexual relations at certain definite times with a woman allotted to him, as has been the case in certain regions of France and Germany. This system, too, is to be condemned as against the natural law, or at least the divine positive law, for it promotes selfish gratification rather than the good of the offspring.

There is, however, a third kind of community of women, which is the system followed by the inhabitants of the City of the Sun. It consists in matching only the best breeders, who will have sexual intercourse only at the time that is most suitable for generation and within certain age limits. This system, remarks Campanella, does not involve a breach of the natural law and is consistent with people who live *in puris naturalibus,* like the citizens in question, who have no knowledge of the divine positive law. Even if such a system were against the natural law, that fact could not be known by reason alone, since it cannot be inferred by way of conclusion from the natural law itself. It can only be known by a specific determination of the positive law, which of its nature is subject to change.[78] Thus the doctrine of the community of women, as propounded in *The City of the Sun,* would become heretical only after the Church's condemnation; and those citizens, whose only rule and guide is the natural law known by reason, cannot be blamed for their conduct in regard to women.[79]

Is this teaching inconsistent with the position that Campanella takes in his other works, such as the *Quaestiones oeconomicae, Oeconomica,* and *Theologia,* where he proclaims that polygamy is against the natural law?[80] Certain statements of the *Quaestiones politicae,* if taken separately, may seem to point toward a real conflict in his teaching. Yet, if we take a closer look at the context, we will see that the conflict is only apparent. In the works that have just been mentioned, where Campanella treats the doctrine of marriage specifically, he maintains that polygamy is only secondarily against the natural law, so that it is possible for God to dispense men from it. In the *Quaestiones politicae* he does not reject explicitly this doctrine; he simply emphasizes the difficulty for the inhabitants of the City of the Sun to discover it by the light of natural reason alone, prior to the positive decree of the Church. That this is Campanella's mind can be inferred from his insistence upon *the state of pure nature* in which those inhabitants are supposed to live, and from his explicit affirmation that the community of women may perhaps be against the natural law, but that this cannot be known by a philosopher.[81]

Before closing this section a final observation is in order. Although *The City of the Sun* is in the mind of its author a poetical dialogue describing an imaginary and hypothetic state, many of the ideas contained in it have a practical value. This was the intention of Campanella, who often refers to the dialogue in later and more serious works. The nature of this study does not allow us to go into a detailed discussion of all the challenging reforms that the work suggests. But even a cursory look at *The City of the Sun* will convince the reader that its author is to be credited with modern views on problems in the social, political, and educational fields. Thus Campanella appears once more as an original thinker and a forerunner of modern times.[82]

III. THE THEOCRATIC STATE

No matter how ingenious and persuasive the scheme of Campanella's ideal state may be, it could hardly represent his plan of a universal reform that would pave the way for that golden age described in glowing terms by prophets, poets, and philosophers which Christ is supposed to have come to restore. The work that best explains this plan, which was the dream of Campanella's entire life, is the *Monarchia Messiae*.[83] As indicated by its author, the main purpose of the treatise is to prove by arguments derived both from reason and from revelation that the Pope, as Vicar of Christ, is the supreme temporal and spiritual ruler of the world,[84] and consequently, that all other rulers are subject to him in spiritual as well as temporal matters.[85] He does this in a systematic way, beginning with some general notions on the nature of dominion and sovereignty.

The only true and absolute owner or sovereign, Campanella says, is one who can *de iure* and *de facto* dispose of the things he possesses in whatever way he pleases and with no restriction whatsoever. This is dominion *per essentiam* and *per se* and it belongs exclusively to

God, on whom all creatures depend for their entire being and operation. On the other hand, an owner *per participationem* and *secundum
quid* is one who can dispose of things and men only to the extent that
he is so empowered by God.[86] On the basis of this distinction, it can
be readily seen that no man is the absolute owner of himself and
other beings inferior to him, much less of his fellow men.[87] Nor can
he rule over other people merely as a man, but only inasmuch as he
is so authorized by God. This may obtain either because of certain
natural qualities with which he has been endowed by the creator or
because of a special supernatural title. In both cases he will act as a
divinized man *(homo divinus)* or a caretaker for God.[88]

Keeping to his principle that the government of one man is better
than the government of many,[89] Campanella now goes a step further
and says that it is proper for a ruler to possess both spiritual and
temporal powers. The concentration of these two powers into one
person is beneficial to citizens as well as to the state. It prevents the
ruler from becoming subservient to secular princes in order to secure
their assistance in time of need, with the consequent danger that laws
will be broken. It also helps to keep him from falling prey to heretics
and pseudoprophets, who otherwise may overcome illiterate laymen
and unarmed priests.[90] Also, citizens are better disposed to obey one
whom they know to be their intercessor before God.[91]

That kingship and priesthood can fittingly be joined in one and
the same person is proved by the fact that this was the situation of
man in the state of natural law prior to any positive determination.
Thus Adam was father, king, and priest of all mankind, as were all
the firstborn after him who are mentioned in the Scriptures.[92] It is
not God but the devil who introduced a multitude of kingdoms in the
world. This is in opposition to the divine plan which provides for
the union of all mankind into one kingdom with but one religion.[93]
It is precisely this kind of kingdom that Christ came to restore, as evidenced by the fact that he has given one universal law for all mankind and has appointed one man to lead the entire world.[94] The
following passage summarizes Campanella's teaching on this point.

Jesus Christ, God and man, Lord of all things, both temporal and
spiritual, established one kingdom *(principatum)* which he placed
above all human kingdoms, with a twofold power in the person of
St. Peter, Prince of the Apostles, and his successors. When the whole
world has been united under this monarchy and all kingdoms and
powers that are not totally and absolutely subject to it have been
eliminated, and all different religions and sects have been sup-

pressed, then will appear that golden age which Christ came to restore, as predicted by prophets, poets, and philosophers. This age already exists at the present time, even though it does not appear to be so.

The Church of God has always been one, and by divine and human right all rulers depend on her head in both temporal and spiritual matters. He [the head of the Church] can give orders to all rulers for some good purpose (ad aedificationem), but cannot take away their kingship unless they rebel against God and the universal Church, or become unfit to rule and thus endanger the common good. If the state can do this [in regard to its rulers], so much more can the Pope.

Yet neither a king nor the Church as a whole can take any action against the head [of the Church], for the Pope is the father, pastor, spouse of the Church, over whom neither sons, nor sheep nor bride have any power. He can make laws binding all men, just as he can change them; he can guide and correct the actions and the life of his subjects in order to direct them to life eternal.[95]

The same doctrine is contained in the *Theologia*, where Campanella devotes an entire chapter to proving that the Pope is king and priest and has universal power over all the kingdoms of the world.[96] Furthermore, the whole of the *Discorsi universali del governo ecclesiastico* is a practical application of the same principle, which he claims to support with many texts taken from Holy Scripture and, among others, a text taken from St. Thomas's *De regimine principum*.[97]

To add further weight to his theory of a universal papal monarchy, Campanella has recourse to his favorite doctrine of Christ as the eternal Reason. Christ, the Word Incarnate, is God's eternal Reason through which the world has been created and redeemed; hence all things belong to Him by right.[98] When He came into this world, He took on all power in both spiritual and temporal matters, and later gave it to the Church so as to fulfill the prophecies.[99] It is true that Christ, as the Second Person of the Holy Trinity, had all power over the world even prior to His incarnation.[100] Likewise, there is no question of the existence of secular powers before the incarnation took place. Yet even these powers were established by Christ, since to be legitimate a power must be based on reason, and Christ is the first essential Reason from which all powers derive.[101] When He came into the world, Christ instituted the Apostolic Church and set it above all secular powers, so that it can direct and control them and help them achieve their end.[102]

That Christ gave to His Church the temporal sword along with the spiritual sword is proved by Campanella in the following way. Since Christ is a most perfect legislator, He must make sure that His law obtains its effect. To be effective, a law must have both a directive and a coercive function. The element of coercion cannot be constituted by the simple threat of hell or of any other spiritual punishment, since men who are truly evil ridicule such things. Hence to enforce His law, Christ must have empowered the Church to use the material sword.[103] It should be clear, then, that the Pope, as the head of the one true Church of Christ, must have inherited from Him all power, both spiritual and temporal, and that he is the supreme ruler to whom all other rulers are subject.[104] To put it another way, the Messias has established but one reign, and this reign has but one head whose power extends over all men and includes all matters, both spiritual and temporal. Hence all other powers and rights, no matter how they have been obtained, depend on the Pope as the Vicar of Christ.[105]

By attributing to the Pope a direct power over secular rulers even in temporal matters, Campanella goes against an established tradition of Catholic theologians, especially that of the Dominican order of which he was a member. He does not conceal this fact, but nevertheless he clings to his opinion and maintains that, despite the contrary teaching of the Thomistic school, his is the only correct interpretation of Aquinas's thought.[106]

What is the position of the secular powers in regard to the papal monarchy? Campanella discusses this question in the last part of the *Monarchia Messiae*. Under the heading of the rights of the emperor and other princes, he writes:

> . . . I affirm that the emperor, as the defender of the Church, the body that rules over the entire world in things spiritual and temporal, is also lord of the whole world, but only in temporal matters . . . and only insofar as he is the defender of the Church . . . When the emperor's strength fails, each one of his princes may share his power, but only to the extent that he is so authorized by the Church.[107]

Applying this principle to the specific case of the New World, Campanella defends the king of Spain's right of conquest on the ground that he acted as the right arm of the Messias and his conquests contributed to the defense of the Christian faith and to the spread of the Gospel.[108] For him there is no doubt that God was behind the Spaniards in their conquests. However, it is the Pope's task to dispose of, and distribute, the newly conquered territory, which belongs to him by divine right. The invasion of the New Hemisphere was in effect carried out under the auspices of Christ the Messias, who was promised dominion over the entire world. On the other hand, Americans, i.e., the natives of the New World, lead such an irrational life that the Pope is completely justified in punishing them until they return to reason, which they share in common with all other men.[109]

With these statements Campanella concludes the formal treatment of his theocratic state.[110] However the idea of a universal papal monarchy so dominates his mind that he never misses an opportunity to stress it and to add some practical suggestions for its realization. Three works represent his practical approach to the problem of a universal monarchy. One is the *Discorsi della libertà e della felice suggezione allo stato ecclesiastico*,[111] which the publisher added as an appendix to the text of the *Monarchia Messiae;* and the other two are the *Discorsi universali del governo ecclesiastico* and the *Quod reminiscentur*. To complete our treatment of Campanella's politics we shall add a brief section on the contents of these works.

The *Discorsi della libertà* attempt to prove two main points. In the first discourse Campanella holds that there is no greater freedom than under the papal monarchy, and in the second he maintains that it is better to be subject to an ecclesiastical ruler than to a secular prince. In discussing the first point he mentions the various types of freedom existing in the papal state: freedom from sin (in the sense that in it there are fewer sins than in other states), freedom from war, freedom from famine, freedom from pestilence, and finally, freedom from all forms of slavery. He compares this situation with the contrary conditions prevailing in secular states and concludes that nowhere in the world can a man be so free, in the true sense of the term, as in Rome under the Pope.[112] The second point, which is the topic of the second discourse, is stated in the following terms: it is political heresy and theological error to doubt that it is better to be subject to an ecclesiastical ruler than to a secular prince. The reason is that a man cannot lead other men unless he himself is led by God. But we know with certainty that the Holy Spirit assists the Pope in a most special way. The conclusion is therefore evident.[113]

To prove his statement Campanella considers ruler, subjects, and the relations existing between the two in both the ecclesiastical and the civil state. The ecclesiastical ruler, especially the Pope, is on many counts superior to a secular prince. He is a high priest consecrated to God and, therefore, more worthy of respect and more reliable; he is usually more mature and experienced and has a greater learning; he has no wife or children to care for; he is not a warrior, and thus has no need to levy heavy taxes to support territorial conquests.[114] The subjects of the papacy ought to consider themselves privileged to be governed by such a wise leader and ought to appreciate the many advantages they enjoy over subjects of a secular state.[115] Finally, there are much better relations between the Pope and his subjects than between a secular prince and his people. The Pope commands with greater authority and his orders are more easily obeyed because of the great veneration people have for him. He is more concerned about their health and defense, and, above all, he administers the state with fairness and justice.[116]

While the *Discorsi della libertà* were written mainly for the benefit of the citizens of the papal state, the *Discorsi universali·del governo ecclesiastico* are confidential reports to the Pope suggesting practical ways and means of governing his state, with a view to establishing the universal monarchy described in the *Monarchia Messiae*.[117] These *Discorsi* are much more elaborate, and their twenty-four chapters contain the essential principles of what may be termed papal domestic and foreign policy. The topics range from general statements concerning the means of obtaining and preserving an empire, which are but repetitions of what we have seen in the *De politica,* to specific problems of the papal state. "All the mistakes committed by the Church leaders," Campanella asserts, "consist in this, that they believe that the same policy that is good for a secular state is also good for the papacy."[118] This belief is evidently incorrect, for the secular state and the papacy are two different types of government, one being concerned mainly with the bodies and the other with the souls of their subjects. One is headed by the Pope who is king, priest, and father, the other is governed by a prince or tyrant; one is built on love and veneration, the other on fear and merciless justice.[119]

To mobilize the whole world and win it over to the cause of a universal monarchy, the Pope need only use a selected group of religious who are young, learned, and the best in each order.[120] They will summon a general council, not only of Christians but of all other peoples as well, and discuss with them the truth of our religion by using the logic of Christ.[121] Furthermore, to preserve the unity of the faith, which is indispensable to a universal monarchy, all heretics should devote their abilities to fields of knowledge other than theology, such as astronomy and the mechanical arts. They should be paid for their services. The brightest among them will be sent to the New World, where they have no time to indulge in theological disputes and can acquire fame in some other way.[122]

To foster the cause of the monarchy, it is important that the Pope establish in Rome a council of all Christian princes or their ambassadors so that they can discuss together all matters pertaining to war and peace among Christians.[123] He should also see to it that the balance of power is preserved among the Christian rulers, so that no one ruler can attack another without his consent. Likewise, any attempt to apostatize must be immediately frustrated. Most of all, the Pope must avoid calling foreigners into Italy, for fear that heresy may creep into the papal state and that his own power be jeopardized and exposed to contempt. Control of Italy is his best assurance of control of the entire world, the aim toward which he should strive with all his power.[124]

The last work to be examined, the *Quod reminiscentur et convertentur ad Dominum universi fines terrae,* is an earnest appeal to all rulers and peoples to join into one great family under Christian law. Thus they will fulfill the prayer of Psalm XXI which provides the title of the book. The work is divided into four parts, which contain messages to Christians, Gentiles, Jews, and Mohammedans. While the general theme is the same, the message to each individual group and respective nation contains points of special interest. In dedicating the work to Pope Paul V, Campanella calls it the epitome and completion of all his studies, for it represents a positive step toward the conversion of all nations under the auspices of the Vicar of Christ.[125] Indeed, it is only through the initiative of the Pope, Campanella states in his message to Paul V, that such a conversion is possible, for all mankind turns to him as the last anchor of hope.[126] Needless to say, many people do not believe in God, much less in the Pope as His representative; but this pitiful state itself cries out for the Pope's intervention, just as disease calls for the cure of a physician even though the sick man may not realize the seriousness of his ailment.[127] Campanella ends his message to Pope Paul V with a passionate appeal to him as Supreme Pontiff and mediator between men and God to fulfill his duty and call all men back to God.[128]

Convinced that the return of mankind to God is not possible without divine grace, Campanella humbly prays to God to show His mercy to men in spite of their sins[129] and begs the nine choirs of angels for their protection.[130] He also entreats the devils to desist from tempting men, since no benefit can come to them from men's damnation.[131] Moreover he beseeches them—a hopeless task indeed!—to recognize their wrong deeds and come back to God, in the hope that because of this act of humility He might restore them to the kingdom they lost on account of their pride.[132]

Quite consistently, Campanella proposes in the *Quod reminiscentur* the same basic principles for Church government that he had already stated in the *De regimine ecclesiastico* and briefly summarized in the *Discorsi universali*.[133] Also, when speaking of the need for the Christian rulers to join forces in order to defend themselves from other rulers and subdue them, he restates his own theory that only the Supreme Pontiff can be their leader, for he alone, as Vicar of Christ, can command their respect and obedience.[134]

All messages to non-Christian leaders, whether Gentile, Jew, or Mohammedan, center on the idea that it is imperative for them to recognize the Christian God as the only true God and Supreme Ruler of the universe. Until this is done, there is no hope for salvation either for them or for the peoples whose government has been entrusted to them. Thus the *Quod reminiscentur* stands out as momentous testimony to the ecumenical spirit of its author, whose plan of a universal papal monarchy is designed as the fulfillment of the psalmist's prophecy: "All the families of the nations shall bow down in His sight; for the kingdom is the Lord's and He has dominion over the nations."[135]

CHAPTER THIRTEEN

Evaluation of Campanella's Moral Philosophy

Campanella's conception of moral philosophy as including ethics, economics, and politics is a clear indication of the importance he attached to man as a moral and social being and to the ethical principles that should guide him both in his private and social life. By nature man tends toward action, and action is always in view of an end. The final end for which man acts can only be his own conservation, for it is inconceivable, says Campanella, that man's supreme good, which is also his final end, should be something different from man himself. But while self-conservation is the goal man must strive to attain in all his acts and operations, both as an individual and as a member of the family and society, it would be wrong to conceive it as a purely egocentric movement that excludes God. Indeed, it is in the conservation of personal existence in God in the next life that man's supreme happiness properly consists.

Despite apparent discrepancies, this teaching is in substantial agreement with the scholastic tradition. What Campanella fails to do is to distinguish between man's intrinsic and extrinsic end, his subjective and objective happiness. He does not identify the two aspects of man's last end, nor does he confuse them, since he states explicitly that God is man's supreme beatitude *ut quod,* while self-conservation is man's own beatitude *formaliter.* Rather, he overemphasizes the subjective and personal element in beatitude without neglecting man's theocentric drive rooted in his inner nature. Only by possessing God through his entire being can man be fully satisfied in his aspirations. Hence Campanella can rightly say that man's ultimate end and supreme good are his own conservation in God, and that this goal can only be attained in a future life. Whether man's possession of God will be mainly through intellect or will, contemplation or love, is a question somewhat extraneous to Campanella's system, where knowledge, love, and power are equated as the three primalities of being. However, even on this highly controversial issue he does not fail to show his preference for the so-called voluntarist trend and to depart once more from the traditional intellectualist position of the Dominican order. For him happiness consists primarily in love, since it is

through the will that man attains formally to the supreme good, and
not through the intellect whose formal object is truth.

The treatise on virtue, which follows immediately upon the discussion of the supreme good, provides Campanella with an opportunity to elaborate his doctrine of the primalities of being in relation
to man's ultimate end. In effect, virtue is the means that enables man
to attain to the supreme good. But in what does this means precisely
consist, or, to put it in more direct terms, what is the nature of virtue? This question is answered by Campanella in an entirely new
way. Virtue, we are told, is not an operative habit, as Aristotle and
the scholastics teach, but a power that proceeds from the intimate
nature of being and manifests itself in the operations˙ of the three
primalities which it helps to perfect. Accordingly, virtue is a guiding
norm of action discovered by the cognitive principle, imposed by the
will, and made possible by power. The habit or facility man acquires
in repeating the same good act is an effect of virtue rather than virtue
itself.

In this conception, virtue acquires a peculiar meaning that is found
neither in scholastic philosophy nor in other philosophies. Instead of
being a quality or perfection of the rational faculties,[1] virtue becomes
an intrinsic power of being, a perfection of the primalities themselves
in which it is supposed to be grounded. Thus virtue takes on the
connotation of power, with which the term was originally associated,
and is conceived as existing in all beings, even though its presence is
more evident in man because of his rational nature. This is another
instance of Campanella's arbitrary use of traditional philosophical
terms to fit into his questionable primalitarian doctrine of reality.
How virtue can be grounded in the primalities and yet be distinct
from their principles of operation *ad extra* is not explained by Campanella. On the other hand, his adverse criticism of the Aristotelian
notion of virtue as a mean between two extremes is unjustified. To
hold against Aristotle the belief that virtue is not the mean between
two extremes, on the ground that in certain things we can go to one
extreme and still be called virtuous, is to forget that the Stagirite
himself had already made it clear that the rule of the golden mean
cannot be applied in all cases, but only when the two extremes are
vicious. In other words, Aristotle teaches that the mean is relative to
us and must be determined by reason and by the virtue of prudence.[2]

Pivotal issues in ethics are the questions concerning the essence of
morality and the norm by which we can gauge the goodness or badness
of human acts. Campanella touches upon these questions only inci-

dentally in his discussion of the relationship between human freedom
and morality, and points out that, to be moral, a free act must be
performed according to the norm dictated by the consideration of
man's relationship to himself, other creatures, and God. He adds
further that a moral act, in contrast with the purely natural act which
belongs to man's nature, must be acquired by practice. It is called
moral because it causes in us a habit or custom of doing things.

These brief statements on the nature and characteristics of the moral
act as distinct from natural act are inadequate for constructing Campanella's doctrine of morality and the norm of morality. What the statements indicate is that, to be a real guide in determining the morality
of an act, a norm must take into consideration man's place in the
entire hierarchy of beings. Yet Campanella does not reveal what this
norm actually is, nor does he offer a definition of morality. His
description of a moral act as a habit-forming act is irrelevant, since
an act can be good or evil apart from its relation to other acts of the
same kind. Habit or custom in the performance of our acts may relate
to virtue or vice, which are traditionally defined as good or bad operative habits, but not to morality as such. Campanella seems to confuse
the two issues.

The classification of virtues based on the different ways in which
the primalities of being tend toward their objects is original and
unique. One may rightly question the doctrine of primalities, but
once this doctrine is admitted—and Campanella's philosophy can
hardly be understood otherwise—it is not difficult to see the ingenuity
of this classification. Some of the virtues named by Campanella, such
as the art of memorizing, counselling, logic, grammar, rhetoric and
poetics, prophecy, and physical exercise, are not virtues in the usual
sense of the term. But one must bear in mind that for Campanella
virtue is not so much an operative habit as it is a guiding norm of
action. However, sanctity cannot properly be called the most important virtue nor sublimity the total of all virtues.

In his treatise on the ethics of the family, Campanella develops
a theory of domestic society so broad as to include servants and animals
as well as parents and children. The family is held to be the simplest
form of society having essentially the same nature as the state. It also
has the same basic purpose, for both family and state help man achieve
his ultimate end of self-preservation in God. But, whereas the state
aims primarily at the preservation of the individual, the family aims
at the preservation of both individual and species.

One might agree with Campanella that the ultimate end of the family and the state is the same, inasmuch as they both help man attain the final purpose for which he was made. In this sense all things cooperate to the glory of God, which is also man's eternal happiness. However, family and state have specifically different purposes which are the immediate causes of their existence and make them into two specifically distinct societies. This fact is not made sufficiently clear by Campanella, who seems to be more interested in showing the common elements existing between the two societies than in highlighting their distinct characteristics.

The importance and value of the family are duly stressed by Campanella, who makes the good and evil of society largely dependent on the family. He suggests some very practical norms for the formation of the domestic society and the government of the household. His conditions for a successful marriage manifest good common sense and unusual psychological insight. While emphasizing the importance of certain physiological factors in choosing a partner, he does not lose sight of the fact that marriage is essentially the union of two persons, and that purely material considerations should never play a primary role in a marriage contract.

As we have already pointed out,[3] Campanella's teaching on marriage in his philosophical writings is completely orthodox. He makes it unmistakably clear that marriage is a contract of the natural law raised by Christ to the dignity of a sacrament. He likewise defends the unity and indissolubility of marriage, even though he admits with all Catholic thinkers that polygamy is against only the secondary precepts of nature.

The advice that Campanella gives to spouses concerning preparation for the generative act, the duties of an expectant mother, and the care of infants reflects his conviction that proper diet and right mental attitudes in the spouses may exert a beneficial influence on the offspring. This conviction does not seem to have the support of modern biology and genetic psychology. However, child psychologists and educators will find it interesting to notice that three centuries ago Campanella warned the parents against any excessive punishments of their children lest they develop a timid and fearful nature.

All in all, the Campanellian treatise on the ethics of the family, imperfect and incomplete as it is, is a valid approach to the complex problem of domestic society in its philosophical and sociological aspects. While undue attention is given to certain minor points dealing with the good of the offspring and the running of the household, the basic questions concerning the nature and purpose of the family and its social function as a primal unit of the state are adequately treated.

Politics is a field of study in which Campanella was deeply involved throughout his entire life. This is so true that he has gone down in history more as a political thinker than as a philosopher. However, in many instances his political theory has been closely associated by historians with *The City of the Sun* or other writings that contain only one phase of his political thought. We believe that we have succeeded in presenting a more realistic and comprehensive view of Campanella's political doctrine. Moreover, it has been our concern to assign each work its proper place and meaning in the development of his varied political theory. We shall now go back to the results of our findings and attempt to pass a judgment on what appear to be Campanella's main positions in the field of politics.

In the introduction to his treatise on politics, which he rightly calls the science of governing the state, Campanella makes two significant statements that characterize his entire approach to the study. He says that politics is subalternate to ethics and that it is a God-given science. This initial attitude toward politics marks Campanella as a strong opponent of Machiavellianism, his most direct target, and of any other system that divorces politics from morality and religion. A state theory based on political expediency, like that propounded by Machiavelli, and the modern state theory of political liberalism are far removed from Campanella's political doctrine. Instead we find in him a conception of a state that attains its full growth and development only in its subjection to the temporal and spiritual leadership of the Pope. In his opinion, the state, like its citizens, has God as its final end; and only the Pope, who combines in his person the temporal and spiritual powers, can properly direct men to their eternal happiness.

While this theory avoids the danger of a secularistic state, it proposes a kind of Church absolutism that could hardly be accepted in Campanella's time and is almost unthinkable in our own time. The doctrine is not so much a theoretical error as it is a practical impossibility. Campanella does not seem to realize the distinct nature and relative independence of the two perfect societies, Church and state, just as he fails to see the possibility of a mutual cooperation between the two without necessarily subordinating one to the other. This is not to say that the Pope has no right to temporal power, or that he cannot have recourse to it for the defense of the Christian faith. The opposite view is correct, and to this extent Campanella is right. But his whole idea of a king-priest ruling over the entire world from which all distinctions of religion and government have disappeared is utopian. Further comment on this point will be made when his notion of a theocratic state is discussed.

The proposal that public officers be appointed on the basis of natural talents and abilities rather than material wealth is wise and practical. So also is the observation that in the state the common good should prevail over the private good. But to hold this and to maintain that the system of private property ought to be abolished and replaced by the system of community of goods is a different thing. Actually, the common good of society is better promoted when due consideration is given to man's natural right to own the products on which he has put the stamp of his own personality. Experience also tells us that man takes more interest in things that belong to him personally, while he is usually careless about the things of the community. Likewise, private profit is the most effective incentive to get men to work. These are but a few considerations that convincingly support the institution of private ownership.

As for the origin of authority in the state, Campanella merely confirms an honored principle of Christian philosophy that all authority comes ultimately from God. He advances no specific theory on the designation of the person to be invested with such authority, although his preference is a system of election rather than one of mere hereditary succession. Monarchy is for him, as for most seventeenth-century thinkers, the preferred form of government, especially in time of war when quick decisions must be made.

The norms Campanella establishes for the selection of a good leader are sound and realistic. He places great emphasis on the previous accomplishments of a candidate for rulership over a small community, and even greater importance on the success with which he has practiced self-control by subjecting lower appetites to intellect and will and both of these to God. This amounts to saying that before being called upon to rule over the destiny of a country, a man must be experienced in posts of lesser responsibility and be of a good moral character.

To be worthy of the name, a citizen must contribute effectively to the welfare of the state to the best of his ability. One who refuses to render any public service forfeits *ipso facto* his right of citizenship. This notion of citizenship is determined by the particular nature of the Campanellian state in which all property is held in common. In such a system it is only natural that an individual cannot enjoy the privileges of the community, including the right of citizenship itself, unless he makes some positive contribution toward the community. But the onerous conditions laid down by Campanella for the right of citizenship are also motivated by social abuses current in his time, especially among the nobility, which he denounces in harsh terms. The open condemnation of a large sector of the nobility offers a sharp contrast to his words of high commendation for the social services of priests as mediators between men and God.

The treatise on law is written on the general lines of scholastic philosophy. All laws are traced back to the eternal law. However, it is a special feature of Campanella's teaching that the eternal law is Christ, the first Reason and the Wisdom of God. Indeed, law is a norm of reason; and so every law, whether positive or natural, must be a participation in, and a reflection of, the eternal Reason.[4] Campanella also identifies eternal law with the divine primalities in the governance of the world, since the primalities constitute a single principle of operation *ad extra,* and wisdom in God is essentially the same as power and love.

In discussing the means for the acquisition and conservation of a state, Campanella says that neither force nor money alone can ensure a lasting empire. Diplomacy must also be used. By force and money one may obtain control over men's bodies and external goods, but their minds can be won only by persuasion. These are very wise words that shed light on the success or failure of many a war of conquest as well as on the rise and fall of many empires.

The idea of the state that Campanella offers us in *The City of the Sun* is in many respects different from his notion of a real state just described. The City of the Sun is Campanella's ideal state ruled by philosophers who have never come into contact with Christian revelation. Its citizens are still *in gentilismo* but ready to accept the Christian doctrine as soon as it is revealed. Small wonder, then, that some of their beliefs and practices conflict with the Christian conscience. A striking example is the system of community of women, an easy target for the attacks of Campanella's critics who cannot resign themselves to the idea of a friar advocating such an immoral practice. Relying almost exclusively on his words, we have shown that the unchristian sexual mores of those citizens in no way reflect Campanella's own convictions about marriage.[5] He sincerely believes that the Catholic Church is right in her interpretation of the natural law, and hence in her condemnation of any sort of sexual promiscuity or polygamous practices. However, he maintains that polygamy is only against the secondary precepts of the natural law, knowledge of which, in contrast with the knowledge of the primary precepts, cannot be attained by people living in the pure order of nature.

In our judgment this is Campanella's teaching in regard to the system of the community of women discussed in *The City of the Sun* and his other works. Yet an observation is in order. While no doctrinal conflict seems to exist between *The City of the Sun* and his philosophical treatises on the problem of the community of women, Campanella exaggerates the inability of the human mind to attain knowledge of the natural law. Although it is true that the secondary precepts of the natural law are not as easy to grasp as the primary ones and may demand a certain amount of training, the high level of culture achieved by the inhabitants of the City of the Sun, evident from their accomplishments in many other fields, should enable them to understand the evils inherent in sexual promiscuity. Hence we do not agree with Campanella's statement that by the light of reason alone a philosopher cannot know that the community of women is against the natural law.

Another defect in Campanella's political theory is his whole attitude toward private property. He holds for the common ownership of goods in his study of an ideal republic as well as in other works of a more serious nature. Apparently he was convinced that private property is the greatest cause of social evils and that, to live better and more natural lives, men should return to the community system of the early Christians. It is the community of goods, insists Campanella, that is in accord with the natural law and not the system of private property.

Campanella's community system, however, is inspired by motives that are quite different from those of Marxist communism. Aside from this, he is completely unrealistic in proposing to extend to an entire nation and even to all mankind, as was his lifelong dream, a way of life that has proved effective only in small communities and with a very selective group, such as men and women dedicated to the religious life, who embrace it on a voluntary basis and from supernatural motives. It is inconceivable that the citizens of an entire nation, let alone all mankind, would renounce basic natural rights to their own possessions and submit to the privations that the system of community of goods involves unless forced to do so, as they are in communistic countries. Heroism may be expected of a few chosen men and women, but not of the community at large. This is what Campanella failed to realize.

It is true that private property can lead to abuses. However such abuses do not suppress the right to private property and its use, when this is demanded by the needs and aspirations of human nature. Abuses call for some control and limitations by the state in view of the common good, inasmuch as private property has to perform a social function; but the institution of private ownership as such must be preserved intact. On this basis Campanella's system of community of goods must be judged unrealistic and utopian as is his conception of the ideal republic in general.

In conclusion it may be asked: What is the purpose of *The City of the Sun?* Does the work have any practical value? The first question has received different answers. We believe that in writing his utopia Campanella wished to depict a republic that would be better than those conceived by philosophers who preceded him from Plato down to Thomas More and Jean Bodin.[6] He did not, and could not, intend to propose his ideal republic as a model for any state then in existence, simply because the conditions prevailing among the inhabitants of the City of the Sun could nowhere be verified. Nor could he have conceived his republic as a substitute for the theocratic state, for this is centered on the papacy and presupposes a well established Christianity. Yet— and this is the answer to the second question—many of the ideas expressed in *The City of the Sun* do have some practical value, since they contain the germs of social, political, and educational reforms that would be beneficial to the state. In this respect Campanella may be considered an original thinker and a forerunner of modern times.

While the ideal republic represents a state devised by philosophers without the aid of revelation, the theocratic state of the *Monarchia Messiae* is conceived on strictly theological grounds with reason and philosophy playing only a secondary and subsidiary role. The central theme of a universal monarchy headed by the Pope is so bold and so vast a project that one is not surprised that Campanella devotes several works to it and uses every opportunity to promote it. The theocratic monarchy represents the last stage of his political plans toward which his unceasing but fruitless efforts to reform society converged.[7] Unrealistic as the plan may be, it was not altogether inconceivable in the political climate of the time, when the papacy enjoyed enormous prestige and played an important role in the political life of the nations. It is in this perspective that the entire scheme of the *Monarchia Messiae* must be seen in order to judge it objectively.

To establish on a seemingly juridical basis the principle that the Pope is by right the supreme spiritual and temporal ruler of the world, Campanella begins by discussing the nature and meaning of absolute dominion and sovereignty. This, he says, belongs exclusively to God, and creatures share in it only to the extent that they are empowered to do so by God. Since the Pope is the Vicar of Christ and God's representative on earth, and since the government of one man is to be preferred to the government of many, it is only natural for the Pope to have all spiritual and temporal powers and for other princes to be subject to him as their supreme ruler. This is all the more true since Christ has established only one kingdom with a twofold power in the person of St. Peter and his legitimate successors.

The fallacy of this reasoning consists in maintaining that the temporal and spiritual powers must be joined together in one person and that this was Christ's intention in founding His Church. There is no evidence in the Gospels that Christ intended to confer on the head of His Church supreme power in temporal matters along with supreme spiritual power. All indications point in the opposite direction. In fact, many Scriptural texts emphasize the spiritual character of the Church and make a sharp distinction between the Church and the secular power, one being concerned with the eternal happiness of men and the other with their temporal welfare.[8] But aside from the teaching of Holy Scripture, Campanella seems to overlook the fact that Church and state are two perfect and distinct societies differing in origin, end, and intrinsic nature, and that each is independent of the other in its own order. It is true that, strictly speaking, absolute dominion belongs only to God and that there is no power that is not a participation in the divine power. But to infer from this that the Pope, as head of the Church, has a direct power over civil rulers in purely temporal matters is a farfetched and unwarranted conclusion. The superiority of the Church and of its end in the hierarchy of ends does not diminish the true sovereignty of the state *in suo ordine* nor alter its nature as a perfect society.[9] Campanella departs from the traditional scholastic doctrine when he asserts the Pope's supremacy over the secular rulers in matters within their jurisdiction. Yet he is not altogether inconsistent with his own teaching on the nature and purpose of the state, which he claims to exist primarily for the worship of God and man's eternal happiness.[10] In this case the end of the state and the end of the Church coincide, and the supremacy of the Pope over civil rulers is more easily understood because of the Pope's superiority in spiritual matters.

To support his theocratic theory Campanella has recourse to the doctrine of Christ the eternal Reason with no apparent success. No one will contest Christ's right to full sovereignty over men both in spiritual and temporal matters, and His power, if He chooses to use it, to transfer this right to His Vicar on earth, the Pope. But the question is whether by His incarnation He actually intended to assume and exercise the twofold power or to confine Himself to the exercise of the spiritual power alone. Again, did He actually choose to transfer the two powers to the head of His Church or to limit papal jurisdiction to spiritual things? Briefly, it is not a question *de iure* but a question *de facto,* and the facts, as evidenced by the Gospels and Christian tradition, speak against Campanella.[11]

The two theses that Campanella attempts to prove in the *Discorsi della libertà,* namely, that nowhere is there greater freedom than within the papal monarchy and that it is better to be subject to a Church ruler than to a secular prince, show Campanella's high concept of the papacy despite the many restrictions to which his own freedom had been subjected by Church authorities. If it is true that the occasion for the *Discorsi* may have been dissemination in Rome of an anonymous libel denouncing the Church government,[12] Campanella's defense of the papal state becomes even more meaningful inasmuch as he places the good of the Church over any personal consideration. It was his love for the Church and his constant dedication to the ideal of a universal papal monarchy that led him to stigmatize as "political heresy" and "theological error" any doubt about the advantages of living under a Church ruler.

The *Discorsi universali del governo ecclesiastico* are a further illustration of Campanella's zeal for the reform of the Church government. His observation that the Church cannot be governed in the same way as the state because of the different traits that characterize the two societies manifests profound knowledge of the weaknesses of contemporary papal politics. His emphasis on the use of spiritual weapons rather than secular ones for the conversion of the world is also an indication of the importance he attaches to spiritual values as opposed to purely material ones. Obviously, he is overly optimistic and somewhat naive in believing that the simple preaching of well trained monks could win the entire world over to Christ. Yet it can hardly be denied that his pioneering efforts in promoting the idea of a college for the training of future missionaries were inspired by highly laudable motives.[13] His suggestion that a council of all Christian rulers be established in Rome for the discussion and solution of the political problems relating to the entire Christian world is another instance of his ingenious and foreseeing political mind. On the other hand, one can hardly share his view that the Pope's control of Italy is the best guarantee for his control over the whole world. The very nature of the Church as a spiritual power seems to rule out world domination by the Popes.

In the *Quod reminiscentur* Campanella's missionary spirit is particularly noticeable. Conceived by the author as a manual for future missionaries, this work is intimately connected with his other political writings and his philosophical system as a whole.[14] By calling it "the epitome and completion of all his studies," Campanella clearly indicated the general scope toward which the philosophical endeavors of his whole life had been directed. One cannot fail to notice how his passionate appeal to Pope Paul V to answer the call of all nations and help them find their way back to God has a striking similarity to St. Bernard's earlier plea to Pope Eugene IV, "From all over the world peoples cry out to you."[15] Indeed, Campanella was convinced that only the Pope could save the world from possible catastrophe. The *Quod reminiscentur* with its inspiring messages to the world leaders may be considered Campanella's spiritual legacy. It is in the light of this work and the *Monarchia Messiae* that his political thought must be viewed, for it is the vision of all mankind united in one fold under one shepherd that gives meaning and unity to his entire political system.

Conclusion

With the exposition and critical evaluation of Campanella's moral theory our study has come to an end. The objective of this work, to give an account of the fundamental positions of Tommaso Campanella in the field of philosophy and to pass judgment on them in the light of sound philosophical principles, has been achieved.

The journey through the maze of Campanellian writings has not been an easy one; and the historians of philosophy, with the exception of a few leading scholars, have made it even more difficult. Yet comfort has been found in the thought that on almost every issue we have been able to support our position with so many original texts that there is little doubt concerning the correct interpretation of Campanella's thought. This is not to assert that the last word on the subject has been said. On many controversial issues the lead of competent historians has been followed. What is meant, is that no stand has been taken that lacks the support of Campanella himself. Whenever a doubt arose as to the exact meaning of apparently conflicting statements, an attempt was made to clear the way for an objective interpretation in the light of other relevant passages to show their agreement with Campanella's thought as a whole.

The results of this inquiry have occasionally led to conclusions that conflict with those of some writers who were perhaps too hasty in their judgments or did not have the opportunity to use all the primary sources now available. In some cases, if they consulted the primary sources, they apparently did so with the set purpose of confirming their own preconceived theories. This is particularly true of certain idealistic thinkers who pretend to find in Campanella a forerunner of their own systems. The same must be said of the Marxist historians who seem to take special pleasure in presenting the Renaissance monk as an early defender of Marxist communism.

This study has also made it clear that, although Campanella subscribed in some degree to naturalistic doctrines current in his time, especially in his earlier writings, he never went so far as to renounce any of the basic truths of the Christian faith. Far from that, he fought throughout his life for the return of all Christians to the Church of Rome, which in turn he wanted to reform and bring closer to the ideal set for it by Christ. It is in this sense that Campanella may be called the philosopher of the Catholic restoration.[1]

However, one would go too far in making him the genuine representative of traditional scholastic philosophy, no matter which school
one may prefer to consider. He does not conform to the Thomistic
school, which he blames on many counts for betraying St. Thomas's
thought and for its close adherence to the pagan philosophy of Aristotle. Nor does he belong, properly speaking, to the Augustinian
school, although Augustinianism greatly contributed to the shaping
of his thought. Campanella's doctrine is truly syncretic. In it elements
of different schools of philosophy are fused to produce a unique and
original synthesis, with principles drawn mainly from Augustinian,
Thomistic, and naturalistic streams of thought.

Such is the general character of Campanella's philosophy. What of
his place in the history of philosophy or, to put it in a slightly different
way, did he have any definite influence upon succeeding philosophers?
This question has been discussed at some length by Blanchet,[2] Cassirer,[3] and De Mattei;[4] and others have touched briefly upon it.[5] To
summarize the results of their findings, we may say that apart from
Campanella's relationship to Descartes, to which we have given extended consideration, perhaps the philosopher most directly influenced
by Campanella's thought was Leibniz, who held him in great esteem,
mentioned him repeatedly in his works, and quoted him in support of his own doctrine on God and the theory of monads.[6] The influence of Campanella upon Giambattista Vico is not to be disre-
garded,[7] and some of his doctrines may have affected the thought of
Gassendi and Spinoza.[8] Whether Malebranche and Berkeley owe anything to Campanella is not clear, since they may all be indebted to
the same sources for the theories they hold in common.[9]

Whatever the complete extent of Campanella's influence may be, it is
not proportionate to the number, length, and quality of his writings.
Nor is his reputation comparable to that of other thinkers who have
gained a greater name in the history of philosophy but are inferior
to him in many respects. The reasons for this apparent neglect and
discrimination on the part of historians are manifold. Some are intrinsic to Campanella's system, which lacks solidity of doctrine and
unity of thought; and some are due to external factors and circumstances which he himself helped to create. Furthermore, Campanella
never held a chair in any school or university where he could form
disciples to continue his thought and make it known to the chief cultural circles of his day. In addition, he was confined to prison for the
best years of his life, with a consequent loss of reputation and prestige

and with the added difficulty of disseminating his ideas or even obtaining permission for the publication of his works.

It is the writer's opinion that lack of interest in Campanella, both as man and as thinker, can be traced principally to conflicts between his views and the personal convictions of historians of philosophy. Catholic historians are evidently disturbed by the unrestrained freedom—often with manifest lack of understanding—with which Campanella criticizes certain well established doctrines of scholastic philosophy and for which he offers very poor substitutes. Non-Catholic writers, on the other hand, may well be offended by Campanella's continuous attacks on Protestantism as the source of many evils within Christianity, and also for his doctrine of a universal monarchy headed by the Pope.

In his *Historia de la filosofía* Cardinal González suggests an additional reason why many writers do not pay as much attention to Campanella as, for example, to Bacon and Descartes. He holds that in spite of his shortcomings, Campanella was always faithful to the Christian spirit in his principles, if not in his conclusions, and constantly repudiated the rationalism on which the doctrines of Bacon and Descartes were based.[10]

Be that as it may, indifference to Campanella is now being replaced by a growing interest in his thought and personality. Scholars of different persuasions have felt a need to re-evaluate his entire work on a more objective basis and in the light of more recent findings. It was with this intention that the present work was undertaken. It is the writer's hope that his efforts will help promote understanding of a complex and fascinating figure of the Italian Renaissance who for centuries has perplexed historians of philosophy.

NOTES

INTRODUCTION

1 Etienne Gilson, "Notes sur Campanella," *Annales de philosophie chrétienne*, XV (1912-13), 491.

CHAPTER ONE

1 The following works, arranged in alphabetical order, have been used as basic sources for the preparation of this chapter: Jacob Burckhardt, *The Civilization of the Renaissance in Italy* (2 vols.; New York: Harper Torchbooks, 1958); Cleto Carbonara, *Il secolo XV* (Milan: Bocca, 1943); E. Cassirer, P. O. Kristeller, and J. H. Randall, Jr., *The Renaissance Philosophy of Man* (Chicago: University of Chicago Press, 1948); Vittorio Cian, *Umanesimo e rinascimento* (Florence: Le Monnier, 1941); Frederick Copleston, S.J., *A History of Philosophy* (Westminster, Md.: The Newman Press, 1953), III, 207-334; Guido De Ruggiero, *Storia della filosofia*, Part III, Vols. I-II, *Rinascimento, riforma e controriforma* (Bari: Laterza, 1930); Giovanni Di Napoli, "La filosofia nei secoli XV-XVI," in *Storia della filosofia*, ed. Cornelio Fabro (Rome: Coletti, 1954), pp. 299-389; Wallace K. Ferguson, *The Renaissance in Historical Thought: Five Centuries of Interpretation* (Boston: Houghton Mifflin, 1948); Francesco Fiorentino, *Bernardino Telesio, ossia studi storici su l'idea della natura nel risorgimento italiano* (2 vols.; Florence: Successori Le Monnier, 1872-74); Eugenio Garin, *La filosofia* (2 vols.; Milan: Vallardi, 1947); Giovanni Gentile, *Il pensiero italiano del rinascimento* (3d ed. rev. and enlarged; Florence: Sansoni, 1940); Carlo Giacon, *La seconda scolastica* (3 vols.; Milan: Bocca, 1944-50); Myron P. Gilmore, *The World of Humanism, 1453-1517* (New York: Harper, 1952); Paul O. Kristeller, *Renaissance Thought: The Classic, Scholastic, and Humanist Strains* (New York: Harper Torchbooks, 1961); Francesco Olgiati, *L'anima dell'umanesimo e del rinascimento* (Milan: "Vita e Pensiero," 1924); Augustin Renaudet, *Humanisme et renaissance* (Geneva: Droz, 1958); Giuseppe Saitta, *Il pensiero italiano nell'umanesimo e nel rinascimento* (3 vols.; Bologna: Zuffi, 1949-51); Bertrando Spaventa, *Rinascimento, riforma, controriforma e altri saggi critici* (Venice: "La Nuova Italia," 1928); Giuseppe Toffanin, *La fine dell'umanesimo* (Turin: Bocca, 1920); The same, *Che cosa fu l'umanesimo?* (Florence: Sansoni, 1929); The same, *Storia dell'umanesimo* (3d ed.; Bologna: Zanichelli, 1943; enlarged in 3 vols.; Bologna: Zanichelli, 1950); Vladimiro Zabughin, *Storia del rinascimento cristiano in Italia* (Milan: Treves, 1924).
2 This is, for example, the opinion of Gentile: "L'Umanesimo è la preparazione o, se si vuole, l'inizio del Rinascimento." *Il pensiero italiano*, p. 17.
3 Cf. Bertrando Spaventa, *La filosofia italiana nelle sue relazioni con la filosofia europea* (3d ed.; Bari: Laterza, 1926), p. 85: "Campanella è l'ultimo filosofo del Risorgimento."
4 For a description of the traits that distinguish Renaissance philosophy from Humanism cf. the articles on "Rinascimento" and "Umanesimo" by Cleto Carbonara in *Enciclopedia filosofica* (Florence: Sansoni, 1957), Vol. IV, cols. 134-41 and 1373-79. See also Ernest H. Wilkins, "On the Nature and Extent of the Italian Renaissance," *Italica*, XXVII (1950), 67-76.

5 See A. Campana, "The Origin of the Word 'Humanist,'" *Journal of the Warburg and Courtauld Institutes,* IX (1946), 60-73; Walter Rüegg, *Cicero und der Humanismus* (Zurich: Rheinverlag, 1946), 1ff. Cf. also Paul O. Kristeller, "The Place of Classical Humanism in Renaissance Thought," *Journal of the History of Ideas,* IV (1943), 59-63; Roberto Weiss, *The Dawn of Humanism in Italy* (London: Lewis, 1947); Wallace K. Ferguson, "The Revival of Classical Antiquity or the First Century of Humanism: A Reappraisal," *The Canadian Historical Association, Report of the Annual Meeting Held at Ottawa, June 12-15, 1957,* pp. 13-30.

6 For a history of the concept of "Renaissance" see Delio Cantimori, "Sulla storia del concetto di Rinascimento," *Annali R. Scuola Normale Superiore di Pisa,* 1932.

7 The nature of the Renaissance as a philosophical movement and its relationship to the Middle Ages have been the object of many studies. Arranged in alphabetical order, some of them are: Hans Baron, *The Crisis of the Early Italian Renaissance,* (2 vols.; Princeton, N.J.: Princeton University Press, 1955); William J. Bouwsma, *The Interpretation of Renaissance Humanism* (Washington, D. C.: Service Center for Teachers of History, 1959); Ernst Cassirer, *Das Erkenntnisproblem in der Philosophie und Wissenschaft der neueren Zeit* (Berlin: Verlag Bruno Cassirer, 1922); The same, *Individuum und Kosmos in der Philosophie der Renaissance* (Berlin: Teubner, 1927); D. Durand, H. Baron, and others, "Discussion on the Renaissance," *Journal of the History of Ideas,* IV (1943), 1-74; Wallace K. Ferguson, "Humanist Views of the Renaissance," *American Historical Review,* XLV (1939-40), 1-28; the same, "The Interpretation of the Renaissance: Suggestions for a Synthesis," *Journal of the History of Ideas,* XII (1951), 483-95; Etienne Gilson, "Humanisme médiéval et Renaissance," in his *Les idées et les lettres* (Paris: Vrin, 1932), pp. 171-96; Tinsley Helton (ed.), *The Renaissance: A Reconsideration of the Theories and Interpretations of the Age* (Madison: The University of Wisconsin Press, 1961; Johan Huizinga, "Das Problem der Renaissance," in his *Wege der Kulturgeschichte,* trans. Werner Kaegi (Munich: Drei-Masken Verlag, 1930), pp. 89-139; The same, *The Waning of the Middle Ages* (New York: Doubleday, 1954); Paul O. Kristeller and John R. Randall, Jr., "The Study of the Philosophies of the Renaissance," *Journal of the History of Ideas,* II (1941), 449-96; Paul O. Kristeller, *Studies in Renaissance Thought and Letters* (Rome: Edizioni di storia e letteratura, 1956); Henry S. Lucas, "The Renaissance: A Review of Some Views," *The Catholic Historical Review,* XXXVIII (1952-53), 397-409; Theodor E. Mommsen, *Medieval and Renaissance Studies,* ed. Eugene F. Rice (Ithaca, N. Y.: Cornell University Press, 1959); Berthold L. Ullman, *Studies in the Italian Renaissance* (Rome: Edizioni di storia e letteratura, 1955); Herbert Weisinger, "The Renaissance Theory of the Reaction against the Middle Ages as a Cause of the Renaissance," *Speculum,* XX (1945), 461-67.

8 "Habent Aristotelem pro Christo, Averroem pro S. Petro, Alexandrum pro S. Paulo." Quoted in Olgiati, *L'anima dell'umanesimo,* p. 527.

9 For a detailed account of the Averroistic school of Padua cf. Erminio Troilo, *Averroismo e aristotelismo padovano* (Padua: Cedam, 1939); Bruno Nardi, *Saggi sull'aristotelismo padovano dal secolo XIV al XVI* (Florence: Sansoni, 1958).

10 Garin, *La filosofia,* II, 39.

11 The Alexandrist school, with special emphasis on the teaching of Pomponazzi, has been studied by Francesco Fiorentino in his work, *Pietro Pomponazzi. Studi storici su la scuola bolognese e padovana del secolo XVI* (Florence: Le Monnier, 1868). See also Andrew H. Douglas (eds. Charles Douglas and R. P. Hardie), *The Philosophy and Psychology of Pietro Pomponazzi* (Cambridge, England: The University Press, 1910); Bruno Nardi, *Studi su Pietro Pomponazzi* (Florence: Le Monnier, 1965).

12 This is the opinion of Emilia Verga in her study, "L'immortalità dell'anima nel pensiero del card. Gaetano," *Rivista di filosofia neoscolastica*, Supplement to Vol. XXVII (1935), 21-46. For more details on the Thomistic school at the time of the Renaissance cf. Carlo Giacon, *La seconda scolastica*, I, 37-162.

13 Kristeller, *Renaissance Thought*, p. 38.

14 An objective presentation of these views can be found in Efrem Bettoni, O.F.M., *Duns Scotus: The Basic Principles of His Philosophy*, trans. and ed. Bernardine Bonansea, O.F.M. (Washington, D. C.: The Catholic University of America Press, 1961). For a better understanding of the Thomistic school, especially during the nineteenth century, see the present writer's study, "Pioneers of the Nineteenth-Century Scholastic Revival in Italy," *The New Scholasticism*, XXVIII (1954), 1-37.

15 Kristeller, *Renaissance Thought*, p. 48.

16 For a study of the philosophy of Marsilio Ficino and the Italian Renaissance Platonism the following works may be consulted: Giuseppe Saitta, *Marsilio Ficino e la filosofia dell'umanesimo* (3d ed. rev.; Bologna: Fiammenghi e Nanni, 1954); Nesca A. Robb, *Neoplatonism of the Italian Renaissance* (London: Allen and Unwin, 1935); Bohdan Kieszkowski, *Studi sul platonismo del Rinascimento in Italia* (Florence: Sansoni, 1936); Paul O. Kristeller, *The Philosophy of Marsilio Ficino*, trans. Virginia Conant (New York: Columbia University Press, 1943); Michele Schiavone, *Problemi filosofici in Marsilio Ficino* (Milan: Marzorati, 1957).

17 Paul O. Kristeller, "Renaissance Philosophies," in *A History of Philosophical Systems*, ed. Vergilius Ferm (New York: The Philosophical Library, 1950), p. 234. For the thought of Giovanni Pico della Mirandola see Eugenio Garin, *Giovanni Pico della Mirandola* (Florence: Le Monnier, 1937); Avery Dulles, S.J., *Princeps Concordiae: Pico della Mirandola and the Scholastic Tradition* (Cambridge, Mass.: Harvard University Press, 1941); Giuseppe Barone, *L'umanesimo filosofico di Giovanni Pico della Mirandola* (Milan: Gastaldi, 1949); Pierre Marie Cordier, *Jean Pic de la Mirandole, ou la plus pure figure de l'humanisme chrétien* (Paris: Nouvelles Editions Debresse, 1958); Various Authors, *L'opera e il pensiero di Giovanni Pico della Miraandola nella storia dell'umanesimo* (2 vols.; Florence: Istituto nazionale di studi sul Rinascimento, 1965).

18 A very good synthesis of Cusanus's philosophy can be found in Copleston, *A History of Philosophy*, III, 231-47. For a more extensive study see: Henry Bett, *Nicholas of Cusa* (London: Methuen, 1932); Paolo Rotta, *Il cardinale Nicolò da Cusa: la vita e il pensiero* (Milan: "Vita e Pensiero," 1928); The same, *Niccolò Cusano* (Milan: Bocca, 1942); Renata Gradi, *Il pensiero del Cusano* (Padua: Cedam, 1941); Maurice P. de Gandillac, *La philosophie de Nicolas de Cues* (Paris: Aubier, 1941); Peter Mennicken, *Nikolaus von Kues* (Trier: Cusanus Verlag, 1950).

19 Cf. Kristeller, "Humanism and Scholasticism in the Italian Renaissance," in *Renaissance Thought,* pp. 92-119 *passim.*

20 Copleston, *A History of Philosophy,* III, 250.

21 The philosophy of Bernardino Telesio has been the object of many studies, among which are: Francesco Fiorentino, *Bernardino Telesio, op. cit.;* Giovanni Gentile, *Bernardino Telesio* (Bari: Laterza, 1911); Erminio Troilo, *Bernardino Telesio* (2d ed.; Modena: Formiggini, 1924); Neil Van Deusen, *Telesio, the First of the Moderns* (New York: Columbia University Press, 1932); The same, "The Place of Telesio in the History of Philosophy," *The Philosophical Review,* XLIV (1935), 417-34; Nicola Abbagnano, *Telesio* (Milan: Bocca, 1941); Giacomo Soleri, *Telesio* (Brescia: "La Scuola," 1944); Giovanni Di Napoli, "Fisica e metafisica in Bernardino Telesio," *Rassegna di scienze filosofiche,* VI (1953), 22-69.

22 Referring to Patrizi's *Discussiones peripateticae,* Bruno says: "Sterco di pedanti, mostra aver molto del bestiale e dell'asino," sì che basta leggere il suo libro per vedere "in quanta pazzia e presuntuosa vanità può precipitare e profondare un abito pedantesco." Quoted in Garin, *La filosofia,* II, 132-33.

23 A presentation of Patrizi's thought can be found in Fiorentino, *Bernardino Telesio,* I, 364-414; II, 1-19; 365-91; De Ruggiero, *Rinascimento, riforma e controriforma,* II, 105-109; Garin, *La filosofia,* II, 131-34; Saitta, *Il pensiero italiano,* II, 521-67.

24 Cf. Augusto Guzzo, "Giordano Bruno," *Enciclopedia filosofica,* 1957, Vol. I, col. 814.

25 According to William K. Wright, *A History of Philosophy* (New York: Macmillan, 1941), pp. 31-33, Bruno seems to have wavered between three different interpretations of the notion of God and his relation to the world. One of these interpretations is neo-Platonic. The world is an emanation from the Deity on which it depends, just as light was thought by Plotinus to emanate from the sun without affecting or in any way diminishing the power of the sun. The second interpretation is that the Deity is at once the efficient cause of the world and its inward essential principle. In this conception God is immanent in the world and yet transcendent to it. The third interpretation advanced by Bruno is similar to what is now called "pluralism." The world would consist of an infinite number of ultimate individual units or "monads" which are at once spiritual and material in their nature. The absolutely small "minima," as well as our own souls and God, are immortal. Moreover, each minimum is included within larger units without losing its own distinctive identity, while all are included within God.

Much has been written on Bruno's philosophy. Here are the principal works: Erminio Troilo, *La filosofia di Giordano Bruno* (Vol. I, Turin: Bocca, 1907; Vol. II, Rome: Artero, 1914); Leonardo Olschki, *Giordano Bruno* (Bari: Laterza, 1927); Edoardo Fenu, *Giordano Bruno* (Brescia: Morcelliana, 1936); Giovanni Gentile, *Giordano Bruno e il pensiero del Rinascimento* (3d ed. rev.; new title: *Il pensiero italiano del Rinascimento,* Florence: Sansoni, 1940); Antonio Corsano, *Il pensiero di Giordano Bruno nel suo svolgimento storico* (Florence: Sansoni, 1940); Luigi Cicuttini, *Giordano Bruno* (Milan: "Vita e Pensiero," 1950); Dorothea W. Singer, *Giordano Bruno; His Life and Thought* (New York: Schuman, 1950); Gerardo Fraccari, *Giordano Bruno* (Milan: Bocca, 1951); Erminio Troilo, *Prospetto, sintesi, commentario della filosofia di Giordano*

Bruno (Rome: Accademia Nazionale dei Lincei, 1951); Irwin I. Horowitz, *The Renaissance Philosophy of Giordano Bruno* (New York: Coleman-Ross, 1952); Augusto Guzzo, *Giordano Bruno* (Turin: Edizioni di Filosofia, 1960).

26 George H. Sabine, *A History of Political Theory* (3d ed.; New York: Holt, 1961), p. 338.

27 *The Prince,* chap. XV, trans. N. H. Thomson, in *The Harvard Classics* (New York: Collier, 1910).

28 *Ibid.,* chap. XVII.

29 *Ibid.,* chap. XXV.

30 *Ibid.*

31 *Discourses on the First Ten Books of Titus Livius,* I, 12; trans. Christian E. Detmold, in *The Historical, Political, and Diplomatic Writings of Niccolò Machiavelli* (4 vols.; Boston: Osgood, 1891).

32 Sabine, *A History of Political Theory,* p. 351.

33 For a comprehensive study of Machiavelli's political thought the following works are suggested: Pasquale Villari, *The Life and Times of Niccolò Machiavelli,* trans. Linda Villari (2 vols.; rev. ed.; London: Unwin, 1892); Luigi Russo, *Machiavelli* (Rome: Tumminelli, 1945); John H. Whitfield, *Machiavelli* (Oxford: Blackwell, 1947); Goffredo Quadri, *Nicolò Machiavelli e la costruzione politica della scienza morale* (Florence: "La Nuova Italia," 1948); Achille Norsa, *Machiavelli* (Milan: Genio, 1948); John K. Ryan, "Niccolò Machiavelli: The Prince," in *The Great Books: A Christian Appraisal* (New York: The Devin-Adair Co., 1949), I, 50-59; Pierre Mesnard, *L'essor de la philosophie politique au XVIᵉ siècle* (2d ed.; Paris: Vrin, 1951); Herbert Butterfield, *The Statecraft of Machiavelli* (New York: Macmillan, 1956); John W. Allen, *A History of Political Thought in the Sixteenth Century* (London: Methuen, 1957); Federico Chabod, *Machiavelli and the Renaissance,* trans. David Moore (Cambridge, Mass.: Harvard University Press, 1958); Leo Strauss, *Thoughts on Machiavelli* (Glencoe, Ill.: Free Press, 1958); George H. Sabine, *A History of Political Theory* (3d ed.; New York: Holt, 1961), pp. 331-53; Giuseppe Prezzolini, *Machiavelli,* trans. Gioconda Savini (New York: Farrar, Straus and Giroux, 1967).

CHAPTER TWO

1 Cf. Tommaso Campanella, *Lettere,* ed. Vincenzo Spampanato (Bari: Laterza, 1927), p. 402: "io vivo come scrivo."

2 Cf. Tommaso Campanella, *De libris propriis et recta ratione studendi syntagma,* ed. Vincenzo Spampanato (Milan: Bestetti e Tumminelli, 1927).

3 Ernestus Salomon Cyprianus, *Vita et philosophia Th. Campanellae* (Amsterdam: Apud Christianum Petzoldum, 1705). We shall quote from the reprint of the second edition (Traiecti ad Rhenum: Apud Stephanum Neaulme, 1741).

4 Jacobus Échard, "Vita Campanellae," *Scriptores Ordinis Praedicatorum,* II, 505-521. Reproduced by E. S. Cyprianus in the second edition of his work. Cf. Cyprianus, *op. cit.,* Appendix III, pp. 90ff. It is to this Appendix that we shall refer for Échard's account of Campanella.

5 Cf. Michele Baldacchini, *Vita e filosofia di Tommaso Campanella* (2 vols.; Naples: A. Manuzio, 1840-43). Baldacchini defends Campanella against groundless accusations made by Pietro Giannone, whose political ideas prevented him

from passing a fair judgment on a man holding views different from his own. Cf. Pietro Giannone, *Dell'istoria civile del regno di Napoli libri XL* (4 vols.; Naples: N. Naso, 1723).

6 Louise Colet, *Oeuvres choisies de Campanella, précédées d'une notice* (Paris: Lavigne, 1844).

7 *Ibid.*, Avant-propos, p.1.

8 *Opere di Tommaso Campanella scelte, ordinate ed annotate da Alessandro d'Ancona, e precedute da un discorso del medesimo sulla vita e le dottrine dell'autore* (2 vols. Turin: Cugini Pomba, 1854).

9 Cf. Bertrando Spaventa, *Rinascimento, riforma, controriforma e altri saggi critici* (Venice: "La Nuova Italia," 1928), pp. 1-122.

10 Domenico Berti, "Lettere inedite di T. Campanella e catalogo dei suoi scritti," *Atti della R. Accademia dei Lincei* (Rome, 1878); *Nuovi documenti su T. Campanella tratti dal carteggio di Giovanni Fabbri* (Rome: Tipografia Bodoniana, 1881). Berti's catalogue of Campanella's works has been judged by Luigi Firpo ·as confused, very incorrect, and worse than that of Échard. Cf. Luigi Firpo, *Bibliografia degli scritti di Tommaso Campanella* (Turin: V. Bona, 1940), p. 7.

11 Luigi Amabile, *Fra Tommaso Campanella. La sua congiura, i suoi processi e la sua pazzia* (3 vols.; Naples: Morano, 1882); *Fra Tommaso Campanella nei castelli di Napoli, in Roma ed in Parigi* (2 vols.; Naples: Morano, 1887). They will be quoted henceforth as *Congiura* and *Castelli*, respectively.

12 Jan Kvačala, *Thomas Campanella, ein Reformer der ausgehenden Renaissance* (Berlin: Trowitzsch und Sohn, 1909). Kvačala is also known for his contribution to the Campanellian bibliography. His studies are not always accurate and have now been surpassed.

13 Enrico Carusi, "Nuovi documenti sui processi di T. Campanella," *Giornale critico della filosofia italiana*, VIII (1927), 321-59.

14 Rodolfo De Mattei, *Studi campanelliani* (Florence: Sansoni, 1934).

15 Luigi Firpo, *Ricerche campanelliane* (Florence: Sansoni, 1947).

16 Léon Blanchet, *Campanella* (Paris: Alcan, 1920). The work of Blanchet was until a little over two decades ago the best known study on Campanella.

17 Cecilia Dentice D'Accadia, *Tommaso Campanella* (Florence: Vallecchi, 1921). This monograph is not a scholarly work. Its main contribution consists in a list of 208 works on Campanella which is far from being complete. Paolo Treves in his work *La filosofia politica di Tommaso Campanella* (Bari: Laterza, 1930) added 244 entries without filling all the gaps.

18 Giovanni Di Napoli, *Tommaso Campanella, filosofo della restaurazione cattolica* (Padua: Cedam, 1947). Di Napoli's work is the most comprehensive study on Campanella. The author shows a thorough knowledge of all the primary and secondary sources as well as a remarkable ability to organize the vast mass of material at his disposal.

19 Romano Amerio, *Campanella* (Brescia: "La Scuola," 1947). In this work the author makes use of the results of several years of studies on Campanella that appeared in various periodicals, especially the *Rivista di filosofia neoscolastica* of the Sacred Heart University of Milan. Amerio shows a penetrating insight into Campanella's thought, which he presents with clarity and rare competence. He deserves special credit for his edition of the *Theologia*, of which several volumes have already been published.

20 Firpo is well known for his biographical and bibliographical contributions in the field of Campanellian studies. In addition to his *Bibliografia degli scritti di Tommaso Campanella, op. cit.*, which contains a critical account of all Campanella's works, his introduction to the first volume of the critical edition of *Tutte le opere di Tommaso Campanella* (Milan: Mondadori, 1954) is particularly valuable. It presents the main features of Campanella as a thinker and historical figure (pp. XI-LXII), and has a detailed chronological report on Campanella's life and works (pp. LXIII-XCIX). Among Firpo's other contributions in the field of Campanellian bibliography the following deserve to be mentioned: "Contributo alla bibliografia campanelliana," *Rivista di storia della filosofia*, III (1948), 183-211, which contains all Campanellian literature from 1930 to 1947 in continuation to the previous catalogues of Dentice D'Accadia and Treves; "Cinquant'anni di studi sul Campanella (1901-1950)," *Rinascimento*, VI (1955), 209-348, with 761 entries, including those of the preceding study; "Campanella nel Settecento," *Rinascimento*, IV (1953), 105-154, with 172 entries, also printed in the form of extract (Florence: Sansoni, 1953); "Campanella nel secolo XIX," *Calabria nobilissima*, VI (1952), 235-42; VII (1953), 31-38, 75-82, 193-202; VIII (1954), 11-24, 125-33; IX (1955), 104-119; X (1956), 42-62, with a total of 502 entries, also printed in the form of extract (Naples, 1956); "Un decennio di studi sul Campanella (1951-1960)," *Studi secenteschi*, I (1960), 125-64, with 213 entries.

For Campanella's bibliography in the United States of America cf. Francesco Grillo, *Tommaso Campanella in America: A Critical Bibliography and a Profile* (New York: S. F. Vanni, 1954). It contains 209 entries for the years 1794 to 1954; the same, *A Supplement to the Critical Bibliography* above mentioned (New York: S. F. Vanni, 1957), with 91 entries, six of which are revisions of works previously listed. Grillo misrepresents the present writer's interpretation of Campanella's thought, and shows little knowledge of Campanella's philosophy.

21 *Syntagma*, p. 11.

22 *Ibid.*, p. 12.

23 *Ibid.*

24 Amabile, *Congiura*, I, p. 11. It is reported that after a heated argument with his professors, one of Campanella's classmates warned him, "Campanella, Campanella, you will not end up happily." *Ibid.*

25 *Phil. sens. dem.*, Praef., p. 1.

26 Th. Campanella, *Disputationum in quatuor partes suae philosophiae realis libri quatuor: Quaestiones physiologicae* (Paris: Typographia D. Houssaye, 1637), p. 513: "Quadam nocte in adolescentia mea eas [rationes pro immortalitate animae] perpendens quam fragiles sint, plorare coepi."

27 *Phil. sens. dem.*, Praef., p. 4: "summopere laetatus sum quod sotium haberem, vel ducem cui dicta mea apponam."

28 *Syntagma*, p. 13.

29 Bernardini Telesii, *De rerum natura iuxta propria principia*, ed. Vincenzo Spampanato (3 vols.; Vol. I, Modena, 1910; Vol. II, Genoa, 1913; Vol. III, Rome, 1923).

30 *Phil. sens. dem.*, p. 4.

31 *Syntagma*, p. 13; *Phil. sens. dem.*, p. 4.

32 Cf. Échard, "Vita Campanellae," in Cyprianus, *op. cit.*, p. 92.

33 Jacobus A. Marta, *Pugnaculum Aristotelis adversus principia B. Telesii* (Rome: Typis Barth. Bonfandini, 1587).

34 It is interesting to note the contempt with which Campanella speaks of G. A. Marta: "Pervenitque ad manus eorum liber quidam scioli Peripatetici Iacobi Antonii Martae, de utroque iure, Philosophia et Theologia se iactantis, et nullam veritatem scientis. . . Non quod fuerit dignus homuncio ut apud pugnas Philosophorum nominetur, etc. . . ." *Phil. sens. dem.*, Praef., p. 5.

35 *Ibid.*

36 Th. Campanella, *Philosophia sensibus demonstrata et in octo disputationes distincta* (Naples: Apud Horatium Salvianum, 1591).

37 *Ibid.*, Praef., p. 14. The book was published two years after, thus marking the beginning of Campanella's career as a writer that—as his confrere Échard puts it—came to an end only with his last breath. Cf. Échard, "Vita Campanellae," in Cyprianus, *op. cit.*, p. 92.

38 *Phil. sens. dem.*, p. 6.

39 *Ibid.*, pp. 7-8.

40 *Ibid.*, p. 10.

41 Cf. Cyprianus, *op. cit.*, pp. 4-5, for a detailed report on the legend of Campanella's relationship with the Jewish rabbi. See also Amabile, *Congiura*, I, 18-20, for a critical evaluation of the legend.

42 It was lost with other treatises by Campanella. Amabile, *Congiura*, I, 40.

43 *Syntagma*, p. 14. There are two editions of Campanella's *De sensu rerum et magia* and one critical edition of the Italian version *Del senso delle cose e della magia*, also written by Campanella. The latter was edited by Antonio Bruers (Bari: Laterza, 1925) with the variants from the codices and the two Latin editions.

44 This is the *Metaphysicae novae exordium*, which was later developed into the most important of Campanella's works, *Universalis philosophiae, seu metaphysicarum rerum, iuxta propria dogmata, partes tres, libri 18* (Paris: Apud Dionysium Langlois, 1638). Cf. Firpo, *Ricerche campanelliane, op. cit.*, pp. 76-77, for information about the publisher, who does not appear on the front page.

45 Cf. Syntagma, pp. 14-18, for the above information.

46 Cf. *Lettere*, p. 107: "Quinquies citatus in iudicium, primo caussam dixi interrogantibus: 'Quomodo literas scit, cum non didicerit? ergone demonium habes?' At ego respondi me plus olei quam ipsi vini consumsisse; et mihi ab eis dictum fuisse sacra suscipienti: 'Accipe Spiritum sanctum.' De quo certi sumus quod docet omnia, teste Ioanne; de demone autem incerti unde acceperim, et stultos esse illos qui, in se hunc spiritum non sentientes, negant aliis, quod dant et tribuunt diabolo sapientiam caeteraque dona Dei." Cf. also *Syntagma*, p. 17. The belief that Campanella was possessed by an evil spirit on account of his unusual talents later spread among the people in Calabria. They even thought they had found out the place where the spirit was residing, namely, in Campanella's fingernails. The reason for this strange belief was Campanella's habit of looking at his nails. Cf. Amabile, *Congiura*, I, 158.

47 The Provincial's sentence on Campanella was found by Vincenzo Spampanato in the *Registro di Provincia in Napoli*, "Monasteri soppressi," Vol. 582, c. 189 r. Cf. Di Napoli, *op. cit.*, p. 113, where the text of the sentence is reproduced in its entirety.

48 Cf. T. Campanella, *Del senso delle cose e della magia*, ed. Bruers, p. 31; *Syntagma*, p. 17.
49 *Lettere*, p. 107.
50 *Syntagma*, p. 18.
51 *Syntagma*, pp. 19-20.
52 *Lettere*, p. 107.
53 The documents on Campanella's trials, edited by Msgr. Enrico Carusi, are the principal source of information for Campanella's dealings with the Holy Office. Cf. Carusi, "Nuovi documenti," *op. cit.*
54 The *Compendium de rerum natura* was edited by Tobias Adami under the title *Prodromus philosophiae instaurandae* (Frankfort: I. Bringerus, 1617). The *Epilogo magno* was edited by Carmelo Ottaviano (Rome: R. Accademia d'Italia, 1939). Cf. Firpo, *Ricerche campanelliane, op. cit.*, pp. 100-103, for his critical remarks on Ottaviano's edition of the *Epilogo magno*.
55 The *Poetica* was edited by Luigi Firpo (Rome: R. Accademia d'Italia, 1944).
56 Cf. Di Napoli, *op. cit.*, pp. 124-26, for the whole discussion. The *Monarchia di Spagna* is Campanella's best known political work. The aim of Campanella in writing that work has also been a matter of discussion among his biographers. There is an English translation of the *Monarchia di Spagna*. Cf. T. Campanella, *A Discourse Touching the Spanish Monarchy*, trans. Edmund Chilmead (London: P. Stephens, 1654).
57 The supposed conspiracy against the Spanish government is the Gordian knot of Campanella's biography. Luigi Amabile has no doubt that there was an actual plot by Campanella "for the establishment of a State along the lines of what he will describe later as the *City of the Sun*." Cf. Amabile, *Congiura*, I, 220ff. Other writers, both before and after Amabile, express varying opinions, although the number of those who are inclined to see a real conspiracy on the part of Campanella seems to have increased slightly since Amabile's works. It is neither the intention nor within the competency of the present writer to pass judgment on either side of the question. There are too many factors involved in the solution of this problem and too many conflicting statements. (Cf. D'Ancona, *op. cit.*, I, p. LXXXIV). However, after a careful reading of both the primary and secondary sources relating to this particular point, it seems to the writer that a conspiracy in the sense admitted by Amabile is at least highly questionable. For a discussion of the various opinions cf. Di Napoli, *op. cit.*, chapters I and III, and especially pp. 136-37, where the author denies a real conspiracy on the part of Campanella. Luigi Firpo calls Di Napoli's presentation "a complete misunderstanding of Campanella's juvenile rebellion." Cf. Luigi Firpo, "Nota bibliografica [on Campanella]," in *Scritti scelti di Giordano e di Tommaso Campanella* (Turin: UTET, 1949), p. 262.
58 Cf. "Narratione della historia sopra cui fu appoggiata la favola della congiura," in Amabile, *Castelli*, II. See also Amabile, *Congiura*, II, p. 67.
59 Amabile, *Congiura*, II, p. 298. Cf. Firpo, *Tutte le opere di Tommaso Campanella*, Introduction, pp. LXXIV-LXXVI, for the exact dates of Campanella's tortures.
60 *Lettere*, p. 107: "Vide, quaeso, simne asinus ipsorum qui quidem iam in quinquaginta carceribus hucusque clausus afflictusque fui, septies tormento durissimo examinatus. Postremumque perduravit horis quadraginta, funiculis arctissimis ossa usque secantibus ligatus, pendens manibus retro contortis de fune super

acutissimum lignum qui carnis sextertium in posterioribus mihi devoravit et decem sanguinis libras tellus ebibit."

61 *Phil. realis: Quaest. physiol.*, p. 529. See also T. Campanella, *Teologia*, ed. Romano Amerio (Milan: "Vita e Pensiero," 1936), p. 351.

62 Campanella was never convicted of being either a conspirator or a heretic. We have already discussed the question of his conspiracy (cf. n. 57). Was he really guilty of heresy? If we were to rely on the testimony of the witnesses as reported in the proceedings of his trials, the answer would be, yes. But we know that the witnesses were not always telling the truth; moreover, the trials were vitiated by many irregularities. For his part, in his letters to the Pope and to cardinals, Campanella speaks of his attempt to escape the civil tribunal by means of an accusation of heresy, so that he could be referred to the ecclesiastical tribunal in Rome. The plan did not materialize because of the stubbornness of the Spanish authorities, as may be seen from a letter of the Spanish representative in Naples to his king: "La inquisición quería llevados a Roma, y yo·ó tenido tiesso, que no me an de salir de aquí sino ahorcados o quemados." (Amabile, *Congiura*, II, 298). On the other hand, if we examine Campanella's works, both before and after his imprisonment, we can find hardly any really heretical teaching, although it is true that he speaks in several places of his own conversion. Did this conversion affect only his life, or both his life and his doctrine? This question will be dealt with more extensively in the next section of the present chapter.

63 The best edition of Campanella's *Aforismi politici* is that by Luigi Firpo (Turin: G. Giappichelli, 1941). A very good *Introduction* precedes the text.

64 Cf. the critical edition of the *Città del Sole* by Norberto Bobbio (Turin: Einaudi, 1941), which also contains the Latin text. After the critical edition was published, Firpo made a few corrections and changes based mainly on new MSS unknown to Bobbio. Later Firpo published his own edition of the *Città del Sole* in *Scritti scelti di Giordano Bruno, etc., op. cit.* An English translation of the *Civitas Solis* or *City of the Sun* appears in the following collections: *Ideal Commonwealths; Plutarch's Lycurgus, More's Utopia, Bacon's New Atlantis, Campanella's City of the Sun and a Fragment of Hall's Mundus Alter et Idem;* with an Introduction by Henry Morley (6th ed.; London-New York: G. Routledge & Sons, 1893); *Ideal Commonwealths; comprising More's Utopia, Bacon's New Atlantis, Campanella's City of the Sun, and Harrington's Oceana,* with Introductions by Henry Morley (rev. ed.; London-New York: The Colonial Press, 1901); *Ideal Empires and Republics* (Washington and London: M. W. Dunne, 1901); *Famous New Deals of History* (New York: W. H. Wise and Company, 1935); *Famous Utopias of the Renaissance,* with Introduction and Notes by Frederic R. White, *University Classics* (3d Printing; New York: Hendricks House, 1948). The same imperfect and incomplete translation by Thomas W. Halliday is used in all these works. A new but likewise incomplete translation by William J. Gilstrap is found in *The Quest for Utopia: An Anthology of Imaginary Societies,* edited by Glenn Negley and J. Max Patrick (New York: Schuman, 1952).

65 The final draft of the *Metaphysica* was edited under the title *Universalis philosophiae, seu metaphysicarum, etc., op. cit.* For the various drafts of the work see R. Amerio, "Nota sulla cronologia dell'opera metafisica di T. Campanella," *Sophia,* III (1935), 195-202.

66 *Lettere,* p. 102: "Ego tanquam Prometheus in Caucaso detineor"; T. Campanella, *Poesie,* ed. Mario Vinciguerra (Bari: Laterza, 1938), pp. 113-14. There is
   an English translation of some of Campanella's *Poesie* in *The Sonnets of Michael
   Angelo Buonarroti and Tommaso Campanella,* translated into rhymed English
   by John Addington Symonds (London: Smith, Elder, & Company, 1878).
67 *Poesie,* pp. 114-17.
68 Cf. Firpo, *Ricerche campanelliane,* pp. 36-38.
69 Cf. "Canzone a Berillo di pentimento desideroso di confessione ecc.," *Poesie,*
   p. 157. There is no reason to accept Dentice D'Accadia's view, *op. cit.,* pp. 126-
   27, that Campanella's contrition was not genuine. Her statements that "Campanella has lost entirely the Christian conscience of sin. . . . The sincerity of
   his contrition is, as it were, wholly esthetic, not religious," *ibid.,* have no foundation.
70 *Syntagma,* p. 33. The original title of the *Atheismus triumphatus* was *Recognitio
   verae religionis secundum omnes scientias contra anti-Christianismum Machia-
   vellisticum.* Gaspar Schopp, a friend of Campanella, changed the title, which
   was later approved by Campanella himself. The edition of the *Atheismus
   triumphatus* used in the course of this study is that of Paris (Apud Tussanum
   Du Bray, 1636), which includes also the *De gentilismo non retinendo* and the
   *De praedestinatione et reprobatione et auxiliis divinae gratiae. Cento Thomisti-
   cus.*
71 Cf. preceding note.
72 Romano Amerio is working on a critical edition with an Italian translation
   of all the thirty books of Campanella's *Theologia,* or *Theologicorum libri XXX.*
   The work is being published by the *Centro internazionale di studi umanistici*
   in Rome, and is part of the *Edizione nazionale dei classici del pensiero italiano.*
   The MS is preserved in the general archives of the Dominican order at St.
   Sabina in Rome and is one of the only two extant copies of the original. The
   other copy is kept in the Bibliothèque Nationale at Paris and is known as the
   Mazarin MS (1077-1078). The original, like many other of Campanella's
   autographs, has been lost. The Paris MS contains many corrections and
   additions that Campanella himself introduced into the original text but is
   not complete. It contains only Vols. VI-XV (differently numbered from the
   Rome MS) and Vols. XX-XXIII (same enumeration). So far, the following
   books of the *Theologia* have been published: Book I, *Dio e la predestinazione*
   (2 vols.; Florence, 1949 and 1951), previously published in one volume with
   only the Latin text under the title *Teologia* (Milan: "Vita e Pensiero," 1936);
   Book II, *De sancta Monotriade* (Rome, 1958); Book III, *Cosmologia* (Rome,
   1964); Book IV, Part II, *De homine* (Rome, 1961); Book XIII (Book XII of
   Rome MS), *Della grazia gratificante* (Rome, 1959); Book XIV (Book XIII of
   Rome MS), *Magia e grazia* (Rome, 1957); Book XVI, *Il peccato originale* (Rome,
   1960); Book XVIII, *Cristologia* (2 vols.; Rome, 1958); Book XXI *Vita Christi*
   (Rome, 1962); Book XXIV, *I sacri segni* (5 vols.; Rome, 1965—); Book XXVI,
   De antichristo (Rome, 1965); Books XXVII-XXVIII, *La prima e la seconda
   resurrezione* (Rome, 1955). Unless otherwise stated, for Book I of the *Theologia*
   we shall quote from the "Vita e Pensiero" edition.
73 The seventh book of the *Astrologicorum* was added by Campanella in 1626 on
   the occasion of Pope Urban VIII's illness.
74 *Lettere,* pp. 163-69.

75 The *Apologia pro Galilaeo* has been translated into English. Cf. *The Defense of Galileo of Thomas Campanella*, trans. and ed., with Introduction and Notes, by Grant McColley (Northampton, Mass.: Department of History of Smith College, 1937). The original title of the work, written by Campanella at the request of Cardinal Bonifacio Caetani (see, however, Firpo below), was *Disputatio in utramque partem*. In it Campanella discusses the arguments for and against Galileo's heliocentric theory, which he himself holds as probable but not certain, and comes to the conclusion that neither Holy Scripture nor the Church Fathers can be quoted against it, since they do not intend to approve or disapprove any particular cosmological system. The title *Apologia pro Galilaeo mathematico florentino* under which the *Disputatio* is known, was coined by Tobias Adami, editor of the work when it was first published at Frankfort in 1622. For a discussion of the relationship between Galileo and Campanella cf. Romano Amerio, "Galilei e Campanella: la tentazione del pensiero nella filosofia della riforma cattolica," in *Nel terzo centenario della morte di Galileo. Saggi e conferenze* (Milan: "Vita e Pensiero," 1942), pp. 299-326. See also Jerome J. Langford, O.P., *Galileo, Science and the Church* (New York: Desclée Company, 1966), pp. 82-86, where a brief summary of the *Apologia* is given. A new Italian translation of the *Apologia* from the original Latin, with an Introduction and Notes, has been edited by Luigi Firpo. Cf. Tommaso Campanella, *Apologia di Galileo* (Turin: U.T.E.T., 1968). Stressing the fact that Campanella was the only person in Italy openly to defend Galileo immediately after his condemnation in 1616, Firpo discusses anew the relationship between Campanella and Galileo (pp. 6-26) and questions the truth of Campanella's statement that the *Apologia* was written at the request of Cardinal Caetani (p. 33, n. 2).

76 The full title of the work is *Quod reminiscentur et convertentur ad Dominum universi fines terrae. Volumen quatripartitum*. The first two books have been edited and published in one volume and under the same title by Romano Amerio (Padua: Cedam, 1939). The other two books have also been edited by Romano Amerio but appeared separately and under different titles. Book III: *Per la conversione degli Ebrei* (Florence: L. S. Olschki, 1955); Book IV: *Legazioni ai Maomettanti* (The same, 1960). Unless otherwise specified, reference to the *Quod reminiscentur* will mean the 1939 Padua edition of the first two books.

77 In the *Quod reminiscentur* Campanella proposes the erection of a college to prepare missionaries for apostolic work in all parts of the world. His idea was given consideration by Church authorities and may have exerted some influence on the establishment of the Congregation *De Propaganda Fide* by Pope Gregory XV (1622), as well as on the erection of the *Propaganda Fide* College (1627). Cf. R. Amerio, "L'opera teologico-missionaria di T. Campanella nei primordî di Propaganda Fide," *Archivum Fratrum Praedicatorum*, V (1935), 175-93; G. B. Tragella, "T. Campanella e l'idea missionaria," *Il pensiero missionario*, XIII (1941), 302-313.

78 *Syntagma*, p. 39. The *Defensio* occupies the first place in the 1637 Paris edition of Campanella's *De sensu rerum et magia*. It is important for a better understanding of the latter.

79 Cf. n. 70.

80 In his writings Campanella calls Father Riccardi "the Monster," a nickname

originally given to him by King Philip III of Spain because of his extremely comprehensive knowledge.

81 Cf. Luigi Amabile, *Fra T. Pignatelli, la sua congiura e la sua morte* (Naples: Morano, 1887).

82 *Lettere*, p. 259.

83 This is the seventh book of the *Astrologicorum*, written by Campanella on the occasion of Pope Urban VIII's disease. Cf. n. 73.

84 Échard, "Vita Campanellae," in Cyprianus, *op. cit.*, p. 110.

85 Amabile, *Congiura*, I, 4.

86 Angelo Zavarrone, in *Bibliotheca calabra, sive illustrium virorum Calabriae, qui literis claruerunt, elenchus* (Naples: De Simone, 1753), p. 129, describes Campanella as follows: "[Campanella] fuit staturae procerae, optimique temperamenti. Caput habebat aesopium, peponis instar, variis segmentis distinctum, capillos hispidos, oculosque castaneos." Quoted in Baldacchini, *Vita e filosofia di Tommaso Campanella, op. cit.*, I, 145-46, n. 1.

87 *Lettere*, p. 15; *Theol.*, I, Praef., p. 7.

88 *Lettere*, p. 144.

89 *Poesie*, p. 15: "Di cervel dentro un pugno io sto, e divoro
           Tanto, che quanti libri tiene il mondo
           Non saziâr l'appetito mio profondo:
           Quanto ho mangiato! e del digiun pur moro!"

90 *Lettere*, p. 144: "Ego enim cum libros lego, ita lectione afficior ut verba et res memoriae deinde semper quasi inhaereant." This is one of the reasons advanced by Campanella to excuse the many barbarisms of his style. *Ibid.*

91 Di Napoli, *op. cit.*, p. 228.

92 *Lettere*, p. 76.

93 *Poesie*, p. 18: "Io nacqui a debellar tre mali estremi:
           Tirannide, sofismi, ipocrisia."

94 Letter to the Grand Duke Ferdinand II De' Medici from Paris, July 6, 1638. Cf. *Lettere*, p. 389.

95 *Lettere*, p. 406.

96 Campanella's love for his own land and people is reflected both in his campaign for the liberation of Calabria from Spanish domination and in his writings, particularly the *Philosophia sensibus demonstrata*. In the preface to this work, which, as has been mentioned, is an answer to the attacks on Telesio by Marta's *Pugnaculum Aristotelis*, statements like the following can be found: "Calabria is the best and oldest of almost all lands. Because of the fertility of its soil it was first inhabited by Aschenax, Noah's nephew, in the vicinity of Reggio. It was called Ausonia on account of its production of all sorts of goods, just as now it is called Calabria, which means abundant region. Likewise, it was called Enotria, Morgetia, Sicilia, and Magna Graecia to distinguish it from the other Greece, which it surpassed in every way. It was also called Italia, from which the present Italy as a part of Europe took its name." *Ibid.*, p. 12. And a little further: "Every branch of knowledge flourished among the Calabrians; and all sciences, including those sciences that are now taught in the schools, originated with them. Plato, and Aristotle, his disciple, were students of the Calabrians. For Plato went to Calabria from Athens, and there he learned everything." *Ibid.*—"Whatever Aristotle has of good he learned it from Plato, who in turn was taught by the

Calabrians." *Ibid.*, p. 13.—"Pythagoras, whom Cicero in his book *De senectute* calls the prince of the philosophers as by universal consent, was from Calabria, wherefrom all sciences and schools of philosophy have been derived." *Ibid.*

97 Campanella displayed his apostolic zeal principally in Paris, where he tried very hard to convert heretics and atheists to the Catholic Church. To better achieve his purpose, he put up posters throughout the city inviting all people to come to discuss religious matters with him. "Everybody comes to listen to me," he wrote from Paris, "and they say that they are satisfied. Otherwise, I would not let them go away." *Lettere,* p. 344. See also *ibid.*, p. 337.

98 Baldacchini, *op. cit.*, I, p. 5.

99 For a full exposition of the judgments passed on Campanella from the 16th century to the present time, see Di Napoli, *op. cit.*, pp. 3-59, where the author places special emphasis on the interpretation of Campanella's life and religious doctrines. He deals extensively with the conflicting views on Campanella's supposed conspiracy against the Spanish domination. The writer is indebted to Di Napoli for some of the data the original sources of which were unavailable to him. Credit will be given in each case.

100 *Phil. sens. dem.,* Aloysii Bresci Badolatensis, in authoris laudem epigramma: "Cumque hominum nulli faveat sic docta Minerva
Ingenio hic cunctos vincit in orbe vivos."

101 Amabile, *Congiura,* III, 14.

102 Cyprianus, *op. cit.*, pp. 36-37.

103 Cf. Preface to *Prodromus, op. cit.*

104 Cyprianus, *op. cit.*, Appendix IV, p. 196: ". . . ingenio potuit qui vincere cunctos, diversam a cunctis possidet effigiem."

105 Quoted in Di Napoli, *op. cit.*, p. 4:
"Communem rebus sensum facis omnibus esse.
Quod commune facis, dic cur eo ipso cares?"

106 Quoted in Cyprianus, *op. cit.*, p. 65: "Librum Campanellae *De sensu rerum et magia,* et quoscumque alios ei similes, dignissimos esse puto, qui flammam sentiant, et fumo incantentur."

107 *Ibid.*, p. 64.

108 Theophilus Raynaudus, S.J., *Cyriacorum censura, Diatriba IV,* p. 90. Cited by Échard, "Vita Campanellae," in Cyprianus, *op. cit.*, p. 172: "[Campanella] revera est ignorantissimus, ita ut ne ipsos quidem terminos sive philosophicos sive theologicos intelligat. . . Haereses crassae in eius libris tam multae et tam inexcusabiles occurrunt, ut mirum sit adeo pinguem scriptorem superioribus annis invenire potuisse laudatores."

109 Card. Sforza Pallavicinus, *Vindicationes Societatis Jesu, quibus multorum accusationes in eius institutum, leges, gymnasia, mores refelluntur* (Rome, 1649), chap. 27.

110 Cyprianus, *op. cit.*, pp. 1-2.

111 *Ibid.*, Praef, pp. 4-5.

112 Échard, "Vita Campanellae," in Cyprianus, *op. cit.*, pp. 111, 139 and *passim.*

113 Giannone, *op. cit.*, 1. XXXIV, c. VIII. Quoted in Di Napoli, *op. cit.*, p. 13.

114 *Vita e filosofia di Tommaso Campanella,* cf. n. 5 above.

115 *Oeuvres choisies de Campanella,* cf. nn. 6 and 7.

116 *Opere di Tommaso Campanella,* cf. n. 8.

117 Quoted in D'Ancona, *op. cit.*, I, p. CCCVII: "Quid Cartesio in physicis, Hobbio in moralibus acutius? At si ille Baconio, hic Campanellae comparetur, apparet illos humi rapere; hos magnitudine cogitationum, consiliorum, imo destinationum assurgere in nubes, ac pene humanae potentiae imparia moliri. Illi ergo tradendis principiis, hi conclusionibus ad usum insignibus eliciendis meliores."

118 Georg W. F. Hegel, *Lezioni sulla teoria della filosofia*, trans. E. Codignola and G. Sanna (Florence: "La Nuova Italia," 1934), III, 212.

119 *Oeuvres de Victor Cousin*, Vol. I, *Introduction à l'histoire de la philosophie* (Bruxelles: Société Belge de Librairie, 1840), p. 209.

120 Antonio Rosmini, *Il rinnovamento della filosofia in Italia*, edited by Dante Morando (Milan: Fratelli Bocca, 1941), I, 23 (Vol. XIX of *Opere edite e inedite di Antonio Rosmini-Serbati*, Rome-Milan, 1934-1954).

121 D'Ancona, *op. cit.*, I, pp. XLIV-XLV.

122 Charles Déjob, "Est-il vrai que Campanella fût simplement déiste?", *Annales de la Faculté des lettres de Bordeaux, Bulletin italien*, XI (1911), 124-40; 232-45; 277-80.

123 Spaventa, *Rinascimento, riforma, controriforma, op. cit.*, p. 3.

124 *Ibid.*, p. 17.

125 *Ibid.*, p. 22. It should be noted that in his interpretation of Campanella's thought Spaventa relies to a great extent on Heinrich Ritter whom he frequently quotes, even though he disagrees with him on certain specific points. Ritter had already pointed out the mixture of old and new elements in Campanella's philosophy in his *Geschichte der neueren Philosophie* (Hamburg: Perthes, 1851), Part II, p. 61. See pp. 3-62 for the whole section on Campanella.

126 Cf. Francesco De Sanctis, *Storia della letteratura italiana* (new ed. by Benedetto Croce; Bari: Laterza, 1912), II, 253.

127 Cf. Francesco Fiorentino, *Bernardino Telesio, ossia Studi storici su l'idea della natura nel risorgimento italiano* (Florence: Le Monnier, 1874), II, 132-210.

128 Cf. Ernst Cassirer, *Das Erkenntnisproblem in der Philosophie und Wissenschaft der neueren Zeit* (Berlin: Bruno Cassirer, 1922), I, 240: "Die widerstreitenden Tendenzen, die das Zeitalter der Renaissance bewegen, treten sich bei ihm noch einmal in all ihrer Energie und Schroffheit entgegen." For Campanella's theory of knowedge see pp. 240-57.

129 Giovanni Gentile, *Il pensiero italiano del rinascimento* (3d ed. rev. and enlarged; Florence: Sansoni, 1940), p. 49.

130 *Ibid.*, p. 385.

131 Guido De Ruggiero, *La filosofia contemporanea* (6th ed.; Bari: Laterza, 1951), pp. 363-64. For a more extensive exposition of Campanella's doctrines cf. G. De Ruggiero, *Storia della filosofia*, Part III, *Rinascimento, riforma e controriforma* (Bari: Laterza, 1930), II, 233-61.

132 Giuseppe Saitta, *Il pensiero italiano nell'umanesimo e nel rinascimento* (Bologna: Zuffi, 1951), III, 187-291. Saitta's presentation of Campanella's philosophy is vitiated by the author's preconceived idealism. We shall have the opportunity to point out some of Saitta's inconsistencies in the course of this study.

133 Cf. n. 11 above.

134 For a summary exposition and refutation of Amabile's view see Romano Amerio, "Attualità di Tommaso Campanella," *Convivium*, XIII (1941), 554-74, especially pp. 555-56; Di Napoli, *op. cit.*, pp. 22-26 and pp. 58-59. Amabile's

opinion has been made the object of a severe criticism by Raffaele Mariano in his article, "Fra T. Campanella del prof. Amabile; saggio critico-storico," *Atti della R. Accademia di scienze morali e politiche di Napoli,* XXIII (1889), 151-229, and by Pio Carlo Falletti in his study, "Del carattere di Fra Tommaso Campanella," *Rivista storica italiana,* VI (1889), fasc. II, also printed in the form of extract (Turin: Bocca, 1889).

135 Giovanni Sante-Felici, *Die religionsphilosophischen Grundanschauungen des Thomas Campanella* (Halle, 1887), a doctoral dissertation which was later developed into the larger work, *Le dottrine filosofico-religiose di Tommaso Campanella, con particolare riguardo alla filosofia della Rinascenza italiana* (Lanciano: Carabba, 1895).

136 Cf. Amerio, "Attualità di T. Campanella," *art. cit.,* p. 556.

137 Blanchet, *op. cit., passim.*

138 Amerio, *Campanella, op. cit.,* p. 219. Cf. also his "Attualità di T. Campanella," *art. cit.,* for the refutation of Blanchet's opinion.

139 Dentice D'Accadia, *T. Campanella, op. cit., passim.*

140 Francesco Olgiati, *L'anima dell'umanesimo e del rinascimento* (Milan: "Vita e Pensiero," 1924), pp. 731-76.

141 For Amerio's interpretation of Campanella cf. his "Attualità di T. Campanella," *art. cit.,* especially pp. 557-58; "Il problema esegetico fondamentale del pensiero campanelliano," *Rivista di filosofia neoscolastica,* XXXI (1939), 368-87; *Campanella, op. cit.,* pp. 221-25; and "Un'altra confessione dell'incredulità giovanile del Campanella," *Rivista di filosofia neoscolastica,* XLV (1953), 75-77, where he defends his opinion of a philosophical metanoia in Campanella against the criticism of G. Di Napoli—to be discussed presently—by bringing forth a new text from the manuscript of Campanella's *Theologia.*

142 Luigi Firpo, "A proposito del 'Quod reminiscentur'," *Giornale critico della filosofia italiana,* XXI (1940), 268-79.

143 Di Napoli, *op. cit.,* Pref., p. VI.

144 *Ibid.,* p. 59.

145 *Ibid.,* p. 523.

146 Antonio Corsano, *Tommaso Campanella* (Bari: Laterza, 1961), pp. 8-9; 242-43.

147 *Ibid.,* p. 243.

148 Nicola Badaloni, *Tommaso Campanella* (Milan: Feltrinelli, 1965), pp. 34-35.

149 *Ibid.,* chap. 4, "La religione magica," pp. 254-343.

150 *Ibid.,* p. 286.

151 *Ibid.,* p. 347. For a review of Badaloni's work cf. Luigi Negri, "Di una recente interpretazione del pensiero campanelliano," *Filosofia e vita,* IV (1967), 376-89.

152 Salvatore Femiano, *Lo spiritualismo di Tommaso Campanella* (2 vols.; Naples: Istituto Editoriale del Mezzogiorno, 1965). Vol. I. La teorica dell'ente; Vol. II. Il problema di Dio. See *Bibliography* for 1968 revised edition in one volume.

153 *Ibid.,* Vol. I, pp. 79-80.

154 *Ibid.,* pp. 81-84.

155 *Ibid.,* pp. 105-115.

156 *Ibid.,* p. 91.

157 *Ibid.,* Vol. II, p. 159.

158 To show how apropos are the two foregoing observations, we refer the reader to an unpublished doctoral dissertation written in the Department of Philosophy in the Graduate School of Indiana University, 1935, by George Cooper Reeves,

under the title *The Philosophy of Tommaso Campanella, with Special Refer-ence to His Doctrine of the Sense of Things and Magic*. The principal part of the work consists in a translation of the first two books of Campanella's *Del senso delle cose* (ed. Bruers). Only a summary of books 3 and 4 is given. The translation is not always faithful, and even the subtitle has been misunderstood and given an erroneous interpretation. Reeves' work is not original. His only personal contribution consists in an interpretation of *Del senso delle cose*, which is often wrong. Moreover, the importance of *Del senso delle cose* is exaggerated, while practically no attention is paid to Campanella's *Metaphysica*, his most important philosophical work. Reeves mentions the *Metaphysica* on p. 83 but does not give precise references: perhaps an indication that he did not use the actual work. A further proof of the inadequacy of the study, or at least of the inappropriateness of the dissertation's title, is the fact that throughout the work no hint is made of Campanella's most fundamental philosophical doctrine, the theory of the *primalities* of being. Credit must be given, however, to Reeves for being the first to attempt a translation into English of Campanella's *Del senso delle cose*. The translation should be revised and completed.

Reeves' study closes with an extensive bibliography of 479 entries, including 110 of Campanella's own works, taken mostly from Dentice D'Accadia, *op. cit.*, and Treves, *op. cit.*, as the author acknowledges. The "Glossary of Technical Terms" shows the author's lack of a proper background in the history of philosophy.

159 The writer does not intend to enter into the debated question whether it is possible or not to write a history of philosophy without a philosophy of one's own. (Cf. Armando Carlini's review of Giovanni Di Napoli's *Tommaso Campanella*, in *Giornale di metafisica*, III (1948), 533-35, where the issue is incidentally raised). He wishes only to stress the point that even if one adheres to a particular philosophical system, he should never try to project, as it were, his own ideas into the mind of the man whom he has undertaken to study. He must confine himself to exposing the latter's thought as warranted by the texts, which he should try to interpret in the light of the cultural environment in which they were written. Unfortunately, this criterion of sound criticism has frequently been violated in the case of Campanella, who, like many other philosophers, has been forced into the mold of a preconceived system. It is an attitude typical of many Italian idealists both in the past and at present, although the gradual decline of idealism in recent years has brought a change even in this respect.

CHAPTER THREE

1 *Met.*, Letter to D. Claudio De Bullion, *regi christianissimo*, p. ã ii: "haec Philosophia, quam voco universalem et Metaphysicam, ad omnes scientias et artes inventas et inveniendas ut officina et fons ipsarum referri potest." This and all following translations from Campanella's works are the author's.

2 *Ibid.*, I, 1, 1, Prooemium, p. 4a: "de principiis rerum primis et finibus atque de scientiarum fundamentis erit doctrina haec, quam Metaphysicam appellamus, propterea quod Physicas excedit et communem Philosophiam, propterea quod

circuit omnes et ad primas causas erigitur et ad supremam, unde causationem et cognitionem omnium gradatim contuemur."

3 *Ibid.*, p. 4b: "nulla scientia tractat de rebus cunctis prout sunt, sed prout apparent et sunt nobis."

4 *Ibid.*, I, 5, 3, 1, p. 351a-351b: "Metaphysica vero tractat de omnibus prout, et quatenus sunt, et nihil praesupponit, nisi apparere quaedam quae vera et falsa esse possunt. . . . Distinguitur autem ab omnibus, quia de rebus omnibus prout sunt, et de primo ente mox principalius tractat, et de proprincipiis, propartibus, et propassionibus entis in cognoscendo, vel essendo."

5 *Ibid.*, I, 5, 2, 1, p. 346b.

6 *Ibid.*, I, 1, 8, 2, p. 66b: "Metaphysica autem est scientiarum domina."

7 *Ibid.*, I, 5, 2, 2, p. 346b.

8 *Ibid.*, p. 347a; *Theol.*, I, 4, 1, p. 98.

9 *Met.*, Letter to D. Claudio De Bullion, p. ã ii: "Codex iste, si ut decet confectus est (id quod posteritas iudicabit) appellari potest Biblia Philosophorum, sapientia seientiarum, divinarum et humanarum rerum Arx; omniumque quaestionum de cunctis rebus actualibus et possibilibus, stimulantium mentes hominum, resolutio; ita ut omnes gentes scientiarum legumque suarum veritates et errores radicitus ex hoc codice explorare valeant."

10 *Ibid.*: "Ego, qui nunquam mea laudavi opera, hoc unum pro veritate ad nationum utilitatem laudare cogor, cum rite agnitum sit omnes humanos libros ad istum esse quasi pueriles notitiae ad provectas."

11 *Lettere*, p. 142: "Profecto cum Metaphysicos meos legeris, non tibi videbuntur ab homine sed omnino ab angelo conscripti."

12 *Ibid.*, p. 320: "Galeno, S. Agostino, S. Tomaso e tanti altri che scrisser assai, son letti assai da chi n'ha voglia; cosí saró io nella *Metafisica.*"

13 *Ibid.*, Letter to Rudolf II of Austria, p. 87: "nam [metaphysici libri] digni sunt Caesare."

14 *Ibid.*, p. 142: "Excellunt enim [Metaphysici] hosce quos iam accepisti libellos, sicut omnibus in coelo sol praemicat aureus astris."

15 *Ibid.*

16 *Met.*, I, 1, 1, Prooemium, p. 2b.

17 *De gentilismo non retinendo*, p. 3.

18 *Ibid.*, p. 6.

19 *Ibid.*, p. 12.

20 *Ibid.*, p. 14: "Haeresis ergo est dicere Aristotelem invenisse veritatem, neque nos posse ultra philosophari." To say this and to say that the Aristotelian philosophy as a whole is a heresy are two quite different things. Hence the author cannot explain how Saitta, *op. cit.*, p. 203, could confuse one thing with the other. The conclusion that he draws from Campanella's statement of the need of a new philosophy is even more inaccurate than the interpretation of the text just mentioned: "La verità è infinita e come tale essa è una novità continua. Questo concetto *che è squisitamente cristiano e moderno, è il Campanella per il primo a fissare* con una precisione e ricchezza di particolari davvero sorprendenti" (italics are the author's). There is nothing farther from Christian philosophy than a concept of truth as something that is continuously new. Campanella, as will be seen in the course of this study, did not depart from Christian tradition in his definition of truth.

21 *Ibid.*, p. 16.

22 *Ibid.*, pp. 60-61.

23 *Ibid.*, p. 52.

24 *Met.*, I, 1, 1, Prooemium, p. 5a.

25 *Ibid.*: "[Aristoteles] cum proposuisset dicere de causis altissimis, XI libros consumit in prooemio. Duodecimus est metaphysicus, ubi tot impietates et deliria scribit, quot propositiones scribit."

26 *De gentilismo*, p. 10.

27 *Met.*, I, 1, 1, Prooemium, p. 2b.

28 *Prodromus*, p. 27: "Duce sensu philosophandum esse existimamus. Eius enim cognitio omnis certissima est, quia fit obiecto praesente. Signum est quod aliae cognitiones dubiae ad sensum recurrunt pro certitudine." See also *Del senso*, pp. 143-44.

29 *Met.*, I, 1, 1, Prooemium, p. 2b.

30 *Ibid.*, p. 3b. Cf. also *Theol.*, I, 17, 3, p. 349: "nos principium hoc ˈmetaphysicum statuimus: credendum esse testificantibus magis quam opinantibus."

31 *Met.*, I, 1, 1, Prooemium, pp. 3b-4a.

32 *Ibid.*, p. 6b.

33 Romano Amerio, "Forme e significato del principio di autocoscienza in S. Agostino e T. Campanella," *Rivista di filosofia neoscolastica,* Supplement to Vol. XXIII (1931), 98.

34 *Met.*, I, 4, 1, 1, p. 331a-331b: "Rerum naturas cognoscere difficile quidem est; ac modum cognoscendi longe difficilius. Idcirco plurimi de rebus dixerunt, de modo vero pauci, qui et in hoc valde hallucinantur, dum vel proprio arbitratu ipsum effingunt, vel aliorum decreto . . . Quapropter labor nobis nimius in scientiarum fundamentis propalandis et stabiliendis relictus est."

35 *Ibid.*, I, 1, 1, Prooemium, p. 5b.

36 It is true that the *Discours de la méthode* was published in 1637, one year before Campanella's *Metaphysica*. However, Campanella had finished his work at least as early as 1623, and it is most probable that the passages referring to the methodic doubt were contained in some of the previous drafts of the *Metaphysica*.

37 *Met.*, I, 5, 3, 1, p. 351a.

38 *Syntagma*, p. 67: "metaphysicus . . . nihil praesupponit, sed omnia dubitando perquirit. Nec enim praesupponet se esse veluti sibimetipsi apparet, nec dicet se esse vivum aut mortuum, sed dubitabit."

39 The exposition of the *dubitationes*, the *praeambula responsionum,* and the *responsiones* take up the entire first book of the *Metaphysica* covering eighty-eight double column pages *in quarto*. It may be interesting to know that the *Metaphysica* is made up as follows: Pars I, libri I-V, pp. 1-352; Pars II, libri VI-X, pp. 1-296; Pars III, libri XI-XVIII, pp. 1-274. Total number of pages, 922; total number of words, over 900,000.

40 *Met.*, I, 1, 1, 1, pp. 6-7.

41 *Ibid.*, a. 2, pp. 7-10.

42 *Ibid.*, a. 3, pp. 11-13. In Campanella's works *sapientia* stands either for wisdom or for science or knowledge.

43 *Ibid.*, a. 4, pp. 13-14.

44 *Ibid.*, a. 5, p. 15.

45 *Ibid.*, a. 6, pp. 15-16.

46 *Ibid.*, a. 7, pp. 16-19.

47 *Ibid.*, a. 8, pp. 19-20.

48 *Ibid.*, a. 9, p. 20.

49 *Ibid.*, a. 10, pp. 21-23.

50 *Ibid.*, a. 11, p. 23.

51 *Ibid.*, a. 12, pp. 24-27.

52 *Ibid.*, a. 13, pp. 27-28.

53 *Ibid.*, a. 14, pp. 28-29.

54 Cf. St. Augustine, *De vera religione*, XXXIX, 73. The same argument is also developed at length in St. Augustine's *Contra Academicos*, III.

55 *Met.*, I, 1, 2, 1, p. 30.

56 *Ibid.*, I, 1, 3, 2 [Wrong enumeration; it should be either c. 2, a. 2, or c. 3, a. 1], pp. 30-31.

57 *Ibid.*, a. 3 [It should be either c. 2, a. 3, or c. 3, a. 1], p. 32a: "sternenda est via ex certissimis et notissimis nobis et naturae, infallibilibusque."

58 *Ibid.* The passage quoted by Campanella is taken from St. Augustine's *De civitate Dei*, XI, 26. The quotation is not absolutely exact, but the content is substantially the same.

59 *Ibid.* He refers to St. Thomas, *Sum. Theol.*, I, q. 87, a. 1: "ad primam cognitionem de mente habendam, sufficit ipsa mentis praesentia, quae est principium actus ex quo mens percipit seipsam. Et ideo dicitur se cognoscere per suam praesentiam."

60 *Ibid.* Quotation *ad sensum* from *De civitate Dei*, XI, 26.

61 *Ibid.*: "sternenda est via ex certissimis et notissimis nobis et naturae, infallibilibusque. Haec autem sunt universalissima ut ens, entisque primalitates, potentia, sapientia et amor unicuique propriae, quae nec ignorari, nec per deceptionem incerta fieri posse . . . notum est."

62 *Ibid.*

63 *Theol.*, I, 11, 1, p. 194.

64 The term *notitia abdita* was apparently suggested to Campanella by Henry of Ghent, who speaks of a certain *abditum intelligere* (cf. *Theol.*, I, 11, 1, p. 198). Other philosophers closer to him, such as John Pico della Mirandola and Agostino Donio, with whom he was certainly acquainted, had most probably a more direct influence upon him both for the selection of the term and for the doctrine of self-consciousness. Thus John Pico della Mirandola, in his *Apologia* (ed. 1601), II, 62, writes as follows: "Anima nihil actu et distincte intelligit, nisi seipsam. Hanc [propositionem] declarando, dixi quod intelligebam de *intelligere abdito*" [italics are the author's]. Quoted in Blanchet, *Campanella, op. cit.*, p. 269, n. 1. Agostino Donio, from Cosenza, in his *De natura hominis* (Basel, 1581), repeats more or less the same doctrine in connection with the vital spirit when he says: "Quod quidem sui ipsius [spiritus] statusque sui abditam in se intellectionem, esse quoque sensum atque adeo primum sensum, jure opinor aliquis dicere posset, et ex intentione in sese fieri atque constare." Quoted in Fiorentino, *Bernardino Telesio, op. cit.*, I, 329, n. 1.

65 *Met.*, I, 1, 3, 3, p. 32a-32b.

66 *Ibid.*, II, 6, 8, 5, p. 64b: "Non ergo requiritur ut cognoscens patiatur, vel immutetur a seipso, sed ut sit seipsum ad hoc ut noscat seipsum."

67 *Ibid.*, a. 1, p. 59a: "videtur Telesio esse perceptio illatae passionis omnis cognitio. Nos autem aliter sapimus."

68 *Ibid.*, II, 6, 6, a. 9, p. 36a: "ut autem intelligat se intellectus non indiget pati a

se, nec fieri ipsemet; est enim; quod autem est, non fit; ergo seipsum novit per essentiam, et notio et intellectio est sua essentia; et verum est in angelo et in anima idem esse intellectum, intellectionem, et intelligentem sui ipsius primordiali innata [notitia], non autem illata et reflexa."

69 *Ibid.*, p. 36b. For the doctrine of St. Augustine in this connection cf. *De Trinitate*, X, 11, 18; IX, 4. See also Etienne Gilson, *Introduction à l'étude de Saint Augustin* (2d ed.; Paris: Vrin, 1943), pp. 289-90 and notes for the commentary on those passages.

70 *Met.*, II, 6, 8, 8, p. 67a: "Nec recte dicunt intellectum non posse seipsum intelligere, quia pura potentia est. Aristoteli enim est potentia ad intelligere, non ad intelligi; cum enim sit de ordine immaterialium, multo magis potest intelligi ipse quam species materiales defoecatae a phantasmatibus, quoniam ipse per se defoecatus est."

71 Cf. Aristotle, *Metaphysica*, XII 7, 1072b, 20-23: "Seipsum autem intelligit intellectus secundum transumptionem intelligibilis. Intelligibilis enim fit attingens et intelligens: quare idem intellectus et intelligibile. Susceptivum enim intelligibilis et substantiae, actuatur autem habens." (S. Thomae Aquinatis, *In duodecim libros Metaphysicorum Aristotelis expositio*, Turin-Rome: Marietti, 1950, *Textus* Aristotelis, n. 1073). Commenting on that passage St. Thomas writes: "[Aristoteles] dicit, quod hoc est de ratione intellectus, quod intelligat seipsum inquantum transumit vel concipit in se aliquid intelligibile; fit enim intellectus intelligibilis per hoc quod attingit aliquod intelligibile . . . Intellectus . . . comparatur ad intelligibile sicut potentia ad actum." *Ibid.*, *Commentarium S. Thomae*, nn. 2539-40.

72 *Met.*, II, 6, 8, 4, p. 63a: ". . . cognitio sui [animae] est impedita a cognitione aliorum; sumus enim inter contraria geniti, et patimur a calore et a frigore et ab innumeris obiectis continuo; et ideo quasi in aliorum esse transimus, quoniam pati et immutari est fieri aliud; ergo quasi in sui oblivionem et inscitiam cadit anima, quia alienorum viribus exagitatur semper."

73 *Ibid.*: ". . . quia non [est anima] in sua puritate, sed in externorum obiectorum mistura, quae ipsam exagitat, idcirco notitia reflexa videtur ipsi propria magis pro praesenti statu." Cf. also *Met.*, II, 6, 6, 9, p. 36b.

74 *Met.*, III, 14, 1, 1, p. 129a. See also *Met.*, II, 6, 8, 1, p. 59b: "anima disquirit diuturnis argumentis quid sit anima, atque ab externis suis actibus, vel aliorum colligit."

75 *Ibid.*, I, 1, 9, 10, p. 74b: "Discrepantia opinionum de animae quidditate et functionibus nascitur ex scientia illata, non ex innata."

76 *Ibid.*, II, 6, 8, 4, p. 63b: "nequaquam omnino seipsam ignorare animam assero; si enim est sua quidditas, suam novit quidditatem." Ritter's reference to Campanella's passage in *Met.*, III, 17, 3, 1, p. 246b: "Eo quod noscit alia, [anima] reflectitur ad cognoscendum se cognoscentem se," is not complete. Campanella adds immediately after: "Hoc autem falsum est: quinimo ex hoc enim quod potest, et scit, et amat se, potest, scit, et amat alia, ut probatum est supra." Cf. Ritter, *op. cit.*, p. 52, n. 2. On the other hand, Campanella himself is not always exact in his own statements. Thus, when writing in *Met.*, III, 13, 3, 1, p. 127b: "neque seipsam novit anima nisi abdita notitia," he apparently forgot all that he had said before concerning the soul's reflex knowledge.

77 *Ibid.*, III, 14, 4, 1, p. 138a: "Animae ergo est scire, et posse, et appetere quatenus ens, non quatenus anima."

78 *Ibid.*, II, 6, 9, 6, p. 73b: "Utrum autem sit melior sapientia innata quam adscita . . . Respondeo quod sapientia innata est primalitas et a Deo, idcirco nobilior, verior et certior. Nec enim circa primalitates erramus, nec circa ens et universalia."

79 Colet, *op. cit.*, p. 45. (The translation is the author's.) Mme. Colet quotes a passage from Baillet's biography of Descartes to the effect that Descartes did not envy the reputation that Campanella had acquired nor the discoveries that he claimed to have made in his study of nature. *Ibid.*, p. 45f., n. 1. In 1638, when returning to Père Mersenne one of Campanella's works—the name of the work is not mentioned—Descartes complains about the author's bad style and then goes on to say: "As far as the doctrine [of Campanella] is concerned, I read the *De sensu rerum* and other works by the same author fifteen years ago. It may be that the present work was one of them. However, I found then such scant soundness of doctrine in those works, that I did not try to remember anything of them. . . . I have nothing else to say now except this, that in my opinion those who lose their way by pretending to follow some extraordinary paths, seem to be much less excusable than those who go astray by travelling in company with others and following the same path that many others did." *Ibid.*

80 Cf. Blanchet, *Les antécédents historiques du "Je pense, donc je suis"* (Paris: Alcan, 1920), pp. 175-76, where the points of resemblance between the two works, both in structure and in the philosophical systems presented, are well stated.

81 See nn. 37 and 38 above.

82 *Met.*, I, 5, 2, 1, p. 346b: "Metaphysica autem ex toto, ut Physicae ex parte quatenus sunt sapientiae, de omnibus quaerit et quidditatem et existentiam, praesertim ubi omnibus non patent sensibus; quaerit etiam utrum pateant, et quid sit sentire et intelligere, ut noscamus num vere sciatur: quod nos hoc in libro observamus; praesupponit autem tanquam notum sensibus multorum, et non omnium existentiam, et quod multa apparent; quaerit tamen num quae apparent vere [erroneously written "verae"] sint, et quid sint: et an secundum naturam vere sint, an solum apparenter."

83 *Ibid.*, a. 2, pp. 346b-347a: "ad hanc [scientiam metaphysicam] . . . spectat principia scientiarum enucleare et stabilire; et rebus secundum naturam nomina imponere, et ordinem, et fines omnium declarare."

84 Di Napoli, *op. cit.*, pp. 257-58.

85 *Met.*, I, 1, 9, 2, p. 67a: "Cum autem quaeritur cuius est scientia, singularium ne, an universalis, respondeo quod *inventiva* tractat singularia, *doctrinalis* universalia ex singularibus collecta similibus." And a little further: "scientia inventiva tractat singularia, ex quorum similitudine reale resultat in mente universale, quod est principium scientiae, ut ars est et docens, non ut sciens, et a quo est rei ens." *Ibid.*, p. 67b.

86 *Ibid.*, I, 5, 1, 1, p. 343b [erroneously numbered 143].

87 *Ibid.*, p. 343a.

88 The interpretation of the text of the *Syntagma* that we have offered seems to be the only one that makes sense. This is apparent from a reading of the full original text: "Qui autem inventivas tradit scientias, modum quo ad eas pervenit viamque aperiet, nec aliquid praesupponet nisi universalissimum esse; quapropter metaphysicus qui communem cunctis scientiis philosophiam tractat, nihil praesupponit, sed omnia dubitando perquirit. Nec enim praesup-

ponet se esse veluti sibimetipsi apparet, nec dicet se esse vivum aut mortuum, sed dubitabit . . ." *Syntagma,* p. 67.

89 Cf. preceding n. 58. See also Gilson, *Introduction à l'étude de Saint Augustin, op. cit.,* chap. 3, as well as his other work, *René Descartes, Discours de la méthode* (Paris: Vrin, 1947), p. 298, where he says: "Il existe, depuis saint Augustin, une tradition ininterrompue, qui fait de la connaissance immédiate de l'âme par elle-même la première et la plus évidente de nos connaissances."

90 In his work, *Distinguer pour unir, ou Les degrés du savoir* (5th ed.; Paris: Desclée de Brouwer, 1946), pp. 150-51, Jacques Maritain has demonstrated that a universally real doubt is impossible, for it would end up in a vicious circle. Canon Fernand Van Steenberghen has illustrated the same point in his *Epistemology,* trans. Rev. Martin J. Flynn (New York: Joseph F. Wagner, 1949), p. 79. He says that "every attempt to doubt or deny will encounter this evident affirmation: A consciousness exists." That Descartes' doubt was only a methodic one seems to be very well established on the basis of the text itself of his *Discours de la méthode.* However, this does not mean that he really did not doubt things that were not certain to him. Cf. Gilson, *René Descartes, Discours de la méthode,* pp. 285-86.

91 For Descartes' teaching on this point cf. his *Principia philosophiae,* I, 10, quoted in Gilson, *René Descartes, Discours de la méthode,* p. 287. Campanella clearly admits the absolute validity of the principle of noncontradiction in his *Metaphysica.* Here are two pertinent passages: "Res quatenus est non potest non esse." *Met.,* I, 1, 9, Def. Metaph., p. 79b. "Inter esse et non esse non datur medium; ergo non possunt verificari, aut falsificari propositiones contradictoriae." *Ibid.*

92 Cf. n. 82 above.

93 Blanchet, *Les antécédents historiques,* p. 241. Blanchet's conviction rests on the fact that certain of Campanella's works where the critical problem is either implicitly or explicitly stated and tentatively solved were written before Descartes' *Discours de la méthode.* Among such works he mentions: *Metaphysica, De sensu rerum et magia, Poesie, Atheismus triumphatus,* and *Syntagma.*

94 *Ibid.,* pp. 258ff.

95 *De sensu rerum,* Title.

96 Etienne Gilson, *Études sur le rôle de la pensée médiévale dans la formation du système Cartésien* (Paris: Vrin, 1930), pp. 262-67.

97 Amerio, "Forme e significato del principio di autocoscienza in Sant'Agostino e Tommaso Campanella," *art. cit.,* n. 17, p. 106. See also his monograph, *Campanella, op. cit.,* pp. 49-51.

98 Annibale Pastore, "Autocoscienza e intuizione lirica in T. Campanella," *Sophia,* XV (1947), 50-59. Cf. also his previous article, "Anticipazioni cartesiane e sviluppi lirici in S. Agostino e Campanella," *Atti della R. Accademia delle Scienze di Torino,* LXXV (1939-40), II, 89-106.

99 Di Napoli, *op. cit.,* pp. 261-62.

100 Gilson, *Études sur le rôle de la pensée médiévale, op. cit.,* p. 267.

101 See, for example, Spaventa, *Rinascimento, riforma, controriforma, op. cit.,* pp. 54-56, where he states that Campanella's principle of self-consciousness consists in the identity of thought and being. For him "Campanella is truly the forerunner of Descartes; but between the two formulations of the principle of

self-consciousness there is a necessary relationship of progress which corresponds to the development of the life of the spirit." *Ibid.*, p. 55.

102 Francesco Olgiati, *I fondamenti della filosofia classica* (Milan: "Vita e Pensiero," 1950), p. 127. Cf. likewise his other monographs, *Cartesio* (Milan: "Vita e Pensiero," 1933), and *La filosofia di Descartes* (Milan: "Vita e Pensiero," 1937), where the author defends his viewpoint at length and in a very forceful way.

CHAPTER FOUR

1 The trichotomic structure of man is taught by Campanella in all of his works where the subject is discussed, from the *Philosophia sensibus demonstrata* to the *Metaphysica.* For our purpose it suffices to quote the following passages: "Triplici vivimus substantia, corpore scilicet, spiritu et mente." *Prodromus,* p. 83. "Homo enim constat corpore, spiritu et mente." *Met.*, III, 14, 5, 4, p. 148b. Campanella mentions St. Augustine as sponsoring the same doctrine (*Met., loc. cit.*), and quotes St. Paul's teaching in confirmation of it: "L'anima dunque umana si appella mente quella che Dio infonde, quella che con le bestie abbiamo commune, spirito. Onde san Paolo dice che *se lo spirito ora, la carne ora e la mente è supervacante senza effetto,* perchè lo spirito nasce dalla carne e dal sangue, e noi di spirito, carne e membra siam composti" (*Del senso,* p. 153). Actually, the trichotomic doctrine has its origin in Greek philosophy, especially among the Epicureans. Lucretius is the first to call the rational part of the soul *animus* or *mens,* and the irrational part *anima* (cf. Lucretius, *De rerum natura,* III, 94ff.). However, Campanella took over the doctrine directly from Telesio, as is evidenced from the *Philosophia sensibus demonstrata* (cf., e.g., p. 85), and parted company with his master only in regard to the meaning and function of the intellective soul (*Phil. sens. dem.*, pp. 517-18).

2 *Prodromus,* p. 83; *Epilogo,* pp. 418-19; *Del senso,* p. 93.

3 *Prodromus,* p. 83; *Del senso,* pp. 154-55. Spirit embraces also the vegetative power. This is not a distinct power in Campanella's biological system, where plants are classified as animals of inferior quality.

4 *Lettere,* p. 113; *Epilogo,* p. 419.

5 *Del senso,* p. 90; *Epilogo,* p. 402.

6 *Met.*, I, 1, 4, 3, p. 37b: "Sanguis enim ligat corpus cum spiritu; spiritus vero sanguinem cum mente."

7 *Ibid.*, I, 1, 5, 2, p. 45a: "est spiritus mobilis, tenuis, lucidus, calidus, secundum naturam obiectorum; et insuper sentiens, appetens, atque potens, ex participio primalitatum."

8 *Ibid.*

9 *Ibid.*, p. 45b.

10 *Del senso,* p. 93; *Met.*, I, 1, 4, 3, p. 37a.

11 *Met., loc. cit.:* "Arist. et Aphrod. [Alexander of Aphrodisias] in periphrasi argumentantur: ergo abeunte anima remaneret corpus, sicut navi egresso nauta . . . Respondeo vere esse consequentiam (primam). Palam enim, abeunte anima, corpus remaneret idem, ut patet in Christo et in multis denuo subitoque per miraculum resuscitatis. Quod si manu tenueris morientem, comperies resolutionem usque ad materiam primam minime fieri, sed eosdem oculos, et carnes, et ossa permanere in sua forma."

12 *Ibid.*, III, 14, 4, 1, p. 138b. Here is Campanella's full statement: "ex corpore et anima non fit unum simpliciter, ut ex potentia, sapientia, et amore, neque ut compositum similare ex materia et forma, ut ex calore et tenui corpore ignis, et ex aere et circulo aes: sed unum decompositum, ut molendinum ex aqua et lapidibus molaribus et homine; et textrinum ex texente et tela et filis et radio et casside et caeteris partibus. Quapropter frustra quaeritur unitas in animali simplex, in quo apparet multiformitas; sed unum est de compositione, ut et recte Scotus advertit. Verum quia haec decompositio est naturalis substantialisque in unam formam totius propter finem, datur unitas maior quam pistrino: licet et in hoc conveniant omnes partes in unam formam totius propter finem."

13 *Lettere*, p. 113; *Del senso*, p. 91: "il principio senziente . . . è uno per continuazione, come l'aria nei canali suonanti."

14 *Met.*, I, 1, 4, 5, p. 39b.

15 *Ibid.*, I, 1, 5, 2, p. 48a.

16 *Del senso*, pp. 154-55.

17 *Met.*, I, 1, 4, 3, p. 37a.

18 *Ibid.*, I, 1, 5, 2, p. 45a.

19 *Ibid.*, I, 1, 4, 5, p. 40b: "Nec anima sentit qua corporeitatem participat, sed qua primalitates." Cf. *ibid.* and p. 41a where Campanella tries to refute the arguments of the Aristotelians against the corporeal nature of the sensitive soul. Another passage in which he shows that the sensitive soul has the power of perception insofar as it is a being with the primalitarian structure is found in *Met.*, III, 14, 4, 1, p. 138a-138b: "Anima ergo non sapit sensu vel intellectu, quatenus est corpus . . . Ergo quatenus ens, quoniam omne ens sentit."

20 *Met.*, I, 1, 4, 5, p. 40b: "Concedo fieri [ex parte animae] operationes cum corpore, ut navis cum remigante: non tamen cogitationes et intellectiones."

21 Cf., e.g., *Del senso*, p. 111, where he states: "Ne gli animali senso, memoria, discorso e giudizio sensitivo trovarsi, ma non mentale razionale umano." And on p. 116 of the same work: "intendiamo dicendo razionali, cioè mentali, quando diciamo gli uomini esser razionali animali."

22 The term *mens* is used by Campanella to distinguish the human or intellective soul from the spirit and corresponds to the Greek *nous*. However, he often calls it simply *anima*. The context has therefore to be examined in each case in order to determine the exact meaning attached to the term *anima*, which sometimes stands for the sensitive soul.

23 *Epilogo*, p. 418: "Poscia che lo spirito forma il corpo e distinguelo nelle sue parti et si fa queste vie et stromenti di sentire, vede Dio finito sì bel lavoro con molta eccellenza più che ne i bruti, laonde di quello si compiace: però gl'infonde l'anima immortale, la qual debba perfettionare tutto l'artificio et le sue operationi. Et insiememente ella si fa forma di tutto l'huomo, il quale innanzi alla sua infusione è composto di spirito, d'humido et di solido." And *Met.*, III, 14, 6, 2, p. 152a: ". . . dicimus mentem uniri corpori naturaliter, et cum infertur: ergo non a Deo: negamus consequentiam. Deus enim et Natura sunt agentia subordinata, sicut principale et instrumentarium, a quibus idem effectus manant. Neque dicimus violenter immitti, neque sponte sua in corpus, sed naturaliter, quia sic nascitur et creatur a Deo ut in corpore humano habitet."

24 *Prodromus*, p. 83.

25 *Epilogo,* p. 423; *Lettere,* p. 113; *Del senso,* pp. 154-55: ". . . ella [mens] è incorporea e non può stare unita alla corpolenza senza un mezzo, onde Trismegisto chiamò questo spirito veicolo della mente, e sant'Agostino dice che senza sangue non può stare l'anima perchè al secco corpo la sua spiritualità è troppo dissimile, ma non all'umido." Saitta's claim that this passage contains an implicit denial of the soul's spirituality and immortality is entirely arbitrary. The same lack of seriousness can be noticed in his attempt to present Campanella's religious convictions on this matter (*Del senso,* pp. 153-55) as a well thought device to deceive the churchmen's credulity. (Cf. Saitta, *op. cit.,* pp. 231-32).

26 *Del senso,* p. 155.

27 *Met.,* III, 14, 4, 2, p. 139a; *Del senso,* p. 95.

28 *Del senso, loc. cit.* This text, which is fundamental for the understanding of Campanella's psychology, has been completely distorted by Reeves in his English translation of *Del senso delle cose e della magia.* Cf. n. 158 of chap. II.

29 The definition of the Council of Vienne (1311-12) reads: "Definientes . . . quod quisquis deinceps asserere, defendere, seu tenere pertinaciter praesumpserit, quod anima rationalis seu intellectiva non sit forma corporis humani *per se* et *essentialiter,* tanquam haereticus sit censendus." H. Denzinger, *Enchiridion symbolorum,* n. 481.

30 The traditional opinion that Peter J. Olivi's doctrine of information was the object of condemnation of the Council of Vienne is opposed by L. Jarraux, O.F.M., and E. Müller, O.F.M. They claim that Olivi's doctrine of information, as it stands in his authentic writings, was neither discussed in the Council of Vienne nor condemned. Olivi's doctrine was only the occasion for the Council to define the Church's standpoint on the union of soul and body in man. Cf. L. Jarraux, "P. J. Olivi. Sa vie, sa doctrine," *Études Franciscaines,* XLV (1933), 129-53, 277-98, 513-29, and E. Müller, *Das Konzil von Vienne (1311-12). Seine Quellen und seine Geschichte* (Münster in Westph.: Aschendorff, 1934), pp. 387ff. This opinion is criticized by B. Jansen, S.J., "Die Seelenlehre Olivis und ihre Verurteilung auf dem Vienner Konzil," *Franziscanische Studien,* XXI (1934), 297-314, and by L. Amorós, "De mente Concilii Viennensis in causa P. I. Olivi," *Archivum Franciscanum Historicum,* XXVII (1934), 408-420. Müller answers Jansen's criticism in his other article, "Olivi und seine Lehre von der Seelenform auf dem Konzil von Vienne 1311-1312. Eine Erwiderung an P. B. Jansen," in *Kirchengeschichtlichen Studien P. Michel Bihl als Ehrengabe dargeboten* (Kolmar, 1941) pp. 96-113. Whatever the case may be, it is not correct to say, as Di Napoli states in his monograph on Campanella, *op. cit.,* p. 363, that in the Council of Vienne the Church defined against Olivi the doctrine of the soul as form of the body. Olivi never denied that the intellective soul is the form of the body. What he did deny is that the intellective soul is the form of the body *per se* and *essentially.* He taught that there are three formal parts in the human soul, the vegetative, the sensitive, and the intellective; and that all of them are united in one spiritual matter in such a way that they constitute all together and, as it were, by a mechanical addition, one total form. Accordingly, the intellective part of the soul becomes the form of the body only by means of the vegetative and sensitive parts. All this is against the mind of the Council. Cf. Zacharias Van de Woestyne, O.F.M., *Cursus philosophicus* (Malines: Imprimerie St. François, 1925), II, 605ff., n. 2, where the

author gives a good summary of Olivi's doctrine on the union of soul and body as well as a substantial bibliography on the subject.

31 *Theol.*, IV, 3, 2: "Mentem humanam . . . nec esse formam nisi largo modo et non radicatam sed independentem." MS quoted in Di Napoli, *op. cit.*, p. 364.

32 Campanella's teaching on the relationship of the *mens* to spirit and body has been the object of various interpretations. What surprises the writer is that even Di Napoli is rather confused in his treatment of this question (cf. Di Napoli, *op. cit.*, pp. 363-64). He discusses Campanella's doctrine on the relationship between the *mens* and the other two components in man and, without making any distinction, he quotes certain passages from Campanella's works which explicitly refer to the union of the body with the *sensitive soul.* (See his reference to *Met.*, I, 2, 4, 7, p. 144a, which reads: "Nec fingamus *animam sensitivam* esse animalis formam, cum non sicut forma insit, sed sicut operator in suo operatorio substantialiter unitus," and his other reference to *Met.*, I, 1, 4, 3, tit., p. 37: "*Animam sentientem* . . . esse tenuissimum corpus habitans in crasso ad operationes vitales concinnato, sicut nauta in navi"). In the same connection, Di Napoli cites the following text from Campanella's *Phil. realis: Quaest. physiol.*, p. 539: "Quod autem dicunt non fieri unum simpliciter, nisi ex potentia et actu, Peripateticum est, non verum," and objects to it on the ground that it endangers the unity in man guaranteed by the peripatetic doctrine of act and potency adopted by the Council of Vienne. Campanella's statement, insofar as it denies the strict application of the peripatetic theory of act and potency to the human composite, cannot be rejected unconditionally, and certainly not in the name of the Vienne Council. It is well known that in defining the soul as *per se* and *essentially* the form of the body, the Council of Vienne did not intend to apply necessarily to the human composite the strict peripatetic theory of act and potency, or form and primary matter. In other words, the Council did not want to take sides in the famous scholastic dispute about the unicity or plurality or forms in man, which is a purely philosophical question. Consequently, Campanella's statement mentioned above cannot be condemned *as such,* but may be accepted or not according to one's own philosophical opinion in this matter.

33 *Del senso,* p. 134.

34 *Met.*, III, 14, 2, 1, p. 133b: "Divina ergo res est homo."; *Del senso,* p. 135: "è divinissima la natura dell'uomo."

35 *Met.*, III, 14, 2, 1, p. 133b: "Homo inquirit de Deo, de angelis, de rebus divinis et disputat et tractat; ergo eius animus divinitatis proles est."

36 *Ibid.*, I, 1, 5, 2, p. 47a.

37 *Ibid.*, III, 14, 6, 2, tit., p. 152: "Mens unitur corpori propter bonum futurum, non praesens."

38 *Ibid.*, I, 1, 5, 2, p. 47a: "si anima ex elementatione veniret, sicut spiritus brutorum, nequaquam ultra elementa aut supra erigeretur: neque enim ulla forma aut vis corporea extra corpus suum vagatur, nec ullus effectus supra causam erigitur, nec pars supra totum." See also *ibid.*, III, 14, 2, 1, p. 132b.

39 *Ibid.*, III, 14, 4, 2, p. 139a: "mens extenditur extra corpus et extra mundum corporeum."

40 *Phil. realis: Quaest. physiol.*, p. 531: "Anima autem supra coelum se erigit et intelligit alios mundos et soles et res divinas in infinitum."

41 Campanella also uses the spirituality of the soul as an argument for the soul's immortality.

42 His argumentation in this connection is not very effective; moreover, it presupposes some of his epistemological and metaphysical notions that have not yet been discussed. The full text in *Met.*, II, 6, 6, 13, p. 39a, reads: ". . . D. Augustinus probat intellectum et voluntatem esse ipsam animam, et non accidentia eius; quoniam accidens non transilit subiectum suum; amamus autem et intelligimus extra nos. Ergo S. Augustinus ex ea ratione, qua probant alii facultates animae esse accidentia, ipse probat esse substantiam, et iure quidem meliori. Non enim convenit accidentia infinitae virtutis amplitudinisque facere; substantiam vero unde fluunt, et in qua radicantur, coarctare. Ergo si amamus extra nos, virtute Mentis substantialis amamus; quoniam Mens Divinitatis particeps, in qua movemur et sumus et intelligimus et possumus et volumus, ita potest amare et intelligere; et non habet hoc a potentia, seu facultate, quae sibi sit accidens, sed potius potentia, seu facultas habet hoc ab essentia, seu essentialitatibus mentis. Unde mirum quo pacto probant intelligere intelligendique facultatem accidentia esse infinita; animam vero eiusque essentiam finitam. Nec nos docent unde haec infinitas accidentibus; si enim a se dicas, stultum est responsum; si ab anima ex qua fluunt, ergo falsum est quod anima sit finita et accidentia eius infinita; vel oporteret utrumque infinitare, ideoque simul identificare."

43 He praises Durandus of Saint Pourçain, who, without knowing the doctrine of the primalities, holds the same point of view: "Hic laudo Durandum, qui intellectum et voluntatem non distingui realiter contendit tanquam duas potentias sed esse unam. Et verum dicit absolute, non terminative, nec de primalitatum manationibus quidquam scivit." *Theol.*, I, 3, 12, p. 91.

44 *Phil. sens. dem.*, p. 352: "Omnem notitiam a sensu oriri palam est."

45 *Epilogo*, p. 490: "tutta la scienza umana sta nel senso."

46 *Ibid.*, p. 457.

47 *Met.*, I, 1, 1, Prooemium, p. 3b: "Veritas enim est rei entitas sicuti est, non autem sicut imaginamur nos; sensus autem testatur de rebus uti sunt, imaginatio vero uti nos putamus esse."

48 *Del senso*, pp. 115-16.

49 *Ibid.*, p. 144.

50 *Ibid.*, p. 145.

51 *Met.*, I, 1, 9, 3, p. 69a.

52 *Ibid.*, I, 1, 4, 4, p. 38b.

53 *Phil. sens. dem.*, p. 28.

54 See, for example, *Phil. sens. dem.*, p. 29, where he speaks of *sensata ratio*, and p. 66, where it is stated that we must follow *sensum vel rationem*. Likewise, on p. 204 of the same work, he asserts that we have to reason *sensu et rationibus sensibus confirmatis*.

55 *Ibid.*, p. 66: "vera intellectio est, cui sensus, unde ipsa est et certificatur, non contradicit, et experientia favet."

56 *Epilogo*, p. 490: "tutta la scienza umana sta nel senso: non ne gli organi, ma nello spirito senziente per loro, il quale è atto a ritenere et conferire quel che apprende una volta."

57 Campanella seems to have difficulty in understanding how Aristotle, who teaches the multiplicity of the senses, actually does not admit more than five

senses in man. In his opinion, other senses, too, such as the *sensus Veneris,*
the sense of hunger, the sense of thirst, etc., ought to be admitted along with
the five senses commonly accepted, for each one of them has an organ and a
function of its own. (Cf. *Met.,* I, 1, 6, 3, p. 51a; *Del senso,* p. 92). Unlike
Aristotle, he also claims, quite in agreement with modern physiology, that the
principal organ of perception is the brain, not the heart. (Cf. *Phil. realis:
Quaest. physiol.,* p. 363).

58 *Met.,* I, 1, 6, 3, tit., p. 51: "Unam esse substantiam sentientem in omnibus
organis, et unum realiter sensum: sed plures sentiendi modos ob pluralitatem
obiectorum." *Ibid.,* p. 51a: "Quinque sensus exteriores secundum substantiam
sentientem idem sunt. Secundum vero organa plures sunt, et secundum
obiecta, quae pluribus organis hauriuntur." *Prodromus,* p. 81: "Nos autem
[admittimus] sensum unum, at sensationes, organaque sentiendi plura."

59 *Met.,* I, 5, 1, 3, p. 334a-334b.

60 *Ibid.,* p. 334a: "Prima notitia est sensus, quae notio est praesentis obiecti."
See also *Del senso,* p. 68.

61 *Del senso,* p. 143.

62 *Prodromus,* p. 27: "sensatio praeterita . . . dici solet memoria"; *Epilogo,* pp.
458-63; *Del senso,* p. 98; *Met.,* I, 1, 6, 4, tit., p. 52; *ibid.,* I, 5, 1, 3, p. 344a.

63 *Met.,* I, 5, 1, 3, p. 344a: "reminiscentia nobis sensus renovatus dicitur"; *ibid.,*
I, 1, 6, 4, tit., p. 52.

64 *Prodromus,* p. 27.

65 *Met.,* I, 5, 1, 3, p. 344a: "fides . . . est sentire et intelligere alieno sensu, vel
intellectu"; *Epilogo,* pp. 463-65.

66 *Met.,* I, 5, 1, 3, p. 344a: "discursus . . . est sentire in simili similia"; *Epilogo,*
pp. 465-70; *Del senso,* p. 68.

67 *Prodromus,* p. 27.

68 *Met.,* I, 5, 1, 3, p. 344b: "intellectus, notitia nimirum intus legens et colligens
ea quae singulae praeviae cognitiones deforis ostendunt." More clearly the
Epilogo, p. 470, ed. *P* in note: "Intelligere est intus legere in rebus sensibilibus
id quod foris latet, et per discursum ex his quae patent." For the full treatise
on the intellect cf. *ibid.,* pp. 470-80.

69 *Met.,* I, 5, 1, 3, p. 344b: "imaginatio . . . fingit ideando, fabricando imagines
novas per divisionem et copulationem praeteritarum; in quibus aliquando
attingit quod optat, aliquando delirat"; *ibid.,* II, 6, 8, 2, p. 60a; *Epilogo,* pp.
481-90; *Del senso,* p. 101.

70 *Met.,* I, 1, 6, 6, tit., p. 53: "Animam imaginantem eandem esse sentienti,
memoranti et ratiocinanti, contra Aristotelem et Avicennam, et eorum rationes
contrarium probantes vanas esse."

71 *Del senso,* p. 105: "L'anima senziente pur intendere."

72 *Prodromus,* p. 83: "Cum ergo notum sit spiritum sentire intelligereque, vanum
putamus aliam propter hoc substantiam esse intellectum."

73 *Del senso,* p. 105, n. 1: "Sensum intellectumque, Aristoteli notum, esse idem."

74 *Ibid.,* p. 111, n. 4: "Esse in brutis sensum, memoriam, disciplinam, discursum, et
intellectum universalis."

75 *Met.,* I, 1, 8, 1, p. 60a-60b: "Sensus autem noster in ratione nostra est illa
notitia quam Theologi intuitivam vocant."

76 *Ibid.,* p. 61b: "Sensus ergo sive mentis sive spiritus gustativa, seu mavis, quasi

intuitiva est sapientia, unde nascitur discursiva ex eo quod non omnia intueri licet, nec simul et semel nobis, sicut Deus."

77 *Del senso*, p. 152. The same idea is expressed in *Met.*, I, 1, 4, 4, p. 39a: "patet sensum esse notitiam innatam sui, et per hoc perceptionem obiecti praesentis, et sapientiam partis eius obiecti."

78 *Met.*, I, 1, 8, 2, p. 65a [erroneously numbered p. 66]: "sensibus primo convenit sapientia . . . Et mens quatenus sentit, sapit, non quatenus ratiocinatur."

79 *Ibid.*, a. 1, pp. 60b-61a.

80 *Ibid.*, a. 2, p. 66a.

81 *Ibid.*, I, 1, 4, 4, p. 38a-38b: "sensus est partis sapientia; totius vero similium est scientia, ratio et syllogismus . . . ."

82 *Ibid.*, II, 6, 9, 6, p. 73b: "Utrum autem sit melior sapientia innata quam adscita . . . Respondeo quod sapientia innata est primalitas et a Deo, idcirco nobilior, verior et certior. Nec enim circa primalitates erramus, nec circa ens et universalia . . . Circa particularitates et nonens erramus: quae noscuntur scientia illata adscititiaque, in qua non solum homines errant, sed etiam bruta, quidquid dicant inertes . . . Verum est quod scientia extensior est sapientia innata; sed non posset extendi nisi ex innata extenderetur; scimus enim alia per hoc quod scimus nos ab aliis motos et affectos."

83 *Ibid.*, I, 2, 1, 1, p. 89a: "Sapientia in nobis ab auctore naturae inest essentialiter, et datur sicut potentia et amor essendi; scientia vero per sapientiam, extrorsum obiecta-entia respicientem, accidentaliter acquiritur."

84 *Ibid.*, I, 1, 8, 1, p. 61a: "omnis cognitio ad sapientiam refertur."

85 *Del senso*, p. 149: "ogni scienza al senso s'appoggia, non dico all'occhio, orecchio, ma alla senziente conoscenza."

86 Cf., for example, Saitta, *op. cit.*, pp. 230-31, where Campanella is presented as leaning heavily towards rationalism and naturalism.

87 *Phils. sens. dem.*, p. 27: "Coniuncta est autem spiritui caduco divina anima, ut eius opera perficiat, et imperet, cui unita est, a quo movetur."

88 *Prodromus*, p. 83: "Cum ergo notum sit spiritum sentire, intelligereque, vanum putamus aliam propter hoc substantiam esse intellectum. Sed ipsum quo nomine Mens vocatur, immistum esse a Deo, ut corporis spiritusque opera perficiat, et felicitatis capacia reddat."

89 *Phil. realis: Quaest. physiol.*, p. 532: "palam est habere animam operationes per se, quibus non communicat sensui."

90 *Del senso*, p. 154, n. 5: "Quapropter eius est [mentis] frenare perficereque cognitionem operationemque omnem."

91 *Epilogo*, p. 473: "Contemplar l'Idee, che sono diverse participalità della prima Idea, è proprio della mente divina all'huomo infusa."

92 *Met.*, I, 1, 6, 3, p. 51a-51b: "Mens autem quidquid operatur sentiens anima, et ipsa operatur cum ea: sentit enim, memoratur, reminiscitur, imaginatur, ratiocinatur circa naturalia, et insuper operationem habet propriam erga transnaturalia per se, ad quam [erroneously written "quem"] etiam rapit spiritum sensitivum."

93 *Ibid.*, III, 14, 4, 2, p. 141b: "licet alibi nos nullam propriam operationem dederimus animae humanae quae spiritui corporeo communis non sit, tamen cognoscere quod res non sunt sicut nobis apparent, non datur brutis, et intelligentiam divinorum, et extasim ut propriam damus." Blanchet makes use of this text, which he compares with another passage from *De sensu rerum et*

magia (ed. 1637; 1. II, c. XXX, p. 109: "Potestque [mens a Deo indita] plura temperamenta actuare, sed principaliter in spiritu habitare, nec operationem habere propriam"), to strengthen his opinion of a double theory of knowledge in Campanella. (Cf. Blanchet, *Campanella, op cit.*, p. 294 and n. 3). Here an observation is in order. Campanella's statement that elsewhere he did not attribute to the human soul any operation which is not common to the spirit, does not mean necessarily that he formerly *denied* such an operation to the soul. It may simply mean that in his previous approach to the question he did not treat the subject thoroughly. This can be evidenced from a further reading in the very chapter of *De sensu rerum et magia* quoted by Blanchet, where we find that Campanella repeats the statement that the soul has no operation of its own, and then he adds, almost incidentally, "excepta [operatione] quam a superis immediate accipit." (Cf. *Del senso*, p. 154, n. 5.) The soul has, there-fore, even according to *De sensu rerum et magia*, an operation of its own. The contradiction between *De sensu* and the *Metaphysica* is only apparent, although in the latter work Campanella's doctrine is developed more fully.

94 *Met.*, II, 7, 6, 2, p. 150a.

95 *Epilogo*, p. 481, note; *Del senso*, p. 151, n. 8; *Met.*, I, 5, 1, 3, p. 344b: "Imagi-natio mentalis, non sensualis, est inventrix scientiarum per ideationem."

96 *Epilogo*, p. 483, ed. *P* in note: "Imaginatio enim mentis potius ideatio dici potest."

97 *Ibid.*, pp. 482-83, note: "Consideratio est ratiocinium multa conferens ad iudicium, ut sidera astrologus, unde nomen sortitur. Contemplatio est multorum simul attenta intellectio intuitiva. Cogitatio et meditatio ad imaginativam pertinent, quae laborat ubi ex praedictis certitudo haberi non potuit, prop-tereaque ut plurimum ideales causas consulit aut fingit." *Ibid.*, p. 483, ed. *P* in note: "Animali divino de naturalibus scientia et iudicium insufficiens erat, nisi Deus illi virtutem ideativam addidisset, per quam tot res et mundos et systemata fere facit imaginaria, quot Deus faceret realia."

98 *Met.*, I, 1, 6, Appendix, pp. 57-58.

99 Di Napoli, *op. cit.*, p. 278.

100 *Met.*, I, 1, 4, 4, p. 39b: "alia est ratio et intellectus sensualis, in quo thesaurizat Aristoteles sapientiam: et aliud mentalis unde assurgimus ad invisibilia et aeterna, de quo Theologi et meliores Philosophi loquuntur." Cf. also *Del senso*, p. 105, n. 1.

101 *Met.*, III, 12, 10, 2 [erroneously written a. 5], p. 99a: "Intellectus vero est intrinsece naturam rei legere: et si totam et in se legit, vocatur intuitiva intellectio, qua similis est sensui percipienti partem. Si vero non totam, sed quatenus similem alii, vocatur abstractiva; ex eo quippe quod cognosco Petrum esse hominem similem Paulo, abstractive nosco eum, quod etiam discursus est. Sed quatenus nosco hunc hominem Petrum cum suis conditionibus, intuitive intelligo; *intelligere ergo in hoc a sensu differt, quod totam naturam cognoscit, sensus partem*" (italics are the author's).

102 *Epilogo*, p. 470, ed. *P* in note: "Intelligere est intus legere in rebus sensibilibus id quod foris latet, et per discursum ex his quae patent: et hoc obscurum est in brutis, in homine mirificum et clarum. At vulgo intellectio reputatur illa diminuta cognitio, quae abstractione constat, non quidem facta ab mente activa purificante obiecta, ut putant (hoc Deus enim solus posset), sed a diminutione cognoscibilitatis et impotentia cognoscentis: sicut oculus potest sentire colorem

pomi non sentiendo saporem, at non quia abstrahit active illum ab hoc, sed quia non potest etiam hunc sentire vel sentitum retinere; et hoc proprium est puerorum et bestiarum et a longe sentientium. Intellectus enim, qua intellectus est, intus legit omnia, etiam minimas singularitates (alioquin intellectus Angelicus et Divinus istas non sentirent), et non solum universalitates, immo et universalem Ideam, nedum universale ideatum; et hoc inest homini. Sed imbecillitas est spiritus animalis ista abstractio, quam non recte vocant intellectum, cum non legat intus latentia et plene sicut Angelus, sed extrinseca communiaque sicut puer: quare potius apprehensiva virtus dici deberet."

103 *Epilogo*, p. 475: "L'intelletto adunque dell'Idea come suggello è della mente, e dell'Idea come suggellata è del senso interiore."

104 *Met.*, I, 1, 6, 7, p. 56b.

105 *Ibid.*, I, 1, 6, Appendix, p. 58a: ". . . et divus Thomas cogitativam vocat intellectum rationemque in secunda secundae." The reference is to St. Thomas's *Sum. Theol.*, II-II, q. 49, a. 2: "Utrum intellectus sit pars prudentiae." Cf. *Epilogo*, p. 488, ed. *F* in note. See also *Del senso*, p. 153.

106 *Met.*, I, 1, 6, Appendix, p. 58b.

107 *Del senso*, p. 116, n. 9: "hominem rationalem mentalem intelligimus, bruta vera ratione sensitiva donamus: quam D. Thomas vocat aestimativam, *quae per essentiam est sensus, participatione ratio*" (italics added).

108 Cf. St. Thomas, *In II De anima*, lect. 13, n. 395ff.; *Quaest. disp. De anima*, a. 13 c; *Sum. Theol.*, I, q. 78, a. 4 c.

109 *Ibid., passim.*

110 *Epilogo*, pp. 488-89.

111 *Met.*, III, 13, 3, 1, p. 126a: "triplex est universale: aliud in causando iuxta quodcumque genus causae, sicut sol causa est sublunarium; aliud in essendo, sicut angelus est eminenter omnia quae novit, et quae sub ipso sunt; aliud in praedicando, sicut similitudo multorum essentialis vel accidentalis uno donata nomine."

112 *Ibid.*

113 *Ibid.*, p. 126a-126b. See also *Phil. realis: Quaest. physiol.*, p. 531.

114 *Met.*, I, 2, 3, 3, p 106a-106b: "Nos autem dicimus in re esse universale, idest, ideam a qua oritur similitudo, quae est unitas singularium; et hac ratione non dari in singularibus, quae sola sunt in natura inferiori, aptitudinem essendi in multis per se, nisi per ideam; . . . universale in repraesentando ubique est, scilicet in re et in intellectu; praedicatur autem quatenus in intellectu formaliter, sed in re fundamentaliter."

115 *Theol.*, I, 11, 9, pp. 248-49: "Universale platonicum est idea individuorum et causa praecellens res materiales, et non posterius: est (enim) sicut domus in mente artificis; aristotelicum vero sicuti domus in sensu a longe spectantis fabricatam ideatam ab artifice: illud dat esse et scire, hoc vero est effectus inspectionis et languidae cognitionis, sed signum illius posterius quoddam."

116 *Phil. realis: Quaest. physiol.*, p. 531.

117 *Met.*, III, 13, 2, 5, p. 118b: "Plato ergo elevat hominem ad perfectam scientiam, et ad divinorum notionem a sensibilibus . . . Aristoteles vero in sensibilibus haeret, tanquam semper addiscens et nihil intelligens."

118 *Ibid.*, I, 1, 4, 7, p. 43a-43b: "recte Durandus sustulit intellectum agentem quoniam abstrahere species universales non est actus alicuius agentis causae,

sed debilitas obiecti in singularitatibus, et fortitudo in communitatibus." See also *Epilogo,* pp. 477-78, where Campanella argues against Aristotle's agent intellect.

119 *Epilogo,* p. 475.

120 *Del senso,* p. 148; *Met.,* I, 1, 4, 4, p. 39a.

121 *Theol.,* I, 11, 3, p. 210: "cognoscere in universali est confusum imperfectumque."

122 *Met.,* I, 1, 4, 4, p. 39b; *Epilogo,* p. 474; *Del senso,* p. 106. See the same example in St. Thomas, *Sum. Theol.,* I, q. 85, a. 3 c.

123 *Met.,* I, 1, 6, 7, p. 55b: "tam sensus quam intellectus apprehendunt universale."

124 *Ibid.,* p. 55a: "profecto illum intellectum universalis, quem Aristoteles hominibus tribuit, magis convenire brutis palam est."

125 *Ibid.,* I, 1, 4, 4, p. 39b: "Sic et canes et equi universalia norunt magis quam particularia."

126 *Epilogo,* p. 474 and note; *Del senso,* p. 106.

127 *Epilogo,* p. 476. The same example is used in *Del senso,* pp. 105-106; *Theol.,* I, 11, 9, p. 248. It is found in almost the same terms in St. Thomas, *Sum. Theol.,* I, q. 85, a. 3 c.

128 *Theol.,* I, 11, 9, p. 248: "universale aristotelicum non fit ab abstractione, sed languore cognoscentis."

129 *Phil. realis: Quaest. physiol.,* p. 533.

130 *Met.,* I, 1, 5, 1, p. 45b: "universale Peripateticum crassi spiritus apti sunt percipere, inepti ad singularitates. Tenues vero purique universale Platonicum, et ideas rerum in se percipere et imaginari possunt magis ac simul rerum singularitates, et una cum mente ad divina levari."

131 *Ibid.,* II, 6, 8, 2, p. 60a: "idem sensus particulare et universale novit, similiter et intellectus."

132 *Ibid.,* I, 1, 6, 7, p. 55a: "idem est universale et particulare. Petrus enim est homo, et hic homo: idem ergo est obiectum, ergo eadem facultate cognoscitur. Si asseris cognosci posse universale non cognito particulari, falleris. Intellectus enim non capit obiecta extrinsecus, sed intrinsecus a sensu delata; ergo sensus iam percepit utrumque."

133 *Ibid.; Del senso,* p. 106.

134 *Met.,* I, 1, 6, 7, p. 56a: "quando intellectus abstrahit universale a singularibus, praecognoscit singularia: alioquin abstraheret falso, sicut ex pluribus pomis singularibus abstraheret speciem pyri, vel peponis."

135 *Ibid.:* "anima separata et Deus et angelus cognoscunt singularia. Ergo non erat intellectus noster faciendus aliud a sensu, propterea quod cognoscit singularia, cum illi non repugnet, quatenus intellectus est eadem nosse; immo eo magis ipsi convenit, quo magis corpori inhaeret singulari."

136 *Ibid.:* "Propterea Scotus et Durandus, Theologi primates, dicunt intellectum cognoscere singularia, etiam directe. Nos autem ostendimus quod sensus cognoscit etiam universale. Ergo eadem est anima utrumque noscens."

137 *Ibid.,* I, 1, 9, 2, p. 67a: "Cum autem quaeritur cuius est scientia, singularium ne, an universalis. Respondeo quod inventiva tractat singularia, doctrinalis universalia ex singularibus collecta similibus."

138 *Ibid.,* p. 67b: "dicimus universale non fieri a nobis, nisi virtute ideae in qua sunt unum particularia quo similia."

139 *Del senso,* p. 106.

CHAPTER FIVE

1 *Met.*, II, 6, 14, 1, p. 99a: "Sapientiae autem obiectum dicimus ipsam veritatem. *Est veritas* (ut aiunt) *adaequatio rei et intellectus*"; *Phil. sens. dem.*, p. 64: "veritas est adaequatio rei ad intellectum."

2 *Epilogo*, p. 482, note: "veritas nostra est aequatio intellectus ad rem, et rei ad divinam potentiam." Cf. also *Theol.*, I, 12, 1, p. 254.

3 *Met.*, II, 6, 14, 1, p. 99a: "duplex est intellectus, alius noscens, producens veritatem ut divinus; alius non producens sed noscens, ut intellectus creatus. Res ergo cunctae dicuntur verae quatenus adaequantur intellectui divino, a quo habent esse; quatenus vero adaequantur intellectui nostro, non sunt verae, sed faciunt veritatem in nobis; sed nos veri sumus si rem intelligimus sicuti est. Sin autem intelligimus sicuti non est, sumus falsi. Igitur in rerum natura non est falsitas aliqua, sed veritas omnino, quia res non possunt esse nisi sicut voluit Deus ut sint." See also *Epilogo*, p. 482.

4 *Met.*, II, 6, 14, 1, p. 99a-99b.

5 *Ibid.*, p. 99b.

6 *Ibid.*: "Igitur non videtur Aristoteles recte posuisse falsitatem solum in intellectu humano, quoniam et in re est quatenus deficit ab esse . . ." This statement is in apparent contradiction with another statement of *Del senso delle cose*, which reads as follows: "nel mondo non ci è bugia, perchè ogni cosa è qual'è in se stessa, ma non in noi" (*ibid.*, p. 66). The contradiction disappears when we consider that in *Del senso* Campanella prescinds entirely from the notion of nonbeing as opposed to being, which he developed later, and wants only to emphasize the transcendental character of truth in things in conformity with the scholastic principle that every being is true. Furthermore, in *Del senso* he speaks of "lie" or "deception," whereas in the *Metaphysica* he speaks only of "falsity," attaching to this word the connotation of lack of perfection in being. The two texts under discussion can therefore be explained without admitting a real contradiction in Campanella's teaching.

7 *Met.*, II, 6, 14, 1, p. 100a: "Veritas et falsitas in rebus simplicibus sunt esse et nonesse, et semper mistae sunt, quoniam nullum esse respondet ideae prorsus."

8 *Ibid.*: "Neque posset [esse] in intellectu veritas, nisi esset prius in re. Intellectus enim noster est verus quando est conformis rebus, falsus quando difformis." *Ibid.*, a. 3, p. 102a: "antequam cognoscatur res est vera, sicuti antequam appetatur est bona; obiectum enim omne praevenit potentiam cuius est."

9 *Theol.*, I, 12, 1, p. 252.

10 *Ibid.*, pp. 252-53: "Res autem naturales verae sunt, si imitantur divinas ideas, a quibus oriuntur. Et quoniam Deus non potest errare in operibus suis, omnis res est vera. Idcirco verum et ens convertuntur."

11 *Ibid.*, p. 253.

12 *Ibid.*, pp. 255-56: "patet quoniam est una veritas prima invariabilis, et omnia quae sunt vera, ad eius exemplar vera sunt."

13 *Commentaria super poëmatibus Urbani VIII*, p. 403: "Intellectus humanus non mensurat res, quarum non est auctor; sed mensuratur a rebus, et est verus quum illis prorsus assimilatur, ut intelligat sicuti sunt; non autem aliter. Res autem sunt verae non quatenus a nobis intelliguntur, sed quatenus a Deo, et sunt sicut a Deo esse acceperunt, falsae autem cum aliter." MS quoted in Di Napoli, *op. cit.*, p. 264.

14 *Met.,* II, 6, 14, 1, p. 100b: "Veritas enim et falsitas sunt in re ipsum ens et nonens, simplex vel compositum. In intellectu vero humano veritas est conformatio eius ad res; cum enim aliquid intelligimus, in illud mutamur et esse eius suscipimus . . . In hac autem immutatione est iudicium subito praestoque de re immutante. At si iudicat prout est, veritas est in iudicante intellectu. Si prout non est, ipsum immutans falsitas est in intellectu."

15 Cf. Aristotle, *Met.,* VI, 4, 1027b 25; IX, 10, 1051b 3-4; St. Thomas, *Sum. Theol.,* I, q. 16, a. 2; q. 17, a. 2; *De veritate,* q. 1, a. 9.

16 *Met.,* II, 6, 14, 3, p. 101b: "Concedimus nos in intellectu esse verum et falsum, sicut in cognoscente; sed non formaliter, ut ipsi volunt, quoniam in rebus est formaliter veritas et falsitas . . . Et est etiam causaliter, quatenus facit ut oratio et intellectus noster sit verus et falsus. Praeterea dicimus in intellectu et sensu esse verum et falsum, quatenus sunt res quaedam; et causaliter et formaliter sic in eis est verum et falsum, et non modo cognoscitive. Sicut enim res adaequata ideae est vera, inadaequata falsa, ita intellectus adaequatus rei est verus, inadaequatus, falsus, licet et hoc habeat amplius, quoniam etiam potest cognoscere verum et falsum directe, et suum reflexe: quod et sensui competit."

17 *Ibid.,* p. 102a: "cognoscere aut dicere verum facit intellectum veracem sed non constituit rei veritatem."

18 *Ibid.,* "intellectus est verus quando adaequatur, non quando cognoscit adaequationem."

19 *Ibid.*

20 *Ibid.,* p. 102a-102b: "Quapropter alia est veritas iudicii, alia est rei, alia est conformationis cognoscentis ad cognoscibile, licet haec sit quoque rei, veluti omnes aliae immutationes."

21 *Phil. sens. dem.,* pp. 28, 61, 63, 68; *Epilogo,* pp. 191-200; *Del senso,* pp. 37-41; *Met.,* I, 2, 5bis, 9, pp. 199ff.

22 St. Thomas, *In Libros Sententiarum,* I, d. 40, q. 1, a. 1, ad 1 (Parma ed.).

23 For Aristotle's doctrine on sensation and intellection see his treatises *De anima,* II-III, and *De sensu et sensato.*

24 *Del senso,* p. 10; *ibid.,* pp. 78-79; *Met.,* I, 1, 4 (erroneously written c. 5), 7, p. 42a, and especially *Met.,* II, 6, 8, 1, p. 58a.

25 For all Campanella's arguments against the so-called Aristotelian theory of information cf. *Del senso,* pp. 79-80, text and note; *ibid.,* pp. 84-89; *Epilogo,* p. 478; *Met.,* II, 6, 8, 1, p. 58b.

26 *Del senso,* p. 81; *Prodromus,* p. 83.

27 *Met.,* I, 1, 4, 2, p. 35a: "cum species intentionales in sensibus recipi dicunt, se ipsos seducunt. Aut enim sunt intentionales, quia sola intentione nostra considerantur, et hoc stultum est: nam nos et bruta sentimus absque intentione Peripatetica; vel quia sunt reales, sed exiliter, et non constantes, ut color iridis, et hoc nos dicimus: at non semper, nam aliqua obiecta fortia imprimunt se ita sensibus ut expelli vix queant."

28 *Epilogo,* p. 478.

29 *Del senso,* p. 89, n. 2.

30 *Epilogo,* p. 413; *Del senso,* p. 81.

31 *Del senso,* p. 89.

32 Democritus followed Leucippus, the founder of the atomistic school, in explaining the process of sensation as well as of knowledge in general from a purely mechanical standpoint. Since in his opinion the soul is composed of atoms like

every other being, sensation is nothing but the impact of atoms of the external objects on the atoms of the soul, while the sense organs are merely passages through which these atoms are introduced. Hence vision, for instance, does not consist in the actual seeing of the objects themselves but only of their "images" (δείκελα, εἴδωλα), which objects are constantly shedding. The images, however, do not reproduce the objects exactly; for they are subject to distortion by the intervening air. For this reason things at a distance are not clear and distinct to us. Differences of color are due to the smoothness or roughness of the images. A similar explanation is given of the other senses, which are all reduced, in the last resort, to the sense of touch. For a further exposition of Democritus' theory of knowledge cf. John Burnet, *Greek Philosophy: Thales to Plato* (London: Macmillan and Co., 1950), pp. 196-99.

33 *Del senso*, p. 82 and notes; *Epilogo*, p. 400.

34 *Met.*, II, 6, 8, 1, p. 58a; *Del senso*, p. 10.

35 *Met.*, I, 1, 4, 1, p. 33a: "sentire est pati. Nulla enim res sentitur quae non possit agere in sentientem vim. Ea enim quae sunt in America nos Itali non sentimus, quoniam in nos non agunt; sed maxime sentimus quae maxime in nos agunt, ut frigus maximum et calorem potentissimum. Sensus ergo videtur esse passio, per quam scimus quid est quod agit in nos, quoniam similem sibi entitatem in nobis facit."

36 *Ibid.*; *Del senso*, p. 10.

37 *Met.*, I, 1, 4, 1, p. 33b: "In hoc ergo fundatur scientia, quia simile sibi facit omne agens. Et cognoscimus illud quid sit, quoniam similes illi efficimur, vel ex parte: . . . si autem simile non facit simile, nihil scimus." Cf. also *Del senso*, p. 89.

38 *Del senso*, p. 10; *Epilogo*, p. 367; *Met.*, I, 1, 4, 2, p. 35a: "non enim sensus est ipsa passio nobis, sicut Peritateticis, sed perceptio passionis, immo actus est iudicantis de passione percepta"; *ibid.*, I, 1, 5, 1, p. 44a: "Ergo non sola immutatio est sensus, sed immutationis perceptio. Videtur tamen magis actus esse vitalis iudicativus, qui rem perceptam prout est cognovit." See also *Theol.*, I, 11, 1, p. 196.

39 *Met.*, I, 1, 5, 1, p. 44b; *ibid.*, I, 1, 4, 4, p. 38a; *ibid.*, I, 1, 6, 6, p. 54a: "Ex modica autem immutatione sensus iudicat de toto obiecto immutante." Cf. also *Epilogo*, p. 367.

40 *Del senso*, p. 65.

41 *Met.*, I, 1, 9, 9, p. 73a: "dicimus sapientiam formaliter non esse passionem, sed perceptionem et iudicium de passione, ac proinde de obiecto passionem inferente."

42 *Epilogo*, p. 367.

43 *Met.*, II, 6, 8, 1, p. 59a. In this place Campanella reports the doctrine on sensation mentioned above as Telesio's teaching. There is no doubt that he shared the same opinion in his previous writings and never departed from it entirely, not even in the *Metaphysica*, where he speaks in terms of a new explanation of knowledge different from that of Telesio.

44 These same concepts are repeated over and over through *Del senso delle cose e della magia*, thus making all further references useless. But since it is our claim that Campanella holds to this teaching also in the *Metaphysica*, we shall quote a few passages from this work in confirmation of our view. Thus in *Met.*, I, 1, 4, 2, p. 35a, when speaking of the kind of change that takes

place in sensation, he says: "non propterea erit immutatio intentionalis et
non realis, quia realiter alterata non sentiunt: non enim sensus est ipsa passio
nobis, sicut Peripateticis, sed perceptio passionis, immo actus est iudicantis de
passione percepta." A little further (*Met.*, I, 1, 4, 4, p. 38a), he emphasizes the
kind of change and transformation that takes place in the sentient subject in
the following terms: "Quando igitur sentiens patitur anima a re aliqua immutatur in illam, sed non totaliter, alioquin moreretur in se et fieret res illa a qua
immutatur, ut lignum fit ignis; sed neque a tota re immutatur, quoniam
impossibile est. Tum quia non ab interioribus et cunctis obiecti partibus tangi
potest: sensus autem omnis tactus est et fit tangendo, ut dictum est. Tum quia
si a vehementibus viribus rerum potentium tangeretur, in illas immutaretur
et iudicium praecedens amitteret et novum acquireret; . . . spiritus paululum
immutatur ab obiecto, sapit illum paululum, et ex illo paululo sapit reliquum
per discursum a simili." Finally (*Met.*, I, 1, 5, 1, p. 44a-44b), he stresses the
notion of sensation as a perception of passion and a judging act of the sense
by saying: "Licet ostenderimus sensum esse passionem realem contra Peripa-
teticos, haud tamen nunc consentimus eis quod sit passio. Videtur enim nobis
passionis potius esse perceptio. . . . Ergo non sola immutatio est sensus, sed
immutationis perceptio. Videtur tamen magis actus esse vitalis iudicativus, qui
rem perceptam prout est cognovit, nam et bruta multa percipiunt absque
iudicio, similiter et delirantes. . . . Ex eo enim modico quod sentimus de
caeteris iudicamus. Qui autem non recte sentit, nec recte iudicat."

45 *Del senso*, p. 68: "Tutti li sensi esser tatto, ma li sensorii e modi differire";
   Met., I, 1, 4, 2, p. 34b: "Omnis enim sensus tactus est."

46 *Del senso*, p. 68, n. 5; *Epilogo*, p. 368.

47 Here is the full text as reported in the *Epilogo*, p. 368, ed. *P* in note: "Quoniam
   ad sentientem spiritum quae ex rebus ad nos veniunt non poterant admitti,
   oportuit organa admittentia fieri, in quibus assistens spiritus sentiat, non ut
   forma organi, sed operator per illa, a quibus etiam recedit in somno et accedit
   in vigilia. Et quoniam diversum non patitur, ergo nec sentitur a diverso, neque
   simile persimili: idcirco tot sensoria fabrefecit spiritus, Deo duce, quot a rebus
   ad se entitates consimiles in natura, sed non in gradu, communicantur. Et
   quoniam spiritus est lucidus, subtilis, calidus, mobilis, propterea aedificata sunt
   illi organa alia, quibus lucem admittit simplicem et coloratam, ut oculus; alia
   quibus motum et hunc promoventia obiecta, ut auris; alia quibus tenuitatem
   exhalantem, ut nasus; alia quibus substantiam temperatam calore, ut lingua. In
   toto autem voluit calorem et frigus, tanquam semper et ubique agentia, sentiri
   tactione. Aliud a rebus non advenit, et si advenit, non est perceptibile nobis;
   neque haec nisi in gradu potentiori, ut possint agere in minus potens. Etsi
   enim sensus non sit passio, tamen ex passione sequitur. Et ideo sunt alia per
   sensilia, ut calor et lux et odor et sapor et sonus; alia per aliud, ut calida,
   illuminata, odorantia, saporosa et sonantia; alia per accidens mista his, ut
   homo, campana, arbor, caelum, corpus, substantia et anima et amicitia, ad
   quae ex sensatis discurrendo sensum extendimus, eaque quasi sentire videmus."

48 *Met.*, II, 6, 8, 1, pp. 58b-59a: "Deferunt vero se se obiecta ad sentientem
   animam, vel quia sunt per se activa, ut calor, et frigus, et lux, vel cum alterius
   actione miscentur, ut quantitas illuminata, et substantia calida, et frigida, et
   mobilis, et exhalans, ad sensoria deferuntur a calore, vel frigore, vel a luce,

vel ab aëre, motum communicante auribus; vel eorum tenuitas subit nares. Ita quod omnis sensatio per tactum fit et per immutationem corpoream."

49 In addition to the texts already quoted in this connection, reference is made to *Met.*, I, 1, 5, 2, p. 45a: "assimilatio autem fit per passionem realem a realitatibus, non ab intentionalibus obiectorum." See also *Met.*, II, 6, 8, 7, tit., p. 66.

50 Cf., for example, *Epilogo*, p. 367: "Sente lo spirito le cose e le conosce toccandole dolcemente, viene da esse cose sensibili mutato tanto che può discernere le forze loro"; *Met.*, I, 1, 5, 2, p. 45a: "necesse est animam sentientem rem corpoream esse quae patiatur a corporibus, et qualitatibus, et viribus corporum, habeatque cum illis et symbolum et commune subiectum, quibus *patitur receptive ut materia, et perditive ut calor a frigore, et acquisitive ut tepiditas a calore potiori*" (italics added).

51 In a passage in *Del senso* Campanella also ridicules the opinion of Lucretius, as though the material object, when seen by the sense, would be stripped of its superficial likeness (*ibid.*, p. 90).

52 *Met.*, I, 1, 4, 2, p. 35b: "cum aiunt non esse colorem Petri neque Petrum in oculo, concedimus; at non sequitur, ergo non movetur visus realiter suo ab obiecto. Nam Petrus non est obiectum visus, neque color, sed lux. Lux autem realiter intrat oculos: color ergo videtur per lucem ipso faedatam, et figura per colorem, et Petrus per utrumque syllogismo quodam sensuali. Dicimus ergo ab his quae obiecta propria non sunt moveri sensum realiter, sed per accidens: ideoque non ipsa, sed aliud, cui mixta sunt, sentiri. Id autem palam realiter movet." Cf. also *Del senso*, pp. 83, 89-90; *Theol.*, I, 11, 1, pp. 195-96.

53 The immediateness as well as the mediateness of the object to the sense organs in the process of sensation is taught by Campanella in many passages of his works. This teaching is contained in the texts of the *Physiologia* and *Metaphysica* quoted above in nn. 47 and 48, and is also clear from the following passage in *Met.*, I, 1, 4, 2, p. 35b: "Neque enim odor, neque sapor, neque sonus, neque calor, nisi intrinsecus recipiantur sentiuntur. Cum vero a longe in nos agunt, ab aëre deferuntur, si aërem afficere potentes sunt. Palam enim ignis calefacit nos, *non tactu modo immediate, sed per intermedium quoque aërem, calorem effundendo; magis tamen cum sine medio tangitur*" (italics ours).

54 Cf. n. 32 above.

55 Thus he writes in *Del senso*, pp. 89-90: "Qui ti puoi guardare dalla sciocchezza d'alcuni Aristotelici che delle cose le similitudini o specie venire al senso dicono." And in the *Met.*, I, 1, 4, 5, p. 40b: "non enim suscipit anima rerum species, sed motum quo a rebus afficitur; neque totius, sed partis, per quam sentit totum discurrendo." Cf. also *Theol.*, I, 11, 1, p. 198. One cannot fail to notice that in the foregoing passages Campanella speaks always of *the species of things.*

56 This is clear from the following text of the *Met.*, I, 1, 9, 5, p. 71b: "Hinc advertere licet quod Peripatetici non recte docent speciem receptam in oculo non esse quod sentitur, sed quo sentitur; nisi enim ipsa sentiretur non esset causa ut id, unde advenit, sentiatur. Sic nisi calor receptus in manu sentiretur, neque causa esset ut ignis sentiatur: propter quod enim unumquodque est et illud magis; est ergo lux colorata in oculo, quae vere sentitur, *ut quod;* et quia ipsa sentitur, et similis est rei coloratae ex qua reflectitur, est simul *quo* res

colorata sentitur." The same idea is expressed in the *Theol.*, I, 11, 1, pp. 195-96.

57 Here are some of the passages in which Campanella seems to admit the species of things: *Del senso*, p. 98: "dunque la medesima virtù [la memoria] sente le spezie e le riserba"; *Theol.*, I, 5, 7, p. 122: ". . . cogniti in cognoscente non est essentia sed simulacrum: non enim lapis [est] in oculo aut in mente, sed lapis species: fit enim cognoscens simile cognoscibili per illam"; *ibid.*, I, 11, 2, p. 207: "cognoscimus enim res per speciem vel mutationem nostri a rebus factam."

58 That Campanella rejects the idea of the species coming directly from the objects has been amply demonstrated in the course of our discussion. The texts quoted above in n. 55 are a further confirmation of it. His acceptance, on the other hand, of *some kind* of species also seems well established. As a matter of fact, in the very places where he denies that the species of things are received in the senses, he admits that some sort of species is involved in the process of sensation. Thus in dealing with sight in *Del senso*, p. 89, he mentions "the light dyed with the species," and then he adds immediately, "ma *questa specie* non informa tutto il senziente spirito, ma solo lo muove a giudicare il suo oggetto, donde viene." The same thing can be observed in the *Met.*, I, 1, 4, 5, p. 40b, where he states that the sensitive soul "et amicitiam et incorporea *per species corporeas* imaginatur." In the *Theol.*, I, 11, 1, p. 195, it is likewise explicitly affirmed that in sight "lux tincta colore lapidis tingit spiritum sentientem in oculo, qui affectus tali mutatione discit lapidem." This is in perfect agreement with our interpretation of Campanella's thought.

59 Although a new approach to the problem of knowledge can be noticed in the *Metaphysica*, we read nowhere in Campanella's works of a change of his mind in regard to the doctrine of the species.

60 *Del senso*, pp. 83-84.

61 *Ibid.*, p. 84, n. 1.

62 *Met.*, II, 6, 8, 1, p. 59a. Because of the importance of the text, we report it in full: "Nos autem aliter sapimus, videlicet sensum, seu sapientiam pertinere ad ipsum esse rerum; et sentiri et cognosci unumquodque quia est ipsa natura cognoscens. Nam cum sensatio sit assimilatio, et omnis cognitio fiat propterea quod ipsa essentia cognoscitiva fit ipsum cognoscibile, et cum factum est ipsum cognoscibile perfecte illud cognoscit, quoniam iam est illud, ergo *cognoscere est esse;* ergo quodcumque ens plura est, plura cognoscit, quod pauca, pauca."

63 The soul in fact, Campanella says, is not a mere potency, like primary matter, but a being in act which, because of its simplicity, can be affected by a plurality of entities: "anima sentiens non est potentia pura sicut materia, sed ens actu: at quidem simplex, ideoque pluribus potest entitatibus effici" (*Met.*, I, 1, 4, 6, p. 41a).

64 *Met.*, I, 2, 5, 1, p. 153b: "cum autem [anima] res obiectas intelligit, non res illas intelligit, sed seipsam ab illis mutatam in illas."

65 *Ibid.*, II, 6, 8, 2, p. 61b: "palam est omnem cognitionem esse entitatem rei cognitae, in quam res cognoscens mutatur, vel potius esse entitatem rei cognoscentis, vel quam acquirit, vel quam habet."

66 *Ibid.*, II, 6, 9, 1, p. 69a-69b: "Nos autem neque actionem, neque passionem esse cognitionem dicimus, sed quid longe divinius, et entitatis praeeminentiam vocamus vocabulo novo . . . ac primalitatem, et pertinere ad esse."

67 *Ibid.*, II, 6, 8, 1, p. 59a.

68 *Ibid.*

69 *Ibid.*

70 *Ibid.*, p. 59a-59b. For Aristotle's teaching on this point cf. his *De anima*, III, 427a; 429a-433a. See also Averroës' commentary on the same treatise for the latter's viewpoint.

71 *Met.*, II, 6, 8, 1, p. 59b.

72 *Ibid.*, a. 4, p. 62a-62b.

73 *Ibid.*, p. 62b.

74 *Ibid.*, a. 1, p. 59b: "nullum cognoscibile est idem cum cognoscente, nisi esse nativum ipsius cognoscentis."

75 The objectivity of the external world as independent of our minds can be further documented by passages in which Campanella states, for instance, that we do not sense things as they are: "quia [sentiens vis] sentit alias res propter hoc quod sentit se immutatam ab illis, propterea non sentit sicuti sunt" (*Met.*, I, 1, 8, 1, p. 60a); or that we know things only in part, and to the extent that we are affected by them: "palam est nos scire ex parte, et non prout sunt res, sed prout afficimur" (*ibid.*, I, 1, 9, 13, p. 86a); or finally, when he affirms that things in nature are different from what they are in us: "Omne ergo quod videtur est in natura et in nobis: sed aliter utrique" (*ibid.*, a. 12, p. 78a). Cf. also the *Epilogo*, pp. 475-76, where he says that man does not make things, but only knows them.

76 It is true that Campanella does not deal with these various aspects of the problem under discussion in a clear and distinct way. This could hardly have been expected of him in his time when epistemology was not considered a distinct branch of philosophy. Thus, while we are ready to admit that he sometimes uses language suggestive of idealism, we are far from agreeing with those who try to present him as the forerunner of modern idealism.

77 Cf. n. 62 above.

78 *Met.*, II, 6, 8, 2, tit., p. 60: "Cognitionem sensitivam, imaginativam, memorativam in eo consistere quod cognoscens est esse cogniti, vel fit. Ergo in facto esse, vel innato esse, essentiari, et non immutatione, aut informatione omnino."

79 *Ibid.*, a. 4, p. 62b: "notitia sui est esse suum, notitia aliorum est esse aliorum."

80 *Ibid.*, a. 2, p. 61b: "Constat ergo seipsa omnia entia sentire, quoniam seipsa sunt absque eo quod fiant; realiter ergo et fundamentaliter cognoscere est esse; formaliter vero distinguitur; quia est iudicatum esse."

81 Cf., e.g., Di Napoli, *op. cit.*, p. 268.

82 The distinction between these two types of knowledge of the extramental world is clearly indicated in many passages of Campanella's works. See, for instance, *Met.*, II, 6, 8, 2, p. 60b: "Nec oportet spiritum fieri res ipsas quando sentit, sed modicam ipsarum entitatem; ex qua de reliqua iudicat, quoniam quasi et reliqua fit, dum modica illa consimilis fit et est"; *ibid.*, III, 12, 10, 2 (erroneously written a. 5), p. 99a: "quoniam esse aliud quam quod sumus nobis impossibile est ex toto, sed tantum ex parte, ideo scientia nostra est discursus."

83 In fact Campanella states that in knowledge by inference or through judgment the spirit "*quasi* et reliqua fit" (cf. first text quoted in n. 82), which is tantamount to saying that it is only in a very imperfect manner that the spirit becomes the object known.

84 *Met.*, II, 6, 8, 4, p. 63a: "Animam et cuncta entia seipsa pernosse primo et essentialiter, caetera vero secundario et accidentaliter inquantum norunt seipsa mutata et facta aliqualiter ea, a quibus immutantur."

85 *Ibid.*, II, 8, 4, 2, p. 160a: "Non enim scimus neque volumus nisi quod sumus essentialiter, ut nosipsos, vel accidentaliter, sicut quae extra nos volumus et scimus; quae sane intantum volumus et scimus, inquantum nos illa res scita et volita facti sumus." Cf. also *ibid.*, I, 2, 5, 7, tit., p. 160.

86 *Ibid.*, II, 6, 6, 9, p. 36b.

87 See n. 80 above.

88 Cf. *Met.*, II, 6, 11, 10, p. 93a-93b, where the Scotistic formal distinction is applied to the proprinciples in God, in opposition to their real distinction in creatures. The present writer does not agree with Di Napoli in interpreting the *formaliter vero distinguitur* of Campanella's text mentioned in n. 80 as a mere qualification of the extramental knowledge as such ("formalmente, *come conoscere,*" *op. cit.*, p. 268). He believes, on the contrary, that the adverb *formaliter* stands in this connection for *formal distinction.* Cf. Blanchet, *Campanella, op. cit.*, p. 275, where the same view is expressed.

89 *Met.*, I, 1, 4 (erroneously written c. 5), 7, p. 44b; *ibid.*, I, 1, 9, 9, p. 73b.

90 *Ibid.*, I, 1, 4, 1, p. 33b: "Putamus enim obiecta sciendi occasionem praebere, non scientiam"; *ibid.*, I, 2, 2, 2, p. 96b: "obiecta ergo non dant id quod est primalitatum, sed specificant et occasionem praebent ita exercendi se"; *ibid.*, I, 2, 3, 1, p. 100a: "res cognoscimus propterea quod earum similitudines in nobis imprimuntur, ut Peripatetici autumant, aut quia excitantur, ut Platonici, aut quia specificantur, ut nos."

91 Amerio, *Campanella, op. cit.*, p. 141.

92 *Theol.*, IV, 5, 2: "credo quod anima per modum unius habet omnia obiecta et non distinguit nisi de foris excitata ab ideatis obiectis." MS quoted in Amerio, *Campanella, op. cit.*, p. 141.

93 *Met.*, II, 6, 9, 1, p. 69a-69b: "passionem intervenire [in cognitione] quatenus esse fluens dicit; et hoc esse fluens quatenus additur ab obiectis cognoscenti essentiae non parere notitiam, sed notitiae radicali occasionem se se manifestandi praebere . . . in adventu novae entitatis, iuxta acceptionem vel refutationem, [notitia] comparere solet accidentaliter, ut ignis ex percusso lapide."

94 *Ibid.*, I, 1, 9, 9, p. 73b.

95 *Ibid.*, I, 2, 2, 2, p. 96b: "Intelligibile . . . non movet intellectum ad intellectionem, neque dat illi ut intelligat, sed ut hoc intelligat occasionem offert."

96 *Ibid.*, I, 1, 9, 9, p. 73b: "scientia non acquiritur, sed scibilia acquiruntur."

97 *Ibid.*, II, 6, 9, 1, p. 69b: "sic intelligo aliquid inexplicabile verbo hominis."

98 Di Napoli, *op. cit.*, pp. 271-72.

99 *Met.*, I, 1, 8, 1, p. 59a.

100 *Ibid.*, II, 6, 8, 4, p. 63a.

101 Cf. nn. 67 and 70.

102 *Met.*, II, 6, 9, 1, p. 69b: "quanto plura scimus, tanto plura sumus; unde qui omnia est, omnia scit; qui pauca est, pauca scit." The direct relation between growth in being and growth in knowledge is taught in St. Thomas's *Summa Theologica*, I, q. 14, a. 1, to which Campanella refers the reader.

103 *Theol.*, I, 11, 2, p. 207: "cognoscimus enim res per speciem vel mutationem nostri a rebus factam, quibus extrinseci sumus, nec causa"; *ibid.*, II, 1, 5: "ex modica specie impressa seu passione intelligimus totum movens per iudica-

tionem." MS quoted in Di Napoli, *op. cit.*, p. 277. Same text in Amerio's critical edition, *De sancta Monotriade*, p. 42.

104 *Met.*, I, 1, 8, 1, p. 59a-59b; *ibid.*, p. 60a; *ibid.*, II, 6, 9, 1, p. 69a.

105 *Ibid.*, II, 6, 8, 6, p. 64b. The *Liber de causis* cited by Campanella is really the *Institutio theologica* of Proclus. Cf. Frederick Copleston, S.J., *A History of Philosophy* (Westminster: The Newman Press, 1950), II, 188.

106 Cf., e.g., *Met.*, I, 1, 9, 13, p. 86a: "palam est nos scire ex parte, et non prout sunt res, sed prout afficimur." See also *ibid.*, I, 1, 8, 1, pp. 59b-60a.

107 *Ibid.*, I, 2, 5, 1, p. 153b; *ibid.*, II, 6, 9, 1, p. 69a-69b.

108 St. Thomas, *Sum. Theol.*, I-II, q. 9, a. 1 c: "obiectum movet, determinando actum, ad modum principii formalis, a quo in rebus naturalibus actio specificatur, sicut calefactio a calore."

109 *Met.*, III, 12, 10, 2 (erroneously written a. 5), p. 100a: "Nos autem diximus [animam] excitari et specificari quoniam in confuso scit omnia, quatenus primalitatibus constat." Cf. also *Theol.*, IV, 5, 2. MS quoted in Amerio, *Campanella, op. cit.*, p. 140.

110 This is evident from the many passages quoted in the second section of this chapter. Cf., e.g., nn. 25, 26 and 27. See also *Theol.*, I, 11, 1, *passim*.

111 See n. 103 above.

112 The fact that in the texts of the *Theologia* under discussion Campanella states that we know things *per speciem vel mutationem nostri a rebus factam*, and that the understanding of a being through reasoning is *ex modica specie impressa seu passione*, shows well enough that he does not attach to the term *species* the Aristotelian-Thomistic connotation.

113 *Theol.*, IV, 5, 2: "Mens humana apta est discurrere ad ignota et nosse omnia quoniam est participatio quaedam Dei qui est omnia et cognoscit omnia. Igitur sunt in mente rationes rerum sicuti est lumen Dei eas continens omnes. Igitur intelligit res in rationibus aeternis et propterea recte docuit Telesius quod scientia est in anima et discere est revocare animam ab aliis curis ad considerationem scibilium, et Plato et Augustinus quod sit quoddam reminisci, non tamen quale fit ab obiectis noviter acceptis per alia similia postmodum occurrentia, sed qualis fit innatae scientiae per illatam, ut cum anima reflexe noscens excitat se ad directam sui notionem quam habebat . . .; igitur anima res potest scire quoniam eas habet in rationibus aeternis, quarum ipsa est particeps dum Dei in se omnia continentis est particeps." MS quoted in Amerio, "Forme e significato, etc.," *art. cit.*, n. 20, pp. 112-13.

114 *Ibid.*: "neque enim [anima] ideas habet sicut Deus, cum ipsa non sit creatrix rerum, sed sicut res imitans Deum, cuius est particeps." MS quoted in Amerio, *Campanella*, p. 141. Here again, as one can readily see, we have a direct denial of the idealistic principle according to which the subject creates its own object of knowledge.

115 *Ibid.*: "[intellectus] excitatur ad obiecta perpendenda per confusas idearum participationes innatas, quatenus ipse est participatio divini intellectus omnia in se scientis." MS quoted in Amerio, *Campanella*, p. 140.

116 *Ibid.*: "Sicut enim per aërem et lucem omnia sentiuntur, sic per divinum lumen omnia intelliguntur." MS quoted in Amerio, "Forme e significato, etc.," *art. cit.*, n. 20, p. 113.

117 *Ibid.:* "neque enim sufficiunt rationes illae [aeternae] in animo, nisi per totum universum divina radiatio in rerum primalitatibus coaptaret rerum notitias et noscibilia cum cognoscentibus." MS quoted in Amerio, *art. cit.,* n. 20, p. 113.

118 *Ibid.:* "Deus ergo est intellectus ille activus de foris in cuius lumine intellectus videt sicuti oculus in lumine solis et non eius usus propter abstractiones sed propter illuminationes. Fit ergo sensatio et intellectio in nobis sed communi-cando cum exterioribus sub lumine Dei in primalitatum participatione." MS quoted in Amerio, *art. cit.,* n. 20, p. 113.

119 *Theol.,* IV, 5, 3, as reported by Amerio, *Campanella,* p. 56.

120 *Theol.,* I, 11, 2, tit., p. 201: "nos quoque in Deo omnia cognoscere etiam in vita mortali." See also *Met.,* III, 13, 2, 5, pp. 118b-119a, where Campanella quotes St. Augustine as saying the same thing.

121 *Theol.,* I, 5, 6, p. 118.

122 *Theol.,* IV, 5, 5: "regulariter anima a sensibilibus acquirit scientiam ut a causa adiuvante et materia causae, non ut formaliter facientibus scire. Hoc enim faciunt rationes aeternae, quibus anima participat, ut docet Augustinus, *non quae intuetur: nemo enim, nisi beatus, potest eas in Deo intueri, sed solum in se"* (italics added). MS quoted in Amerio, *Campanella,* pp. 56-57.

123 *Met.,* I, 1, 9, 1, p. 66.

124 *Ibid.,* a. 2, p. 67.

125 *Ibid.,* a. 3, pp. 68-69.

126 *Ibid.,* a. 4, pp. 70-71.

127 *Ibid.,* a. 5, pp. 71-72.

128 *Ibid.,* a. 6, p. 72.

129 *Ibid.,* a. 7, p. 72.

130 *Ibid.,* a. 8, p. 73.

131 *Ibid.,* a. 9, pp. 73-74.

132 *Ibid.,* a. 10 (erroneously written a. 5), pp. 74-75.

133 *Ibid.,* a. 11, pp. 75-76.

134 *Ibid,* a. 12, pp. 76-77. The answer to the twelfth objection is followed by a few paragraphs in defense of metaphysics and logic (pp. 78-79), mathematics (pp. 79-83), and physiology (pp. 83-86).

135 *Ibid.,* a. 13, p. 86.

136 *Ibid.,* a. 14, pp. 86-88.

CHAPTER SIX

1 Ernst Cassirer, *Das Erkenntnisproblem in der Philosophie und Wissenschaft der neueren Zeit, op. cit.,* I, 240.

2 In his commentary on Aristotle's *De anima,* Averroës writes: "Aristoteles est regula et exemplar, quod natura invenit ad demonstrandam ultimam perfec-tionem humanam . . . Aristotelis doctrina est summa veritas, quoniam eius intellectus fuit finis humani intellectus." Quoted in Francesco Olgiati, *L'anima dell'umanesimo e del rinascimento, op. cit.,* p. 112.

3 Olgiati shows very well the difference between "abstraction," as used in meta-physics, and "abstractionism," or the lack of sense of reality. The former is a legitimate and necessary *process of knowledge* whereby the human intellect grasps the nature or essence of things, leaving aside their individual notes;

the latter is a deplorable *method of action* that takes into consideration neither the nature of things nor their particularities. "Abstractionism," as a method, as well as the so called system of the αὐτὸς ἔφη—which Petrus Ramus (1515-1572) did not hesitate to call *Scholasticus morbus* instead of what was better known as *Aristotelicus morbus*—can be ascribed to certain scholastics of the Renaissance, but not insofar as they represent the great traditions of the Middle Ages. St. Thomas, whose system of philosophy owes so much to Aristotle, always maintains an absolute independence of judgment, and does not hesitate to part company with him in many essential doctrines. He teaches in this connection that "the argument from authority based on human reason is the weakest" (*Sum. Theol.*, I, q. 1, a. 8, ad 2), thus showing an attitude of intellectual freedom that is quite admirable. Nor does he use the method of abstraction in such a way that he deserves the ridicule of the anti-Aristotelians of the Renaissance. His philosophy of reality is indeed far from being a system of "abstractionism." Olgiati, *L'anima dell'umanesimo e del rinascimento*, pp. 168-69; 487-88.

4 Spaventa, *Rinascimento, riforma, controriforma*, p. 19.

5 *Ibid.*

6 Blanchet, *Campanella*, p. 140: "il faut avouer que la plupart des écrits de Campanella ne témoignent nullement du souci dominant de l'observation."

7 Cf. *Le Opere di Galileo Galilei*, edizione nazionale, IV, 738. Quoted in Blanchet, *Campanella*, p. 140. Amerio seems to take exception to Blanchet's statement that Campanella's writings do not show a great concern for scientific observation. There are indications, on the contrary, of Campanella's daily experiments on chickens and fish. He even tried to ascertain the supposed dissolution of a dying man into primary matter! (Amerio, *Campanella*, p. 36.) Perhaps one can bring the diverging statements into agreement by placing Campanella's experiments in the time of his freedom. Campanella's interest in scientific observation is revealed in one of his letters where he asserts, not without some exaggeration, that "he learns more from the anatomy of an ant and a blade of grass than from all the books written since the beginning of the world" (*Lettere*, p. 134).

8 The priority of epistemology over metaphysics in the systematization of the various branches of philosophy can be conceived without sharing the idealistic tenets that all reality is reduced to thought. Hence Campanella's modernity is not to be understood in the sense attached to it by the idealists, as though he considered epistemology the basis and essence of all philosophy.

9 Cf. Van Steenberghen, *Epistemology, op. cit.*, pp. 32-33. For the text of St. Thomas see his commentary *In duodecim libros metaphysicorum Aristotelis*, III, 1, n. 343: "ista scientia [metaphysica] sicut habet universalem considerationem de veritate, ita etiam ad eam pertinet universalis dubitatio de veritate."

10 Cf. St. Thomas, *Sum. Theol.*, I, q. 87, a. 1: "Non ergo per essentiam suam, sed per actum suum se cognoscit intellectus noster." In the same article of the *Summa*, and most probably in the same text referred to by Campanella in his claim for Aquinas's teaching of the soul's essential cognition through self-presence, we read: "ad primam cognitionem habendam, sufficit ipsa mentis praesentia, *quae est principium actus ex quo mens percipit seipsam*" (italics ours). This kind of self-cognition on the part of the soul is therefore the beginning of an act whereby the soul perceives itself. To dispel any doubt about St. Thomas's precise teaching on this matter, the writer wishes to quote

another passage from the same article: "Intellectus autem humanus . . . in sua essentia consideratus, se habet ut potentia intelligens. Unde ex seipso habet virtutem ut intelligat, *non autem ut intelligatur, nisi secundum id quod fit actu.*"

11 *Met.*, II, 6, 8, 1, p. 59a.

12 The difference of opinions among philosophers about the nature of the soul is also asserted by St. Thomas in the *Summa Theologica*, I, q. 87, a. 1: "multi naturam animae ignorant, et multi circa naturam animae erraverunt."

13 Cf., e.g., St. Augustine, *De fide et symbolo*, X, 23; PL 40, col. 193: "tria sunt quibus homo constat: spiritus, anima et corpus."

14 Gilson, *Introduction à l'étude de Saint Augustin*, p. 56, n. 1. Here is St. Augustine's full text in support of the Scriptural meaning attached by him to *spiritus:* "Et quoniam tria sunt quibus homo constat, spiritus, anima et corpus, quae rursus duo dicuntur, quia saepe anima simul cum spiritu nominatur; pars enim quaedam eiusdem rationalis, qua carent bestiae, spiritus dicitur; principale nostrum spiritus est; deinde vita qua coniungimur corpori, anima dicitur; postremo ipsum corpus quoniam visibile est, ultimum nostrum est" (*De fide et symbolo*, X, 23; PL 40, cols. 193-94).

15 Cf. Gilson, *loc. cit.*, pp. 56ff.

16 For a refutation of the doctrine of the spirit or any other corporeal element as a necessary link between soul and body in man cf. St. Thomas, *Sum. Theol.*, I, q. 76, a. 7.

17 Cf. Blanchet, *Campanella*, pp. 265-66.

18 See chapter II for the various opinions on Campanella's supposed spiritual crisis.

19 Cf. n. 87 to n. 97 of chapter IV of the present study.

20 *Met.*, I, 5, 2, 2, p. 346a: "principia scientiarum sunt nobis historiae."

21 Spaventa, *Rinascimento, riforma, controriforma*, pp. 50-51.

22 For Aristotle's doctrine on the nature of the intellect and its object of knowledge cf. *De anima*, 427a; 429a-433a and St. Thomas's commentary on it.

23 Cf. chapter IV, n. 128.

24 *Ibid.*, n. 130.

25 *Met.*, I, 2, 3, 1, p. 100a: "prima cognitio confusa est entis et universalis, in quo conveniunt plurima quatenus similia." *Ibid.*, I, 2, 1, 1, p. 89a: "Ens autem sensibile est quod primo obiicitur cognosciturque confusa notitia . . . Quidditas ergo sensibilis est primo notum distincte, si tamen ad exactam definitionem pervenire et ad totius notitiam totaliter quis possit."

26 Cf., e.g., St. Thomas, *Sum. Theol.*, I, q. 16, arts. 1 and 2. St. Thomas attributes the definition of truth as "adaequatio rei et intellectus" to Isaac Israeli, the author of the *De definitionibus.* However, several passages in Aristotle may have inspired that definition. Cf. Louis De Raeymaeker, *Philosophie de l'être* (Louvain: Institut Supérieur de Philosophie, 1947), p. 93, n. 1.

It is worth noting that some scholastics hold that truth is the conformity between the judgment and the concept that the intellect has made of the thing or reality. Cf. Card. D. J. Mercier, *Critériologie générale* (8th ed.; Louvain: Institut Supérieur de Philosophie, 1923), pp. 27-32; R. P. Sertillanges, *La philosophie de St. Thomas d'Aquin* (Paris: Aubier, 1940), II, 161ff.

27 These concepts are developed extensively by St. Thomas in his *Summa Theologica*, I, q. 16, arts. 5 and 6; q. 21, a. 2; *De veritate*, q. 1, arts. 1 and 2.

28 *Met.*, I, 1, 9, Def. Metaph., p. 78a: "principia entis finiti, seu potius proprincipia sunt ens et non-ens."

29 St. Thomas, *Sum. Theol.*, I, q. 17, a. 1, ad 2; *De veritate*, q. 1, a. 10 c.

30 Aristotle, *Metaphysica*, 1027b, 20-30; St. Thomas, *In Metaph.*, VI, 1. 4, nn. 1233, 1236. Some scholastics, like Ferrariensis † 1528), Molina (1535-1600), and more recently, Hugon and Zigliara, hold that truth can be found even in the simple apprehension of the mind. Cf. Joseph Gredt, *Elementa philosophiae* (9th ed.; Barcelona: Herder, 1951), II, 46; R. P. Phillips, *Modern Thomistic Philosophy* (Westminster, Md.: The Newman Press, 1950), II, 119-20.

31 P. Coffey, *Epistemology* (New York: Peter Smith, 1938), II, 39-40.

32 St. Thomas, *Sum. Theol.*, I, q. 84, a. 5.

33 St. Thomas, *De veritate*, q. 11, a. 1; q. 16, a. 1.

34 St. Thomas, *Contra gent.*, 1. III, c. 47.

CHAPTER SEVEN

1 *Met.*, I, 5, 3, 1, p. 351a.

2 *Ibid.*, I, 1, 9, 12, p. 78b: "aliquo modo omnia sunt, et idola quae somniamus intus."

3 *Del senso*, p. 66: "Perchè ogni cosa del mondo è, [lo spirito] disse tutto ente"; *Epilogo*, p. 472: "perchè tutti sono, [lo spirito] li dice enti, in nome communissimo."

4 *Met.*, I, 1, 9, 12, p. 78a-78b.

5 *Ibid.*, I, 2, 1, 1, p. 89a: "Vox ergo Ens prima est, primae notionis confusae index"; *ibid.*, I, 2, 3, 1, p. 100a: "prima cognitio confusa est entis et universalis, in quo conveniunt plurima quatenus similia."

6 *Ibid.*, I, 2, 3, 3, p. 107a: "Ens non habet definitionem, sed per seipsum diffinitur, scilicet est habens esse, vel quod est."

7 *Ibid.*, I, 2, 1, 1, p. 89a: "Vox . . . ens . . . nominaliter sumpta dicit quid et essentiam rerum seu quidditatem; verbaliter vero quia et actum essendi, hoc est, esse seu existentiam. Existentia vero est esse in alio et extra causam, uti et veteres monuerunt." Cf. also *ibid.*, I, 2, 15, 1, p. 290a-290b: "essentia dicitur de finita et de infinita, potius autem de infinita, quae excludit existentiam, vel dicit idem cum sua existentia. . . . Ens participialiter sumptum dicit essentiam finitam, quoniam participium dicit essentiam cum actu existentiae. Ergo dicit essentiam extra suam causam, ergo finitam; quidquid enim extra est, finitum est."

8 *Ibid.*, I, 2, 1, 1, pp. 89b-90a.

9 *Ibid.*, III, 13, 3, 2, p. 127a.

10 Scotus, *Opus Oxoniense*, I, d. 3, q. 2, a. 4, n. 5; Vivès ed., Vol. IX, p. 18a.

11 For a comparative study of St. Thomas's and Scotus's concept of being the following works may be profitably consulted: Efrem Bettoni, *Duns Scotus: The Basic Principles of His Philosophy*, trans. and ed. Bernardine Bonansea, O.F.M. (Washington: The Catholic University of America Press, 1961), pp. 25-46; Cyril L. Shircel, O.F.M., *The Univocity of the Concept of Being in the Philosophy of Duns Scotus* (Washington: The Catholic University of America Press, 1942); Allan B. Wolter, O.F.M., *The Transcendentals and Their Function*

in the Metaphysics of Duns Scotus (Washington: The Catholic University of America Press, 1946); Etienne Gilson, *Jean Duns Scot. Introduction à ses positions fondamentales* (Paris: Vrin, 1952), especially pp. 84-115, where the author presents Scotus's concept of being as meaning essence rather than existence. The same point of view is held in his previous work, *The Spirit of Mediaeval Philosophy*, trans. A. H. Downes (New York: Charles Scribner's Sons, 1940), pp. 263ff. However, in *God and Philosophy* (New Haven: Yale University Press, 1941), p. 69, n. 17, Gilson is careful to remark that "The existential character of being has been powerfully stressed by Duns Scotus," referring the reader to Parthenius Minges, O.F.M., *Ioannis Duns Scoti doctrina philosophica et theologica* (Florence: Quaracchi, 1930), I, 14-17.

12 *Met.*, I, 2, 3, 3, pp. 104b-105a.

13 *Ibid.*, p. 106b.

14 *Ibid.*, pp. 106b-107a.

15 *Ibid.*

16 *Ibid.*

17 *Ibid.*

18 *Ibid.*, p. 107a-107b.

19 *Ibid.*, p. 107b.

20 *Ibid.*: "potest ergo univocum dici ens ex ea parte qua similitudo ab intellectu in cunctis rebus consideratur, et nomine et ratione entis donatur."

21 *Ibid.*

22 *Ibid.*, II, 7, 2, 3, p. 124a-124b: "ens dicitur de Deo et de qualibet re univoce, si imperfectionem rei sequestres intellectu. Nam si intellectu a lapide sequestraverimus defectum entitatis, sapientiae, potentiae, et amoris, et obiectorum suorum, tunc ipse lapis habebit tantum esse suum, et quidem infinitum; si enim finitur nonente, hoc sequestrato, remanebit Ens infinitum."

23 *Ibid.*, p. 124b: "et si hoc intellexisset Scotus univocationem penitius et verius in ente posuisset."

24 *Ibid.*, I, 2, 3, 3, p. 107b: "ex parte errat Scotus quod univocum fecit ens et non item genus propter rationem minus hoc probantem."

25 *Theol.*, I, 5, 5, p. 114.

26 *Ibid.*

27 *Ibid.*, p. 115.

28 In his exposition of Scotus's teaching Campanella does not distinguish properly between the real order and the logical order. As Gilson has pointed out, nothing is more contrary to Scotus's mind than to make *ens rationis* the subject of metaphysics. Scotus himself has clearly stated that, although in a certain sense the logician considers the totality of being in the same way the metaphysician does, they do not talk about the same kind of being. The logician speaks of *ens rationis*, whereas the metaphysician speaks of *ens reale*. Thus, not only does Scotus differentiate between the two orders, but he explicitly warns against confusing them. *Jean Duns Scot, op. cit.*, p. 107.

Femiano's presentation of Scotus's doctrine of univocity contains several inaccuracies, chief among which is the interpretation of Scotus's concept of being on a purely logical level. (Cf. Salvatore Femiano, *Lo spiritualismo di Tommaso Campanella*, I, 288-93). When he says that in regard to the concept of being, or rather the relation between essence and existence in being, Campanella accepts Scotus's *distinctio formalis a parte rei* "in a purely logical sense, not in a metaphysical sense" (*ibid.*, p. 288), he also confuses the issue. Indeed, the Scotistic formal distinction implies of its nature a distinction in the thing itself (*a parte rei*) and not merely a logical distinction or a distinction made by the mind alone. For an accurate and authoritative presentation of Scotus's doctrine of univocity cf. Timotheus A. Barth, "Being, Univocity, and Analogy according to Duns Scotus," in *John Duns Scotus, 1265-1965*, ed. by John K. Ryan and Bernardine M. Bonansea (Washington, D. C.: The Catholic University of America Press, 1965), pp. 210-62.

29 *Met.*, I, 2, 3, 3, p. 107b.

30 *Ibid.*, II, 7, 2, 5, tit., p. 125.

31 *Ibid.*, I, 2, 3, 3, pp. 107b-108a; *ibid.*, II, 7, 2, 5, p. 125a-125b.

32 *Ibid.*, I, 2, 3, 3, p. 108a.

33 *Ibid.*, II, 7, 2, 5, p. 125b.

34 *Ibid.*

35 *Theol.*, I, 3, 8, p. 79: "Ens ergo dicitur de Deo et de creaturis analogice, sicut de causa et effectu: prius autem de Deo, postea de creaturis."

36 *Met.*, II, 7, 2, 2, p. 123b.

37 *Ibid.*, I, 2, 3, 3, p. 108a.

38 *Theol.*, I, 5, 5, p. 115.

39 *Met.*, I, 2, 3, 3, p. 108b.

40 *Theol.*, I, 5, 5, p. 114.

41 *Ibid.*, p. 115: "Hinc conclude contra Rabbinum quod pure aequivoce nihil de Deo et creaturis dicitur."

42 *Met.*, II, 6, 7, 1, p. 39a: "Omne . . . ens constat potentia essendi, sensu essendi, et amore essendi, sicut Deus, cuius imaginem aut vestigium gerunt"; *ibid.*, II, 6, 11, 1, tit., p. 83: "Omnia entia constitui amore, sapientia et potestate tanquam ex tribus principiis eminentialibus."

43 T. Campanella, *Realis philosophiae epilogisticae partes quatuor*, ed. Tobias Adami (Frankfort: Ex typis Egenolphi Emmelii, 1623), p. 3: "totus mundus et quaelibet particula illius constituitur ex sapientia, potentia et amore."

44 *Met.*, I, 1, 6, 2, p. 50a: "Neque ad momentum duraret tota natura, vel eius particula, si non posset esse, aut non sentiret esse, aut non amaret esse."

45 *Ibid.*, pp. 49b-50a: "res cunctae . . . constituuntur ex primi entis participio."

46 *Ibid.*, II, 6, 7, 1, p. 43b.

47 *Theol.*, I, 3, 12, p. 90.

48 *Met.*, II, 6, 11, 4, tit., p. 87.

49 *Ibid.*, p. 87a.

50 *Ibid.*

51 *Ibid.*: "Quoniam igitur entis cuiusque constitutio ad haec principia reducitur; nec ullum absque horum constantia invenitur, et priora his non sunt ulla; et omnia fiunt ex eis factione eminentiali, quae est esse, et non motus: manifestum restat haec esse proprincipia rerum. Nam etsi alii assignarunt principia alia, non tamen his priora, quae ob hoc vocamus primalitates, et primordia, et praeeminentias." Cf. also *ibid.*, II, 6, 11, 3, p. 86a. To better express his ideas, Campanella does not hesitate to coin new terms. A few of these terms have already been mentioned; many more will follow. With a view to reproducing his thought as faithfully as possible, we shall try to give a literal translation of such terms, even if an accepted English word does not result.

52 *Ibid.*, II, 6, 11, 3, p. 86a.

53 *Ibid.*, p. 86a-86b.

54 *Ibid.*, I, 1, 2, 1, p. 93a: "Primalitas est unde ens primitus essentiatur."

55 *Ibid.*, I, 2, 2, 4, p. 99a: ". . . [primalitates] sunt aeque prima [sic] tempore, dignitate, et natura, et unum omnino propter identitatem realem, et coessentialem coentitatum mutuam in se ipsis: non enim essentiae sunt, sed essentialitates eiusdem essentiae, quam essentiant absque gradu: et haec identitas est summa unitas, et omnia essentiantur per analogiam ad ipsam. Etenim nisi sint unum, essentiam non habent unam." *Ibid.*, II, 7, 1, 2, p. 113a: "unalitates unius dici possent."

56 *Ibid.*, II, 6, 11, 3, p. 85a.

57 *Ibid.*, II, 6, 11, 6, tit., p. 89: "Quamvis ex alterutris procedant ipsa primordia, aeque tamen proprincipiant seu primordiantur; quoniam non sunt materialiter aut essentialiter procedendo divisa, sed quodlibet in quolibet remanet, et procedens praeest in eo a quo procedit; et id a quo procedit communicatur procedenti, et totaliter, idcirco comprincipia sunt."

58 *Ibid.*, p. 90b: "manifesta est identitas et comprincipiatio ipsorum [proprincipiorum], quoniam non fit per participationem, sed per toticipationem et coessentiationem." The same idea is expressed in *Met.*, I, 2, 2, 4, p. 99a, in regard to the "essentiation" of being: "Essentiatio tandem est entis constitutio intrinseca, simplicissima, prima, toticipatione, non participatione, ergo nec mutatione constituentium essentialitatum, nec constituti essentiati."

59 *Ibid.*, I, 2, 2, 4, p. 99b: ". . . [amor] a potentia et sapientia non recedit cum procedit."

60 *Ibid.*, p. 99a-99b, *passim.* See also *Met.*, II, 6, 11, 2, p. 85a-85b.

61 *Ibid.*, II, 10, 2, 1, p. 250a.

62 *Ibid.*, II, 6, 11, 9, p. 93a-93b.

63 *Ibid.*, I, 2, 2, 4, p. 99a: "[Essentiatio entis est] celeberrima secundum se, nobis vero ineffabilis."

64 *Ibid.*, II, 6, 11, 1, p. 83a: "Distinctionem . . . originis inter haec ipsa [primalitates et primordia] inveniri." Cf. also *ibid.*, II, 6, 11, 6, p. 89a.

65 *Ibid.*, I, 2, 2, 4, p. 99b; *ibid.*, II, 6, 11, 1, p. 83a-83b.

66 *Ibid.*, II, 6, 11, 10, p. 93a: "si considerentur ut quod procedit et ut a quo procedit, [primalitates] distinguuntur relationibus realibus."

67 Cf. Campanella's pertinent discussion in *Met.*, II, 6, 11, 10, p. 93a-93b. The discussion ends with these words: "Idcirco [primalitates] tres realitates esse dicimus distinctas ex natura rei formaliter, non autem realiter." The idea of a distinction *ex natura rei* in the primalities is also expressed in *Theol.*, I, 3, 12, pp. 89-90: "non enim video quomodo potestas, voluntas et intellectus non sint distincti ex natura rei, quandoquidem alius ab alio est, nec possunt quae sic se consequuntur non distingui secundum naturam aliquo pacto." For a proper understanding of Scotus's formal distinction cf. Maurice J. Grajewski, O.F.M., *The Formal Distinction of Duns Scotus* (Washington: The Catholic University of America Press, 1944).

68 *Theol.*, I, 3, 12, p. 89: ". . . in Logicis vocavimus distinctionem rationis eam quae sola ratione fit: realem quae in rebus ante ratiocinationem nostram. Quam vero Scotus ex natura rei dicit, nos idealem nuncupavimus, ne videamur facere compositionem rerum, quam Thomistae non immerito aversantur."

69 Thus Campanella writes in *Met.*, I, 2, 3, 9, p. 133b: "cum entitates plures faciunt unum ens, et tamen definitiones patiuntur plures, fundant hanc

distinctionem, quam Scotus vocat ex natura rei, Thomistae secundum rationem ratiocinatam. Nos autem rationum vocavimus distinctionem et idealem, quia alteram ideam alterumque conceptum et rationem in nobis pariunt cum apprehenduntur."

70 Campanella's full text, as it stands in *Theol.*, I, 3, 12, p. 91, reads: "Distinctio autem ista primalitatum non est realis tanquam rerum, sed tanquam realitatum eiusdem rei, *nec erit solius rationis nostrae, sed, ut dicit Scotus, ex natura rei, at non totaliter, quia non fundamentaliter, sed terminative distinguuntur:* ergo ex natura rei seu idealiter terminative tantum, et haec distinctio nec pluralitatem facit numeralem nec compositionem, sed realitatum essentiationem et unitatem perfectissimam. Illae enim emanationes non sunt motus, nec cum tempore, nec separatione, sed coaevae essentialitates unius essentiae seu entis unius et in uno."

The present writer does not agree with Femiano's interpretation of Campanella's *distinctio idealis* as something different from Scotus's *distinctio formalis* or *ex natura rei*. (Cf. Femiano, *Lo spiritualismo di Tommaso Campanella*, Vol. II, pp. 208-210). As the above text indicates, Campanella identifies the two kinds of distinction when he says, *ex natura rei seu idealiter terminative tantum.* Clearly, a distinction that is neither real nor merely logical can only be Scotus's formal distinction, no matter what one may wish to call it.

71 *Met.*, II, 6, 11, 6, p. 89a.

72 *Ibid.*, I, 2, 2, 3, p. 98a: "sapientia, potestas, amor, principia rerum etiam ad extra unum sunt." Cf. also *ibid.*, II, 10, 3, 1, p. 252a.

73 Cf. *Met.*, I, 2, 3, 9, p. 133b, where Campanella discusses the distinction among the primalities of being and the attributes of God, and concludes the discussion by saying: "sic omnes quaestiones dissolvuntur inter Scotistas et Thomistas, qui inter rem et realitatem distinguere perperam non satagerunt." Campanella fails to realize that the distinction between *res* and *realitas* is precisely the basis for Scotus's formal distinction.

74 *Ibid.*, II, 6, 5, 1, p. 20b.

75 *Ibid.*, II, 6, 6, 3, p. 27b: ". . . potentiam essendi esse principium constitutivum ipsius esse." The same doctrine is taught in *Met.*, II, 6, 6, 5, p. 29a.

76 *Ibid.*, II, 6, 6, 7, p. 31b.

77 *Ibid.*, II, 6, 5, 1, p. 20a: "Ens nullum videtur esse, nisi quia potest esse. Quod enim esse nequit, non est, quatenus esse non potest."

78 *Ibid.*: "Quemadmodum . . . in actionibus reperitur potentia, ita et in esse."

79 *Ibid.*, II, 6, 5, 2, p. 21a.

80 *Ibid.*, II, 6, 5, 3, p. 21a.

81 *Ibid.*, p. 21a-21b.

82 *Ibid.*, p. 21b: "patet falsum esse quod aliquid sit in potentia, nisi habeat aliquod esse; potentia ergo est essentialitas ipsius esse."

83 *Ibid.*, II, 6, 6, 7, p. 31b: "talis potestas [i.e., potentia quae facit ut res sint tam ad intra quam ad extra] est ipsum esse, prout est, vel prout futurum est."

84 *Ibid.*, II, 6, 6, 3, p. 26b.

85 *Ibid.*, p. 27a.

86 *Ibid.*, II, 6, 6, 8, p. 33b; *ibid.*, II, 6, 13, 1, p. 97a-97b.

87 *Ibid.*, II, 6, 6, 13, p. 38a: "potentia et actus non distinguuntur realiter in eis quae non sunt purus actus: quoniam cuiusque potentia essendi id, quod est, est ipsemet actus."

88 *Ibid.*, II, 6, 6, 3, p. 26a.

89 *Ibid.*, II, 6, 5, 3, p. 22a.

90 *Ibid.*, II, 6, 6, 5, p. 29a.

91 *Ibid.*, II, 6, 5, 1, p. 20b; *ibid.*, II, 6, 6, 5, p. 30b.

92 For the various kinds and specific meanings of the *potentia operandi* cf. *Met.*, II, 6, 5, 1, p. 20a-20b; *ibid.*, II, 6, 6, 7, p. 31a. Sometimes Campanella uses *potentia activa* to mean simply the *potentia agendi.* Cf., for example, *Theol.*, I, 10, 1, p. 187.

93 *Met.*, II, 6, 6, 8, tit., p. 32: "Potentiam activam esse idem cum potente agere."

94 *Ibid.*, p. 32a.

95 *Real. phil. epil.*, p. 30: "Operatio est inditus rerum actus, quo ipsae in suo esse conservantur."

96 *Ibid.*: "deficiente operatione deficit et ipsum esse per illam actuatum conservatumque."

97 *Ibid.*

98 *Met.*, II, 6, 6, 3, p. 26a; *ibid.*, II, 6, 6, 10, p. 36b.

99 *Real. phil. epil.*, p. 30: "Actusque extensus in patiens est actio."

100 *Ibid.*, pp. 30-31: "Actio est effusio similitudinis agentis in patiens, quod oportet ergo illi esse contrarium aut diversum. Si enim simile est omnino, non patitur ab eo; quoniam agere est quoddam assimilare sibi quod est dissimile." See also *Epilogo*, p. 226. Campanella is not always consistent in his use of the terms *operation* for an internal act and *action* for an act *ad extra.* In each case the context has to be examined. However, the specific meaning of the two terms is indicated above.

101 *Met.*, I, 2, 6, 2, p. 233a: "dicimus enim actionem esse communicationem similitudinis agentis causae in aliud inquantum aliud." This statement, as well as the statement mentioned in the preceding note, while helping to clarify the notion of action, makes it clear that active potency and its object are two distinct things. Hence, as far as the question under discussion is concerned, no pantheistic or idealistic implications can be found in Campanella's system. It should be noted, however, that what we are discussing here is not the relationship between power and its object, but rather the relationship between cause or active power and action, inasmuch as it is through the latter that the agent attains its object. The two questions are entirely different.

102 *Ibid.*, I, 2, 6, 2, p. 233b; *ibid.*, I, 2, 7, 3, p. 244a.

103 *Ibid.*, II, 6, 6, 9, tit., p. 33: "Actionem essentialiter esse ipsam virtutem agentem et causam agentem; et differre solum per accidens quatenus superaddit fluxum et respectum ad patiens."

104 *Ibid.*, II, 6, 6, 11, p. 37a.

105 *Ibid.*, II, 6, 6, 10, p. 36a: "operari enim est esse."

106 *Ibid.*: "operari in alio est esse in alio."

107 *Ibid.*, II, 6, 6, 9, p. 35b.

108 *Ibid.*

109 *Ibid.*, II, 6, 6, 10, p. 36a: "operatio transiens non differt ab esse operantis nisi dum est in patiente; et tunc differt solo numero, non autem specifica essentia."

110 *Ibid.*, III, 13, 2, 5, p. 116b: "essentia formalis est ab idea."

111 *Ibid.*, II, 6, 6, 7, p. 31a.

112 *Ibid.*, II, 6, 5, 1, p. 20b.

113 *Ibid.*, II, 6, 5, 4, p. 23b.

114 *Ibid.*

115 *Ibid.,* II, 6, 6, 7, p. 31a.

116 *Ibid.,* II, 6, 5, 4, p. 22b: "potentia eatenus est potentia, quatenus ad ideam et agentem respicit causam."

117 *Ibid.,* II, 6, 6, 9, p. 35a: "potentia receptiva in se considerata secundum id quod est fundamentaliter non est ipsa receptio; sed considerata in ordine ad receptibile fit recipiens et receptio simul."

118 *Ibid.,* II, 6, 6, 3, p. 26a.

119 Campanella has still another division of *potentia* based on the causes of being. (*Met.,* II, 6, 5, 5, p. 23a.) Since this new division is intimately connected with the doctrine of the causes of being to be discussed later, we do not think it advisable to mention it here.

120 Cf., for example, *Met.,* II, 6, 7, 1, p. 40a.

121 As previously stated (chap. IV, sect. II), although strictly speaking *sapientia* stands for intuitive knowledge, the same term is used by Campanella to mean either simple knowledge, science, or wisdom.

122 *Met.,* II, 6, 7, 1, tit., p. 39: "Entia omnia sensu sui esse et conservationis donata esse; et esse, conservari, operari, et agere, quia sciunt."

123 *Ibid.,* II, 6, 9, 4, p. 70b: "[Sapientia] est . . . essentialitas constitutiva entis; cuiusmodi autem entia sunt, videlicet indivisibilia vel divisibilia, eiusmodi est sapientia."

124 *Ibid.,* II, 6, 9, 3, p. 70a.

125 *Del senso,* subtitle. Because of its importance, we report the full original text: "Parte mirabile d'occulta filosofia dove si mostra il mondo essere statua di Dio viva e bene conoscente, e tutte sue parti e particelle loro avere senso chi più chiaro chi più oscuro quanto basta alla conservazione loro e del tutto in cui consentono e si scuoprono le ragioni di tutti li segreti de la natura."

126 It is worth recalling that one of the charges brought against Campanella in Rome was precisely his pansensistic doctrine in *De sensu rerum et magia.* In order to clear himself of this charge, he wrote the *Defensio* of this latter work, where he assembles arguments taken not only from philosophy but also from other fields of knowledge, such as the natural sciences and theology.

127 *Defensio,* pp. 13-14; *Met.,* II, 6, 7, 1, p. 39a-39b.

128 *Del senso,* p. 1; *Defensio,* p. 10; *Met.,* II, 6, 7, 1, p. 40a; *ibid.,* II, 6, 7, 6, tit., p. 50.

129 This doctrine will be better explained when the theory of the five worlds is discussed in connection with the treatise on God.

130 *Defensio,* p. 46: "quicquid est in inferioribus creaturis, est in superioribus eminentiori modo, et per essentiam ut in Deo, vel per participationem, ut in intelligentiis mentibusque rationalibus. Quicquid vero in superioribus e converso est in inferioribus obscurius tamen, et exiliori participio, ut S. Thomas et S. Dionysius declaraverunt, et ordo Naturae suffragatur."

131 *Del senso,* p. 15; *Met.,* II, 6, 7, 1, p. 43b.

132 *Met.,* II, 6, 7, 1, p. 40a-40b.

133 *Del senso,* p. 13; *Defensio,* p. 16.

134 *Del senso,* p. 13.

135 *Met.,* II, 6, 7, 1, p. 40b: "in plantis manifestae sunt operationes sapientiae; siquidem ipsae nutriuntur et vegetant"; *ibid.,* p. 41a: "ergo et plantis est

sapientia principium essendi, et operandi, et agendi manifeste." Cf. also *Del senso*, p. 213; *Atheismus*, p. 23.

136 *Epilogo*, pp. 316-18; *Del senso*, p. 215; *Met.*, II, 6, 7, 3, p. 44a.

137 *Met.*, II, 6, 7, 1, p. 41a; *Del senso*, pp. 208ff.; *Atheismus*, p. 23.

138 *Del senso*, p. 74: "Ossa, peli, nervi, sangue e spirito tutti sentire, contra Aristotile."

139 *Met.*, II, 6, 7, 1, p. 41a-41b. Evidently, Campanella speaks here of death from the empirical point of view, leaving intact the doctrine of the immortality of the human soul, which he asserts whenever he deals with it expressly. The spirit, according to his trichotomic theory, is a corporeal substance which enters as a third element to compose animals and man and is subject to dissolution at the time of death. Cf. chap. IV, sect. I, of this study.

140 *Ibid.*, II, 6, 7, 1, p. 41b; *Del senso*, pp. 38-39.

141 *Met.*, II, 6, 7, 1, p. 41b; *Del senso*, pp. 26-30.

142 *Met.*, I, 1, 6, 2, tit., p. 49: "Omnia entia participio sensus praedita aliquo modo esse."

143 *Del senso*, p. 134.

144 *Ibid.*, p. 31: "Il mondo essere animale"; *Poesie*, p. 14: "Il mondo è un animal grande e perfetto." The belief in the world as a huge animal is also shared by the inhabitants of the City of the Sun. Cf. *Città*, p. 454.

145 *Del senso*, p. 161.

146 *Epilogo*, p. 336: *Del senso*, pp. 1-2; *Città*, pp. 454-55.

147 *Del senso*, p. 161. Campanella admittedly took the doctrine of the world soul from Plato. Commenting further on such a doctrine, he writes: "It is foolish to think that the world does not sense because it has no legs, eyes, or hands. These instruments are useful to the animal spirit enclosed in gross matter which it must move with the help of them, just as it can sense only by means of openings. But, as far as the world is concerned, the round figure is sufficient for its motion; the rays and active powers are hands diffused to operate without being closed up in heavy arms; the stars and luminaries are eyes that see and make us see." *Ibid.*, p. 34.

148 *Del senso*, p. 17.

149 *Met.*, I, 1, 6, Append., p. 58a: "quamvis omnia entia ut entia essentientur primalitatibus, tamen gradibus specialibus distinguuntur."

150 A detailed classification of the various types of sense can be found in the *Defensio*, pp. 8-9. There Campanella states that "sense is quintuple," but he actually mentions six different types of sense. Another classification is to be found in *Met.*, II, 6, 7, 1, p. 43b, where the *vegetative* sense is not mentioned at all. The omission of the vegetative sense as something distinct from the animal sense may be due to the fact that plants, according to Campanella, are imperfect animals. Other places where the sixfold classification is made are *Met.*, I, 1, 6, Append., p. 58a, and II, 6, 9, 6, p. 73a. In these two places, however, Campanella speaks of *sapientia* rather than *sensus*. The two terms, it is worth repeating, are used by him indiscriminately.

151 *Defensio*, p. 9.

152 *Met.*, I, 1, 6, Append., p. 58a; *ibid.*, II, 6, 9, 6, p. 73a.

153 *Del senso*, p. 45, n. 1: "sensus esse perceptionem passionis in ipso tamen spiritu vividiorem."

154 *Del senso,* p. 73: "ogni sensazione farsi per contatto e . . . la diversità nasce dalla grossezza e sottilezza della materia."

155 *Met.,* II, 6, 7, 3, p. 44a: "etsi entia omnia sentiant, non tamen omnia sunt animalia."

156 *Ibid.,* II, 6, 7, 1, p. 42b: "Nec quia elementa et caelum et venti et plantae carent oculis et auribus et lingua, non sentiant, ut Peripatetici stulte contendunt"; *Del senso,* p. 44; *ibid.,* p. 181; *Epilogo,* p. 334.

157 *Del senso,* p. 217: "ogni senso è tatto, e chi ha questo non si può insensato dire."

158 *Del senso,* p. 330: "Il mondo, dunque, tutto è senso e vita e anima e corpo, statua dell'Altissimo, fatta a sua gloria con potestà, senno e amore."

159 In the *Defensio,* p. 51, Campanella speaks of life in natural things in these terms: "error est, et materialis saltem haeresis, negare vitam animasticam rebus naturalibus; haeresis autem formalis contra omnes scripturas negare vitam et sensum omni modo."

160 The term "colchodea" is used by Campanella several times in *Del senso delle cose e della magia* and *Metaphysica,* and is attributed by him to Avicenna. Its meaning is somewhat like Anaxagoras's *mens,* Alexander of Aphrodisia's *intellectus agens,* and the Platonists' *anima mundi.* From the context it is clear that Campanella identifies the "colchodea" with Avicenna's "active intellect" or "active intelligence," the last of the "separate intelligences" in a decreasing order. However, such a term is not to be found in Avicenna's original works or in their Latin translations, nor is it mentioned by any medieval writer. It is quite probable that Campanella took it from the Averroistic writings of either Marco Antonio Zimara or Agostino Nifo. This latter is supposedly responsible for the coinage of the term "colchodea," which was meant to signify Avicenna's agent intellect in its strict function of *dator formarum.* Campanella extended its use to mean other functions of the agent intellect as well. Cf. *Del senso,* Append., pp. 339-41, for a summary of Prof. C. A. Nallino's study on the subject which appeared in *Giornale critico della filosofia italiana,* VI (Jan., 1925), under the heading "La 'Colcodea' d'Avicenna e T. Campanella."

161 *Del senso,* p. 9; *ibid.,* pp. 14ff.; *Met.,* II, 6, 7, 4, tit., pp. 45ff.

162 *Del senso,* p. 15; *Defensio,* p. 18.

163 *Del senso,* p. 16.

164 To be more exact, one should speak of a natural tendency in things rather than of a natural instinct. Scholastics, whose opinion Campanella is reporting, distinguish very clearly between the natural tendency in things in virtue of their own nature and the instinct of animals, which is a sensitive power. If occasionally they use the term "appetite" in connection with material things, they do so only analogically.

165 *Del senso,* pp. 17-18; *Defensio,* p. 14; *Epilogo,* pp. 339-40.

166 *Del senso,* p. 19; *Epilogo,* p. 340.

167 *Met.,* II, 6, 7, 4, pp. 47b-48a.

168 *Del senso,* p. 14, n. 1: "Rerum operationes in quibus ipsarum manifestantur sensus, non a Deo, nec ab angelis, nec ab anima mundi, nec ab intellectu agente, ut alii opinantur, sed ab ipsis formis naturalibus, attamen non sine Deo fieri." Cf. also *Defensio,* p. 14; *Met.,* II, 6, 7, 4, p. 45b.

169 *Met.,* II, 6, 10, 1, p. 74a.

170 *Ibid.*, II, 6, 10, 4, p. 77a.

171 *Ibid.*, p. 77b: "Patet ergo quod amare seipsum est esse seipsum, nec distingui ab esse nisi ratione et notione."

172 *Ibid.*, p. 77a: "Amare . . . aliud est fieri aliud."

173 *Ibid*, p. 77b.

174 *Theol.*, I, 13, 1, p. 258.

175 *Met.*, II, 6, 10, 4, p. 77b.

176 *Ibid.*, p. 78a: "sicut notitia nostri reflexa evidentior est nobis quam notitia abdita, ita amor nostri reflexus adscititiusque evidentior est nobis quam amor abditus."

177 *Ibid.*, II, 6, 10, 8, p. 82a: *Theol.*, I, 13, 2, p. 262.

178 *Met.*, II, 6, 10, 4, p. 78a.

179 *Theol.*, I, 11, 9, p. 246: "Definitio enim est epilogus scientiae uniuscuiusque rei per essentialia."

180 *Met.*, II, 6, 10, 6, p. 80b. Cf. also *Theol.*, I, 13, 1, p. 259, where Campanella emphasizes the point that love is not simply an act of the will but also an essential primality of all beings. It is called natural tendency or appetite in things in nature, animal appetite in animals, and will in rational creatures.

181 *Met.*, II, 6, 11, 1, p. 83a: "manifestum esse debet potentiam, sapientiam et amorem primordia esse altissima constitutiva non modo rerum compositarum, sed et simplicissimarum. Quinimo in eis et ex eis consistere omnium esse."

182 *Ibid.*, II, 6, 11, 7, p. 90a: "Omne ens est quod potest esse, et quod scit esse, et quod vult esse."

CHAPTER EIGHT

1 *Met.*, I, 2, 2, 1, pp. 93b-94a: "Ex primalitatibus extantibus, seu extra respicientibus, oriuntur principia vocata facultates a philosophis"; *ibid.*, II, 10, 2, 1, p. 250a: "ex . . . primalitatibus, ut respicientibus ad extra exterioritate naturae, non loci, manant facultates seu principia."

2 *Ibid.*, I, 2, 2, 1, p. 94a: "quoniam tres sunt primalitates, tria etiam sunt principia extantia erga principiata, videlicet Potestativum, Cognoscitivum et Volitivum."

3 *Ibid.*, II, 10, 2, 1, p. 250a.

4 *Ibid.*, p. 250a-250b.

5 *Ibid.*, I, 2, 2, 1, p. 94a; *ibid.*, II, 6, 17, 2. p. 110b; *ibid.*, II, 10, 2, 1, p. 250b.

6 *Ibid.*, I, 2, 15, 1, p. 289a-289b; *Theol.*, I, 4, 1, p. 97.

7 *Met.*, II, 6, 13, 1, p. 97b: "Obiectum . . . est id ad quod primo et per se respicit virtus, cuius dicitur obiectum, et cuius ratione caetera respiciuntur."

8 *Ibid.*

9 *Ibid.*, p. 97a.

10 Cf. *Met.*, II, 6, 14, 1, pp. 99ff.; *Theol.*, I, 12, 1, pp. 252ff.

11 *Met.*, II, 6, 15, 1, p. 102a-102b.

12 *Ibid.*, pp. 102b-103a.

13 *Ibid.*, p. 103a-103b. Cf. also *Theol.*, I, 14, 1, pp. 282ff.

14 *Met.*, II, 6, 16, 1, p. 107a; *Theol.*, I, 15, 1, p. 300.

15 *Met.*, II, 6, 16, 1, p. 107a; *Theol.*, I, 15, 1, p. 300.

16 *Theol.*, I, 15, 1, p. 301.

17 *Ibid.*, p. 300.

18 *Ibid.; Met.*, II, 6, 16, 1, pp. 107b-108a.

19 *Met.*, II, 6, 16, 1, p. 107a.

20 *Theol.*, I, 15, 1, p. 300: "Pulchrum ergo est obiectum cognitionis a longe."

21 *Ibid.*, p. 301: "Deus sibi ipsi non est pulcher: non enim a longe sese aspicit, sed sibi ipsi est idem: ergo fruitur seipso, non autem admiratur, neque nobis pulcher apparet, quoniam non videtur in se. At in creaturis eius relucet bonitas, cuius relucentia et flos est pulchritudo."

22 *Met.*, II, 6, 16, 1, p. 108a.

23 *Ibid.*, p. 108b.

24 *Sum. Theol.*, I, q. 5, a. 4, ad 1.

25 *In Dion. De Divin. Nom.*, c. IV, lect 5.

26 *Sum. Theol.*, I-II, q. 27, a. 1, ad 3.

27 *Ibid.*

28 *Sum. Theol.*, I, q. 39, a. 7.

29 *Ibid.*, I-II, q. 27, a. 1, ad 3.

30 *Sent.*, I, d. 31, p. 2, a. 1.

31 Aristotle, *Met.*, XIII, c. 3, 1078a 36.

32 *Poetics*, c. 7, 1450b 37.

33 *Gorgias*, 506d.

34 The combined term $\kappa\alpha\lambda o\kappa\grave{\alpha}\gamma\alpha\theta\acute{o}\nu$ is a typical example of the identification of the beautiful with the good among the Greeks. Although commonly understood to mean that the beautiful is good, Plato, following Socrates, interpreted the term as meaning that *the good is beautiful*.

35 *Met.*, II, 6, 16, 1, p. 108b.

36 *Ibid.*

37 *Ibid.*

38 *Epilogo*, p. 433: ". . . il bello è fior del buono divino o naturale o artificiale."

39 *Met.*, II, 6, 17, 1, p. 109b.

40 *Ibid.*, II, 6, 17, 2, p. 110a: "Falluntur [Peripatetici] etiam in eo quod dicunt metaphysicum non considerare ens rationis, sed ens reale tantum; utrumque enim considerat, quoniam omnes scientias regulat et eorum principia investigat, et probat reprobatque, et artes scientiasque rationales ipse constituit."

41 St. Thomas, *Sum. Theol.*, I, q. 11, a. 1, ad 1.

42 *Met.*, II, 7, 1, 1, p. 111a-111b.

43 *Ibid.*, p. 111b.

44 *Ibid.*, pp. 111b-112a.

45 *Ibid.*, p. 112b.

46 *Ibid.*

47 *Ibid.*

48 *Ibid.*

49 *Ibid.*, II, 7, 1, 1, tit., p. 111.

50 *Ibid.*, II, 7, 1, 2, p. 113a: ". . . cuiusmodi entitas, eiusmodi unitas est in rebus . . . Tolle unitatem, non datur ens unum nec multitudo: quae eatenus est quatenus constat unitatibus."

51 *Ibid.*, II, 6, 17, 1, p. 109b.

52 *Ibid.*, I, 2, 15, 1, p. 289b; *ibid.*, II, 6, 17, 2, p. 110a-110b; *Theol.*, I, 4, 1, pp. 97-98.

53 Cf. *Met.*, II, 10, chaps. 5-7, pp. 261-68, where Campanella deals extensively with the categories of the supreme transcendentals, such as *praeesse, subesse, substare, inesse, praeinesse, adesse, subsistere, extare, inexistere, coinesse; vere praeesse, vere subesse,* etc.; *bonum vere praeens, bonum vere substans,* etc.

54 *Epilogo,* pp. 473, 480.

55 *Met.,* I, 2, 3, 6, p. 118b.

56 *Ibid.,* pp. 118b-119a. Blanchet calls the treatise of generic predicaments "la partie la plus ingrate de la philosophie de Campanella." *Campanella, op. cit.,* p. 306.

57 *Met.,* I, 2, 15, 1, p. 289a.

58 *Ibid.,* pp. 289b-290a.

59 *Ibid.,* I, 2, 15, 2, p. 290a.

60 *Ibid.; Phil. rat.: Dial.,* p. 73. The definition of substance is given in *Met.,* I, 2, 15, pars 2, a. 3, p. 294a-294b: "Substantia est quae proprie, principaliter, et maxime secundum se, et non secundum aliud, substat."

61 *Theol.,* I, 3, 6, p. 75; *Epilogo,* p. 190, Avvertimenti c; *Phil. rat.: Dial.,* p. 79.

62 *Met.,* I, 2, 15, 2, p. 290a.

63 *Ibid.,* I, 2, 15, pars 3, a. 1, pp. 294b-295a.

64 *Ibid.,* I, 2, 5, pars 3, a. 2, p. 202a; *ibid.,* I, 2, 15, pars 3, a. 3, p. 295a.

65 *Ibid.,* I, 2, 15, 2, p. 290a; *ibid.,* I, 2, 15, pars 3, a. 3, p. 295a; *ibid.,* I, 2, 15, pars 4, a. 1, p. 296a.

66 *Ibid.,* I, 2, 15, pars 4, a. 1, p. 296b.

67 *Ibid.,* I, 2, 15, 2, p. 290a.

68 *Ibid.*

69 *Ibid.,* p. 290a-290b.

70 *Ibid.,* p. 290b.

71 *Ibid.*

72 *Ibid.,* I, 2, 11, 2, p. 284b. In *Met.,* I, 2, 11, 1, p. 283a, Campanella speaks of accident in these terms: "Accidens dicimus quidquid entibus particularibus accidit praeter essentiam, aut potentiam, aut intentionem, aut voluntatem, aut ordinem naturalem, aut consuetudinem. Quoniam ergo est praeter essentiam, non est genus, neque differentia, neque proprietas essentialis eius cui accidit. Licet in se sit haec omnia."

73 *Ibid.,* I, 2, 11, 4, p. 286a-286b.

74 *Ibid.,* I, 2, 15, 2, p. 290b. Campanella's transcendental and generic predicaments may be listed one beside the other in the following order:

TRANSCENDENTAL PREDICAMENTS	GENERIC PREDICAMENTS
1. Essence	Substance
2. Finitude	Quantity
3. Quality	Form or figure
4. Power	Faculty
5. Act	Operation
6. Communication, emanation or effusion	Action
7. Reception, change or alienation	Passion
8. Addition, existentiality and circumstance	Accident
9. Unity	Similarity
10. Plurality or number	Dissimilarity or opposition

75 It might be observed that the notion of being and nonbeing, which dominates Campanella's entire philosophy of finite things, would have been discussed more logically before the subaltern transcendentals and immediately after the supreme transcendentals. Such an arrangement would no doubt have had the advantage of presenting Campanella's thought more organically. But, for the sake of clarity, we have preferred to group all the transcendentals under a single heading, especially because the subaltern transcendentals do not necessarily include finite beings alone, as their predicaments do.

76 *Met.*, I, 1, 9, Def. Metaph., p. 79b; *ibid.*, I, 2, 3, 4, p. 109a.

77 *Ibid.*, I, 1, 9, Def. Metaph., p. 78a; *ibid.*, II, 6, 12, 3, p. 95a.

78 *Ibid.*, II, 6, 3, 1, p. 11a. Cf. also *Real. phil. epil.*, p. 29.

79 *Met.*, II, 6, 3, 2, p. 12a.

80 *Ibid.*, II, 6, 3, 3, p. 13a: "Considerandum tamen est huiusmodi compositionem [ex ente et nihilo] non esse physicam, sed transcendentalem, non tamen quae pertingat ad Deum, nisi ut a nobis capitur." See also *ibid.*, pp. 13b-14a.

81 *Ibid.*, II, 6, 3, 3, p. 13a.

82 This represents substantially Campanella's teaching as contained in the following texts: *Met.*, II, 6, 12, 1, p. 94a; *ibid.*, II, 6, 3, 5, p. 15a; *ibid.*, II, 6, 3, 6, p. 16b.

83 *Ibid.*, II, 6, 3, 7, p. 16a.

84 *Ibid.*, II, 6, 3, 3, p. 13a: "essentia quaelibet cuiuslibet rei absque existentia est nihilum."

85 *Ibid.*

86 *Ibid.*

87 *Ibid.*, II, 6, 3, 7, pp. 16a-16b and 17a.

88 *Ibid.*, II, 6, 3, 2, p. 12b.

89 *Ibid.*, II, 6, 3, 7, p. 17b: "nihilum ab ente terminari asserimus ex una parte, ex altera vero infinitum esse."

90 *Ibid.*, II, 6, 3, 5, p. 15b.

91 *Ibid.*, II, 6, 3, 5, p. 14a.

92 *Ibid.*, II, 6, 3, 7, p. 17a-17b; *ibid.*, II, 6, 3, 5, p. 14a.

93 *Theol.*, I, 12, 1, p. 254: "Non quidem potest concipi nihilum a nobis, nisi per ens: idcirco formamus propositiones de eo tanquam de ente, et cum dico: *verum est nihilum non esse,* ly *verum* non de nihilo dicitur quatenus nihilum, sed quatenus a nobis concipitur per speciem entis, et sic est ens rationis. Et sic formantur de eo propositiones etiam verae, cum tamen verum de solo ente dicatur."

94 *Met.*, II, 6, 3, 3, p. 13b: "ubi est aliqua entitas non est purum nihil, quippe cum nihilo ens sit admistum, et non purum."

95 *Ibid.*, II, 6, 3, 7, p. 17a-17b.

96 Cf. Plato's *Sophist,* 256e.

97 *Met.*, I, 1, 9, Def. Metaph., p. 78a; *ibid.*, I, 2, 2, 4, p. 99b; *ibid.*, II, 6, 12, 1, p. 94a.

98 *Ibid*, II, 6, 12, 1, p. 94a; *ibid.*, II, 6, 12, 3, p. 95a.

99 *Ibid.*, II, 6, 12, 2, p. 95a.

100 Cf. *Met.*, II, pp. 97-107, for an extensive treatment of the objects of the primalities of nonbeing along with the corresponding objects of the primalities of being.

101 *Ibid.*, II, 6, 15, 3, p. 105a.

362 TOMMASO CAMPANELLA

102 In *Met.*, II, 6, 12, 3, pp. 95b-96a, Campanella makes it clear that nonbeing and its first primality, impotence, are responsible for change and mutation in things.
103 *Theol.*, I, 3, 9, p. 82: "dicimus existere quod extra suas causas est."
104 *Met.*, I, 2, 15, pars 2, a. 1, p. 292a: "Est autem essentia id quod ens proprie, principaliter, et maxime est secundum quod ipsum, et non secundum aliud."
105 *Ibid.*, pp. 292a and 293a-293b.
106 *Ibid.*, I, 2, 15, pars 6, a. 1, p. 300a: "ipsa essentia, ut est, vocatur actus"; *ibid.:* "actus essendi non distinguitur ab essentia nisi ratione."
107 *Ibid.*, II, 6, 2, 2bis, p. 4a; *ibid.*, II, 6, 2, 4, p. 10a.
108 *Ibid.*, II, 6, 2, 2bis, p. 5a-5b; *Theol.*, I, 3, 9, pp. 81-82.
109 *Met.*, I, 2, 15, pars 11, a. 1, p. 303a.
110 *Ibid.*, II, 6, 2, 4, p. 10a.
111 *Ibid.*, p. 10b: ". . . [existentia] quatenus habet esse ad essentiam spectat; et quatenus non esse, ad nihilum."
112 *Ibid.*, II, 6, 2, 4, p. 8b: "ita verum est esse contrahi ab essentia, sicut essentiam ab esse; etenim essentia communissimum est nomen, et contrahitur ad substantiam, ad quantitatem, ad figuram, ad operationem, et ita esse contrahitur ad esse quantum, ad esse materiam, ad esse formam, ad esse operationem, ad esse hominem; haec autem contractio non fit neque ab esse, neque ab essentia, ut Peripatetici docent, sed a nihilo, quo utitur ipsum ens primum ad distinctionem rerum."
113 *Ibid.*, II, 6, 2, 2bis, p. 4a.
114 *Prodromus*, p. 28: "res . . . in causis est causa, vel exemplar, et idea, sed essentiam non habet, nisi in actu sit, et e rebus."
115 Cf. our treatise of the first primality of being, chap. VII, sect. III, 1.
116 *Met.*, II, 6, 2, 2bis, p. 4a: "cogitatio enim nostra mensuratur, non mensurat."
117 *Prodromus*, p. 28: "Esse rerum, essentiam et existentiam unum idemque existimo."
118 *Met.*, II, 6, 2, 4, p. 9a.
119 *Ibid.*, II, 6, 2, 2bis, p. 4a.
120 *Prodromus*, p. 28: "Tunc enim res video habere esse cum existunt, et existunt cum habent essentiam et econtra: et quae non habent existere, non habent esse."
121 *Theol.*, I, 3, 9, p. 81: "quando ad exterius esse deducitur per voluntatem et opus artificis, dicitur contrahi ad talem existentiam materialem: non ergo advenit esse ut quid nobilius, sed ut contrahens essentiam, quae habet esse eminens commune, ad particulare et concretum: et simul esse contrahitur ad hanc essentiam. *In re autem exteriori non differt essentia ab existentia intrinsece"* (italics ours).
122 *Met.*, II, 6, 2, 2, p. 3a; *ibid.*, II, 6, 2, 2bis, p. 4b.
123 *Ibid.*, I, 2, 15, pars 6, a. 1, p. 300a-300b. In his presentation of Campanella's doctrine concerning the relationship between essence and existence, Di Napoli *(Tommaso Campanella,* p. 245) fails to distinguish between *actus existendi* and *actus essendi.* These two, as we explained in the course of our discussion, have in Campanella a meaning different from that used in scholastic philosophy. Of the two texts which Di Napoli brings forth to support the thesis, which is basically true, that Campanella denies the real distinction between essence and existence, one is not correct, for it reads *"actus . . . essendi"* instead of *"actus . . . existendi,"* and the other is not to the point, since the context shows that the *actus essendi* refers to essence rather than to existence.

124 *Met.*, II, 6, 2, 2bis, p. 5a.

125 *Ibid.*, II, 6, 2, 4, p. 7a.

126 Reference is made particularly to Heidegger's concept of the *Dasein*, which later was taken up and developed in their own way by J. P. Sartre and other existentialist philosophers.

127 *Met.*, I, 2, 2, 1, p. 93a: "Causa est unde aliquid fit."

128 *Ibid.*, I, 2, 2, 1, p. 93a; *ibid.*, I, 2, 2, 2, p. 94a-94b; *ibid.*, I, 2, 2, 3, p. 97a: "Causatio vero est effectio, id est, extra factio, hoc est suae participationis ad existentiam per mutationem deductio."

129 *Ibid.*, I, 2, 2, 1, p. 93a.

130 *Ibid.*, I, 2, 2, 1, p. 93a: "Semen est compendium causarum et principiorum et elementorum et primalitatum in effectus substantiam veniens." *Ibid.*, I, 2, 2, 3, p. 97a: "seminatio est emissio compendii causarum ad novum numero ens, per propriam existentiam producibile."

131 *Ibid.*, I, 2, 2, 1, p. 94a.

132 *Ibid.*, I, 2, 2, 1, p. 94a-94b; *ibid.*, I, 2, 9, p. 271b.

133 *Ibid.*, II, 10, 2, 1, p. 250b.

134 *Ibid.*, I, 2, 2, 2, p. 94a-94b.

135 *Ibid.*, p. 95a.

136 *Ibid.*

137 *Ibid.*

138 *Ibid.*: "Semen . . . est omnes istae causae in unum redactae, seu causarum omnium simul participatio non remotissime, nec remote, nec propinque, sed proxime."

139 *Ibid.*

140 *Ibid.*, I, 2, 2, 2, p. 95a; *ibid.*, I, 2, 5, 1, p. 152b.

141 *Ibid.*, I, 2, 2, 2, pp. 95a-97a; *ibid.*, II, 10, 2, 1, p. 250b.

142 *Ibid.*, I, 2, 5, 4, p. 155a.

143 *Ibid.*, I, 2, 5, 6, p. 159a.

144 *Ibid.*, I, 2, 5, 4, p. 155b.

145 *Ibid.*, p. 156a: "Causatio metaphysica est quando aliquid agit non quatenus elementum aut elementatum physicum, sed vi primalitatum."

146 *Ibid.*: "Primalitas longius extendit vires quam activitas, et longius activitas quam materialitas; imo nec materia agit, nisi impellente aut cogente activitate; nec vis activa, nisi primalitate praestante ac movente."

147 *Ibid.*, I, 2, 5, 5, p. 158b.

148 *Ibid.*, I, 2, 5, 6, p. 159a. Whether a formal action could take place without any intermediary means of communication, such as the transmission of the sunlight to the earth without the medium of the air, Campanella says it is difficult to decide. *Ibid.*

149 *Ibid.*: "Metaphysicam vero actionem etiam per vacuum transire affirmamus. Sunt enim in vacuo primalitates."

150 *Ibid.*, I, 2, 2, 2, p. 96a.

151 *Ibid.*, I, 2, 9, 1, p. 272.

152 *Ibid.*, I, 2, 9, 2, p. 273b.

153 *Ibid.*

154 Amerio, *Campanella*, p. 168.

155 *Met.*, I, 2, 3, 2, p. 102b.

156 *Ibid.*, III, 13, 1, 1, p. 107a-107b.

157 *Ibid.*, III, 13, 2, 5, p. 116b: "essentia formalis est ab idea."

158 *Ibid.*

159 *Ibid.*: "dicimus ideam esse formam non formatam sed formantem, id est, instar cuius fit formatio, ideo separatur ab ideato; et est in ideato, non secundum totam sui essentiam, sed secundum participationem."

160 *Theol.*, I, 11, 9, p. 242.

161 *Ibid.*, p. 244: "Est ergo idea forma rerum praeter res ipsas existens, quam artifex cognoscendo, cognoscit res, et operando imitatur."

162 *Ibid.*

163 *Ibid.*

164 Cf., e.g., David Ross, *Plato's Theory of Ideas* (Oxford: Clarendon Press, 1951), pp. 43-44, 90, 235-39, where further evidence is produced against a possible Neo-Platonic interpretation of Plato's doctrine of ideas. It is worth mentioning in this connection that Ross's work induced Frederick Copleston to change the attitude he had expressed in *A History of Philosophy, op. cit.*, I, 193, toward Plato's doctrine of ideas. Cf. Copleston's review of Ross's *Plato's Theory of Ideas*, in *The Month* (July, 1952), pp. 54-57.

165 *Epilogo*, pp. 187-88.

166 *Ibid.*, p. 188; *Prodromus*, p. 28: "Locum dico substantiam primam incorpoream, immobilem, aptam ad receptandum omne corpus." Campanella does not make any distinction between space and place; actually he identifies one with the other. Thus, when speaking of the creation of the world, he writes: "il primo Architetto nel principio della successiva duratione o vicenda delle cose . . . stese uno spatio presso che infinito per locar questa sua statua. *Questo è il luogo*, base dell'essere, dove il bel lavoro, cioè il Mondo siede." *Epilogo*, pp. 187-88.

167 *Epilogo*, p. 188, note: "Hic est mundus mathematicus interior et anterior ad omnia corporalis mundi systemata."

168 *Prodromus*, p. 28.

169 *Theol.*, I, 3, 2, pp. 57-58.

170 *Del senso*, p. 29.

171 *Epilogo*, p. 189.

172 *Ibid.*, pp. 191-92.

173 *Phil. sens. dem.*, p. 63: "Stabilimus igitur firmissimum nobis a sensu fundamentum, quod materia sit idem quod corpus, nec esse in re nisi nominis differentiam."

174 *Epilogo*, p. 193.

175 *Met.*, I, 2, 5, pars 2, a. 2, p. 177a: ". . . natura materiae est ut sit corpus universale, informe et iners, aptum ad recipiendas formas, et operationes et numeros. Moles enim corporea est subiectum ex quo res fiunt, et in quod resolvuntur."

176 *Ibid.*, I, 2, 5, pars 2, a. 9, pp. 199b-200a.

177 *Del senso*, p. 37; *Epilogo*, p. 193.

178 *Prodromus*, p. 32: "Dixi materiam corpus, quia sine corpore nihil est ipsa, nisi chimera Aristotelis."

179 *Met.*, I, 2, 5, pars 2, a. 9, p. 200a-200b.

180 *Ibid.*, I, 2, 15, pars 5, a. 4, p. 299b.

181 *Ibid.*, II, 6, 5, 4, p. 22a-22b.

182 *Ibid.*, II, 6, 5, 4, p. 23b.

183 *Prodromus*, p. 37: "Nemo Peripateticorum exponunt bene primum *Physicorum*.

Nam intelligunt privationem nihil, et materiam ens inanime, et formam quae nascitur, non quae facit nasci de gremio materiae, esse principia. Quae quippe chimerica sunt, et non entia, ex quibus realia entia effici nequaquam possunt."

184 *Met.,* I, 2, 4, 1, p. 134a-134b.

185 *Ibid.,* p. 134b: "Forma igitur in sua communitate analogica considerata, est modus seu qualitas cuiusque rei."

186 *Ibid.,* pp. 134b-135a.

187 *Ibid.,* p. 135a.

188 *Ibid.:* "Est . . . materia principium distinguibilitatis; . . . individuationis principium est ipsa formalitas et signatio talis; materia enim de se non signatur, nec a dimensionibus, sed a forma tantas dimensiones requirente ut regnet in materia; ergo si materia signata est principium individuationis, ergo ut formatione insignitur, sic et essentia."

189 *Ibid.,* I, 2, 3, 7, p. 123a: "facit autem unitatem numeralem formaliter haecceitas, quae est singularitas, et indivisibilitas, et particularitas."

190 *Ibid.,* p. 124a.

191 *Ibid.,* pp. 124a and 125a-125b.

192 *Ibid.,* p. 125a.

193 *Ibid.,* I, 2, 4, 1, p. 135b.

194 *Ibid.,* I, 2, 4, 2, p. 136a.

195 *Ibid.,* I, 2, 4, 6, p. 143b.

196 *Ibid.:* "Essentiam ergo aliud esse a forma volumus; istam enim partem, illam totum."

197 *Ibid.,* II, 6, 7, 8, p. 53a: "ex materia prima, quae omni caret forma, stupidissime formas educunt Peripatetici."

198 *Ibid.* Cf. also *Del senso,* p. 41, where Campanella adds that if form were hidden in matter, this latter would always be informed and could no more be pure potency, as the Peripatetics claim it to be.

199 *Phil. sens. dem.,* p. 28.

200 *Epilogo,* p. 197, Avvertimenti a.

201 *Ibid.,* pp. 194-97.

202 *Ibid.,* p. 199.

203 *Ibid.,* p. 200.

204 *Phil. sens. dem.,* p. 68.

205 Hence the present writer does not agree with Di Napoli's statement (*Tommaso Campanella,* p. 340) that in Campanella's teaching the Aristotelian hylomorphism is substantially preserved. What Campanella preserves of Aristotle is his terminology and a dualistic conception of reality which does not go beyond an external kinship with the Stagirite's hylomorphic theory.

206 To convince oneself of the role played by imagination in Campanella's theory of nature, it is enough to read his account of the supposed struggle that went on in the beginning of the world between heat and cold for the possession of space (*Epilogo magno,* pp. 194-97). Rather than a scientific exposition of the origin of the world, it sounds like poetry or fiction.

207 Cf. Ottaviano's *Preface* to *Epilogo magno,* p. 63.

208 Aristotle, *Physics,* 219b.

209 *Ibid.,* 223a 21-29.

210 *Prodromus,* p. 30; *Met.,* II, 6, 12, 3, p. 96a.

211 *Prodromus*, p. 30; *Theol.*, I, 7, 2, p. 154; *Met.*, II, 6, 12, 3, p. 96a; *ibid.*, II, 8, 3, 1, p. 158a-158b; *Epilogo*, p. 211.
212 *Prodromus*, p. 30; "non existente anima adhuc tempus est."
213 *Met.*, II, 8, 3, 1, p. 157a: "Tempus . . . est duratio successiva rei, principium, finemque habens." Cf. also *ibid.*, II, 6, 12, 3, p. 96a; *Prodromus*, p. 30; *Epilogo*, p. 190; and *Theol.*, I, 7, 2, p. 153, where the same definition of time is given, although the wording is somewhat different.
214 *Met.*, II, 8, 3, 1, p. 157a; *Epilogo*, p. 190.
215 *Met.*, II, 8, 3, 1, p. 157a-157b.
216 *Ibid.*, II, 10, 1, 9, p. 247a; *ibid.*, II, 10, 1, 11, p. 249a. This is in accordance with Campanella's theory of the five worlds to be discussed in the next chapter.
217 *Ibid.*, II, 10, 1, 9, p. 247a. The distinction between time, perpetuity, and vicissitude is not so much emphasized by Campanella as the distinction between time, eternity, and aevum. Thus in *Theol.*, I, 7, 2, p. 153, he speaks of time and vicissitude in the same terms.
218 *Met.*, II, 8, 3, 1, p. 158a.
219 *Theol.*, I, 7, 2, p. 153: "tempus componitur ex ente et nonente succedentibus."
220 *Met.*, II, 8, 3, 1, pp. 157b-158a.
221 *Ibid.*, p. 158a: "tempus est ipse fluxus, et quia omnis fluxus est fluentis formae vel rei, ipsum Nunc est ipsa forma fluens, vel eius entitas." Cf. also *Theol.*, I, 7, 2, p. 153.
222 *Ibid.*: "singula entia habent singula tempora, et Nunc propria."
223 *Ibid.*: "tempus universale est ipse coeli motus tanquam deferens omnes mutationes, et Nunc est mobile, ut sol."

CHAPTER NINE

1 *Met.*, I, 5, 3, 1, p. 351a-351b. Cf. the full text in n. 4 of chapter III of this study.
2 Cf. F. Van Steenberghen, "Réflexions sur la systématisation philosophique," *Revue néoscolastique de philosophie*, XLI (May, 1938), 185-216, for a discussion of the problem both from the historical and philosophical points of view.
3 *Theol.*, I, 2, 1, tit., p. 40: "Deum esse et secundum se et secundum nos per se notum notitia innata, illata vero non esse per se notum nobis, sed secundum se tantum. Propterea posse demonstrari."
4 *Ibid.*, I, 2, 1, p. 40.
5 *Met.*, II, 6, 9, 6, p. 73a.
6 *Theol.*, I, 2, 1, p. 40: "Deum esse ita per se notum est in natura, ut nihil magis, si non brutali more consideres quaecumque vides. Et quidem, cum sit maxime ens maximeque activum, maxime movet et afficit cognoscentem animam, ut non possit latere, et ubicumque rerum est aliqua cognitio, seu naturalis, seu animalis, seu mentalis, ibi prius ante omnia cognoscitur Deus."
7 *Met.*, II, 6, 9, 6, p. 73a.
8 Cf. *De fide orthodoxa*, I, 3; PG 94, 794. Quoted in St. Thomas, *Sum. Theol.*, I, q. 2, a. 1.
9 Cf. *De libero arbitrio*, II, 12, 13; PL 32, 1259-61; *Soliloquia*, I, 1, 3; PL 32, 869-74. Campanella brings in St. Augustine's argument from truth to prove his thesis of the soul's innate knowledge of God. Cf. *Met.*, II, 6, 9, 6, p. 73a.

10 *Theol.*, I, 2, 1, p. 41: "Non enim Deus illata notitia nos afficit, cum praeveniat omnia et sit rebus intrinsecus. Propterea dicitur invisibilis et insensibilis, sed ratione intelligibilis, quatenus ex visibilibus rebus ad ipsum syllogizando adsurgimus. Et quidem ita nobis ignotus est illata cognitione, sicuti nos vermibus qui intra ventrem nostrum gignuntur, qui ob sui exiguitatem et nostram magnitudinem, quod simus nos animalia non percipiunt, pungunt intestina et vivunt intra nos, quasi intra corpus insensatum habitantes. Sic omnia sunt in Deo et intra Deum, cumque sit infinitus excedens capacitatem et proportionem nostram, videtur nobis ignotus, cum tamen secundum sui naturam sit notissimus, uti homo notior est quam pediculus aut vermis intra ipsum latens."

11 *Met.*, II, 7, 1, 6, tit., p. 116.

12 *Theol.*, I, 2, 2, p. 42; *Met.*, II, 7, 1, 6, p. 116a-116b.

13 *Theol.*, I, 2, 2, p. 42; *Met.*, II, 7, 1, 6, pp. 116b-117a.

14 *Met.*, II, 7, 1, 6, p. 117a; *Theol.*, I, 2, 2, p. 43; *Atheismus*, p. 24.

15 *Met.*, II, 7, 1, 6, p. 117a-117b.

16 *Theol.*, I, 2, 2, p. 43; *Met.*, II, 7, 1, 6, p. 117b.

17 *Met.*, II, 7, 1, 6, pp. 117b-118a.

18 *Ibid.*, p. 118a. For a comprehensive study of the theistic argument from eternal truths cf. the present writer's article, "The Ideological Argument for God's Existence," *Studies in Philosophy and the History of Philosophy*, ed. John K. Ryan (Washington, D. C.: The Catholic University of America Press, 1961), I, 1-34.

19 *Met.*, p. 118a-188b.

20 Although Campanella does not emphasize this argument any more than the preceding ones, since he places it at the end of the *rationes metaphysicales*, we can consider it the total of all his metaphysical arguments. He words it thus: ". . . omnibus entibus potest addi aut minui aliquid, quoniam non pure perfecta sunt. Datur ergo primum perfectum, cui neque additio neque minutio fieri potest, perfectionum legislator, super omnem sese expandens finem ubique absque fine." *Met.*, II, 7, 1, 6, p. 118b.

21 Cf. *Met.*, II, 7, 1, 7, tit., p. 118, where Campanella calls the arguments of a physical order *rationes efficacissimae* and likens them to the metaphysical arguments previously mentioned.

22 *Theol.*, I, 2, 2, tit., p. 42: "Deum esse sensatis invictissimisque rationibus demonstratur, a Peripateticis vero nonnisi sophistice."

23 *Met.*, II, 7, 1, 7, p. 118a.

24 *Ibid.*

25 *Ibid.*

26 *Ibid.*: "Datur ergo primum efficiens, a cuius primi efficientia ventum est ad praesentes causarum effectiones."

27 *Ibid.*

28 *Ibid.*, p. 118b; *Theol.*, I, 2, 2, pp. 43-44.

29 *Met.*, II, 7, 1, 7, p. 119a.

30 *Ibid.*; *Theol.*, I, 2, 2, p. 43.

31 *Met.*, II, 7, 1, 7, pp. 119a and 120a; *Theol.*, I, 2, 2, p. 44.

32 *Met.*, II, 7, 1, 7, p. 120a.

33 *Ibid.*, p. 120a-120b; *Theol.*, I, 2, 2, p. 44.

34 *Met.*, II, 7, 1, 7, p. 120b. A comparatively recent and original development of the theistic argument based on man's knowledge of, and desire for, the infinite

can be found in Maurice Blondel's "integral realism." Cf. the present writer's study, "Maurice Blondel: The Method of Immanence as an Approach to God," in *Twentieth-Century Thinkers,* ed. by John K. Ryan (Staten Island, N. Y.: Alba House, 1965), pp. 37-58.

   In his *Theologia* Campanella mentions other arguments for the existence of God, such as the consideration of the heavenly system (*Theol.,* I, 2, 2, p. 45), the universal consent of men (*ibid.,* p. 46), and the witness of many holy and wise men, like Moses, the prophets, the apostles, etc. (*ibid.*).

35 Cf. René Descartes, *The Method, Meditations, and Philosophy,* trans. John Veitch (Washington: W. Dunne, 1902), pp. 242ff.

36 *Ibid.,* p. 243.

37 *Ibid.*

38 To support our statement, we report Campanella's argument in full: ". . . anima hominis eam [divinam causam] intelligit. Nam infinita meditatur et cupit; quomodo autem possit hoc facere, nisi infinitum ens reperiatur? Absit enim ut anima, quae est particula mundi, plus cupiat quam sit in veritate rerum. Neque enim pars ulla excedit suum totum; nec effectus supra causas suas elevatur." *Met.,* II, 7, 1, 7, p. 120b. Put in the form of short syllogisms, Descartes' and Campanella's arguments read as follows:

   Descartes —I have the idea of an infinite substance or a most perfect being. But a finite being cannot have such an idea unless a most perfect being produce it in his mind. Therefore, a most perfect being, which we call God, must exist.

   Campanella—I have the knowledge of, and the desire for, an infinite good. But a limited being cannot have such a knowledge and desire unless an infinite being exists as their cause. Therefore, an infinite being, which we call God, must exist.

Reduced to this simple form, the two arguments appear to be substantially the same.

39 *Sum. Theol.,* I, q. 2, a. 3 c.

40 Van Steenberghen's *Ontology, op. cit.,* p. 149, may be worth reading in connection with St. Thomas's argument from motion: "If we wish the *prima via* to lead to an explicit affirmation of the one true God, we must be prepared to make use of Thomas' development up to that point. This added deduction will consist in showing that all finite beings are changeable and that consequently only the infinite and unique Being can be the unchangeable mover or First Mover." For Duns Scotus's criticism of the argument cf. Roy R. Effler, O.F.M., *John Duns Scotus and the Principle "Omne quod movetur ab alio movetur"* (St. Bonaventure, N. Y.: The Franciscan Institute, 1962).

41 *Theol.,* I, 2, 2, pp. 46-47.

42 Our exposition of Campanella's criticism of the Aristotelian principle "quidquid movetur ab alio movetur" is based on *Met.,* I, 2, 10, 6, pp. 280-81; *ibid.,* II, 7, 1, 7, pp. 120b-121a.

43 *Theol.,* I, c. 5, Introd., p. 101.

44 *Enneads,* III, 8, 9; V, 4, 1; VI, 8, 9.

45 *De divinis nominibus,* I, 1, 5, 6; PG 3, 585-96; VII, 3; PG 3, 869-72; *De coelesti hierarchia,* II, 3; PG 3, 139-42.

46 *Sum. Theol.,* I, q. 12, a. 12, ad 1; *ibid.,* q. 13, a. 8, ad 2. For the interpretation of St. Thomas's thought in regard to our knowledge of God's nature cf. F. X.

Maquart, *Elementa philosophiae* (Paris: A. Blot, 1938), t. III, v. 2, pp. 355-56; A. Horvath, *La sintesi scientifica di S. Tomaso d'Aquino* (Turin: Marietti, 1932), pp. 293-313; Ch. Journet, *Conoscenza e inconoscenza di Dio* (Milan: Comunità, 1947); C. B. Daly, "The Knowableness of God," *Philosophical Studies*, IX (Dec., 1959), 90-137. See also the present writer's article, "God—7. Existence of God in Philosophy," *New Catholic Encyclopedia*, 1967, VI, 547-52.

47 *Theol.*, I, 3, 9, pp. 82-83: "Sed quaerimus quo pacto cognoscimus Deum existere, non tamen quid sit: ergo differt existentia a quidditate seu essentia. Respondet S. Thomas quod scimus Deum esse, quatenus propositionis copulam ly *esse* dicit, non quatenus quidditatem. Sed copula non est inanis significatu: ergo dicit existentiam Dei, quae cum sit idem quod essentia, sequitur quod cognoscamus Deum quidditative."

48 *Ibid.*, p. 83.

49 *Ibid.*

50 *Ibid.*, I, 5, 2, p. 103.

51 *Ibid.*, I, 5, 1, p. 101; *Met.*, II, 7, 6, 2, p. 149a.

52 *Met.*, II, 7, 6, 2, p. 149a.

53 *Theol*, I, 5, 2, p. 104.

54 Cf. chap. VII of this study for Campanella's notion of being. See also *Met.*, II, 7, 2, 2, p. 123a-123b.

55 *Theol.*, I, 5, 3, p. 107: ". . . Deus cognoscitur ut creaturae ipsum repraesentant, et ita nominatur ex eis: ergo formaliter et substantialiter dicuntur nomina eius significantia similitudinem cum creaturis: at imperfecto modo."

56 *Met.*, II, 7, 6, 2, pp. 149a-149b and 150a.

57 Because of its beauty, we cite Campanella's text in full as it stands in *Met.*, II, 7, 6, 2, pp. 150b-151a: ". . . in nobis est Deus, et nostri causa latet, non sui; ipse enim manifestissimus est, nos autem occultati in opaco, putamus illum occultatum; multo autem stultius cum dicimus luce sua occultari. Non enim lux occultat, sed manifestat; sed nos imbecilles ad intuitum eius in luce occultari dicimus Deum potentissimum. Quapropter transgresso syllogismo iam intuiti paululum sumus nostro vel alieno intellectu primum Ens unum in luce sua. Assuefactio requiritur ex parte nostra, et dispositio Primalitatum nostrarum, maxime autem Amoris. Deus enim praesto, nec in Amore secundus erit."

58 We should rather say, "what is usually considered as St. Thomas's position," because of the various statements in which Aquinas seems to exclude any quidditative knowledge of God. Cf., for example, P. Sertillanges, *Somme théologique* (Paris: Desclée, 1942), *Dieu*, Vol. II, p. 383, where the author presents St. Thomas's opinion in these terms: "Nous ne savons nullement, en rien, à aucun degré, ce que Dieu est." Gilson does not seem to think otherwise. Cf. *The Christian Philosophy of St. Thomas Aquinas*, trans. L. K. Shook, C.S.B. (New York: Random House, 1956), p. 107.

59 *Theol.*, I, 2, 3, p. 48.

60 *Ibid.*, I, 3, 1, pp. 55-56; *Met.*, II, 7, 2, 6, p. 127b.

61 *Theol.*, I, 3, 2, tit., p. 57; *Met.*, II, 7, 2, 6, pp. 127b-128a.

62 *Theol.*, I, 3, 3, tit., p. 59.

63 *Ibid.*, I, 3, 4, tit., p. 61; *ibid.*, pp. 66-67.

64 *Ibid.*, I, 3, 5, tit., p. 68.

65 *Ibid.*, I, 3, 6, pp. 73-75.

66 *Ibid.*, I, 3, 7, p. 76.

67 *Ibid.*, I, 3, 8, p. 78.

68 *Ibid.*, pp. 78-79.

69 *Ibid.*, p. 79: "Deus est omnis natura, seclusa imperfectione et contractione . . .
Deus est omnia non formaliter, quoniam eorum formis contractis constitueretur,
Deus autem est forma omnium formarum idealis et causalis, non ideata et
causata: est autem omnia causaliter, quia causat omnia: sed non posset causare,
nisi eorum similitudines haberet. Habet Deus omnium esse virtualiter, et
tandem eminenter, quoniam non contractus."

70 *Ibid.*, pp. 79-80.

71 *Ibid.*, I, 3, 9, p. 82.

72 Cf. chap. VIII, sect. III, of this study.

73 *Met.*, II, 8, 1, 2, p. 154a-154b; *Theol.*, I, 3, 9, p. 82.

74 *Theol.*, I, 3, 10, p. 85.

75 *Ibid.*, I, 3, 11, pp. 86-87. "Deus nulla res est, quatenus imperfecta est et
nihilitatis participativa et contradictionis, et est omnis res, quatenus entitatis
et perfectionis." *Ibid.*, p. 87. See also *Met.*, II, 7, 6, 1, p. 148a.

76 *Met.*, II, 7, 6, 1, p. 148a.

77 *Theol.*, I, 3, 12, p. 91: ". . . sunt idem potestas, sapientia et amor fundamentaliter et absolute."

78 *Ibid.*: "multo minus in Deo facient compositionem primalitates, si nullibi
ipsam faciunt."

79 *Met.*, II, 6, 11, 10, pp. 93b-94a.

80 *Ibid.*, p. 94a-94b.

81 *Ibid.*; *Theol.*, I, 3, 12, p. 91.

82 *Met.*, II, 6, 11, 10, tit., p. 93: "Proprincipia distingui ex natura rei formaliter
fundamentaliter in primo Ente."

83 *Theol.*, I, 3, 13, p. 94.

84 Unity does not belong to the class of *praedicata negativa* with which this section is primarily concerned. However, we wish to follow the order set out by
Campanella in his *Theologia*, where unity and being in God are discussed
before the *praedicata supereminentia*, on the ground that they are better understood and respond more properly to the question *an sit* than to the question
quid sit. Cf. *Theol.*, I, 6, Introd., p. 128.

85 *Theol.*, I, 6, 1, p. 130: "quo Deus est, unum est, et quo unum, etiam [ens est],
et ideo maxime unum, quia maxime ens."

86 *Ibid.*, I, 2, 3, p. 51.

87 *Met.*, II, 7, 5, 5, p. 143a.

88 *Theol.*, I, 2, 3, p. 51: "Quatenus ergo sunt, unum sunt omnes res: quatenus
non sunt, plura sunt. Si autem unum est, plura non sunt, quatenus plura, sed
quatenus unum; et revera contrahuntur ad hoc et illud esse per non esse alia."

89 *Met.*, II, 7, 5, 5, p. 143a; *Theol.*, I, 6, 1, p. 130: "divisio enim nihilitatis participium."

90 *Theol.*, I, 6, 2, p. 132.

91 *Ibid.*

92 *Ibid.*, pp. 132-33.

93 *Ibid.*, I, 6, 3, p. 135; *Met.*, II, 7, 5, 2, p. 141a.

94 *Met.*, II, 7, 5, 4, p. 143a.

95 *Theol.*, I, 6, 3, pp. 137-38.

96 Cf. the last argument of the physical order in the preceding section of this chapter, as well as n. 69 above. This basic similarity between the two arguments is even more manifest in the parallel text of the *Metaphysica*, where Campanella makes use of our idea of the infinite to prove that infinity is an attribute of God as well as to demonstrate that an infinite being must exist. He writes: "nos imaginamur infinitum: et quidem anima nostra est intra pusillum cerebri limitata; ergo infinitum existit. Neque enim pars potest supra totum elevari; si ergo anima quae particula mundi est, ens infinitum extra mundum concipit, videtur quid incredibile et stultum omne dogma contra infinitum." *Met.*, II, 7, 5, 4, p. 143b.

97 *Theol.*, I, 6, 3, p. 138: "Ergo Deus necessario est infinitus ex hoc quod anima infinitum cogitat. Et hoc argumentum superat omnia argumenta et demonstrat quasi digito Dei infinitatem veram."

98 *Ibid.*, I, 6, 4, p. 141: "Ens aliquod alicubi est: ens simpliciter ubique."

99 *Ibid.*: "Ubique autem simpliciter est, cuius totalitas est ubique."

100 Cf. *Glossa super Cant. Cantic.*, 5, 17; PL 113, 1157 BC. The author of the *Glossa* is Walafridus Strabo († 849), but the doctrine to which Campanella refers, following the scholastic tradition, is found in the works of St. Gregory the Great *passim*. Cf. St. Thomas, *Sum. Theol.*, ed. P. Caramello (Turin: Marietti, 1950), I, Appendix I, Adnotationes ad Primam Partem, q. 8, a. 3, p. 564.

101 *Theol.*, I, 6, 4, p. 142; *Met.*, II, 8, 2, 2, p. 156a.

102 *Met.*, II, 8, 2, 2, p. 156a; *Theol.*, I, 6, 4, p. 142.

103 *Met.*, II, 7, 5, 5, p. 144a.

104 *Ibid.*, II, 7, 6, 1, p. 148b: "Intimior est nobis Deus quam ipsi nobis, tanquam prior et primus essentiarum dator et conservator."

105 *Ibid.*, II, 8, 2, 1, pp. 155b-156a.

106 *Ibid.*, II, 8, 4, 4, p. 161a: "Dicimus autem extra Deum esse res, non loco extra, nec scitu, nec potestate, aut voluntate, aut scientia, quoniam omnia sunt in ipso et ab ipso: sed essentia et natura. Etenim quia Deus est ens summum infinitumque, quidquid finitum reputatur extra ipsum: finitur enim a nonesse: nonesse autem non est in Deo, sed in nobis, idcirco reputamur extra Deum."

107 Ritter did not understand Campanella correctly when he wrote: "Aber alle Geschoepfe sind doch ihrer Wahrheit nach in Gott. Denn ausser dem unendlichen Gott ist nichts moeglich. Wenn wir von Dingen ausser Gott reden, so wollen wir damit nur sagen, dass sie ein Nichtsein an sich tragen, welches in Gott nicht sein kann." *Geschichte der neueren Philosophie*, p. 36. Ritter's quotation from Campanella's *Metaphysica* is somehow faulty and misleading. The last sentence reads: "non esse autem non est in Deo, sed in nobis, idcirco *reputatur* extra Deum." It must read: "idcirco *reputamur* extra Deum." The same faulty text was reproduced by Spaventa, *Saggi di critica filosofica, politica e religiosa* (Naples: Ghio, 1867), I, 123, n. 1, and later by Fiorentino, *Bernardino Telesio, op. cit.*, p. 171, n. 2. This confirms once more our opinion that both Spaventa and Fiorentino based their interpretation of Campanella's thought more on Ritter's account than on Campanella's original works.

108 *Theol.*, I, 7, 1, pp. 146-47.

109 *Ibid.*, pp. 147, 149; *Met.*, II, 8, 3, 1, pp. 158b-159a.

110 *Theol.*, I, 7, 1, p. 149.

111 *Ibid.*: "quia [Deus] solus est immutabilis, solus quoque est aeternus."

112 *Met.*, II, 8, 3, 1, p. 159a-159b: "Deus ergo aeternitas est."

113 *Theol.*, I, 7, 1, p. 150.

114 *Ibid.*

115 *Ibid.*, I, 3, 12, p. 88: "Cum autem Deus sit summum ens, ex summa potentia, summa sapientia summoque constat amore, exclusis oppositis constitutivis nihilitatis."

116 *Ibid.*, I, 8, 1, tit., p. 158.

117 *Ibid.*, p. 160. In the *Metaphysica* Campanella explains why the primalities in God are infinite: "Posse autem Dei infinitum est in eo quod ipse potest semper esse, et omnia esse. . . Similiter scientia Dei est infinita, quia scit seipsum infinitum, et voluntas infinita eadem ratione." *Ibid.*, II, 8, 4, 3, p. 160a.

118 *Theol.*, I, 9, 1, tit., p. 162; *Met.*, II, 7, 2, 6, pp. 126-27.

119 *Theol.*, I, 9, 2, p. 165.

120 *Ibid.*, p. 166.

121 *Ibid.*, I, 9, 3, p. 168.

122 *Ibid.* In the *Metaphysica* Campanella speaks of a double power in God in His action *ad extra*, one speculative and one practical. The text where the reasons for, and the meaning of, the twofold power are pointed out follows: ". . . assero Deum quae facit ad extra non necessario facere, nec necessario posse; sed duplex potestas hic consideratur, sicut duplex voluntas et scientia iam patefacta est. Altera scilicet potentia speculativa, altera practica et operativa (loquor per similitudinem ad scientiam, quoniam caremus expressioribus vocabulis); potentia speculativa est qua omnia potest absolute in se, et respondet scientiae simplicis intelligentiae et voluntati speculativae. Potentia vero practica est quae ad opus exterius porrigitur. At Deus non potest operari nisi quod vult, quoniam cogi ad nullum opus potest. Non vult autem nisi quod per sapientiam novit esse volendum. Cum autem vult, libere vult et non necessario; ergo potest libere et non necessario; ergo potest non posse, quia potest non velle; ergo quae non facit, non potest facere; quia non vult; quoniam haec potestas mista [sic] est voluntati et scientiae." *Met.*, II, 8, 4, 6, p. 162b.

123 *Theol.*, I, 9, 3, p. 170.

124 *Ibid.*, pp. 171-72: "actio Dei non distinguitur ab eo, nisi prout est in effectu, et sic est passio vel terminus."

125 *Ibid.*, I, 9, 4, p. 173; *Met.*, II, 7, 5, 4, p. 143b.

126 *Met.*, II, 8, 4, 7, p. 163a. See also *Theol.*, I, 9, 5, p. 182.

127 *Theol.*, I, 9, 5, p. 180.

128 *Met.*, II, 8, 4, 5, p. 161a: "Deus omnia potest quaecumque dicunt esse, quoniam est summum ens, foecundissimum omnis entitatis."

129 *Theol.*, I, 10, 1, p. 187.

130 *Ibid.*, p. 190.

131 *Ibid.*, I, 11, 1, p. 194.

132 *Met.*, II, 7, 6, 1, p. 148a.

133 *Theol.*, I, 11, 1, p. 196.

134 *Met.*, II, 8, 5, 4, p. 167a.

135 *Theol.*, I, 11, 1, p. 199. Cf. also *Met.*, II, 8, 5, 4, p. 167a-167b.

136 *Met.*, II, 8, 5, 6, p. 168b.

137 *Ibid.*: "Aristoteles qui negat mundum esse factum a Deo, negat ideas rerum in mente Dei; et putat Deum vilescere, si respiceret extra se; et recte, sed iuxta dogma impium." Cf. also *Theol.*, I, 11, 2, p. 203, where the criticism of

the Stagirite's position is concluded with this sharp remark: "Quapropter videtur Aristoteles in rebus magnis semper crassus, in paucis subtilis."

138 *Met.*, II, 8, 5, 7, p. 169a-169b.

139 For the exact meaning of Scotus's doctrine on this point cf. his *Opus Oxoniense,* I, d. 35, q. unica, n. 10. See also Van de Woestyne, *op. cit.*, II, p. 772, and Bettoni, *Duns Scotus,* pp. 153-56.

140 *Theol.*, I, 11, 2, pp. 204-205. Campanella concludes the discussion thus: "Nos autem diximus Deum scire res omnes in sua essentia, quatenus a rebus in tali gradu est participabilis, quae nihil aliud sunt quam umbrae et participationes divinae essentiae. Verum res habent esse et hoc esse, quod limitatur per nonesse, cuius participatione fit numerus et limes, sicut Dei primi entis participatione fit unitas et esse. Tunc dico quod, cognoscendo propriam essentiam, cognoscit earum entitates, et sicuti cognoscit quod tantum participant et non plus, cognoscit differentias et nonentitates."

141 *Ibid.*, p. 207: "Ut autem entia sunt in Deo, relucent antequam fiant; et cum fiunt et cum facta sunt, etiam in eo sunt et non extra, quatenus sunt. . . Deus autem est intrinsecus et causa et cognoscit ut dans, non ut recipiens."

142 *Ibid.*, I, 11, 3, title and the whole article, pp. 209-212. Cf. also *Met.*, II, 8, 5, 7, p. 171a.

143 *Theol.*, I, 11, 4, tit., p. 214.

144 *Ibid.*, I, 11, 5, p. 218. Father Remer, S. J., points out that the *scientia simplicis intelligentiae,* as the name indicates and as Campanella states, is really only a subdivision of the *scientia conditionalium.* Cf. Remer-Gény, S. J., *Theologia naturalis* (5th ed.; Rome: The Gregorian University, 1926), p. 140.

145 *Theol.*, I, 11, 5, pp. 219-21; *Met.*, II, 8, 4, 6, p. 162a.

146 *Theol.*, I, 11, 5, p. 222.

147 Cf. St. Augustine, *De Trinitate,* XV, c. 13; PL 42, 1076.

148 St. Thomas, *Sum. Theol.*, I, q. 14, a. 8.

149 *Theol.*, I, 11, 6, pp. 222-23.

150 St. Thomas, *Sum. Theol.*, I, q. 14, a. 13 c; *I Periherm.*, lect. 13, n. 11.

151 *Theol.*, I, 11, arts. 7 and 8, pp. 226-40; *Met.*, II, 8, 5, 8, p. 171a-171b; *ibid.*, II, 9, 3, 4, p. 182a-182b.

152 *Theol.*, I, 12, 1, p. 252; "Est quidem veritas adaequatio ideati ad ideam."

153 *Ibid.*, pp. 255-56.

154 *Ibid.*, p. 256: "Deus autem, ut intelligens et ut intellectum, sibi ipsi non solum est conformis, sed unum, et intellectus eius non ideatur a sua idea, sicuti noster, sed identificatur: solum (enim) ratione discernuntur, ut patet. Verum ergo et veritas est identitas Dei, ut obiecti, cum seipso, ut intelligente."

155 *Ibid.*, I, 13, 1, tit., p. 257.

156 *Ibid.*, pp. 258-59.

157 *Met.*, II, 8, 5, 8, p. 173a; *ibid.*, II, 8, 7, 1, p. 174a-174b, **Resp.**; *Theol.*, I, 13, 2, p. 264.

158 *Theol.*, I, 13, 2, p. 267: ". . . cum Deus sit omnino infinite bonus et intensive et extensive, non habet unde velit aliquod bonum aliud a se: extra infinitum enim nihil esse potest: quod si fieri extensio potest, illud non vere infinitum fuit nec adaequavit proprium amorem, sicuti cum homo vult alia a se, extendit volitionem extra, quoniam finitus est cui potest addi. *At quomodo Deo potest addi? Hoc opus, hic labor*" (italics ours).

159 *Met.*, II, 8, 6, 2, p. 173a-173b.

160 *Theol.*, I, 13, 2, p. 265: "licet in Metaphysica dixerim ex amoris exuberantia Deum amare alia extra se per hoc quod amat se . . . nunc tamen huic responsioni non satis acquiesco."

161 *Ibid.*, p. 267: "Equidem hoc unum scio vere: quod latet nos arcanum hoc. Tamen, data licentia balbutiendi, dico extra infinitum non posse exuberantiam bonitatis et perfectionis reperiri: sed haec intra Deum sciri et amari. Et quia scientia Dei et amor est activus, non passivus, et liber, non coactus, puto hoc esse eius amare et scire, dare scilicet rebus scientiam et amorem et esse."

162 *Ibid.*, I, 14, 2, p. 289.

163 *Ibid.*, I, 17, 1, p. 311.

164 *Met.*, III, 11, 1, 1, pp. 1-2.

165 *Ibid.*, III, 11, 2, 1, pp. 2-3; *ibid.*, III, 11, 2, 2, pp. 3-4; *ibid.*, III, 11, 3, 1, pp. 10-11.

166 *Ibid.*, III, 11, 3, 2, pp. 11-15; *ibid.*, III, 11, 3, 3, pp. 15-18; *ibid.*, III, 11, 5, 3, pp. 25-26. This same doctrine is held by Campanella in other works, such as *Phil. sens. dem.*, pp. 16-25, *passim; Epilogo*, p. 193, ed. *F; Real. phil. epil.*, p. 29. Campanella's statement that the inhabitants of the City of the Sun are uncertain as to the actual origin of the world (*Città*, p. 452) is by no means an indication of his own attitude toward the doctrine of creation, as Firpo maintains (*ibid.*, n. 146). The statement simply describes the supposed mentality of a people who never came in contact with Christian revelation, and who are therefore unable to explain by the light of natural reason alone the creation of the world from nothing. A discussion of the scholastic notion of creation, with special emphasis on its relationship to the findings of modern science, can be found in the present writer's study, "A Prime Instance Where Science Needs Religion," in *Science and Religion*, ed. John Clover Monsma (New York: G. P. Putnam's Sons, 1962), pp. 93-102.

167 *Met.*, II, 7, 3, 1, p. 129a.

168 *Ibid.*, II, 7, 4, 3, p. 136a-136b.

169 *Ibid.*, II, 6, 7, 6, p. 52b.

170 *Ibid.*, II, 7, 3, 1, tit., p. 128. Cf. also *Defensio*, p. 10.

171 *Met.*, III, 11, 3, 2, p. 13b: "Ens primum fecit omnia ex se et non ex alio ente, non tamen ex substantia sui, quoniam essent similiter infinita et aeterna. Non potest autem esse nisi unum infinitum et unum aeternum . . . ergo per quandam a se emanationem, ex nihilo materiali facit omnia: et sicut lux a sole emanat, et non est sol, ita res a Deo emanant, et non sunt Deus, sed quasi quidam radii et splendores eius." It is clear, then, that by calling creation *quandam a se emanationem* Campanella does not intend to say that the world is but an outpouring of God's substance. On the contrary, he explicitly excludes that doctrine. Hence no trace of pantheism is to be found in his teaching on creation. "Creatio," he affirms in another text of the *Metaphysica*, "addit supra fieri productionem ex nihilo, et emanatio dici solet." *Ibid.*, I, 2, 1, 2, p. 90a.

172 *Met.*, II, 7, 4, 4, p. 137a: ". . . limitationem formaliter non esse a Deo, sed a nihilo; nec factam fuisse, quoniam nonens non fit, sed a Deo usum in hoc accepisse, *qui vocat quae non sunt tanquam ea quae sunt.* Ad constitutionem enim materiae non solum requiritur esse, sed nonesse Angelum, nec formam, nec locum; et ad esse hominis non solum requiritur esse, sed non esse asinum, non esse lapidem, non esse gladium, etc. Quapropter asserimus omnia quae

sunt, in quantum sunt, unum esse, et non plura, sed inquantum non sunt, plurificari." *Ibid.*, p. 137b: "Cum autem quaeritur quare Deus fecit mundum, et unde limitata est eius actio, et quomodo nihilum potuit impedire ipsum ens, respondemus ipsum ens infinitum non impediri, quoniam Deus est in Deo; ipsum vero finitum necessario impediri ne sit infinitum, quoniam extra Deum reperiri infinitum non potest."

173 For St. Thomas's doctrine on this point cf. *In Met.*, XII, lect. 5; *Sum. Theol.*, I, q. 46, arts. 1 and 2; *Cont. gent.*, II, 31-38; *De aeternitate mundi contra murmurantes* (Opusc.).

174 *Met.*, III, 11, 3, 2, p. 13a: "Implicat . . . contradictionem dicere esse factum et aeternum, ut patet ex ratione terminorum."

175 *Ibid.*, III, 11, 5, 3, pp. 25a-25b and 26a. See also *ibid.*, III, 11, 3, 2, pp. 12a and 13a; *Phil. sens. dem.*, pp. 23-24. In his *Ontology*, trans. Rev. Martin J. Flynn (New York: Joseph F. Wagner, 1952), pp. 242-43, Van Steenberghen repeats substantially Campanella's reasoning when he states: "The hypothesis of an evolution without a starting point involves a contradiction. This contradiction has been often demonstrated. A typical *reductio ad absurdum* follows. If the time past were eternal and if, as Aristotle thought, the revolutions of the stars were eternal, then an infinity of days would have elapsed up to the present time. In that case we would have to say that any 'past' day lies at a finite distance from today, and consequently that no one of them is infinitely removed. But then the past is finite, because there would be a day located at a finite distance from today which would yet be the furthest away of all, and consequently the first day. Or we would have to say that one or several days of the past are at an infinite distance from today. How then can we conceive the passage from the days which are infinitely removed to the days which are located at a finite distance from us? This leaves us in complete confusion."

176 *Met.*, III, 11, 5, 3, pp. 25a-25b and 26a; *Theol.*, I, 7, 1, p. 151. To support his own opinion, Campanella wrongly appeals in *Met.*, III, 11, 5, 3, p. 26a, to St. Thomas's *Quodlibetum Quintum*, q. 1.

177 *Met.*, III, 11, 5, 3, pp. 25a-25b and 26a, *passim.*

178 *Ibid.*, II, 10, 1, 3, p. 243a-243b: "In primo Ente ponimus mundum Archetypum, immensum et infinitum sibi simillimum, longe excedentem limites et numeros mundi corporei, et realius, et verius, et melius: et quidem in sua entitate innumerabiles absque fine mundos corporeos praehabentem et praecellentem."

179 *Ibid.*, II, 10, 1, 1, pp. 241b-242a.

180 *Ibid.*, II, 10, 1, 9, p. 247a; *ibid.*, II, 10, 1, 11, p. 248a-248b.

181 *Ibid.*, II, 10, 1, 4, p. 243a: "In . . . mundo Archetypo profecto inexistunt Angeli, Virtutes, Intellectus, et Numina vocati, si corporei non sunt." In *Met.*, II, 10, 1, 10, p. 248, a scheme of the five worlds is to be found, where each world is represented by a circle. In the explanation that follows the scheme Campanella says: "In secundo circulo a centrali locavimus mundum mentalem, qui est angelicarum et humanarum mentium, ex solis primalitatibus, finitis tamen, constitutum, potentia nempe, sapientia et amore: ubi posuimus aeviternitatem et metaphysicas entitates." *Ibid.*, II, 10, 1, 11, p. 249a. Cf. also *Met.*, II, 10, 1, 9, p. 247a.

182 *Ibid.*, II, 10, 1, 5, p. 245a: "In mundo Mentium fundatur basis mundi corporalis,

quae est mundus Mathematicus praecedens omnia: in quo mentes tanquam in posteriori sibi ente faciunt figuras, lineas, puncta imaginesque omnes mathematicas." *Ibid.*, II, 10, 1, 11, p. 249a: "In tertio circulo inscripsimus mundum mathematicum, hoc est, spatium universale, basim corporum intraneam, in quo imaginans vis ideat omnes figuras et corpora commensurat." See also *Met.*, II, 10, 1, 9, p. 247a.

183 *Ibid.*, II, 10, 1, 6, p. 245a: "Intra, seu supra, seu potius in mundo Mathematico contractior mundus locatur corporalis, seu materialis: posuit enim Deus corpoream molem intra mathematicam, ut locus esset formarum activarum, quarum pugna factus est mundus corporeus." *Ibid.*, II, 10, 1, 11, p. 249a: "In quarto circulo interiori et exteriori ponitur mundus materialis, videlicet moles corporea, in qua extruitur mundus situalis per formarum distinctionem." See likewise *Met.*, II, 10, 1, 9, p. 247a.

184 *Ibid.*, II, 10, 1, 7, p. 246a: "Post mundum corporalem, imo (dicam melius) in mundo corporali locatur mundus situalis noster, genitus quoad situationem ab agentibus causis, calore scilicet et frigore, dum simul pugnant pro corporeae molis possessione, sine qua subsistere non possunt, sicuti neque materia sine spatio." *Ibid.*, II, 10, 1, 11, p. 249a: "In quinto multicolori circulo ab utrisque extremis est mundus situalis ab omnibus circumplexus, et intus compenetratur, penetrans ipse nullos. In quo est materia basis, et spatium continens, et mens ideatrix, et divinitas creatrix et conservatrix; et coexistentia corporalia systemata mutuis officiis sese servantia, et tempus in eorum mutabilitate." Cf. also *Met.*, II, 10, 1, 9, p. 247a.

Here is a scheme of the five worlds:

ORDERS OF BEINGS	TYPES OF WORLDS	CHARACTERISTICS
1. God	Archetypal	Eternity
2. Angels and human minds	Mental	Eviternity
3. Universal space	Mathematical	Perpetuity
4. Bodily mass	Material	Vicissitude
5. Organized bodies	Localized	Time

185 *Met.*, II, 10, 1, 8, pp. 246-47.

186 *Ibid.*, II, 10, 1, 11, p. 249b: ". . . [disseremus] quomodo in hoc mundo mirificentissime Deus coadunavit res physicas corporeas, et mathematicas et metaphysicas tanquam in Epilogo omnium; et quomodo mens humana physicae materiae vinculis communis vitae miscetur, et faciat Microcosmum. In homine enim est spatium intraneum, corporea moles, vires activae ad situales partes distinguendas. Solidum terrae, humidum maris, spiritus coeli, mens divinitus immissa, Deus immittens et conservans, angelus custodiens. E quibus mutuis utilitatibus ista continentur in homine omnium mundorum Epilogo." For man's knowledge of God and the eternal ideas cf. our previous discussion on sense and supersensible knowledge in chap. IV, sect. II, of this study.

187 *Ibid.*, III, 12, 2, art. unic., p. 82a-82b.

188 *Ibid.*, p. 83b.

189 *Ibid.*, III, 12, 3, 4, p. 87a.

190 *Ibid.*, III, 12, 7, 1, pp. 91a and 92a. It is worth noting that even the inhabitants

of the so called City of the Sun admit the existence of good and bad angels.
Cf. *Città*, p. 455. This fact shows once more Campanella's belief that human
reason, even when unaided by Christian revelation, can prove the existence
of angels.

191 *Theol.*, I, 17, 1, p. 311.

192 *Ibid.*, p. 314.

193 *Ibid.*, I, 17, 3, p. 339; *Met.*, II, 9, 11, 2, p. 225b; *Città*, p. 458.

194 *Met.*, III, 11, 6, 2, p. 34b; *ibid.*, III, 15, 1, 1, p. 155b.

195 *Theol.*, I, 17, 1, p. 313: "Providentiae influxus magnos esse tres, videlicet
necessitatem, quae oritur ex potentia, fatum, quod (ex) sapientia, harmonia,
quae ex amore . . . Et sine his nihil potest fieri."

196 *Ibid.*: "Est ergo necessitas influxus potentiae divinae ad faciendas (et) movendas
causas in finem."

197 *Ibid.*, I, 17, 3, tit., p. 339; *Met.*, II, 9, 1, art. unic., p. 177b.

198 *Theol.*, I, 17, 1, p 313: "Fatum vero est series causarum et concausarum ordi-
natissima fluens a sapientia Dei." See also *Met.*, II, 9, 4, 1, p. 186a-186b.

199 *Met.*, II, 9, 7, 3, tit., p. 209.

200 *Epilogo*, p. 206: "Se non piacesse questo nome di fato e destino a theologi,
benchè io habbia dichiarato ch'egli sia il voler divino e l'accordo de tutte le
cause agenti in virtù della prima, si può mettere il nome di conordinamento
[sic] overo coordinazione."

201 *Theol.*, I, 17, 3, tit., p. 339; *Met.*, II, 9, 1, art. unic., p. 177b.

202 *Theol.*, I, 17, 1, p. 313: "Harmonia est influxus divini amoris, quo res propriis
finibus et hos supremo tandem adaptantur." Cf. also *Met.*, II, 9, 8, 1, p. 211a.

203 *Theol.*, I, 17, 3, tit., p. 339; *ibid.*, p. 342; *Met.*, II, 9, 1, art. unic., p. 177b.

204 *Met.*, II, 9, 2, 4, p. 179b; *Theol.*, I, 17, 3, pp. 344-45.

205 *Met.*, II, 9, 11, 2, p. 224a: "Non enim res faciunt quod vellent, sed quod velle
coguntur; sed ex quo volunt voluntate naturali aut libera coactionem exuunt."
See also *Theol.*, I, 17, 3, pp. 344-45.

206 *Theol.*, I, 17, 3, pp. 352-53: "Non ergo dicam quod Deus movet voluntates
physice: quod si Patres moderni aliquando dicunt, intelligitur realiter: nec
dicam solum moraliter, tanquam obiectum bonum, ut alii, nec solum persuasive
et erudiendo, ut Pelagiani, sed metaphysice: qui (modus) includit moralitatem
et persuasionem et illustrationem et aliquid plus, non tamen quod possit
facere, ne anima possit reluctari: sic enim statim libertas perit: sed ut velit
prout vult."

207 *Ibid.*, I, 17, 3, tit., p. 339: "voluntates [hominum] . . . possunt Deo resistere
ex suppositione et in volendo, non in exequendo."

208 *Met.*, II, 9, 11, 2, p. 224a. Femiano's enthusiastic appraisal of Campanella's
solution of the problem of divine providence and human freedom does not
seem to be justified. (Cf. Femiano, *Lo spiritualismo di Tommaso Campanella*,
Vol. II, p. 152).

209 *Theol.*, I, 17, 3, pp. 349-50. In his ardor for the defense of freedom of the will
Campanella brings in a personal experience from his prison life: "Ego quadraginta horas de fune pependi tortus brachia, et funiculis secantibus ossa, et
ligno acuto devorante posteriora, terebrante, lacerante et sanguinem bibente,
ut cogerer iudicibus dicere verbum unum vel leve, nec dicere volui, *ut probarem
me esse liberae voluntatis.* Quomodo suavitas Dei aut stellarum motus sine vi
poterunt libertatem tollere, quam violentia tanta non aufert?" He concludes his

observation with this strong finale: "Merentur in bestiarum numero haberi, qui se liberos esse negant." *Theol.*, I, 17, 3, p. 351. For anyone who denies the freedom of the will not only lacks metaphysical training but shows also a complete lack of common sense. *Ibid.* The doctrine of freedom of the will is also mentioned in *Città del Sole*, p. 463.

210 *Met.*, II, 7, 5, 8, p. 147a-147b.

211 *Ibid.*, II, 9, 10, 3, p. 221a. To show how seemingly physical evils may work for a definite purpose of divine providence, Campanella brings forth, among others, the example of the formation of a woman's body. Nature, he claims, always intends to produce its best, that is, a male. By accident, however, and because of lack of power for the formation of a male's body, a woman is born, which is an imperfect being, nay, a monster of nature, as Aristotle calls her. Yet, if we consider the mission of a woman in the world, i.e., the generation and education of the offspring and man's companionship, we shall have no difficulty in recognizing that she fits very well into the general plan of divine providence. *Ibid.* See also *Del senso*, p. 151, and *Epilogo*, p. 434, for the same teaching. Campanella's low concept of woman should not surprise anyone who is acquainted with the slow development that the Christian notion of womanhood received in the course of history. His doctrine may very well have been inspired by St. Thomas, *Sum. Theol.*, I, q. 92, a. 1; I, q. 99, a. 2, ad 1 and 2.

212 *Met.*, II, 7, 5, 8, p. 147b.

213 *Ibid.*

214 *Ibid.*, II, 9, 5, 6, p. 196b; *ibid.*, II, 9, 13, 1, p. 230a-230b; *ibid.*, II, 9, 13, 2, p. 231a-231b; *Theol.*, I, 17, 8, p. 441.

215 *Theol.*, I, 17, 8, p. 442; *Città*, pp. 455-56.

216 *Met.*, III, 14, 4, 2, p. 138b.

217 *Ibid.*, p. 139a.

218 *Ibid.*, p. 139b.

219 *Ibid.*

220 *Ibid.*, pp. 139b-140a. The doctrine of the immortality of the soul is also taught in *Del senso*, pp. 118-27; *Atheismus*, c. VII, pp. 65ff.; *Theol.*, III, 3, 3 (cf. Amerio, *Campanella*, p. 148). The same doctrine is held as certain by the inhabitants of the City of the Sun. Cf. *Città*, p. 455.

221 *Met.*, II, 9, 13, 1, p. 229b; *Theol.*, I, 17, 4, pp. 359, 362, 375; *Lettere*, pp. 404-405.

222 *Theol.*, I, 17, 4, p. 371.

223 *Ibid*, p. 374; *Met.*, III, 15, 1, 2, p. 158b.

224 *Met.*, II, 9, 13, 1, p. 229b: "Illud autem inconcusse sustineo, esse in nobis libertatem ad volendum et nolendum, et auxilium ut entitas addita est, non fieri a nobis efficax; nullam enim entitatem nos dare possumus, nisi a primo Ente et cum primo; ergo fieri efficax a Deo effective, a nobis vero meritorie tantum." In an attempt to explain this difficult doctrine, Campanella writes: ". . . dicerem, salvo meliori iudicio, quod Deus concurrit ad actus pios praeveniendo et cooperando, ut dicunt nostrates, ad malos vero solum permittendo et cooperando cum causa, et non in causas, auxilio generali, non speciali, nec praedeterminasse hosce actus, sed praevidisse et ordinasse ad bonum: non enim possum audire quod homo in actu homicidii a Deo et a diabolo simul iuvatur et excaecetur et impellatur, nec Origenes (nec) Ambrosius nec quispiam ex Patribus. Solum dicam cum S. Thoma quod Deus dicitur movere ad peccatum,

quatenus aliqua bonitas apprehensa a peccante ipsum movet, ex parte obiecti et physice."
225 *Theol.*, I, 17, 9, p. 446.
226 *Ibid.*, p. 448: "Quae si non potes capere, melius est sic, quam tuo metiri sensu arcana Dei et per vocabula repugnantia loqui, meliusque est satagere ne delearis a libro vitae."

CHAPTER TEN

1 Cf. *De natura generis*, c. I; *De veritate*, q. 1, a. 1, ad 3 in contr.
2 *Quodlibetum II*, a. 3.
3 See chap. VIII, sect. III, of this study.
4 See chap. VII, sect. III, par. 1, of this study.
5 In Campanella's system the term "existence" often has a different connotation from its commonly accepted meaning in scholastic philosophy. It stands for everything that is not nothing, and belongs even to a potential being in the mind of God or in our minds. This arbitrary use of the term "existence" may save him from some of the inconsistencies we have pointed out, but will hardly excuse him from the confusion and misunderstanding his teaching is likely to cause in the mind of the reader.
6 Cf. above chap. VI.
7 Cf. Aristotle's *De anima*, 411a 7, where Thales, the founder of the Milesian school, is described as believing that "all things are full of gods." John Burnet makes some reservations on the value of Aristotle's interpretation of Thales. He cautions that it is not safe to regard an apothegm as evidence of the teaching of a particular philosopher. The chances are that the saying, "all things are full of gods," belongs to Thales as one of the Seven Wise Men, rather than as founder of the Milesian school. Moreover, such sayings are, as a rule, anonymous to begin with, and are attributed now to one sage and now to another. *Early Greek Philosophy* (4th ed.; London: Adam & Charles Black, 1952), p. 50. See the present writer's articles, "Hylozoism" and "Panpsychism," in the *New Catholic Encyclopedia*, for a historical survey of the two systems.
8 Reference is made here particularly to Giordano Bruno, whose system is often presented as a naturalistic pantheism. Bruno, however, never rejected the transcendence of God.
9 Cf. above chap. VII, n. 158.
10 Cf. above chap. VIII, n. 9. See also our observation in n. 5 of the present chapter.
11 *De veritate*, q. 1, a. 1.
12 It may be interesting to report in this connection what an outstanding present-day scholastic philosopher says concerning the application of the potency and act theory to the composition of essence and existence in finite things. "We do not think that it is either exact or opportune to compare the composition of essence and existence to a composition of potency and act. To avoid any equivocation, it would seem better to restrict these notions of potency and act to the dynamic order, as Aristotle himself did." Van Steenberghen, *Ontology*, p. 113.

13 "Averroès présente la théorie d'Avicenne comme si ce dernier faisait de l'existence un accident prédicamental, ce qui n'est pas exact. Les scolastiques reprennent à leur compte cette interprétation d'Averroès et, dès lors, même les partisans de la distinction réelle, par exemple S. Thomas, se déclarent adversaires de cette thèse prétendument avicenienne." Louis De Raeymaeker, *Philosophie de l'être* (Louvain: Institut Supérieur de Philosophie, 1947), p. 147, n. 5.

14 "Pour exprimer le caractère adventice de l'existence de l'être fini, Avicenne se sert du terme arabe 'lazim' (concomitans, accidens). Pour le sens de ce terme, cfr. A. M. Goichon, *La distinction de l'essence et de l'existence d'après Ibn Sina (Avicenne)*, Paris, 1937, pp. 112-23." *Ibid.*, p. 145, n. 2.

15 Cf. St. Thomas, *Sum. Theol.*, I, q. 14, a. 9; *Cont. gent.*, I, 66.

16 *Sum. Theol.*, I, q. 14, a. 16; *ibid.*, q. 15, a. 3.

17 *Ibid.*, I, q. 14, a. 13 c.

18 Cf. *De Civitate Dei*, XI, 4, 5, 6; PL 41, 319-22.

19 *Ibid.*, X, 31; PL 41, 311.

20 *Monologium*, c. 8; PL 158, 156 c.

21 *Sum. Theol.*, I, q. 46, a. 2, ad 1; *De aeternitate mundi*.

22 Cf. Van de Woestyne, *Cursus philosophicus, op. cit.*, Vol. II of new edition, *Ontologia* (Malines: Typographia S. Francisci, 1933), pp. 48-49, for a list of scholastic philosophers, from the time of St. Albert the Great to our own time, who deny the possibility of creation from eternity. References are also given in n. 1, p. 49.

23 St. Thomas, *Sum. Theol.*, I, q. 46, a. 2, ad 1. For a detailed notion of creation in St. Thomas cf. James F. Anderson, *The Cause of Being* (St. Louis-London: Herder, 1952).

24 *Sum. Theol.*, I, q. 46, a. 2, ad 7; *De veritate*, q. 2, a. 10.

25 The importance that the problem of predestination had assumed in Campanella's time may be judged from his statement in *Met.*, II, 9, 13, 2, p. 231a: "Hoc argumentum vexat hodie totum genus humanum."

26 The following text from *Theol.*, I, 17, 4, p. 368, will confirm our position: "Etsi praedestinatio universalis non fit ex meritis praevisis, ut dictum est, sed sola liberalitate Dei, *specialis* tamen post praevisum peccatum fit, *praevisis meritis et demeritis:* non tamen sunt ratio praedestinationis (illa enim iam facta erat pro omnibus), sed permanentiae in praedestinatione et ruinae ab ea, quod reprobatio dicitur. Ergo *in voluntate consequenti* est reprobatio, *in antecedenti et consequenti* est praedestinatio" (italics ours).

CHAPTER ELEVEN

1 *Met.*, I, 5, 2, 4, p. 349a-349b: "Scientia . . . moralis dividitur in Ethicam, Politicam, et Oeconomicam: illa regimus proprios mores, Politica Rempublicam et Imperium, Oeconomica familias . . . Sed re vera unica scientia est, divisa per nostram imbecillitatem in plures. Principia autem ipsarum in sensu actionum

et passionum humanarum fundantur. Et conservationem respiciunt: quoniam istae scientiae praxim respiciunt. Quaecunque ergo conservant nos in nobis, et in Republica, et in fama, utilia et honesta dicuntur; quae vero obsunt et destruunt, e contra. Est autem unus homo pars familiae. Familia vero Reipublicae; ergo Ethica est oeconomiae pars: oeconomia Politiae."

2 *Ibid.,* I, 5, 3, 1, p. 351.

3 Cf. *Disputationum in quatuor partes suae philosophiae realis libri quatuor. Quaestiones super secunda parte philosophiae realis, quae est Ethicorum* (Paris: Ex typographia Dionysii Houssaye, 1637), pp. 1-60 (independent enumeration), henceforth to be referred to as *Quaest. mor.,* whereas the treatise on *Ethics* that follows immediately after the *Quaestiones morales* and goes from p. 1 to p. 70, will be referred to as *Ethica.*

4 *Quaest. mor.,* p. 1.

5 *Ibid.*

6 *Ibid.*

7 *Ibid.,* pp. 2-10.

8 *Ibid.,* pp. 10-17.

9 *Ibid.,* p. 19: "Opinio . . . Aristotelis de summo bono puerilis et mollis videtur."

10 *Ibid.:* "Recte quidem assumit [Aristoteles] primo felicitatem esse finem, et optimum, cuius gratia omnia facimus, et perfectum, et nullius indiguum. Haec enim ex Philebo excripsit. At cum ait, uniuscuiusque finem esse operationem, probe mentitur: operatio enim non sui gratia, sed vitae tuendae, est . . . Quapropter imperite Aristoteles ponit felicitatem in operatione: cum haec semper alterius sit gratia: et ipsa propter hominem, non homo propter ipsam."

11 *Ibid.:* "neque enim quia scio bona, gaudeo illis, sed quia fruor; est ergo contemplatio propter sui consecutionem et mali vitationem, non propter se unquam."

12 *Ibid.,* pp. 19-20.

13 *Ibid.,* pp. 20-21. See also *ibid.,* p. 23, where he states: "confessi sumus summum bonum esse virtutem, quatenus praestat vitam beatam. Vita autem beata non est, nisi sit aeterna." In *Ethica,* p. 10, he states further: "Attamen quoniam virtus vitam aeternam in se non habet, sed aliunde illam optat, clarum est non beare, sed ad bonum beans nos perducere."

14 *Ethica,* p. 8: "Entia cuncta propriam beatitudinem appetunt, eamque certum est esse, cuius gratia omnes affectiones et operationes fiunt. Fiunt autem propter sui ipsorum esse conservationem; quapropter proprium esse seu vita est unicuique beatitas, quae est summa possessio Boni, possibilis illis . . . In se autem et non in alio beatitatem haberi palam est; alioquin si in alio meliori, tunc omnia destrui et in illud melius converti cuperent."

15 *Ibid.:* "Triplex videtur hominis conservatio, in se, in filiis, in fama et creditur quarta post mortem in Deo."

16 *Ibid.,* p. 9.

17 *Ibid.:* "[Homo] cum cupit esse semper, et ubique, et omnia posse, omnia scire, et omnibus frui, tunc cupit esse Deus; quod cum non possit per essentiam, participio et consortio Dei deificetur aequum est." See also *Epilogo,* pp. 514-15.

18 Campanella himself refers the reader to his *Metaphysica* for a more complete treatise on the supreme good. Cf. *Quaest. mor.,* p. 1.

19 *Met.*, III, 1. 17, c. 4 (erroneously written 2), a. 1, title, p. 244: "Beatitudinem, quae est conservatio entitatis humanae, in summo Ente consistere, in unione secundum potentiam, sapientiam, et amorem: nec consummari, nisi in fruitione, quae praesupponit habere et sapere."

20 *Ibid.*, p. 244a.

21 *Theol.*, I, 14, 2, pp. 291-92: "omne ens, dum se amat, Deum amat, cuius ipse est participatio; item non se, sed magis Deum. Cum enim sit finitum loco et tempore, amat tamen esse infinitum utroque modo, idest ubique esse et semper immortaliter, et hoc plusquam esse hic et nunc: esse autem ubique et semper est divinum: ergo appetit plus esse divinum quam proprium naturaliter."

22 *Ibid.*, I, 18, 1, p. 455: "Non solum Deus est sua beatitudo obiective et formaliter, sed etiam omnium rerum: omnia enim modulo quodam suo beantur aliquo bono: Deus autem est omnis boni causa efficiens et exemplaris, omneque bonum est effective et obiective."

23 *Ibid.*, VII, 2, 7: "Deum obiective et active esse summam hominis beatitudinem ut quod, virtutem et gratiam active et dispositive ut quo, conservationem vitalis esse hominis esse formaliter beatitudinem; actus vero eius esse conditionem sine qua impossibilem esse homini adeptionem Dei." MS quoted in Di Napoli, *op. cit.*, p. 376.

24 *Met.*, III, 17, 4 (erroneously written 2), a. 2, p. 245a: "Quando ergo quaeritur utrum beatitudo consistat in visione, quae est actus intellectus, aut in fruitione, quae est actus voluntatis, aut in comprehensione, quae est actus potestatis, quaestio nulla est apud nos: etenim est in unione, seu possessione, quae est actus potestatis, qua primo attingimus bonum, et sine qua non sequitur cognitio, nec voluptas . . . Est ergo in comprehensione, potentiae actu, sicut dicit Apostolus: *Sic currite ut comprehendatis;* est in sapore, actu intellectus, sicut dixit Iesus: *Haec est vita aeterna, ut cognoscant te verum Deum.* Est et in voluptate, actu nimirum voluntatis, sicut dixit David: *Torrente voluptatis tuae potabis eos.* Siquidem nulla primalitas est extra essentiam, et nulla expers beatitudinis, aut minus particeps." See also *Theol.*, I, 18, 1, p. 453.

25 *Theol.*, I, 18, 1, p. 453.

26 *Met.*, III, 17, 4 (erroneously written 2), a. 2, p. 245a: "consummatio beatitudinis consistit in fruitione; adsecutio fit per comprehensionem; profundatio per intellectionem. Ergo per omnem primalitatem; et quatenus sunt unum, quia omnes sunt in omnibus; et quatenus sunt plures, quoniam non nisi per actus omnium beamur. Et profecto beatitudo est summum bonum, quod est obiectum voluntatis, licet per intellectum proponatur et percipiatur, non tamen ut intellectum beat, sed ut volitum; sed tamen volitum ut intellectum. Item cognoscere et sapere est propter delectationem; et non e contra. Et quamvis actus voluntatis non sit primum volitum, sed obiectum intellectum ut bonum, tamen illud non beat, nisi ut volitum."

27 *Theol.*, I, 18, 1, p. 453. For an understanding of the scholastic views on the nature of beatitude cf. the present writer's study, "Duns Scotus' Voluntarism," in *John Duns Scotus, 1265-1965*, ed. by John K. Ryan and Bernardine M. Bonansea (Washington, D. C.: The Catholic University of America Press, 1965), pp. 83-121.

28 Cf. n. 13 above.

29 *Quaest. mor.*, pp. 34ff.

30 *Ibid.*, p. 36.

31 *Ibid.*, p. 38f.

32 *Ibid.*, pp. 39ff.

33 *Ibid.*, p. 42: "cum enim res cunctae ex potentia, sapientia, et amore essentientur: sitque virtus essentiae conservativa quam bonam facit: bonum enim
est esse cuique suum, esse autem bonum virtus facit, quae servat esse et operationem; hoc enim est bonum facere suum possessorem et opus, uti cuncti
fatentur: consequens est, quod virtus sit illa qualitas quae ex potentia, sapientia,
et amore essendi in unoquoque resultat ente, quam alii dicunt potentiam ad
operandum: sed ubi est appetitus et sensus, non sufficit dicere potentiam;
contingit enim posse et nolle: vel velle et nescire: quia res cunctae impurae
sunt, nec iuste ad suam ideam correspondent. Ideoque virtutem perfectam
existimabo, cum ex his integratur."

34 *Ibid.*, pp. 43-44. The idea that virtue belongs to the very nature of man and
is not something conventional is also expressed in *Met.*, III, 16, 7, 1, p. 209a-
209b: "Videtur quibusdam virtus et vitium non constare natura, sed prout
homines decernunt: nam idem actus apud alias nationes reputatur virtuosus,
apud alias vero vitiosus." *Ibid.*, pp. 209b-210a: "Nos autem putamus secundum
naturam ista decerni etiam si homo viveret solitarius." *Ibid.*, pp. 210b-211a:
"Quapropter habemus virtutes et vitia, non ex arbitratu cuiuscunque fieri, sed
ex naturali sapientia, potentia, et voluntate constitui, dum finem praestituunt
bonum, aut malum: et media parant aequa fini bono, vel malo."

35 *Quaest. mor.*, p. 45: "Virtus ergo est naturalis vigor regulatus sapientia, et
decreto voluntatis firmatus ad regendas affectiones, notiones, passiones et
operationes humanas pro consequutione summi boni." A simpler definition of
virtue is given in *Ethica*, p. 3: "Virtus ergo regula est passionum, notionum, et
affectionum animi, et operationum ad certe acquirendum verum bonum, et
fugiendum verum malum." In *Met.*, I, 5, 2, 4, p. 349b, Campanella simply
states that "Virtus est regula conservandi individuum."

36 *Ethica*, p. 4: "[Virtus] est regula et decretum ab intellectivo inventum in
se vel extra se in aliis, a volitivo acceptatum, a potestativo imperatum, et
executioni per omnes primalitatum facultates, prout licet, mandatum, et per
operationes declaratum et illustratum."

37 *Ibid.*: "Vitium vero est enormitas affectionum et operationum erga malum,
tanquam in bonum ferens."

38 *Quaest. mor.*, p. 45.

39 *Ibid.*, p. 43: "Habitus autem nulli sunt, qui sint virtutes et vitia, sed sunt
effectus virtutis et vitii, et stabilitas." *Ethica*, p. 3: "virtus non est habitus
acquisitus per operationem, antequam enim acquiratur habitus, oportet per
virtutem regulare affectionem et operationem." See also *Quaest. mor.*, p. 46,
and *Epilogo*, pp. 515-16.

40 *Ethica*, pp. 3-4; *Quaest. mor.*, pp. 47-48. Campanella's teaching that virtue does
not consist in a mean between two extremes represents a change of attitude
from the position taken in the *Epilogo magno*, an earlier work, where he states
explicitly: "Perciò ella [la virtù] consiste nella mediocrità, di cui il più e il
manco chiamo vitij." *Epilogo*, p. 510.

41 *Quaest. mor.*, p. 48; *Ethica*, p. 4. Campanella's teaching in this respect is in substantial agreement with his stand in the *Epilogo magno,* where virtue is called normative wisdom (*ibid.*, p. 505), is identified with wisdom itself (*ibid.*, pp. 510, 514), and is further said to be the norm or decree of the soul governing the passions and operations of the spirit for the pursuance of man's end, namely, his self-conservation in God (*ibid.*, pp. 510, 514-15). Hence Ottaviano's statement that the *Epilogo magno* contains a descriptive naturalistic ethics that is "the first and original attempt of a phenomenology of the moral life . . . from a physiological or physical point of view" (Preface to *Epilogo magno,* pp. 149-50), does not seem to agree with Campanella's teaching. Moreover Ottaviano seems to contradict himself when he affirms, a few lines after the preceding statement, that for Campanella virtue is "a norm according to which the soul or mind or the first ordering reason attempts to rectify and discipline the spirit." *Ibid.*, p. 150.

42 *Quaest. mor.*, p. 49; *Ethica*, p. 4. It is worth noting that in the *Epilogo magno,* written at a time when Campanella was still largely under the influence of Telesio's philosophy, he seems to endorse the latter's viewpoint on the nature of virtue. He calls virtue "the purity of beings" (*ibid.*, p. 512), and human virtue "the purity of the human spirit" (*ibid.*, p. 513). A being, in Campanella's philosophy, is pure when it is exactly what it is supposed to be according to its nature and nothing else. Accordingly, man is pure when he has everything that belongs to the human nature, including the rational soul. It is in this sense that Campanella's foregoing expressions must be understood. Incidentally, he speaks of "human spirit,' and not merely of "animal spirit." This latter, according to his trichotomic theory, is the second component of man and is distinct from the rational soul. Cf. chap. IV, sect. I, of this study.

43 *Ethica*, p. 4; *Quaest. mor.*, pp. 49-50. "Nos in Theologicis ostendimus virtutem integrari ex primalitatibus. Non enim quia scio bonum, illud facio: nec quia volo, illud facio, cum saepe laudemus et velimus bonum, deterioraque sequamur, ut ait Horatius; sed quia scio cognoscitivo, et volo volitivo, et impero potestativo, aggredior bonum, ut nemo non experitur. Insufficientes ergo sunt Philosophi istas primalitates ignorando." *Ibid.*, p. 50.

44 *Ethica*, pp. 5-7. See also *Quaest. mor.*, pp. 24ff.

45 *Quaest. mor.*, pp. 50ff. "Quapropter non est immorandum in dictis Aristotelis neque terendum tempus ad distinctiunculas vanas et inanes: sed docendi sumus iuxta S. Scripturam et rerum naturam, omnes virtutes in cognitione esse intellectuales, in operatione vocari practicas." *Ibid.*, p. 52.

46 *Ibid.*

47 *Ibid.*, p. 58.

48 *Ibid.*, pp. 58-59.

49 We refer to the systematic classification of virtues, with their opposite vices, that takes up the entire art. 3 (it should read art. 4) of chap. I of Campanella's *Ethica*, p. 12. We shall report here below the classification, which we have arranged in the form of a scheme, keeping the original Latin terms. For the classification of virtues in the *Epilogo magno,* which is prior to, and less complete than, the one contained in the *Ethica,* cf. *Epilogo,* pp. 154-55, where sixteen virtues and thirty-two opposite vices are presented in a diagram by Carmelo Ottaviano, editor of the work.

CAMPANELLA'S CLASSIFICATION OF VIRTUES

(Cf. *Ethica*, p. 12)

A. EX SUIS FONTIBUS

I. *Ex Potestativo*

1. Fortitudo	{ timor / audacia	9. Imperiositas	{ ira / pavor
2. Strenuitas	{ debilitas / ferocitas	10. Clementia	{ crudelitas / misericordia
3. Constantia	{ rigiditas / flexibilitas	11. Tolerantia	{ impatientia / insensibilitas
4. Alacritas	{ promptitudo / lentor	12. Mansuetudo	{ iracundia / asinitas
5. Opportunitas	{ acaedia / pernicitas	13. Verecundia	{ impudentia / erubescentia
6. Confidentia seu Fiducia	{ diffidentia / parvipensio	14. Celsitudo	{ tumor / despicientia
7. Spes	{ praesumptio / desperatio	15. Diligentia	{ negligentia / sollicitudo
8. Comprehensio	{ irruptio / recessio	16. Aequalitas	{ arrogantia / abiectio

II. *Ex Intellectivo*

1. Prudentia	{ scientia / ignorantia	7. Studiositas	{ curiositas / incuria
2. Fides seu Credibilitas	{ incredulitas / credulitas	8. Veritas	{ mendacium / ironia
3. Ars memorandi	{ memoria / oblivio	9. Prophetia	{ divinatio / improvidentia
4. Consilium et Logica	{ perplexitas / praecipitatio	10. Solertia	{ inertia / anxietas
5. Grammatica Rhetorica et Poetica	{ occultatio et declaratio / suasio et dissuasio	11. Benevolentia	{ manifestatio / obtumescentia
6. Vigilantia	{ animadvertentia / inadvertentia	12. Disciplinabilitas	{ ruditas / sciolorum vitium

III. *Ex Volitivo*

1. Sanctitas	{ circa finis amorem et impetum	7. Liberalitas et Parsimonia	{ avaritia prodigalitas
2. Charitas	{ erga parentes et patriam	8. Moderatio	—regula luxuriae
3. Castitas	—erga uxorem	9. Honorificentia	{ ambitio vilitas
4. Dilectio	—erga filios	10. Benignitas	{ malignitas amor
5. Benevolentia	—erga amicos	11. Attemperatio	{ voluptas dolor
6. Temperantia	{ regula cupiditatis	12. Aemulatio	{ invidia applausus

B. CIRCA MODOS CONSERVANDI

I. *In nobis*
  1. Fortitudo
  2. Exercitium
  3. Solertia
  4. Prudentia
  5. Probitas
  6. Liberalitas

II. *In filiis*
  Castitas

III. *In amicis*
  1. Beneficentia
  2. Benedicentia

IV. *In republica*
  Iustitia

V. *In Deo*
  Sublimitas

C. AB OBIECTIS
  1. Castitas
  2. Sobrietas

D. EX PRINCIPATU

I. *Per se*
  1. Fortitudo
  2. Prudentia
  3. Sanctitas

II. *Ad alios*
  1. Benevolentia
  2. Benedicentia
  3. Beneficentia

50 *Ethica*, p. 13: "Sanctitas . . . est prima virtus, quae Deum patrem nobis sancit, et ad eum omnia dirigit, a quo sunt." In the *Epilogo magno* wisdom is mentioned in the first place, not sanctity. This latter does not figure as a distinct virtue, nor is it treated as such. The reason for this omission may be that in the *Epilogo magno* Campanella identifies wisdom with the norm of our affections and operations and the first ordering reason (cf. *ibid.*, p. 505). It should not be forgotten, on the other hand, that the *Epilogo magno* represents only the second stage in the development of his doctrine on virtue, which receives its complete treatment in the *Quaestiones morales* and *Ethica*. The first stage is represented by the *Prodromus philosophiae instaurandae*, one of the earliest of Campanella's writings.

51 *Ethica*, p. 13: "Tenetur igitur homo simulac mens compos fuerit sui usumque libertatis acceperit de fine, ad quem omnes dirigat affectus et operationes, sancire, longe magis, quam de arte quae vitam sustentet."

52 *Ibid.*, p. 15.

53 *Ibid.*, p. 17. Speaking of *studiousness* and some of the opposite vices, such as curiosity and vanity, Campanella writes: "Alii scire volunt ut sciant, et hi curiosi; alii ut sciantur, et hi ambitiosi; alii ut lucrentur, et hi avari; alii ut meliorentur, et hi studiosi." *Ibid.*

54 *Ibid.*, p. 18. Were it not for the purely physiological aspect from which Campanella looks at man in judging about his aptitude for a particular field of study or occupation, the following would be quite practical: "Ad scientias autem apti non sunt qui spiritus habent obtusos ex crassitie; perplexum discursum ex fuligine intervolante, praecipitem ex subtilitate nimia, inhabilemque in discursu, obliviosum ex flexibilitate multa; eos igitur applicabit scientiis, qui [spiritum] lucidum, purum, moderatum in calore et tenuitate sortiti sunt, quod facile ex physionomia, et motu, et loquela, et oculorum luce, et modis istorum, et actibus agnoscitur. Artibus mechanicis eos qui spiritu crasso et multo abundant; curam Reipublicae mediis inter istos. Neque enim tenuissimi spiritu, neque crassi, sunt apti administrationi: illi quia mutant omnia ut meliorent, et speculationi praxis non respondet: isti quia inepti ad multarum rerum circumspectionem." *Ibid.*

55 *Ibid.*, p. 20.

56 *Ibid.*

57 *Ibid.; Epilogo*, pp. 518-19.

58 *Ethica*, p. 23.

59 *Ibid.*

60 *Ibid.*, p. 24; *Epilogo*, p. 520.

61 *Ethica*, p. 24; *Epilogo*, pp. 521-22.

62 *Ethica*, p. 25.

63 The treatment of these and like virtues can be found in *Ethica*, pp. 26-30. Physical exercise and fortitude are also dealt with in the *Epilogo magno*, pp. 526-28 and pp. 545-47, respectively.

64 *Ethica*, p. 32; *Epilogo*, pp. 523-25. In the *Epilogo magno* Campanella emphasizes the law of monogamy. *Ibid.*, p. 525.

65 Cf. *Ethica*, pp. 33-59, for a detailed discussion of these virtues and others of the same category. See also *Epilogo*, pp. 554-67, for a similar treatment.

66 *Ethica*, pp. 59-64; *Epilogo*, pp. 549-50.

67 *Ethica*, pp. 64-70; *Epilogo*, pp. 564-67.

68 *Met.*, III, 16, 5, 1, p. 207: "Homo est animal sociale."

69 Cf. *Philosophiae realis pars tertia, quae est de politica in aphorismos digesta*, ed. by Luigi Firpo under the title *Aforismi politici* (Turin: Libreria Scientifica G. Giappichelli, 1941), pp. 145-46. See also *Oeconomica, Philosophiae realis pars quarta in aphorismos digesta*, p. 190. This work will henceforth be referred to as *Oeconomica*.

70 Cf. *Quaestiones in quartam partem philosophiae realis, quae sunt oeconomicorum seu de re familiari*, p. 172. Hereafter the work will be referred to as *Quaestiones oeconomicae*.

71 *Oeconomica*, p. 191.

72 *Ibid.*, p. 189.

73 *Quaest. oecon.*, p. 171: "Propterea sciendum est quod finis alius supremus et extrinsecus, qui est Deus, et vita aeterna in Deo, et hic finis communis est hominis, et familiae, et civitatis, et regni, et toti speciei humanae."

74 *Ibid.*: "quia familia potior est ad generationem quam civitas, ibi enim elementa sunt mas et femina, hic vero familiae et cives: videtur magis secundum naturam oeconomia quam politica, illa enim utrique utilis conservationi: haec autem soli individuorum. Cum quo fit, ut species etiam melius conservetur: utriusque ergo idem finis est conservatio, sed non idem modus et forma."

75 *Oeconomica*, p. 192.

76 *Quaest. oecon.*, p. 175.

77 *Oeconomica*, p. 193: "Quamobrem ii modo, qui ad praefatos fines idonei sunt, copulandi essent matrimonio ex physicorum prudentumque senum consultatione; non secundum dotes exterioresque divitias: sed secundum animi corporisque bona . . . Natura enim naturale vinculum fecit: politica illud honestavit: Autor gratiae sacramentavit. Propterea nec contra naturam, nec contra politicam, nec contra religionem debet celebrari."

78 In his *Atheismus triumphatus* Campanella states explicitly: "Matrimonium contractum naturalem esse nemo negat." *Ibid.*, p. 126.

79 Cf. "Città del Sole," in *Scritti scelti di Giordano Bruno e Tommaso Campanella, op. cit.*, pp. 415-16, 429-30.

80 The Latin text reads: "Utrum expediat unam tantum uxorem ducere, an plures secundum naturam, omissa lege." *Quaest. oecon.*, p. 173.

81 *Ibid.*, p. 174. Campanella does not use the expression "secondary precepts of the natural law," but his statement, "sic secundario, et aliquo pacto poligamia adversatur naturae," amounts to the same thing.

82 Cf. *Oeconomica*, p. 198, where Campanella defends unity in marriage and brings forth arguments from the accepted laws among the Christians, the Romans, and the Greeks, as well as arguments from reason and divine revelation. However, since polygamy is only against the secondary precepts of the natural law, he can say: "Haud propterea damnamus, quasi contra naturam uxorum multitudinem, praesertim si quis insterilis [sic] copulam impegit, quandoquidem David et Patriarchae plures habuere uxores et concubinas."

83 See, for example, *Theol.*, XXIV, 17, 22: "Contra naturam poliandria primario, poligamia secundario"; *ibid.*: "poligamiam non esse contra naturam primario sed secundario nec totaliter, meliorem tamen et magis secundum naturam esse monogamiam, et hanc esse secundum Evangelium, illam potius contra Evangelium." MS quoted in Di Napoli, *op. cit.*, p. 396. Cf. also *Quaestiones politicae*, pp. 108-112.

84 *Quaest. oecon.*, p. 178; *Oeconomica*, p. 199.

85 *Oeconomica*, pp. 202-203.

86 *Ibid.*, p. 203.

87 *Ibid.*, pp. 195-97. Campanella's argument against Aristotle on the nature of man's dominion over his servants is as follows: "Ad Aristotelem dicimus non esse hominem hominis instrumentum simpliciter operis, sed socium: nam et mulier est adiutorium. Teste Deo, concedo tamen non secundum naturam, sed post corruptelam naturae factum esse ut homo homini dominetur secundum quid, non simpliciter, ad bonum utriusque et non solius dominantis. Potiusquam regimen dici debere: nos diximus dominium in textu: sed intelligo politicum et secundum quid. Inter individua enim eiusdem ideae non potest

esse per se et simpliciter relatio dominii, nisi quis praecellat quantum pastor oves." *Quaestiones politicae,* p. 86.
88 *Oeconomica,* pp. 191-92; 194.
89 *Ibid.,* pp. 205-206.
90 *Ibid.,* p. 206.
91 *Ibid.,* pp. 207-208.
92 *Ibid.,* p. 208.
93 *Ibid.,* pp. 208-211.

CHAPTER TWELVE

1 Prof. Firpo classifies Campanella's political works into four groups. The first group includes Campanella's youthful writings glorifying the Spanish government, namely, the *Discorso sui Paesi Bassi* (1594), the *Discorsi ai Principi d'Italia* (written in 1593 and revised in 1607), and the *Monarchia di Spagna* (1598-1601?). The second group comprises the *Aforismi politici* (1601), the *Città del Sole* (1602), and the *Quaestiones politicae* (1609 ff.), all of which are part of the *Philosophia realis.* To the third group belong all the writings having to do with Campanella's theory of a universal theocratic monarchy, such as the *Monarchia Christianorum* (1593), which has been lost, the *Discorsi universali del governo ecclesiastico* (1593-95), the *Dialogo politico contro Luterani, Calvinisti ed altri eretici* (1595), the *Monarchia del Messia* (1605), the *Discorso dei diritti del Re Cattolico sul Mondo Nuovo* (1605), the *Discorsi della libertà e della felice suggezione allo stato ecclesiastico* (1625-26), and the *De regno Dei* (1630). The fourth group embraces some minor works, especially those favoring the French government. They are: the *Antiveneti* (1606), the *Arbitrî sopra l'aumento delle entrate del Regno di Napoli* (1608), the *Oeconomica* (1614-15), the *Avvertimenti al Re di Francia* (1628), the *Dialogo politico tra un Veneziano, Spagnuolo e Francese* (1632), the *Aforismi politici per le presenti necessità di Francia* (1635), the opuscule *Se al tempo nostro possa e debba trasmutarsi l'impero Romano* (1635), and the *Documenta ad Gallorum nationem* (1635). Cf. Firpo, *Aforismi politici,* Introduction, pp. 6-9. Certain dates have been corrected according to more recent discoveries made for the most part by Firpo himself. Although the authenticity of the *Discorso sui Paesi Bassi* has been questioned by Firpo, he admits nevertheless that the material is basically of Campanellian origin. Cf. Luigi Firpo, "Appunti campanelliani. XXII: Un'opera che Campanella non scrisse: il 'Discorso sui Paesi Bassi'," *Giornale critico della filosofia italiana,* XXXIII (1952), 331-43.
2 For detailed information on the present textual situation of Campanella's political writings cf. Firpo, *Aforismi politici, loc. cit.;* the same, *Scritti scelti di Giordano Bruno e di Tommaso Campanella,* pp. 263-66; the same, *Bibliografia degli scritti di T. Campanella,* under the title of each political work mentioned in the *Aforismi politici.*
3 The complete title of the treatise is *Thomae Campanellae, Suae philosophiae realis pars tertia, quae est de politica in aphorismos digesta.* It is part of the *Philosophia realis,* an extremely rare book, published in Paris in 1637. We shall quote *De politica* from Firpo's *Aforismi politici,* where it runs from p. 143

to p. 225. Firpo's edition contains also the critical text of the Italian *Aforismi politici* (pp. 87-142), which is like a preview of Campanella's later treatise *De politica*. The *Aforismi* are preceded by a very enlightening introduction (pp. 5-52) and a discussion on the relationship between Campanella and Hugo Grotius (pp. 53-85). The latter's *Observata in Aphorismos Campanellae politicos* are also included in Firpo's edition (pp. 227-45).

4 The version was made by Campanella himself in 1618 from the original Italian text of the *Monarchia del Messia*, written in 1605. There are only a few extant copies of the *Monarchia Messiae*, published at Iesi by Gregorio Arnazzini in 1633. For fear that the work might not be well received by the contemporary secular rulers, the Master of the Sacred Palace, Father Riccardi, ordered that the entire edition of 1500 copies be withdrawn from circulation. Reportedly, the book fell an easy prey to rats and worms in the Dominican monastery of Minerva in Rome. Cf. Tommaso Campanella, *Discorsi della libertà e della felice suggezione allo stato ecclesiastico*, ed. Luigi Firpo (Turin, 1960), Introduction, pp. 5-6. The 1633 edition of the *Monarchia Messiae* with the *Discorsi della libertà, etc.*, has been reissued in facsimile reprint by Luigi Firpo (Turin: Bottega d'Erasmo, 1960).

5 Cf. *Syntagma*, p. 24: "Scripsi praeterea *Aphorismos politicos*, quos deinde in capitula distinxi et politicam scientiam condidi."

6 Cf. Firpo, *Scritti scelti*, pp. 465-523, where the critical edition of the *Discorsi universali del governo ecclesiastico* is contained. The text of the *Discorsi universali, etc.* that has come down to us is the abstract of the *De regimine Ecclesiae*, a much larger work which was lost and which Campanella himself was never able to recover. He wrote the abstract in question by relying entirely on his prodigious memory. He was so pleased with it that he called it "better" than the lost original. *Ibid.*, p. 265. We shall refer to Firpo's *Scritti scelti* for the *Discorsi universali*.

7 The *De regno Dei* is a short political treatise that Campanella wrote to take the place of the *Monarchia Messiae* which had been withdrawn from circulation. (Cf. Di Napoli, *Tommaso Campanella*, p. 475). It is included in the *Philosophia realis*.

8 The *Quaestiones politicae* extend from pages 71 to 112 of the *Philosophia realis* and it is only by mistake that they were inserted before the *De politica*.

9 Here are the principal studies on Campanella's politics: Rodolfo De Mattei, *La politica di Campanella* (Rome: Anonima Romana Editoriale, 1927); Paolo Treves, *La filosofia politica di Tommaso Campanella* (Bari: Laterza, 1930); Kurt Sternberg, "Ueber Campanellas Sonnestaat," *Historische Zeitschrift*, 148 (1933), 520-71; Walther Ducloux, *Die metaphysische Grundlage der Staatsphilosophie des T. Campanella* (Speyer am Rhein: Pilger Druckerei, 1935); Norberto Bobbio's critical edition of *La Città del Sole*, with an introduction, pp. 9-51 (Turin: Einaudi, 1941); Gioele Solari, "Di una nuova edizione critica della Città del Sole e del comunismo del Campanella," *Rivista di filosofia*, XXXII (1941), 180-97; The same, "Filosofia politica del Campanella," *Rivista di filosofia*, XXXVII (1946), 38-63. See also Giovanni Di Napoli, *Tommaso Campanella, op. cit.*, chap. XI, "La politica," pp. 401-428; Romano Amerio, *Campanella, op. cit.*, "Etica e politica," pp. 171-214; Antonio Corsano, *Tommaso Campanella* (Bari: Laterza, 1961), chap. VI, "Morale e diritto," pp. 189-237.

10 *Lettere*, p. 7: "Non mi scema la scienza con la quale si governano gli stati."

This statement contained in a letter that Campanella wrote to Ferdinand I de' Medici was apparently overlooked by Treves, who affirms that he could find a definition of politics in none of Campanella's works. Cf. Treves, *op. cit.*, p. 48.

11 See n. 1 of preceding chapter.

12 *Atheismus,* p. 243: "Politica dependet ab ethica tanquam a subordinante."

13 *Monarchia di Spagna,* in D'Ancona's edition of *Opere di T. Campanella, op. cit.,* II, 163.

14 *Atheismus,* p. 236: "Respublica non potest stare absque religione."

15 *Met.,* I, 5, 2, 4, p. 349b: "Machiavellistica politica pessima est, quoniam discordat a primo Rectore, quem ipse non agnoscit, ergo et a toto mundo et a fato: ergo sibi et aliis perniciosa, dum prodesse credit, veluti puerorum astutia, medico et magistro, et patri familias repugnans, perdit eos."

16 *Articuli prophetales,* in Amabile, *Congiura,* III, doc. 401, p. 489: "Nullum Imperium aut Regnum sola prudentia politica stetit."

17 *Atheismus,* p. 226: "Machiavellum omnium scientiarum fuisse ignorantissimum, excepta historia humana; et politicam suam non per scientias, sed per astutiam et peritiam practicam examinasse." In his unrestrained contempt for Machiavelli, Campanella calls him "porcus et pecus," *ibid.,* p. 238, as well as "scandalo, rovina, tosco e fuoco di questo secolo." *Antiveneti,* ed. Luigi Firpo (Florence: L. S. Olschki, 1945), p. 49.

18 *Aforismi,* pp. 145-46: "Naturaliter consociantur quaecunque reciprocum bonum copulat naturale. Igitur . . . septima [communitas] plurium provinciarum in uno regno. Octava, plurium regnorum sub uno imperio. Nona, plurium imperiorum in variis climatibus sub una monarchia. Decima, omnium hominum sub specie humana et Papatu."

19 *Ibid.,* p. 145: "Mens Prima necessitatis stimulis homines, cum nemo sibi sufficiens esset ad tuendam vitam ab externis internisque malis nec ad speciem propagandam, copulavit in unum fere corpus in quo alii regerent, alii regerentur, alii scientiae agendorum, alii agendis pro communi bono operam darent, mutuisque officiis innumeris, ob innumeras necessitates, sese iuvarent in vita, ad finem propter quem Deus Dominum dominantium creavit hominem ordinata."

20 *Monarchia Messiae,* p. 78: "Finis reipublicae non est rex, nec eius commoda, nec procerum, nec populi, sed cultus Dei propter regnum aeternum." *Quaestiones politicae,* p. 72: "Finis autem reipublicae est Dei cultus, ut Plato agnovit, non autem rex, aut libertas, aut divitiae: his enim positis finibus tyrannides fiunt."

21 *Aforismi,* p. 187. Cf. also *ibid.,* p. 176, where Campanella states: "Quoniam dominium hominis est divinae potestatis participatio, nemo potest fundare et retinere imperium nisi vere missus et authorizatus a Deo, vel creditus missus et authorizatus a Deo immediate vel mediate. Religio ergo quae Deo homines religat est causa imperandi."

22 *Ibid.,* p. 188.

23 *Ibid.,* p. 189.

24 *Ibid.,* pp. 193-96.

25 *Ibid.,* p. 175: "Quapropter errant quicunque gladium solummodo spiritualem, non etiam temporalem Papae tribuunt. Sic enim eius Monarchia diminuta

esset, cui hoc tutamen deficit, et Christus Deus legislator diminutus esset, quod imprudenter et haeretice affirmatur."

26 *Ibid.*, pp. 196-98. The *De monarchia Christianorum* was written by Campanella in 1593, when he was in Padua. The MS has been lost, but it is possible to reconstruct its general theme from Campanella's references to the work in his other writings. In Firpo's view, the *De monarchia Christianorum* is "a fundamental work for the understanding of Campanella's complex [political] system." *Bibliografia, op. cit.*, p. 177. In it Campanella expounds "the supreme ideal of his life: the unification of the world under one civil and religious law." Cf. Luigi Firpo, *Introduzione e cronologia premesse al primo volume delle opere di Tommaso Campanella nell'edizione Mondadori, Estratto, 1953*, p. LXIX. In Di Napoli's opinion, the *De monarchia Christianorum* contains the scheme of "a true and proper *Society of Nations* presided over by the Pope and having its seat in Rome." Di Napoli, *op. cit.*, p. 117.

27 *Aforismi*, pp. 198-202.

28 *Ibid.*, pp. 203-204.

29 *Ibid.*, p. 153.

30 *Ibid.* Campanella distinguishes between *ius, dominium,* and *beneficium,* three acts that in accordance with his doctrine of primalities correspond to the triple operation *ad extra* of every being. It belongs to the potential principle *(principium potestativum)* to dominate, to the cognitive principle *(principium cognitivum)* to rule, and to the loving principle *(principium amativum* or *volitivum)* to help others by loving them, speaking well of them, and doing good to them. The *ius* exists among equals, the *dominium* between a superior and his subjects, and the *beneficium* between a possessor and a needy person. *Ibid.*, pp. 147-49.

31 *Ibid.*, p. 155: "Natura imperat qui virtute praestantior est; natura servit qui virtute inferior vel vacuus est. Ubi contra fit, dominium violentum est. Praestantia in politicis aut est secundum virtutem animi, aut corporis, aut utriusque. Melius dominatur qui in utraque praecellit."

32 *Ibid.*, p. 158.

33 *Monarchia Messiae*, p. 10: "Optimus est si non populorum, sed Dei auctoritate [praeponitur Princeps]."

34 *Ibid.*, p. 9: "Magis secundum naturam est Princeps unus per electionem, quam per successionem adscitus."

35 *Ibid.*: "Naturalius est hominibus regi ab uno."

36 *Met.*, I, 1, 9, 12, p. 85b.

37 *Theol.*, XIV, 6, 3. MS referred to in Di Napoli, *op. cit.*, p. 411.

38 Cf. *Città del Sole,* in Firpo's *Scritti scelti,* p. 412.

39 *Aforismi*, p. 158.

40 *Ibid.*, pp. 158-59. See also *Monarchia di Spagna*, p. 107; *Quaestiones morales*, p. 13.

41 *Aforismi*, p. 160.

42 *Ibid.*, p. 161.

43 *Ibid.*

44 *Ibid.*: "Indiget communitas lege semper."

45 In his *Met.*, I, 5, 2, 4, p. 439b, Campanella states: "Virtus est regula conservandi individuum: lex est virtus conservans speciem, id est rempublicam." In *Theol.*, XIV, 1, 1, he defines law as "regula voluntaria rationis efficacis ad

bonum commune per rectorem promulgata." MS quoted in Di Napoli, *op. cit.,* p. 385.

46 *Aforismi,* p. 162.

47 *Ibid.,* pp. 162-63. See also *Met.,* III, 16, 7, 5, pp. 216b-217a. The relationship between the law of nations and natural law is pointed out by Campanella in *Theol.,* XIV, 4, 1, where he states: "Convenit ius gentium in iure naturali in hoc, quod utrumque est cunctis commune nationibus quatenus rationalibus, et utrumque deducitur ex fundamentis naturalibus; sed immediate ius naturale, gentium vero mediante naturali." MS quoted in Di Napoli, *op. cit.,* p. 388.

48 *Atheismus,* p. 107.

49 *Aforismi,* pp. 162-63; *Theol.,* XIV, 3, 1, and XVII, 6, 6. MS quoted in Di Napoli, *op. cit.,* p. 387.

50 *Aforismi,* p. 164.

51 *Ibid.,* pp. 172-74.

52 *Ibid.,* p. 177: "Ad [imperium] acquirendum lingua, ad defendendum arma, ad conservandum pecunia videntur proficere magis."

53 The island of Taprobane is now known as Ceylon. In placing Taprobane under the equator rather than north of it, Campanella was apparently influenced by Botero's *Relazioni universali* (Rome, 1591-96), which Prof. Firpo calls "the main source of Campanella's geographic information." Firpo, *Scritti scelti,* p. 407, n. 3. The mistake is due to an error of the ancient maps which led the first sailors to identify Taprobane with Sumatra. In all probability it was Sumatra that Campanella had in mind when he described the City of the Sun. *Ibid.,* p. 408.

54 Authors are not of one opinion as to the source for this name. It is possible that in calling his ideal republic *The City of the Sun* Campanella was influenced, at least remotely, by the text of Isaias, XIX, 18: "In that day there shall be five cities in the land of Egypt . . . One shall be called the city of the sun"; or by Pliny's *Solis insula (Hist. nat.,* X, 2), which the Roman historian estimates as a four-day voyage from India, close to Taprobane. A more direct influence could have been exerted on Campanella by Botero's description of the cult of the sun among the natives of Mexico and Peru, or, as Firpo is inclined to believe, by the *Civitas Solis* or *Paradisus* dreamed of by the Grand Duke of Tuscany, of which mention is also made in Botero's work, *Delle cause della grandezza delle città* (Rome, 1588, chap. I, 2). Cf. Firpo, *Scritti scelti,* p. 408, n. 4. Di Napoli, on the other hand, cites as Campanella's proximate sources for the title of his ideal republic St. Francis' "Canticle of Creatures," where the sun occupies a prominent place, and the abbot Joachim of Flores, who had decreed that his monks should praise creation by singing hymns to the sun. Cf. Di Napoli, *op. cit.,* pp. 155-56.

55 For this outline of *The City of the Sun* we have used Firpo's critical edition of the Italian text in *Scritti scelti,* pp. 405-464, as well as the English translations by Thomas W. Halliday in *Ideal Commonwealths* (rev. ed.; London-New York: The Colonial Press, 1901), pp. 141-79, and William J. Gilstrap in *The Quest for Utopia* (New York: Schuman, 1952), pp. 317-47.

56 We refer especially to the study of Paul Lafargue, "Campanella. Étude critique sur sa vie et sur la Cité du Soleil," *Le devenir social,* I (1895), 305-320, 465-80, 561-78. The same study, with some minor additions, appeared also in German under the title "Die beiden grossen Utopisten: T. More und T.

394   TOMMASO CAMPANELLA

Campanella," *Geschichte des Sozialismus in Einzelndarstellungen,* ed. E. Bern-
stein and K. Kautsky, Vol. I, Part II: "Die Vorlaüfer des neueren Sozialismus"
(Stuttgart: Dietz, 1895), Sect. IV, 469-506. Lafargue's thesis has been slavishly
accepted and reproduced by Andrea Calenda di Tavani in his work *Fra T.
Campanella e la sua dottrina sociale e politica di fronte al socialismo moderno*
(Nocera Inferiore: Angora, 1895). The foregoing publications offered to Benedetto Croce the opportunity of discussing the nature and import of Campanella's political reform in his study, "Intorno al comunismo di T. Campanella,
a proposito di recenti pubblicazioni," *Archivio storico per le provincie napoletane,* XX (1895), 646-83, where he strongly denies any doctrinal similarity between Campanella's political thought and modern communism. This has not
prevented the Russians from portraying Campanella as an early representative
of their communistic ideology. Cf. *The Living Age* (New York), CCCXLVI
(1934), 453-54, where an anonymous writer, under the heading "A Dominican
Communist," reviews a new Russian translation of Campanella's *City of the
Sun* with a commentary by F. A. Petrov and an introduction by V. P. Volghin
(Moscow: Akademia, 1934). In the course of his review the writer speaks of
the prominent place Campanella occupies in the history of communism and
refers to an article in the *Izvestia,* where A. Djivelegov hails Campanella as a
harbinger of Marxist communism.
57 This, to mention only a recent writer, is the opinion of Norberto Bobbio,
the editor of the first critical edition of the Italian text of *The City of the Sun.*
Cf. T. Campanella, *La Città del Sole,* a cura di Norberto Bobbio, *op. cit.,* p. 17.
58 *Ibid.,* pp. 32-33. Similar views have also been expressed by Treves, who believes that *The City of the Sun* represents the last stage of Campanella's political dream. The work, in Treves' opinion, is not merely a *Dichtung,* as it has
been labeled, but "the logical and necessary consequence of the philosophical
premises of Campanella's political system." Cf. Treves, *La filosofia politica di
T. Campanella,* p. 54.
59 Bobbio, *La Città del Sole,* p. 16.
60 Cf. Prof. Firpo's Italian edition of *The City of the Sun* in *Scritti scelti,* p. 407.
61 The 1637 edition of *The City of the Sun* carries the following remark: "Defensio huius dialogi est in politicis quaestionibus, quarta quaestio, ubi osten-
ditur esse catechismum Gentilium ad politiam et fidem Christianam pure
apostolicam." Cf. Bobbio, *La Città del Sole,* p. 117, note.
62 *Quaest. pol.,* p. 101.
63 *Ibid.:* "Nos autem fingimus illam [Rempublicam] non tamquam a Deo datam,
sed Philosophicis syllogismis inventam et quantum potest humana ratio, ut
hinc elucescat veritas Evangelii esse naturae conformis. Quod si aliquibus ab
Evangelio deviamus, vel videamur deviare, hoc non impietati adscribendum,
sed imbecillitati humanae, quae multa putat recte fieri ante revelationem,
quae postmodum haud sic se habent, ut dicemus de communitate coniugum;
proptereaque fingimus hanc Rempublicam in gentilismo, quae expectat revelationem melioris vitae, ac meretur de congruo ipsam habere, dum quod
naturalis dictat ratio observat vitae institutum. Unde sunt quasi in Catechismo
ad vitam Christianam, veluti Cyrillus dicit in libro contra Iulianum, datam
esse gentilibus Philosophiam tanquam Catechismus ad fidem Evangelicam."
64 It is true that the inhabitants of the City of the Sun are reported as having
some knowledge of Christ, the Apostles, the Christian martyrs, Adam's sin,

etc. However, such knowledge is vague and superficial and does not amount to a real understanding of Christian doctrine. For them Christ is just one among other great legislators, even though he occupies a prominent place among them.

65 Thus Campanella says immediately after the passage quoted in n. 63: "Nos ergo Gentiles docemus ut recte vivant, si a Deo velint non negligi, et Christianis suademus vitam Christi esse secundum naturam." *Quaest. pol.*, p. 101. And a little further in the same article he answers the objection raised against the practical value of his ideal republic by saying: ". . . et si ad tuam exactam Reipublicae ideam pervenire non possumus, haud propterea superflui sumus, dum exemplum ponimus imitandum quantum possumus. At etiam possibilem esse talem vitam ostendit Christianorum in principio communitas sub Apostolis, teste Luca et S. Clemente. Et in Alexandria modus vivendi eiusmodi sub S. Marco observatus, teste Philone et S. Hieronimo. Item vita Clericorum usque ad Papam Urbanum I, immo etiam sub S. Augustino, et nunc vita Monachorum quam tanquam possibilem in tota civitate optat S. Chrysostomus." *Ibid.*, p. 102. Again: "Qui autem ipsam [Rempublicam] negant Aristotelizando, dicunt sub statu innocentiae potuisse servari, non nunc. At Patres etiam nunc servabilem faciunt, et Christum illius status reparatorem." *Ibid.*

66 *Ibid.*: ". . . ergo futuram [Rempublicam] spero post ruinam Antichristi ut in Prophetalibus." Reference is here made to his other work, *Articuli prophetales*, *op. cit.*, where the theme of his future ideal republic is discussed.

67 *Quaest. pol.*, p. 103: "Dico hanc Rempublicam et seculum aureum ab omnibus desiderari, et peti a Deo, ut fiat voluntas eius in terra sicut in caelo. Non tamen in praxi ob principum malitiam, qui sibi non summae Rationi imperium submittunt. De usu autem dictum et experimentoque probatur esse possibilem: sicut magis secundum naturam est vivere ratione quam sensuali affectu, et virtuose quam vitiose, teste Chrysostomo. Et quidem Monachi id probant, et nunc Anabaptistae in communi viventes: qui si dogmata Fidei recta haberent, in hoc magis proficerent; nam exemplum facerent huius veritatis: sed nescio qua stultitia quod melius est respuunt."

68 *Ibid.*, pp. 104-106. Cf. Di Napoli, *op. cit.*, pp. 392-93, for a short critical appraisal of the texts in question.

69 *Quaest. pol.*, p. 107: "Concedimus ergo Ecclesiam fecisse posse divisionem permissive potius quam effective, et ex proposito: sed, ut ait S. Augustinus, mavult habere claudos quam mortuos clericos, idest proprietarios, quam hypocritas . . . Dicimus Ecclesiam posse divisionem facere et permittere illam: et meretrices tolerare ut minus malum, sicuti claudos potius quam mortuos, ut dicit S. Augustinus."

70 *Ibid.*, p. 106.

71 *Ibid.*, p. 105: "Quapropter certo certius est de iure naturae omnia esse communia."

72 *Ibid.*, p. 104: "Quapropter haeresis est damnare vitam communem, aut contra naturam dicere."

73 *Ibid.*, p. 105.

74 In several places in *The City of the Sun* Campanella portrays the citizens as friars in a monastery. They eat in common refectories while one of them reads aloud (*Città del Sole*, in Firpo's *Scritti scelti*, p. 420); they dress in the

same way *(ibid.,* pp. 421-22); their leader and main officers are priests *(ibid.,* pp. 411, 447); regular confession of sins is practiced *(ibid.)*; young men are called "friars" *(ibid.,* p. 416); etc.

75 *Quaest. pol.,* p. 106: "Neque enim quis potest recusare dum omnia ratione tractantur, immo amat unusquisque id quod sibi connaturale est aggredi, uti fit in hac Republica."

76 For a discussion of Campanella's socialism vs. Marxist communism cf. Benedetto Croce, *art. cit.* in n. 56 above, and Treves, *op. cit.,* pp. 181-82. Croce's article was published again in *Materialismo storico ed economia marxista* (5th ed.; Bari: Laterza, 1927), pp. 177-223.

77 "Utrum communitas mulierum sit convenientior secundum naturam ac generationi utilior, quam proprietas uxorum et natorum: ac proinde simul toti reipublicae." *Quaest. pol.,* p. 108, heading of art. 3, quaest. 4.

78 *Ibid.,* pp. 109-110: "Sic nunc dico quod communitas mulierum a nobis posita non est contra ius naturae: aut si est, non potest cognosci a puro philosopho: non enim deducitur per modum conclusionis ex iure naturali: nec determinationis, nisi a longe: determinatio autem variari potest, cum iuris sit positivi." For a detailed description of the three kinds of community of women or *concubitus* cf. *ibid.,* p. 109.

79 This is substantially the teaching that can be gathered from the following texts: "Communitas mulierum in concubitu non est contra ius naturae, praesertim quomodo a nobis posita est, sed maxime videtur ea congruere propter quod non est haeresis docere illam in puris naturalibus, sed tamen post ius divinum aut ecclesiasticum positivum." *Ibid.,* p. 109. "Quod autem lex sanxit, ut sua sola uxore quisque utatur quamvis sterili, non potest a philosopho facile cognosci naturaliter: propterea ego hoc unum contendo, quod qui instituunt Rempublicam cum tali communitate mulierum, non peccant in naturam, antequam a lege Dei doceantur sic non faciendum esse." *Ibid.* "Manifestum est pluralitatem uxorum non esse contra naturam: immo omnia animalia, excepta forsan turture, pluribus miscentur. Columbus autem soli sorori. Nec quidem in Republica ista, quae ex naturalibus, non ex revelatis gubernatur legibus, id cognosci potest." *Ibid.,* p. 111. "In Republica vero solari fit commistio tam celebris ex philosophia et astrologia, ut generatio sit melior et abundantior: ergo secundum naturam: ergo non est haeresis nisi postquam ab Ecclesia condemnatur." *Ibid.,* p. 112.

80 Cf. preceding chapter on *Ethics of the Family,* nn. 80-83.

81 Cf. nn. 78 and 79 above.

82 For the originality and modernity of Campanella's political thought cf. Treves, *op. cit.,* pp. 54-55, where he is called, although with some reservation, "a forerunner of modern democratic theories." Campanella's pioneering efforts in the field of education are discussed by Alfio and Antonietta Nicotra in their modest work, *Tommaso Campanella* (Florence-Catanzaro: Guido Mauro, 1948). The authors compare Campanella to Rabelais, Montaigne, and especially Comenius. *Ibid.,* pp. 87-94.

83 That Campanella held this work in great esteem is evident from his remark in the preface: "Propterea de messiae monarchia prioribus libris, liber iste connectitur, super omnes utilissimus pluribus causis." *Mon. Mess.,* p. 1.

84 *Ibid.,* title: ". . . Compendium scripti secundi, in quo per philosophiam divinam et humanam demonstrantur iura Summi Pontificis, Christianorum

Patris et Capitis, super universum orbem in temporalibus et spiritualibus."

85 *Ibid.*, p. 21: ". . . omnes Principes dependent ab eiusdem [Ecclesiae] Capite in temporalibus et spiritualibus."

86 *Ibid.*, p. 5.

87 *Ibid.*, pp. 5-6.

88 *Ibid.*, p. 7: "Potest homo naturaliter dominari ac regere homines, non in quantum homo, sed in quantum est a Deo, vero dominatore auctorizatur; accipiens ab eo fundamentum, aut titulum superioritatis, per naturam, aut per gratiam. Hic autem non quatenus homo, sed quatenus homo divinus, imperabit, et quatenus locumtenens Dei."

89 *Ibid.*, pp. 9-10. See first section of this chapter for pertinent quotations, especially nn. 35ff.

90 *Ibid.*, p. 10.

91 *Ibid.*, p. 11.

92 *Ibid.*

93 *Ibid.*, p. 14.

94 *Ibid.*, p. 19, title of chapter IV: "Iesum Messiam, ac Dominum nostrum, venisse in mundum ad restituendum saeculum beatum, proptereaque dedisse legem universalem, et praefecisse caput universale in toto mundo, super omnes leges et applicationes illarum."

95 *Ibid.*, p. 21.

96 *Theol.*, XXII, 3, 7, tit.: "Papam esse regem et sacerdotem super omnia regna mundi in omnibus." MS quoted in Amerio, *Campanella*, p. 202.

97 Cf. *Discorsi universali*, in Firpo's *Scritti scelti*, p. 469. St. Thomas's text used by Campanella is: "Papa habet potestatem in temporalibus et spiritualibus super omnes reges de iure divino, naturali et positivo." *De regimine principum*, III, 10. It is now commonly agreed upon by commentators that Books III and IV, as well as the last twelve chapters of Book II of the *De regimine principum*, were not written by Aquinas but by his disciple Ptolemy of Lucca, bishop of Torcello. Campanella himself was aware of the doubtful authenticity of the work. Cf. *Mon. Mess.*, p. 24.

98 *Mon. Mess.*, p. 25, heading of chapter VII: "Christum esse Rationem aeternam, et in tempore tandem incarnatam. Ideoque esse Dominum universorum aeternaliter et temporaliter." The chapter begins with the following statement: ". . . assero Christum esse Sapientiam, Verbum, seu Rationem Dei aeternam, per quam creavit mundum et gubernavit semper, et tandem in genere humano instauravit eum cum esset corruptus." To support his statement Campanella brings forth ten arguments from the Scriptures.

99 *Ibid.*, p. 27, heading of chapter IX: "Christum fuisse Regem in spiritualibus et temporalibus, et ambas potestates assumpsisse, et easdem in Ecclesia reliquisse, ut adimplerentur omnia iura naturalia et prophetiae et expectationes." See also *Theol.*, XXIII, 2, 4, tit.: "Christum assumpsisse dominium in spiritualibus et temporalibus et harum dignitatum functiones ostendisse in se exemplariter easque in Ecclesia reliquisse." MS quoted in Amerio, *Campanella*, p. 201. The same basic principle is affirmed in the *De regno Dei*, p. 213: "Christus iure creationis est Rex regum . . . et iure redemptionis."

100 *Mon. Mess.*, p. 28: "Deus ante etiam erat Dominus in temporalibus et spiritualibus. Ergo Christus cum sit Deus, de iure habet et temporale Regnum."

101 *Theol.*, XXIII, 2, 4, tit.: "Christum instituisse principatus saeculares et militiam

etiam ante incarnationem suam." MS quoted in Amerio, *Campanella,* p. 201. *Mon. Mess.,* pp. 27-28: "Quoniam Christus est ipsa ratio prima essentialis aeterna: omne autem dominium fundatum est super ratione, ergo pendet ab eo, sicut splendet a sole, et membra a capite."

102 *Theol.,* XXIII, 2, 4, tit.: ". . . postea vero [Christus] eis [principatibus saecularibus] praefecisse dignitatem apostolicam ad correctionem et meliorationem, cui etiam addidit potestatem evellendi priores principatus et iudices et instituendi novos." MS quoted in Amerio, *Campanella,* p. 201.

103 *Mon. Mess.,* p. 36.

104 *Ibid.,* p. 45, heading of chapter XII: "Christianismum esse unum et non plures: unumque caput, regem ac iudicem supremum in spiritualibus et temporalibus habere, cui omnes principatus et dignitates subsint per prophetiam, naturam, et propter beneficium principum et vassallorum et universi."

105 *Ibid.,* p. 65: "Regnum Messiae unum esse unumque habere caput, Dominum omnium in temporalibus et in spiritualibus; et omnes dominorum titulos, sive electionis, sive successionis, sive emtionis, sive iusti belli, a Papa dependere ut Christi Dei Vicario."

106 *Ibid.,* p. 63: "Quapropter ego in Thomistarum choro non potui assentire dicentibus quod indirecte Papa habet potestatem super laicos reges etiam in temporalibus: sed dixi, secundario in temporalibus; in spiritualibus vero principaliter, ut videtur docere Bernardus . . . et D. Thomas . . . ." This statement is contained in an Appendix that runs through pp. 63-64 of the *Monarchia Messiae* in which Campanella defends himself against charges of error He quotes several texts from St. Thomas to support his own viewpoint.

107 *Ibid.,* p. 74.

108 *Ibid.*

109 *Ibid.,* pp. 86-87: "Nunc ex his assero: Proculdubio a Deo missos fuisse Hyspanos ad punitionem alterius Hemispherii per instinctum, sicuti Cyrus, Alexander, Nabucodonosor, Romani, et alii, ac subinde bona certaque iura in natura eos habere contra praefatos Barbaros, hoc est arma propria, et barbarorum scelera. Itaque quicquid Rex sub auspiciis Christi occupat ad Papam disponere spectat, ab eoque praedictorum Regnorum possessionem, sive, ut dicunt, investituram largiri iure divino certum est, cum enim Messiae mundi Imperium promissum fuerit: et dictum: Gens et Regnum quod non servierit tibi peribit; cumque sit Messias Ratio summa incarnata; et illi Americani contra rationem tam impie vivant, proculdubio potest D. Papa eos iure iudicare castigatione dignos nisi rationi obedierint, cuius capaces participesque sunt naturaliter." For a more detailed discussion of the right of the Spaniards to conquer the New World see Campanella's *Monarchia di Spagna.*

110 A more proper term for it is "hierocratic state," i.e., a state governed by ecclesiastics. But since the term "hierocratic" is not very popular, and, on the other hand, the Pope is supposed to head the universal monarchy as the representative of God, we prefer to use the term "theocratic."

111 Firpo asserts that the *Discorsi della libertà* are to be reckoned among the least known pages of Campanella. Even the date of their composition is uncertain. He places them between 1625 and 1626. Cf. Introduction to the *Discorsi,* p. 8.

112 *Discorsi della libertà,* Firpo's edition, p. 36: "Dunque è vero che in nessun imperio di uno principe, nè di molti, nè di tutti si trova viver più libero d'ogni sorte di vera libertà, come in Roma sotto il papato."

113 *Ibid.*, p. 37: ". . . è eresia politica ed errore teologico dubitare che non sia meglio sottostare all'ecclesiastico [imperio], sendo certi che l'uomo non può guidare gli altri uomini, se non è guidato da Dio . . . Noi sapemo che l'assistenza dello Spirito Santo in abondanza sopra tutti sta nel papato: *ergo ecc.*"

114 *Ibid.*, pp. 37-39.

115 *Ibid.*, p. 40.

116 *Ibid.*, pp. 40-41.

117 That this was the purpose of Campanella in writing his *Discorsi* is clear from the title and subtitle of the work: *"Discorsi universali del governo ecclesiastico per far una gregge e un pastore. Secreto al Papa solo, con modi non soggetti alla contradizione de' Prencipi."* Firpo, *Scritti scelti*, p. 467. Furthermore, in his introduction to the *Discorsi* Campanella refers the reader to his *Monarchia Messiae*. *Ibid.*, p. 469.

118 *Ibid.*, p. 472.

119 *Ibid.*, pp. 472-73.

120 *Ibid.*, p. 474: "Per tirar il mondo alla monarchia universale l'opera dell'eloquenti religiosi basta." *Ibid.*, pp. 474-75: "Di tutti ordini di religione del mondo il Papa deve eligere i più dotti giovani per predicare la renovazione del secol felice in una gregge e un pastore, e segnarli con un segno suo papale, ma con gli abiti dell'ordini loro, e mandarli a diverse legazioni."

121 *Ibid.*, p. 475.

122 *Ibid.*, p. 493.

123 *Ibid.*, p. 497. The formation of a senate of all Christian rulers in Rome under the presidency of the Pope is the central theme of the *Monarchia Christianorum*, a fundamental political work written in 1593 that unfortunately has been lost. Campanella refers to it frequently in his writings.

124 *Ibid.*, p. 506: "Quando il Papa sarà signore d'Italia, sarà anche del mondo; però deve procurar ogni via di arrivar a questo." The remaining pages of the *Discorsi universali* are of no particular interest to us. They contain for the most part practical suggestions for the election of the Pope and the appointment of cardinals, archbishops, bishops, and other prelates of the Roman Curia.

125 Cf. *Quod reminiscentur*, p. 3: ". . . scripsi volumen hoc sat elaboratum, tanquam epitomen et colophonem et finem studiorum meorum, quo omnium nationum conversio facile perficiatur tuis auspiciis, sanctissime Vicarie Christi."

126 *Ibid.*, p. 31: "Vox totius generis humani clamantis ad te, sanctissime pastor." These are the initial words of Campanella's message to Pope Paul V.

127 *Ibid.*

128 *Ibid.*, p. 34: "Exurge, vigilantissime pastor, qui inter Deum et homines pontem Pontifex facis, qui mediator inter nos et Deum, ministerium tuum imple, et caetera omnia adiicientur vobis. Hanc igitur humani generis sequentem legationem perlectam aggredere, et coram Deo, cui proximus es, ipse fungere. Nos in atrio sanctuarii expectabimus, donec tu Moyses noster, imo Melchisedech noster, responsum salutare reportes et iuxta exemplar, quod tibi in monte Dei in vertice montium, ad quem confluent gentes, monstrabitur, ita fac."

129 *Ibid.*, pp. 35-40.

130 *Ibid.*, pp. 40-42.

131 *Ibid.*, p. 43.

132 *Ibid.*, pp. 43-44: "Quapropter convertimini et agnoscite Deum vestrum: sic

enim erit ut humilitas regnum solidum vobis resarciat, quod superbia tantopere constituit inane . . . Vel ergo vestrum studium superbiendi vos admoneat, ut revertamini, unde cecidistis. Quod si non vultis, coniuro vos per Deum vivum, per Deum verum, per Deum sanctum, ut desistatis ab hominum infestatione, nec hanc, quam paramus, reminiscentiam audeatis impedire."

133 *Ibid.,* pp 57-60. The fourteen points that make up the article contain, in Campanella's words (*ibid.,* pp. 57-58), the substance of the *De regimine Ecclesiae.*

134 *Ibid.,* pp. 68-71. In the course of the article reference is made to the *Monarchia Messiae.*

135 Psalm XXI, 28-29. These two verses, which follow immediately upon the words of Ps. XXI that make up the title of the book, are cited by Campanella as a subtitle of Book II of the *Quod reminiscentur* containing his messages to the Gentiles.

CHAPTER THIRTEEN

1 On the nature of virtue cf. Aristotle, *Nichomachean Ethics,* 1105b-1107a 26; St. Thomas, *Sum. Theol.,* I-II, qq. 55-56.

2 Cf. Aristotle, *Nichomachean Ethics,* 1106b 36-1107a 26.

3 Cf. Section II of Chapter XI, "Ethics of the Family," and Section II of Chapter XII, "The Ideal State."

4 *Atheismus,* p. 107: "Omnis quippe lex Ratio est vel rationis regula; ergo lex omnis est participium et splendor primae Rationis, Sapientiae Dei."

5 Cf. Di Napoli, *Tommaso Campanella,* pp. 156ff., where evidence is produced against any possible heretical doctrine in *The City of the Sun.*

6 This seems to be the implication of the text from the *Syntagma* where Campanella speaks of *The City of the Sun* in the following terms: ". . . adiecique ideam reipublicae quam voco Civitatem Solis, longe praestantiorem quam sit Platonica aut alia quaevis." *Ibid.,* p. 24.

7 The present writer cannot share Treves' view that the *Monarchia Messiae* represents Campanella's last step in the construction of his political theory only before *The City of the Sun* was written (Treves, *op. cit.,* pp. 164-65). To subordinate Campanella's ambitious plan of a universal papal monarchy to a utopian conception of society in the order of pure nature is a complete misunderstanding of Campanella's thought. The same misunderstanding is evident in Treves' remark that the *Monarchia Messiae* is an objectification of a philosophical and political ideal rather than the effect of a genuine Christian zeal. *Ibid.,* p. 175. Other unfair and quite arbitrary statements by the same author are that the God of Campanella is not the God of the Gospels and the Apostles, *loc. cit.,* and that the papacy of the *Monarchia Messiae* is not the real papacy but an ideal and rationalized one, as in the last analysis are every dogma and institution of the Church. *Ibid.,* p. 176.

8 The institution of the Church as a religious body independent of the state and extraneous to any purely temporal interest is an important factor of

Christ's social and religious reform. "En créant une société chargée des intérêts religieux des fidèles et en déclarant cette société indépendante de tout État temporel en même temps qu'étrangère à tout intérêt temporel, le Christ a introduit dans le monde une réforme redoutable, mais si géniale que les incroyants même, semble-t-il, devraient reconnaître un des éléments primordiaux du progrès humain." Jacques Leclercq, *Leçons de droit naturel*, Vol. II, *L'état ou la politique* (Louvain: Société d'Études Morales, Sociales et Juridiques, 1948), p. 120.

9 Cf. Heinrich A. Rommen, *The State in Catholic Thought* (St. Louis, Mo.: Herder, 1950), p. 583. Campanella's theory of the Pope's direct power over the state rulers had been defended by John of Salisbury (*c.* 1115-80) and the curialists in the twelfth century. For a comprehensive study of the relationship between Church and state from the historical and juridical points of view see the entire Part III of Rommen's work mentioned above, extending from p. 505 to p. 612. A full treatment of the problem from the historical viewpoint can be found in Luigi Sturzo, *Church and State* (New York: Longmans, Green and Co., 1939). See also *The State and the Church*, ed. John A. Ryan and Moorhouse F. X. Millar, S.J. (New York: Macmillan, 1924), where the contributors discuss specific problems with special emphasis on the relationship between Church and state in the United States of America. More recent works on the subject are: *Church and State Through the Centuries*, ed. S. Z. Ehler and J. B. Marrall (London: Burns and Oates, and Westminster, Md.: Newman Press, 1958); *Church and State*, by Douglas Woodruff, Vol. 89 of the *Twentieth Century Encyclopedia of Catholicism* (New York: Hawthorn Books, 1961).

10 See chap. XII, n. 20, of this study.

11 It is worth noting here that, following St. Thomas's principles of political philosophy, the doctors of late scholasticism had already clearly propounded the thesis of the true sovereignty and independence of the secular power in temporal matters. Thus Bellarmine and Suarez refute the medieval curialist theory of the unrestricted power of the Pope *in temporalibus*, a thesis that became untenable after St. Thomas demonstrated that the state is based on natural law. Bellarmine and Suarez develop instead the theory of the indirect power of the Pope in things temporal. This means that by divine institution the Pope has no temporal power nor any direct authority in the field of secular political life. However the Pope may rightly acquire temporal power and exercise political sovereignty in a territory, i.e., the Church state, as a political necessity for the effective independence of the spiritual power. The Pope also has the right to interfere in the field of the temporal power if acts of a secular ruler injure or endanger the superior end of the Church, which is the salvation of souls. Rommen, *op. cit.*, pp. 547-50, *passim*.

12 This is Prof. Firpo's opinion as given in the introduction to his critical edition of the *Discorsi della libertà*, p. 8, where he takes exception to the view that the occasion for the *Discorsi* had been the widespread discontent of the subjects of the pontifical state.

13 It is well known that Campanella tried very hard but apparently with no immediate success to convince Pope Urban VIII of the necessity of establishing

in Rome a college where the best talents of Europe (cf. letter to Urban VIII, Sept. 29, 1631), or at least the best talents from among the Dominicans of Calabria (cf. letter to Cardinal Francesco Barberini, Sept. 14, 1630), could be trained for their future missionary work among the gentiles. Cf. Firpo, *Scritti scelti*, p. 475, n. 4. See also chap. II, n. 77, of this study for pertinent literature on the subject.

14 This is also the opinion of Romano Amerio. Cf. his introductory article to the critical edition of the *Quod reminiscentur* which appeared in *Sophia*, VII (1939), 419-53, under the heading: "Circa il significato delle variazioni redazionali nell'elaborazione del 'Reminiscentur' di Fra Tommaso Campanella."

15 "Appellatur de toto mundo ad te." St. Bernard, *De consideratione*, III, 2; PL 182, col. 761.

CONCLUSION

1 This, it should be recalled, is the title that Spaventa gives to Campanella. Cf. chap. II, sect. II, of this study. Di Napoli thought it well to use it as a subtitle of his work *Tommaso Campanella, filosofo della restaurazione cattolica*. That Campanella considered himself a champion of the Catholic faith can be gathered from his own words, "la chiesa non ha maggior difensor di me." *Lettere*, p. 406.

2 *Campanella, op. cit.*, pp. 523-56.

3 *Das Erkenntnisproblem, op. cit.*, II, pp. 36, 79-84.

4 *La politica di Campanella, op. cit.*, chap. X: "Varia fortuna del pensiero del Campanella," pp. 210-22.

5 Cf. especially D'Ancona, *Opere di Tommaso Campanella, op. cit.*, pp. CCCX-CCCXIII; Benedetto Croce, *Storia della età barocca in Italia* (Bari: Laterza, 1929), pp. 240-42; Armando Carlini, "Riduzione del sistema leibniziano alla sua idea cosmologica fondamentale," *Giornale di metafisica*, I (1946), 490-92, 496.

6 Blanchet, *Campanella*, pp. 549-54.

7 Cf. D'Ancona, *op. cit.*, p. CCCXI, n. 5; Antonio Sarno, "Campanella e Vico," *Giornale critico della filosofia italiana*, V (1924), 138-54; Croce, *Storia della età barocca in Italia*, pp. 228-29; Gentile, *Il pensiero italiano del rinascimento*, p. 385, n. 1. See also S. Scimé, S.I., "Tommaso Campanella e Gian Battista Vico," *La civiltà cattolica*, XCIX (1948), I, 295-99.

8 Cf. Blanchet, *Campanella*, pp. 531-32, 538-49; Cassirer, *Das Erkenntnisproblem*, II, pp. 36, 79-84.

9 Cf. Blanchet, *Campanella*, pp. 530-31.

10 Zeferino González, *Historia de la filosofía* (2d ed.; Madrid: A. Jubera, 1886), III, 212.

BIBLIOGRAPHY*

I. PRIMARY SOURCES

Campanella, Tommaso. *Philosophia sensibus demonstrata*. Naples: Apud Horatium Salvianum, 1591.

——————. *Prodromus philosophiae instaurandae*. Edited by Tobias Adami. Frankfort: Ioannes Bringerus, 1617.

——————. *Poesie*. Edited by Mario Vinciguerra. Bari: Laterza, 1938.

——————. *De Monarchia Hispanica*. Editio novissima, aucta et emendata. Amsterdam: Apud Ludovicum Elzevirium, 1653.

——————. *Della Monarchia di Spagna*. Edited by Alessandro d'Ancona in *Opere di Tommaso Campanella*. Vol. II, pp. 77-229. Turin: Pomba, 1854.

——————. *Del senso delle cose e della magia*. Edited by Antonio Bruers. Bari: Laterza, 1925.

——————. *De sensu rerum et magia*. Edited by Tobias Adami. Frankfort: Apud Egenolphum Emmelium, 1620.

——————. *Idem*. Paris: Apud Ioannem Du Bray, 1637. It contains the *Defensio libri sui De sensu rerum*, pp. 1-92.

——————. *Apologia pro Galilaeo*. Edited by Eugenio Alberi in *Le opere di Galileo Galilei*. Vol. V, pp. 495-558. Florence: Società Editrice Fiorentina, 1846.

——————. *Apologia di Galileo e Dialogo politico contro Luterani, Calvinisti ed altri eretici*. Edited by Domenico Ciampoli. Lanciano: Carabba, 1911.

——————. *Apologia di Galileo*. Edited by Luigi Firpo. Turin: U.T.E.T., 1968.

——————. *Epilogo magno*. Edited by Carmelo Ottaviano. Rome: Reale Accademia d'Italia, 1939.

——————. *Realis philosophiae epilogisticae partes quatuor*. Edited by Tobias Adami. Frankfort: Ex typis Egenolphi Emmelii, 1623. It contains the *Civitas Solis*.

——————. *Disputationum in quatuor partes suae philosophiae realis libri quatuor*. Paris: Ex typographia Dionysii Houssaye, 1637: *Physiologia*.

——————. *Idem: Quaestiones physiologicae*.

——————. *Idem: Ethica*.

——————. *Idem: Quaestiones morales*.

——————. *Idem: Quaestiones politicae*.

——————. *Idem: Oeconomica*.

——————. *Idem: Quaestiones oeconomicae*.

---

*This bibliography contains only writings of and about Campanella and basic studies in the Renaissance. For studies on individual Renaissance thinkers treated in this work the reader is referred to the notes for Chapter I.

—————————. *Idem: De regno Dei.*

—————————. *Aforismi politici.* Edited by Luigi Firpo. Turin: Giappichelli, 1941. It contains the text of the *De politica*, pp. 143-225.

—————————. *La Città del Sole.* Italian and Latin text edited by Norberto Bobbio. Turin: Einaudi, 1941.

—————————. *Idem.* Edited by Luigi Firpo in *Scritti scelti di Giordano Bruno e di Tommaso Campanella*, pp. 405-464. Turin: U.T.E.T., 1949.

—————————. *Astrologicorum libri VII.* Lyons: Sumptibus Iacobi, Andreae et Matthaei Prost, 1629.

—————————. *Atheismus triumphatus.* Paris: Apud Tussanum Du Bray, 1636.

—————————. *De gentilismo non retinendo.* Attached to the *Atheismus*.

—————————. *Della necessità di una filosofia cristiana (De gentilismo non retinendo).* Translation with an Introduction by Romano Amerio. Turin: Società Editrice Internazionale, 1953.

—————————. *De praedestinatione et reprobatione et auxiliis divinae gratiae. Cento Thomisticus.* Attached to the *Atheismus*.

—————————. *Monarchia Messiae.* Aesii: Apud Gregorium Arnazzinum, 1633. Reissued in facsimile reprint by Luigi Firpo. Turin: Bottega d'Erasmo, 1960.

—————————. *Discorsi della libertà e della felice suggezione allo stato ecclesiastico.* Extract from Luigi Firpo's edition of the *Monarchia Messiae*. Turin: Bottega d'Erasmo, 1960.

—————————. *Medicinalium iuxta propria principia libri septem.* Edited by Jacques Gaffarel. Lyons: Ex Officina Ioannis Pillehotte, 1635.

—————————. *Philosophiae rationalis partes quinque.* Paris: Apud Ioannem Du Bray, 1638: *Grammatica.*

—————————. *Idem: Dialectica.*

—————————. *Idem: Rhetorica.*

—————————. *Idem: Poëtica.*

—————————. *Idem: Historiographia.*

—————————. *Universalis philosophiae, seu metaphysicarum rerum iuxta propria dogmata partes tres, libri 18.* Paris: Apud Dionysium Langlois, 1638. Reissued in phototype by Luigi Firpo. Turin: Bottega d'Erasmo, 1961.

—————————. *Metafisica.* Edited by Giovanni Di Napoli. 3 vols. Bologna: Zanichelli, 1967. Latin text with an Italian translation of selected questions from Campanella's *Metaphysica*.

—————————. *De libris propriis et recta ratione studendi syntagma.* Edited by Vincenzo Spampanato. Milan: Bestetti e Tumminelli, 1927.

—————————. *Discorsi ai Principi d'Italia ed altri scritti filo-ispanici.* Edited by Luigi Firpo. Turin: Chiantore, 1945.

—————————. *Articuli prophetales.* Edited by Luigi Amabile in *Fra Tommaso Campanella. La sua congiura, i suoi processi e la sua pazzia.* Vol. III, pp. 489-498. Naples: Morano, 1882.

—————————. *Discorsi universali del governo ecclesiastico.* Edited by Luigi Firpo in *Scritti scelti di Giordano Bruno e di Tommaso Campanella*, pp. 465-523. Turin: U.T.E.T., 1949.

——————————. *De regimine Ecclesiae.* Edited by Luigi Amabile in *Fra Tommaso Campanella nei castelli di Napoli, in Roma ed in Parigi.* Vol. II, pp. 75-97. Naples: Morano, 1887.

——————————. *Antiveneti.* Edited by Luigi Firpo. Florence: L. S. Olschki, 1945.

——————————. *Quod reminiscentur et convertentur ad Dominum universi fines terrae. Volumen quatripartitum.* Edited by Romano Amerio. Padua: Cedam, 1939. It contains the first two books.

——————————. *Per la conversione degli Ebrei (Quod reminiscentur,* Book III). Edited by Romano Amerio. Florence: L. S. Olschki, 1955.

——————————. *Legazioni ai Maomettani (Quod reminiscentur,* Book IV). Edited by Romano Amerio: Florence: L. S. Olschki, 1960.

——————————. *Theologicorum libri XXX.* The MS is preserved in the general archives of the Dominican order at St. Sabina in Rome and is a copy of the original. The other extant copy of the original is kept in the Bibliothèque Nationale at Paris and is known as the Mazarin MS (1077-1078).

——————————. *Teologia, Book I of Theologicorum libri XXX.* Critical edition with an Introduction by Romano Amerio. Milan: "Vita e Pensiero," 1936.

——————————. *Dio e la predestinazione. Theologicorum liber I.* Critical edition with an Introduction and Italian translation by Romano Amerio. 2 vols. Florence: Vallecchi, 1949-1951.

——————————. *De sancta Monotriade. Theologicorum liber II.* Critical edition with Italian translation by Romano Amerio. Rome: Centro internazionale di studi umanistici, 1958.

——————————. *Cosmologia. Theologicorum liber III.* Critical edition with Italian translation by Romano Amerio. Rome: Centro internazionale di studi umanistici, 1964.

——————————. *De homine. Theologicorum liber IV, Pars II.* Critical edition with Italian translation by Romano Amerio. Rome: Centro internazionale di studi umanistici, 1961.

——————————. *Della grazia gratificante. Theologicorum liber XIII.* Critical edition with Italian translation by Romano Amerio. Rome: Centro internazionale di studi umanistici, 1959.

——————————. *Magia e grazia. Theologicorum liber XIV.* Critical edition with Italian translation by Romano Amerio. Rome: Fratelli Bocca, 1957.

——————————. *Il peccato originale. Theologicorum liber XVI.* Critical edition with Italian translation by Romano Amerio. Rome: Centro internazionale di studi umanistici, 1960.

——————————. *Cristologia. Theologicorum liber XVIII.* Critical edition with Italian translation by Romano Amerio. 2 vols. Rome: Centro internazionale di studi umanistici, 1958.

——————————. *Vita Christi. Theologicorum liber XXI.* Critical edition with Italian translation by Romano Amerio. Rome: Centro internazionale di studi umanistici, 1962.

——————————. *I sacri segni. Theologicorum liber XXIV.* 5 vols. Critical edition with Italian translation by Romano Amerio. Rome: Centro internazionale di studi umanistici, 1965—.

——————. *De antichristo. Theologicorum liber XXVI*. Critical edition with Italian translation by Romano Amerio. Rome: Centro internazionale di studi umanistici, 1965.

——————. *La prima e la seconda resurrezione. Theologicorum libri XXVII-XXVIII*. Critical edition with Italian translation by Romano Amerio. Rome: Fratelli Bocca, 1955.

——————. *Poetica*. Edited by Luigi Firpo. Rome: Reale Accademia d'Italia, 1944.

——————. *Commentaria super poëmatibus Urbani VIII*. The MS is in the Vatican Library, Cod. Barb. XXIX, 262.

——————. *Lettere*. Edited by Vincenzo Spampanato. Bari: Laterza, 1927.

——————. *Opuscoli inediti*. Edited by Luigi Firpo. Florence: L. S. Olschki, 1951.

——————. *Tutte le opere di Tommaso Campanella*. Vol. I. Edited by Luigi Firpo. Milan: Mondadori, 1954. This is the first of the projected three-volume series of Campanella's "Scritti letterari." It contains a general introduction to Tommaso Campanella (pp. XI-LXII)), a *Cronologia della vita e delle opere di T. Campanella* (pp. LXIII-XCIX), and the text of the *Poesie*, the *Poetica* (juvenile Italian redaction), the *Grammatica*, the *Rhetorica*, the *Poëtica* (Latin redaction), and the *Historiographia*.

English Editions

Campanella, Tommaso. *A Discourse Touching the Spanish Monarchy*. Translated by Edmund Chilmead. London: Printed for P. Stephens, 1654.

——————. *The Sonnets of Michael Angelo Buonarroti and Tommaso Campanella*. Translated into rhymed English by John Addington Symonds. London: Smith, Elder, and Co., 1878.

——————. *The Defense of Galileo of Thomas Campanella*. Translated and edited, with Introduction and Notes, by Grant McColley. Northampton, Mass.: Department of History of Smith College, 1937.

——————. *Ideal Commonwealths; Plutarch's Lycurgus, More's Utopia, Bacon's New Atlantis, Campanella's City of the Sun and a Fragment of Hall's Mundus Alter et Idem*. 6th ed. London and New York: G. Routledge and Sons, 1893.

——————. *Ideal Commonwealths; comprising More's Utopia, Bacon's New Atlantis, Campanella's City of the Sun, and Harrington's Oceana*. Revised edition. London and New York: The Colonial Press, 1901.

——————. *Ideal Empires and Republics; Rousseau's Social Contract, More's Utopia, Bacon's New Atlantis, Campanella's City of the Sun*. Washington and London: M. W. Dunne, 1901.

——————. *Famous New Deals of History; Rousseau's Social Contract, Sir Thomas More's Utopia, Bacon's New Atlantis, Campanella's City of the Sun*. New York: W. H. Wise and Co., 1935.

————. *Famous Utopias of the Renaissance.* Introduction and Notes by Frederic R. White. *University Classics.* 3d Printing. New York: Hendricks House, 1948. It includes *The City of the Sun* (pp. 158-204), trans. by T. W. Halliday, with a short Introduction (pp. 155-157) on the life and works of Tommaso Campanella.

————. *The Quest for Utopias: An Anthology of Imaginary Societies.* Edited by Glenn Negley and J. Max Patrick. New York: Schuman, 1952. It contains *The City of the Sun* (pp. 317-347), trans. by William J. Gilstrap, with a short Introduction (pp. 314-317).

II. SECONDARY SOURCES

A. *Studies on Campanella*

Amabile, Luigi. *Fra Tommaso Campanella. La sua congiura, i suoi processi e la sua pazzia.* 3 vols. Naples: Morano, 1882.

————. *Fra Tommaso Campanella nei castelli di Napoli, in Roma ed in Parigi.* 2 vols. Naples: Morano, 1887.

————. "Campanella," in *Fra T. Pignatelli, la sua congiura e la sua morte.* Naples: Morano, 1887. Pp. 3-13, 27-30, 59-60, 78-79, 151-53, 157-59 and *passim.*

Amerio, Romano. "La politica di Campanella," *Rivista di filosofia neoscolastica,* XX (1928), 311-28.

————. "Ritrattazione dell'ortodossia campanelliana," *Rivista di filosofia neoscolastica,* XXI (1929), 410-30.

————. "Le dottrine religiose di T. Campanella," *Rivista di filosofia neoscolastica,* XXII (1930), 435-61.

————. "Forme e significato del principio di autocoscienza in Sant'Agostino e Tommaso Campanella," *Rivista di filosofia neoscolastica,* XXIII (1931), Suppl., 75-114.

————. "La diagnostica della religione positiva in T. Campanella," *Rivista di filosofia neoscolastica,* XXIV (1932), 174-97.

————. "Su alcune aporie dell'interpretazione deistica della filosofia campanelliana al lume degli inediti," *Rivista di filosofia neoscolastica,* XXVI (1934), 605-615.

————. "L'opera teologico-missionaria del Campanella nei primordi di Propaganda Fide," *Archivum Fratrum Praedicatorum,* V (1935), 175-93.

————. "Nota sulla cronologia dell'opera metafisica di T. Campanella," *Sophia,* III (1935), 195-202.

————. "Il problema esegetico fondamentale del pensiero campanelliano," *Rivista di filosofia neoscolastica,* XXXI (1939), 368-87.

————. "Circa il significato delle variazioni redazionali nell'elaborazione del 'Reminiscentur' di Fra Tommaso Campanella," *Sophia,* VII (1939), 419-53.

————. "Attualità di Tommaso Campanella," *Convivium,* XIII (1941), 554-74.

————. "Galilei e Campanella: la tentazione del pensiero nella filosofia della riforma cattolica," in *Nel terzo centenario della morte di G. Galilei. Saggi e conferenze.* Milan: "Vita e Pensiero," 1942. Pp. 299-326.

——————. "L'ultima forma del mito solare nella teologia politica di fra T. Campanella. Nota intorno a una nuova edizione della 'Città del Sole' con appendice di testi inediti," *Jahrbuch der Schweizerischen philosophischen Gesellschaft,* IV (1944), 28-59.

——————. *Campanella.* Brescia: "La Scuola," 1947.

——————. *Introduzione alla teologia di Tommaso Campanella.* Turin: Società Editrice Internazionale, 1948.

——————. "Un'altra confessione dell'incredulità giovanile del Campanella," *Rivista di filosofia neoscolastica,* XLV (1953), 75-77.

Anonymous. "A Dominican Communist," *The Living Age,* CCCXLVI (July, 1934), 453-54.

Arabia, Francesco. *Tommaso Campanella. Scene.* Naples: Tipografia della R. Università, 1877.

Badaloni, Nicola. *Tommaso Campanella.* Milan: Feltrinelli, 1965.

Baldacchini, Michele. *Vita e filosofia di Tommaso Campanella.* 2 vols. Naples: All'insegna di A. Manuzio, 1840-1843.

——————. *Vita di Tommaso Campanella.* Naples: All'insegna di A. Manuzio, 1847.

Berti, Domenico. "Lettere inedite di Tommaso Campanella e catalogo dei suoi scritti," *Atti della R. Accademia dei Lincei,* Serie III, Classe di scienze morali, II (1878), 439-507.

——————. "Tommaso Campanella," *Nuova antologia di scienze, lettere ed arti,* Serie II, Vol. XL (1878), 201-227; 605-616; Vol. XLI (1878), 391-415.

——————. *Nuovi documenti su Tommaso Campanella tratti dal carteggio di Giovanni Fabbri.* Rome: Tipografia Bodoniana, 1881.

Blanchet, Léon. *Campanella.* Paris: Alcan, 1920.

——————. *Les antécédents historiques du "Je pense, donc je suis."* Paris: Alcan, 1920.

Bonansea, Bernardino M. *The Theory of Knowledge of Tommaso Campanella. Exposition and Critique.* Ph.D. Dissertation. Washington, D.C.: The Catholic University of America, 1954.

——————. *The Theory of Knowledge of Tommaso Campanella. Exposition and Critique.* Philosophical Series. Abstract No. 14. Washington, D.C.: The Catholic University of America Press, 1954.

——————. "Campanella as Forerunner of Descartes," *Franciscan Studies,* XVI (March-June, 1956), 37-59.

——————. "The Concept of Being and Non-Being in the Philosophy of Tommaso Campanella," *The New Scholasticism,* XXXI (Jan., 1957), 34-67.

——————. "Knowledge of the Extramental World in the System of Tommaso Campanella," *Franciscan Studies,* XVII (June-Sept., 1957), 188-212.

——————. "The Political Thought of Tommaso Campanella," *Studies in Philosophy and the History of Philosophy,* edited by John K. Ryan. Washington, D.C.: The Catholic University of America Press, 1963. Vol. II, pp. 211-48.

——————. "Campanella, Tommaso," *The Encyclopedia Americana*, 1967, Vol. V, pp. 273-74.

——————. "Campanella, Tommaso," *The Encyclopedia of Philosophy*, 1967, Vol. II, pp. 11-13.

——————. "Campanella, Tommaso," *New Catholic Encyclopedia*, 1967, Vol. II, pp. 1110-11.

Botta, Carlo. *Storia d'Italia in continuazione del Guicciardini fino al 1789*. Capolago: Tipografia Elvetica, 1832. Vol. IV, pp. 312-23.

Bréhier, Émile. *Histoire de la Philosophie*. Paris: Presses Universitaires de France, 1951. Vol. I, *L'antiquité et le Moyen Age*, Book 3, pp. 782-85.

Bruers, Antonio. *Pensatori antichi e moderni*. Rome: Bardi, 1936. Pp. 95-135.

Calenda di Tavani, Andrea. *Fra Tommaso Campanella e la sua dottrina sociale e politica di frônte al socialismo moderno*. Nocera Inferiore: Angora, 1895.

Calogero, Giuseppe. *Tommaso Campanella, Prometeo del Rinascimento*. Messina: Samperi, 1961.

Carlini, Armando. "Riduzione del sistema leibniziano alla sua idea cosmologica fondamentale," *Giornale di metafisica*, I (1946), 490-92; 496.

——————. Review of G. Di Napoli's "Tommaso Campanella, Filosofo della restaurazione cattolica," *Giornale di metafisica*, III (1948), 533-35.

Carusi, Enrico. "Nuovi documenti sui processi di T. Campanella," *Giornale critico della filosofia italiana*, VIII (1927), 321-59.

Cassirer, Ernst. *Das Erkenntnisproblem in der Philosophie und Wissenschaft der neueren Zeit*. Berlin: Verlag Bruno Cassirer, 1922. Vol. I, pp. 240-57; Vol. II, pp. 79-84.

Colet, Louise. *Oeuvres choisies de Campanella, précédées d'une notice*. Paris: Lavigne, 1844.

Corsano, Antonio. *Tommaso Campanella*. New ed. revised. Bari: Laterza, 1961.

Croce, Benedetto. "Intorno al comunismo di T. Campanella, a proposito di recenti pubblicazioni," *Archivio storico per le provincie napoletane*, XX (1895), 646-83. Published again in *Materialismo storico ed economia marxista*. 5th ed. Bari: Laterza, 1927. Pp. 177-223.

——————. "Alcune osservazioni sulla filosofia del Campanella," *La critica*, XL (1942), 51-55.

Cyprianus, Ernst Salomon. *Vita Th. Campanellae*. 2d ed. Trajecti ad Rhenum: Apud Steph. Neaulme, 1741.

D'Ancona, Alessandro. *Opere di Tommaso Campanella scelte, ordinate ed annotate*. 2 vols. Turin: Pomba, 1858.

De Carolis Pilotti, Laura. *Tommaso Campanella, poeta*. Florence: Sansoni, 1942.

Déjob, Charles. "Est-il vrai que Campanella fût simplement déiste?", *Annales de la Faculté de Lettres de Bordeaux. Bulletin italien*, XI (1911), 124-40, 232-45, 277-80.

De Mattei, Rodolfo. *La politica di Campanella*. Rome: Anonima Romana Editoriale, 1927.

——————————. *Studi campanelliani*. Florence: Sansoni, 1934.

Dentice d'Accadia, Cecilia. *Tommaso Campanella*. Florence: Vallecchi, 1921.

——————————. "Campanella, Tommaso," *Enciclopedia Italiana Treccani*, Vol. VIII, pp. 567-70.

De Ruggiero, Guido. *Storia della filosofia*. Parte Terza. *Rinascimento, Riforma e Controriforma*. Bari: Laterza, 1930. Vol. II, pp. 233-61.

De Sanctis, Francesco. *Storia della letteratura italiana*. New ed. by Benedetto Croce. Bari: Laterza, 1912. Vol. II, pp. 244-62.

Di Napoli, Giovanni. *Tommaso Campanella, filosofo della restaurazione cattolica*. Padua: Cedam, 1947.

——————————. "Campanella, Tommaso," *Enciclopedia Cattolica*, Vol. III, 1949, cols. 449-56.

——————————. "Il problema dell'ortodossia campanelliana," *Euntes docete* (Rome), XVI (1963), 55-104.

Ducloux, Walther. *Die metaphysische Grundlage der Staatsphilosophie des Thomas Campanella*. Speyer a. Rh.: Pilger Druckerei, 1935.

Échard, Jacobus. "Vita Campanellae," *Scriptores Ordinis Praedicatorum*, II, 505-521. Reprinted in Ernst Salomon Cyprianus, *Vita Th. Campanellae*. 2d ed. Trajecti ad Rhenum: Apud Steph. Neaulme, 1741. Appendix III, pp. 90ff.

Falletti, Pio Carlo. "Del carattere di Fra T. Campanella," *Rivista storica italiana*, VI (1889), 209-290. Reprinted in the form of extract. Turin: Bocca, 1889.

Femiano, Salvatore. *Lo spiritualismo di Tommaso Campanella*. 2 vols. Naples: Istituto Editoriale del Mezzogiorno, 1965. Vol. I. La teorica dell'ente; Vol. II. Il problema di Dio. Revised and published as one volume under the title *La metafisica di Tommaso Campanella*. Milan: Marzorati, 1968.

Fiorentino, Francesco. *Pietro Pomponazzi. Studi storici su la scuola bolognese e padovana del secolo XVI*. Florence: Le Monnier, 1868. Pp. 391-405.

——————————. *Bernardino Telesio; ossia Studi storici su l'idea della natura nel risorgimento italiano*. 2 vols. Florence: Successori Le Monnier, 1872-1874. Vol. II, pp. 122-210.

——————————. *Studi e ritratti della rinascenza*. Bari: Laterza e Figli, 1911. Pp. 377-421.

Firpo, Luigi. "I primi processi campanelliani in una ricostruzione unitaria," *Giornale critico della filosofia italiana*, XX (1939), 5-43.

——————————. *Bibliografia degli scritti di Tommaso Campanella*. Turin: V. Bona, 1940.

——————————. "A proposito del 'Quod reminiscentur'," *Giornale critico della filosofia italiana*, XXI (1940), 268-79.

——————————. *Ricerche Campanelliane*. Florence: Sansoni, 1947.

——————————. "Contributo alla bibliografia campanelliana," *Rivista di storia della filosofia*, III (1948), 183-211.

——————————. "Per il testo critico della 'Città del Sole' di T. Campanella," *Giornale storico della letteratura italiana*, CXXV (1948), 245-55.

——————————. "Appunti Campanelliani," *Giornale critico della filosofia italiana*, XXIX (1950), 68-95.

—————————. "Appunti Campanelliani, XXII: Un'opera che Campanella non scrisse: il 'Discorso sui Paesi Bassi'," *Giornale critico della filosofia italiana,* XXXIII (1952), 331-43.

—————————. *Introduzione e cronologia premesse al primo volume delle opere di Tommaso Campanella nell'edizione Mondadori.* Estratto, 1953.

—————————. "Campanella nel Settecento," *Rinascimento,* IV (1953), 105-154. Reprinted in the form of extract. Florence: Sansoni, 1953.

—————————. "Campanella nel secolo XIX," *Calabria nobilissima,* VI (1952), 235-42; VII (1953), 31-38, 75-82, 193-202; VIII (1954), 11-24, 125-33; IX (1955), 104-119; X (1956), 42-62. Reprinted in the form of extract. Naples, 1956.

—————————. "Cinquant'anni di studi sul Campanella (1901-1950)," *Rinascimento,* VI (1955), 209-348.

—————————. "Un decennio di studi sul Campanella (1951-1960)," *Studi secenteschi,* I (1960), 125-64.

Gardner, Edmund G. *Tommaso Campanella and His Poetry.* Oxford: The Clarendon Press, 1923.

Garin, Eugenio. *La filosofia.* Milan: Vallardi, 1947. Vol. II, pp. 247-83.

Gentile, Giovanni. *Il pensiero italiano del rinascimento.* 3d ed. revised. Florence: Sansoni, 1940. Pp. 357-92.

Gheorgov, Ivan A. "Roger Bacon und Tommaso Campanella," in *Bericht über den III. Internationale Kongress für Philosophie zu Heidelberg.* Heidelberg: C. Winters, 1909. Pp. 233-39.

Giannone, Pietro. *Dell'istoria civile del Regno di Napoli libri XL.* Naples: Naso, 1723. Vol. IV, *passim.*

Gilson, Etienne. "Notes sur Campanella," *Annales de philosophie chrétienne,"* XV (1912-1913), 491-513.

—————————. "Descartes, Saint Augustin et Campanella," in *Études sur le rôle de la pensée médiévale dans la formation du système cartésien.* Paris: Vrin, 1930. Pp. 259-68.

González, Zefirino. *Historia de la filosofía.* 2d ed. Madrid: A. Jubera, 1886. Vol. III, pp. 203-215.

Grillo, Francesco. *Tommaso Campanella in America: A Critical Bibliography and a Profile.* New York: S. F. Vanni, 1954.

—————————. *A Supplement to the Critical Bibliography.* New York: S. F. Vanni, 1957.

Hoeffding, Harold. *A History of Modern Philosophy.* Trans. by E. B. Meyer. London: Macmillan, 1900. Vol. I, pp. 149-58.

Illari, Francesco. *Sintetismo e fenomenismo nella filosofia di Tommaso Campanella.* Ph.D. Dissertation. Milan: Università del S. Cuore, 1951.

Italiener, Bruno. *Die Gotteslehre des Thomas Campanella.* Peine: Herzberg und Macke, 1904.

Jacobelli Isoldi, A. Maria. *Tommaso Campanella: la crisi della coscienza in sè.* Milan: Bocca, 1953.

Kvačala, Jan. *Thomas Campanella, ein Reformer der ausgehenden Renaissance.* Berlin: Trowitzsch und Sohn, 1909.

Lafargue, Paul. "Campanella. Étude critique sur sa vie et sur la Cité du Soleil," *Le devenir social,* I (1895), 305-320; 465-80; 561-78.

Mandonnet, Pierre. "Campanella, Thomas," *Dictionnaire de théologie catholique,* Vol. II, cols. 1443-47.

Mariano, Raffaele. "Fra T. Campanella del professore Amabile. Saggio critico-storico," *Atti della Reale Accademia di scienze morali e politiche,* XXIII (1889), 151-229. Reprinted in *Fra libri e cose di storia, arte, religione e filosofia.* Florence: Barbera, 1906. Pp. 167-224.

Mondolfo, Rodolfo. "T. Campanella e il suo pensiero," in *Figure e idee della filosofia del Rinascimento.* Florence: "La Nuova Italia," 1963. Pp. 162-219.

Negri, Luigi. "Di una recente interpretazione del pensiero campanelliano," *Filosofia e vita,* IV (1967), 376-89.

Nicotra, Alfio and Antonietta. *Tommaso Campanella.* Florence and Catanzaro: Mauro, 1948.

Olgiati, Francesco. *L'anima dell'umanesimo e del rinascimento.* Milan: "Vita e Pensiero," 1924. Pp. 731-76.

Pastore, Annibale. "Anticipazioni cartesiane e sviluppi lirici in S. Agostino e Campanella," *Atti della R. Accademia delle Scienze di Torino,* LXXV (1939-1940), II, 89-106.

—————————. "Autocoscienza e intuizione lirica in T. Campanella," *Sophia,* XV (1947), 50-59.

Reeves, George C. *The Philosophy of Tommaso Campanella, with Special Reference to His Doctrine of the Sense of Things and of Magic.* Ph.D. Dissertation. Bloomington, Ind.: Indiana University, 1935.

Ritter, Heinrich. *Geschichte der neueren Philosophie.* 4 vols. Hamburg: Perthes, 1850-1853. Vol. II, pp. 3-62.

Rixner, Th. A., and Siber, Th. *Leben und Lehrmeinungen berühmter Physiker am Ende des XVI. und am Anfange des XVII. Jahrhunderts, als Beyträge zur Geschichte der Physiologie in engerer und weiterer Bedeutung.* Book VI: *Thomas Campanella.* Sulzbach: J. E. von Seidel, 1826.

Rossi, Mario M. *T. Campanella, metafisico.* Florence: Carpigiani e Zipoli, 1923.

Saitta, Giuseppe. *Il pensiero italiano nell'umanesimo e nel rinascimento.* Bologna: Zuffi, 1949-1951. Vol. III, pp. 187-291.

Sante-Felici, Giovanni. *Die religionsphilosophischen Grundanschauungen des Thomas Campanella.* Ph. D. Dissertation. Halle: Plötz'sche Buchdruckerei, 1887.

—————————. *Le dottrine filosofico-religiose di Tommaso Campanella, con particolare riguardo alla filosofia della rinascenza italiana.* Lanciano: Carabba, 1895.

Sarno, Antonio. "Campanella e Vico," *Giornale critico della filosofia italiana,* V (1924), 138-54.

Scimé, Salvatore. "Tommaso Campanella e Gian Battista Vico," *La civiltà cattolica,* XCIX (1948), 295-99.

Solari, Gioele. "Di una nuova edizione critica della 'Città del Sole' e del comunismo del Campanella," *Rivista di filosofia,* XXXII (1941), 180-97.

——————. "Filosofia politica del Campanella," *Rivista di filosofia*, XXXVII (1946), 38-63.

Spaventa, Bertrando. *Saggi di critica filosofica, politica e religiosa*. Naples: Ghio, 1867. Vol. I, pp. 3-135.

——————. *Rinascimento, riforma, controriforma e altri saggi critici*. Venice: "La Nuova Italia," 1928. Pp. 1-122.

Sternberg, Kurt. "Ueber Campanellas Sonnestaat," *Historische Zeitschrift*, CXLVIII (1933), 520-71.

Testa, Aldo. *T. Campanella*. Milan: Garzanti, 1941.

Tragella, Giovan Battista. "T. Campanella e l'idea missionaria," *Il pensiero missionario*, XIII (1941), 302-313.

Treves, Paolo. *La filosofia politica di Tommaso Campanella*. Bari: Laterza, 1930.

Valeri, Nino. *Campanella*. Rome: Formiggini, 1931.

B. *Studies in the Renaissance*

Allen, Don Cameron. *Doubt's Boundless Sea: Skepticism and Faith in the Renaissance*. Baltimore: Johns Hopkins University Press, 1964.

Allen, John W. *A History of Political Thought in the Sixteenth Century*. London: Methuen, 1957.

Artz, Frederick Binkerd. *Renaissance Humanism, 1300-1550*. Kent, Ohio: Kent State University Press, 1966.

Baron, Hans. *The Crisis of the Early Italian Renaissance*. 2 vols. Princeton, N.J.: Princeton University Press, 1955.

Bouwsma, William J. *The Interpretation of Renaissance Humanism*. Washington, D.C.: Service Center for Teachers of History, 1959.

Bréhier, Émile. *The Middle Ages and the Renaissance*. Trans. by Wade Baskin. Chicago-London: University of Chicago Press, 1965.

Burckhardt, Jacob. *The Civilization of the Renaissance in Italy*. 2 vols. New York: Harper Torchbooks, 1958.

Burke, Peter. *The Renaissance*. London: Longmans, 1964.

Campana, Augusto. "The Origin of the Word 'Humanist'," *Journal of the Warburg and Courtauld Institutes*, IX (1946), 60-73.

Cantimori, Delio. "Sulla storia del concetto di Rinascimento," *Annali della R. Scuola Normale Superiore di Pisa*, Ser. II, Vol. I (1932), 229-68.

Carbonara, Cleto. *Il secolo XV*. Milan: Bocca, 1943.

——————. "Rinascimento," *Enciclopedia Filosofica*, 1957, Vol. IV, cols. 134-41.

——————. "Umanesimo," *Enciclopedia Filosofica*, 1957, Vol. IV, cols. 1373-79.

Cassirer, Ernst. "Some Remarks on the Question of the Renaissance," *Journal of the History of Ideas*, IV (1943), 49-56.

——————. *The Renaissance Philosophy of Man*. Joint edition with P. O. Kristeller and J. H. Randall, Jr. Chicago: University of Chicago Press, 1948.

——————. *The Philosophy of the Enlightenment*. Trans. by Fritz Koelln and James Pettergrove. Princeton, N.J.: Princeton University Press, 1951.

——————. *The Individual and the Cosmos in Renaissance Philosophy.* Trans. with and Introduction by Mario Domandi. New York: Barnes and Noble, 1964.

Chabod, Federico. *Scritti sul Rinascimento.* Turin: Einaudi, 1967.

Cian, Vittorio. *Umanesimo e Rinascimento.* Florence: Le Monnier, 1941.

Copleston, Frederick, S.J. *A History of Philosophy.* Westminster, Md.: The Newman Press, 1953. Vol. III, Part II, "The Philosophy of the Renaissance," pp. 207-334.

Croce, Benedetto. *Storia della età barocca in Italia.* Bari: Laterza, 1929.

Di Napoli, Giovanni. "La filosofia nei secoli XV-XVI," in *Storia della filosofia,* edited by Cornelio Fabro. Rome: Coletti, 1954. Pp. 299-389.

Durand, D., Baron, H., and others. "Discussion on the Renaissance," *Journal of the History of Ideas,* IV (1943), 1-74.

Fallico, Arturo Biagio, and Shapiro, Herman (eds. and trans.). *Renaissance Philosophy.* Vol. I, *The Italian Philosophers: Selected Readings from Petrarch to Bruno.* New York: Modern Library, 1967.

Ferguson, Wallace K. "Humanist Views of the Renaissance," *American Historical Review,* XLV (1939-1940), 1-28.

——————. *The Renaissance in Historical Thought: Five Centuries of Interpretation.* Boston: Houghton Mifflin, 1948.

——————. "The Interpretation of the Renaissance: Suggestions for a Synthesis," *Journal of the History of Ideas,* XII (1951), 483-95.

——————. "The Revival of Classical Antiquity or the First Century of Humanism: A Reappraisal," *The Canadian Historical Association, Report of the Annual Meeting Held at Ottawa, June 12-15, 1957,* pp. 13-30.

——————. *Renaissance Studies.* London, Ontario: Humanities Department of the University of Western Ontario, 1963.

Garin, Eugenio. *Medioevo e rinascimento.* Bari: Laterza, 1954.

——————. *La cultura filosofica del rinascimento italiano.* Florence: Sansoni, 1961.

——————. *Italian Humanism; Philosophy and Civic Life in the Renaissance.* Trans. by Peter Munz. New York: Harper and Row, 1965.

Gentile, Giovanni. *Il pensiero italiano del rinascimento.* 3d ed. revised. Florence: Sansoni, 1940.

Giacon, Carlo. *La seconda scolastica.* 3 vols. Milan: Bocca, 1944-1950.

Gilmore, Myron P. *The World of Humanism, 1453-1517.* New York: Harper, 1952.

Gilson, Etienne. "Humanisme médiéval et Renaissance," in *Les idées et les lettres.* Paris: Vrin, 1932.

Gundersheimer, Werner L. (ed.). *The Italian Renaissance.* Englewood Cliffs, N.J.: Prentice-Hall, 1965.

Hearnshaw, Fossey John (ed.). *The Social and Political Ideas of Some Great Thinkers of the Renaissance and the Reformation.* New York: Barnes and Noble, 1967.

Helton, Tinsley (ed.). *The Renaissance: A Reconsideration of the Theories and Interpretations of the Age.* Madison: The University of Wisconsin Press, 1961.

Huizinga, Johan. *The Waning of the Middle Ages.* New York: Doubleday, 1954.

——————. "Das Problem der Renaissance," in his *Wege der Kulturgeschichte.* Trans. by Werner Kaegi. Munich: Drei-Masken Verlag, 1930. Pp. 89-139.

——————. *Men and Ideas: History, the Middle Ages, the Renaissance; Essay.* Trans. by J. S. Holmes and H. Van Marle. London: Eyre and Spottiswoode, 1960.

Kieszkowski, Bodhan. *Studi sul platonismo del Rinascimento in Italia.* Florence: Sansoni, 1936.

Kristeller, Paul O., and Randall, John H., Jr. "The Study of the Philosophies of the Renaissance," *Journal of the History of Ideas,* II (1941), 449-96.

Kristeller, Paul O. "The Place of Classical Humanism in Renaissance Thought," *Journal of the History of Ideas,* IV (1943), 59-63.

——————. "Renaissance Philosophies," in *A History of Philosophical Systems.* Ed. by Vergilius Ferm. New York: The Philosophical Library, 1950. Pp. 227-39.

——————. *Studies in Renaissance Thought and Letters.* Rome: Edizioni di storia e letteratura, 1956.

——————. *Renaissance Thought: The Classic, Scholastic, and Humanist Strains.* A revised and enlarged edition of *The Classics and Renaissance Thought.* New York: Harper Torchbooks, 1961.

——————. *Eight Philosophers of the Italian Renaissance.* Stanford: Stanford University Press, 1964.

——————. *Renaissance Philosophy and the Mediaeval Tradition.* Latrobe, Pa.: Archabbey Press, 1966.

Lucas, Henry S. "The Renaissance: A Review of Some Views," *The Catholic Historical Review,* XXXV (1950), 377-407.

Lucki, Emil. *History of the Renaissance, 1350-1550.* 5 vols. Salt Lake City: University of Utah Press, 1963—.

McGuire, Martin R. P. "Mediaeval Humanism," *The Catholic Historical Review,* XXXVIII (1952-1953), 397-409.

Mazzeo, Joseph A. *Renaissance and Revolution: The Remaking of European Thought.* New York: Pantheon Books, 1966.

Mesnard, Pierre. *L'essor de la philosophie politique au XVIe siècle.* 2d ed. Paris: Vrin, 1951.

Mommsen, Theodor E. *Medieval and Renaissance Studies.* Edited by E. Rice. Ithaca: Cornell University Press, 1959.

Nardi, Bruno. *Saggi sull'Aristotelismo Padovano dal secolo XIV al XVI.* Florence: Sansoni, 1958.

Phillips, D. "Ferguson's History of the Periodic Conception of the Renaissance," *Journal of the History of Ideas,* XIII (1952), 266-80.

Plumb, John H. *The Italian Renaissance. A Concise Survey of Its History and Culture.* New York: Harper and Row, 1965.

Randall, John H. *The School of Padua and the Emergence of Modern Science.* Padua: Editrice Antenore, 1961.

Renaudet, Augustin. *Humanisme et Renaissance.* Geneva: Droz, 1958.

Robb, Nesca A. *Neoplatonism of the Italian Renaissance.* London: Allen and Unwin, 1935.

Rüegg, Walter. *Cicero und der Humanismus.* Zurich: Rheinverlag, 1946.

Sabine, George H. *A History of Political Theory.* 3d ed. New York: Holt, 1961.

Saitta, Giuseppe. *Filosofia italiana e umanesimo.* Venice: "La Nuova Italia," 1928.

——————————. *Il pensiero italiano nell'umanesimo e nel rinascimento.* 3 vols. Bologna: Fiammenghi e Nanni, 1954.

Spaventa, Bertrando. *La filosofia italiana nelle sue relazioni con la filosofia europea.* 3d ed. Bari: Laterza, 1926.

Symonds, John Addington. *The Renaissance in Italy.* 5 parts in 7 volumes. New York: Holt, 1887-1908.

Toffanin, Giuseppe. *La fine dell'umanesimo.* Turin: Bocca, 1920.

——————————. *Che cosa fu l'umanesimo?* Florence: Sansoni, 1929.

——————————. *History of Humanism.* Trans by Elio Gianturco. New York: Las Americas Publications Co., 1954.

Troilo, Erminio. *Averroismo e Aristotelismo padovano.* Padua: Cedam, 1939.

Ueberweg, Friedrich. *Grundriss der Geschichte der Philosophie.* Vol. III, *Die Philosophie der Neuzeit bis zum Ende des XVIII Jahrhunderts.* 13th ed., prepared by Max Fischeisen-Koehler and Willy Moog. Basel: Schwabe, 1953.

Ullman, Berthold L. *Studies in the Italian Renaissance.* Rome: Edizioni di storia e letteratura, 1955.

Weisinger, Herbert: "The Renaissance Theory of the Reaction against the Middle Ages as a Cause of the Renaissance," *Speculum,* XX (1945), 461-67.

Weiss, Roberto. *The Dawn of Humanism in Italy.* London: Lewis, 1947.

Wilkins, Ernest H. "On the Nature and Extent of the Italian Renaissance," *Italica,* XXVII (1950), 67-76.

Windelband, Wilhelm. *A History of Philosophy.* Trans. by James H. Tufts. Revised ed. Vol. II, *Renaissance, Enlightenment, and Modern.* New York: Harper Torchbooks, 1958.

Wright, William K. *A History of Modern Philosophy.* New York: Macmillan, 1941.

Zabughin, Vladimiro. *Storia del rinascimento cristiano in Italia.* Milan: Treves, 1924.

INDEX OF NAMES

417